Studies in the History of Music • 1

Lewis Lockwood and Christoph Wolff, General Editors

Music and Culture in Italy from the Middle Ages to the Baroque *A Collection of Essays*

Nino Pirrotta

Harvard University Press
Cambridge, Massachusetts, and London, England 1984

Publication of this book has been aided by a subvention from
the American Musicological Society

This book is printed on acid-free paper, and its binding materials have been chosen
for strength and durability.

Library of Congress Cataloging in Publication Data

Pirrotta, Nino.
Music and culture in Italy from the Middle Ages to the Baroque.

(Studies in the history of music; 1)
Includes index.
1. Music—Italy—History and criticism—Addresses,
essays, lectures.   I. Title.   II. Series.
ML290.1.P57   1984   780'.945   83–12827
ISBN 0–674–59108–9

To my children,
Dilli, Vincenzo, Silvia, and Sergio

⇥Foreword

There could be no better or more appropriate overture than this book to what we hope will be a distinguished series of studies in the history of music. Nino Pirrotta's writings have been a model of musicological discourse of broad-ranging intellectual scope, and will remain a challenge for generations to come. The twenty-two essays gathered in this volume represent a cross-section of Pirrotta's scholarly work on Italian music and its changing cultural background from the Middle Ages through the Settecento. His exemplary scholarship demonstrates how archival and philological research, analytical and critical study—all of this overlaid upon an interdisciplinary viewpoint—can form a unified approach to historical material and illuminate it for a modern audience. The inaugural volume of Studies in the History of Music sets a standard for the series that will be difficult to match but that we certainly hope to emulate in later volumes.

Nino Pirrotta, now both Walter W. Naumburg Professor of Music, Emeritus, at Harvard University and Professor Emeritus at the University of Rome, wrote most of the essays in the present volume during his memorable Cambridge years, 1956–1972. That these lines are written in the month in which he celebrates his seventy-fifth birthday is not entirely a coincidence. It gives us the welcome opportunity to pay a visible and lasting tribute to a great scholar and writer, an admired teacher and colleague, and a true friend.

Lewis Lockwood
Christoph Wolff

Cambridge, Massachusetts
June 1983

Preface

Friends have on occasion suggested that I select some of my scattered essays for publication in one volume. The project has been delayed, but now two such collections are being published, the present one by the press of the university where I taught for many years, the other in my own country, Italy. The latter is restricted to medieval topics up to the transition to the Renaissance, but the essays collected here should provide a wider sampling of the areas I have touched upon during nearly fifty years of musicological activity. I wanted this new presentation to be as faithful as possible a reflection of the originals—a reflection, and not merely a replica, because it involved a considerable amount of translation, as well as additions to the notes to bring them up-to-date. The texts have remained basically unaltered, except for the correction of some mistakes. In two instances I have added new information in a postscript; in every case I have striven to keep the distinction clear between my old statements and the new additions. The musical examples have been photographically reproduced from the original articles. Some illustrations that appeared with first publication have been omitted here, and a few have been added.

The process of rereading, selecting, and supervising the translations inevitably has become an occasion for self-searching. While it is gratifying to think that my writings may still be of interest, the sobering thought came to me that my work may belong to the past. To this rather pessimistic intimation I reacted by thinking of the essays, half a dozen or so, that I produced during this past year. But these thoughts added to my realization that my published work consists mainly of relatively short pieces—lectures, papers related to the special topics of conferences or symposia, articles for periodicals and, lately, for *Festschriften*—all written to record fresh impressions and observations and for immediate purposes.

Perhaps I have been less than a regular musicologist, for which I would like to give (mainly to myself) a number of reasons. I came to musicology at a relatively late age and without any previous training; this limited my work for a time to the restricted area of the Italian Ars nova. I worked for many years, as long as I remained in my native Sicily, in isolation from most musicological sources—hence my inured reliance on my own thinking and direct observation. I started my teaching career in a foreign country whose language I was just beginning to learn, and I learned mostly through my teaching. Yet I am aware that this is not all; deeper contributing factors to my writing style must have been my compulsive need to stay close to the concreteness of particular documents and individual works and my annoyance with the requirements of larger works, including the systematic exposition and rediscussion of already established facts and generalizations.

I recognize and willingly accept my vocation—to some extent also a literary vocation—as an essayist; but it does not follow that I consider my work to consist simply of unrelated fragments. As early as 1935, when I started to deal with the Italian sources of fourteenth-century polyphony, the thought struck me that the pieces they had preserved were like objects on the visible face of the moon. Because of the technical requirements of precise performance, those pieces, like all polyphonic works, were precisely formulated and written down and thus were placed on the lighted side. The flexible ways of monophonic music, on the other hand, from its humblest popular expressions to the most refined traditions of chivalric sung poetry, were doomed to darkness and oblivion by their almost complete disregard for notation. Although it is impossible to reconstruct an obliterated past, I have attempted on many occasions at least to assess the full visibility that monophonic music must have enjoyed in its own days as the most widespread and most immediately effective way of music making. To these attempts belong two more recent essays, one on Ars nova and Stil novo and the other on Dante (actually two lectures dating from the poet's centennial celebrations of 1965), both of which are included in this volume.

Also on the same basic theme, some of my essays have endeavored to recapture whatever "glimpses" of the unwritten tradition we may catch through what was written, through some surprising *siciliane* of the early fifteenth century and through such reflections of reflections as Bedingham's O *rosa bella* and Willaert's reelaborations of Neapolitan *canzoni villanesche*. On the other hand, I have written about my characterization of polyphony as the expression of a learned minority—clergymen and

those who shared an educational curriculum designed mainly for ec-
clesiastics—in a number of essays, including the one on the poetics of
Guido d'Arezzo and large sections of the already mentioned essay on
Dante. To go one step further, such a characterization became the leitmotif
of two longer surveys, "Music and Cultural Tendencies in Fifteenth-
Century Italy" and "Novelty and Renewal in Italy: 1300–1600," in which
I maintain that a humanistic rejection of polyphony as a scholastic art,
paralleled by the glorification of such masters of the unwritten tradition as
Leonardo Giustinian and Pietrobono dal Chitarrino, must have been a
principal cause of the seeming lack of music during one century of Italian
life—the so-called secret of the quattrocento.

To a completely different train of thought belong my operatic studies,
first started when I moved to Rome and, as a music librarian, had access to
practically all the available sources for the initial phase of the new genre
and its Roman developments. An unpublished edition of Peri's *Euridice*,
which I prepared and commented on for a radio broadcast in 1951, was
my first move to stress the importance that Peri, Caccini, and Cavalieri had
achieved, each in his own way, on the positive side of competitive
creativity, and to dismiss the assumption of their collective participation in
the theorizing of the so-called Florentine Camerata and of a unity of intent
deriving from such theorizing. Of the various writings in which I have
criticized the leveling implications of this deceptive term, I take particular
pride in the one included in this collection, "Temperaments and Tendencies in the Florentine Camerata," originally conceived as a lecture for the
Santa Cecilia Academy in Rome, which became my first English article
when its text came into the hands of Nigel Fortune, who graciously offered
to translate it for publication in *The Musical Quarterly*.

From the beginning of opera I moved in two different directions. I
looked back, to the intellectualistic and figuralistic polyphonic *maniera*
which had been still prevailing in the art music of the sixteenth century, for
signs of the new striving for emotional expression of which the discussion
of Bardi's Camerata had been but one symptom, though an important one.
The essays on Marenzio and Tasso and on Monteverdi's choice of poetic
texts for his madrigals (this essay also derived from a centennial celebration) are late representatives of this line of thought. Following a natural
chronological order, I proceeded to Monteverdi's contributions to opera,
aiming to go beyond their remote glow as masterpieces to explore their
relationship to contemporary life and art and the concrete problems of
their conception and realization, including stage realization. Two essays
show this concern in their titles, but Monteverdi is present in three other

essays as well, dealing with the facts of theatrical life as reflected in some early Venetian libretti, with the politics of rival opera houses ("The Lame Horse and the Coachman" refers to Cavalli acting as an impressario), and with one problem we now take for granted, the location of the orchestra for a theatrical performance. Monteverdi is even present in the essay on early *cavatina*, even though Falsirena was a creation of a Roman composer, Domenico Mazzocchi, in *La catena d'Adone* of 1626. The last essay in this volume gives a broad description of opera as a social phenomenon that owes its success only in part to the quality of its music; in this essay I point to a number of analogies and parallels between the operatic world (we might say "il teatro alla moda"), its performers, and its companies, and those of another successful theatrical genre, *commedia dell'arte*. I have personal reasons for attachment to this article, which also originated as a lecture, written in French for Brussels and Charles van den Borren, then translated into Italian for Rome, and retranslated by Lewis Lockwood to become my second English article. This was long ago, but Lewis has remained a dear friend, and he is one of the two people—the other being Christoph Wolff—to whom I owe my thanks for having encouraged and assisted in the publication of this book. I also want to thank the other translators of my Italian essays, particularly my friend Lowell Lindgren, who carefully checked some of my statements.

Finally, I gratefully acknowledge the assistance of the editorial staff of Harvard University Press, particularly that of senior editor Margaretta Fulton, always generous with keen interest and expert advice, and of Peg Anderson, understanding and resourceful in polishing my own prose and that of my translators.

Contents

Music and Culture in Italy
from the Middle Ages to the Baroque

1   *Musica de sono humano* and the Musical Poetics of Guido of Arezzo

Not much love was lost during the Middle Ages between music theorists and performers. The theorists arrogated to themselves the name of *musici,* while stressing that instrumentalists took their names from their instruments, the *citharoedus* from the *cithara,* the *lyricen* from the *lyra,* the *tibicen* from the *tibia,* and so on. They stated that "in every art or discipline reasoning is naturally honored above the *artificium* that is practiced by hand and toil," or even that "what takes place in instruments has nothing to do with the science and understanding of music."[1]

It seems natural that they should have had a low opinion of the instrumentalists, who as jugglers or minstrels were often assimilated into the scum of society. Anyway, the classical bias was applied to them, by which the *artista,* who possessed the knowledge of one or more of the liberal arts, took preeminence over the *artifex,* who exercised his manual skill and industry in a mechanical art. Less natural was the extension of the same bias to singers, for although Boethius considered the human voice to be an instrument, like a pipe or a bell, and included singing in the class of *musica instrumentalis,* it seems farfetched to see a singer as a mechanical worker. Yet music theorists, whose judgment of the instrumentalists was expressed in dispassionate terms, became harsher, even emotional, when they spoke of singers.

We must realize that the men we list as music theorists were usually scholars with broader interests as well. They were often abbots or bishops, or at least the *scholastici* or *praecentores* in a monastery or episcopal church, responsible in every case to some degree for the singing and teaching of music in their own institutions.[2] They had in mind their own singers, part and parcel of their daily life, and were aware that even in the ecclesiastical world, the gift of a good voice usually magnifies the ego of the owner more or less in the measure to which it dulls, if not his head, his willingness to take advice. Just as St. Jerome and St. Ambrose had once complained of singers who were in the habit of dyeing and curling their hair, Guido of Arezzo several centuries later opened his *Regulae musicae de ignoto cantu* with the passionate outburst: "In our times singers are foolish above all other men."[3]

Granted that the theorists' concern was real, the reasons they gave for complaint were mostly intellectual snobbery. Singers were blamed because "they think they can sing well just by practice, with no knowledge of the *ars;* but they do not know how to answer when asked the numerical ratio of an interval."[4] It did not matter that they could sing without mistakes and come to the proper end of a melody; despite this, their performance was compared to the "coming home of a drunkard" or to the attempts made by a blind man to hit a running dog.[5] Sternest of all was another pronouncement by Guido of Arezzo, a poetic one, which was quoted again and again by generations of theorists:

> Musicorum et cantorum magna est distantia;
> Isti dicunt, illi sciunt, quae componit Musica.
> Nam qui facit quod non sapit diffinitur bestia.[6]

But snobbery defeats itself when a theorist compares a singer to a nightingale yet refuses to recognize him as a *peritus cantor,*[7] or when another writer states that "whoever is utterly ignorant of the power and rationale of musical science boasts the name of singer in vain even though he is able to sing very well."[8]

The truth is that singers were good or bad without much help from theory. In fact, for many centuries theory had little to offer that applied to practice. Even when it went beyond its metaphysical statements about *musica mundana* and *humana*—the music of the spheres and the accord of man's soul and body—it dealt with problems either removed from actual music making or handled in an abstract way, in the apparent belief that every problem was solved for which one could give rational explanations, most often in the form of numerical ratios. More specifically, references to numerical ratios had little to do with the new problem which writers from the eighth to the eleventh century were most involved with, the definition of modal patterns and the classification of liturgical melodies according to them.

Nor were all melodic deviations from such patterns actually to be blamed on singers' faulty or arbitrary interpretations. This was the very time when the modal system, whether derived from the classical *harmoniae*, from the Byzantine *echoi*, or from both, was being used to channel toward uniformity a variegated repertory of melodies (or, should we say, melodic habits) which had been evolving during many centuries through the procedures, and in the fluid conditions, of an oral tradition. To be sure, classification and codification of the melodies was the most effective way to achieve a unified musical liturgy, short of a precise notation of pitch, which was still in the process of being perfected. Nevertheless, it must be admitted that the whole operation, a turning point in the history of Western music, was an intrusion of the theorists (representatives, we might say, of "the system") in a field which had been for centuries the exclusive domain of singers. However, numerical ratios were of no help when a decision had to be made concerning any given melody, whether the most orderly succession of pitches and intervals according to the modal theory, or the most effective according to the singers' experience and taste, should be preferred. It is most likely that the big display theorists made of them was merely intended to impress the *cantor artis expers*.[9]

Once in a while, the stiff intellectualistic approach was softened by a more sympathetic view of the facts of musical life. The example I have in mind is that of Regino, abbot of Prüm, the author of an *Epistola de harmonica institutione*, of a *Chronicon* covering events from Christ's birth to the year 906, and of a work *De synodalibus causis et disciplinis ecclesiasticis*.[10] To me, Regino is a good representative of a ninth-century Renaissance, if there was such a Renaissance. Many other theorists were polymaths and polygraphs, but few let the variety of their interests and readings show in a single work as those of Regino transpired in his *Epistola*, with the added bonus of a certain humanistic fervor and flavor.[11] This does not help the *Epistola* to be a model of organization, nor is it entirely free of the usual statements asserting the superiority of the *musicus*.[12]

It is refreshing, however, that this particular *musicus* did not pretend to have all the answers. Much as he was conversant with all the works produced to date by medieval theorists (of which there were not too many) and with the available classical literature, Regino believed that "as Music keeps most of itself concealed from both those who know and the ignorant, it is as if it was lying in a depth dense with fog."[13] A little earlier he compared the *musica institutio* to a forest, "immense and very thick, obscured by so much fog that it seems to withdraw from human recognition,"[14] an almost Dantesque topos.

What gives Regino's work such feeling? It has all the current intellectualistic equipment, mostly gathered from Boethius;[15] however, it is
selective in its use. It does not repeat, for instance, the usual tripartition of
music into *mundana, humana,* and *instrumentalis.* It does not reject it,
either, but cuts across it, dividing music into *naturalis* and *artificialis.*[16]
The latter is the equivalent of Boethius' *musica instrumentalis,* minus the
vocal music—of instrumental music, then, in a modern sense. But Regino's *musica naturalis* comprises Boethius' *musica mundana* plus a
modified view of *musica humana,* basically coinciding with what we call
vocal music—the *musica de sono humano* of my title.[17]

As a matter of fact, Regino first uses the expression *musica naturalis* in
referring to the "cantilena, quae in divinis laudibus modulatur," that is, to
plainsong.[18] Only after a description of the ecclesiastical modes does he
come back to it with a more comprehensive definition: "Natural music
does not sound because of any instrument made by man, or because of any
action of fingers, or because of any human touch or percussion, but shapes
sweet melodies by divine inspiration, with the sole guidance of nature;
such music exists in the motion of the sky and in the human voice."[19] We
have long since untuned the sky and no longer care for the cosmic aspect of
natural music. As for plainsong, if it is "Gregorian" chant, it fits the
definition, for it was thought to have been created by Saint Gregory, with
the assistance of the Holy Ghost.[20] But in our progress through Regino's
text we are brought to realize that the human side of *musica naturalis* is by
no means restricted to plainsong. "No one who is aware of himself," he
wrote, "can question that music naturally exists in conjunction with all
men, all ages and all sexes. Which age or sex does not enjoy musical
songs? . . . Children and youths as well as old people are taken by musical
modulations with such a spontaneous feeling that no age exists that has
not enjoyed sweet songs." He even goes on to quote the case of people who
cannot sing, yet "sing disagreeably something agreeable to them."[21]

How such a propensity is built into human nature, and how it works, is
what, I think, Regino regarded as an enigma, and a mystical one, for his
work seems to imply that a divine inspiration is inherent in the act by
which the soul is created. It never mentions the Boethian rational explanation that a numerical ratio links or attunes soul and body in a consonant
relationship, "quaedam coaptatio et veluti gravium leviumque vocum
quasi unam consonantiam efficiens temperatio."[22] I shall not investigate
which theological reasons are behind Regino's rejection, but rather will
content myself with stressing that trends of musical theory existed in
which musical practice was seen not only as a question of rules and skills,
but also as something related to an innate ingenuity of the human spirit.

A Christian refusal of the rationalizing interpretation of man's musical nature (now referred to Plato) was stated by Aribo, a German *scholasticus* about two centuries younger than Regino: "Quamvis non vere, verisimiliter tamen tractat Plato de animae genitura. Cum enim dupla proportio, sesquitercia, sesquialtera, sesquioctava, iucunditatem mentibus intonat, potest a gentilibus credi non incongrue animas ex eisdem proportionibus consistere."[23] Aribo was still convinced of the superiority of the *musicus*, for, as he stated, "By means of *ars*, what Mother Nature has borne rough and unpolished is made more refined."[24] But his recognition of a natural, spontaneous creativity, here merely implied, is more clearly asserted in such paragraphs as the following: "We can best appreciate how very much music is part of our blood and nature from the fact that even the jugglers, totally unaware of the *ars musica*, can warble any secular song without fault, offending no rule whatsoever in the varied disposition of tones and semitones, and reaching correctly the final note."[25] Nor was he the only writer to express such an ambivalent attitude, a mixture of admiration and disapproval, in regard to popular, instinctive ways of music making.[26]

I have used Regino's and Aribo's reluctant recognition of musical spontaneity to set the stage for the most important, indeed almost unique, musical poetics I know from the Middle Ages. Chapter 15 of the *Micrologus de disciplina artis musicae* by Guido of Arezzo[27] is a chapter most widely discussed (for reasons, however, entirely different from mine) both by medieval theorists, including Aribo, and by modern scholars. Old writers thought a few passages needed clarification;[28] more or less the same passages have been used by modern scholars to support, in turn, each one of the various theories about the rhythm of plainsong: mensuralism, proportionalism, and free rhythm.[29] The only argument I need to worry about concerns the title of the chapter. The old edition by Gerbert gives it as follows: "De commoda componenda modulatione";[30] but the latest editor, Josef Smits van Waesberghe, has found that the majority of the sources add a small word, making it: "De commoda vel componenda modulatione."[31] Smits van Waesberghe also maintains that the word "componenda" must not be taken in a modern sense and interprets it as "coniunctim ponenda."[32] His interpretation might very well fit such precepts as Guido addressed to performers, were they not already covered by the adjective "commoda." I do not see that anything short of the modern sense of composing may apply to other aspects, and I hope my reader will agree when we come to read the text of the chapter.

The word added to the title makes the translation slightly more difficult; the best I can think of is, with some freedom: "Of a good melody or how to make one." As I read it, the title already gives the gist of Guido's poetics: a new *modulatio* must be made in imitation of the best available models. Needless to say, Guido's taste was conditioned by his lifelong concern with plainsong; his idea of what makes a melody *commoda*—that is, *cum modo,* or in good taste—was too obviously dependent on what he most admired in the liturgical repertory. This was so much so that his chapter became the main source for the most essential part of a fundamental work on the aesthetics of plainsong.[33] It is pertinent to my purpose, however, to observe how he endeavored to explain in the rational terms of a medieval *ars* what he admired because of an inner feeling of beauty, as art, then, in the modern sense of the word. This I propose to do by reading through the prose of Guido's chapter, of which I have tried to render the clarity and precision in an English translation. I might have referred to the text established by Smits van Waesberghe in his critical edition, but I believe in the interpretive (and provocative) value of a translation.[34]

Just as in metrical poetry there are letters and syllables, feet and *partes* and lines, similarly also in vocal music[35] there are *phthongi,* that is, sounds, one, two, or three of which are combined to make syllables; and these [syllables], singly or in pairs, form a *neuma,* that is, one *pars* of the *cantilena;* and one *pars,* or more, make a *distinctio,* that is, a suitable place for breathing. Concerning which things, the following needs to be observed, that the whole *pars* must be written and uttered all together (*compresse*), the syllable even more so (*compressius*). But the *tenor,* that is the sustaining (*mora*) of the last note (which is short in the syllable, longer in the *pars,* and very long in the *distinctio*), is the mark in them of their division.

This is a preamble, in which a description is given first of the components of a melody and then of the longer and shorter stops marking their articulation.[36] For the former, an analogy which had already been hinted at by other theorists is not only enlarged but specifically referred to metrical poetry, whereas it had been previously referred to language in general.[37] The purpose of this shift will become apparent when the analogy is resumed in the next section, which is, I must warn, the most controversial in the whole chapter.

And thus, the *cantilena* ought to be scanned as if it were in metrical feet, and certain sounds ought to have a lengthening (*morula*) twice as long or twice as short as others, or else a *tremula,* that is a *varius* [vibrato?] *tenor,* which sometimes is shown to be long by a horizontal line placed above the letter.[38] And by all means such a distribution of the *neumae* ought to be observed (the *neumae* being formed either by the repetition of the same sound or by the connection of two or more) as to let them always be related to each other, either in the number of sounds or in the proportion of the *tenores,* and respond [to each other] now like equal to equal, now like double, or triple, to simple, and others in a *sesquialtera* or a *sesquitertia* proportion.

With all respect to eminent scholars who have given this matter much more thought than I have, it is my impression that controversy has unnecessarily arisen around this passage out of a comprehensible eagerness to take advantage of every available bit of information to foster the solution of a very important musicological problem. But can precise conclusions be inferred from an analogical description? Guido repeatedly stresses that the parallel with metrical poetry is an analogy, evidently intended to justify his rationalization of the kind of balanced proportion he would have liked to find in a good melody. The suggestion made in the paragraphs I have just quoted is that a balance or proportion should already be present in the number of sounds forming each *neuma;* if not— and this might be a suggestion addressed to performers—it should be forced on the *neumae, partes,* and *distinctiones* by means of different lengths given to their *tenores.*

What is most important for our purpose (and further clarifies the motive dictating the analogy) is once more that an ingrained habit of the medieval mind translates the artistic need for balance into precise numerical ratios. Not surprisingly, those mentioned by Guido are the very ones by which perfect consonances are produced between two pitches: *porportio dupla,* producing the octave; *tripla,* producing the fifth above the octave, that is, the twelfth; *sesquialtera,* producing the fifth; and *sesquitertia,* producing the fourth. The connection is made even more evident by Fig. 1.1.[39] Thus, the same principle by which the harmony of the cosmos, the orderly succession of the seasons, and the *coaptatio* of soul and body are ruled must also be applied by the *melopoieta* to the temporal ordering of his melody.

The sentences I am going to quote next give evidence, if any is needed, that composing in the modern sense was very much in Guido's mind. Then comes a rare moment of truth in which he seems about to admit that not everything is crystal clear in the would-be all-rational world of his *ars.* The disturbing thought, however, is immediately supplanted by a brilliant sophism, adroitly reconciling reason and aesthetic pleasure.

Let the *musicus* propose to himself in which of these divisions he will make his *cantus* proceed, just as the *metricus* [proposes to himself] in which feet he will cast his verse, except that the *musicus* will not bind himself to an equally stringent law,

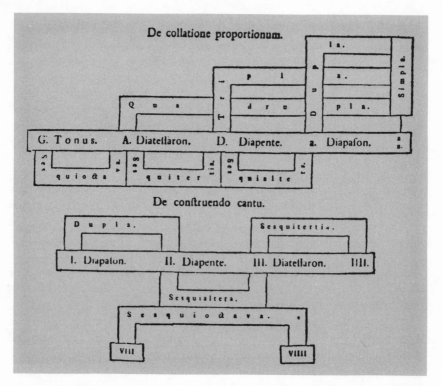

Fig. 1.1 "De construendo cantu," according to Gerbert, *Scriptores ecclesiastici de musica*, vol. II, p. 15.

for his *ars* diversifies itself in everything with a rational variety in the disposition of sounds. We may often not understand such rationality, *yet that is thought to be rational in which the mind, the seat of reason, takes pleasure.* But such things and similar ones are better shown in spoken words than in writing.

It is a narrow escape, after which Guido, having settled the point of what we can describe as a quantitative balancing and proportioning of melodic parts, has much easier going in prescribing procedures by which a qualitative balance, that is, a unified melodic style, can be achieved:

Therefore, it is convenient that the *distinctiones* be comparable among them like *versus* and sometimes repeated just the same, or else modified by some small variation; and then[40] they would be very beautiful if they were repeated having *partes* not too different, and if similar ones were changed in regard to their modes, or were made (*inveniantur*) similar but higher or lower. Also [it is convenient] that a *neuma reciprocata* should go back the same way it came and by the same steps; and also that, whatever turn or line one [*neuma*] makes in leaping from the high range, the second should repeat just the same, but from an inverted direction, answering from the low range, as happens when we watch our image reflected in a well. Also [it is convenient] that one syllable should have at times one or more *neumae,* and that one *neuma* should be split at times into many syllables. These and indeed all *neumae* shall be diversified, some being made to begin from the same note, others from one that is different according to different qualities of gravity and acuity. Also [it is convenient] that almost all *distinctiones* should move toward the principal note, that is, the *finalis* [of the mode], or toward any note related to it which they may have chosen in its stead; and that the same note [the *finalis* or its substitute], as it ends [all] the *neumae* [that is, ends the melody] and many *distinctiones,* similarly should sometimes also begin them;[41] which things, if you are curious, you may find in Ambrose.

I shall not embark on a detailed comment on the techniques by which, according to Guido's sharply worded advice, variety should be afforded and integrity of melodic style still preserved. All but two of the devices he prescribes can be easily verified in the liturgical repertory,[42] the two exceptions being, as far as I know, those that later came to be known as, respectively, crab canon (Guido's *neuma reciprocata*) and mirror canon (Guido did not have a name for it, but the later term is clearly fore-shadowed by his reference to the image reflected in a well). Even these are so vividly described that I surmise there should be models for them somewhere, even though they have not been recognized.

In the following sentences the parallel with metrical poetry is insisted upon—actually even buttressed by a second one with prose—and yet confirmed to be an analogy, not an identification. And thus we come to the passage in which Guido, having previously defined his ideal of harmonious quantitative balance, adds to it the requirement of qualitative consonance, unifying the melodic style of the new composition:

To be sure, there are *cantus* resembling prose which pay less attention to such things and in which it does not matter whether larger and smaller *partes* and *distinctiones* are found everywhere without a rule, in the manner of proses. On the contrary, I speak of metrical *cantus* because we often sing in such way as to seem to be scanning *versus* into feet, as when we sing real *metra*. In which [*cantus*] we must avoid having too many two-syllable *neumae* follow each other without a mingling of three- or four-syllable ones. For, just as the lyrical poets combine sometimes certain feet, sometimes others, similarly those who make a *cantus* combine *neumae* rationally selected and diversified. In fact, there is a rational criterion when a moderate variety of *neumae* and *distinctiones* is so arranged that *neumae* respond to *neumae* and *distinctiones* to *distinctiones,* always in consonance because of some resemblance, that is, in such way as to create a *similitudo dissimilis,* in the manner of sweetest Ambrose.[43] In fact, there is no little resemblance between *metra* and *cantus*—if the *neumae* stand in place of feet, and the *distinctiones* of lines—inasmuch as the *neuma* flows in a dactylic, that one in a spondaic, the other in an iambic meter, and you can see that the *distinctiones* are now tetrametrical, now pentametrical, and at another place, as it were, hexametrical, and many other things likewise.

One last point I wish to bring to the reader's attention is what Guido has to say about the relationship between words and music:

Also [it is convenient] that the *partes* and *distinctiones* of [both] *neumae* and words should end at the same time. Nor should a long *tenor* on some short syllables, or a short one on some long [syllables], give offense, which fact, although unusual, shall be taken care of. Also [it is convenient] that the effect of the *cantio* [on the audience] be in imitation of the topic (*rerum eventus*), so that the *neumae* shall be grievous in sad matters, pleasant in quiet things, joyous in happy ones, and so on.

It would have been difficult to explain rationally what makes the *neumae* grievous, pleasant, or joyous, but Guido goes on to the next topic without even attempting to settle this one, with another of his masterly sophisms. Previously, it seems to me he gave vent to the concern for prosodic observance of the classically oriented grammarian in support of his own aesthetic need for harmonious proportions; here he just pays lip service to some faint, though persistent, reminiscence of the classical ethos.[44] As I have already pointed out, Guido's poetics, like his aesthetics, were those of plainsong; the melodies he spoke about, whether models or newly composed imitations, were meant for liturgical use. Now I am aware I am about to make a generalization, bound, like all generalizations, to have exceptions; yet it seems to me that liturgical music was not so much intended to express the contrition of the sinner or the suffering of the martyr as to exalt the power bestowed on the Church to bring salvation to the former and celestial glory to the latter. Liturgical music essentially celebrates the celebration and seldom has any need for the kind of emotionalism which became the artistic concern of later times. Accordingly, Guido's prescriptions, fashioned on his models, need to be taken with a grain of salt; the equivocal assimilation of *effectus* and *affectus* is still far off in the future.

More tangible than a concern for emotional intensity is Guido's deep feeling for the effectiveness of the performance. His advice is now mainly addressed to the singers, in whose behalf such time-honored musical devices as *crescendo, diminuendo,* and *rallentando* are described with clarity and no attempt at rationalization.[45] Less familiar to us, the singing of liquescent sounds on liquescent syllables is brought nearer to our experience as a kind of *portamento,* which also makes Guido's wary attitude toward such graces easier to understand. The final sentence of the chapter is one last appeal to the intuitive *discretio* of good taste.

Also, we often superimpose an accent, grave and [or?] acute, on the sounds, for we often utter them with greater or lesser force, to such extent that the repetition of the same sound often seems to be a raise or a descent.[46] Also [it is convenient] that the sounds come near to the place of breathing, at the end of the *distinctiones,* in the manner of a running horse, as if they were dragging tiredly to get a rest. Of which dragging the arrangement of the written notes (*notae compositae*) might often give a hint, if they are set thickly or sparsely as needed.[47] Finally, sounds, like letters, become often liquescent, so that the initial pitch of one, trespassing smoothly into the other, does not even seem to be ending. Hence, we place a dot like a spot on the liquescent note.[48] But if you want to pronounce it more fully, and not liquescent, it does no harm, for this is often liked better. And do all that we have said neither too seldom nor too often, but with good judgment.

Even though Guido's writings enjoyed wide distribution, his poetics remained to a great extent isolated. Among the theorists who followed him, Aribo included extensive quotations from, and commentaries on, Chapter 15 of the *Micrologus* in a chapter entitled "De oportunitate modulandi" of his own *De musica;* but he was mainly concerned with prescriptions made by Guido in order to introduce, or improve, quantitative proportions in a melody—that is, with the performance aspect. In this regard Aribo's first sentence sounds like one of approval: "The beauty of singing is doubled if the *neumae* and the *distinctiones* are proportionally related in the way in which the sounds of the monochord are arranged, as taught by dom Guido."[49] Yet only a little later, he comes to the conclusion that such practices, beautiful as they may be are a thing of the past: "In former times, great attention was paid, not only by the composers of *cantus,* but also by the singers themselves, that they should invent and sing everything applying proportions. Such consideration died long ago, [and] indeed is buried."[50] In a later addition to his treatise, also dealing with Guido's chapter, Aribo hints of some "obscuras Guidonis sententias," argues about them with an earlier commentator, but never comes to terms with the real substance of Guido's poetics.[51]

After Aribo, or about the same time, Johannes Affligemensis comes nearer to Guido's intentions in two chapters (XVIII and XIX) of his *De musica,* entitled, respectively, "Praecepta de cantu componendo" and "Quae sit optima modulandi forma."[52] His skepticism in regard to

Guido's passionate striving for artistic poise and balance (or at least in regard to the ways to achieve them) can be gathered *ex argumento silentii*. In Johannes' chapter XVIII, the basic prescription comes first that the *cantus* should be varied "secundum sensum verborum," but also according to which audience they are meant to please (gone is Guido's dedication to an ideal of liturgical beauty).[53] Then the "laudis cupidus modulator" is warned against monotony, or, in Johannes' words, against the "vitium similium tonorum," parallel to the "vitium similium casuum" avoided by the poets.[54] Chapter XIX touches lightly upon the need for the melody to pause "ubi sensus verborum distinctionem facit," then plunges into a lengthy discussion of which sounds and intervals ought to be preferred in each mode, partially a duplication of previous chapters.[55] Nothing is left of the poetic afflatus sweeping through Guido's prose and its rationalizations. Even much later, Machaut's *Remède de Fortune* or the *Règles de seconde rhétorique* dealt with matching musical and poetic forms, but had little to say about music itself.

Guido's isolation is partly explained by the changing times and musical taste. The creation of new liturgical offices was a rare event, while new forms of ecclesiastical music, such as the sequence and the monophonic conductus, were becoming fashionable and were ruled by different poetics—not to speak of polyphony, which was soon to capture the main interest of music theorists. New tastes may have brought about new confrontations between the humanistic principle of *dulcedo* and *subtilitas*, or the sophistication of music through symbolic or rationalizing devices, but few theorists were as pragmatically motivated as Guido to come out of their ivory towers and let their feelings for beauty transpire through the intellectualizing equipment of music theory.[56] Guido not only did it, but he came near to adding a new expression, *irrationalis ratio*, to such favorite medieval oxymora as *concordia discors* or his own *similitudo dissimilis*.

2 Dante *Musicus:* Gothicism, Scholasticism, and Music

In recent years I have spoken several times on the subject "Notre Dame, University, and Music," without ever committing my ideas to paper. The fact is that I found it quite easy to stress the coincidence of date and purpose that existed between the building of the new Parisian cathedral, begun in 1163, and the composition of a polyphonic cycle for use there during the liturgical year. It was also relatively easy to point out internal and external evidence showing that the further development of that polyphony and its main outgrowth, the motet of the thirteenth century, were under the powerful cultural influence of the newly institutionalized University of Paris. But it was clear to me that I was avoiding the more difficult and necessary task of recognizing the spiritual congruity and cultural continuity that must have existed between those expressions of a single society, a Gothic cathedral, a scholastic approach to knowledge and faith, and the then new style of music now variously labeled Notre Dame polyphony or Ars antiqua.

Having planned such an attempt, not without some hesitation, as an homage to Dante in the seventh centennial of his birth,[1] and having selected "Gothicism, Scholasticism, and Music" as a possible title, I suddenly realized I might have already found some guidance for the still uncharted progress of my writing. It occurred to me that there was a study—one I had read years ago—in which the relationship between "Gothic Architecture and Scholasticism" had been investigated.[2] This relationship—I cannot do better than quote—"is more concrete than a mere 'parallelism' and yet more general than those individual (and very important) 'influences' which are inevitably exerted on the painters, sculptors or architects by erudite advisers."[3] I thus realized the subconscious plagiarism of my title, a plagiarism of which I was by no means ashamed when it became conscious. On the contrary, I was and am happy to acknowledge the author of that valuable essay as my Vergil in the present venture.

I must warn my reader, however, that any easy parallelism with the parallel-avoiding study of Erwin Panofsky is immediately barred by both the nature and status of medieval music. Medieval architecture was always the creation of a high-ranking and highly cultured patron and of the architect, or a small body of master builders. Philosophy, too, was the concern of a small minority, even if we include teachers and students of logic and dialectics. But music, at least medieval music, had two sides, on one of which—that of sounding music—everybody seemed to have some claim, while only learned people had any knowledge of the other, no less important side, of music theory. Nor do the differences end there. The cathedral, once it had been erected under the direction of the few (its formal cause), stood there in its majestic presence, offering to the many the age's most impressive example of man-made durability, a model whose artistic lesson deeply affected the taste of entire generations. Scholastic thinking, too, a refinement and deeper realization of the universal process of thought, always descended from the highest speculation to influence and permeate everyday and everyone's thought through aphorisms, proverbs, and innumerable applications to practical matters. From the dichotomy of music, on the other hand, a gap originated at this very time between art music, the music of and for the few, and everyone's music, a gap no following age has ever succeeded in bridging.[4] To this double dichotomy between music and its theory, and between the artistic and common practice of music, we must finally add that whatever piece of music has reached us from the past has done so in the form of a faint, imprecise impression on the unyielding medium of musical notation, while its actual sound must have acted on the souls of its listeners as a vibration does on a responsive string.

As a man of culture Dante was keenly aware of the first dichotomy. Indeed, he knew music, first of all, as one of the liberal arts. Its invention, attributed by a classic tradition to Pythagoras, by the followers of a patristic trend to Tubalcain, was never meant as the invention of song, playing, and dance, which humanity had enjoyed since creation. Rather, it was meant as the beginning of a mathematical appraisal of those activities. In turn, the mathematical appraisal of music appeared to be the clue to an all-pervading system of numerical relationships, underlying, signifying, and unifying the physical and metaphysical structure of the universe. Thus

Music took her place among the mathematical arts of the Quadrivium, second only to Arithmetic, which is the science of *multitudo per se,* or numbers in themselves, while the others are sciences of *multitudo ad aliquid,* or applied numbers. Yet, such was the magnitude of Music's *aliquid* that she could have claimed for herself the crown among the arts as a source of universal knowledge. According to the most common pattern of classification,[5] the first of her great divisions was *Musica mundana,* the music of the universe, dealing with the harmonious numerical relationships of planetary and stellar orbits, or of the quintessential crystalline spheres supporting those orbits. Consideration of the four elements and the four seasons also came under the heading of *Musica mundana,* while the harmonious coexistence of soul and body and their various faculties was the subject of *Musica humana,* the music of human nature. Last, and least, came *Musica instrumentalis* or *organica,* under which were considered the character and effects of musical sound produced either by the natural instrument of the human voice or by various artificial means, such as strings, pipes, or percussion instruments.

In practice, however, the greatest portion of this domain was stripped away from Music. Legitimately, the mathematical aspects, that is, numerical proportions, fell under the teaching of Arithmetic. But much larger sections of both *Musica mundana* and *humana* were usurped by the extensive, more detailed, and more "applied" treatment they received under the two branches of Astronomy, *astrologia de motibus* and *astrologia de effectibus,* the study of stellar motions and of their influence on the character and actions of men. With minor parts of Music also falling under the domain of meteorology and ethics, it was left to her to deal with either or both of two items: first, the mathematical determination of musical pitches and intervals, called "the Monochord" from the instrument on which they could have been practically demonstrated, and second, the analysis and classification of plainchant melodies, clearly a medieval addition.

This sharply defines not only the foundation but also the limits under which the artistic practice of music was to be conceived for many centuries. Liturgical music was a tradition not only officially sanctioned by the Church but also believed to have been dictated to Saint Gregory by divine inspiration. Yet its tradition was not absolutely inflexible; it admitted local variants and did not entirely repress creativity, musical as well as verbal, as is attested to by tropes and sequences, by the history of some parts of the Ordinary of the Mass, and by the occasional addition to the liturgical repertory of newly composed offices for newly canonized saints.[6] It left outside, however, the much larger fields open to musical creativity in extraliturgical activities such as sacred drama, *lauda,* and all kinds of secular music, including some that we should like, indeed, to consider artistic manifestations, as, for instance, troubadour song.

I doubt that even the latter could qualify as artistic under any interpretation of the medieval concept of *ars.* I need only recall the Boethian distinction, faithfully insisted upon during the Middle Ages and never challenged until the fifteenth century, according to which three categories of men have to do with music: *cantores,* including all kind of performers, instrumentalists as well as singers; *poetae,* who blend together words and melody; and finally *musici,* the true artists, that is, the music theorists.[7] Only to the latter do knowledge and reason give a real understanding of musical things; the others are guided only by usage or mechanical skill or, in the case of poets, by some inborn, intuitive faculty that leads them, without their knowing why, to reproduce the harmonious ways of macrocosm and microcosm, of nature and soul. Dante's *De vulgari eloquentia* is an attempt to raise the legacy of troubadour music to the level of an art, either as union of words and music, or as purely verbal music, *musica rhythmica.*[8]

The man who, about one century before Dante's birth, first laid the foundations on which the main tradition of artistic polyphony was to be built must have deemed himself a *musicus,* not merely a *cantor.* A quirk of fortune has preserved his name but no precise indication of the way in which he may have been attached to the strange world of the chapter of Notre Dame in Paris.[9] In 1182, however, when the choir of the new cathedral had just been vaulted and closed by its chancel, and the main altar consecrated, Magister Leoninus must have already presented his bishop with the original body of the *Magnus Liber Organi de Graduali et Antiphonario,*[10] a collection of two-voice polyphonic settings, or *organa,*[11] for the Graduals, Alleluias, and Vesper responsories of the major feasts in the Parisian liturgical calendar.[12]

In many ways Leoninus' work was a product of *Ars musica.* Essential to it, and spiritually vital, was the continued presence of the proper liturgical melodies. Yet they are slowed down to the point of losing their melodic impact and cast in long-sustained notes, which suggested the name *tenor*—the voice that holds, but also the voice that guides—for the part that carried them, leading then modern writers to compare these long-held notes of the *tenores* to pillars supporting the melodic arc of the *vox organica,* the newly composed voice.[13] The latter, though freely invented, had to provide a basically concordant comment to the plainchant, involving naturally all the numerical proportions corresponding to consonant intervals: 1 / 1 for the unison, 2 / 1 for the octave, 3 / 2 for the fifth, 4 / 3 for the fourth. Even more striking are the temporal aspects. As the architectural plan of a medieval cathedral was oriented with intentional symbolism toward the rising sun, similarly the plan of the musical cathedral opens with the season of Nativity and encompasses the year according to the cycle of the liturgical, not merely the seasonal, calendar. Newer, however, than this attunement to the rhythm of macrocosm is the introduction of rhythmic "modes" to give an "order" to the succession of musical sounds.

Musicologists, though they may disagree on details, agree that the plainchant had what we describe as a free rhythm. A regularity of rhythm may have existed in some forms of popular song or dance music. But whoever first thought of casting polyphony into *ordines* determined by certain *modi* had in mind no secular or popular tastes but the desire, characteristic of the time, to introduce *ars,* that is, rationality, into whatever had to do with serious subjects. That such rationality was not already present in the plainchant did not matter, for plainchant was revelation, inscrutable to the human mind. An authoritative source for the tight system of *modi* and *ordines* may have been, though we lack precise evidence, a great name and a great work, Saint Augustine's *De musica.*[14] And the trend of Augustinian thought that led to it may have been suggested by the school of Saint Victor, with which the chapter and the founder of Notre Dame, Maurice de Sully himself, entertained friendly relationships.

I can only outline here the development of artistic polyphony. As in the case of many a stone cathedral, the design of the musical one had already been enlarged and partially modified at the turn of the twelfth century by a second and even more prolific composer, a Magister Perotinus.[15] Perotinus is said to have shortened some of Leoninus' settings and to have composed settings for more feasts and new substitutes for the old ones, no longer in two-voice, but in three- and even four-voice polyphony. We may say—if I am allowed to continue my metaphor—that Perotinus expanded the ideal musical apse by doubling the *circulus anni* and raising its vaulting higher. In contrast to Leoninus, said to have been "melior organista," Perotinus is described as "melior discantista," which means that even more than Leoninus he strengthened the aspects of precise rhythm and temporal rationality.[16]

Little was added to the main structure of the Notre Dame polyphonic repertory after Perotinus,[17] but the new generations attended to its decoration with ardor. There are passages in Leoninus' and Perotinus' *organa* in which a long melisma on a single syllable in the basic plainchant melody allows the composer to involve even the liturgical *tenor* in the strict rhythmic and melodic organization of the other parts. Organized repetitions of such fragments of the *tenor* expanded the *clausulae,* as these special sections were called. It became an accepted practice to make the *clausulae* into independent sections, interchangeable with others in which the same melismatic segment of the *tenor* was differently organized and harmonized to new melodies of the other parts, so that while the tradition of the *Liber organi* was faithfully observed and continued, an element of artistic novelty was always made possible by the introduction of newly composed *clausulae.*[18]

The special attention paid to the *clausulae*—not by the public at large but by the ecclesiastic "coetus"[19]—is made even more evident by the next step by which it became customary to provide them with a new text, according to a procedure no different from that, well known to the medievalists, of troping. Should we want to push our architectural metaphor further, we might compare the troped *clausulae* to windows in which stained-glass figurations were inserted, were not the transparency of those figurations clouded by the fact that, while the basic plainchant remained untroped, different tropes were added to each of the other voices of the polyphonic composition.[20] In the case of three-voice or four-voice polyphony, two or three different texts were superimposed simultaneously on the liturgical one. For, as each voice had its individual melody (or individual melodic trope), it seemed rational that each should have its individual verbal expression; in the same line of reasoning, as the different melodic lines were woven into a consonant polyphonic texture, it seemed proper that their verbal tropes should voice variations of the same basic meaning, forming, texturally as well as musically, a diversified concordance, a *concordia discors.*

In the final step of this process the sharply delimited and interchangeable troped *clausulae* came to be considered independent compositions, or *moteti,* which were not always, or even seldom, performed in their original liturgical frame.[21] Long before the late thirteenth century or the beginning of the fourteenth century, when we presume Dante visited Paris, the motet had ceased being a liturgical composition, although sacred motets could still be used in the liturgy. It had become essentially a secular genre, often using vernacular texts, and reflecting the polemics, the meditations, and even more often the sports of the masters and students of the now independent university.[22] But just as the university still preserved the traces of its origin in the cathedral schools, the motet, while it portrayed the modes and moods of its composers and listeners, still betrayed its liturgical origin in the almost constant use of plainchant melodies as its *tenores* and in the constant symbolism, at times a sly one, which binds the chosen *tenor* to the concepts expressed in the various texts of the other parts.[23]

I have already acknowledged Professor Panofsky as my Vergil. His study analyzes the *modus operandi* of some Gothic architects and, comparing it to the *modus operandi* of scholastic thinkers, proceeds inductively to assert the identity of their *modus essendi*. Following in his path, I have tried to reach similar conclusions from the *modus operandi* of the Gothic musicians. There is no want, in their case, of theoretical writings in the usual forms of "Positiones," "Lucidaria," "Specula," and "Summae," all giving unequivocal evidence of scholastic dialectics in their arguments. I have therefore preferred to insist on the image of the musical cathedral, but also to insist on calling it a metaphor, not a parallelism.[24] For if it has been useful to stress the synchronism of the musical events, the building of Notre Dame, and the emancipation of the university, more essential than the superficial and arbitrary resemblances is the identity of the *forma mentis,* interlacing the constant urge for rationality with a persistent recourse to symbolic analogies. The nature of this writing prevents me from going into technical details but gives me one advantage over Panofsky's path-finding essay. It makes it possible to indicate *per essemplo* what can hardly be reached through a purely analytical procedure. This is the strong determination of the great Gothic artist behind the lucidity of his rationalization, the heat of his passion behind the power of his will, and in turn, closing the circle, the clarity of the truth—gained through either knowledge or faith—that stirred his passion and sharpened his will.

No human rational process can ever be totally free of emotional elements—not even the computer's, for the monster "feeds" on human blood. But it is in the nature of the Gothic artist, in his *modus essendi,* to identify his faith with his passion, and his passion with the hard-won conquest of a rational truth. From which, reversing the process, his *modus operandi* descends, engaged in the challenge of the most arduous technical problems the more the truth to be expressed is dear to him.

Music ranks high in Dante's set of values, if we may judge from the wealth and variety of the images he derives from it. It would appear, according to a well-known passage of *Il convivio,* that the sound of music cast a spell on him comparable only to the power of abstraction exerted by the exalted imagination of his fantasy, by the

> ... imaginativa che ne rube
> talvolta sì di fuor, ch'om non s'accorge
> perché d'intorno suonin mille tube.
>   (*Purgatorio,* XVII, 13–15)

Above and beyond the poignancy of his personal musical experiences, Dante was aware, however, that the effects exerted by sounding music on him and on most human beings (as well as, according to myths constantly repeated and cherished, on animals and inanimate objects) were but consequences of a superior truth, weakly reflected by the opaqueness of man-made music. It is not, therefore, from one or another pointed musical image, it is not from "lo guizzo della corda," the quivering immediacy of the similes with which the great *citarista* "catches the eye to possess the mind" that we may judge the place of music in the complex system of his thought, but mainly from the considered care with which music is structured in the structure of the *Comedia.*

Rightly there is no reference to music in the first *cantica*. Inferno, the physical center of Dante's universe, but the farthest from the spiritual center that lies outside the orderly physical cosmos, is by definition the realm of disharmony. In the words of Dante, who combines the ideas of eternal confinement and lack of harmony with his usual forcefulness, Inferno is a "cattivo coro" (*Inferno,* III, 37). Its jarring noise is described just after the lines that proclaim the inexorable sentence engraved on its gates:

> Parole di dolore, accenti d'ira,
> voci alte e fioche, e suon di man con elle,
> facevano un tumulto, il qual s'aggira
> sempre in quell'aria senza tempo tinta,
> come la rena quando turbo spira.
>   (*Inferno,* III, 25–30)

The sound of Limbo is only a prelude, yet it is so fierce that the poet is forced to weep. Later on in the descending journey, a musical instrument is recalled, but only to describe the abhorrent shape of a lost soul, Master Adam of Brescia (*Inferno,* XXX, 49–51). Even deeper, at the bottom of the chasm, the parody of a liturgical hymn—more symbolic than ironic according to one interpretation[25]—heralds the presence of the prince of darkness: "Vexilla regis prodeunt inferni" (*Inferno,* XXXIV, 1).

It is by no means accidental that music regains its voice when the stars shine again on Dante's head, for from their power, "received from above and imparted below" (*Purgatorio*, II, 123), diversity is created according to a design, diversity and design from which music arises. The Purgatory is full of sounding music—*musica instrumentalis,* according to the Boethian distinction already mentioned. Yet it is not a proper place for the pleasures of music. Cato's harsh reproaches soon break the spell of Casella's song (*Purgatorio*, II, 106–120), and thereafter only such *musica instrumentalis* is heard as is instrumental to the purgation and perfection of the soul, to the full realization of the highest values of *musica humana.* Thus, prevailing in the Purgatory is either the sound of psalms or, still attuned to the stern recitation of psalm tunes, that of other religious texts, mainly derived from Saint Matthew's account of the Sermon on the Mount. Yet, in spite of the accent he places on penance and hope, Dante finds opportunity to give examples of all the ways in which music affects the human soul. Dante's own *canzone, Amor che nella mente mi ragiona,* the song of Casella mentioned earlier, indicates music's power of soothing and diverting the mind; the hymn *Te lucis ante terminum,* properly sung at Compline in the Valley of the Princes, brings comfort to the souls and fortifies them against the nocturnal temptations; on the other hand, the dream of the Siren warns against the spiritual dangers of music's misuse; and finally, the singing of Lia is a symbol of the power given to music of stirring and spurring men to action.

Hardest, as we all know, is the approach to Paradise. Dante, no longer content with the assistance of the Muses, invokes the help of Apollo, the full light of knowledge. The *artes,* too, are at his side: Astronomy to suggest the world's geocentric structure and the order of the planets, and Geometry to help him repeatedly to locate himself in his journey. He seems to dispense with Arithmetic, for a poet is seldom bound to exact figures; but we know that his neglect is only apparent, for figures and numerical symbolism are essential and central to the structure of the poem. I shall not investigate, however, the musical analogies or implications into which this demiurgical aspect of Dante's numerology might lead us. More obviously the higher level of music, *musica mundana,* makes its appearance from the very beginning of the heavenly journey, for Dante's "trasumanar," his experience, in the first canto of *Paradiso,* of a transcending beyond humanity that "cannot be expressed in words," has as its first connotation the perception of the divine illumination and of the harmony that rules the world. The terms in which the latter is described, "con l'armonia che temperi e discerni" (*Paradiso,* I, 78), are strictly technical, for "temperi" indicates the action of tuning, and "discerni" is a precise reference to the "numerus discretus" by which each musical pitch is determined.[26]

Commentators have interpreted this line as referring to a sounding music of the spheres, and the following passage, in which "the novelty of the sound" is mentioned, as confirming their interpretation. From the general context, however, it seems evident to me that "la novità del suono e 'l grande lume" (*Paradiso*, I, 82) can refer only to the realm of fire through which Dante and Beatrice are swiftly moving in their ascent. No other passage of the last *cantica* gives even a hint of a musical sound produced by the heavenly spheres. Moreover, the concept of a powerful yet monotonous and, after all, unmusical "music of the spheres" had been disclaimed by two of Dante's most admired authorities: Aristotle and Saint Thomas.[27] In Dante's Paradise the concept of an audible cosmic harmony is again denied by the silence reigning in the seventh heaven, the sphere of Saturn, which, we should remember, he had associated with Astronomy in *Il convivio*. Here, in canto XXI of *Paradiso*, he makes it the abode of the contemplative saints, experiencing the ideal harmony of divine perfection through spiritual sublimation, not through their senses. The harmony of the divine conception of the universe is not expressed by a single, gigantic chord, powerful as its sound might be, but by spiritual proportions and by the fitness—*coaptatio* is the scholastic term—of all its infinite components. On the basis of this lesson we should list under the heading of *musica mundana* the concordant diversity, the *coaptatio*, in the *Comedia* of everything that aims to convey the idea of the divine, and all the parts of its poetic structure that are modeled after the symbols of divine perfection. Again, I shall not attempt such a global task, but only try to reach conclusions from the music that sounds, from heaven to heaven and from canto to canto, in Paradise.

Needless to say, the accent is on *ars*. After Cacciaguida has asserted himself as the most fluent speaker in the three *cantiche*, a Florentine in all aspects, Dante calls on him to show "qual era tra i cantor del cielo artista" (*Paradiso*, XVIII, 51), how great an artist he was among the heavenly singers. Again and again the idea of melodic perfection is combined with the image of a revolving circle: "cosi la circulata melodia / si sigillava" (*Paradiso*, XXIII, 109–110) is said of the singing of Gabriel to the Virgin,[28] that singing so ineffably beautiful that

> Qualunque melodia più dolce suona
> qua giù, e più a sé l'anima tira,
> parrebbe nube che squarciata tuona,
> comparata al sonar di quella lira.
> (*Paradiso*, XXIII, 97–100)

It is no mere chance that the heavenly singing is for the first time associated with a threefold circular dance of fulgent lights in canto X, when the first ring of theologians surrounds "with looks of love" the symbol of divine truth, Beatrice. Reason and exalted imagination make musical perfection most meaningful and most perfectly expressed when associated with the splendors of illumination and the perfection of circular motion, the whole attuned to the mystic perfection of the ternary number. Now I do not need to stress that ternary rhythm, as the one that better expressed divine perfection, was one of the basic tenets of thirteenth-century polyphony, strenuously asserted in theory and in practice against the wantonness, the *lascivia,* of binary rhythm.[29] Even more evocative is that the idea of a concentric motion, with a low and slow *tenor,* and the various parts added to it moving the higher the faster,[30] seems to have dictated, at least for a certain time, the overall rhythmic structure of the polyphonic motet. We may describe it in Dante's words:

> E come cerchi in tempra d'orioli
> si giran sì che 'l primo a chi pon mente
> quieto pare, e l'ultimo che voli,
> così quelle carole differente-
> mente danzando, della sua ricchezza
> mi faceno stimar, veloci e lente.
> (*Paradiso,* XXIV, 13–18)

The idea of circular motion is present unequivocally in the polyphonic *rota,* as well as in the earliest form of the Italian *caccia,*[31] in both of which the various voices chase each other along the lines of a melody common to all and eventually resume it from the beginning in what could become virtually a perpetual circling motion. Some suggestion of a similar polyphonic performance is offered by Dante at the beginning of the twelfth canto of *Paradiso,* when to the first singing circle of theologians a second adds its wheeling, "matching motion with motion and song with song" ("e moto a moto, e canto a canto colse," *Paradiso,* XII, 6), or later, when the triad of Dominions, Virtues, and Powers

> perpetualemente "Osanna" sberna
> con tre melode, che suonano in tree
> ordini di letizia onde s'interna.
> (*Paradiso,* XXVIII, 118–120)

Similarly, the wheeling and singing of the three burning flames, the Apostles Peter, James, and John, are described as "the sweet blending of

sound made by the threefold breath" ("il dolce mischio/che si facea nel
suon del trino spiro," *Paradiso,* XXV, 131–132).

Nor are these the only hints of polyphony, to which the third *cantica*
refers most clearly, although only in the form of a poetic simile, in canto
VIII: "e come voce in voce si discerne /quando una é ferma e l'altra va e
riede" (*Paradiso,* VIII, 17–18). This passage, recalling as it does Leoninus'
organa with the description of one voice that holds while the other now
moves away, now comes near, may indicate that Dante's experiences with
polyphony consisted mainly of his Parisian reminiscences. Yet, we must
not forget that a few French motets are included in a Florentine *laudario,*[32]
and polyphonic music still survives that was sung in the cathedral of Padua
during Dante's own time.[33] Nor are these the only examples of early
polyphonic music in Italian sources. At any rate, even though Dante's
exposure to polyphony may not have been too extensive, his mind was
certainly impressed with the realization that more musical knowledge was
required for its making than for any of the more familiar monophonic
genres.

We must assume that for Dante, as for the musicians of Notre Dame,
polyphony is the exalted projection of plainchant, no longer limited in
Paradise to recitative tones or penitential texts, but ranging through the
whole scale of divine praise, with tunes that are sweeter, more vivid, and
more joyous than any song in our earthly experience:

> canto che tanto vince nostre muse,
> nostre sirene, in quelle dolci tube,
> quanto primo splendor quel ch'ei refuse.
>   (*Paradiso,* XII, 7–9)

More florid, too, must have been the tunes, yet this is not merely a choice
or display of *ars.* While in the lower spheres singing accompanies symbolic
pageantry or elaborates on theological concepts, the higher we ascend the
more it centers on simpler, purely exclamatory texts, such as "Gloria,"
"Sanctus," and "Hosanna."

Again, an Augustinian thought underlies this use of music, a thought
most eloquently expressed in a passage that is appropriate to conclude our
musical excursus: "The sound of jubilation signifies that love, born in our
heart, that cannot be spoken. And to whom is such jubilation due if not to
God; for He is the ineffable One, He Whom no words can define. But if you
cannot speak Him into words, and yet you cannot remain silent, what else
is left to you if not the song of jubilation, the rejoicing of your heart beyond
all words, the immense latitude of the joy without limits of syllables."[34]

Like reason and philosophy, the *artes* are no longer of any avail when the soul nears the central mystery of its faith. Similarly, the poet's song, as the architect's building, and—why not?—the philosopher's *Summa*, need to reach beyond the rationale of their *artes* to attain beauty that is born in their hearts, not merely prescribed by a set of rules.

3   Ars Nova and Stil Novo

Musicology is a recent word—one that would have surprised Dante and one many people are not too happy with. It is modeled, as others are, after the old and glorious name of philology. But whoever invented the older name set the accent on love—love of beauty in speech; every subsequent derivation has emphasized instead the *logos* component, with inelegant verbosity and, in the name of objectivity, with a detached, almost aggressive attitude toward its purported subject. Lovely and loving Philology was deemed by a poet the worthy bride of Mercury; I can think of Musicology only as a maiden, whose secret love for no lesser deity than Apollo will never have a chance until she gets rid of her heavy glasses, technical jargon, and businesslike approach and assumes a gentler, more humanistic manner.

To be fair to my lady Musicology, I must admit that the magnifying glasses, the analytical approach, even statistics, are at present indispensable tools to her work. She acquired her status among the historical disciplines as late as the second half of the last century, at which time, alas, euphoric generalizations and rationalizations were made, quite often on the basis of only scanty documentary evidence. Musicology and musicologists are still reacting to those generalizations, and that is why we are so strictly bound to the document, to the manuscript source, to the early music print, of which an enormous quantity still must be inspected before we can establish new values.

It is refreshing, then, to raise my head from the microfilm reader, if only for a short while, and I am grateful to the Dante centennial for the opportunity to glance at a wider horizon. But the brief respite brings with it a concern which has haunted my musicological career from its very beginning, a concern with the dangers implied in our bondage to the written document.

The history of music, as outlined by our founding fathers and also as we are now trying to rewrite it, is essentially the history of written music. Now it is true that the development and extensive use of a system of notation is one of the important features of our musical tradition; it is true that notation, originating as a guide and an aid to the performer, often reacted on the composer himself and conditioned his musical thinking; it is even true that at times elaborate notation has become almost more important to the composer than the actual sound of his music. Yet we fail to recognize that for all its importance, written music represents only one aspect, and a very special one, of our musical tradition. The fact that we have little hope of reconstructing what music existed beyond it is no justification for ignoring the gap that exists in our knowledge. To reach a proper balance in assessing what we know, we should make every possible effort to explore the extent of that gap. Instead, we tend either to forget it or, in the most favorable case, to minimize it by assuming that the unwritten tradition was the expression of inferior layers of culture. I do not need to consider how valid this assumption would be, if it were true. I know it is untrue, at least for the Middle Ages and most of the Renaissance.

In a paper delivered at a musicological convention I tried to dramatize this view by stressing the difference between the obscurity in which fifteenth-century Italy kept—for almost thirty years—one of the greatest composers of all time, Josquin des Prez, and the fame, at the time, of a certain Pietrobono dal Chitarrino, as shown by the medals cast by Pisanello and by the scores of Latin epigrams and vernacular poems written in his honor.[1] Josquin, as everybody knows, was a composer of polyphonic—written—music; Pietrobono was a singer and a lutenist of whose repertory not a single note has reached us. Nor is this case an exception. Poliziano, having described in a letter to Pico the accomplishments of his former pupil Piero dei Medici, tersely added: "Canit etiam, vel notas musicas, vel ad cytharam carmen."[2] Obviously he considered at least equal in importance to written music (*notas musicas*) the unwritten songs of the kind Piero, like Pietrobono and many others before and after them, used to sing "ad citharam," "ad lyram," or "ad violam"—to the accompaniment of a string instrument.

If we go back to the fourteenth century, we find a similar dichotomy between the written tradition of the so-called Italian Ars nova and the widespread custom of sung poetry, which not only was cultivated without the help of any kind of notation, but seems to a certain extent to have intentionally avoided the strictures of notation.

The written tradition of the fourteenth-century polyphonic Ars nova was one of the most dazzling meteors in the history of music. The sudden outburst of creative energy it represented, with about six hundred settings of secular vernacular texts, has been accepted as natural only because it happened in the century that was inaugurated by Dante and Giotto and then resounded with the voices of Petrarch and Boccaccio. For the preceding centuries, a recent important discovery has doubled the number of early polyphonic pieces in Italian manuscripts, bringing the total to some two dozen, all on Latin religious texts and many of recognizably French provenance.[3] Yet this lack of any important manifestation of polyphonic activity preceding the Ars nova does not seem to have much disturbed the historians; it has been all too easy, although certainly mistaken, to find an explanation for it in the torpor of medieval life. Only the falling of a new curtain of darkness after the short act of the Ars nova has aroused surprise; only a new lapse of silence, covering almost completely the century of Alberti and Leonardo and dividing the island of the Ars nova from the solid continent of later Italian music—only this has come to be considered a disquieting puzzle or, to quote the title of a well-known book, "the secret of the Quattrocento."[4]

It is not surprising to me that no attempt to solve the case of the missing Quattrocento music has led to a satisfactory answer. It has been my contention that the secret, if there is one, is in the island, not in the gap that divides it from the continent. For the island is largely a mirage of our historical perspective, a tiny object magnified by our faith in the written tradition, at best a floating island, not only surrounded but also supported by the waves of a sea now opaque to our eye, once full of light, of life, and of sound—the sound of unwritten music.

I am said to be a specialist of the Italian Ars nova, though a very special one, who has been planning to write a book to reduce the topic to size. Let me state briefly then, the main features and positive values of the Ars nova, in my opinion. It was essentially a polyphonic art or, as they said, *cantus mensuratus*; it required that the length of every sound be precisely determined so that the different voices could proceed on schedule and fall precisely into the combinations of sound and rhythm desired by the composer. As a polyphonic art it was heavily indebted for its technical equipment to the French tradition of artistic polyphony. In spite of this, however, the Italian Ars nova was able to find its own sound and its own solutions to both technical and artistic problems. At the end of its short life, those solutions, having been absorbed by several foreign musicians who were active in northern Italy during the early decades of the fifteenth century, had a modest impact on the development of the artistic poly-phony, again French-dominated, of the following century.

The highest merit of the Italian Ars nova was in reaching and maintain-ing a rare balance between refinement, even subtlety (though never complexity) and freshness and directness of expression. Nevertheless, it is my strong conviction that its polyphony remained practically unnoticed by contemporaries. A few Ars nova texts do refer to such lords as Luchino Visconti and his brother the archbishop Giovanni or to the brothers Alberto and Mastino della Scala, but these references might only be signs of sporadic interest on their part, not evidence of a continued custom of courtly polyphonic performances. In fact, in any reference to music in contemporary sources or any description of a musical performance, the reference is never to polyphonic madrigals or *cacce*, but to the many genres of unwritten music, from the street song to the troubadour lyric, from dance music to religious vernacular *laude*, from the *canto camerale*, restrained in expression and sound (which Francesco da Barberino de-scribed as proper for a young lady of high station) to the narrative and satirical tirades of mountebanks, through which shrewd politicians spread rumors and popular commotion. Casella, the musician conjured with deepest affection by Dante in the second canto of *Purgatorio*, was not a polyphonist; nor was Floriano da Rimini, to whom Petrarch addressed two of his *Familiares*, extolling him as a new Orpheus; nor did Boccaccio, describing the social entertainments that frame the telling of stories in the *Decameron*, include any music that could possibly be construed as polyphonic.

The composers of the Ars nova were all monks, priests, canons, or church organists, although the texts they set to music were secular, or even amorous. I have come to consider their activity as a private hobby, appreciated only by a few connoisseurs. The most conspicuous exception was Francesco Landini, mentioned and praised in a number of literary sources; he too was a church organist in Florence, but he was also the friend of such early humanists as Filippo Villani, Coluccio Salutati, and Leonardo Bruni. To his merits as a gifted and prolific composer we may possibly add that through such connections he helped preserve most of the music of the Ars nova; almost all the manuscripts containing it are Florentine, and they belong, with one exception, to the fifteenth century, thus coinciding in time and place with the trend of ideas in defense of Dante and of vernacular poetry, which ran from Bruni's dialogues "ad Petrum Istrum" to the *certame coronario* of 1441.

The term Ars nova is one of those expressions which, once hit upon by a writer, seems to become indispensable. The term was actually the title— or, better said, part of the title—of a treatise by Philippe de Vitry; for this reason it has been proposed recently that it be applied only to the French music of the fourteenth century, excluding the Italian. For my part, I can think of a few good pedantic reasons to strip it away not only from Italian but also from French music, but I shall continue to use it as an extremely useful and convenient label for both.[5]

I must add that Hugo Riemann, who first introduced the term Ars nova at the beginning of this century, spoke of Florence as its cradle; in choosing the term he was probably influenced by its assonance with the "dolce stil novo." I like that assonance, and I shall defend it. However, this does not mean that I am too easily inclined to accept Riemann's implicit suggestion of a factual connection between the two phenomena. In fact, I have denied that connection for many years, and only in recent times have I become more amenable to consider it a possibility.

Let us review first the circumstances that seem to exclude any connection. The first should be evident, after all I have said about the two traditions of music, for the Ars nova belongs to the tradition of written music, while the music to which the poems of the stil novo were sung has long since disappeared, swallowed up in the oblivion of all things unwritten. The next reason is the discrepancy in time. The ideals of the stil novo had already received full formulation in the last twenty years of the thirteenth century, but only by stretching can we set the date of the earliest known Ars nova compositions at just after 1330. Those fifty years of difference meant little to Riemann fifty years ago, but today they seem significant to us, thus indicating how great a difference fifty years can make; the difference becomes even greater if you add that Florence, far from being the cradle of the Ars nova, came relatively late into its picture. The last, but not least compelling, reason is the discordance between the metrical forms used in the stil novo and the Ars nova. We may dismiss the sonnet, which, in spite of its musical name, was no longer a musical form; but *canzoni* and *ballate* often suggested to the poets of the stil novo the image of tender, trembling new creatures waiting to receive from the musician their final attire. Against these essentially lyrical forms, the main form of the early Ars nova was the madrigal, a short epigrammatic, encomiastic, or satirical text, objective even when its topic was love, with a tendency for description which found an even better outlet in the *caccia*, a modified form of the madrigal.

If I were considering only the discrepancies, I would have no excuse for bringing the topic of the Ars nova into a Dante celebration. But I have listed them to justify my previous skepticism and to indicate that even now my attempt to find a different solution can be only a tentative one. Reflections of the stil novo abound in the poetry of the Ars nova, but they have no meaning, indicating only that a new poetical fashion had been established as common property. What we may want to know is whether the sudden emphasis on musical creativity represented by the Ars nova received any impulse from the original thoughts and aspirations of the stil novo. For this I must dare, even though I am not a historian of literature, to look at the stil novo.

It seems evident to me that we can find but little help in the consideration of what Dante called *stile tragico* and of the poetic form in which it was to be used, the *canzone*. Although all that is said about them in the incomplete second book of *De Vulgari Eloquentia* is full of musical references and expressions, we must be extremely cautious and discriminating in interpreting them. Some are undoubtedly metaphoric—the eternal metaphors of poetry as song and of the poet's tools as plectrum and strings, which are insidious traps to any musicological investigation. A few others are obviously references to, let us say, *musical* music. But most of them, along with Dante's quest of the *volgare illustre*, and all his poetical work, as well as that of the other poets of the stil novo, clearly point out the concept of poetry as primarily verbal music. With this we are no longer on metaphorical ground but on that of a persistent medieval doctrine, only too frequently overlooked by those theorists who had a professional interest in *musical* music. No words of mine could better express it than a short quotation from Roger Bacon's *Opus tertium*. "If we consider that part of music that consists in sound produced by man (musica de sono humano)," he wrote, "well, it is either *melica*, or *prosaica*, or *metrica*, or *rhythmica*."[6] Only *melica musica*, he then explains, consists in singing; prose, metrical verse, and rhymed poetry are also music "because they conform themselves to the singing and to the instruments, in similar [temporal] proportions, for the pleasure of the ear (quoniam conformantur cantui et instrumentis proportionibus consimilibus, in delectationem auditus)."

Some scholars have gone so far as to interpret Dante's theory of the *canzone* as completely excluding actual music;[7] to me, the details he gives about repetition or lack of repetition in the melody of the stanza and about the *diesis*, that is, the passage from one melodic phrase to another at the conjunction of the two parts of the stanza, indicate that he considered it not only possible and normal, but even desirable, to have a melody added to the poem.[8] I must admit, however, that the depth and intensity of thought Dante entrusted to the *canzone*, and its various levels of interpretation as discussed and exemplified in his *Convivio*, strongly favor, as equally important alternatives, not only spoken recitation but also the purest and most spiritual of all sounds, that of mental recitation by an admiring and thoughtful reader. Whether that mental recitation might have included the accompaniment of an equally spiritualized mental melody, I do not know. All I know is that if and when music was added to the *canzone*, the length of the poems and the need for clear perception of the words must have imposed a strictly syllabic and, in a certain sense, recitative style.

What is said of the *stile tragico* does not need to be extended to the mediocre or comic style or to the humble, elegiac style. We would have a better basis for judgment if Dante had written the missing book of *De Vulgari Eloquentia*, which was to have dealt with the *ballata*. As it is, the regular, refined *ballata*, whose stanzas are a miniature replica of those of the *canzone*—interlaced, however, with a refrain unknown to the *canzone*—would seem to be on the whole a more elaborate form; yet it is considered inferior to the *canzone* by Dante and implicitly by all the other poets of his group.

According to a theory of mine, the regular *ballata*, as we know it, is essentially a creation of the stil novo, a creation at the same time poetic and musical, giving an artistic rule to the unruled, even chaotic practice of the earlier dance song. On purely literary grounds the complex structure of the *ballata* would be a strange and unnatural accomplishment for the stil novo, for a school, that is, which professes to repudiate the twisting of thoughts determined in the older style by some traditional or self-imposed canon of rhyme and verse. Actually, the new *ballata* was first introduced as a literary translation of the alternation between soloist and chorus, as a refinement of the dance song, soon transferred to purely lyrical poems mainly because of its musical effectiveness.

Dante himself at least once went out of his way just for the sake of music. This is the case of the *ballata* "Per una ghirlandetta," admittedly written to take advantage of the graceful melody of another poem, as stated in its final stanza:

> Le parolette mie novelle,
> che di fiori fatto han ballata,
> per leggiadria ci hanno tolt'elle
> una veste ch' altrui fu data:
> però siate pregata,
> qual uom la canterà,
> che li facciate onore.[9]

> These few novel words of mine, / forming a *ballata* about flowers, / for the sake of beauty have accepted / a [musical] dress once already given to another: / for this reason I pray you, / whoever will sing it, / that you do honor to it.

There must have been among the graces of the unknown composition a change of rhythm between the refrain (*ripresa*) and the beginning of the stanza and again, within the stanza, between its first part and the *volta* which resumed the melody of the *ripresa*; but the repeated shift between seven-syllable and nine-syllable lines, divested of the melody for the sake of which it was introduced in the *ballata*, produces to my ear rhythmic disharmony and inconvenience of parts.[10]

Even though we cannot have too much faith in a tradition crediting Dante with musical skills, there can be no doubt that he was extremely receptive to music. The *Comedia*, alas, is not the place to look for the evidence we are after: not the *Inferno*, by definition the realm of disharmony and discordance; not the *Paradiso*, where idealized song and dance poetically replace the concept, discarded by Dante as a philosopher, of the music of the spheres; not the *Purgatorio*, resounding with liturgical melodies in which the words of penance and hope are stressed by the poet far more than the musical sound. Yet the only occasion on which Dante indulges in his deepest feeling for music is clearly enough to show the nature of that feeling. This happens, of course, in the second canto of *Purgatorio*, when the meeting with Casella reminds him once more of a most poignant musical experience. Highly significant are the words with which he first addresses his friend and then describes the singing of one of his own most famous *canzoni*:

> ... Se nuova legge non ti toglie
> Memoria o uso all'amoroso canto
> Che mi solea quetar tutte mie voglie,
> Di ciò ti piaccia consolare alquanto
> L'anima mia, che con la sua persona
> Venendo qui, è affannata tanto.
> "Amor che nella mente mi ragiona"
> Cominciò egli allor sì dolcemente
> Che la dolcezza ancor dentro mi suona.

> If the memory or skill has not been taken / away from you of that singing of love / by which all my desires were once appeased, / be kind to give with it / some respite to my soul, which coming here / within her body has made so full of grief. / "Amor che nella mente mi ragiona" / He then began, and was his song so sweet / that the sweetness rings within me still.

The following ecstatic pause, the spell that the singing casts not only on Dante, but on Vergil and on the other listeners, the souls who have just landed on the shore of Purgatorio who should have been hastening toward their penance, is best explained by Dante himself, although in a quite different context. In *Convivio*, book II, chapter 13, he attempts to describe the effects of music in terms of medieval psychology:

Ancora, la musica trae a sè gli spiriti umani, che sono quasi principalmente vapori del cuore, sicchè quasi cessano da ogni operazione; si è l'anima intera quando l'ode, e la virtù di tutti quasi corre allo spirito sensibile che riceve il suono.

Besides, music summons to herself the spirits of man, which essentially are the vapors of his heart, so that they almost desist from any action; his soul is all united the while he listens, and the power of all the many spirits rushes, as it were, to join the sensitive spirit that receives the sound.

Those two passages, unavoidable whenever the question arises of Dante and music, provide more than we need to prove that the highest standards of the most severe among the "faithfuls of love" accepted music, and not only verbal music, as a most desirable ornament, as long as it was fit and proper to the nature and to the aim of each poem. We may also agree that the preference accorded to the *ballata* by the other representatives of the stil novo indicates that the pleasure of music was possibly less highly praised, but certainly more eagerly sought after than the raptures of philosophical meditation. The next and more conclusive point to be made is whether or not the other representatives may also have accepted and sought to add more musical ornaments to the ornament of music.

I have already indicated that the proper melodic style for a *canzone* must have been a very simple one, nearly consistent with its poetic rhythm. Was it possible that other genres allowed greater expansion to the flowing of melody? I see evidence for this in the growing fashion of short lyrical poems, at first in the form of isolated strophes of *canzone*—such as Guido Cavalcanti's *Se m' à del tutto obliato Merzede* or Dante's *Lo meo servente core* and *Madonna, quel signor che voi portate*—and later, when the possibility arose of using the *ballata* as a lyrical piece, also in the form of short *ballate*: either a single stanza preceded and followed by its *ripresa* (rather frequent among the poems of Cino da Pistoia), or a few miniature strophes of the kind called by later theorists *ballata minore* and *minima*. The first of Dante's two *coblas esparsas* (*Lo meo servente core*) has an accompanying sonnet (*Se Lippo amico se' tu che mi leggi*) with which the poet sent it to another of his musician friends (probably Lippo Pasci de' Bardi), requesting him to give the poem its proper musical setting.[11] Dante also wrote a single-strophe *ballata, Deh, Violetta che in ombra d'amore*, with which the name, or surname, of a third musician is associated, that of Scochetto.[12]

I cannot see any other reason for this reduced poetic scope than the need or desire to make allowance for the slower pace of recitation associated with a florid, melismatic melody. Support for this assumption comes also from other quarters. Only two manuscripts have preserved melodies of the religious vernacular songs called *laude*, for the singing of which hundreds of companies or congregations were founded in almost all Italian towns. In the older *laudario* from Cortona, partially reflecting the practice of the last decades of the thirteenth century, syllabic melody prevails—one note for each syllable; in the Florentine *laudario*, some thirty years younger, syllabic recitation very often alternates with chains of melodic flourishes that must have required considerable virtuosity on the part of the performers.[13]

The form of the *ballata*, principal vehicle of musical expression in the stil novo, is also the only common ground with the Ars nova. I have listed the madrigal and *caccia* as the most typical forms of Ars nova, yet its earliest surviving repertory also includes a small but significant group of *ballate*. However, they are not polyphonic *ballate*, although their known composers were polyphonists; they are one-voice pieces, requiring the help of mensural notation because of their melodic floridity and rhythmic refinement. Being monophonic and sung by a single performer, they still preserved the flexibility of delivery and the sensitivity to nuances that were needed in a lyrical genre. Only much later, around 1370, did the polyphonists dare to write polyphonic *ballate*, at first with some hesitation, then with such great enthusiasm that the practice of madrigal and *caccia* soon became obsolete.

The line I have traced between written and unwritten tradition may be too sharp. On one hand the composers of written music had their ears open also to unwritten music; on the other, the quest for melodic refinement, as well as the desire to discard the old blind rules of usage and to establish new rules according to "art" and reason, may have led the representatives of the stil novo to seek an unprecedented contact with the depositaries of the "art" of music. The main feat of the Ars nova, French as well as Italian, was its merging of formal elements and expressive ideals deriving from the old feudal tradition of troubadour song with the more technical tradition—more "artistic" in medieval terms—of polyphonic music.

The main ground for this merging was the university. I have for many years characterized polyphony as an ecclesiastical art, but again I must confess a slight but not insignificant shift in my thinking. I have come to consider artistic polyphony a scholastic tradition—not scholastic in a strictly philosophical sense, of course, although some of that sense is there, but in the sense of the tradition connected with the type of education imparted in the universities or similar institutions. What place music held in an academic curriculum is hard to determine. As one of the mathematic arts, the principles of numeric relationship behind every musical phenomenon, as well as their neo-Pythagorean implications, must have been quickly dispatched by the instructors in charge of the Quadrivium—mathematicians, astronomers, physicians, or, more often, a mixture of all those. A second set of rules, concerned with the analysis and classification of plainchant melodies, had probably been absorbed by the young clerics as part of their training as choirboys, long before they were sent to any university. Most difficult to place, although most important to our purpose, is *musica mensurabilis*, the part of music theory concerned with the length of each sound and with the signs by which their length could be precisely indicated on paper. Although it is difficult to place it in the curriculum, the theory of *musica mensurabilis* was certainly fostered by the sudden glowing and growing of an impressive tradition of artistic polyphony mainly centered in Paris. This tradition was represented by a chain of theorists mostly connected with Paris and its university, from Johannes de Garlandia to Philippe de Vitry and Johannes de Muris.

For the Italian Ars nova, is it just a coincidence that its earliest theorist was Marchettus de Padua, and that the most famous composer in its first generation was one Jacopo da Bologna, both of whom derived their names from the sites of great Italian universities? Two sonnets by a minor poet of the stil novo, Nicolò de Rossi, who lived in Treviso after graduating from Bologna in 1317, gives a list of musicians, including the best-known names of the unwritten tradition, from Garzo, an ancestor of Petrarch, to Casella, Lippo, and Scochetto, all connected with Dante, to Confortino and Floriano, later associated with Petrarch. Highest in Rossi's opinion is one Ceccolino, whom he knew in Bologna and whom he praises, significantly, as "plen d'aire nuovo a tempo et a mesura" (full of new melody with precise rhythm and measure) and describes in the act of "notare," of writing down the music of his *ballate*.[14] Also in Bologna, Giovanni da Ravenna was reported to have felt strongly encouraged to show his prowess as a singer of vernacular songs, including madrigals, and to have become famous for it.[15] On the side of Ars nova, the confluence of the two traditions finds confirmation in a madrigal set by Iacopo da Bologna that mentions Floriano da Rimini as an authority along with Philippe de Vitry and Marchettus de Padua; the text of the madrigal complains that at the time too many singers boasted supreme mastery, so that "tutti èn Floran, Filipotti e Marchetti" ("they all [think they] are a Floriano, a Philippe, a Marchettus").[16]

All the major figures of the stil novo had contacts with scholastic milieus. Brunetto Latini, if we may include him, lived in Paris for several years; Guido Guinizelli from Bologna certainly studied there, and Cino da Pistoia not only studied but also taught there; Dante may not have attended the university, but he must have visited Bologna in his early youth; at any rate, he and his "first friend," Guido Cavalcanti, must have attended either the Franciscan schools or the Dominican *studium* in Florence, which must have reflected much of the Parisian curriculum.

Even in scholastic milieus, deep involvement with the rules of *musica mensurabilis* may have been reserved for those few who intended to become either performers or composers of polyphonic music. All the layman needed was some general knowledge of the kind given in the only surviving chapter of an anonymous and compendious tract on music. Its author somehow mistreats the technical terms, but manages to describe for each poetic form, although in a rather confused way, the rules of its correspondence to musical phrases. Interestingly enough, he starts with the dance forms—*ballate*, so-called "quia ballantur" ("because they are danced"), and *rondeaux*; he then goes on to the French polyphonic motet, and traces his way through polyphonic madrigal and *caccia*, back to the *ballata* form, now called "sonus," and described this time as a freer lyrical monophonic song unrelated to dance.[17] This was probably the work of an Italian grammarian at the beginning of the fourteenth century; some of the most remarkable writing on *musica mensurabilis* of the preceding century had also been the work of a grammarian, Johannes de Garlandia.[18]

I may not have reached a conclusion, but I must come to a final cadence. Only through conjectural work, taking leave for a while from my lady Musicology's stern rule of objectivity, I can suggest that a connection existed between the creative impulse of the stil novo and the quickening activity of the Ars nova. Only a possible connection, but one deserving attention, for it adds urgency to the need to consider the Italian and French *Artes novae* as parallel expressions of a single, basically united spiritual process. As Dante's *De Vulgari Eloquentia* has its counterpart in the French writings on *seconde rhétorique*, which trace their point of departure back to Vitry, similarly a hint of Dante's proclamation of the stil novo may be found in a French motet by one of the forerunners of the Ars nova. Says Pierre de la Croix, in a work which is an intentional assertion of new musical trends:

> Aucuns on trouve chant par usage
> Mais a moi en donne occasion
> Amour qui resbaudit mon courage.[19]

> Many have found their songs just by usage/but to me the occasion is given/by Love who enhances my daring.

The fact that in both cases the Italian manifestation preceded the French, thus reversing a long tradition of dependence, is a mark of the burning flame of Dante's passion, will, and knowledge.

4 ⟩⟩⟩⟩⟩ Polyphonic Music for a Text Attributed to Frederick II

B eginning in the fourteenth century, we hear rather frequently about singing of *siciliane*,[1] but two well-known literary documents of the first half of the fifteenth century stand out because of their more abundant, if not more precise, particulars. The first is a passage of the so-called *Paradiso degli Alberti*, attributed to Giovanni da Prato, in which the ride of the elegant company of the Count of Poppi is rendered more pleasurable by the singing of "Andreuolo Dandolo, giovane non meno di costumi, che di generazione nobile e famoso, piacevole e gentile, della famosissima città Veniziana" (Andreuolo Dandolo, a pleasant and courteous young man from Venice, as noble and famous for his habits as for his descent); he is a Venetian who sings *siciliane* in a Tuscan milieu.[2] In the other text the geographical situation is reversed: it is a banquet of exiled Florentines in Venice, at the end of which, after various other music, "juvenis quidam nomen Cosmas, in Sicilia diutius commoratus, nonnullas Siculas symphonias et cantilenas modulari et cantari cepit" (a certain youth by name Cosmas, who had long sojourned in Sicily, started to play and sing some Sicilian "symphonies" and songs). The description is by Giannozzo Manetti.[3]

In both texts it is not clear how the singing was performed. In Giovanni da Prato's text, Andreuolo Dandolo "fu comandato ... che quale delle leggiadre contesse a lui piacesse, in compagnia una canzonetta delle sue leggiadrissime siciliane, che da Francesco Vannozi apparato avea, eleggesse a cantare"(was ordered to select whichever of the attractive countesses he preferred to sing with him one of his most graceful Sicilian *canzonette*, which he had learned from Francesco Vannozi). But the text does not further state whether the young countess Margherita di Poppi,

Andreuolo's choice, sang with him simultaneously, that is, polyphonically, or alternately, in the way of amoebean singing, so common in
Sicilian poetry.[4] There is no reference to instruments. From Giannozzo
Manetti's Latin as well, we can only surmise that the "simphoniae" were
polyphonic and the "cantilenae" were monodic; since Manetti does not
say that someone besides Cosma participated in the singing, we also must
surmise that, at least in the "simphoniae," he accompanied himself with an
instrument. Perhaps this is the meaning of the repeated distinction between "modulari" and "cantare."

Although rich in superlatives, the praises are generic, in the first case of
the "dolcissima ermonia" (very sweet harmony) and in the second case
of the "incredibilis modulandi et canendi dulcedo" (incredible sweetness of playing and singing), by which the listeners had been downright
"titillati" (tickled). A more positive element is that Andreuolo's singing
went "con dolcissimi accenti nelle piatose e leggiadre parole ... dimos-
trando quanto fa grandissimo male e incomparabile ingiuria chi amato si è
non amare, e con quanta gloria è de' ferventi amare e essere amato"
(showing with sweetest tones in its sorrowful and graceful words what a
wrong it is for him who is loved not to love and what a glory it is for those
inflamed to love and be loved). The singing, therefore, had to be in tune
with the pathetic situation described by its text. Probably the same should
be said about Cosma's songs, since everybody praised above all the fact
that by them was "imitato e riprodotto, per così dire, il siculo compianto
delle prefiche" (imitated and, so to speak, reproduced the Sicilian complaint of female mourners).[5] If we compare the two examples with the
Sicilian song reported by Boccaccio (*Decameron*, IV, 5), *Quale esso fu lo
malo cristiano*, a pathetic tone and situation appear to be a frequent, if not
downright typical, element of *siciliane*.

The music of a *siciliana*, perhaps similar to those Francesco di Vannozzo
was teaching his Venetian pupils,[6] survives in the most ancient section—
mostly Italian in content, and probably originating from the Veneto
region—of the Codex Reina (manuscript Paris, Bibliothèque Nationale,
nouv. acq. frc. 6771, usually abbreviated PR).[7] The composition is on the
verso of fol. 29 and is part of a group of works that, besides being
anonymous, do not appear in any other manuscript. Among the various
reasons that induce me to recognize it as a *siciliana*—reasons that will
become clear in the course of this essay—the most exciting is the possibility of attributing the text to Frederick, the first king of Sicily of that name,
the second of the ultramontane emperors.[8] We have little hope of ever
knowing the author of the music, but we can easily exclude that it goes
back to the time of Frederick II.

The composition is usually listed under the incipit *Dolce lo mio drudo* and classified as a two-voice *ballata*.[9] It has the *ballata*'s two-section division, but no other indication that the two sections corresponded to the *ripresa* and the first *piede* of a *ballata* and had to be repeated in inverse order for the second *piede* and for the *volta*, according to the formal habit of the *ballata*. There is no further text in the codex besides what is written below the notes of both voices; neither section has an ending differentiated between *aperto* (usually leading to a repetition) and *chiuso* (more strongly conclusive cadence); nor is the ending of one section more conclusive than the other, for the simple reason that they are identical.

Notwithstanding this, we would have few reasons to doubt the *ballata* form, except that a similar text exists in the form of a *canzone* in a source very well known to scholars of Italian poetry of the early centuries, codex Vaticano 3793, and this *canzone* is preceded by the inscription "Re federigo." It is not up to me to judge how valid is the attractive attribution to a king and emperor poet, an attribution tenaciously defended by some, contested by others. Whether the Vatican text was written by him, or by Frederick of Antiochia, his natural son, or by any other of the poets of the "magna curia," what is important for us is that it goes back to the thirteenth century and to one of the poets whom Dante himself called Sicilian.[10] The text consists of five stanzas outlining one of the pathetic situations that, as we have seen, were predominant in the generic concept of the *siciliana*. It is a dialogue, this too a typical feature, between a lady afflicted by the nearing departure of her beloved one and a *messere*, whose state duties impose the departure.

I reproduce here the first stanza, according to the codex's diplomatic edition given by Francesco Egidi,[11] and followed by the text of PR, with all its extra syllables, but not the repetitions caused by the music:

> Vat. 3793 Dolze meo drudo e uatène.
> Meo sire, a dio t' acomano,
> che ti diparti da mene,
> ed io tapina rimanno.
> Lassa, la uita m' è noia,
> dolze la morte a uedere,
> ch' io nom penssai mai guerire
> menbrandone fuori di noia.

Oh my sweet lover, do go. My lord, I entrust you to God, you who are departing from me, and I am left in misery. Poor me, life is sorrow for me, death is a sweet thing to envisage; I did not think I might ever recover to remember you without pain.

> PR Dolce lo mio drudo e uaitende.
> E misere, a dio t' arecomando.
> ....
> ....
> Molto rimango dogliosa
> de sì lontano partire,
> ma non spero zamay guarire
> e minbrandome de uuy, fior de çoya.

Oh my sweet lover, do go. My lord, I entrust you to God ... I am left in great sorrow by such departure for far away, but I have no hope ever to recover while thinking of you, flower of joy.

The similarity of the two first and the two last lines leaves no doubt about the fundamental identity of the two texts, although they are rather different from each other as well as, probably, from the original version. The omission in PR of lines 3–4, which should be sung to the same music of lines 1–2, and the omission of the stanzas that follow the first are not surprising to those who have experience with musical manuscripts and with how easily they drop, totally or in part, the text's so-called *residua*. But even though incomplete, the PR version does not totally lack philological values: "e vaitende" in line 1 confirms a linguistic conjecture of Oliva Joh. Tallgren;[12] "fior de çoya" in line 8 confirms an amendment of Camillo Guerrieri Crocetti and makes "menbrandone" more plausible.[13] Paradoxically, even the most important differences, those of lines 5–6, are proof of identity; at some time in the history of the PR text the two lines, corrupted and by then senseless, must have demanded a restoration, which was done by resuming and almost literally repeating the contrast "ti diparti"—"io rimanno," which is the foundation of lines 3–4 and of the whole *canzone*.

The way the lines were restored influences once again our judgment on the form of the poem, and helps us see that notwithstanding its origin as a *canzone*, PR's text may have been interpreted, or misinterpreted, as a *ballata*. Naturally such a misinterpretation could have happened only during the fourteenth century, when the *canzone* had ceased to be a form habitually associated with music and had been replaced as such by the *ballata*.

In the *canzone* the fourteenth-century rhymers used to mark the *diesis*— that is, according to Dante's terminology, the point of passage from the first to the second part of the stanza—giving an identical rhyme to the last line of one and the first of the other. The same procedure is usually applied by analogy within the stanza of the *ballata*, where the *volta* is united to the second *piede*. The *ballata*, though, has another *diesis* (the extension of the term is mine), the one between *ripresa* and stanza. To mark it (discarding the solution of repeating the rhyme, which would have "tied" all the stanzas to the same rhymes), the most ancient *ballate*, and also some of popular tone in the fourteenth century, adopted at least in the first stanza the repetition, at the beginning of the *piede*, of the most characteristic words or the idea of the *ripresa*. The restoration of PR's lines 5–6 in fact uses this popular and *ballata*-like way of marking the *diesis*.

One can object that this theory presupposes that the restorer knew lines 3–4 and therefore the whole first stanza's original metric form. But this is not enough to exclude the possibility that by mistake or intentionally he considered it a *ballata* form: a *ballata* with a double *ripresa*. One must remember that the term *ripresa* (in Latin *responsum* or *responsiva*) derives from the fact that in the dance the refrain was proposed at the beginning by a soloist and immediately repeated—"ripreso"—by a chorus of all the dancers.[14] The immediate repetition was eventually dropped when the *ballata* structure was used for purely lyric chants by a single singer, but it left its trace in a small number of *ballate* with a double *ripresa*.[15]

The last obstacle to interpreting *Dolce lo mio drudo* as a *ballata* is that the music of lines 5–8, which would be the *piedi* and the *volta* (the entire stanza) of the *ballata*, is written in full; but although this is unusual, it is not without precedent and justification. The articulated repetitions of the *ballata*, crystallized by learned versification and usually punctiliously respected by artistic polyphony, reflect the *canzone* structure, but they were not essential to the practice of dance, in which it was enough to alternate a choral refrain and a solo stanza. It happened, therefore, that freer forms, in which the stanza structure deviated from the better-known one, continued to exist beside more elaborate forms. On the other hand, we will soon see that although written in full, the music of the second section of *Dolce lo mio drudo* contains repetitions that reconcile it with the regular scheme.

What first catches the eye about the music is the singularity of its relationship to the text, whose lines are broken into small fragments, which fragments, often breaking in the middle of a word, are insistently repeated and introduced by the syllable *e* without any other value than as a vocal start or *attacco*. Broken words and repetitions are frequent in polyphonic Italian or Italianate *ballate* of the first decades of the fifteenth century, but there the repetition is usually to dramatize the line, as in the accompanying example by Andrea dei Servi (Ex. 4.1), made more effective because it is sung by a single voice before the others begin their counter-

Deh che fa _ rò?   deh che fa_rò, si _ gno_   re?

Ex. 4.1

point. Or the repetition may have the purpose of repeating the line in all its recitative evidence after a beginning slowed by melodic effusion. But in *Dolce lo mio drudo* the repetition does not result in a more effective or more understandable rendition of the text; on the contrary, it so fragments and stutters it that any meaning is lost, except as a pretext for the melody which submerges it. In the first section of the *ballata* seven textual fragments are used for as many musical phrases:

	Dolce dolce lo mio dru	= a	
	drudo e uay	= b	
	e uaitende	= c	
Ripresa	e misere	= d	A
	e misere a dio	= e	
	a dio t' a	= f	
	a dio t' arecomando	= g	

The same melodic elements, or almost the same, also form the second section, the stanza:

1st piede	Molto riman	= f'	
	rimango dogliosa	= b'	B'
	E dogliosa	= h	

2nd piede	De si lonta	= f'	
	lontano par	= b'	B
	E partire	= d	

	Ma non spero	= i	
	spero ça	= b	
	zamay guarire	= c'	
Volta	E minbrando	= d	A'
	e minbrandome	= e	
	de uuy	= f	
	de uuy fior de çoya	= g	

The *ballata* form is evident: *ripresa*, followed by the first *piede* (line 5) with an *ouvert* cadence; the second *piede*, which repeats the same music of the first with a *clos* cadence; and the *volta* (lines 7–8, the first of which marks the *diesis*, repeating the rhyme of the second *piede*) with the same music as the *ripresa*, with an *ouvert* at the beginning. Since phrases *f'*, *b'*, and *c'* differ from *f*, *b*, and *c* only in the addition of an upbeat note, the only new musical elements are *h* and *i*. In spite of an almost regular metric form, a grave deviation from the normality of both monodic and polyphonic *ballate* of the Ars nova is represented by using again in the *piedi* some of the musical material of the *ripresa;* this, too, is related to popular types of *ballate*.[16]

The analysis of *Dolce lo mio drudo*'s polyphonic language confirms the presence of a tradition that was refined in its own way and did not completely ignore the Ars nova tradition, but was substantially different. Every phrase is essentially formed by the syllabic declamation of a textual fragment by the two voices in "contrapunto" (that is, note against note), which is then expanded and projected toward a cadence by the minute vocalization of the upper voice, soberly sustained by the lower one. The "contrapunto" is in turn characterized by alternating parallel and contrary motion. Besides the beginning in unison on four consecutive notes, which has already been noted by Kurt von Fischer,[17] also in unison are the beginnings of the second section, of line 6 (the repetition of the former), and of fragment *c'*. Doubling the melody in the two voices adds emphasis to the initial melodic gesture and furthermore allows reaching the most convenient position to start the rather rigid, simple procedure that is at the bottom of this polyphony: contrary motion, either diverging from unison to the third and from the third to the fifth, or converging from the fifth to the third and from the third to unison. Usually the two voices get no more than a fifth apart, and unison and fifth (in some cases, as in phrase *g*, several parallel fifths) are the dominant simultaneous intervals. The third occurs in the transition from one to the other in the note-against-note recitative passages; it is, moreover, the pivot around which moves the melisma in the vocalized passages of the upper voice. One cannot ignore in these last passages the tendency, so insistent as to reveal an intention or complacency, to use the fourth in an accented position and often to give it an upward resolution. Also frequent, especially in the proximity of cadences, is the strong discordant friction of the major or minor second, this, too, often resolved in an upward motion. In one instance only, in phrase *d*, the two voices, moving from an interval of a fifth, diverge through the sixth to the octave, and then converge back through a vocalized passage to a cadence in unison.

What can be said of the music of *Dolce lo mio drudo* (Ex. 4.2.)? As already stated, we can exclude any idea that in it may survive the melody

Ex. 4.2   Anonymous *ballata* (PR, fol. 29v).

Ex. 4.2   Continued

Ex. 4.2   Continued

Ex. 4.2   Continued

originally associated with the *canzone* about the middle of the thirteenth century. The formal scheme, which is substantially the scheme of a *ballata,* denies it, and it is organized on a version of the text that has the characteristics of a *ballata.* Furthermore, the original melody, whatever its quality, must have allowed the text to carry it through its five stanzas of dialogue; in the PR version only one stanza of the text survives, weak and lifeless, a mere pretext for the music. In spite of that, the upper voice of PR's composition gives the impression of being a received melody, even if not very old, because the successive unisons and fifths that it forms with the other voice have a plausible explanation only if one admits that the upper voice was a *res prius facta* that had to be respected. In fact, the polyphony of *Dolce lo mio drudo* is a very simple and rather mechanical accompaniment technique, and its procedures are closely analogous to the technique (more diffused than artistic polyphony) of the improvised or semi-improvised "contrapunto" on liturgical melodies. In our case, the *res prius facta* is a melody for which the origin of the text could justify the name of *siciliana.* A certain flavor of Sicilianity remained attached to the text with the persistence of southern linguistic forms like "vaitende" and "t' arecomando," which are not otherwise justifiable in a codex whose copyists were probably from Veneto and certainly northerners. If and to what extent a Sicilian flavor was present also in the music, we cannot judge.

Objectively considered, the music of *Dolce lo mio drudo* is a mixture of primitive and refined elements. One refined element is the melismatic vocalization, but it is primitive in that the melody is formed by brief isolated fragments, aligned without real necessity and continuity, like glass beads, taken more or less by chance from the unknown composer's storeroom of expressive elements to make a necklace. It is possible that the performer's emphasis could give to each fragment the sad pathos of the *siciliana* (notwithstanding the text it is given, I tend to think of the lower voice as an instrumental accompaniment and support); but it is unlikely that the performer could succeed in giving it what it lacks: a design, an artistic development. It was not art, therefore, but musical handicraft.

5 — New Glimpses of an Unwritten Tradition

In the minds of most musicians the word *siciliana* is associated with elegant baroque tunes whose composers in most cases had never set foot on the island, or with a certain melody by a Tuscan of Leghorn which is impressive when heard from behind the curtain at the beginning of *Cavalleria rusticana* but which only vaguely resembles a real Sicilian song. To a native the popular songs of Sicily are a different, deeper experience; I may be forgiven, then, if I preface my discussion with a few samples of their fast-disappearing tradition.

The first is a song from S. Agata, on the northern shore of the island, on a text which has—or should have— the *a b a b a b a b* rhyme scheme of a *strambotto*.

> Quannu passu di ccà, provu un duluri:
> ti viu e nun ti pozzu salutari.
> Tu ti cridissi ch'è lu picca amuri;
> lu fazzu pi li genti nun parlari.
> E l'occhiu di la genti su' balestri;
> tradiscinu lu cori di luntanu.
> Sa' chi ti dicu, carissimu amuri?
> statti ferma cu mia, nun dubitari.[1]

Its melody (Ex. 5.1), as usual with most Sicilian songs, sets the first two lines and is then repeated with variants and adjustments for the following ones. Less usual here is the fact that the first large melodic unit embraces not only the first but also half of the second line of text; the latter is repeated and brought to its conclusion with the second melodic phrase.[2]

Typical of the brooding mood of most Sicilian lyricism is the slow pace

Ex. 5.1 *Santagatisa* (Favara, *Corpus*, no. 441).

of the melody, whose flexible rhythm is more determined at the beginning of each melodic segment and then slackens into ecstatic sustained notes embroidered at will by the performer. The relaxed flexibility of the melody does not disguise the strong polarization of its two main sections toward two different tonal goals, represented in this case by the same note at a higher and lower octave. It must be noted that the first phrase comes to a strong cadence on an interrupted sentence ("I see you and cannot . . .") and that the second breaks on the first syllable of a word and then resumes with the second syllable used as an upbeat to the new melodic segment.

The strong major flavor of this song, only slightly tempered by the minor third at the end, may seem to indicate a fairly recent origin. However, the two largely different versions of my second example will show how tonal inflections may have encroached on a preexisting outline conceived in a nontonal idiom. Both versions are from Salemi, inland toward the western tip of the island, and are set, as was the first song, to a *strambotto*-like text.

> (E) 'nti stu curtigghiu c'è un peri di rosa;
> nun la tuccati nuddu, ch'è la mia.
> C'è qualchidunu chi pretenni cosa,
> si lu livassi di la fantasia.
> D'unn'avi li peri la testa ci posa;
> ieu ci lu giuru pi la parti mia.
> M'arriccumannu a tia, peri di rosa,
> ca sta 'mputiri to' la vita mia.[3]

The two versions of the music (Ex. 5.2, *a* and *b*), again set to the first two lines, parallel each other up to the end of the first line, cadencing respectively on A and B, and then again in the section corresponding to the second line of text, descending to a cadence on low E. A major difference is

Ex. 5.2   Laundress song, versions *a* and *b* (Favara, *Corpus*, nos. 293 and 294).

the melodic fragment repeating the second half of the first line of text ("un peri di rosa"), which is present only in version *a*. The insertion does not have any particular chronological intimation; yet version *a,* insisting as it does on the triad of E major, sounds somewhat more modern than the playing with clustered semitones and the double *diabolus in musica* (at "rosa" and "la mia") of version *b*.[4] Once more we may notice the splitting of words between the end of one melodic segment and the beginning of the following one ("nud-du" in version *a;* "ro-sa" and "nud-du" in version *b*), as well as the initial conjunction "E," present in both versions but absolutely unnecessary from the standpoint of either sense or meter. Its function as a way for the singer to start his melody, or one fragment of it, becomes more evident in the last of my prefatory examples, a "motet" of a more melismatic character from Partanna, near Salemi (Ex. 5.3).[5]

I shall not deny that I have been indulging in a nostalgic feeling for one aspect of my native island's past that is in the process of being irretrievably erased by the wave of modernization. But my offering such an exotic bouquet may also have some less morbid and more scholarly reasons,

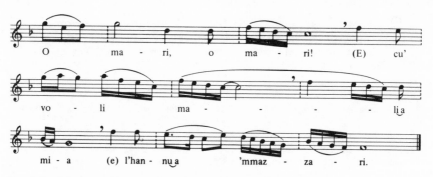

Ex. 5.3   *Muttettu* (Favara, *Corpus*, no. 317).

which shall be presently indicated by a sudden plunge of my recording pen from the vibrations of open-air singing to the flat austerity of dusty bibliographical information.

The older section of the well-known Codex Reina (Paris, Bibliothèque Nationale, nouv. acq. frç. 6771—henceforth designated with the usual abbreviation, PR)[6]—includes between fascicles I and II, dedicated respectively to works by Jacopo da Bologna (fols. 1–12) and Bartolino da Padova (fols. 13–24), and fascicle V, whose first pages (fols. 49–52) contain works by Francesco Landini, two more fascicles (fols. 25–48); these were left, or inserted, as a repository for (1) additional works by the three composers represented in the adjacent fascicles; (2) works by seldom-mentioned composers such as Dompnus Paulus, Henricus, Jacobelus Bianchus, and Johannes Baçus Correçarius;[7] and (3) a number of anonymous settings for which PR is the only known source. The last have more and more attracted my attention in recent years because of the possibility that their heterogeneous gathering may include samples of what I call the unwritten tradition of music, the importance of which—per se and for the assessment of the written tradition—I have also pointed out with possibly tedious insistence.[8]

Written and unwritten tradition are broad generalizations, or polarizations, between whose extremes there is ample space for exceptions, hybrids, and borderline cases—almost the only hope we may have of catching some glimpse of the vast uncharted domain of unwritten music. I had this in mind when I commented, in another essay on one piece in PR, *Dolce lo mio drudo e vaitende* (fols. 29v–30), which I singled out because its text reworks as a *ballata* the first strophe of a *canzone* attributed in an earlier source to "Re federigo" (either Emperor Frederick II, king of Sicily and Jerusalem, or his son, Frederick of Antiochia).[9] Accordingly, the North Italian compilers of PR may have had good reasons to consider it as a specimen, exotic also to them, of a genre that was spreading among the practitioners of unwritten music: the *siciliana*.

Another possible *siciliana*, at least from the point of view of its text, is the following, also a *ballata:*

> (E) vantènde, segnor mio, (e) vatène, amore;
> con ti via se ne vene l'alma (mia) e 'l core.
>   (E) gli ochi dolenti piangon sença fine
>   cha vedèr el paradisso e soa belleza.
>   A cuy ti lasso, amore, ché no me meni?
>   l'alma me levi e 'l cor e l'alegreça.
>   La bocha cridava che sentiva dolceça;
>   amarà lamentarse, oymé, topina!
> Altro signor zamay non voglio [avere]
> perch'io non troverey del suo vallore.
>   (E) vantène, segnor mio [etc.][10]

Already the first line has in common with *Dolce lo mio drudo* the peculiarly southern form "vantènde";[11] later on, such rhymes as "fine,' "meni," and "topina" can be made regular only when reduced to corresponding dialectal forms ("fini," "mini," and "taupini," the last a conjectural plural instead of the feminine singular of PR). The poetic theme, the emotional farewell of two lovers, is similar to the situation in *Dolce lo mio drudo*. Furthermore, both texts are irregular *ballate,* the irregularity here consisting in the presence of two extra lines, 7 and 8; we do not know whether to consider these as a third *piede* or a doubling of the *volta* (in *Dolce lo mio drudo* the irregularity consisted in the probable existence of a double *ripresa*).

Translated into musical terms, the problem of interpreting the two extra lines raises the question whether they should be sung to the music of the *piedi* (second section) or the *ripresa* (first section). A quick glance at the music shows that the decision is irrelevant, for the two sections are but two versions of the same music, the first slightly expanded, the second more concise and also more balanced (Ex. 5.4).[12] This helps me answer a question I left open when writing on *Dolce lo mio drudo*, whether a Sicilian flavor is present in the music as well as in the text. My answer is decidedly yes in the case of *E vantènde*. Considering that the *ballata* form is foreign to the tradition of Sicilian poetry, in which the norm is a series of lines of equal length set two by two to a single melodic element, a strong

Ex. 5.4 Anonymous *ballata* (PR, fol. 38v).

E glio-chi do-len-ti pian-go...
A cu-y ti las-so, a mo -

E glio-chi do-len-ti pian-go -
A cu-y ti las-so, a mo -

piangon sen-ça fi - - -
- mor ché no me me - - -

no... piangon sen-ça fi - -
re... a-mor ché no me me - -

- - - ne? Cha ve -
ni? L'al - ma

- - - ne Cha ve -
- - - ni? L'al - ma

dèr el pa-ra - dis - - so...
me le-vi e'l co - - re...

dèr el pa-ra - dis - so...
me le-vi e'l co - re...

pa-ra-dis - so e so'... e soa bel-le -
e il cor e l'a... e l'a - le - gre -

pa-ra-dis - so e so'... e soa bel-le -
e il cor e l'a... e l'a - le - gre -

- - - - - za.
- - - - - ça.

Da capo
al Fine

- - - - - za.
- - - - - ça.

case can be made for the thesis that the text and music of PR have recast into a *ballata* form the text *and* music of an authentic Sicilian song, recorded on paper at least some five hundred years earlier than any of the available collections.

Recorded, yes, but where, by whom and, even more important, from which source? We can give approximate answers to the first two questions: the songs were probably written down in the Venetian inland rather than in Venice itself[13] by the compilers of the older section of PR. As for the third question: although the presence of Sicilians is not unlikely—among the students in Padua and among the clergy or in various trades elsewhere—I am inclined to think these melodies were received from non-Sicilian singers, to whom all the accounts reporting the singing of *siciliane* invariably refer. Two such accounts, which I quoted in writing on *Dolce lo mio drudo* (see essay 4), present as performers, respectively, a Venetian singing in Tuscany, who had learned his *siciliane* from Francesco di Vannozzo (probably born in Padua, he never went to Sicily),[14] and a Florentine singing in Venice, who at least had been on the island (his singing, however, took place forty to fifty years later than the recording of *E vantènde* in PR).[15] We may add to them Sollazzo, the hero of a well-known poetic description of social entertainments and a literary character whose skills certainly reflect the experiences of his creator, Simone Prudenzani of Orvieto. Sollazzo's repertory includes, with old polyphonic madrigals and more recent *ballate* (the time is during the second decade of the fifteenth century), popular songs from many places, including "strambotti de Cicilia a la reale."[16] Finally, we should also remember that the adjective *Sicilian* had two meanings: the first more specifically regional, indicating a connection with the island of Sicily; the second more general, applying to anything pertaining to the kingdom of Sicily, that is, to all southern Italy.

It thus becomes apparent that the singing of *siciliane,* or would-be *siciliane,* represents only one element, although a prominent one, in a vogue of eclectic exoticism that was spreading among professional and semiprofessional singers.[17] Accordingly, we may expect that even a song of authentic Sicilian provenance would be filtered, so to speak, through the habits and needs of non-Sicilian singers. More easily preserved in this process were the external features of the song, the declamatory beginning of phrases, the unhurried progress, the breaking of lines and words and their resumption in a new melodic start, the love of suspended vocalization, and even the preference for certain cadences, particularly those on E and B (the mode on E with strong cadences on the tonic and fifth degree is still prominent in the modern collections of Sicilian popular songs).[18]

Many of these elements are present in *E vantènde* and even more in *Dolce lo mio drudo,* in the latter to such an extent that it seems to me an unnatural and unauthentic ostentation of Sicilianity. In spite of the lack of cadences on E, the melody of *E vantènde,* in which neither pauses nor digressions ever cancel the strong tension toward the melodic goals A and G, sounds more authentic to my ear.

In another *ballata* (PR, fol. 39v) a disappointed lover scolds his former beloved:

> Donna fallante, mira lo to aspetto.
> Ti mostri vergognosa,
> e (tu) stari 'nchiusa / ve par[r]ia dilletto.
>> Dilletto ve par[r]ia u' l'ascossa magione,
>> donna de fallo piena.
>> Tuo cuor getta' con falsa ragione
>> cridar sera e matina.
> Tu, stella fina, / ché mi day spiandory?
> por chi luce ormay?
> Scuro lo troveray / al to soççetto.
>> Non av[e]rò çamay consolamento,
>> né riso, né sperança,
>> poi che falçasti lo (tuo) dolci talentu,
>> tornasti falsa amança.
> Or doncha dança / cum pianti e rispeti.
> Por chi luci ormay?
> Scuro lo troveraj / al to sogetto.[19]

Again the imperfect final or internal rhymes "vergognosa-'nchiusa" and "piena-matina" become regular when retranslated into "virgugnusa-'nchiusa" and "china-matina"; furthermore, the scribe of PR forgot to modify the Sicilian endings of "dolci talentu" (both Tuscan and Venetian parlance would have had "dolce talento") and preserved at the end of the two stanzas a typically southern pleonastic construction with two objects, the second of them preceded by the preposition "a" ("lo" and "al to sogetto"). Archaic or popular traits in this text are the repetition of the last words of the *ripresa* at the beginning of the first *piede* (lines 3 and 4) and the refrain-like recurrence of two lines at the end of both stanzas.

The text of *Donna fallante* may have originated with a Sicilian poet; however, it cannot belong to the popular tradition because of its un-equivocal *ballata* form. Thus, the popular traits we have observed in it seem to be an intentional display, which is reflected with no lesser determination by the music (Ex. 5.5). In the latter, something of the

Ex. 5.5   Anonymous *ballata* (PR, fol. 39v).

Ex. 5.5 Continued

characteristic playing with semitone inflections can be introduced, or reinstated, merely by applying some simple rule of *musica ficta;* see, for instance, the upper part at the words "aspetto" and "stari 'nchiusa."

The verbal repetition between the *ripresa* and the first line of the following *piede* is paralleled by the music: compare the last measures of the first section with the three measures of the second section on the words "u' l'ascossa magione." The shift of the latter to the upper fifth is part of the higher melodic and tonal range often exhibited by the *piedi* section in the more popular types of *ballata* (for instance, in the monophonic *laude*), echoing the alternation between chorus and soloist of the original dance songs. Another repetition occurs at the end of the *piedi* section, where the music on "Donna" strongly resembles that set to the same word at the beginning of the piece. Such repetitions, however, although they can be considered popular features in the poem, become in the music a subtle procedure for which no popular singer, accustomed as he was to readjusting the same melody to a number of texts, would have cared.

More instances of *siciliane,* or would-be *siciliane,* are present in PR; I cannot examine them within the limits of this essay. They are by no means the only pieces that were crystallized into a written record instead of being left in the fluid state of the unwritten tradition. Others are set to texts having a definite Venetian flavor, which made better sense to the compilers of PR than the texts of presumably Sicilian origin. One, however, gives a curious testimony of both the embarrassment of northern scribes when confronted with southern texts they did not fully understand and the frequency with which such confrontations occurred. The poem reads quite correctly in PR, fol. 39:

> Strençì li labri c'àno
> d'amor melle ch'a zucaro someglia,
> et alçì quey dolci cigli / chi m'alcide.
>   Tu say cum quanta angossa quanta pena
>   sosteni per to amore
>   inançi che ver mi fossi piatossa;
>   poi per pietà solgisti la cathena
>   che me ligasti el core,
>   che dì e note e' non avea may possa;
> e la vita angosossa
> mi festi ritornare in gran dolceça,
> sì che toa zentileça / vince amore.
>   Strençì li labri [etc.]

But in another, nonmusical manuscript, the charming incipit is misread "Strengi le lapre piano, l'amor mio";[20] the scribe, evidently conditioned in his reflexes by having dealt with a number of southern texts, interpreted "chi àno" (that have) as one word, which he translated into "piano" (soft), and took the first syllable of "melle" (honey) as the equivalent of "mio" (mine). This, plus some lines missing in his version, shows how badly the works committed to the ways of the unwritten tradition could fare—a risk nobody worried about, for one of the most fascinating aspects of the tradition was the freedom it left to continuous reinterpretation or even re-creation.

Although the text of *Strençì li labri* is affected by Venetian idioms ("strençì," "alçì," "m'alcide," and so on), its music (Ex. 5.6) strongly resembles that of the previous examples, whose texts were tainted with Sicilianisms. Even stronger than theirs (with the exception of *Dolce lo mio drudo*) is the acceptance of the mannerisms that, we have seen, are typical of much later Sicilian singers: the breaking and / or repetition of words and short phrases, the insertion of supernumerary vowels and (less generally) the insistent cadences on E. In *Strençì li labri* the cadences almost invariably allow the singer to indulge in a favorite melismatic formula, the only instance in the piece of a multiple use of the same musical material (comparable to the insistent repetition and variation of the initial melisma of *Donna fallante*).

My comments up to this point have centered on the popular features exhibited by the upper parts of the unusual anonymous pieces of PR, but the samples I have given must already have told my reader that they are even more pointedly set apart from the standard of contemporary art music by their peculiar polyphonic procedures. Once more, *Dolce lo mio drudo* is such an exhaustive compendium of these procedures that I only need repeat what I wrote of them in essay 4. Most musical phrases in these pieces consist of the simultaneous declamation of a fragment of text by the two parts, note against note (that is, in counterpoint)—declamation which leads rapidly to a climax; from there on, the upper part usually descends with relaxed vocalizations toward a cadential note (off which the melodic wave often softly rebounds), sedately supported in this process by a few notes of the lower part. Parallel unisons and fifths are predominant in the declamatory beginning, after which contrary motion sets in, with the two parts diverging from unison to third and from third to fifth, or, inversely, converging toward the unison, on which most cadences take place (with the result that no extraneous note interferes with the melodic goal toward which the upper line has been directed). Only occasionally is the diverging contrary motion expanded to reach the octave. The upper part embroiders this simple harmonic skeleton with passing notes, showing an evident taste for dissonant intervals (such as perfect or augmented fourths) placed on strong beats, quite often with ascending resolutions. Also frequent, particularly near cadences, is the strong friction of a minor or major second in the form of either an ascending appoggiatura or an anticipation of the cadential note.

I see in this technique an unorthodox style of accompaniment subservient to the intended message contained in the upper parts—an accompaniment doubling and therefore emphasizing the emphatic declamatory

Ex. 5.6   Anonymous *ballata* (PR, fol. 39).

Ex. 5.6   Continued

passages, giving rhythmic as well as harmonic support to the flourishes of the singer and then converging toward the cadential sounds that give the melody its structural direction. Eventually, when the outline of the upper part makes the favorite contrary motion impossible, there is again recourse to parallel unisons and fifths, until a position is reached from which contrary motion can be comfortably resumed. Generally avoided are parallel thirds, whose frequency in *Donna fallante* is one more element that places it halfway between unorthodox practice and regular artistic polyphony. Although the lower parts are given full texts in PR, I am inclined to think that they were conceived for instrumental performance of the kind to which Prudenzani refers when speaking of Sollazzo:

> Con la chitarra fe' suoni a tenore
> Con tanta melodia che a ciascuno
> Per la dolceza gli alegrava 'l core.
> Con la cetera ancor ne fece alcuno . . .[21]

> With his guitar he performed *ballate* with a tenor, with so much melody that he cheered everybody's heart with its mellowness. With his zither, too, he performed some . . .

Of course, singing with a stringed instrument is nothing new; what is new is the intimation that the instrumental accompaniment could take the form of a popular kind of polyphony.

The evidence I have assembled seems to indicate that a Sicilian style of singing was practiced and imitated in northern Italy, where it either determined or merged with a more general trend of the unwritten tradition of music; eventually, it became accepted in its own right, with no further reference to its exotic provenance. Although it adopted a polyphonic accompaniment, its popular accent redeemed it from the growing disaffection among some of the most sophisticated listeners for what I call the scholastic tradition of music, art polyphony. Thus it became part of the stylistic and cultural background from which at least one type of so-called *giustiniana* was to emerge a few years later.[22]

We may go one step further and suggest that the style of unaccompanied and accompanied melody initiated by the vogue of authentic and synthetic *siciliane* may not only have affected the humanistic taste of Leonardo Giustinian but may also have impressed some of the representatives of the scholastic tradition of music. Two of the *doctores subtiliores* of the Franco-Italian mannerist school of polyphony will serve our purpose and

Ex. 5.7   Antonellus Marot de Caserta, *Ballata* (Mn, no. 39).

also hint at the vein of romanticism that was one component of that complex phenomenon. The transition from mannerism to a Sicilianate style may have been easier for Antonellus Marot de Caserta because he was, after all, a southerner, although probably active in northern Italy. Of Antonellus' Italian pieces, several exhibit the broken and suspended treatment of the text we have become familiar with.[23] In the one I have selected (Ex. 5.7), however, a faster delivery of the text was probably intended, so that neither breaking nor repetition of words occurs.[24] Nevertheless, it seems to me that the composer recaptured the rhythmic flexibility of popular singing[25] and reproduced some of the techniques of popular polyphony.

Among the Italian pieces of Johannes Ciconia—a northerner from beyond the Alps who spent his last years in Padua—several, including *O rosa bella* on a text that might be by Giustinian, represent a post-Sicilian style of music practiced in the Venetian region during the first decade of the fifteenth century, just after the approximate date of compilation of the older section of PR.[26] In spite of a keen naturalistic spirit of observation, Ciconia was too refined a polyphonist to accept at face value the rather crude and mechanical techniques of popular polyphony, except for their expressive dissonances. The piece I am giving (Ex. 5.8), however, is notated in the *octonaria* measure that is typical of the slow florid pieces we have been discussing and has a text (eight lines, with rhymes so similar that it might almost be considered to be monorhyme) which deals with the familiar themes of unhappiness and forced separation.[27] Its airy major somewhat recalls, after so many pieces in the minor, the mode of my initial example—one added musical reason for selecting it to round out my own verbiage on words and music.

Postscript, 1983

The putative *siciliane* examined in this essay do not exhaust the list of known pieces whose musical features may have been intended to suggest a Sicilian style of singing. To them four more two-voice *ballate* must be added which are also present in the same section of Codex Reina: *Fenir mia vita me convien cum guay* (fol. 26r), *Con lagreme sospiro* (fol. 27v), *Troveraço mercè* (fols. 28v–29r), and *Amore, a lo to aspetto* (fol. 38r). The first of them, *Fenir mia vita*, has also been found in a somewhat modified version in a newly discovered fragment in the Archivio di Stato in Padua (MS S. Giustina 553); a second two-voice *ballata* in the same fragment, *Par che la vita mia*, is also to be added to our list.[28]

Ex. 5.8 Johannes Ciconia, *Ballata* (Mn, no. 54).

Ex. 5.8 Continued

Giulio Cattin, who discovered the Paduan fragment among the pasted leaves supporting an old binding, has shown that it is related to the Paduan abbey of Santa Giustina and to documents belonging to a Rolando da Casale, a humanist monk and a music copyist long active in that abbey and in one of its dependencies.[29] This confirms the role of Padua as one center where *siciliane* or would-be *siciliane* were sung. Commenting on Cattin's discovery, F. Alberto Gallo has pointed out that the text of *Par che la vita mia* (a text lamenting departure and separation, in which it is possible to spot some hints of an original in the Sicilian dialect) is also given in a more complete version in the literary MS Florence, Biblioteca Nazionale Centrale, Magliabechi VII 1040, fol. 55r, and labeled there "cieciliana."[30] To this confirmation of my ideas on the early singing of *siciliane*, Gallo adds the precious observation that *Fenir mia vita* is referred to in one of the sonnets of Simone Prudenzani's *Liber Solatii* in a line reading: "*Finir mia vita* de Cicilia pruôno" ("they rehearsed *Finir mia vita* from Sicily").[31]

Last but not least (to me), my hypothesis that Ciconia's *ballata Poy che morir mi convien per to' amore* might have been intended to recapture what was then considered in Padua to be a Sicilian style of music finds some confirmation in the strong resemblance I notice between its beginning and the beginning of the confirmed "cieciliana" *Par che la vita mia.*[32]

6   The Oral and Written Traditions of Music

My arriving at the conference on fourteenth-century Ars nova in Certaldo without a written text, and thus being obliged to "improvise" the presentation reconstructed here, became, without my intending it, an example of the *modus operandi* of the unwritten tradition. I do not mean to establish an absolute or exact identity between improvisation and unwritten tradition; however, there can be no doubt that the lack of a written text leaves the door open to improvisation, either where the memory (to which the text is entrusted) has a lapse, or where the occasion or a sudden whim impels the performer to diverge from a prearranged plan. On the other hand, what we know as improvisation usually is possible only because the "improviser" has stored within himself an assemblage of materials from which he may borrow; he builds with elements drawn from this storehouse, combining, reshaping, and coloring them as directed by his imagination and the occasion. I found myself in such an improviser's role, because in my presentation I proposed to discuss themes which I had previously dealt with in other contexts.

My principal theme, which had appeared in several of the papers already delivered at the Certaldo conference, was a proposition that I had repeatedly called to the attention of my colleagues.[1] The music from which we make history, the written tradition of music, may be likened to the visible tip of an iceberg, most of which is submerged and invisible. The visible tip certainly merits our attention, because it is all that remains of the past and because it represents the most consciously elaborated portion, but in our assessments we should always keep in mind the seven-eighths of the iceberg that remain submerged: the music of the unwritten tradition. Moreover, it is sometimes possible to go beyond the generic, essentially negative notion we usually have of the submerged mass by identifying some elements in the written tradition that provide a glimpse of those below the surface.

Such elements are found in a composition dating from the end of the fourteenth century (based on a much earlier text, which has been attributed to Emperor Frederick II as well as to his son, Frederick of Antiochia), discussed in an article that I wrote some years before it was first published in 1968, under the imprint of the esteemed Centro di Studi of Certaldo.[2] In my estimation this work mirrors a musical repertory different from that represented by the cultivated pieces normally entered in manuscripts, indeed different from the bulk of pieces entered in the codex in which it is found (the so-called Codex Reina, Paris, Bibliothèque Nationale, nouv. acq. frç. 6771, known as PR). The primary distinguishing characteristic of this composition is the interaction of the two voices, which often begin their phrases by moving in unison (or, more rarely, in parallel fifths), then continue like a bellows, expanding via contrary motion from the unison to the third, the fifth, and occasionally the octave, then contracting back to the fifth, the third, and the unison. The same bellows-like polyphony is found elsewhere, for example in a "Verbum caro" for two voices, the beginning of which has been transcribed in an article by Kurt von Fischer.[3] It is an obviously mechanical procedure, compared to the more skillful and varied procedures of artistic polyphony. Yet I believe that church musicians resorted to it for improvised polyphonic performances to permit them to add with ease a "contrappunto alla mente" (mental counterpoint) to a melody already written; on sporadic occasions such counterpoint was preserved in writing.

Aside from its singularly mechanical polyphony, the composition in the Codex Reina is set apart by its unusual way of stating the text, fragmenting it into small segments which are repeated several times, often introduced by an interpolated vowel ("E" or "O"); these interpolations, which create a vocalized approach to a segment of text but which interrupt and corrupt the poetic meter, are a common feature among popular and popularizing singers. Nor is my example unique: the Codex Reina includes others, some of which are treated in another essay.[4] Since the first example is undoubtedly "Sicilian" (the quotation marks will be explained later), and the others also have a southern linguistic complexion, even though the codex containing them all is probably Venetian,[5] I have linked them with the singing of *siciliane* which, as we know from literary sources, were in vogue for quite a while in northern Italy.[6]

Siciliane were rarely performed by singers who were themselves Sicilian;

usually they were sung by persons who had learned them from someone who had obtained them from sources that were more or less Sicilian—a typical transmission in an unwritten tradition. In confirmation of the assumption that my unusual polyphonic pieces were indeed related to the *siciliane,* I did provide examples (see essay 5) of monophonic, folkloristic Sicilian songs, in which are found the same alternation of text statement with vocal melisma, the same habit of insistent repetition of the text, and the same custom of interpolating introductory vowels which are extraneous to the poetic meter. I must avow, however, that although my examples come from Sicily, the exemplified traits might be found in some other regions or countries as well. Moreover, my being of Sicilian birth does not blind me to the fact that during the period represented by the Codex Reina, "Sicilian" corresponded somewhat to "regnicolo" (native of the Kingdom), referring to the kingdom (later known as the Kingdom of the Two Sicilies) which the Normans had first established in Sicily but had then enlarged until it included all of southern Italy. This entire area, which Frederick II inherited, is implied when Sicily is named in connection with my examples, whether folkloristic or polyphonic.

One characteristic of polyphonic *siciliane* is a tendency to reuse the same musical elements several times in a composition. A popular singer tends toward maximum economy of means; like the improviser (and the two endeavors often coincide), he must memorize a vast repertory, and he is therefore likely to simplify it, to reduce anything he memorizes to what seems indispensable. Among the compositions in the Codex Reina, the piece which best typifies such an attitude is a *ballata,* the text of which is as follows:[7]

(E) vantènde, segnor mio, (e) vatène, amore,	A
con ti via se ne vene l'alma (mia) e'l core.	
(E) gli ochi dolenti piangon sença fine	B
cha vedèr el paradisso e soa belleza.	
A cuy ti lasso, amore, chè no me meni?	B
l'alma me levi e'l cor e l'alegreça.	
La bocha cridarà che sentiva dolceça;	?
amarà lamentarse, oymè topina!	
Altro signor zamay non voglio [avere]	A
perch'io non troverey del suo vallore.	
(E) vantène, segnor mio, [etc.]	A

The exhortative form *vantènde,* which this text shares with that attributed to Frederick II, is southern rather than distinctively Sicilian. Even more

noteworthy is the irregular form of this *ballata,* which has two extra lines
(7 and 8). Since they do not clearly constitute either a third *piede* (B
section) or a doubling of the *volta* (second A section), the singer had to
choose whether to sing them to the music of the *piedi* or to that of the
ripresa (first A section). This decision, however, was of little importance,
because the two sections are very similar musically; the first sixteen and the
last five breves (preceding the closing note) of section B basically reuse the
music of the *ripresa;* the central span of eight breves is different, but only
somewhat different, in each section.

At this point in my talk, my improvisation took flight and I embarked on
general considerations of the concept of economy and of the advantages it
offers to an improviser who, by having a simple melodic formula ready in
his memory, can concentrate more easily on improvising a text appropriate to the circumstances. Economy of means and memorization of melodic
formulas may well have been among the secret components of the fabled
"secret of the Quattrocento." At its base, however, the "secret" featured a
divorce, verified in the course of the century, of humanistic from musical
culture. To humanists the *ars musicae* appeared irremediably tied to
scholastic traditions, so they tended to reject it as something too close to
medieval sophistry, outmoded, and far from the classicism and simplicity
which they aspired to reestablish. The humanists' indifference to the
polyphony of their time is discussed elsewhere.[8] Close to the end of the
fifteenth century, Angelo Poliziano was most explicit in expressing not
only indifference, but even distrust. In a letter the poet refers to having
heard in Rome a boy who performed with other "experts" (therefore in
polyphony) "quaedam ... notata accentiunculis musicis carmina." This
phrase is charged with irony concerning both the experts and those "small
scrawls of music" in which their songs were written; indeed, the poet does
not praise the music, but only the beauty of the boy's voice. His admiration
knows no bounds, however, when he refers to the adolescent's singing "to
a lyre," a form of solo song typical of the unwritten tradition. Poliziano
rapturously describes the power of such song to enthrall, exalt, or soothe
the souls of listeners and does not hesitate to compare the singer's effective
recitation with that of an actor, terming the singer "a diminutive Roscius
on the stage."[9]

With this citation, my improvisation approached its final point: that we
can and should perceive in the *frottola* repertory, which dates from the end
of the fifteenth century, the surfacing in written tradition of forms and
modes which until then had been employed in oral tradition. Among the
so-called frottolesque forms, the *strambotto* had during the fifteenth

century an importance comparable to that of the madrigal during the following century; although there were certainly popular types of the *strambotto,* its courtly and refined formulation was esteemed above all others. Serafino Aquilano, the brightest star in Italian music at the end of the century, was especially admired for his singing of *strambotti,* seen at that time as the ne plus ultra of music, although we now tend rather to discredit their texts as baroque before their time. *Strambotti,* including those found in musical manuscripts and prints, are among the most remarkable examples of musical economy: the setting for the first two lines is simply repeated for each of the next three distichs, with nothing more than slight modifications, which—although not notated—were certainly introduced by performers in order to adjust the same melodic line to varying verbal accentuations. When a number of stanzas—each of them an eight-line *strambotto*—were sung, the musical unit would have been repeated for each distich in every stanza. To our astonishment, we find that this practice still held sway at Florence in 1539, at the time of the wedding of Cosimo dei Medici to Eleonora of Toledo. The print containing music performed on that occasion includes a series of polyphonic madrigals sung in honor of the betrothed by groups impersonating the various cities of Tuscany; the groups were presented by a singer, personifying Apollo, who sang "to the lyre" as many as forty eight-line stanzas. The print gives the text but not the music, which was still submersed in the unwritten tradition.[10]

Analogous compositional procedures were employed for the *capitolo* and the *oda,* both related to the poetic category known as *sirventese* in the fifteenth century; in them the musical setting for the first three-line unit was repeated for the following symmetrically constructed units.[11] We find greater variety in the sonnet, either because the written examples belong to a period in which new solutions concerning the relationship between poetry and music were already in the air, or because the relative brevity of the form (fourteen lines) lent itself to through-composed settings written especially for particular texts rather than for generic use. Nevertheless, the prevailing procedure, especially in the "arie da cantar sonetti" (airs for singing sonnets) was economical in that the music for three lines served for the entire poem: only the first, second, and fourth lines were set to music. Since the third rhymes with the second, it reuses the second musical phrase; the same three phrases likewise serve for the second quatrain and—without repetition of the second phrase—for the two tercets.

By far the predominant form in the musical prints of Petrucci is that which is often called the *frottola* by musicologists and the *barzelletta* by literary scholars. For a long time I have wondered whether it might be possible to make a distinction between *frottole* and *barzellette,* and what that distinction might be. I have now come to the conclusion that the most precise term is *barzelletta* and that its etymology is most probably that which came to my mind twenty years ago while dealing with *belzeretta,* which is found in some letters written by Isabella d'Este.[12] The term was derived from *bergerette,* which in fifteenth-century France designated an intermediate form between the *virelai* and the *rondeau.* The *barzelletta* likewise stands between the *ballata* and the *rondeau* in that it has the verse structure of the *ballata* (although with a distinct preference for an eight-syllable line with a popular flavor in place of the eleven- and seven-syllable lines of the literary *ballata*), while like the *rondeau* its stanza employs musical material borrowed from the *ripresa.* Not all the *barzellette* in Petrucci's collections correspond completely to this description, yet it would not be difficult to demonstrate statistically that it is the most common type. The *frottola* "Oimè el cor, oimè la testa," which opens the collection of *Frottole libro primo* (Venice, 1504), may serve as an example. My transcription (Ex. 6.1) is, however, taken from the later arrangement by Franciscus Bossinensis, found in *Tenori e contrabassi intabulati col sopran in canto figurato per cantar e sonar col lauto Libro primo* (Venice, 1509). As in Petrucci's prints, the text of the four-line *ripresa* is given with the music; the problem of how the eight-line stanza is fitted to the music is solved as follows:

Oimè, Dio, che error fece io	A
ad amar un cor fallace;	B
oimè, Dio, ch'el partir mio	A
non mi dà per questo pace.	B
Oimè, el foco aspro e vivace	B
mi consuma el tristo core.	C
Oimè, Dio, ch'el fatto errore	C
l'alma afflicta mi molesta.	A
Oimè el cor, ohimè la testa [etc.]	A—B'—B"

The first two phrases of the melody are used for the first two lines and then repeated for the next two lines, which rhyme with the first two.[13] The next phrase, which follows the first set of repetition signs, is used for line 5 and is musically identical with the second phrase (relating to the fact that the line rhymes with lines 2 and 4). A new phrase serves for line 6 and is repeated for line 7 (which rhymes with 6). Line 8, which rhymes with line 1 of the *ripresa,* is set with the opening musical phrase, and hence it

Ex. 6.1 Marchetto Cara, *Frottola*

Ex. 6.1   Continued

foreshadows the abbreviated return of the *ripresa*.[14] Thus for the *barzelletta,* as for other frottolesque forms, only three musical phrases are needed in order to sing any number of stanzas.

The first decades of the 1500s saw the beginning of a period which is marked in the literary world by a conscious orientation toward the linguistic and metric forms of fourteenth-century poetry, and in the musical world by a search for "artistic" solutions. Yet some practices of the preceding period still remained in compositions with *canzona* texts (usually Petrarchan), in which the recurrence of a rhyme sometimes invited the repetition of a musical phrase; even in the early years of the madrigal, any text that was reminiscent of a *canzona* strophe, with its symmetrical *piedi* and a *sirima,* was often similarly treated by a composer, in that the setting of the first *piede* was repeated for the text of the second. These sixteenth-century pieces were performed "a libro" (that is, with music in hand or, as Poliziano would have said, from those "small scrawls of music"), and their musical repetitions are therefore disengaged from any practical necessity related to memorization. However, we should not ignore their derivation from the practices of the unwritten tradition which had prevailed during the preceding century.

7 ⊱ Music and Cultural Tendencies in Fifteenth-Century Italy

A singer employed at the Duomo of Milan from 1459 to 1472 has been identified with the great Josquin des Prez, and to my knowledge the identification suggested by Claudio Sartori[1] has never been challenged. Nor do I see why it should be, for there seems to be a real continuity between the record of "Judocho de frantia," the obscure singer at the Duomo, and what had been considered up to now as the beginning of the career of the *princeps musicorum*—his presence in the newly established and decidedly ambitious chapel of Galeazzo Maria Sforza. The thirteen years of service rendered by Josquin No. 1 ended at the very time when the activity of the ducal chapel was gaining momentum, attracting several singers of the Duomo. The name of Josquin No. 2 is then present in all the extant lists of ducal chaplains.[2]

To be sure, this continuity does not provide absolute certainty about the identity of the two musicians; nevertheless, the coincidence of names, places, and dates is too significant to be dismissed without evidence to the contrary. If a gap exists anywhere, it is between the last known document connecting Josquin with the Milanese court—a safe-conduct released to him in 1479 for a three-month journey to St. Antoine de Vienne in southern France[3]—and his admission to the papal chapel in 1486.[4] However, the latter followed only two years after the arrival in Rome of the newly elected Cardinal Ascanio Sforza, Galeazzo Maria's younger brother.[5] It is possible that the ties with the Sforza family had never been severed and that we should admire the skill and savoir-faire of the young cardinal, who so quickly succeeded in placing on the pope's payroll a musician whose close association with the cardinal's own household had made him known as "Jusquin d'Ascanio."

Moving the beginning of Josquin's career to 1459 simply accentuates the anomaly that only a small number of his surviving compositions can be tentatively dated before 1480. At this time he would have been about thirty years old according to the old chronology, almost forty on the basis of the newer findings. Although Josquin may have acted in later years to suppress the works of his youth that no longer satisfied his demanding taste, he could have effectively disposed only of compositions that had never enjoyed popularity nor met any standard of taste. If we also consider that the singer who entered the Sforza chapel after 1472 was over thirty, yet was regularly named almost at the bottom of every list of the members of the chapel and paid the lowest monthly salary among his colleagues,[6] there seems no way to escape the conclusion that for all his potential gifts, Josquin had a late start as a composer.

Josquin's biography is not my present concern, however. I do hope, indeed, that future discoveries may help to determine what personal factors and vicissitudes played a part in his belated start. Yet my purpose in citing his conspicuous case here is chiefly to draw attention to the more general factor of environment. Whatever may have diverted the brilliant and enterprising young man from the path which would later commit his name to history, his example dramatically raises the question of the degree to which the atmosphere of the Italian courts and towns during the second half of the fifteenth century was actually favorable to the artistic development of a young composer of polyphonic music.

It is well known that Italy did not produce any active polyphonist of renown after the second or third decade of the fifteenth century, and it has been generally assumed that the country welcomed and fostered the activity of many foreign composers. In turn, their presence is related to the quickening pulse of the Italian Renaissance and to that extravagant yet impressive mixture of intellectual alertness and selfish exhibitionism, the generous artistic patronage of many—too many—Italian courts.

Should we accept such a view, it would still remain to be explained why the age that saw an enormous display of native ingenuity in architecture, the fine arts, and all minor artistic crafts should have leaned so heavily on foreign talent only for music. The undisputed prestige of the French musical tradition cannot be made to account alone for the imbalance. On the one hand, the stylistic charms of the Italian Ars nova had attracted such foreign artists as Ciconia and Dufay, and on the other hand, a number of Italian composers had been successful in mastering the skills required for the adoption of the French forms and styles of polyphonic composition.

I confess to have indulged (possibly more than it deserved) in the thought that the lack of permanent institutions like the later chapels, where young people could receive an adequate musical training, might have been a factor in the anomalous situation. But the same conditions had prevailed during the previous century without preventing the appearance of the composers who are responsible for the Italian Ars nova. No matter how these composers had learned their craft, there is no reason why the same sources—churches, monasteries, or individual teachers—should not have met, at least partially, an increased demand for composers of polyphonic music in the fifteenth century as well.

As a matter of fact, the first part of that century was a time of intense international polyphonic activity, reflected in a number of well-known sources that are of primary importance for our knowledge of the music of this period. The geographical distribution of these sources along the valley of the river Po and the vast arc of the Alps—from Aosta and Brescia to Trent, Munich, and Cividale—and the unprecedented emphasis on the Ordinary of the Mass, and on hymns, Magnificats, and antiphons for the Offices, call for an explanation that cannot be found in the music performed in churches.

Scanty as the information in our possession may be, what we know of such major centers as Milan, Padua, and Florence does not seem to explain so extensive a repertory, and there is even less explanation for the presence of so many composers. Cathedral churches in those towns were often served by only one or two singers; three or four was a maximum sometimes reached but seldom sustained.[7] Among those church singers whose names are known to us, only Prepositus Brixiensis in Padua and Beltrame Feragut in Milan were composers of some merit.[8] Nor do we have any evidence of the existence at that time of large seigneurial chapels. Among the forty-five persons forming the retinue of Nicolò d'Este in his pilgrimage to the Holy Land in 1413, music was possibly represented by one Rodolfo da l'Alpa [sic], by the trumpeters Janni and Santo, and by "el capellano con un compagno," who may or may not have formed a polyphonic duo.[9]

In my opinion, only the high ranks of the Church can be credited with an extensive use of artistic polyphony. Between 1406 and 1443 the Roman popes actually resided most of the time north of Rome, in Lucca, in Florence, and even more often in Bologna. In the same period the crisis inaugurated by the Great Schism and unresolved even by its conclusion called for—in rapid succession—the Councils of Pisa, Cividale, Constance, Pavia-Siena, Basel, Ferrara, and finally Florence, which brought into the precise geographical region mentioned earlier an unusual concentration of the leading figures of the Church. The Councils were also attended by the representatives of the highest political powers in Europe, which too were more often than not selected from the ecclesiastical ranks.[10]

More often than we think, these dignitaries had musicians in their *familiae*, not so much for any public display as for the daily private celebrations required by their ecclesiastical status. It is recorded, for instance, that bishops arriving in Basel dismissed their singers in deference to the Council.[11] The Council had its own singers (Fig. 7.1), whose salaries soon became a source of periodic embarrassment to the financial committee.[12] Yet it is my contention that the singers who were dismissed by the bishops and rehired by the Council were only a part, and possibly the least significant part, of the musicians involved in the creation and performance of the polyphonic repertory.

We may be handicapped in our attempts to establish the biographies of musicians by a mental habit of seeing them too exclusively as musicians. We marvel at their accomplishments in other fields—that Binchois had been a valiant soldier; that Dufay may have had a degree "in decretis"; that Gilles Joye was possibly a distinguished theologian, certainly an effective church administrator who could afford a portrait by such a fashionable and expensive painter as Hans Memlinc.[13] But this is precisely what they were: a soldier, a counselor, an influential and affluent canon—high court or church officers who added the refinement of musical skills to the cultural training that enabled them to be employed in administrative, political, or diplomatic tasks.

Individual musicians sometimes possessed all the ecclesiastic qualifications to become full members of a Council, that is, "fathers of the Church." Thus it happened, for instance, that on December 10, 1434, a petition was recorded in the acts of the Council of Basel, by which Johannes Brassart requested retention of all his rights as a member of the Council even though he might have to absent himself, being a "familiaris et capellanus" of Emperor Sigismund of Austria.[14] The same may have been the case in 1437, when Dufay took part in an embassy sent by the duke of Burgundy to the Council, the Curia, and the emperor.

An analogous fallacy may lie in our consideration of the institutions in which musicians operated. While some court chapels were already in the process of becoming the purely musical institutions we know from later times, they still retained a number of other features. Like the *familia* of a bishop, the *capella* of a prince combined the tasks of providing daily celebrations of private religious services with those of a "cabinet," a body

Fig. 7.1   Canonization of Brigitta of Sweden, February 1, 1415, from U. von Richental's Chronicle of the Council of Constance (ms. Constance, Rosgarten Museum, circa 1460, fols. 32v–33r). The papal singers of John XXIV wear their

furred surplices (*superpellicia*); on the stalls are three nonsinging members of the chapel. (Courtesy of the Rosgarten Museum.)

of competent assistants and advisers, working in close association with their masters.[15] In the chapel of the dukes of Burgundy, Jacques de Templeuve was chosen as first chaplain in 1418, not because of musical skill but in consideration of past administrative services, namely in establishing an inventory of jewelry and furniture.[16] For all his artistic merits Binchois never reached a similar position in the chapel, nor did he take precedence over Fontaine, a much weaker composer.[17]

If we assume that the sole purpose of having boys in a chapel was to enjoy the clear sound of their voices, then we do not understand the intent of the dukes of Burgundy, who so often sent the boys attached to their chapel to study in Paris or elsewhere for years.[18] Information coming from the chapel of the Aragonese kings of Naples around the middle of the century may help us to understand, for it stresses the role of a chapel as a teaching institution.[19] Providing an education for the sons of faithful servants was a reward to their parents and an investment in future loyalties. This may also explain the title of *magister capellae*, which does not seem to have had anything to do with conducting at this time,[20] and was occasionally given—Dufay again is an example—to men who did not even reside with the chapel.[21]

All of this may seem not to apply to the papal court, where the needs of an enormous centralized bureaucracy had led to the creation of specialized groups: the *abbreviatores* or secretaries, the *notarii* and *protonotarii*, the *advocatura apostolica* for legal advice, the *camera apostolica* for financial transactions.[22] Yet, although the chapel was thus restricted to its liturgical functions and their musical complement, its *magister capellae* was usually a bishop, not a musician,[23] and the choice of its members was so strongly felt to be the personal concern of the pontiff, with whom they lived in close association, that Eugene IV was able on his accession to almost completely renew the membership of his chapel.[24]

As evidence for the importance and quality of the papal singers, I may mention a decree of Pope Martin V, in which the rights and privileges that the pope had granted after his election to the doctors and masters of art of the University of Paris are said to apply "naturally" to his own *cantores capellani*.[25] This particular point is of special significance to me, since my purpose is to portray the greater and better part of the polyphonists of this time, either singers or composers, not as the mercenary professionals they became later, but as ecclesiastical dignitaries who had received academic training and who combined their musical skills and gifts with many other talents, capacities, and ambitions. They were still the successors of Philippe de Vitry—a royal officer and later a bishop who had strong cultural ties with the university—and of Machaut—a royal secretary and later a canon who would have styled himself a *rhétoriqueur* rather than a musician. They belong to a broad cultural type, the product of an educational pattern especially designed to prepare for an ecclesiastical career, represented at its best by the curriculum of the University of Paris. Even the fact, often stressed, that the emergence (neither as sudden nor as exclusive as claimed) of the so-called School of Cambrai coincides with the episcopacy of Pierre d'Ailly, formerly chancellor of the Parisian university, may indicate that the strong emphasis on music at Cambrai was only one facet of a strong emphasis on "scholastic" education.[26]

My aim is all too transparent: to contrast the cultural type I have just outlined—which we may define as scholastic, using the term in its broader acceptance—with the new breed of educated men, the humanists. But first I need to describe the sharp decline of polyphonic practice in Italy after 1437, relating it to the diminished influx of foreign prelates. In that year the Council still assembled in Basel was condemned by the pope; it lost ground rapidly even among its sympathizers because of its extremist attitudes and continued its work in a political vacuum. A new Council opened in Ferrara in the same year and then continued in Florence to work out a short-lived reunion of the Greek and Roman churches; it had much less resonance among the Western powers and a smaller attendance, more humanistically than scholastically oriented.

A policy of austerity adopted by Eugene IV also affected musical practice, reemphasizing plainchant, or polyphony strictly dependent upon it.[27] Establishing new seminary schools in Florence, Turin, and Urbino, the pope prescribed the study of plainchant but never mentioned measured music, that is, polyphony.[28] If we take the lists of members of the papal chapel as an index, none is known as a composer of polyphonic music in the years following Dufay's final departure in 1437;[29] Johannes Fede stayed in the chapel only a few months in 1443–44.[30] Under Eugene's successors only one polyphonic composer, Johannes Pullois, was present in the chapel from 1447 to 1469.[31] One senses the impact of the demands for ecclesiastical reform that were then so strongly insisted upon by the Councils, and that at all times (except our own) have led to condemnation of the "artificiality" of polyphonic invention and a renewal of enthusiasm for the venerable simplicity of plainchant.

An even more important factor in the long run was, in my opinion, the process by which the representatives of the old cultural type were being replaced, in the Curia as in the executive ranks of every Italian court or town government, by the followers of the *studia humanitatis*.[32] By this process those who had practiced polyphony as a creative, liberal activity, as well as those who could best appreciate it, were being eliminated. What remained was on one side the hired singer—the *cantor*, not the *musicus*—and on the other side an indifferent audience.[33]

It is true that the difference between the old scholastic and the new humanistic type of culture was not a basic one. Much of the old curriculum was maintained or even expanded. Differences existed, however, derived in part from the less speculative and more pragmatic tradition of the Italian communal universities, in part from the emphasis put on the study of classical models as a necessary approach to the art of composing all types of documents, letters, and speeches, and, even further, as an ideal guidance to every aspect of human life. Music apparently held its place in the curriculum. Commencement speeches by Francesco Maturanzio[34] and Filippo Beroaldo the Older[35] include it among the arts that were considered as the foundation of a liberal education and describe at length its pervasive presence in every order of physical and spiritual phenomena. But what is said of *sounding* music is restricted to extensive lists of its effects on men, animals, or inanimate objects, with examples drawn without exception from mythology or ancient pseudo-historical anecdotes. Similar passages occur frequently in other fifteenth-century writings wherever their authors felt that a display of encyclopedic knowledge was appropriate to round out the treatment of any topic.[36] They are obviously derived from a few classical models, particularly from the writings of Quintilianus, Censorinus, and Martianus Capella.

Dressed in more classical garb, those passages are similar in content to the initial paragraphs, dealing with *musica mundana* and *humana*, of most scholastic treatises on music.[37] One gets the impression, however, that a humanist seldom read beyond the initial paragraphs; beyond the general concept of numerical proportions underlying musical phenomena, he had no use for a more detailed study of modes, rules of notation, or rhythmic proportions. Even Ficino, whose vivid interest in music was artistically as well as philosophically motivated, appears to be extremely insecure as soon as he ventures into technical descriptions.[38]

Younger humanists gave definite evidence of their distrust of a technical tradition of music that was too closely associated in their minds with medieval Latin and the French vernacular. A letter of Ermolao Barbaro, dated 1488, describes an attempt he had made to fit the terminology of the "great system" of Greek ancient music theory to the Guidonian hand. This, Barbaro states, had been suggested to him by a "poor book" he was reading—poor not because of its contents, but for being written in an "alien" language.[39] To this disparaging allusion, which I interpret as referring to scholastic Latin, he later adds a criticism of the Guidonian syllables of solmization for their "barbaric" sound and for their derivation from a poem that had little or nothing of Latin elegance, the Hymn to Saint John. One has to tolerate them, he concludes, "until something more refined and more elegant is invented."[40] Along the same line of thought, Giorgio Valla wrote an extensive treatise on music, published posthumously in 1501, in which only classical Greek sources seem to have been used.[41]

The most usual attitude of a humanist, however, seems to me to be not one of distrust or contempt toward the most technical aspects of music, but simply one of ignorance for lack of exposure. His musical experience is chiefly empirical, concentrating on the most immediate aspects of this art, on soloistic singing, dance tunes, flourishes of trumpets, lulling sounds of harps and flutes, and perhaps some display of instrumental virtuosity on the lute or on a keyboard instrument. We need not be surprised by this if we consider how large a part is given to these same aspects of music also in contemporary French descriptions of musical events. But French writers often indicate that they were also aware of the existence and merits of contemporary polyphonists; the Italian humanists recall all the mythical powers of music to describe the accomplishments of singers or instrumentalists who would be completely unknown to us but for the exalted praise of their humanist friends.[42]

We must wait until almost the end of the century to find a similar eulogy addressed to a polyphonist. To my knowledge, the earliest example is one that takes us back to the musician with whom we were first concerned; it is the well-known sonnet addressed by Serafino Aquilano about 1490 to "Jusquino, suo compagno musico d'Ascanio" (Josquin, his fellow musician under Ascanio).[43] If we are shocked by the equation implied in this title between the art of Josquin and Aquilano's own musicianship, we should consider that a fifteenth-century man who had little familiarity with polyphony may not have been prepared to include Josquin's works at all in his notion of music.[44]

Humanist writers often accented the performance of music at a banquet as one point on which contemporary habits happily coincided with the custom of the ancients.[45] A nice example of such habits, the description of the banquet following the wedding of Francesco Sforza and Bianca Maria Visconti, is included in the ninth book of La Sfortiade, a long manuscript poem by Antonio Cornazano, better known to musicologists as a writer on the dance.[46]

The stage is Cremona, given to the bride as part of her dowry. The year is 1441, and the language vernacular, yet the poem aims to recreate the flavor of Homeric times, probably known to the poet through Vergil's *Aeneid* or through some snatch of Homeric translation provided by another Milanese courtier, Francesco Filelfo.[47] Cornazano does not indulge in the usual enumeration of elaborate courses and of their musical and theatrical *entremets*, which were the fad at this time.[48] Contrary to our expectation, he dismisses the banquet itself in a few lines and swiftly moves on to describe the mood of relaxation following the meal.

Then, as in the second book of the *Aeneid*, "conticuere omnes"; all become silent while the protagonist himself, Sforza, tells of an episode of war and of mercy on the vanquished. After him one of his captains, whose name, Troilo, happens to have a classical ring, recalls past adventures and perils. Only when the pathos of reminiscence has reached its peak[49] is the musician introduced, "whom the stars have endowed with the power of soothing and pacifying."

I have summarized about 140 lines of the "Descriptio conuituj," as it is labeled on fol. 104 *bis* of the ms. The following section, rubricated "Laudes Petri Boni Cythariste," I have rechecked with the original[50] and given as Appendix 1 to this essay. As Telemachos says in the first book of the *Odyssey*, "The song people praise is always the latest thing." Our singer, too, is careful "to sing in well-ordered verses, to the *cythara*, the love stories of modern people that are [most] praised." So eager is he to keep up to date that he includes in his singing the love affairs of Sigismondo Malatesta, lord of Rimini, with Isotta degli Atti, and of Alfonso of Aragon, king of Naples, with Lucrezia d'Alagno; neither of these affairs had yet taken place at the supposed time of the performance in 1441.[51] It is unlikely that either Cornazano (who was eleven in 1441) or the musician he describes (although he was somewhat older) attended Sforza's wedding. In his poem, finished in 1459, the year of Josquin's arrival in Milan, Cornazano simply describes some performance that must have taken place in 1456, when the musician in question, the then famous Pietrobono dal Chitarrino of Ferrara, was lent to the court of Francesco Sforza for a short period.[52]

Surprisingly, Pietrobono, whom we know better as a lutenist, is described by Cornazano as a singer accompanying himself on an unidentified string instrument classically named a "cetra," while the performer himself is called "el primo cithareo" (rhyming with "prestante deo" and "Orpheo"). Although the reason for this choice is quite evident, for there was no place in Cornazano's revival of the Homeric climate for anything less than a classical rhapsodist, we must admit that also in real life Pietrobono was a "cantore a liuto" as well as a lutenist.[53]

A few years later the same kind of singing to a string instrument charmed Galeazzo Maria Sforza, still a boy, on the occasion of a visit he made to Florence. The singer this time was a favorite of the Medici, Antonio di Guido, not as famous to us as his contemporary Antonio Squarcialupi, but much admired in his own day.[54] Even later, singing "a liuto," or "alla viola," or "alla lira" was still in high fashion. Poliziano, who mentions it more than once in letters describing the accomplishments of his pupil Piero dei Medici, is himself reported to have met his death while singing to the lute.[55] The Brandolini brothers, Baccio Ugolini, and Bernardo Accolti (called "l'Unico aretino")—to name only a few—were all famous for their singing.[56] At the Milanese court the style of singing of a Neapolitan gentleman, Andrea Coscia, deeply impressed the most famous practitioner of this genre, Serafino Aquilano, and affected his own style.[57] About the turn of the century, according to Vincenzo Calmeta (Beatrice Sforza's secretary and Aquilano's follower and biographer), the customary way for a poet to make his new poems known was to have them sung by a "citaredo."[58]

The trend was rapidly changing, however. The appearance among militant music theorists and polyphonists of such humanists as Gafori, Tinctoris, and possibly Josquin himself, the daily exchanges established in Rome between the papal singers and the hosts of poets and orators haunting the Curia, and finally the creation of a new poetic sense of polyphonic language, in which again Josquin had a major part, led to a better understanding between humanists and polyphonic composers. A growing appreciation for the art of polyphony is evident in the praise given to Josquin as the outstanding composer of polyphonic Masses, and to Isaac and Obrecht as eminent in the lesser genre of the motet, in Paolo Cortese's *De cardinalatu libri tres*—once more an encyclopedic treatise on the rules of behavior fitting a "senator" of the Church, that is, a cardinal.[59] Cortese's utterances specifically refer for support to the authority in musical matters of the young Cardinal Medici, later Pope Leo X, who certainly played an important role in this as well as in later musical developments, together with his younger relatives Giuliano, Giulio (later Clement VII), and the younger Lorenzo, and with another future pope, Alessandro Farnese.[60]

Yet a remnant of the humanists' mixed feelings toward polyphony can still be detected in Cortese's dealing with music (Appendix 2 to this essay includes a translation of this section). His praise of Josquin as a composer of Masses constitutes in his mind the highest honor, based, however, on the excellence of the genre rather than of the composer. The songs accompanying the sacrifice of the Mass, which he classically calls [*carmina*] *litatoria*, are highest in his esteem because of the humanist's prejudice that the importance of the text essentially determines the esthetic value of its music. He downgrades the motets—not only Josquin's motets—because their texts are less directly concerned with the most essential part of the ritual sacrifice. Their *ad libitum* nature,[61] left to the decisions of the *praecentor*, and perhaps a suspicion of the latter's showmanship, seem to have suggested the term *praecentoria* by which they are designated. Finally, in spite of all that precedes, Cortese's section on music still concluded with an emphatic eulogy of Serafino Aquilano as the star of secular music. Polyphonic *chansons*, either by Josquin or by others, are simply ignored.

Cortese is remembered for having been possibly the initiator of modern literary criticism—which he refused to apply to his contemporaries unless they were already dead[62]—and for a mild and not at all unkind polemic exchange with Poliziano. The latter's flexible use of Latin antagonized his own sense of respect for the golden model of the most classic writers.[63] As a fervent Ciceronian he makes it a point to describe even contemporary musical instruments and practices in the most classical terms. He deliberately ignores the time-honored word for "organ" and replaces it with an elaborate circumlocution: "those pneumatic genres in which tin pipes are assembled together, usually in the shape of a castle"; the lute, which some medieval writers had called "lembutum," becomes "that genre that looks like a cutter," for "lembus" in Latin means an agile ship. *Missae* and *moteti*, other typically medieval terms, are replaced, as already observed, by *litatoria* and *praecentoria*, both implying the noun *carmina*; but *carmina*, with no need for a qualifying adjective, is Cortese's term for the poems sung "ad lembum," whose origins he traces back to Petrarch. Even more drastically, the misuse of ancient terms perpetuated in the medieval theory of church modes is swept away by Cortese with a new arbitrary classification in which the Gregorian chant as a whole is said to belong under the Dorian ethos. More faithful to the letter than to the spirit of classicism, Cortese reverses the relationship between mode and ethos and makes the determination of the former depend on the latter.

Passages from Cortese's chapter (or section of a chapter) on music have been occasionally quoted in recent writings. Yet its general context, and the evidence it gives for the history of musical taste during the Renaissance, seem to me far more revealing than the information given on individual musicians. Here I shall take advantage only of its title, which can be rendered in a somewhat free translation: "How passions should be avoided, and music enjoyed after dinner." Of all the mythical powers of music, only one seems to have been most familiar to the humanists, that of diverting the mind and bringing relaxation. For the rest, they still seemed to rely on their own forte, the power of words.

Appendix 1

"Laudes Petri Boni Cythariste" from Antonio Cornazano's *Sforziade*, canto VIII (Codex Paris, Bibliothèque Nationale, nouv. acq. 1472, fols. 106v–107v).

> Qui el choro, al suo parlar stato suspeso
>   sulle vivande a quel che havea parlato,
>   facto già fine, in pede si fu reso.
> A questo alto triumpho era chiamato
> 5   un Piero Bono da lontana via,
>   che in musica le stelle havean dotato
> pascer l'orechia di dolçe armonia.
>   Non havrà el mondo el più prestante deo,
>   ni accender fiama in cor, ch'el là non sia.
> 10 Ancho di forma el primo cithareo
>   è questi, apena cavo fu vivendo,
>   excepto Apollo, el bel corpo d'Orpheo.
> E per quanto da lui de ciò m'intendo
>   a soa comparation nullo reservo,
> 15 e l'armonie che i ciel fano suspendo.
> Quest'un già puote col percosso nervo
>   svegliar gli corpi nelle sepolture,
>   et adolcire ogn'animo protervo;
> gli attracti sensi da tucte altre cure
> 20 subvertir puote e con sue voci liete
>   fermar gli fiumi e dar strada a le mure.
> Quasi ebriati nel fonte di Lethe
>   trava a sè i cor la man sì dolc'e dotta
>   e convertia ciascun a Anaxarethe.
> 25 Cantava in cetra ad ordinata frotta
>   l'amor d'alcun moderni chi s'appretia:
>   come el Signor d'Arimini hebbe Ysotta.

Laudava la marina de Venetia
    ov'ella naque, e quinçi entrava in canto
30   come el re d'Aragona hebbe Lucretia.
A questa de le belle dava el vanto,
    e dicea, in aer più d'altro superno,
    de Viola novella el fine e 'l pianto.
Mettea costei dannata al campo Averno
35   e comendava el giustissimo amante
    che andò a vederla fino entro lo 'nferno.
D'una madonna assai poco constante
    dicea l'ardor con la corrente spanna,
    e per coprirla molto andava errante;
40   pur s'intendea la regina Giohana,
    e fra gli suoi amator par che mettea
    el magno Sforça chi la vide a canna.
Molto mostrava che tacito ardea,
    ma a ciò che pervenisse el cuore ardente
45   lassò in dubio el si e 'l no, s'el la tenea.
Per singular cançone estremamente
    dicea d'un'altra l'inflamationi,
    passando el Conte sotto Aquapendente.
E la guidava tucta in semitoni,
50   proportionando e sincoppando sempre,
    e fugiva el tenore a i suoi cantoni.
Tanto expedite, chiare e dolce tempre
    s'udiron mai, oymè ch'io el posso dire:
    qual cor sì temprato è che amor non stempre?
55   Quinçi scendeva in languido finire,
    tal che fe' ponto fino in su la rosa
    e una pausa per duol vene a tegnire.
Di questa, a lui palese, ad altri ascosa,
    la sententia era e fiori e non viole
60   d'una seconda madre e d'una sposa.
In ta' mellodie docto, al mondo sole,
    soleva ascoltatissimo a lor farse,
    dando col suon vivissime parole.
Allor, retracto in altro adoperarse,
65   hebbe el cerchio amoroso a ballo spinto
    e gli portici voti a copie sparse,
quale Amphion in meço all'Arachinto
    con la cava testude, a Thebbe intorno,
    de comandati sassi el muro ha cincto.

Commentary. Pietrobono, mounted on a high bench (l. 4), is compared to Apollo and Orpheus (ll. 6–12); his music rivals the heavenly harmonies, can revive the dead, turn rivers and stones, and even change people into statues (ll. 13–24; for the last accomplishment Cornazano refers to Ovid's *Metamorphoses*, XIV, ll. 698–760). His singing includes the love stories of: Isotta degli Atti and Sigismondo Malatesta (ll. 27–29); Lucrezia d'Alagno and Alfonso of Aragon (ll. 30–31); Viola Novella and Malatesta Ungaro (ll. 32–36); Johanna II of Naples and Attendolo Sforza, father of Francesco (ll. 37–45); and an anonymous lady, who had seen Francesco himself near Acquapendente (ll. 46–51). The latter is a tactful hint to Giovanna, called la Colombina, who followed Sforza for years, and bore to him Polissena (1428), Sforza Secondo (1433; Cornazano addressed to him the second version of *L'arte del danzare*), Drusiana (1437), and two other children who did not live long. Lacking texts and music of these stories, we would like to know at least their meter, but all Cornazano tells us is that Pietrobono "sang to the *cetra* in a well-ordered *frotta*." *Frotta* may have meant a *ballata* form, and a *ballata* actually exists telling of Viola Novella, killed by her jealous husband and visited in hell by her faithful lover—a romance built around the historical feat of a pilgrimage to St. Patrick's well, accomplished by Malatesta Ungaro in 1358 (see for extensive references and comments M. A. Silvestri, *art. cit.*, in *Miscellanea di storia, letteratura e arte piacentina*, pp. 157–161, n.2). *Frottola*, a diminutive of *frotta*, means a *ballata* form, yet it has also a second meaning indicating a poem consisting of an irregular succession of long and short lines. Accordingly, Cornazano's, and Pietrobono's "ordinata frotta" may have meant any of the narrative meters which usually replace the narrative *ballata* during the fifteenth century: the *capitolo* or *terza rima* (the meter of each canto of Cornazano's *Sfortiade*), the *sirventese*, and finally the *ottava rima*, which was later to prevail as the meter of Boiardo's, Ariosto's and Tasso's epic poems. Lines 49–57 of Cornazano's description of Pietrobono's last narrative poems give details about the music. Yet we cannot give them too much faith; although we are told that Pietrobono's last song was a "singular cançone," it is hard to believe that it was "tucta in semitoni," made extensive use of proportions and syncopations, and had its tenor fugally imitated on the lower strings of the accompanying instrument. It seems to me that we have here one more instance of a poet (Cornazano) using technical terms just because of their sound or even inventing them, for I have never before found the lower strings of an instrument called *cantoni* (Cornazano must have derived this term from *cantino*, a diminutive of *canto*, which is the proper name for the upper string). Cornazano gives another example of his cavalier treatment of technical terms in the following lines 52–60, cryptically referring to the feelings "of a second mother and of a wife." He describes the languid descending end of the song as coming to a "fine point on the 'rose' "; but of course the nearer Pietrobono's fretting fingers came down to the "rose" of his instrument, the higher must have been the sounds produced by the strings. Should we suppose that what Cornazano had in mind was the converging motions of a descending vocal part and an ascending instrumental accompaniment? Pietrobono's transition to dance music, described in the final lines (64–69), gives Cornazano the opportunity for another classical comparison, particularly reminiscent of Vergil's *Eclogue* II, l.24.

Appendix 2

From Paolo Cortese, *De cardinalatu libri tres* (Castel Cortesiano, 1510), book II: the final section (from the last three lines of fol. 72r to fol. 74v) of the chapter "De vitandis passionibus deque musica adhibenda post epulas" (how passions should be avoided, and music used after meals) is given in facsimile, followed by a translation. Notice the running title, "De victu quotidiano," for the section on music.

DE VITANDIS PASSIONIBVS.   LXXII

Recte $\bar{q}$ etiam affirmari poteſt ⁄ut cauendum ſit ⁄ne ſpes aut deſpe⁄ **Spes** ·7·
ratio in ſenatorem cadat:nec.n.homines debent ea$\bar{x}$ arduarum for⁄
tuita$\bar{x}$ $\bar{q}$ rerum expectatione duci⁄quibus inanius aut a⁄mentis agita⁄
tatione aut a⁄commodorum ſuorum utilitate auocentur : nam cum
certa eſt adhibita ſpei incoſideratę ratio⁄ quæ iudicando doceat⁄id
quod expectatur⁄fieri nullo modo poſſe ⁄ facile tum exiſtimandum
eſt⁄cauſam deſperandi dari:ex quo futurum ſit⁄ut eo naſcatur moe
ſtitia improuiſa maior⁄quo ſpes erat opinata firmior: ut ſi Hermo ⁄ **Hermolaus Bar**
laus Barbarus homo probus⁄ & diſertus ⁄ eo certius ſperaret ſe in **barus**
ſenatum cooptatum iri⁄quo ſperatę dignitati eſſet doctrinæ preroga
tiua propior⁄cauſa ei daretur dolendi grauior⁄ ſi experiundi occaſo
ne cognouiſſet⁄minus uirtuti in ſenatum patere ſolere uiam ⁄ ex quo
iudicandum ſit⁄eum eatenus in erumna futurum fuiſſe⁄quoad ab eo
eſſet inſidenti opinationi obuiam animi magnitudine & humilitate **Remedium ſpei**
itum:qua$\bar{x}$ una eſt improuidę ſpei moderatrix ⁄ altera deſperationis
opinatę malum deprimendo &obtundendo leuat: atc$\bar{q}$ in hoc genere
etiam uitari debet ea audax appetitio ⁄ & is rerum arduarum orſus
ex quo maxime cauſa metuendi ſit⁄ut ſi modo dicamus quempiam **AVDACIA.8.**
conari & moliri uelle⁄ut Baizeto Turcarum Regi aditus ad Italiam **Baizetus Tur ⁄**
opprimendam clandeſtina coniuratione pateat⁄quę ſit tanta floren⁄ **ca$\bar{x}$ Ipator.**
tiſſimorum regum poteſtate cincta⁄nihil abeſſe poſſit⁄quin ei cauſa
timēdi ſit⁄ne re patefacta poenas audacia inconſiderata luat: ex quo
iure medicorum genus multis accidere ſolere cenſet ut in rerum di
ficillimarum conatu⁄periculi magnitudine metu$\bar{q}$ præmente com ⁄
moti ⁄ aut uaria corporis egrotatione contabeſcant ⁄aut in adole ⁄
ſcentia fiat ętate feſtinata ſenes⁄quo magis eſt a ſenatorum genere
cauendum⁄ne ante res difficiles moliri audaci ambitione uelint⁄$\bar{q}$ ſit
animi meditatione prouiſum⁄quorſum ſit rei gerendę caſura ratio : **INVIDIA .9.**
Sed ex his omnibus ualde debet inuidię form dari malum ⁄ nam cū
ea maxime ſoleat aliena preſtātia fortunata angi ⁄ recte affirmatur
eius amara animi cōtractiuncula lędi oportere corpus: Id$\bar{q}$ facile ex
inuido$\bar{x}$hominū genere iudicari poteſt⁄q ſemp lurido colore pallent:
Quod idem eſt de cæteraꝯ perturbationū genere differendū⁄quibus
cum alias ſemper a⁄ſenatore⁄tum maxime hoc ktandi tempore ob
ſiſti debet⁄ne corpus in exterendo cibo⁄aduentitia animi egrotationę

LIBER SECVNDVS

DE MVSICA

Qđ qđã dicunt muſicã eſſe in utilem:

Qđ mu. ē adhi benda delecta/ tionis , morum &diſciplinę cau ſa

elidatur:Quare cum hoc interim tempore maxime ſint ea poſtulan da,quibus animi hilaritas excitari ſoleat,quęri multũ hoc loco po / teſt,num maxime ſit muſices ſuauitas adhibenda:Siquidem multi a cõmunium ſenſuum natura auerſi.non modo eam praua quadam na ture peruerſitate reſpuunt/ſed eam etiam inutilem eſſe opinãtur:pro ptereaꝗ ea quędam ſit ignauæ uoluptatis inuitatrix / maximeꝗ eius iucunditate ſoleat libidinum excitari malum:contra autem · multi eã tanꝗ diſciplinam quãdam adhibendam eſſe uolunt,quę in ſympho nię moɖ̃ꝗ cognitione uerſetur/nos uerò hoc tempore eam non modo delectationis , ſed etiam diſciplinę moɖ̃ꝗ cauſa dari debere cenſemus:nam cum ludus ſit uacationis cauſa repertus / ceſſationiꝗ delectatio annexa inſit/proptereaꝗ uacatio eius urgētis moeſtitiæ me dicina dicatur quę ex negociorum laborumꝗ aſſiduitate dimanat,fa cile affirmamus,eius rei ceſſationem,ex qua animi moeſtitia naſcat ſuapte natura uideri debere iucundam:cum autem diſciplina,quæ eſt quoddam ratione pręeunte intelligendi munus,non modo beni expe tendi,ſed etiam conſentaneę delectationis rationem nanciſcatur , conſentaneum eſt,quicquid intelligendi cauſa expetendum ſit , de lectationemꝗ ſuapte natura conſequatur,id ludendi diſciplinęꝗ cau ſa debere quęri : at qui cum muſice ſuapte ſit natura iucunda,uimꝗ contemplandi nãciſcatur ,dubitari non debet,quin fatendum ſit/ iure eã delectationis diſciplinęꝗ cauſa debere quęri:eodemꝗ modo dicendum eſt,eam morum cauſa eſſe expetendam,ſiquidem conſue ſcere đ eo iudicare,quod ſimile moɖ̃ rationi ſit,nihil aliud uideri po teſt ꝗ cõſueſcere de moɖ̃ ratione iudicare,ĩ eoꝗ exerceri imitãdo,atꝗ cum muſices numeroſi modi omnes habitus moɖ̃/cunctosꝗ pertur bationũ uideantur imitari motus,dubitatione nõ habet,ꝗn modoɖ̃ tē perata collatione delectari,nõ ſit cõſueſcere de moɖ̃ ratiõe iudcare: idꝗ oſtēdi argumēto poteſt,cũ pſpicuũ ſit,oēs habitus animiꝗ mo tus,in modoɖ̃ natura reperiri,qua aut fortitudinis , aut temperan / tię,aut irę,ſiue manſuetudinis ſimilitudo oſtendatur ,facileꝗ notari udicando poſſit,perinde hominum mentes ad eos deduci ſolere mo tus,ut modorum permotione concitantur:nec.n.dubium eſſe poteſt, quin res inter ſe ſimiles ad ueri iudicium eadem finitima propinqui tate aſtringantur:ſed cum duplex ſit modorum utendorum genus ,

Qđ mu. ē adhi benda propter mores

Qđ mu. ſit ſimi litudine habituũ & motuum ani mæ

Qđ duplex eſt muſica:

DE VICTV QVOTIDIANO LXXX

unum quod manu conficitur, alterum quod canendi ratione conſtat intelligendum eſt ſenatores debere in ſonantiũ genere audiendo uer ſari, quo ratio certior in modorum collatione metienda ſit, men, ſ₃ fiat iudicando abſolutior : quo circa cauendum eſt, ne in hoc præparato ad muſicen ocio, ea genera adhibeantur, in quibus non modo uideatur aurium obtundi ſenſus, ſed etiam maxime auerſa, a, morum ratione ſint, quo in genere barbiti & pẽtades nu, merari ſolent, qui teretes aures uocum inſolentia ſonoq; perturba, to ledunt : Itaq; ſenatoribus illa pneumatica genera utiliora eſſe poſ ſunt, in quibus fiſtulæ ſtamneæ quaſi in arcis figuram coagmen, tari ſolent, quæ cum ſint aptiſſimę ad ſpiritum hauriendum & fun, dendum factę, graues & acutos amplificant referendo ſonos : in quorum quidem tractatione multum Iſachius Argyropyli pe, ripaterici filius conſtanti modorum collatione præſtat : nam qui Dominicum Venetum, aut Danielem Germanum maxime mi, rantur, hoc excipere in eorum laudatione ſolent, ꝙ intemperan, tius effuſa percurſione uterentur, qua uarie aurium ſenſus explere, tur, non ſcienter artificioſi diſtinguerentur modi : quin etiam ea genera laudari poſſunt, quæ ex ligno ad ſimilitudinem dimidia, ti antiqui uaſis extruuntur, ex quibus digitorum pulſu cordarum diſtincti eliciuntur ſoni : ſed qui longe a, pneumaticorum grauita, te abſint, cum eorum ſit percuſſio ſoluta celerior, breuioremq; referat in terminando ſonum : in quo quidem genere maxime eſt Laurentii Cordubenſis facilitas interpuncta nota : Atq; in hunc quoq; numerum illa genera referuntur, quæ quaſi lembtorum quo, rundam ſimilia uideri poſſunt, quæq; maxime iucunda aurium menſione iudicantur : nam illi certi digitorum curſus, tum itera, tio, tum concluſio, tum uocum extenuatio & quaſi interductio facile in hominum mentes irrepere exquiſita ſuauitate ſolent: quod quidem genus ſcientius eſt, a, noſtris artis terminatione renoua, tum, cognitumq; primum quomodo ſtructum & nexum poſſet ſonandi celebrari genus, idq; primum Balthaſar & Ioánem Ma riam Germanos inſtituiſſe ferunt, quo ſimplex antiquorum per hyperboleon iteratio ab hypate ſingulorum coagmentatione iun, geretur, ex eaq; effloreſceret ſymphonia ſociata ditior : antea

.K.i.

Muſica iſtrumẽ talis

Barbiti :
Et pentades.
Organa .i.

Iſaac Bizantius:

Dominicus Ve, netus:
Daniel Germa ꝫ nus.

Grauecordiũ .2.

Laurentius Cor dubenſis
Lembi .3.

Balthaſar Cer ꝫ manus.
Io. Maria Cerꝫ manus.

LIBER SECVNDVS

P.Bonus Ferra
riensis

Lyra hispana.4

CANENDI
RATIO:

Ratio phrygia
Ratio Lydia
Cantores palati
ni

Hispani

Versus Virgilii
Ferdinadus .ii.4
Caritheus poeta

Cātus firmus.S.
Gregorii
MISSE:
MOTETI
CANTILENe
Io.Ca.Medices

Iuschinus Gallg

MOTETI

enim Petrus Bonus Ferrariensis & hi qui ab eo manarunt , fre,
quenter , per hyperboleon iteratione utebantur , nec dum erat co,
gnitus hic singulorum colligădox, modus , quo maxime aurium ex,
pleri sensus cumulata suauitate potest : quod idem fere esset de hi,
spana lyra dicendum , nisi eius equalis lentaç; suauitas soleret au ,
rium satietate sperni , longiorç; similitudo uideretur , q̃ expectari
aurium terminatione possit : canendi autem ratio tripertita descrip,
tione secernitur , ex qua una phrygia , altera lydia , tertia dori,
ca nominatur , phrygia enim est , qua animi audientium acriori
uocum contentione abalienari solent : ex quo genere illa numera,
tur , qua gallici musici in palatino sacello natalitiis exsuscitatitiisç;
feriis , rituali lege utuntur : lydia autem duplex iudicari potest ,
una quæ coagmentata , altera quæ simplex nominatur : coagmen,
tata enim est , qua inflexo ad dolorem modo , animi ad fletum
misericordiamç; deducuntur : qualis ea uideri potest , qua no,
uendilia pontificia , aut senatoria parentalia celebrari solent : quo
quidem lugubri canendi genere semper est natio hispanorum usa :
simplex autem est ea , quæ languidius modificata cadit : ut eos
. P . Maronis uersus inflexos fuisse uidimus , qui Ferdinando se,
cundo auctore soliti sunt , a , Caritheo poeta cani : at uero dori,
ca ratio multo est æquali mediocritate temperatior : quale illud ge,
nus uideri uolunt , quod est , a , Diuo Gregorio in aberrucato ,
rio sacro stataria canendi mensione institutum : quocirca nostri
omnem canendi rationem in litatoria , præcentoria : & carmina
comparando seiungunt : litatoria enim sunt ea , in quibus omnia
pthongorum , prosodiarum analogicarumç; mensionum genera
uersantur , & in quibus musicorum generi laus cantus præclare
struendi datur : ex quo non sine causa Io . Medices senator ho,
mo in musicis litterata peruestigatione prudens , neminē in præ,
stantiũ musicox numex referendũ esse censet , qui minus gnarus
litatorii modi faciendi sit . Itaç; ob id unum inter multos Iuschi,
num Gallum præstitisse ferunt , proptereaç; ad litatoria cantus
genera plus doctrinæ sit ab eo adiectum , q̃ addi a , recentium
musicorum ieiuna sedulitate soleat : Præcentoria autem ea dicun,
tur , quæ q̃q̃ sint litatorio permixta cantu , ascriptitia tamen & in,

DE VICTV QVOTIDIANO   LXXIIII

fititia uident poffunt, cum in his libera fit commutandi optio, idᵭ
ob eam cafam factum effe uolunt, ne uniufmodi feruarentur in
canendo modi, quibus litætoria continuata cadunt : quo ingene,
re Iacobus Obrechius habitus eft uaria fubtilitate grandis, fed to,   **Iacobus Obrech**
to ftruendi genere horridior, & is a, quo plus fit in muficis acer,
rimæ fuauitatis artificiofa concinnitate fatum, q̃ effet aurium uo,
luptati fatis, ut qui in guftatu ea magis laudare folent, quæ
omphacium, q̃ quæ faccarum fapere uideantur : ex eodemᵭ ftu,
dio   Herricus Ifachius Gallus, maxime eft appofitus ad eiuf,   **Herricus Ifaacᵉ**
modi præcentoria conftruenda iudicatus : nam preterq̃ ꝙ mul,
to eft cæteris in hoc genere fundendo celerior, tum ualde eius il,
luminat cantum florentior in ftruendo modus, qui maxime fatus
communi aurium naturæ fit : fed q̃q̃ hic unus excellat, e multis,
uitio tamen ei dari folere fcimus, ꝙ in hoc genere licentius ca,,
tachresi, modorumᵭ iteratione utatur, quam maxime aures fa,
ftidii fimilitudine in audiendo notent : nec longo quidem interual,
lo Alexander Agricola, Antonius Brunellus, Lodouicus Com   **AlexanderAgri**
pater, Io. Spatarius Bononienfis ab ea mufica laude abfunt :   **cola**
ex quibus q̃q̃ alius alio plus uel artis, uel fuauitatis fit in con,   **An.Brunellus.**
ftruendo nactus, fitᵭ alius alio, aut mutuatione, aut commenti no,   **Lo Compater**
uitate uendibilior, omnes tamen funt fcienter : in hoc præcento,   **Io.Spatarius:**
rio genere uerfati, ex quibus multa ad fenatorium ufum trasfer,
ri poffint : At uero carminum modi hi numerari folent, qui ma,
xime octafticorum, aut trinariorum ratione conftant : quod qui,   **Cantilene**
.dem genus primus apud noftros Francifcus Petrarcha inftituiffe   **F.Petrarcha**
dicit, qui edita carmina caneret ad lembū:nuper aūt Seraphinus Aq   **S.Aquilano**
lanus princeps eius generis renouãdi fuit : a, quo ita eft uerboᵷ &
cantuū cõiunctio modulata nexa:ut nihil fieri poffet eius modoᵷ ra,
tione dulcius:Itaᵭ ex eo tãta imitantiū auledoᵷ multitudo manauit,
ut quicquid in hoc genere Italia tota cani uideatur, ex eius appa,
reat carminum & modorum præfcriptione natum : quare iure af,
firmari poteft, uehementius in hoc genere editis carminibus ani,
morum folere fedari & incitari motus : nam cum uerborum fen,
tentiaᵷᵭ numeri cum modoᵷ fuauitate coniungũtur, nihil caufe
.K.ii.

LIBER SECVNDVS

effe poteft, quin propter aurium uim animiᵭ fimilitudinem maxima
permotio in audiendo fiat, idᵭ tum fere fæpe euenire folet, cum uer
fibus aut turbidi canendo repræfentãt motus, aut animi, morum di,
fciplinᵉᵭ inftitutione admonetur, in qua fita foelicitas humana fit :.

[1] ... The same must be said about the kind of all other passions, against which an adverse position must be taken always by the senator [the cardinal] at other times, but more than ever at this time of recreation, lest his body be prevented from digesting the food by some intervening discomfort of his soul. Wherefore, since at this time those things must be sought after by which a cheerful mood is usually aroused, it may well be inquired whether the pleasure of music should be put to use particularly at this point, inasmuch as many, estranged from the natural disposition of the normal sense, not only reject it [music] because of some sad perversion of their nature, but even think it to be hurtful for the reason that it is somehow an invitation to idle pleasure, and above all, that its merriment usually arouses the evil of lust. On the opposite side, however, many agree to resort to it as to a certain discipline that is engaged in the knowledge of concordance and modes.

[2] Indeed, we are convinced that music should be put to use at this time [after meals] for the sake not only of merriment, but also of knowledge and morals. For if diversion was invented for the sake of vacation, and pleasure is inherent in the suspension [of work], and for that reason vacation is said to be a cure from that oppressive gloom that grows out of continuous involvement in business and work, we can easily establish that the stopping of anything from which sadness arises must be considered joyous by its own nature. Thus, if a discipline—which is a certain function of understanding something with the guidance of reason—is recognized to have a way of seeking not only a profit but also a becoming pleasure, it is proper that whatever must be sought after for the sake of understanding, and results by its own nature in a pleasure, this same should be sought after for the sake of both diversion and learning. Also, nobody who accords to music the faculty of contemplation, while its own nature is cheerful, should hesitate to confess that it must be rightly sought after for the sake of both pleasure and learning.

[3] In the same manner, it must be said that music must be sought after for the sake of morals, inasmuch as the habit of passing judgment on what is similar to morals in its rational basis cannot be considered to be different from the habit of passing judgment on the rational basis of morals themselves, and of becoming expert in this latter judgment through imitation. Also, since the melodious modes of music appear to imitate all the habits of morals and all the motions of passions, there is no doubt that to be entertained by a temperate combination of modes would also mean to get in the habit of passing judgment on the rational basis of morals. This can also be proved, inasmuch as it is evident that all the habits and motions of the soul are found in the nature of the modes, in which nature the similarity to fortitude, or temperance, or anger, or mildness is exhibited, and it can easily be observed and judged that the minds of men are usually brought to those motions just as they are excited by the action of the modes. Nor can there be any doubt that things resembling each other are forced to be such in fact by the very closeness of their affinity.

[4] But, since the kind of modes to be used is twofold, one that is produced by hand, and a second one consisting in the manner of singing, it must be understood that the senators must be engaged in listening to the kind of sounding things [instruments] in which the criterion in the combination of modes can be found

more stable, and the mind is freer in its judgment. Concerning this, one must avoid, in those free moments devoted to music, those genres in which the sense of the ear seems to be stunned, and which are, too, most divergent from the rationale of morals. In this class *barbiti* and *pentades* are usually listed, which offend the discriminating ear with the aggressiveness of their notes and with an inordinate sound. And so, those pneumatic genres [organs] can be more useful to the senators, in which tin pipes are usually assembled as it were in the shape of a castle; the which pipes, while they are made most apt to receive and emit the air, amplify the sounds, repeating them high and low. In touching them Isachius [Isaac of Byzantium], son of the peripatetic Argyropylos, stands out for his regular (*constans*) combination of modes. Those who admire most highly Dominicus Venetus or Daniel Germanus usually in their praise omit the fact that they make intemperate use of quick runs (*effusa percursione*), by which the sense of the ear is filled with variety, but the artful modes cannot be knowingly discerned. Indeed, also those genres [clavichord] can be praised that are made out of wood in the shape of an ancient vase, out of which the pressure of the fingers extracts distinct sounds of strings. Which genres, however, are very far from the gravity of the pneumatic genres, because the percussion on them is sooner released, and ending produces a shorter sound. Most renowned in this genre is the precise agility (*interpuncta facilitas*) of Laurentius Cordubensis.

[5] Also in the same group are placed those genres [lutes] which can be considered as resembling certain fast ships, and are judged to have the most delightful impact on the ear; for those sure-fingered proceedings (*certi digitorum cursus*), now repetition, now stopping, now lessening and almost interlacing of sounds (*vocum extenuatio & quasi interductio*), are in the habit of creeping easily into the minds of men with their exquisite sweetness. Which genre, indeed, has been more knowingly revived into artistic perfection by our generation (*a nostris*), and is acknowledged as the first genre of playing that can be praised for the way in which it is arranged and put together (*structum et nexum*). They say that it was first established by Balthasar and Joannes Maria, both surnamed Germanus, so that the simple repetition in the high region used by the ancients would be joined by a connection of all single sounds from the lower region, and from the latter a combined symphony would flourish more richly. Before them, in fact, Petrus Bonus Ferrariensis [Pietrobono], and those who derived from him, often availed themselves of the repetition in the high region; nor was this [present] mode of harmonizing all the individual [sounds] yet known, by which the sense of the ear can best be filled with perfect sweetness. Almost the same could be said of the Spanish lyre [probably the *vihuela*], were it not that its equal and soft (*lenta*) sweetness is usually rejected by the satiety of the ear, and its uniformity is longer than it could be desired by the limits imposed by the ear (*aurium terminatio*).

[6] The manner of singing, now, is divided into a tripartite description, according to which one manner is called Phrygian, the second Lydian, and the third Dorian. Phrygian is the one in which the spirits of the listeners are usually distracted (*abalienari solent*) by the fiercest straining (*contentio*) of notes. Of which kind is that music of which French musicians make use by traditional rule in the

palatine chapel (*in palatino sacello*) on the holidays of Christmas and Easter (*natalitiis suscitatitiisque feriis*). The Lydian one can be considered to be of two kinds, one that is called complex (*coagmentata*), and the second simple. Complex is the one in which the souls are induced to weeping and compassion by a mode inflected toward sorrows; such may be considered the one in which the papal *novendilia* [nine days of mourning for the death of a pope] or the senatorial *parentalia* [annual memorial services for dead cardinals] is customarily celebrated. Of this lugubrious manner of singing did the nation of the Spaniards always make use. Simple is that manner that results in a rather languid modulation (*languidior modificatio*); thus we saw to be inflected those verses of P. Maro, which used to be sung, on suggestion of Ferdinand II [of Naples] by the poet Caritheus. And finally the Dorian manner is by far more restrained in plain moderation (*aequali mediocritate temperatior*); such, as they say, is to be considered that manner that was established by Saint Gregory in the holy ... (*aberruncatorium?*) in a stately rule of singing.

[7] Concerning these things, our generation (*nostri*) divides and distinguishes the whole manner of singing into propitiatory songs (*litatoria*), precentorial songs (*praecentoria*) and sung poems (*carmina*). Propitiatory songs [Masses] are those in which all kinds of modes (*phtongi*), mensurations (*prosodiae*), and imitations (*analogicae mensiones*) are employed, and in which praise is given to the genus of musicians for devising the singing most admirably (*laus cantus praeclare struendi*); hence, not without reason Cardinal Io. Medices [Giovanni dei Medici], a knowledgeable man in the learned consideration of musical matters, believes that no one should be included in the number of the most eminent musicians, who is not very conversant with the making of the propitiatory (*litatorius*) mode. And so, just for this reason, they say that Iuschinus Gallus [Josquin of France] was the one who excelled among many, because more science was put by him in the propitiatory genres of singing than is usually put into it by the unskilled zeal (*ieiuna sedulitas*) of recent musicians. Then, those songs [motets] are called precentorial which, although mixed with the propitiatory singing, can be seen to be supernumerary (*ascriptitia*) and ingrafted (*astititia*), since for them there is free option of choice; and for this reason it happens, they say, that those modes all of one kind (*uniusmodi modi*), on which the propitiatory songs unremittingly insist, are not preserved [by them]. In this genre Iacobus Obrechius [Jacob Obrecht] is considered great for varied subtlety, but more crude in the whole style of composition (*toto struendi genere horridior*), and also [he is considered to be] the one by whom more of the sharpest agreeableness (*acerrima suavitas*) has been sowed among the musicians than would have been enough for the pleasure of the ear—like, in the field of taste, people who seem to like those things that taste of unripe juice (*omphacium*) better than sugar. For a similar inclination Herricus Isachius Gallus [Heinrich Isaac of France] is judged to be most apt to compose such precentorial songs; for, in addition to being much quicker than all the others in pouring forth this genre, his style of composition brightens the singing so floridly that it more than satiates the ordinary capacity of the ear. But, although he is the one who excels among many, nevertheless we know that it happens to be blamed on him that he

uses in this genre *catachresis* [literally, improper use of words] and repetition of modes more liberally than the most the ear can take without sensing annoyance because of uniformity in what it listens to (*similitudo in audiendo*). Nor are Alexander Agricola, Antonius Brunellus [Brumel], Lodovicus Compater [Loyset Compère], Jo. Spatarius of Bologna far away from such musical praise; although one of them gets more credit than the other for either art or suavity in composing, and one is more acceptable (*vendibilior*) than the other for his borrowing (*mutuatio*) or novelty of paraphrase (*commenti novitas*), all have expertly practiced in this precentorial genre, from which many things can be transferred for the use of the senator.

[8] Finally, those modes are usually listed as [modes] of sung poems [chansons] that mainly consist of the measure (*ratio*) of the octastics or ternaries [possibly *strambotti* and *elegie*]. Which genre Franciscus Petrarcha is said to have first established as he sang his exalted poems on the lute (*ad lembum*). But of late Seraphinus Aquilanus was the originator (*princeps*) of the renewal of this genre, by whom such a controlled (*modulata*) conjunction of words and songs was woven that there could be nothing sweeter than the manner (*ratio*) of his modes. And so, such a multitude of imitative court singers (*auledi*) emanated from him that whatever is seen to be sung in this genre in all Italy appears to be born out of the model of his sung poems (*carmina*) and [melodic] modes. For which reason, it can be rightly said that the motions of the souls are usually appeased and excited with more vehemence by the *carmina* produced in this genre; for, when the rhythms of the words and sentences are combined with the sweetness of the [melodic] modes, nothing can prevent [the audience] from being exceedingly moved because of the power of the ear and of [its] similarity to the soul. And this usually happens quite often when either vehement motions are represented in the singing by the verses, or the spirits are exhorted to the learning of morals and knowledge, on which human happiness is dependent.

Commentary. An attempt could have been made to recreate the Ciceronian flavor of Cortese's text by aiming the translation at a comparable stylistic model. The suggestion, however, was discarded as too ambitious and impractical—as impractical as, at a humbler level, would have been any attempt to preserve the punctuation of the original. Commas and colons, or their equivalent, convey a different message to modern readers than they did to the original readers of the Aldine prints, in much the same way as vertical bars, or the lack of them, have different implications for modern musicians than they had in sixteenth-century scores. Not only was I compelled to use commas and colons in a different way from Cortese, but I have also had to rely heavily on semicolons and periods, much less peremptorily required by the analytical habits of old readers than they are in our age of fast reading. In addition, it seemed advisable to divide and number paragraphs for the sake of clearer order and easier reference.

Yet this is only marginal compared to the continuous need for discretional decisions implied in the choice of English equivalents or approximations of Cortese's Latin words and idioms. It all amounts to the old truism that a translation is no mere reproduction, but an interpretation of the original text—as good and as perceptive an interpretation as a slightly more experienced reader can afford for the benefit of less specialized ones. To be sure, I have here the privilege of giving a facsimile of the original print, against which my translation may be checked and different choices eventually made by my readers. Yet both Cortese's print and my own interpretative translation still leave too many points unclarified, for which I am forced to offer at least tentative explanations.

Paragraph 1 effects the transition between the more general subject of human passions and the special topic of music. I have translated Cortese's "hoc laetandi tempore" as "at this time of recreation," rendering, I hope, his intention if not his classic pun; for *laetari* means to rejoice, but also to fertilize. The main point is, however, that music could be used in many social occasions, but Cortese sees the pause of relaxation after meals as being the very time for its most complete, unconditional enjoyment. Hence we must draw the conclusion that its performance must have been brought to the dining room, where the cardinal and his guests relaxed after dinner. This is a minor point, but it contradicts the illusion I had previously had concerning the existence in Rome, even at this time, of rooms especially designed for listening to music ("Rom," *Die Musik in Geschichte und Gegenwart* [hereafter abbreviated *MGG*], 11, col. 702, to which I shall refer again because it covers the background of Cortese's musical experience). Cortese's description of a "cubiculum musicae," from which my delusion originated (*De cardinalatu*, fol. 51r), stems from the same passages of Vitruvius which, only some thirty years later, spurred Palladio to the construction of the Cornaro odeon.

A series of syllogisms in paragraphs 2 and 3 leads Cortese to the conclusion that music must be used "for the sake of merriment, knowledge, and morals," the latter point supported by the statement that the emotions stirred by music are "similar" to the human passions. Then, after the distinction opening paragraph 4, between instrumental and vocal music, we begin to appreciate the marginal rubrics with which the book was provided by its editor (said to have been Raphael Maffei of Volterra). In these rubrics more allowance is made for nonclassical Latin terms than in the author's main text. (I have inserted translations of some of these rubrics in the text, in brackets.) Without them we might possibly have identified the organ but would have been at a loss to recognize Cortese's wooden instrument "in the shape of an ancient vase" as a "Gravecordium." Also somewhat embarrassing to the translator is Cortese's amphibious use of *genus*; it becomes clearer when one realizes that every instrument is identified with the genre of music played on it, an identification inspired by the classical doctrine of a special ethos attached to each kind of instrument.

Even Raphael Volaterranus was unable to replace such terms as "barbiti et pentades" with the names of contemporary instruments. The *barbiton* is a classic kithara-like instrument, but I have been unable to find any reference to *pentades*; unless this is a misreading for *pektides*, it is my suspicion, enhanced by Cortese's outspoken dislike for the instrument, that it might be a Hellenization of *quinterne* or *guinterne*, unusual names (at least in Italy) for the popular guitar. On the contrary, Cortese displays his best stylistic qualities whenever his appreciation of a given instrument, and the lack of a classical term for it, challenge him into elaborate turns of phrase. Such is his description of the "pneumatic genre" and of its tin pipes "apt to receive and emit the air," in which the indication that the latter "amplify the sounds repeating them high and low" is a clear hint of the most typical feature of Renaissance organs, mixture stops. Equally perceptive is his characterization of the percussive action and short-lived sound of the clavichord.

Of the instrumentalists mentioned by Cortese, Isaac Argyropoulos is fairly well known as a virtuoso on all kinds of keyboard instruments and as an organ builder (Claudio Sartori, "Organs, organ-builders, and organists in Milan, 1450–1476," *The Musical Quarterly* 43 [1957], 60–61). He finally became a *cubicularius secretus* of Pope Sixtus IV (J. Burckard, *Liber Notarum*, ed. E. Celani [Città di Castello, 1906], I, 386), possibly the first hint of the use of keyboard instruments for private ("secrete") entertainment. Dominicus Venetus and Daniel Germanus, both organists, as well as Laurentius Cordubensis, a player on the clavichord, are unknown to me.

It is typical of Cortese's rhetorical training to deal last in each category with what is first in his esteem. This rule also applies to the whole of vocal music, which is dealt with after the instrumental, but is slightly altered in the case of the *lyra hispanica*—plausibly the *vihuela de mano*—the uniform sweetness of which evidently bored Cortese. It is equally evident, however, that he appends the *lyra hispanica* at the end of his account of instrumental music because he sees it as a mere subspecies of the lute, for which, indeed, he has the highest admiration. On the basis of an audition, for which I thank Mrs. Isabel Pope Conant, who sponsored it, and Mr. Robert P. Sullivan, who played both *vihuela* and lute, I fully agree with

Cortese; whatever traditional reasons may have caused the Spaniards to prefer the *vihuela*, the greater technical flexibility and fuller sound of the lute lend themselves to a much richer variety of nuanced effects.

If my interpretation of paragraph 5 is correct, Cortese sharply defines not only the precision and variety of Renaissance lute playing, but also the change which occurred shortly before the end of the fifteenth century in its technique and style. The passage, however, is not as crystal clear as we would like. The distinction is evident between the earlier monophonic ("simplex") manner represented by Pietrobono, and the new, polyphonic ("sociata") way introduced by some German lutenists, but we are left in doubt about the meaning of Pietrobono's "per hyperboleon iteratio." On the basis of Tinctoris' "modulorum superinventiones" also applying to Pietrobono's playing, I wonder whether his "repetition" might not be understood in the sense of the later "double," variations introduced in the upper part. Polyphonic music could also be performed with the old style, but required one instrument for each part; we have no indication which instrument was played by the *tenorista* who usually accompanied Pietrobono in the second part of his musical career, but in another instance (that of a "Janes tedesco," a lutenist of the Milanese court in 1469; see G. Barblan, p. 806) it was a viola (evidently a plucked one, the equivalent of the Spanish *vihuela de mano*). To the basic duo formed by Pietrobono and his *tenorista*, other parts may have been added occasionally, for the same documents which refer to them also often mention viola players.

The change in style cannot have been too abrupt; the older way was still used as late as 1523 by one of the two German lutenists mentioned by Cortese as the representatives of the new style. At a banquet in Rome, on May 20, 1523, "there was Zuan Maria zudio with his three companions, and they all played lute à 4, he himself with the plectrum wonderfully" (translated from Marino Sanudo, *I Diarii* 34 [Venice, 1892], col. 216. The plectrum is never mentioned by Cortese; used in the older style, it was later abandoned in favor of the plucking of more than one string at a time with bare fingers). The career of this Giovanni Maria Dominici (son of Domenico), a converted Jew wanted for murder in Florence in 1492, took him to the office of "castellano" (fortress commander) in 1513, for which he was sometimes addressed as a count. The Medici, to whom he must have been dear for more than his musical gifts (he was even called at times Giovanni Maria Medici), must also have saved him from death in 1492, although this is against the opinion expressed in the most exhaustive account given of him by H. Colin Slim, "The Keyboard Ricercar and Fantasia in Italy, c. 1500–1550" (Harvard University dissertation, 1960), pp. 383–388. Again, I do not find any reason why a lost volume of lute music, printed in 1508 by Petrucci, should be taken away from Giovanni Maria Dominici and given to the already mentioned, and too old, Janes tedesco of the Milanese court (see H. C. Slim, "Musicians on Parnassum," *Studies in the Renaissance* 12 [1965], 158). I am unable to offer an identification for Balthasar Germanus; the name of a German "citaredo," mentioned in a Latin poem as being at the service of Cardinal Ascanio Sforza, was Henricus, not Balthasar (Giuseppe DeLuca, "Il 'libellus carminum' di un poeta sforzesco," *Archivio Storico Lombardo* 54 [1927], iii).

Finally, the humanistic idea of a "revival" of a lost artistic perfection is to be stressed in Cortese's account of the lute genres, as well as the admission that lute music could be appraised not only from the point of view of virtuosity in performance but also for the way in which it was arranged or composed ("quomodo structum et nexum").

Coming, in paragraph 6, to vocal music ("canendi ratio") and to its three "manners" or "rules" (again, "rationes"), Cortese suddenly abandons his previous realistic attitude, firmly based on factual empiricism, and plunges into surprising generalizations. Wary as he is of endorsing medieval theories of music, and yet unable to master the intricacies of the ancient ones, he just disregards any determination of intervals and scales, avoids any such term as *tonoi, tropoi,* or *modi,* and jumps to define each manner of singing again through its ethos, or, better said, through his personal impressions taking the place of ethos. Again, too, the meaning of what he has to say is far from being always clear, even less so since the examples he gives are either unknown or imperfectly known to us.

Evidently Cortese does not like the Phrygian manner, characterized, according to him, by a fierce "contentio vocum." I have conservatively rendered his expression as a "straining of notes," but other meanings are possible, for instance, a "contrast," or an "opposition" of "voices." Furthermore, to a rhetor, *contentio* means the formal arrangement of a speech, and *contentio vocis* was used by grammarians as the equivalent of *arsis.* According to which meaning we select—a genre containing contrasts of voices (double choruses?), or being formally organized, or simply high-pitched—we must also modify our interpretation of the effects of the Phrygian manner on the listeners, for *abalienari* might mean "to be absorbed," or "ravished," as well as "to be distracted." The final decision may depend on the identification of the example mentioned by Cortese, the music customary to French singers in the "palatine" celebrations of Christmas and Easter. I had thought possibly of some traditional piece performed in the chapel of the French kings, but the Roman context of Cortese's life and experience, as well as the normal interpretation of all his togaed expressions as referring to the new Rome of the popes, both point to the papal chapel. There, at least, we know that different national styles were at times exhibited and contrasted in the celebrations of Good Friday ("Rom," *MGG* 11, col. 703).

The songs performed at funerals of popes and cardinals are given by Cortese as examples of the "complex" variety of the Lydian manner, to which, equally lugubrious, the normal style of singing of the Spaniards also belongs. We do not know how much sufferance of the Borgian arrogance and aggressiveness may have influenced Cortese's dislike for the Spanish manners in music. More to his taste was the "simple" variety of the Lydian, represented by a gourmet item for a humanist, the singing of Vergil's poems by Caritheo at the request of Ferdinand II of Naples, a performance which may have taken place only between January 23, 1495, and October 7, 1496.

Third and highest, the Dorian manner of singing is exemplified, according to Cortese, by the whole body of the Gregorian chant. Again and again, Cortese's preferences are for restraint and regularity, as when he blames the aggressiveness of strained voices, or praises the "constans" style of Argyropoulos over the roulades of his competitors. Here, his commending of Gregorian chant for its "uniform mediocrity" needs to be considered in the light of classic standards of taste and of the moral implications of the already mentioned analogy between the effects of music on its listeners and the human passions. The homage paid to Gregory as a saint, and as a champion of classicism against the mounting barbarism of the Dark Ages, is typical of Cortese's age and of its religiosity, which it would be mistaken to deny, no matter how distorted, misplaced, and eventually tainted with superstition its manifestations may have been.

So high was the admiration for Gregory also as a Latin writer that it may have induced Cortese to use a non-Ciceronian word, and one which I have been unable to find in any lexicon of either classic or medieval Latin. The only explanation I can offer for "aberruncatorium" comes from a passage of the "Ordo ad ecclesiam dedicandam" in Gregory's *Liber sacramentorum*: "Deinde incipiat pontifex de sinistro angulo ab Oriente scribens per pavimentum cum cambutta sua A, B, C, usque in dextrum angulum Occidentis" (J. P. Migne, *Patrologiae cursus completus*, series I, 78 [Paris, 1849], col. 155). The letters A, B, C are said to be replaced in some sources by the word Abcturium (that is, abecedary); either misreading and miscopying led to Cortese's *aberruncatorium*, or the latter was a slip of the editor of Cortese's book, who interpreted *abcturium* as an abbreviation.

Unclear is the relationship, if any was intended by Cortese, between the contents of paragraph 6 and the "modern" classification of vocal music which he introduces in paragraph 7. We may add here two more reasons to those already given above for the preeminence accorded by Cortese to the genre, or genres, of the Mass. Motets must have been less frequently performed in Italy than elsewhere, and they were less dependent than the Masses on the use of a *cantus firmus*. If and when the latter was a Gregorian melody, the "uniusmodi modi" attributed by Cortese to the Mass genre may have been a reference to the unifying function of the *cantus firmus* and at the same time to its "stataria" nature (again, an adjective stressing and praising uniformity and moderation) as a Gregorian melody. Cortese's mention of "prosody" among the features of the Mass genre has been interpreted as the requirement of "a special knowledge of language and prosody" on the part of the composer (H. Osthoff, *Josquin Desprez*, I, 37–38). Actually, it is hard to see why the invariable prose text of the *Ordinarium Missae* should have required more attention paid to its prosody than motet texts, which often assumed poetic form and betrayed literary ambitions. From the point of view of a humanist, observance of prosody was an obvious, universal requirement, but Cortese's mention of "prosodiarum . . . genera" seems to me to make better sense in the light of his effort to describe *musical* features by means of classical terms. It is preceded by a reference to "phtongorum . . . genera," another literary term which had a long tradition among the most classically oriented music theorists. I have translated the latter as "modes" on the basis of Hucbald's definition of *phtongi*: "not every sound, but those that are suitable to a melody, being separated from each other by spaces determined by rules" (Martin Gerber, *Scriptores ecclesiastici de musica*, I, 152). Similarly, I interpret "prosodiae" and "analogicae mentiones" as respectively "mensurations" and "imitations"; the latter might also be interpreted as "proportional mensurations." Thus, Cortese's praise of Josquin seems to me to be chiefly aimed at the masterpieces through which the composer had asserted himself in the highly competitive musical milieu of the papal chapel, namely, such compositions as the two *L'homme armé* Masses.

Speaking of Josquin, Cortese always uses a past tense and refers to him, as it were, by hearsay. He resumes his direct approach when he comes to deal with the representatives of the motet genres. We feel then the voice, if not of an expert, of a connoisseur and concert-goer—certain ceremonies may have been attended for the sake of music—or even the after-concert gossip of the would-be well-informed. It is typical of Cortese's own humanistic attitude, however, to praise both Obrecht and Isaac for their good qualities and to blame them at the same time for the abuse of such qualities. I shall leave to whoever is going to "revisit" these composers the task of confirming or denying the "artful abundance of the sharpest agreeableness" attributed to the former, or the excess of "floridity" of the latter, limiting myself to observing that Isaac's productivity and rapidity of composition are confirmed by other sources. For the rest of the group—a highly productive lot of composers, among whom we are surprised to find the theorist Spataro—it would be only a guessing game to decide what merit belongs to whom. I feel more intrigued at this point by Cortese's choice of terms for various features of musical composition. Abuse of "catachresis" and "modorum iteratio" are faults blamed on Isaac. The literal meaning of the first, "improper use of words," may be assumed to stand here for "improper use of pitches"; the blame arises, however, not from the impropriety, but from the insistence on it. Thus, it occurs to me that *catachresis* may be just another classical garb for the ubiquitous *musica ficta*. As for the second, we may exclude that Cortese might have used *modus* in the meaning it normally had in medieval theory; its classical meaning being "melody," its repetitions may have been either melodic "sequences," or "imitations," or both. Similarly, I interpret "mutuatio" as "parody," and "commenti novitas" as novelty of either "paraphrase," or "harmonization," the latter to be taken in the sense of new contrapuntal lines to be adjusted to a *res prius facta*.

I shall not insist on the emphasis accorded in paragraph 9 to the "carmina" and to their hero, lest Cortese should rise from his grave and blame my "intemperantior sedulitas." His praise of Aquilano is equally balanced between the latter's poems (implicitly compared to the "exalted poems" of Petrarch) and melodies, both models for the artistic activity of a host of imitators. It is strange, however, that Cortese makes no reference to Aquilano's activity as an improviser either here or in another passage of his *De cardinalatu* (book III, fol. 164v), where two dead friends of Cortese, Baccio Ugolini and Jacopo Corso, and a living one, Bernardo Accolti, are praised for the wonderful pleasure one could take in their "singing *ex tempore* on the lyre in the vernacular tongue." We must conclude that Aquilano's activity as an improviser was much less prominent than has been commonly assumed. On the genre itself, what Cortese thought of it can be gathered from his comment on Accolti: "Although he recites improvised verses, and although one should be prepared to make allowance for [faults deriving from] the rapidity [of the exploit], most of what he does is commendable, and very little needs to be forgiven; [yet his is] the merit of a prolific but unreflexive talent." A born critic, Cortese never spared reservations, even when he was in his most benevolent mood.

8 Church Polyphony Apropos of a New Fragment at Foligno

As a veteran in the field of Ars nova studies, and one who has spent most of his life among old documents and parchment leaves (or their photographic reproductions), I have occasionally complained to myself that I never had the chance to discover the tiniest fragment of Ars nova music. It is unfair of me to complain, however. I may not possess the invisible feelers that alert and guide the born discoverer, but I have the good fortune of having many friends, and I have been gratified a number of times by their kindness and generosity in bringing to my attention their discoveries. The late Professor Hans David, of the University of Michigan at Ann Arbor, provided an instance of such generosity, which I can repay in kind only by turning the modest results I have derived from it into a joint act of homage to Oliver Strunk, to whom I am indebted for many things, primarily for the gift of his friendship.

I have benefited, too, from the prestige surrounding every kind of specialization. How weak my kind is, however, must have become apparent to Professor David, for I have done nothing, at least ostensibly, by way of commenting on two photographs he gave me some years ago of a new fragment with polyphonic music he had found in my own country, namely, in Foligno. I have not, indeed, kept them under cover for some thunderous release at a favorable moment. On the contrary, I have shared the information they provide with other scholars and have given duplicates of the photographs whenever asked to do so. The sheer truth is that the contents of Professor David's gift have challenged, intrigued, and to a certain extent baffled my specialist's wit. I am reminded, in fact, of a story by Edgar Allan Poe, involving a murder investigation in which witnesses of different nationalities can agree only that the voice of the murderer, which they have all heard, spoke a language different from their own. In the case under consideration here, I am the sleuth and also the first witness. To me, the Foligno fragment, although found in an Italian library and presenting some features that are usually connected with Italian notation, does not suggest the familiar associations of an Italian manuscript.

Whether my reaction is justified or not, the *fauxbourdon* style of one of the pieces in the fragment, combined with some suspicion I have always had of notational collusions between medieval Italy and England, prompted me to seek advice from an acknowledged expert in medieval, and particularly English, music; my second witness was Professor Frank Ll. Harrison, then visiting at Princeton. When he left Princeton for England, Professor Harrison took the photographs with him. Later on he kindly told me that in his opinion, supported by others who had also seen the photographs, the Foligno fragment had nothing to do with England.

My next step was to mail the photographs to a friend in Italy and have them submitted to Professor Renato Piattoli, of the University of Florence. His judgment as a paleographer confirmed my specialist's arrogance in denying an Italian origin; he added the suggestion that the fragment might be French. Thus the photographs once more crossed the Atlantic, this time headed for Paris, where Dr. François Lesure, well-known editor of the *Répertoire international des sources musicales,* expressed the opinion that the fragment might be German, especially if the illuminated capitals in it were of the *sang-de-boeuf* shade of red. At this point, being unable for the moment to verify the shade of the colored initials, and knowing that I would soon have the opportunity to go to Italy, I decided to postpone any announcement of the results—or nonresults—of this very cooperative venture[1] until I had seen the fragment myself.

The fragment is presently kept in a box containing "Frammenti di pergamene antiche" in Sala A of the Biblioteca Comunale of Foligno (see Figs. 8.1, 8.2). It is a vellum double leaf—four pages, that is, each measuring about 252 by 170 millimeters, or 10 by 6¾ inches. According to information provided by Signor Feliciano Baldaccini of the Foligno library, it was formerly the cover of a volume which came to the library from one of the religious institutions suppressed in 1860 by the then-new Italian government. This is confirmed by the inscription "Theophilact. ī E . . ."[2] running across one of its sides at the place which evidently corresponded to the back of the volume. None of the pages preserves any trace of foliation figures (those appearing on the facsimiles are my addition to the photographs); on each of them two vertical lines frame eight pentagrams, leaving rather narrow margins on either side, as well as above and below the staves.

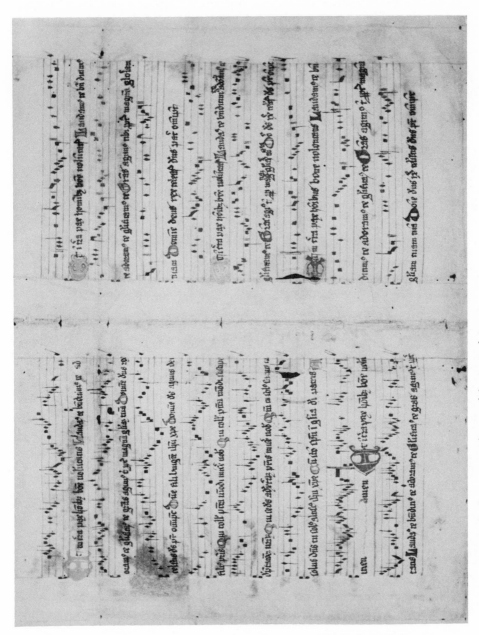

Fig. 8.1   The Foligno fragment, side one, fols. 2v and 1r.

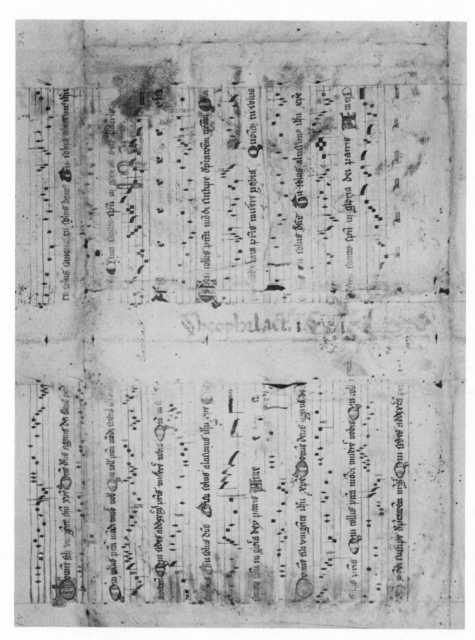

Fig. 8.2   The Foligno fragment, side two, fols. 1v and 2r.

The narrow margins, plus the fact that the staves are completely filled with music and underlined with text (the latter in a rather heavy handwriting full of abbreviations), give the pages a quite crowded appearance. A modest but painstaking decorative effort—including larger and smaller illuminated capitals and touches of red added without any notational significance to the vertical strokes indicating rests in the music—does not overcome the sense of dullness due to the lack of any balanced arrangement on the page. For the record, only a few of the initials are red, and they are much brighter than the *sang-de-boeuf* shade; the others are blue, green, and faded Havana brown, and are distributed in such a way that each individual part of a polyphonic piece is marked with initials all of the same color. The brown ink used for text and music is also faded.

Some figures on the page to the right of the "Theophilact." inscription— probably a library number for the volume—indicate that this was at some time considered the front page. In spite of this, I have preferred to call fol. 1r the page on the right of the other side of the fragment, on which the text and music of three voices of an *Et in terra* run from a miniated initial to the words "deus omnipotens." To me this seems to indicate the beginning of a fascicle, the proper place from which to start the description of the fragment's contents. In fact, the superius part of the same piece continues to its end on fol. 1v, followed by the continuation of the *tenor* part up to the words "Qui sedes ad dexteram patris." The rest of the *tenor* must have appeared on the upper part of the next page, now lost, followed by the completely missing second section of the *contratenor*.

A proof of this arrangement, and a counterpart to it, is found, after a gap of undetermined width, on fol. 2r, where the three upper staves are filled with the end of a tenor part going from "Tu solus sanctus" to "Amen" (again a Gloria text), and the remaining five staves, with the second half of the contratenor of the same piece, from "Qui tollis . . . suscipe" to "Amen." Once more a complete *superius* part, and once more a Gloria text, fill six and a half staves on fol. 2v (the last page of the fascicle beginning on fol. 1r). They are followed on the remaining one and a half staves by another part running from "Et in terra" to "gratias agimus tibi propter . . . ," whose precise relationship to the preceding I would like to leave undecided for the moment.

As far as we can see, fol. 1r was probably not only the front page of a fascicle, but also the beginning of a section of Gloria settings continued on the next fascicle. The arrangement, grouping together settings of each single text of the Mass Ordinary, places our fragment in a category with the well-known manuscript of the Chapter Library at Apt, dating from the second or third decade of the fifteenth century.[3] Dates are not easily assigned on the basis of the rather formal writing in which sacred texts are often cast, and the difficulty is increased in the case of the Foligno fragment by our inability to determine its geographical provenance; yet it seems to me a fair guess to date it also within the first third of the fifteenth century.

This by no means provides a date for the music in the fragment. If we examine the notation of its Gloria No. 1 (fols. 1r–1v), we find that Philippe de Vitry might well never have existed for its composer, were it not for an isolated figure of a minim at its very beginning. As I understand it, the single upward tail applied to a note following two unsigned semibreves indicates, once and for all, the rhythmic meaning of every following group of three, or occasionally four, undifferentiated semibreves in a frame of minor *tempus* and major prolation—that is, ♩. ♩♪ or ♩♪♩♪ , respectively. Other rhythmic interpretations might be possible; this, however, seems most plausible to me because it is in agreement with the prevailing rhythm of most Mass music of this time, representing, after all, a survival, in sound if not in notation, of the old, relaxed first mode. Combined with the use of *puncti* (*divisionis* as well as *perfectionis*), it is consistent with the notational stage of the *Roman de Fauvel*[4] and with the rules given by Marchettus de Padua when he comes to speak "de tempore imperfecto modo gallico."[5] It would place the date of the piece—at least its notational date—at about one century earlier than the fragment itself.

Imperfect *tempus* and major prolation are also omnipresent on the remaining two pages of the Foligno fragment. They are fully spelled out in what survives of the two lower parts of Gloria No. 2 (fol. 2r), by means of upward tails for the semibreves *minimae*. Upward tails alternate on the last page (fol. 2v) with downward ones applied to perfect semibreves whenever there might be some doubt about their being perfect. These features suggest a slightly later date for the music on fols. 2r–2v than for the first Gloria, and for the music on fol. 2v, some analogy with Italian notation.[6]

One consistent feature of the Foligno fragment is that all the parts in all its pieces are texted. In Gloria No. 1—the only one to provide a sample of complete three-voice texture—the three parts move in almost absolute simultaneity (Ex. 8.1). Even a few measures suffice to identify the piece as the one I was referring to when I mentioned the presence of some *fauxbourdon* style. They also give immediate evidence of the lack of accuracy of the version given in the fragment (see the passages marked by asterisks in Ex. 8.1).

I must stress that I do not consider *fauxbourdon* style as being exclu-

Ex. 8.1   Beginning of Gloria Foligno, No. 1, fol. 1r.

sively, or even typically, English. Nor does Professor Harrison, if I correctly interpret his views.[7] Many pages of *Fourteenth-Century Mass Music in France,* edited by Hanna Stäblein-Harder,[8] indicate how common it also was on the continent, although only the Gloria Apt No. 37[9] approaches the insistence on *fauxbourdon* successions displayed in Foligno No. 1. These successions are the result of one of many different *punctus-contra-punctum* techniques, all aimed—whether they were improvised or written down—at obtaining a rich choral sound. This one, that of repeated 6/3 chords, represents a particularly easy way of getting the desired result in melismatic passages. If anything needs to be said here about English polyphony, it is, I think, that its most characteristic feature is not *fauxbourdon* procedures, but rather that even its most refined manifestations always preserved a feeling for a *choral* sound, to which only improvised, or very simple written polyphony remained faithful on the continent.

When I speak of choral sound, I do not necessarily mean the sound produced by more than one singer to a part[10]—we find, after all, that even up to the seventeenth century a group of soloists could still be called a chorus.[11] At the time under consideration, shortly before the beginning of the so-called choral polyphony, the concept of chorus may have been that of a polyphony in which the element of harmonic, vertical *concordia* prevailed over that of contrapuntal (the meaning of the words "contra punctum" has been completely reversed) individualization of lines.[12] Most particularly, this concern for simultaneity and vertical concordance must have been typical of all kinds of improvised *choral* polyphony—and here I use this adjective with still another implication, that is, to indicate performance not by virtuoso singers but by regular members of a monastic or chapter choir.[13]

Coming back to the Gloria Foligno No. 1, the only reason we can produce for not considering it an example of written-down improvisation is that none of its parts has the nature of a preexisting melody on which the *cantus ad librum,* as improvisation was sometimes called, may have been based. It is, then, a truly composed piece, only reminiscent of the sound of improvised polyphony.

While the three voices of Gloria No. 1 are always kept close together, with the *contratenor* constantly in a middle position, the *tenor* and *contratenor* of Gloria No. 2 (its only extant parts) are more widely spaced and eventually cross each other in the Amen.[14] Of the missing *superius* we can only guess that it may have started in a *duodecima* position, occasionally risen to the double octave above the tenor, and stayed always at some distance from the latter, even when contrary motion produced a mutual reapproaching. The general style of the setting, although basically harmonic, and with simultaneous recitation of the text in all the parts, must have given a little more contrapuntal and rhythmic freedom to the voices than did the preceding piece. Short connecting passages, usually two breves in length, appear occasionally either in the *tenor* or in the *contratenor,* marking the conclusion of some section of the text. Similar connecting passages can be seen in the Gloria and Credo of Machaut's Mass, in Apt No. 8 and in Ivrea Nos. 62 and 63, to mention only a few Gloria settings.[15]

The nature and possible relationship of the two Gloria parts appearing on fol. 2v of the Foligno fragment have been left undecided up to this moment because I thought that a more precise knowledge of what preceded might have helped to determine them. At first glance the two parts, both notated with a C clef on the second line, seem to belong to two different settings, since they both begin with a *longa,* the first on G, and the second on F. The starting of two new pieces on fol. 2v, however, would be in sharp contrast with the pattern we have found in the preceding pages, on which the voice parts of one piece (or of a section of it) followed each other, first on the same page, then on the next, beginning from the top. Also, the two *Et in terra* beginning on fol. 2v share a detail of notation that does not appear in the preceding pieces, namely, the downward tails indicating perfect semibreves. An attempt to combine the two parts in spite of the strident clash of their initial *longae* results in further clashes alternating with surprising consonances and combining in even more surprising rhythmic parallelism (Ex. 8.2). Having already seen from No. 1 that the notation of the fragment is far from being flawlessly accurate, I am inclined to consider the music on fol. 2v a badly corrupt version of one single Gloria No. 3.

If this hypothesis is correct,[16] Foligno No. 3 must have been a setting in which a duet of high-pitched voices was supported by one lower voice, probably without text, or by a *tenor-contratenor* duo. One might be tempted to call it a setting in motet style—even more so if the lower part, or parts, had applied isorhythmic techniques. If the missing *tenor* also had a text and had the modest rhythmic activity of the *tenores* in the previous pieces, instead of the holding of notes that often characterizes isorhythmic *tenores* the piece would have assumed a more conductus-like appearance than most ordinary settings that are so labeled.[17] In either case, what survives of the piece seems to indicate a rather early date, at about the middle of the fourteenth century.

Ex. 8.2   Beginning of Gloria Foligno No. 3, fol. 2v.

Conjectural as the dates are of both the fragment and the music it
contains—not to speak of the fact that no plausible conclusion has been
reached in regard to their provenance—an assessment of them is more in
the nature of a tentative opinion than a reasoned conclusion (although
many a reasoned conclusion is nothing more than a reasonable opinion). I
am inclined to think that the Foligno manuscript originated in the chapter
of a provincial monastic, collegiate, or cathedral church, either in Italy
(probably north of Rome) or in southern Germany. Its provincial origin
would account for the lack of characteristics on which a more determined
geographical assignment could be made. As a *church* manuscript, it would
belong in the same category as the already mentioned Apt manuscript, or
the fragment[18] containing the Sorbonne (more properly Besançon)
Mass—to name only the most obvious examples.

Heinrich Besseler once described the Apt manuscript as "ein kirchliches Gegenstück"—a churchly counterpart—of the secular collections of the time.[19] I would not extend that description to the Foligno manuscript without some additional qualifications. One has to do with the secular nature of the counterparts; only a few of the secular collections are secular from every point of view, while many are secular in content but may have been assembled by and for ecclesiastics. On the other hand, the concept I have of the church manuscripts is, I suspect, somewhat more defined than Besseler's vague "kirchliches." In keeping with my *choral* conception, I think they were created, as I have already stated, as polyphonic choirbooks for either monastic, collegiate, or cathedral churches. As such, they should be set apart from those sources in which the selection and arrangement of sacred pieces, and occasionally the mixture of sacred and secular, reflect the more sophisticated, more up-to-date, and also the more mundane taste of clerics exerting their musical skills in private chapels.[20]

If my distinction is correct, the artistic polyphony contained in the latter sources deserves our attention because of its extraordinary significance, not because it represents the common or general practice of that period. It was recorded and preserved with particular care because of its refinement, as a model not easy to imitate and fit into daily common practice, yet inspiring and rewarding. As for the mainstream of church music in the strict sense of the word, it is difficult to make generalizations. First of all, it involves the activity of hundreds or thousands of churches of different types, locations, and importance. Secondly, our attention having been focused until now on the other type of activity, we must unravel the available evidence from passing remarks or devious footnotes and implement it with new and better-focused information.

As I see it in my hypothetical generalization, church practice still considered plainchant as its basic element. This by itself would require some kind of refocused attention, since the performance of plainchant was undergoing considerable change in the direction of rhythmization— occasionally, but not too often, recorded in a curious kind of half-mensural, figured, plainchant notation. To this, one should add a certain amount of creative activity, mainly concerned, as far as I know, with newly composed *Ordinarium* settings.[21]

Polyphony—either written down or unwritten—naturally grew out of that frame as a more elaborate way of fulfilling the liturgical requirements in regard to music. Unwritten polyphony added one or two, seldom more, simple lines to the plainchant, either in its unmeasured version, or, more likely, in its more recent rhythmization. It was called *cantus ad librum* on the assumption that the singers assembled around a choirbook and performed their different parts while reading (or "sighting") the basic melody from it. How much this was the real procedure we shall reconsider after we examine the case of the written-down polyphony. In principle, the writing of a polyphonic sacred setting should indicate that the piece had no plainchant foundation, as in the case of the Gloria Foligno No. 1, or that its construction on a plainchant melody was so elaborate that the piece could not be memorized easily. In fact, some of the pieces thus preserved are pure reflections of improvisational techniques, often of a more elementary kind than the procedures described in most *artes contrapuncti*. Others belong to one of the two categories for which notation seems to be more justified, but they have reached us in bad versions, which would have needed revision if the sources had really been used in performance.

In this connection the clash of G against F at the beginning of Foligno No. 3 (if my interpretation of the two parts as belonging to the same Gloria is correct) is a joy to my musicologist's eye, if not to my ear, as evidence that the writing down of the piece had nothing to do with the requirements of its performance. So are the mistakes in Foligno No. 1 and in many of the Apt readings, as well as in those of other manuscripts. They convey to me the impression that the writing down was, in the type of sources I am trying to describe, a sort of gratuitous gesture in most cases, dictated by a *religio* for the written book, and by an almost ritual habit of assembling around a lectern for the singing. It certainly represents a gift from the usually anonymous ecclesiastical scribe to his unknown, musicologically oriented descendants. Once a piece had been accepted in the repertory of a chapter choir—whatever the ways of and reasons for that acceptance—it was rapidly memorized, so that the written version was soon reduced to the status of a symbol or a vague mnemonic aid, and oral tradition took over. This may also have applied to the so-called improvisations, agreed upon just once (I would like very much to use the baroque term "concertare") and then repeated through the fidelity, and lapses, of memory.

The present writing, largely tentative and scarcely conclusive, has not achieved any positive result—not even regarding the four small pages of music that occasioned it. Yet being in the mood for suggestions, I might repeat one here that I recently expressed verbally,[22] that is, that the kind of polyphony often called "archaic" or "peripheral" (although found in relatively recent and central sources) belongs to the normal practice of polyphony in most churches, large and small, of the Western world. On the other hand, the kind of artistic polyphony we have become used to considering standard for fourteenth- and fifteenth-century sacred music is but the valuable expression of a minority, the advancing standard of a special elite.

Postscript, 1983

The Gloria Foligno No. 1 (Ex. 8.1) has been found to be also present as Gloria No. 1 in another source of the early fifteenth century, Grottaferrata, Badia greca, ms. 197, fols. 1v–2r; see Oliver Strunk, "Church Polyphony apropos of a New Fragment at Grottaferrata," in *L'Ars Nova Italiana del Trecento* (Certaldo, 1970), p. 305ff, and Ursula Günther, "Quelques Remarques sur des Feuillets Récemment Découverts à Grottaferrata," *ibid.*, p. 315ff. A transcription of the piece in the latter article, pp. 355–359, is defective because both sources are incomplete; plausible integrations have been suggested in a new transcription in Kurt von Fischer and F. Alberto Gallo, eds., *Italian Sacred Music,* Polyphonic Music of the Fourteenth Century, 12 (Monaco, 1976), pp. 13–16.

In spite of the slightly more precise notation of the Grottaferrata version, Professor Strunk agreed with my suggestion that the piece is sensibly older than both sources. Our guess finds confirmation in the identification, made by Professor von Fischer (to whom I am indebted for the information), of the Foligno-Grottaferrata Gloria with one (whose beginning is missing) in ms. London, British Museum, Cotton, Titus D. XXIV, fol. 3v, reproduced in facsimile by Ernst Apfel, *Studien zur Satztechnik der mittelalterlichen englischen Musik* (Heidelberg, 1959), II, 26. The disposition with the voice parts in score and the notational features of the Cotton, Titus fragment point to England and to an early Ars nova period.

Our Gloria has been transcribed by Günther, von Fischer, and Gallo according to *tempus perfectum minoris prolationis,* suggested by the Grottaferrata version. Nonetheless, I have not changed my tentative reading of the Foligno version in Ex. 8.1 according to *tempus imperfectum maioris prolationis,* which seems to me more consistent with the ambiguous, old-fashioned notation of the other two sources, with the general style of their music, and possibly with the original intentions of the anonymous composer. The presence of the piece in the Cotton, Titus fragment leaves no doubt about its English origin, while its presence in the Grottaferrata fragment increases the probability that the Foligno fragment is Italian. For the diffusion of the *contenance angloise* and *fauxbourdon* style I must refer to my remarks about the English at the Council of Constance in essay 9.

9   Zacara da Teramo

I have never been to Teramo, but the beauty of the landscape as described by one of its bishops five centuries ago endears it to me: Teramo "is placed between two rivers that lap its walls and converge as soon as they pass the city . . . it expands on a slightly higher level and has the advantage that from a distance one sees it standing above the plain as an island above the sea. Two thousand steps separate it from the mountains, and fifteen thousand from the sea: on the western side are the mountains, whose breeze Teramo gets in the summertime, on the eastern side is the Adriatic gulf, which gives it warmth during the winter. It is neither so near to the sea that summer vapors and southern winds may harm it, nor so near to the mountains to be stiffened by winter cold and snow."[1]

Like many of Giovanni Antonio Campano's letters, this one is addressed to a friend; also a humanist and a prelate, the Cardinal Jacopo Ammannati-Piccolomini, giving an account of the new diocese to which Campano had been nominated on May 23, 1463. I will not repeat all the placid cordiality of his Latin, but it is important to mention what refers to the organization of the cathedral: "There are twenty-four regular priests and they are not ignorant of rites. All of them know the liturgy extremely well. In no other place is the pomp of the ceremonies more solemn. Numerous auxiliary priests officiate at the services of the hours and the breviaries, attending them at night and through the day. They particularly care about music, keeping their predecessors' custom, who, they state, had practiced it honorably. They call their own Zacarus the musician [Zacharus musicus]; they point out his houses, his farms, his younger relatives as well as his disciples; his compositions are considered oracles."[2]

Antonio Zacara da Teramo (Campano calls him "Zacharus," according to the humanistic habit of deriving an adjective from the name of the *gens*) was a composer of secular and sacred compositions, the latest written before 1430 or perhaps even a decade earlier. It is interesting to find that people still remembered him forty or forty-five years later; even more interesting is the claim of his connection with local musical practice. Research would be required to document the statement that music was "honorably practiced" in the Teramo cathedral. Right now I can only accept Campano's statement and compare it with general historical information, which is also documented with less detail than I would like.

Let us consider first the series of bishops, starting with Pietro de Valle of Teramo, nominated in 1363 by Urban V. His successors were Corrado di Melatino, nominated by Boniface IX on March 23, 1396; Antonio di Melatino, to whom Innocent VII entrusted the administration of the diocese on November 19, 1405; Marino di Tocco, nominated by Gregory XII on February 14, 1407; and Stefano da Carrara, nominated by John XXIII on October 13, 1412.[3] The first three were from Teramo, and the order of their succession reflects the events of the bloody fight of their respective families to win leadership of the city. In this fight an even more powerful, external group intervened, helping first one, then another family—the Acquavivas, who were counts and later dukes of Atri. Antonio Acquaviva, who died in 1395, was an accomplice of the Melatinos in the killing of Bishop de Valle's brother; Acquaviva's son, Andrea Matteo (husband of a Tomacelli, Boniface IX's niece) was killed in 1407 by the Melatinos with the tacit approval, it was said, of King Ladislaus of Naples. In 1408 Andrea Matteo's son, Pierbonifazio, took an atrocious revenge on his father's murderers. Probably because of this situation Gregory XII did not ratify the local election of the twenty-year-old priest Antonio di Melatino, nominating instead Marino di Tocco, who was from Abruzzo but a stranger to the Teramo milieu. Even the succession of the last two bishops on the list has some dramatic elements. Marino di Tocco obviously did not reside in Teramo for long; he was in fact with Gregory XII in Gaeta in March 1411 and probably followed him in his flight to Dalmazia and Rimini, after the alliance concluded by King Ladislaus and John XXIII in July 1412.[4] This agreement, together with the fact that Conte da Carrara was ruling Abruzzo in King Ladislaus' name, opened the way to Stefano da Carrara's nomination by John XXIII.

What can we get from this history of municipal, regional, political, and ecclesiastical conflicts? First of all, I think I find confirmation of what I wrote many years ago about the fragmentary codex of the Archivio di Stato di Lucca (*Mn*), which is the principal source of Zacara's secular compositions. Both *Mn* and Prudenzani's sonnets, which were written not later than 1417, represent a polyphonic practice of central Italy, which for lack of a deeply rooted tradition of its own, or because of political events, was much more open than Florentine polyphony to all kinds of external influence, never failing, however, to add its own spice of a markedly popular taste.[5] The people who enjoyed polyphonic music in the milieu of Paolo Guinigi's Lucca knew, first, the Italian repertory prior to the splitting of Italian religious obediences determined by the Pisa Council (this repertory is represented in *Mn* by the works of Bartolino da Padova and Johannes Ciconia) and, second, the typical repertory of the clergy of the Kingdom of Naples, of which Guinigi was a faithful ally. The Abruzzo region around Teramo, where Zacara probably started his activity, was a substantial part of the "kingdom," which was enlarged during Ladislaus' life to include almost all of central Italy.

The reference above to popular style allows me to interrupt the tedium of historical and chronological data with an example of Zacara's music, a *ballata, Rosetta che non cambi mai colore* (*Mn* no. 24, incomplete in that codex, but luckily present, though anonymous, in the manuscript nouv. acq. frç. 4917, Paris, Bibliothèque Nationale, known as *Pz*). The composition (Ex. 9.1) starts, like many others, with the two voices holding long notes in an interval of a fifth; then the higher voice starts to develop its own line, while the *tenor* holds its F like a bagpipe accompaniment; the *tenor* interrupts the F for just a second in order not to be discordant against the strongly accented G of the other voice, then holds the F again for a long time, falling on B flat only when the recitation of the text resumes (bar 9). In this fall, so long prepared for, one might want to see announced the course of the whole composition; the *ripresa* starts, as we saw, on an F chord and ends on B flat, while the section of the *piedi* starts on B flat and goes back to F. But what I wish to stress is the jump of a fifth, repeated two more times during the *ripresa,* which is the result of a harmonic feeling foreign to the usual education of a polyphonist. For him it would have been more natural to move forward to the tonal point of arrival with the *tenor* descending by steps, as happens at the end of the *ripresa* and consequently at the end of the whole composition. A similar case, which also reminds one of the bagpipe is, in modern terms, the fluctuation between perfect and plagal cadences at bars 50–52. All the passages in which the text is recited, furthermore, have a typically popular aria in both the tune and rhythm of the two voices; particularly interesting are the passage on *amar te voglio* at bars 25–29 (where the *tenor* takes the upper hand, enriched by a typical cadential melisma and prolonging its move-

Ex. 9.1   *Rosetta che non cançi* (Pz, fols 20–21), a *ballata*.

Ex. 9.1 Continued

Ex. 9.1 Continued

Ex. 9.1   Continued

Ex. 9.1 Continued

ment beyond the accented syllable), and the one on *Tu me resguardi* (bars 56–59) with a descent by thirds which resumes and continues in the immediately following passage. It seems to me that the frequent convergence of the two voices toward unison, preceded in one voice by anticipation of the tonic and resulting therefore in a clash of seconds (bars 15, 24, 27, 49, 52, 61),[6] also has a popular origin. Similar, although in a different context, is the style of bar 8, where the two voices insist on the interval of a fourth.

Although *Rosetta che non cambi mai colore* may be a good indication of Zacara's artistic qualities, it is not a typical example of his work, in which every composition tends to have some individual characteristics: the canonical beginning of *Un fior gentile,*[7] the double text of *Je suy navvrés* (in which, furthermore, one of the two texts splits in a dialogue between *cantus* and *tenor*),[8] the sharp, angular rhythm of *Spesso, fortuna, cridote,* the syllabic recitation in all the voices of *Ciaramella*. This last (Ex. 9.2) also recaptures, although in a totally different way, the echo of the bagpipe sound (bars 5–8 and 11–14), recalled also by the double entendre of the word *ciaramella,* which indicates both the instrument and a frivolous girl, a flirt.[9] A third example of the variety with which Zacara treated the same theme is given by the onomatopoeic imitation of bagpipe sounds at the end of the *piedi* of *Amor né tossa* (Ex. 9.3b), a *ballata* that also has an amusing madrigalistic hint on the words *Né zoppegar del pe'* (Ex. 9.3a).[10]

On the other hand, Zacara is not simply an intuitive artist. *Rosetta* is written in proportional notation (in a *tempus perfectum* whose perfect *breves* equal the perfect *semibreves* of other compositions), which allows greater rhythmic flexibility than is allowed by normal notation; this is the only example we have of his familiarity with the theory of rhythmic proportion. The same purpose (that is, introducing *tempus perfectum* passages in the composition's prevailing *tempus imperfectum*) is achieved in other compositions as well; for instance, in *Spesso, fortuna, cridote* with other notational means, but above all with the strength of rhythmic progressions. *Rosetta* and *Spesso, fortuna* use a hexachord in the *tenor* that we could call *sub molle* (it goes from B flat to G, a fifth lower than the *molle* hexachord) and it is indicated in both cases by a key signature of two flats in the *tenor*. Finally, the concept of expanding the solmization system with new hexachords (maybe as a justification of *musica ficta* practices) is applied even more extensively in a composition that is rather enigmatic both in its text and in its use of unusual accidentals, the *ballata Deus deorum Pluto.*[11]

Ex. 9.2 *Ciaramella* (Mn, no. 30), a *ballata*.

Ex. 9.2   Continued

Ex. 9.2   Continued

Ex. 9.3 Two fragments of *Amor nè tossa* (Mn, no. 37), a *ballata*.

Neither the speculative side nor the command of technical and nota-tional resources inherited from the so-called manneristic period ever have the upper hand over Zacara's genuinely musical characteristics. He shows in this, as in his obvious interest in naturalistic motifs, a noticeable affinity with Johannes Ciconia. This led me, while working on codex *Mn*, to surmise that Ciconia followed Stefano da Carrara when he was ordained bishop of Teramo in 1412.[12] We now know that Ciconia died a little before Christmas 1411, and Zacara must have left his town at that time also.[13] The stylistic affinities probably derive from influences Zacara was exposed to during his formative years, of which we know nothing. His title of *magister* and the mention in Campano's letter of houses and land make me think he was a cleric of a certain status who perhaps later became canon in the Teramo cathedral. We can also assume that he had a university education and that his musical learning was perfected in a university city—Perugia, Florence, Bologna, Padua?[14]

While almost all of Zacara's secular compositions are in a single manuscript, representing, as I said, the polyphonic culture of "il Regno" (the Neapolitan kingdom),[15] the tradition of sacred works by the "Zacara constellation" encompasses several complex sources that are both extremely varied and highly international; this is explained, according to a favorite theory of mine, by the vast opportunities for cultural and artistic exchange that the Councils made possible.[16] To come directly to the point I will say that Zacara's international musical fame—as well as the present confusion, which must have existed even then, about Zacharias, Zacara, and Nicolaus Zacarie—are connected with the fact that prelates from all over Europe were converging on Constance for the Council, held from the end of 1414 to 1418.

Concerning Zacara, the key to my conjectures is Bishop Marino di Tocco,[17] who, as I have mentioned, was in Gaeta with Gregory XII in 1409. On May 1, 1413, Gregory XII nominated him general vicar of the Recanati diocese, one of the few that still obeyed him.[18] Probably Marino never went back to Teramo, but at the Council of Constance (which Stefano da Carrara did not attend) Marino was always called "episcopus aprutinus," the usual designation for Teramo bishops. It was not easy for a bishop belonging to Gregory XII's following, numerically small and above all, without political and territorial backing, to assert himself in an assembly of the most illustrious representatives of the Church and of Europe's major courts and most famed universities. However, Marino obviously had his authority as bishop reconfirmed after Gregory XII's renunciation (July 4, 1415) and was even given some important tasks by the Council.[19] Later, on July 6, 1418, the new Pope Martino V officially endorsed the position Marino actually had already held for five years, making him bishop of Recanati.[20]

From the little we know about him, we can say that Marino di Tocco was a papal court prelate, a good jurist, and an expert on diplomacy and administration. He was the type of ecclesiastic who could have joined a princely chapel (in the premusical or paramusical sense that we must consider in order to understand the place of such institutions in the musical history of the fifteenth century),[21] and also the type who in turn would appreciate the advantage and prestige of having in his own chapel or episcopal *familia* a clergyman who had musical talent among his other qualities. A hint that Zacara may have followed the restless wanderings of Gregory XII's curia with Marino di Tocco is a *Patrem,* preceded by the inscription "Magister A[ntonius?] Dictus Z[achara?]" of which only the highest voice is extant in the fragment of a polyphonic codex in Cividale. The attribution is not refuted by the style, and the fragment's chronological data point to the time of the brief council assembled by Gregory XII in Cividale in 1409.[22]

The habit of often signing his compositions with a simple "Z" has contributed to our uncertainties and probably also to those of his contemporaries, in distinguishing Zacara from the other two musicians with almost homonymous names. They too, if what we surmise about them is correct, were in Constance, following John XXIII or some bishop loyal to him (for instance the cardinal of Florence, Francesco Zabarella).[23]

I will not try, right now, to solve the problem of attributions. If we eliminate Nicolaus Zacarie, who was Martino V's cantor from 1420 to 1424, and to whom two parts of a Mass are explicitly assigned, and if we do not take into account the Credo in the Cividale fragment (which, as far as I know, is present in no other manuscript), twelve compositions remain to be divided between "Magister Zacharias cantor Domini nostri Papae," who was loyal to John XXIII, and "Magister Anthonius Zachara de Teramo," who was loyal to Gregory XII. It is evident, though, that the majority of settings of Mass movements belongs to the latter.[24] What is important about the compositions is their ecumenism, which confirms my opinion of the importance of the Councils in circulating and fusing stylistic features of the various nations' musical tendencies. The twelve compositions are present in ten manuscripts, the most important being BL (Bologna, Museo Bibliografico Musicale, cod. Q 15, from Piacenza) which has eleven.[25] Among the other codices, one is English (OH, the well-known Old Hall ms. in Ware, Catholic College of St. Edmund, ms. 91),[26] two are German (MüO, ms. 3232a of Munich's Bayerische Staatsbibliothek, and ms. Mus. 40582 of Berlin's Staatliche Bibliothek, which was probably lost or destroyed during World War II).[27] Two other manuscripts are Polish (Kras, ms. 52 of Warsaw's Biblioteka Norodowa, and St P, ms. 695 of Poznan's Biblioteka Universitetu);[28] we must also consider as German the ms. 87 of Trento's Castello del Buon Consiglio (Tr 87).[29]

It is a well-known fact that several of these compositions are titled, and some of these titles refer precisely to Zacara da Teramo's secular compositions (with these I associate a dear personal memory of Federico Ghisi, who first spoke about them at the Congresso Internazionale di Musica Sacra, held in Rome in 1950).[30] Some other titles, though, are not so easily explained. One of them is the inscription "Z. Micinella" set before a Gloria in BL, fols. 16v–17r; it is echoed by "Z. cursor" set before the Credo which immediately follows on fols. 17v–19r of the same manuscript.[31] The two compositions are obviously coupled, having the same disposition and number of voices (four, two of which, tenor and contratenor, are textless), the same D tonality, the same rhythm (tempus imperfectum minoris prolationis), the same rapid syllabic recitation of the text in the two higher voices. Such titles were probably suggested by this last quality, because *micinella* (feminine to agree with *Gloria*) in most dialects of central Italy means "small" (short, therefore), and *cursor* hints at a quick run. But a further suggestion for the second term comes from the fact that John XXIII's court and the Council itself had their own *cursores,* who were messengers or ushers. One other *Gloria* in *BL,* fols. 156v–157r, also has a feminine adjective in the preceding words, "Zacar anglicana." The most likely interpretation is that the piece aimed to follow the suggestions of English polyphonic style, which was then becoming influential.

In Constance among the English representatives were two important figures, the archbishop of Salisbury, Robert Hallam, who already had been at the Pisa Council, and Richard Beauchamp, count of Warwick, a warrior and a gallant man. The English for the first time insisted on their right to decide and vote as a "nation," a right harshly disputed by the French clergy.[32] The establishment of their musical tastes was more pacific. Among the few recorded pieces of information about music during the Council is the record of solemn Vespers celebrated in 1416 in the cathedral on the eve of the feast of Saint Thomas of Canterbury with "sweet English singing," organ, and trombones.[33] As a representative of the "Italian nation" and even more because of the direction of his own musical tastes, Zacara must have given a more hearty welcome to the *dulcedo* of English singing than the representatives of the "Gallic nation," who still had stronger requirements for *subtilitas* where music was concerned.

Postscript, 1971

While I was proofreading this essay I was told that Zacara's name is mentioned by Abruzzo historiographers as Zaccarias, not following Campano (who used the adjective "Zacharus") but rather according to a passage of *Necrologio Aprutino,* a lost manuscript written no later than 1766.[34] From that passage I get the impression that the *Necrologio* could have been written in the sixteenth century but was pretended to be of the first half of the fifteenth century. "Zaccarias Teramnensis" was said to be the composer of many songs "quae *nostra aetate* per Italiam *cantantur,* et Gallis et Germanicis cantoribus in maxima veneratione *habentur*" (which *are sung in our days* all over Italy, and thought of highly by French and German singers).[35] This is confirmed by the manuscript tradition, and therefore the *Necrologio* follows a well-informed source. One suspects, however, a fanciful embellishment in the affirmation that Zacara, *magister* of the papal chapel, received a sumptuous salary. He was probably a follower of Gregory XII, who rarely could afford luxuries; furthermore, it was not for at least another century, if not more, that the office of *maestro di cappella,* or any other kind of "primacy," was given to a cantor.

The newest information is that Zacara was short and had not more than ten digits, counting both hands and feet, possibly because of a birth defect; but his deformity did not stop him from elegant writing. Also of interest is the comment of a Teramo writer on "*Zaccaro,* significante tra noi ... cosa piccola";[36] I have not been able to find confirmation in any Abruzzo or Teramo lexicon, but the possibility that Zacara was a nickname derived from physical characteristics is strengthened by the unusual words of Cividale codex XCVIII: "Magister A. Dictus Z."[37]

Additional Postscript, 1983

A bull of Boniface IX, given in Rome on February 1, 1391, granted "Magister Antonius dictus Zacharias de Teramo" the office of writer in the papal chancery ("scriptor licterarum apostolicarum"). We also learn from this document, the first of a precious series reproduced or quoted in an article by Agostino Ziino,[38] that Antonius was a "laicus licteratus" as well as "uxoratus" (a married laic with a liberal education)[39] and a singer in the papal chapel; the pope, wanting to show his favor, admitted him to the benefits as well as the duties of his new office (to the "onera et emolumenta consueta dicti officii").

This was not just a sinecure: Ziino gives a list of papal bulls written and signed by "A. de Teramo" between July 4, 1391, and June 1, 1407, most dated from Rome, but two written in Viterbo in 1405. Yet their relatively small number seems to indicate, according to Ziino, that Antonius continued to be mainly absorbed by his duties as a singer for three subsequent popes, Boniface IX (1389–1404), Innocent VII (1404–1406), and Gregory XII (1406–1415). Ziino's accurate inspection of the available documents after June 1407 has yielded no further evidence concerning Antonius, for which he suggests three possible explanations: 1) he may have died shortly thereafter, although no document has been found conferring his office on another person; 2) he may have gone back to Teramo, although again Ziino could find no document there attesting his presence; or 3) he may have left Rome on August 9, 1407, following

Gregory XII and his court to Siena. By July 1408 the pope had lost most of his following; in 1409 he and his opponent, Benedict XIII, were deposed by the Council of Pisa and replaced by the newly elected Alexander V (in this period three popes each claimed to be the true pontiff); deposed again in 1415 by the Council of Constance, Gregory finally submitted to its decision.

The third hypothesis best explains the lack of further documents concerning Antonius, since most documents connected with the small circle of faithful followers of Gregory XII were lost during their troubled years of peregrination. It also seems to agree with my earlier conjectures in this essay, only making the role I had attributed to Marino di Tocco less essential, since Antonius was already a singer (we do not know when he began) in the papal chapel. However, my theory was consistent with the assumption that "Magister Antonius Zach*ara* de Teramo" (or "Magister A. dictus Z.") was a different person from "Magister Zach*arias*" ("M. Zach*erias* Cantor Domini nostri pape" in the Squarcialupi codex; all italics are mine), also a composer, whose likely association with the chapel of Alexander V and his successor, John XXIII, I had indicated in an earlier article.[40] Now the papal bull of 1391, speaking as it does of a "Magister Antonius dictus Zac*arias* de Teramo," seems to show that there was just one.

Furthermore, Ziino sees as a likely possibility that the Zacharias mentioned in the 1391 bull, having followed Gregory XII to Siena and eventually to Lucca, may have joined those members of his retinue who defected and went to the Council in Pisa. He would thus take the path I had traced for the other Zacharias; that is, he would have entered the chapel of Alexander V (today considered an antipope), would have followed him to Bologna and served there also under his successor, John XXIII (also now considered an antipope). This path would have brought Antonius Zacharias to Constance (my addition to this theory) in the retinue of John XXIII, who was deposed by the Council in 1415 and died in Florence in 1419.

The images of the two composers (the third, Nicolaus Zacharie, is unaffected, whether or not he was the son of either one) tend further to merge because the only sacred piece attributed to "Zaccharias" in the ms. Modena, Biblioteca Estense, α.M.5.24 (on which my conjectures on "Magister Zacharias" were mainly based) is now given to "M. Antonius" by a newly discovered source.[41] There are only two possible objections to their merging. First, it seems strange (though not impossible), in the face of the copious, brilliant, and highly diversified production of my "Antonius

Zacara" that he should be represented in the Squarcialupi codex only by a few nondescript *ballate* and one not too exciting *caccia* (although the latter presents the unusual feature of an onomatopoeic text in the *tenor*); and second, the ascription of one *Gloria* to "Zacharie maius" in the ms. Munich, Staatsbibliothek, Clm. 14274 (mus. 3232a) and of one *Credo* as "Slowye szacharie mneysche" (work of the minor Zacharias) in Warsaw, Biblioteka Narodowa, Lat. F.I.378[42] once more seems to point to two different composers, whose similar names may have been a source of confusion and misattribution even in their own day.

Whatever the solution to the puzzle, if we reach one, some basic points of the essay remain valid. The impressive stature of Antonius Zacara or Zacharias de Teramo as a composer can only gain from the addition of other works to his production; one of them, the *ballade*(!) *Sumite carissimi* (whose Latin text is itself a puzzle)[43] indicates that he could master the syncopated style and notational intricacies of the late French Ars nova, the so-called *ars subtilior*. Even though Antonius was a laic (and a married man, which makes it more probable that he was the father of Nicolaus Zacharie), his long attachment to papal chapels strengthens my repeated assertion that in the early fifteenth century art polyphony was mainly practiced for the high ranks of the Church. And finally, since both Zacara and Zacharias, whether they are one or two, are likely to have landed in Constance, the puzzle of their identity does not affect my thesis on the importance of the Councils in spreading the polyphonic repertory,[44] especially that of the Council of Constance in introducing the *contenance angloise* on the continent.

10 — *Ricercare* and Variations on *O Rosa Bella*

In a letter addressed to Leonardo Giustinian, Ambrogio Traversari blandly but resolutely inverts, in order to praise his friend, one of the fundamental assumptions of scholastic musical culture, that the *musicus'* knowledge was superior to the *cantor*'s practical skills. He presents instead an outline of musical aesthetics that is implicit in the attitude of humanists until the end of the fifteenth century and even later: "I have known for a long time that your agile and certainly golden mind has succeeded also in those matters that, contrary to ancient custom, are better known to common people than to scholars, such as the ability to sing very sweet arias, [accompanying them] with sound."[1] In order to restore that fabled classical condition in which every free man supposedly practiced singing and playing, scholars would not have to rely upon the *quadrivium*'s *ars musica,* but upon the natural gifts of genius and upon the instinctive resources as they express themselves in the popular musical tradition. We should not be surprised that as the representative of an art founded on such volatile elements, Giustinian was destined to become a mythical figure. He already had had that status for the generation immediately following his own, which called a whole category of songs *giustiniane,* without knowing or wanting to distinguish which ones were really his.

As in musical history, Giustinian is also something of a myth in literary history. The reconstruction of his *canzoniere,* attempted many times with fastidiousness and philological acumen,[2] seems to me a totally hopeless enterprise. It is possible, up to a certain point, to identify a nucleus of poetical compositions which are most probably his, but the problem of distinguishing among originals, author's variations, and external interventions seems insoluble. What is most sure is a negative proposition: that an archetypal *canzoniere* personally collected and organized by the poet never existed.[3] And this is natural, because organizing the canzonets in a *canzoniere* would presuppose the author's recognition of their autonomous literary value, a recognition that does not fit with their intention or the way they were conceived. Born in direct relationship to music, his poems should have been collected, if anything, with their music; but that would have required Giustinian the "composer" (we do not know to what extent he really was one, or if it would not be better to call him a musical "troubadour") to know musical notation methods, and to consider these methods suitable for his music.[4]

I feel that Giustinian's literary ambitions were entirely committed to his speeches, letters, and translations, and maybe to his *laude;* the canzonets, even if he wrote down their texts, had to be "off the record," because their meaning was totally fulfilled only when they were performed, in the union of words, sounds, and that amount of mimicry that is inherent in any musical performance. I apply the same reasoning also to the music, which would probably disappoint us if some precise notation were extant.[5] Just as the texts were poetry for music, the settings, perhaps even more, must have been music for poetry, likely to find expressive fulfillment only in union with a text, and to be both the same and different in combination with different texts, as strophic composition demanded.

The unlikely hypothesis of a rediscovery of the music is not totally idle if it invites us to think how the settings could reflect the nature of the texts with which they were associated. Immediately evident is the distinction between *strambotti,* concluded in the short span of only 8 lines, and *sirventesi* and *ballate,* which could have up to 200 and 400 lines, respectively. The *strambotti* probably had tunes of sober rhythm and *arioso* design, alternating recitative and extended vocalization. The emphasis must have been more musical than recitative, as shown on the one hand by the stops and starts, which were required more by the articulation of the melody than by the very simple text, and on the other hand by the repetition of words or sentences, which allowed a more ample development of the music.[6] Traditionally, the music of the first two lines was repeated for the following distichs, but because of the different recitative accent of every distich and the stimulus offered to the singer by the varying expressive meaning of the text, the repetition must have been rarely precise.[7] In the case of the longer poems, however, the music had more markedly the function of being the text's formal vehicle. This neither excluded the possibility that music could have a distinct melodic individuality nor prevented its adding to the expressive result, provided that it unfolded rapidly; this, of course, minimized the chances that it could indulge in effusions or merely musical ornaments. I do not know if each *sirventese* had its own melody; their metric patterns are simple and generic (the most common are the *terza rima* and the tetrameter with three hendecasyllables and a seven-syllable line), and therefore it would have been easy to use the same tune for different compositions. We must not forget, though, that for the even simpler metric pattern of *strambotti,* the tendency was to use a new tune every time.[8] The preponderance of hendecasyllables and the inclination of the texts toward introspection (sometimes tending, as in Saviozzo's *sirventesi,* to lamentation and despair) suggest a rather grave musical rhythm. Complaints or invocations to the beloved lady (with the exception of *Venite pulzelete,* in which the speaker is a woman) are not addressed directly to her but to her image, once so sweet and inviting, now hard and disdainful; so *Tacer non posso* and *Io vedo ben ch'amore è traditore* are already, two centuries in advance, "lettere amorose in stile recitativo" (love letters in recitative style).

Giustinian's *ballate,* finally, have varied, complex, and sometimes unusual metric structures; the same structure, however, is often repeated in several compositions (for instance, in *Ay quanto e' fu contento, Qual ladra, qual zudea, Qual pensier novamente,* and so on), and in some of them the repetition is associated with the recurrence of a common final rhyme in every stanza (*O done inamorate, Poi che azo perduta, Ayme che son caduto, Essendomi solete*). All these elements taken together imply that for all the *ballate* of that group a single melody was used. The same melody could have been useful also for singing canzonets that have slightly different patterns, as *O canzoneta mia,* which has a pattern slightly different from the two already mentioned groups (it has a seven-syllable line instead of a five-syllable one as the third line of the *ripresa* and of the *volta*), but it has in common with the second group of canzonets the same rhyme at the end of each stanza.

This work of transferring tunes and adjusting lines leads us to imagine Giustinian, the "troubadour," composing his poems not by aligning the syllables on paper but by trying, with the help of his voice and his instrument, to adjust the rhythm of the words to that of the melodic phrases and to match the rhymes to the cadences of the music. Hence the many versification licenses which the music either allows or imposes but always justifies, so that they do not look like defects so long as the line remains associated with the melody. I am presently thinking, besides the many lines with one less or one more syllable, of such cases as the seven-syllable lines accented on the antepenultimate syllable mixing with nine-syllable lines (both accented on the penultimate and on the last syllable) in *Guerriera mia consentimi* (or *Guerriera mia consenti a mi*).[9] In the *ballate*, short lines are prevalent; the longer lines, usually interrupted by a strong caesura, introduce variety in the agile and nervous excitement of a direct and dramatic delivery. Here too the initial motion is almost always that of a serenade, but it rapidly changes from invocation to dialogue and from dialogue to action. In some instances the duet is underlined by the poem's metric pattern, for example by the double *ripresa* and by the stanzas coupled by their final rhyme, as in *Amante e sta fredura*. But it is not necessary to assume that these instances of *opéra* (*comique*) *avant l'opéra* required a second performer; they were musical mimes in which a single actor-singer gave life to the imaginary scene, impersonating each character alternately. These samples too tell us that Giustinian's art achieved its full expression in the performance;[10] the text is little more than the scenario of the mime and the mere notation of the music, even if we had it, would add very little.

It is time now, having tried the tuning of my strings in a speculative *ricercare* on Giustinian, to come to O *rosa bella*, a little *ballata* of one stanza that is not Giustinian's, but was considered a *giustiniana* as far as the poem was concerned.[11] O *rosa bella* is similar in metrics and in poetic language to many other short *ballate* that flourished around 1400 in the Veneto region and faintly echo a minor *stil novo*. Perhaps it had already been sung in a popular vein before Johannes Ciconia from Lièges set it to polyphonic music. Ciconia spent a substantial part of the first decade of the fifteenth century in Padua, where he died sometime between December 15 and 25, 1411.[12] In terms of pure chronology, the text of the *ballata* could have been Giustinian's, since in 1411 he had already been active for some years in public and most probably in literary life. But the shortness of the poem contrasts with the multiplicity of stanzas of Giustinian's most typical *ballate*, and its style is that of a semipopular rhymer who echoes courteous manners, rather than of a patrician who takes over vivid popular expressions and themes.

> O rosa bella, o dolçe anima mia,
> non mi lasar morire, in cortesia.
>
> Ay, lass'a me dolente! deço finire
> per ben servir e lealmente amare.

Socorimi ormai del mio languire,
cor del cor mio, non mi lassar penare.
O idio d'amor, che pena è questa, amare!
vide che io mor tuto hora per questa iudea.

This is the version that appears with Ciconia's music in codex Vaticano Urbinate lat. 1411 (fols. 7v–9r).[13] It represents the copyist's most diligent effort in dealing with an Italian text: of a *ballata* by Dufay (*La dolce vista*) he gives only four lines (*ripresa* and *volta*); he does not even finish the second line of an anonymous composition (*Con dollia me ne vo*); he stops at the incipit of a second and different setting of *O rosa bella,* a late addition which he attributes to Dunstable. Ciconia's *ballata* must have soon been forgotten, since it is found in only one other manuscript (Paris, Bibliothèque Nationale, nouv. acq. frç. 4379, fols. 46v–48r).[14] In contrast, the setting attributed to Dunstable is found, without the composer's name, in a dozen other manuscripts (and in one with a different attribution); furthermore, this setting was the starting point of a certain number of vocal and instrumental arrangements.[15] Even though in most of the manuscripts the text transmission is careless and incomplete, it is evident that this second setting was one of the factors that allowed the text of *O rosa bella* to survive and to be inserted in the first printed collections of poetic texts attributed to Giustinian.

Although the attribution of the second setting is disputed, it is probably the work of an English composer; in fact, the only attribution that differs from that of codex Urbinate—and which comes from a slightly later but no less authoritative manuscript, codex 714 of Biblioteca Comunal in Oporto—attributes it to John Bedingham, who is called elsewhere in the same codex, as if the name were not enough, "Bedyngham de Anglia."[16] I have avoided calling this second setting a *ballata* because the composer, whoever he was, ignored or misunderstood its metric form. Usually the music of a *ballata* is divided into two sections that must be performed first in the order in which they are presented, with the text of the *ripresa* and of the first *piede,* and then repeated in inverted order, with the text (often absent in musical manuscripts) of the second *piede* and of the *volta.* There may or may not be a final repetition of the *ripresa,* but the performance should end with the final cadence of the first section. The composition attributed to Dunstable in codex Urbinate lat. 1411 does not follow this order, however; it is divided into two sections, but it has a final cadence only in the second one.[17] The first section (see Ex. 10.1) ends instead with a temporary, rather dramatic stop on an imperfect consonance; this needs a

Ex. 10.1   Dunstable or Bedinhgam (?), *O rosa bella*.

Ex. 10.1   Continued

resolution, which it finds either by falling back on the initial chord of the composition or by continuing with the opening chords of the second section. Also the graphic indication of the division between the two sections is unusual for a *ballata;* instead of the usual vertical bars through the musical line, a *signum congruentiae* marks in each of the three voices the final note of the first section.[18]

This method is usually employed to distinguish the two sections of the most common form of fifteenth-century polyphony, the *rondeau.* If Dunstable was the author, it would not be surprising if he interpreted O *rosa bella* as a *rondeau quatrain.* Apparently he never came to Italy nor had any connection with Italians; furthermore, his only other secular composition is a *rondeau* on a French text.[19] The performance of a *rondeau quatrain,* though, would require six lines (in a specific rhyme order) added to the four lines of the refrain given with music; however, the most complete version of O *rosa bella* has a total of eight lines, two of which are omitted in all the manuscripts containing the second setting. I believe therefore that the composer, not familiar with Italian metric forms, applied to a *ballata* text the treatment required by a French *ballade;* that is, he immediately repeated (with other lines of text) the music of the initial section. The result, in the version of codex Porto 714, would be the following:[20]

> O rosa bella, o dulze anima mia,
> no me lassar morire, in curtesia.   } A
> O dio d'amor, che pena è questa, am ... }
> vide che moro per questa iudea.   } A
> A, lasso mi dolente! dezo finire
> per ben servir e lialment'amare.   } B
> ....
> ....

The considerations already mentioned for Dunstable apply also to Bedingham, although he probably did spend some time in Italy. The codex that quotes his name most frequently is in fact the Porto manuscript 714, which I believe was written in Ferrara around 1450 and is linked to the presence in that city of French and English musicians, the members of a chapel already founded by Leonello d'Este in his palace around 1445.[21] As in the manuscript Urbinate lat. 1411, in the Porto ms. also the compositions on Italian texts are in the minority and all are by foreign polyphonists, but its copyist was more careful and conscientious in transcribing the texts and in showing their connection with the music. Out of a total of six Italian texts in the codex, only three are more or less *ballate;* only one, *Poi che crudel fortuna* (fols. 65v–67r), seems to have been treated by its composer in the manner prescribed for a *ballata,* even if the copyist neglected to transcribe the text of the *volta.* The composition is attributed to Joye and is the only indication of his possible presence in Italy.[22] I have already mentioned *O rosa bella.* The third text, set to music by a certain Robertus de Anglia, looks like a *ballata* because of the rhyme *ia* recurring at the end of each stanza:

> O fallaze e ria fortuna
> cum la faza or chiara e bruna,
> d'ogni ben sempre degiuna
> tu fai star la vita mia.
>
> O fortuna trista e amara,
> quanto al ben te monstri avara!
> ciascaduno tardi impara
> a cognoscer toa folia.
>
> Talora el rico mandi al fundo,
> talora el tristo fai giocundo,
> e tal golder cred'el mundo
> che tu getti in tenebria.
>
> Chi in te affida soa speranza
> po' ben far la frischa danza;
> questo non è fiaba né zanza,
> ma el vero par senza bosia.

If it is a *ballata* (it could be called a *frottola* because of its popular style and its line length), it lacks the *ripresa.* This English composer also adopted a solution that calls to mind the way a *ballade* was set to music. He composed the first section of music on the first stanza, showing that it should also be repeated for the second stanza, then added to it a second section that encompasses in full the last two stanzas, without making a distinct division between the two. Here too the *signum congruentiae* at the end of the first section produces a stop on an imperfect consonance, which is resolved by going back to the start; after the repetition, the music proceeds beyond the *signum congruentiae* with a brief extension that leads to a more conclusive cadence (Ex. 10.2).[23]

This last procedure is present also in another controversial Anglo-Italian *ballata, Gentil madonna,* which had a remarkable circulation; it is found in no less than nine manuscripts, and in one of them it bears the

Ex. 10.2   Robertus de Anglia, *O fallaze e ria fortuna* (first part).

name of "Jo. bodigham."[24] I will try, as far as possible, to reconstruct this text, mistreated by copyists who were principally interested in its music (in some case they were not even Italian); this reconstruction is necessarily limited to the first stanza:

Gentil madonna, / de non m'abbandonare.
Hame, deb'[i]o / sempre in questo ardore stare?

O pretiosa gemma, / o fiore de margarita,
tu sei colei che tien sempre mia vita
in amorosa fiamma; / de non me far penare.[25]

It is my impression that in this case also the composer picked up the text of an earlier setting that may have had a popular tone.[26] He treated it as described in the previous examples, repeating the music of the first line of the *ripresa* also for the second line ('which originally may not have been part of the *ripresa*), then writing in full the music of the whole stanza, *volta* included.

Besides *O rosa bella*, therefore, other poems—of the kind Bembo would call "composti vinizianamente" (composed in a Venetian fashion) and which already had had a life of their own in the local, semi-learned, literary and musical traditions—were taken up and reinterpreted by foreign musicians from beyond the Alps or beyond the sea.[27] These musicians, who had had a complete education in the technique of polyphonic composition, did not any longer intend to write music for poetry, but music for its own sake. Their tendency was therefore to choose rather short texts or to extract from longer texts as much as was necessary for their purpose. In fact, in accordance with that purpose, their compositions were actually collected as music, in manuscripts which are rarely scrupulous and exhaustive in text transcription. This raises the question, for which there is no easy answer, whether they meant, by turning to those texts (and departing from their national language, English, or from French, the official language of fifteenth-century polyphony), to evoke in a polyphonic language the vivid impressions they had received from those texts or from similar ones, performed in the manner characteristic of unlearned musicians.

If this was the case, they had to reflect two different types of performance: one in which the length of the text prescribe that it be recited rapidly, and another in which the text's shortness allowed indulgence in vocal and melodic effusion. *O fallaze e ria fortuna* (see Ex. 10.2) belongs to the first type; but although the composer may have found it interesting to revive and was rather successful in doing so, it is difficult to imagine that the polyphonic rendering could compete with the amount of textual, musical, and mimic elements present (to go back to the considerations stated above) in Giustinian's canzonets.[28] *O rosa bella* and *Gentil madonna* belong to the second type, which may have echoed the singing of short lyrical *ballate,* or maybe even the singing of *strambotti.* They succeeded, in that these compositions too had a certain fame. *Gentil madonna,* as we saw, was sung with texts of *laude* almost until the end of the century.[29] *O rosa bella* was quoted as an "ayre" well known to everybody: at a banquet offered by Cardinal Pietro Riario in Rome in 1473, "cantosse in uno chitarino *O rosa bella*" (*O rosa bella* was sung to a small guitar); a year earlier, in November 1472, Galeazzo Maria Sforza tried to get from the Savoy court "*Robinetto* notato su l'ayre de *Rosabella*" (*Robinetto* written down in musical notes on the air of *Rosabella*).[30]

The reasons for their charm, evident also to us, are the well-articulated, flexible, and delicately sensuous melody and the persuasive sweetness of harmonic successions circumscribed by the soft counterpoint texture. Such qualities are characteristic of the "contenance angloise" celebrated by a poet of the Burgundian court as a very important contribution of English musicians to the polyphonic art of their times. *O rosa bella,* anyway, be it by Dunstable, Bedingham, or someone else, is a borderline case in the production of the first and an exception in the second;[31] one could therefore suppose that to the usual elements of "contenance angloise" was added (not a new thing in the history of polyphony) the desire of emulating, within the rules of the art, the expressive effectiveness achieved in less "regular" ways by some performer of the "Giustinian type."

The music of *Gentil madonna* is not accessible, as far as I know, in any modern edition, but I abstain from giving its transcription here, relying instead on its publication as part of the entire musical collection of one of the sources in which it is present, codex 871 of the Biblioteca della Badia di Montecassino.[32] Instead I have published *O rosa bella* once again even though it has been published for more than a century,[33] both because all of this essay is based on it and because I hope that my version (see Ex. 10.1) is different and musically more effective.

I base my transcription on the version of manuscript Porto 714, which differs only in some minimal details from the more often used version of codex Urbinate lat. 1411.[34] The major innovation of my transcription is that it alternates ternary (3/4) and binary beats (2/4, sometimes coupled in a 4/4 unity), while the previous transcriptions employ a binary rhythm throughout, changing to the ternary only a little before the end.[35] The same flexibility in the rhythm is found also in *Gentil madonna,* although in a more limited way.

I do not hesitate to admit that one element on which my version is based is musical sensitivity. It has always been my conviction that an editor must give the reader, besides his skill as a musical paleographer, his ampler experience and familiarity with the style of the music presented; he must offer his own personal interpretation of it, of course as a suggestion that does not exclude other possible interpretations. In the case of *O rosa bella,* however, some objective considerations must be added to the subjective ones. Traditional versions rest on the usual interpretation of the *tempus imperfectum* marks present in the sources (but without absolute regularity) at the beginning of *O rosa bella* and the marks of *tempus perfectum* present (with even less consistency) near the end. One must consider, though, that the first of these marks was sometimes used by fifteenth-century composers to indicate normal *tactus* (neither augmented nor reduced, in a period when proportional notation was beginning to be used frequently), whose units (*semibreves* in the original notation, half notes in my transcriptions) follow each other, flexibly regrouping into binary or ternary groups. An example of this use, which was followed also by the English composers of codex Porto 714, is the notation of *O fallace e ria fortuna* (Ex. 10.2), in which the *tempus imperfectum* mark, besides allowing the oscillation between binary and ternary, leaves to the reader's musical intuition the discovery that the subdivision of the *tactus* (that is, the prolation) is ternary.

It must be acknowledged that this habit gives way to uncertainties, and in fact it created uncertainties also among the fifteenth-century readers of *O rosa bella.* The first remedy devised was to add the *tempus perfectum* mark in the composition's final part to show that at least from that point on the rhythm is constantly ternary.[36] A second and more radical device was the proportional notation adopted in codices Trento 89, 90 (Castello del Buon Consiglio), and 93 (Archivio Capitolare); through this the original's *semibreves* are transformed into *breves* under the mark ¢ (therefore with *tactus* to the *breves*); this eludes a strict interpretation of the semicircle mark in the original notation as an indication of binary rhythm, since the new notation allows the *tactus* unities to be freely grouped according to the suggestions of musical feeling. There is no suggestion of a transition to ternary rhythm at the end of the composition, since this too can be done spontaneously under the mark at the beginning.

I will add only one more argument to support my rhythmical interpretation of *O rosa bella*. That the first measure is ternary and the second measure binary (the order is suggested by the *tenor*'s motion) is confirmed by one of the compositions derived from *O rosa bella*, the one attributed in codex Trento 90 (fol. 444v) to an anonymous musician named Hert.[37] Hert began this piece with a canon in which the melody of the higher voice of *O rosa bella*, quoted without alterations, enters as *antecedens* and *consequens* at a distance of five *semibreves*. Other instances to corroborate my thesis could be found in the constellation of compositions that reelaborated *O rosa bella*'s thematic material. But I do not want to get into the longer discussion that these compositions could require and shall be satisfied that the variations referred to in my title be limited to my own.

I have purposely deferred discussion of the author of *O rosa bella*. The attribution to John Dunstable does not convince me, although it has been authenticated by both the first and second editions of the *Complete Works* of the English astronomer, mathematician, and musician. I believe that attribution does not fit with the rhythmical and expressive precision of the text recitation, or with the fact that Dunstable had no direct experience of Italian language and life. Moreover, *O rosa bella*'s rhythmical flexibility is not found in any of the compositions surely written by Dunstable; only the motet *Sub tuam protectionem* approaches it, but without reaching it.[38] Finally, although *O rosa bella*'s counterpoint generally applies Dunstable's controlled harmonic treatment, which Bukofzer defined as "panconsonant," it departs from it in some detail, indulging in spicy frictions of passing notes (see bars 15, 16, 17, 31, 32). The attribution to Bedingham has been denied by Dunstable's supporters, who allege that codex Urbinate lat. 1411 has works by authors active in a period before Bedingham; however, they do not consider that *O rosa bella* is the last composition added to the codex, which itself precedes codex Porto 714 by no more than about ten years. But for Bedingham, too, there is only one composition, *Gentil madonna*, that approaches, although it does not match, *O rosa bella*. After all, Bedingham's artistic stature is indistinct, since there are conflicting attributions for almost all the compositions bearing his name, probably because of his taste for reworking already extant compositions. I would not be surprised if the real author were neither Dunstable nor Bedingham, but a third, certainly English, composer, as yet unidentified.

11 Novelty and Renewal in Italy, 1300–1600

The New Star

Words change their meaning according to the different goals at which they are aimed and the different contexts in which they are used. I wonder what "tradition" means when applied to a short-lived phenomenon for which neither direct antecedent nor direct consequence is known? The music of the Italian Ars nova (I have not given up that expression) appears to have been the equivalent of a nova in the historical firmament: a sudden flash, a short period of brilliance, and a sudden decline. Watching it from light-years of historical distance, we are left to guess what may have been in the darkness before and after that flamboyance.

Tradition derives from *tradere*, we have been recently reminded, yet it is most often used to designate not the action of the verb but its object—whatever is handed down by an older generation and selectively received by a younger one (although such abstractions as "generations" or "layers" of tradition should not be taken too much for granted). I do not object to this transfer of meaning, which is a common procedure of language, but I find it more expedient, in dealing with the Italian Ars nova, to focus on the act itself of *tradere*.

The music of the Ars nova was bound, by its polyphonic nature, to rely on a written tradition, of which six major manuscripts have reached us, plus a number of fragments.[1] Without trying to give them more precise dates (a subject on which I do not always agree with some of my colleagues), it is safe to say that only one large source (represented by the Vatican and Ostiglia fragments) belongs to the fourteenth century. Two others (the so-called Reina and Panciatichi codices) originated about the end of that century. The rest all belong to the first two or three (or even four) decades of the fifteenth century, the final phase of the Ars nova. Geographically, the sources are clearly divided into a Florentine group and a group from northern Italy.

The beauty, size, and numerical predominance of the Florentine group, essentially represented by four complete and meticulously preserved manuscripts, induced the scholars who first dealt with the Ars nova to assign to Florence a leading role, a role I have tried to deny, only to revert in recent years to a more cautious and qualified recognition of Florentine merits. Indeed, the numerical predominance of the Florentine sources has been eroded and finally erased by new findings. As of now the northern representation has been enlarged by a host of fragments, some of which outline the profile of at least three large disbanded sources to be added to the two collections already known (the Reina and Modena manuscripts). More important, Florentine music is practically ignored by the northern sources, with the exception of a few works apparently composed in northern Italy by such migrant Florentines as Giovanni da Firenze and Francesco Landini; on the other hand, all Florentine sources are generous in giving place to the leading composers in the north, Iacopo da Bologna and Bartolino da Padova. These facts explain how I may have been tempted to see a strictly local phenomenon in the Florentine polyphony. They do not, however, tell the whole story; other elements need to be taken into consideration before passing judgment on the relative merits of the two branches of the Ars nova tradition.

The northern sources include both secular and sacred pieces, and works with Latin and vernacular texts. They appear to have been formed by accumulation over a relatively short period of time, collecting works of immediate interest to the scribes or owners either for performance or as models. That is to say, they are repertories reflecting the interests of a certain place at a certain time. The Florentine manuscripts, on the other hand, contain almost exclusively secular pieces with vernacular texts and strive in varying degree toward a pattern of organization grouping their contents by composers and, in a way, by genres. In spite of inconsistencies in the realization, their plan usually gives precedence to the older genres of the madrigal and *caccia,* represented by works of the two older masters (Iacopo da Bologna and Giovanni da Firenze) and of a slightly younger group (Gherardello, Lorenzo, Donato, all Florentines); then the composers are entered who also practiced the younger genre of the polyphonic *ballata,* and finally those (including Landini) who were mainly known for their polyphonic *ballate.*[2] With growing clarity and thoroughness, the

Florentines aimed to give a retrospective view of music and of *poesia per musica* between roughly 1340 and 1415. For the sake of completeness they included the major northern masters, while the northern scribes included Florentine works in their manuscripts only for pragmatic reasons of immediate relevance. Neither branch of the written tradition, however, tells us anything about the origins of the Ars nova, because even the history-minded Florentines were interested only in its ripest fruit.

Older theoretical writings, documents, and sparse polyphonic samples (all of which have been reviewed and increased by Kurt von Fischer) indicate that Italy very early adopted the time-honored practice of church polyphony. As early as the first half of the thirteenth century, we also have lively descriptions of Franciscan friars entertaining themselves with the singing of polyphonic pieces which must have resembled French conductus; according to the same source, the chronicle of Salimbene de Adam, secular clergy indulged in similar amusements. Conductus style seems to have left its mark in the strong tendency of Italian Ars nova polyphony toward all-vocal performance and simultaneous delivery of text in the two (seldom three) parts. Yet the possibility exists of a concomitant derivation from organal *clausulae:* a *clausula,* provided with words, became the matrix of a song, called after it a *carmen matricale.* Whether or not these conjectures are correct, the practice from which the Ars nova derived must have existed long before the fourteenth century; already at the beginning of that century the madrigal (*matriale* in Tuscany, *maregal* or *madregal* in the Venetian region) had become an independent composition on vernacular text, and the original meaning of its name had been completely forgotten. Furthermore, a special system of notation (related to, but somewhat different from the contemporary French usage) had been developed, which gave equal status to binary and ternary rhythms independently of the theories of Vitry and Muris; it was described by Marchettus de Padua in his "Pomerium," circa 1320.

We begin to understand the bias of the later Florentine scribes when we see that the earliest references to the madrigal are tinged with contempt. Francesco da Barberino describes it (circa 1313) as *rudium inordinatum concinnum;* as a literary man he may have objected to the poetry, humble in content (pastoral?) and lacking a definite metrical rule.[3] A few years later a treatise on vernacular poetry (circa 1332) by the Paduan judge Antonio da Tempo explained that the "mandrigal" (taking its name from *mandria*) was formerly a shepherd's song, ennobled only recently by courtly polyphonic practice. However, the examples of madrigal texts offered by da Tempo had not yet attained the metrical form which later came to prevail; nor is it possible to recognize any formal or metrical rule unifying the pieces in the oldest known source of Ars nova music—the above-mentioned Vatican and Ostiglia fragments—a source in which a practice connected with the court of the Scaligeri of Verona is reflected. Such works or their contemporaries do not appear in the late Florentine sources, and similarly excluded are those of a Maestro Piero, who seems to have been the main creator of the genre of the *caccia,* a derivation from and specialization of the madrigal form.[4]

We begin also to realize the fallacy of a unilateral approach based on our experience of music and poetry as independent activities that converge only occasionally. Literature may have provided the impetus which raised the music of a private clerical entertainment to the status of a new art. I have come to think that the rise of the Ars nova was favored by the trends of the *dolce stil novo*—not, of course, by the "tragic" style assigned by Dante to the *canzone* (which rapidly became a purely literary form), but by the "mediocre" style of the *ballata,* enhanced by the poets with all sorts of refinements, to which a similar demand for musical refinement must have corresponded. Most influential (at the time and for the future) was the acknowledgment by Petrarch of the madrigal as an art form; the four madrigals he included in his *Canzoniere* are models of artful variety in the order of rhymes. For one of them we have the music set by Iacopo da Bologna, who was active in Milan from the late 1330s to the 1350s, during which period Petrarch had strong ties with the Milanese court and sojourned in Parma and Milan.[5] A personal relationship is highly probable, but Petrarch's influence was also strongly felt in Florence by poets like Soldanieri, Boccaccio, and Sacchetti, who all contributed texts for the Ars nova composers.

Nor were the musicians merely passive. For one thing, they must have been the authors of many of the texts they set to music (as poets such as Petrarch and Sacchetti are known to have had musical gifts). More important, the earliest-known composers, Iacopo and Giovanni, highly deserved the distinction of being singled out as the "classics" of the Ars nova. Iacopo's skillful control of polyphonic devices and his contrapuntal lines, sharpened with great variety of detail, embody the taste of the northern polyphonists for figuration and contrast.[6] Even Iacopo, however, seems to have derived the overall design of his works from Florentine examples, accessible to him through his personal contacts with Giovanni in Verona and possibly also in Milan. With softer, placidly flowing lines, Giovanni and the Florentines placed the accent on clear definition of each musical phrase (corresponding to a line of text) and on its relationship to the overall musical design. They thus arrived at a balanced strophic structure, based on the optimum number of three phrase-lines, and sealed, after two or three repetitions, by a two-line *ritornello,* in which the real thrust of the short poem found its expression. Most often this heightened meaning was stressed in the music of the *ritornello* with a sudden change of rhythm and tonality. It is thus apparent that the metrical form refined by the poets was the one which best served fundamental needs of musical expression.

The following short-lived course of the Italian Ars nova was enlivened by the interplay between its two main trends. As the northerners had welcomed Florentine formal suggestions, the Florentines derived figural variety from northern models. One quality they had in common, considered to be typical of most Italian music at all times, was the capacity to engage and capture the listener through such factors as the all-vocal sound, the clear, slightly oratorical delivery of the text, and, last but not least, the sense of direction of melodic lines, aptly stressed by the deliberate contour of the supporting *tenor.* The Ars nova composer, while not averse to *subtilitas* in the form of notational expertise and intellectually controlled construction, never gave up the aim of pleasing with sensible qualities, the *dulcedo* of music.

From a social point of view, the political system of republican Florence gave the local polyphony the advantage of modest but continuous support by a small circle of connoisseurs, mostly men engaged in intellectual occupations; in turn, this determined the unity and continuity of its course from Giovanni to Andrea dei Servi and Paolo Tenorista. The northern tradition, mostly bound to courtly activities, which ensured more luster than continuity, tended to fade whenever the support or the supporter was suppressed. Its two major representatives, Iacopo and Bartolino, probably never met and were flanked by only minor figures. Nevertheless, the northern polyphony also achieved a remarkable degree of stylistic coherence, related in all probability to the intellectual reservoir of academic milieus, above all the universities of Bologna and Padua.

Because of its thin social basis, the Italian Ars nova was not, as it could have been, the fountainhead of a stream of tradition. Paradoxically, the measure of recognition it gained about the middle of the fourteenth century was the starting point for the gradual obliteration of some of its traditional features. Raised ambitions intensified the composers' interest in the technical procedures and artistic achievements of French music. In Florence this rapidly resulted in abandonment of Italian notation in favor of a version of French notation adjusted to the simple needs of Florentine rhythm; more sporadic symptoms were the attempts to use different texts in the different voices of a piece, to build on a *tenor prius factus,* and to adopt some isorhythmic procedures. Finally, a number of *ballate* were deemed to be in a French style because of the use of 6/8 or 9/8 rhythms, instrumental *tenor* (and sometimes *contratenor*), *ouvert* and *clos* endings, and musical rhyme between the two sections of a piece. In northern Italy the influence of French music had been felt at an even earlier date; the Vatican fragment includes a polyphonic *rondeau* on an Italian text and a monophonic *ballata* "alla francesca." Yet the Italian notation was not discarded but refined, to accommodate, in the case of Bartolino, even some reflection of the so-called French "mannered" style. Furthermore, social circumstances encouraged the composition of a number of motets—a practice which had almost no counterpart in Florence. Beyond these individual features, the adoption of polyphony for the settings of *ballata* texts, common to both Florentine and northern composers, seems to have been spurred by the desire for an Italian equivalent to the lyrical forms of French polyphony (*rondeau, virelai,* and *ballade*); the madrigal and *caccia,* because of their narrative or descriptive texts, were rather counterparts to the French motet. About 1400 the polyphonic *ballata* had almost completely supplanted the two older forms, only to be itself superseded, during the next two or three decades, by adopted French polyphonic forms and techniques, and often French language for the texts.

The Fifteenth Century and the Unwritten Traditions

Dulcedo, the word most commonly used through the centuries to praise music, does not strictly mean a soft blandishment of the ear, nor have I ever implied that it was an exclusive monopoly of Italian music. I should like to redefine *dulcedo* as an appeal (not necessarily lacking some element of novelty) to a set of expectations determined by the habits and previous musical experiences of the listeners. A certain uniformity of habits and musical experiences existed among the people to whom the music of the Ars nova addressed itself; they were either clergymen themselves (to whom the Ars nova was indebted for its origins) or men of culture, who had received the type of education designed for the upper ranks of clergy. This involved some familiarity with musical theory and intensive exposure to liturgical music, polyphonic as well as monophonic. These people may have been a part of what Carducci liked to call the "mondo elegante" of the fourteenth century, but they formed a special group within that world, a group marked by special tastes and activities, cajoled and patronized for special services they could render or for the luster they could add to a social gathering or a court. What had musical *dulcedo* for them did not necessarily appeal to other people; even the noblest lords did not necessarily have the refined tastes we are inclined to attribute to them. The fact that some Ars nova composers had connections with the Visconti brothers (one of whom was the archbishop of Milan), the Scala brothers, or the Carrara family (one of whose members had been raised for an ecclesiastical career) cannot be taken as indication of a general courtly interest in polyphonic music. Indeed, the musical demands of contemporary society, from its humblest to its most exalted stations, were essentially answered by other types of music and musicians, by singers, players, dancers, and mimes of whose music we have no direct knowledge. We can only define it, because of its more general and regrettably negative feature, as the unwritten tradition of music.

The unwritten tradition embraced a variety of musical activities not always lacking in artistic refinement. One only needs to think of the musical practices descending from the feudal tradition of troubadour art (itself, in my opinion, a part of the unwritten tradition, in spite of the ex post facto notation of a fraction of its music). I have already mentioned the stil novo as an important factor in the rise of the Ars nova. Dante certainly knew some form of polyphony, but he had his lyrical poems set to music by nonpolyphonists and described a performance by one of them (Casella) with touching poignancy. Petrarch, whom I have singled out as having won literary recognition for the madrigal, had friendly relations with practitioners of both the written and unwritten tradition of music: among the former, Ludwig van Kempen (the "Socrates" of his letters), Philippe de Vitry, and possibly Iacopo da Bologna; among the latter, Floriano da Rimini (whom he compared to Orpheus), Antonio da Ferrara, and Confortino (most likely a singer's nickname). Boccaccio had some poems set to music by polyphonists but did not include their way of music making among the musical entertainments described in his *Decameron,* and Sacchetti's more than 250 short stories contain only a single ironic reference to the madrigal, although their author was personally acquainted with the half dozen polyphonists then active in Florence. On the opposite side, I may quote a madrigal text set to music twice[7] by Iacopo da Bologna, "Oselleto salvazo," in which Petrarch's Floriano da Rimini is listed among the highest musical authorities:

> ... tuti se fa màistri:
> fa ballate, matrical e muteti,
> tut'èn Fioran, Filippoti e Marcheti.

The pattern was not different during the fifteenth century. As before, descriptions of musical performances seldom give any hint of polyphonic music; as before, musicians who left no mark in the written tradition are mentioned or enthusiastically praised. From one point of view the fading of the Ars nova during the first decades of that century may be viewed as a minor, almost unnoticed incident, against the background of a much stronger stream of musical life in the ways of the unwritten tradition. Nor is anything "secret" involved in the gap thus created in the written tradition; if anything, it was the previous sudden blooming of the Ars nova from a very thin humus of specialized and private practices that was surprising.

The written tradition of the Ars nova ends in glory with the Squarcialupi codex. This is not a figure of speech, for it is obvious to me that this largest, most consistent with its plan, and most lavishly decorated of the Florentine manuscripts consciously preserves and glorifies an activity in which the compilers took great pride, but which had reached its end. It is also obvious to me that the object of their pride was not so much the music of the Ars nova as the predominantly Florentine line of poetry with which it had been associated. The inspiration is germane to the brand of civic humanism then developing in Florence, in which the cult of classicism was paralleled by admiration for the great Florentines who had developed the local tongue into a refined instrument of artistic expression. The compilation of the Squarcialupi codex is thus related to the celebration of the *certame coronario* in 1441, although it certainly preceded it.[8] What gave its compilers their nostalgic feeling of finality is made clear by the swiftest glance at two polyphonic collections only slightly more recent than theirs: the ample Oxford codex (Canonici 213, seemingly assembled in Venice) and the much smaller Vatican manuscript (Urbinate lat. 1411), once presented to a friend by Piero dei Medici. Their contents, like that of all other Italian sources from about 1440 to 1490, consist essentially of pieces on French texts (Latin in the case of sacred music), with only scattered samples of Italian pieces, either anonymous or by foreign composers. The tide of French music had already been rising during the previous half century, helped by the frequent influx of foreign prelates during the Great Schism and the Councils. As a matter of fact, some of the most flamboyant examples of late musical Gothicism (the so-called "mannered" phase) were composed by Italians during the first two decades of the fifteenth century. The men who had enjoyed the music of the Ars nova belonged to the segment of society most open to international trends and most inclined to intellectual or musical *subtilitas;* it was easy for them to transfer their musical interest to pieces using the international language of polyphony, whatever the language of their texts.

From a musical point of view, then, the Ars nova did not die; it merged with other trends: on a higher technical level with the international, essentially French, polyphonic tradition, to which it contributed some features through such mediators as Johannes Ciconia and Dufay; on a lower technical level with some of the practices of unwritten music. Some Ars nova pieces may have been incorporated in the repertory of more popular singers; this was certainly the case for some *ballate* by Landini, whose texts are occasionally found amid a lyrical repertory of a rather popular, even dialectal flavor. It also appears that a number of singers reared in the ways of unwritten music came to develop or adopt techniques of performance in which the vocal line is supported by some kind of polyphonic accompaniment by a string instrument. A few rather peculiar two-voice pieces found in polyphonic collections[9] might be a written record of normally unwritten practices.

A fact of considerable importance for the history of art polyphony in Italy was a split in the elite minority which had most contributed to its previously rather thin diffusion. With the spreading of humanistic thoughts and attitudes, the new breed of literati came to despise polyphony as a contrived, unnatural form of musical expression, and to see its procedures and theory as typical examples of medieval lore. As a result, art polyphony regressed to its original status of an art entrenched in the most scholastically oriented milieus of monasteries and cathedral chapters, plus, of course, the papal and some princely chapels, for nobody objected to its liturgical uses. For an ornament to their lives and for musical activities better attuned to the fabulous powers attributed to music by classical writers—the power to excite or assuage man's passions, with its ethical implications, and the power to divert his mind from worries and fatigue—the humanists turned to the unwritten tradition. Already in 1429 Ambrogio Traversari praised Leonardo Giustinian for his ability in singing sweet songs to the accompaniment of an instrument, an art which, "contrary to the habit of the ancients, is better known nowadays to the people than to learned men." Giustinian, who had composed his secular songs during the first quarter of the century, soon became a mythical figure; his style was imitated in a category of songs called *giustiniane,* and conversely many later songs (of which, of course, we have only texts) were attributed to him. He is the first in a series of musicians and poets whose names were better known to fifteenth-century Italians than those of Dufay, Ockeghem, or young Josquin. Others were Antonio di Guido in Florence,

Francesco Cieco da Ferrara, Pietrobono dal Chitarrino, and above all
Serafino Aquilano; furthermore, it is a frequent occurrence in humanist
writings that Latin or vernacular poems of precious texture honor musicians whose names and activities are unknown to us.

Songs named for the dialect of their texts (*siciliana, vinitiana,
napoletana,* or *calavrese,* all implying aria or *canzone*) indicate a continuing interest in pieces having popular features of melody or performance,
plus the added advantage of exotic appeal. Apart from these, a number of
new poetic forms come to the fore: the lyrical single-strophe *strambotto,*
only externally related to the narrative sequences of *ottave* (or *ottava
rima*); the *capitolo* or *terza rima* (strophes of three lines), closely related to
the so-called *sirventese* (with strophes of four lines); finally a simplified, or
more popular, form of *ballata,* better known to musicologists as *frottola,*
while literary historians tend to call it *barzelletta.* With the exception of
strambotti, the texts tend to have a large number of strophes (of narrative,
gnomic, or even dramatic content), implying an equal number of repetitions in the music with compact strophic structures and fast, predominantly syllabic delivery. Even the singing of a *strambotto,* judging from
later examples, was based on four repetitions of the same musical unit
(fewer or more may have been needed for *strambotti* having fewer or more
couplets). All this agrees perfectly with two basic, intrinsically related
features of the unwritten tradition: easy memorization of the musical
strophic unit, which eventually enabled the performer to concentrate on
the improvisation of new texts.[10]

The names of singers and instrumentalists (another line of musical
activities that deserves attention), those of new poetic forms, and even the
surviving poems may seem to our distracted ears nothing more than the
faint murmur of an underground brooklet. In the daily life of the fifteenth
century they, not written music, were the elements of a resounding open-
air stream, which gave pleasure and *dulcedo* to every layer of society.

As for sacred music, about which we know more, it continued to have a
secluded life and was only marginally affected by the cultural trends which
were having an impact on secular practice. Cathedral polyphony, because
of its growing complexity, was only possible if the church could afford the
highly skilled performers it required, that is, only in some of the larger
cities. Of greater moment were the activities of court chapels: that of the
Aragonese court of Naples, already in existence before the middle of the
century, and those of the Sforza and Este courts, both created early in the
1470s. But the Aragonese and Sforza chapels were disrupted by political
events before the end of the century, and only the Ferrarese chapel,

brought to international excellence by the musical and religious fervor of its founder, Ercole I d'Este, was left to serve as a model to similar institutions. In any case, both the repertory of sacred polyphony and, to a large extent, its performers belonged to an international musical culture deeply rooted in the French tradition.

The same applies to the papal chapel, in which, however, two still not well understood customs, or traditions, originated, whose beginnings, perhaps related, may go back to the fifteenth century. These are *a cappella* singing and *falsibordoni*. Both practices must be referred to the demands for ecclesiastical reform expressed by the Councils in the early fifteenth century—demands which seem to have had greater impact on the papal chapel than on the chapels of the staunchest supporters of reform, the French kings and the dukes of Burgundy and Savoy. The same influence may have been the cause of the lesser emphasis placed by the Italians on the performance of paraliturgical motets.

The Sixteenth Century: Traditions Lost, Found, and Mixed Up

Written and unwritten traditions, I wrote once, are broad generalizations or polarizations, between whose extremes there is ample space for exceptions, hybrids, and borderline cases. The exceptions, however, become surprisingly numerous toward the end of the fifteenth century; too many pieces which would seem to belong to the unwritten tradition are written down in polyphonic collections. At first, it is mainly *strambotti*, appearing either in manuscripts which may reflect the practice of the Neapolitan court, or in northern sources, where they still preserve some southern flavor in their texts (one more instance of the recurring interest in exotic pieces). Then it is the turn of *frottole;* "Frottole," at the apex of this trend, is the title of eleven printed collections published in Venice by Ottaviano Petrucci from 1504 to 1514. This, however, is an all-inclusive title, covering many types of compositions, among them the declining *strambotto*. A parallel phenomenon is the appearance in Florence of polyphonic settings of *canti carnascialeschi,* normally found only in manuscripts and mostly belonging to the first quarter of the sixteenth century.[11]

In order to assess this large and less than homogeneous body of music from the point of view of tradition, one has to make a distinction between true *frottola* settings, along with masquerade songs and *canti carnasciales-*

chi, and the rest of the repertory. The former group more directly reflects popular custom, taken over and refined for the pleasure of courtiers. The *frottole,* in particular, which outnumber all the other kinds, meet demands for musical entertainment. Set to amorous texts that are either conventionally or caricaturally pathetic, or definitely humorous, their musical interest is centered on the lively rhythm and melodic directness of the upper line, supported by the other parts, sometimes with a certain amount of pseudo-contrapuntal activity, but essentially with a strong chordal and cadential feeling.[12] While the melody lent itself easily to a display of vocal skill on the part of a soloist, the texts often invited gestures or mimicry; accordingly, the one type of performance that still continued the habits of the unwritten tradition—a singer accompanying himself on a stringed instrument—was most often selected from among many possibilities. *Strambotti,* too, met demands for musical amusement and were similarly performed, yet one can easily discern in their texts, alongside a popular vein, a second trend aimed at a more even balance of musical and literary interests. Indeed, the *strambotto* had come to be considered as a suitable form for high poetic expression; those left by Serafino Aquilano, among others, are dismissed by most modern critics as anticipation of baroque bombast, but were praised in their times as precious examples of almost classical epigrammatic brevity.[13] The *strambotto* thus took a middle ground between genres musically motivated and those mainly conceived as vehicles for literary expression. In the latter belonged the *capitolo,* which already in the previous phase had often been charged with sententious content; the strophic *oda* (with either Latin or vernacular texts), whose name and form give a more classical coloration to the older *sirventese;* and finally the sonnet, which for at least the last two centuries had been a purely literary form.

Petrucci further stressed the tendency of some musical genres to be the vehicle for the corresponding poetic form by offering some pieces which he called *aere* or *modo* "per capitoli," "per sonetti," or "per cantar versi latini," and on which all poems having a given metrical structure could be sung. The emphasis was still placed, however, on the performer's effectiveness in delivering music and text—all the more so since poets like Cariteo in Naples, Tebaldeo in Ferrara, and Poliziano in Florence are said to have made their new poems known often through their own singing or through the offices of a professional singer. Nor was there any reason why the settings of such poems should be lacking in musical interest, although the requirement is firmly stated by a contemporary writer that the music be the servant of poetry, its style made simpler the more the quality of the poem deserved attention.

After Naples, whose leading role was soon wiped out by political collapse, the northern epicentrum of the new secular polyphony was Ferrara, whose ruler, Ercole I d'Este, like his brother and predecessor Borso, had been educated in Naples. More than Ercole himself, however (who was mainly interested in sacred music and in the chapel he had created), his children, who had all received good musical training from members of the chapel, took an active role in the new secular trend and were instrumental in spreading it to other allied courts, most directly to those of Mantua, Milan, and Urbino.[14] The composers seldom were foreign members of the local chapels (although men like Compère and Josquin were involved), but rather native musicians, as befitted the very nature of the new polyphony. Nevertheless, they were well acquainted with the technique of international polyphony, having been reared as church singers in such institutions as the "scuola degli Accoliti" in the cathedral of Verona (in which Bartolomeo Tromboncino and Marchetto Cara must have been trained) or similar schools in Padua and Venice.

Along with the new brand of secular music went the spread and better appreciation of church polyphony. This must be related to an impassioned interest in all kinds of artistic expression, first activated by humanistic thoughts, now blossoming in the full vigor of artistic life. Another important place where the representatives of the polyphonic culture (which I have often identified with some residual scholasticism) had daily opportunities for contact with learned men, artists, and art patrons was the papal court in Rome. This was the ground where the artistic stature of Josquin des Prez attained general recognition; it is symptomatic, however, that a Ciceronian writer, Paolo Cortese, while bestowing great praise on Josquin's Masses, still reserved highest honors in the field of secular music to Petrarch and Aquilano.

The sixteenth century poses once more the problem of how to apply the word "tradition." Sacred polyphony, long the privilege of chapels and a few cathedrals, was becoming accessible to larger crowds because of the creation of similar institutions (also called chapels) in many churches.[15] Yet its classic hero (no ancient models were available to musicians) was Josquin, not an Italian; later in the century foreigners like Willaert and Rore were among its most influential masters and, being successful teachers, they dominated the field with a large following of gifted pupils. I can mention only two trends which may have been influenced by Italian inborn preferences. One is represented at its best by the neoclassicist master of Italian sacred music, Palestrina, whose economy of polished counterpoint and purity of vocal sound recall features already observed in the meager body of older Italian polyphony; yet even Palestrina's language is international, and his models are to a large extent French.[16] The same applies, although in a different way, to the practice of polychoral polyphony, in which the distribution of choral groups in different locations contributed to the simultaneous perception of architectural and musical projections. A third trend, the demand for clarity in the enunciation of the liturgical text, was too intertwined with nonmusical factors to be considered as an element of musical tradition. As a whole, sacred polyphony, because of its previous long history and its being rooted in a universal liturgy, was a universal language, hence imposing itself on its listeners and not depending on them or on local traditions. An exceptional artistic personality could have greater impact on its rarefied standards than the taste and expectations of its audiences.

In the field of secular music the surfacing of elements of the unwritten tradition was certainly an impressive phenomenon, even though we have only the vaguest hints about the previous stages of that tradition. Furthermore, the new secular polyphony was associated with another conscious revival, the literary effort to restore the Italian language to the standard of an art medium after the regression it had experienced during many decades of Latin writing. In the new Romance-language humanism, which soon coalesced in a revived Petrarchism, new poets were not content with imitation of the older poet's style and thoughts; they even shaped their collections after the model of the *Canzoniere,* with hundreds of sonnets, plus a number of *canzoni* and a sprinkling of *ballate* and madrigals.[17] Parallel to this was the thought that all these poems could and should be set to music, reviving traditions which, alas, had long been dead and forgotten. We have already mentioned that sonnets were included in the "Frottola" books; settings of *canzoni* and madrigals were discussed in letters and are actually found in prints and manuscripts together with some *ballate.* As a rule, however, the music tended to disregard the internal symmetries of their metrical form; very soon experience taught that the performance of a whole *canzone* with its lengthy strophic repeats was impractical, while even the poets rebelled against the metrical strictures of the old *ballata.*[18] Thus the old forms were replaced by nonstrophic, through-composed settings of new poems, which only occasionally reflected some features of the traditional structures, and all came to be known by the generic name of *canzoni* (songs) or madrigals. The latter name prevailed from 1530 on, and its ascent, as well as the ascent of the genre itself, was not impeded by the further misunderstanding of old traditions it brought with it.

One northern development may have been helped by the 1507 printing of the fourteenth-century treatise on metrical forms of da Tempo. Composers who used popular tunes—as refrains in some *frottole* (where they are usually placed in the *tenor*), or as material for contrapuntal elaboration in the special type called *villota* (somewhat parallel to some French chansons)—may have thought they were reviving the old "mandriale," which had been derived, according to da Tempo, from shepherd songs. At least on one occasion singers masquerading as peasants performed "madrigali alla pavana," that is, madrigals in the Paduan dialect.[19] Thus a realistic, un-Petrarchan strain was being injected into the composite image of the madrigal, whose Petrarchan line was also being subjected to conflicting impulses. Its traditional origin directed it toward soloistic singing accompanied by instruments, but other concepts invited it to a more contrapuntal texture and all-vocal performance. The main thrust in the latter direction must have come from the Medicean patronage in Florence and Rome and must have been supported by the thought that not only the skillful delivery by a soloist, but all the artistic resources of the composer, should be summoned to interpret and convey the poetic message of the text.[20] This thought, aptly summarized in the definition of the madrigal as a "secular motet," opened the way to all kinds of ventures in the field of madrigal and madrigalisms. It also affiliated its genre to a polyphonic tradition which was not altogether foreign because it had been present at all times, but neither did it have altogether a national character.

I am strongly tempted to suggest that the entire development of Italian music during the sixteenth century, sacred as well as secular, should be considered as a deliberate adoption of a polyphonic *maniera*. Within that larger frame innumerable possibilities for individual manneristic expression were available and often exploited, but they were even more remote from any broad feeling of tradition, since they depended on the artist's personality or the patron's whim. This does not mean that traditional elements of temperament and behavior did not still have a part in the tangle of different motivations, but they can only be detected through psychological and critical analysis of individual artists and works.

More evident are the deviations manifesting themselves behind the façade of the official *maniera*, most often in ways of performance. The interest in and admiration of the qualities and skills of performers had a great outlet in the exploits of lutenists, keyboard players, and other instrumentalists, of which we have only a partial record in written music. Also in the vocal field, recourse was often made to ways of performance in which the upper line was sung and the others given to instruments; or else forms were created, like the *villanella* and *canzonetta*, in which the vocal line is specifically conceived to prevail on a subdued, rather chordal accompaniment, be it vocal or instrumental. Even more important, the basic humus of the unwritten tradition was still present to give incentive to new musical forms, of which the *villanesca alla napoletana* is a most typical example. All this and much more (for instance, ostinato bass patterns, new harmonic definitions of tonality, and the protean concept of aria) finally came to converge in a rebellion against the polyphonic *maniera*. Thus the beginning of the seventeenth century brought with it a resounding assertion of the established tradition (or historical delusion?) that each new century be marked by a *nuova musica* of a sort.

12 ⨳ Willaert and the *Canzone Villanesca*

Italy had strong attractions for many foreign musicians during the sixteenth century. Many who went there became so well adjusted to their new life that they stayed for years, even the rest of their lives, and became leading figures in many kinds of music making which we are used to considering as typical of Italian culture and society. One has only to think of the role played by Verdelot and Arcadelt in shaping the madrigal or of the impact of Rore and Wert as forerunners of the *seconda pratica*. But in no other case is the combining of deeply different traditions as startling as in Willaert's meeting with the *canzone villanesca*. One reason for surprise is that except for a short visit Willaert is said possibly to have made to Rome, he spent at least half a century first in the Po Valley and later in the very special climate of the Most Serene Republic of Venice;[1] the *canzone villanesca*, however, came from the south, from Naples, and continued for some time to be called *villanesca alla napolitana*, even though it soon started to mingle with pieces whose dialect and musical language were rooted in northern Italy.[2]

It has been pointed out that the sudden appearance of the *villanesca alla napolitana* on the Italian musical stage must be connected with a flashy political event, the first visit of Emperor Charles V, to his recently secured domain of Naples in January 1536.[3] Much was done on that occasion to honor and entertain the imperial guest, and it was also reported in a letter of the Mantuan ambassador Count Nicola Maffei to his court that groups of musicians, stationed in various sections of the city, had competed with each other in singing "cose villanesche all'usanza di qua e cose de madrigali molto concertatamente" (*villanesca* pieces as they sing them here and madrigal pieces very well concerted).[4] A certain Benedetto di Falco, poet, grammarian, lexicographer, and historian, had already voiced the Neapolitans' pride in their musical traditions in his description of the marvels of Naples and its surroundings, addressed and dedicated to the emperor in view of his forthcoming visit.[5] The first known edition of *Canzoni villanesche alla napolitana,* published with that title in Naples on October 24, 1537, by the German printer Johannes de Colonia,[6] was near enough in time to the emperor's visit to be considered not only as a further expression of Neapolitan pride, but also as an indication that their "cose villanesche" had been a real success and had fully stood the comparison with the most refined and well-concerted madrigals.

Neither a preface nor a dedication explains who or what motivated Johannes de Colonia's edition. The only hint is in a woodcut on the front page of the two surviving part-books, those of *cantus* and *tenor*—the *bassus* part is missing—representing three peasants at work and finding relief from their toil in the singing of polyphonic music. There is no doubt that they are singing polyphony because the tiny figures are labeled "BAS[SUS]," "TEN[OR]," and "CAN[TUS]."[7] The implication seems to have been that the fifteen three-voice pieces on dialectal texts, included in the collection without names of composers, were all part of a popular repertory, whose authorship belonged to no individual but to the whole community.

I am not convinced by the suggestion that this collection had a rural community origin. Not because its repertory is polyphonic, for my colleague and friend Diego Carpitella tells me that harvest songs in two- or three-voice polyphony were sung until recently in the territory of Caserta, not far from Naples. My suspicions are aroused by the presence in the text of some learned idioms, some literary images, and even some Petrarchan language, along with colorful images and realistic expressions in a truly popular vein. The mixture, I believe, is more compatible with an urban tradition of popular song, a tradition that perhaps shared some basic features with the ethnic background of the countryside around Naples, but combined them with the elements of higher culture which even the humblest Neapolitan citizens must have been able to absorb after several centuries of association with, and dependence on, a royal court with its following of noblemen, high officers, and literati.

That this music may have been considered peasant music is no surprise. The *villanesco* is a recurrent topos in the history of western culture, often parallel to, but always sharply distinguished from, the topos of pastoral life. In the latter, a tradition of classical origin, a sophisticated society usually enjoys mirroring itself in an equally sophisticated Arcadian disguise; in the *villanesco,* on the other hand, the main attraction is the exotic flavor, the sudden meeting with a peasant milieu which amuses because of its diversity, crude humor, and realism. There is no lack of such spices in the colloquial texts of the Neapolitan *villanesche,* rich in colorful images and picturesque proverbial lore,[8] but an even greater factor in their success must have been the special accent of their musical language, which I believe had its roots in a popular tradition.

I may be accused of having biased, preconceived ideas about popular musical traditions, or, as I prefer to describe them, traditions of unwritten music, but it is my belief that the *villanesca* actually goes back to a popular tradition, whether urban or rural. Certainly Neapolitan writers of the sixteenth and early seventeenth centuries fondly repeated the names of famous popular singers: Velardiniello, Sbruffapappa, zio Pezillo. They belong to a favorite category of mine, that of musicians very much admired in their time, whose activities are beyond the scope of music history because they had no use for musical notation. The fact is, I feel, that the typical *villanesca* tune has a flavor which sets it apart from both art music and from the examples of northern popular songs which are preserved, usually in the form of quotations, in a number of polyphonic pieces of the late fifteenth and early sixteenth centuries. I may also be biased because I am myself from southern Italy, but I feel the ring of a southern, maybe also Mediterranean, ethnic lore in the humorous delivery of the dialectal texts, in the spirited truncations and repetitions of words, in the sudden slowing and brisk acceleration of tempi, resulting as a whole in a remarkable variety and directness of rhythmic accentuation and expression (Ex. 12.1).

Ex. 12.1   Giovan Domenico da Nola, *Io dich' è sturno* (upper part).

Outside of Naples, the attraction of geographic exoticism was added to the basic exoticism of class inherent in the representation of peasant life and mores. It is no wonder then that the *villanesca alla napolitana* had a sudden vogue, spreading all over Italy at about the same time that the madrigal was spreading. The connection with the latter is that of a complement rather than, as some critics maintain, a polemical and satirical contrast.[9]

The *villanesca* developed along two different lines, initially quite close to each other but then diverging on courses which we can trace in the succession of printed editions published mostly in Venice. One line is represented by the collections of three-voice *villanesche* of Neapolitan origin, bearing names of composers who were actually part of the Neapolitan scene. As far as we know, this line began with the *Canzoni villanesche de Don Ioan Dominico del Giovane de Nola. Libro Primo et Secondo,* published in Venice by Girolamo Scotto. Of this edition the only extant copy was destroyed during World War I, so we have to rely for its contents on the later reprinting as two separate books, also issued in Venice in 1545 by Antonio Gardane.[10] In 1545 and 1546 Gardane also published collections of three-voice *villanesche* by Tomaso Cimello, Vincenzo Fontana, and Tomaso de Maio, all belonging to the Neapolitan circle of composers.[11] Later the three-voice *villanesca* was seldom represented by collections of works of a single composer, but a number of anthologies grouped works of Neapolitan or southern composers, such as Leonardo Primavera, Leonardo dall'Arpa, Massimo Troiano, Stefano Felis, and Pomponio Nenna, to mention only the most famous ones. We may add Orlando di Lasso to the list, who spent most of the formative years of his adolescence in Naples.

The first editions of three-voice *villanesca* music by Neapolitans were soon paralleled by the printing and reprinting of collections representing the other main trend of *villanesca,* that of four-voice pieces by non-Neapolitan composers, surprisingly headed by the master of St. Mark's Chapel, the Flemish-born and naturalized Venetian Adrian Willaert. A collection of his four-voice *villanesche,* first published in 1544, was reissued in 1545, 1548, and 1553; a few of its pieces were again reprinted and a few more added in a posthumous collection in 1563. In the group of Willaert's pupils and followers, the Frenchman naturalized in Venice as Perissone Cambio had one collection printed in 1545; Antonio Barges, one in 1550; Baldissera Donato, who described himself as a "musician and singer in St. Mark's," had a whole series of editions published in 1550, 1551, 1552, 1556, and 1558.[12] Initially their *villanesche* tended to be new arrangements of previous works by Neapolitan composers; soon there appeared other works in which the light touch of the genre was maintained, but the Neapolitan flavor and the popular tone were gradually lost. Even the name for such pieces was first changed into the gentler, more Arcadian form *villanella,* then finally replaced by the generic term *canzonetta.*[13]

The history of Willaert's encounter with the *villanesca* is only a minor episode in his career, but it is representative of some fundamental traits of his character. The head of the Doge chapel in St. Mark's since 1527, he must have been not only highly respected and admired in Venice for his musical artistry, but also loved for his jovial good manners and sense of humor. We have a sample of this feeling in one of Andrea Calmo's bizarre letters, fictitiously attributed to fishermen from the various small villages of the lagoon: "To the blossoming, scented jasmine of Parnassus, Messer Hadrian Willaert, master of the chapel of the Signoria."[14] To his humane qualities Willaert must have added a good dose of prudence and self-respect, and a sense of the proprieties to be observed by the master of St. Mark's, which we find reflected in his approach to the *villanesca.*

For Willaert's major role, the dates speak for themselves. His collections of 1544 and 1545 made him the first non-Neapolitan composer of four-voice *villanesche,* and that status is further strengthened by the fact that he had already had two four-voice *villanesche,* although they were not labeled as such,[15] included with a number of his madrigals in a 1542 collection of works of the printer and composer Scotto, the *Madrigali a quatro voce di Geronimo Scotto con alcuni alla misura di breve.* As the title indicates, it was one of the earliest publications to advertise another novelty, that of music *a misura breve,* also called *a note nere.* It is typical of Willaert to have cautiously introduced two innovations at one time without announcing them, actually hiding the compositions in which novelty was achieved in a collection of madrigals by another man.

Like most four-voice *villanesche* of the earlier phase, Willaert's two pieces of 1542 are thought to be reelaborations of Neapolitan *villanesche* for three voices. In some cases it is possible to determine the models from which the dialectal text and the principal melody have been taken; in other cases, including these two pieces by Willaert, we cannot document the dependence, but the dialectal flavor (clearly recognizable, notwithstanding attenuations or misunderstandings by the Venetian printers) and the stylistic features of the music let us assume the existence of Neapolitan models, either derived from prints unknown to us or from manuscripts.

Willaert's two *villanesche* of 1542 are unrelated to any of Nola's, which could have been made available to him by Scotto's edition of 1541; the problem then arises of how he obtained his models. The fact that "cose villanesche" had been sung in Naples in the presence of the emperor, his court, and of course his musicians must have been known immediately in such cities as Rome, Florence, and Milan, which had closer ties with the imperial court; the connection was less direct with Venice, which was always jealous of its political independence. I have come to think of Florence as the most probable channel by which the Neapolitan *villanesche* could have reached Venice. Many Florentines, including Cosimo dei Medici, had been in Naples in 1536 during the imperial visit; others went there in 1539 to escort back to Florence the daughter of the viceroy, Eleonora of Toledo, the bride of Cosimo, now the duke of Florence; and a Neapolitan retinue would naturally have come with the bride. On Willaert's side, the little we know of his private life seems to point to contacts with the Florentine milieu. Besides his earlier relationships with the younger Lorenzo dei Medici (who died in 1519) and with Leo X (who died in 1521), we know he often contributed to the collections of Philippe Verdelot, the leading composer in Florence between 1520 and 1530. His name is even attached to a selection of Verdelot's madrigals published in Venice in an arrangement for voice and lute, first in 1536 and again in 1540. In the years following 1540, in the period when the *villanesca* was spreading, Willaert directed and organized much-admired concerts held in the house of a Florentine resident of Venice, Neri Capponi;[16] the star performer was Polissena Pecorina, a Florentine singer (her name indicates she was the wife of a Pecori), whose excellence in singing was praised not only by Willaert in his madrigals, but also by another composer who spent many years in Florence, Jakob Arcadelt.[17] Finally, among the many poetic texts chosen by Willaert for his madrigals, one of the very few that is not by Petrarch is by the Florentine Filippo Strozzi.[18]

More pointed clues are found in the editions of Willaert's music. His *villanesche* of 1542 were included, as I have already mentioned, in a collection of pieces *a misura breve,* and it is well known that both Arcadelt and Corteccia, the two leading composers in Florence after Verdelot, had shown an early interest in this new trend. Arcadelt may have visited Venice before arriving at the papal court in Rome in the early 1540s, for like Willaert he wrote a madrigal praising Polissena Pecorina. Even more directly, Corteccia's name is associated with Willaert's in the first of Willaert's collections, the *Canzoni villanesche alla napolitana di M. Adriano Wigliaret a quatro voci,* published by Scotto in 1544. This is only the beginning of a much longer title, which mentions the presence in the collection of some madrigals by Willaert himself and then "the addition of a few other *villanesche alla napolitana* for four voices, composed by M. FRANCESCO CORTECCIA, never seen or printed before, but newly brought to light" (see no. 2 in the Appendix to this essay).

Only a few pages of the *altus* part of this edition are still extant, including one of Willaert's *villanesche* of 1542 and five new ones, but the madrigals by him and the *villanesche* by Corteccia are missing; we have them in another edition, published in 1545 by another printer and composer, the Frenchman Antonio Gardane (Appendix, no. 3). The 1545 collection includes the six *villanesche* we already know from the two previous editions by Willaert and three new ones, which may have been present also in the incomplete 1544 edition, plus three *villanesche* each by Corteccia and Francesco Silvestrino, a pupil of Willaert's. There are no madrigals, so Willaert must have felt that their presence was no longer needed to dignify the otherwise frivolous contents; the *villanesca* was now fully accepted by the public, and collections of *villanesche* by other composers were beginning to appear. Among the many editions of Willaert's *villanesche* (listed in the Appendix), the two of 1548 have a special meaning, having been published in competition by Scotto and Gardane (Appendix, nos. 4–5).

Going back to Corteccia, I think there is something to be gathered from the rise and fall of his name on the title pages of Willaert's collections. It is rather pompously announced in the title of the 1544 edition; in the 1545 edition it is repeated but given last place after the name of the very modest Silvestrino; it is finally dropped from all the later reprints, as are two of Corteccia's three *villanesche,* the third being now consistently attributed to Willaert. I read all this as an indication that Corteccia may have set the pace for the four-voice reworking of the three-voice Neapolitan *villanesche;* however, Willaert dropped his name when he thought he had found a better way to handle such pieces. Actually, Willaert's two *villanesche* of 1542 and the two or three *villanesche* by Corteccia have in common that they all keep the *cantus prius factus,* the melody presumably derived from an earlier Neapolitan model, in the upper part. Willaert soon abandoned this procedure, and his new pieces, as well as those of Silvestrino and of the other Venetian composers, usually have the *cantus prius factus* transposed to the lower fifth and placed in the *tenor* part; the exception is an isolated attempt by Willaert (and after him by Perissone Cambio) to use it as a *vagans,* now in the *tenor,* now in the *cantus* part.[19]

It is quite evident that the whole process of rewriting the three-voice pieces of the Neapolitans into four-voice *villanesche* was meant as an improvement, bringing back a pleasurable but unruly genre into the regularity of *ars musica*. The idea was not new; the custom of using popular tunes as the basis for regular polyphonic compositions had long been present in the Franco-Flemish tradition and was very common in the French *chanson* of the early sixteenth century, to which Willaert himself had contributed a number of compositions. We have in fact an equivalent of the *villanesca* in the so-called *chanson rustique*, so called, as Howard M. Brown has shown, to distinguish it from the *chanson musicale* or *en musique*.[20] This distinction was most aptly formulated in the title of a rather late collection, the *Chansons nouvellement composées sur plusieurs chants tant de musique que de rustique*, published in Paris in 1548,[21] but the concept was so deeply entrenched in the minds of both composers and music lovers that the printer Attaignant long felt the need to advertise a good number of his editions as containing *chansons musicales, motets musicaux*, and even *missae musicales*.[22]

Willaert must also have been acquainted with another equivalent of the *villanesca*, the northern *villota*, whose name once more refers to the topos of peasant life; two of the initiators of this form probably had been men such as Josquin and Loyset Compère. The problem was somewhat different, however, with the Neapolitan *villanesche*; these were not just tunes, linear elements to be worked out in an essentially contrapuntal way, but polyphonic pieces, of which Willaert and his followers intended to fully preserve the most typical features, the brisk irregular rhythms and the spirited, humorous utterance of the dialectal texts. They knew this could be done only by preserving their basic chordal texture, which they expanded in the fuller sonority of the four voices which had become during the last half century the minimum standard of artistic polyphony; they also showed a tendency to reduce whatever small amount of imitation was present in the three-voice version, eliminating the procedures of their models which they considered more irregular.

Speaking of irregular procedures, we immediately think of the notorious successions of three-five chords in parallel motion. Such successions may have been present in the pieces published by Johannes de Colonia in 1537,[23] as they were in later *villanesche*, but they were never too conspicuous in the pieces by Nola, the first to be printed in Venice since 1541, which were used more often than any others as models for some of the four-voice rewritings. In fact, of the two pieces by Nola which I have selected to use as examples with Willaert's corresponding four-voice versions, only one contains a single passage of parallel fifths. (Willaert's four-voice version of

Madonn'io non lo so has two successive twelfths between cantus and bassus.)[24] This means that the notorious parallel fifths were not the only reason—possibly not even the major one—prompting the writing of better versions. As far as we can judge from whatever echo we get of the way such music was perceived by contemporaries, the composers of Willaert's circle must have found fault with the unusual sound of a high-pitched vocal trio formed by a soprano part singing in a medium range and by bass and tenor parts having a range about one fifth higher than usual. Even when not singing in parallel triads, the three voices quite often close on each other to form such triads in root position; and most of the time the two upper voices move in parallel thirds, the exceptions being a fourth followed by a second and its resolution at cadences. It is possible that this unusual texture was originally compounded with some special style of singing peculiar to the tradition of Neapolitan popular singers;[25] it is unlikely, however, that any of those special sounds was ever heard in Venice. Nevertheless, what Willaert saw on paper was enough to suggest to him that he should rewrite the Neapolitan *villanesche* for the madrigalian vocal quartet, whose voices usually encompass a range of two or two-and-a half octaves.

In its first phase the process produced the result one can observe in the two 1542 *villanesche* (Exs. 12.2 and 12.3) which, like those by Corteccia, have the main tune, thought to be a *cantus prius factus* of a previous Neapolitan model, in the soprano part. However, the next step in the process is already hinted at by a direction we find appended to the soprano part of *A quand'a quand'haveva una vicina* (Ex. 12.3) that suggests: "In diapason si placet." To interpret this as suggesting a transposition to the upper octave would bring the part to an impossibly high range (from central F to high D), too far removed from the other parts; the only plausible interpretation is a transposition to the lower octave, and this causes the tune to assume the place and function of a *tenor* part.

Two practical reasons may have made the transposition of the *cantus prius factus* to the *tenor* the final choice for all later reworkings of *villanesche*.[26] One is that *villanesca alla napolitana* tunes, like most monophonic music, tend to come to the final note of every cadence descending by step to the tonic, which is the normal approach of the *tenor* in art polyphony of the fifteenth century, causing the soprano part to ascend by semitone to the octave of the tonic from the raised seventh degree. A second reason may have been the technical problems involved in the task of harmonizing according to the rules melodies that were not intended to lend themselves to such harmonization. Take, for instance, the melody of Nola's *O dolce vita mia* (Ex. 12.4). Had this tune been placed in the upper part of the madrigalian quartet, its range of a minor ninth and its sudden upward leaps would have made it rather difficult to achieve the proper, well-contrived distribution of parts and balanced chordal sonority, which were the most immediate purposes of the four-voice arrangement. The same applies to the tune of *Madonn'io non lo so perché lo fai*, also by Nola (Ex. 12.6), which has the range of an octave (the tunes of Exs. 12.2 and 12.3 have the range of a sixth), this time because of a sudden plunging to low A. All such problems were much more easily dealt with when the tune of the model was moved to the *tenor* part, as shown by Willaert's reworkings of *O dolce vita mia* and *Madonn'io non lo so perché lo fai* (Exs. 12.5 and 12.7).

Ex. 12.2   Willaert, *O bene mio*.

Ex. 12.2   Continued

Ex. 12.3 Willaert, *A quand'a quand'avea.*

Giovan Domenico da Nola

Ex. 12.4   Giovan Domenico da Nola, *O dolce vita mia.*

Ex. 12.5   Willaert, *O dolce vita mia.*

Ex. 12.5 Continued

Giovan Domenico da Nola

Ex. 12.6   Giovan Domenico da Nola, *Madonn'io non lo so.*

Ex. 12.6   Continued

However, along with the solution of technical problems, artistic motivations must be taken into account. Placing the *cantus prius factus* in the *tenor* allowed the four-voice pieces to be no longer considered merely as revisions of three-voice models. They acquired a new status as artistic products of a genre which I think may have come to be classified, by Renaissance standards, under the concept of *imitatio*. Lewis Lockwood has shown that *imitatio* is the word that best fits the compositional procedures we have been used to label as "parody."[27] The relationship to an acknowledged model is much more subtle and refined in the case of a parody piece, but surely the contrapuntal elaboration of a popular tune in a French *chanson rustique* or in a northern Italian *villota* has more than a few points of contact with the practice of *imitatio* or parody. And it seems to me that whether or not the term can be stretched to include the four-voice *villanesca*, this last proposed to its listeners the same game of musical hide-and-seek, the same interplay as the parody between the recognizable identity of a well-known model and the appreciation of new turns given it. When placed in the *tenor*, the identifying element, the tune of the model, becomes to some extent obliterated by two other parts moving in a higher range. The perception of it as a self-possessed melodic line may have varied

Ex. 12.7 Willaert, *Madonn'io non lo so.*

Ex. 12.7   Continued

from one piece to another and even from one to another performance of the same piece. Nevertheless, the *cantus prius factus* still had a way to make its influence felt by impressing its peculiar rhythm and word-tone relationship on the new product as well as by conditioning, with only minor variants, the sequence of harmonic events in a basic pattern quite faithful to the original. We may compare this persistent presence of the original, in spite of a number of changes, to the later relationship between a theme and its variations.

It is now time to mention that Willaert's collections also included under their general title of *Canzoni villanesche alla napolitana* a few pieces which had nothing to do with Naples, for their texts use the Venetian dialect and have a ring quite different from the Mediterranean ring of the *napolitane*. *Un giorno mi pregò una vedovella,* the comic narrative of a love affair compared to a stormy navigation, is present in all the editions of his *villanesche* from 1544 to 1563, as is *Sospiri miei d'oimè doglioririosi,* which plays on the stammering of a comic character, thus anticipating similar *lazzi* in the acting of comedies. The *Canzon di Ruzante,* always advertised on the title pages and yet strangely missing in the 1545 edition, has an even more direct theatrical connection, Ruzante being a well-known Paduan actor as well as the author of dialectal plays which describe peasant life with vigorous realism and bitterness. He died in 1542, and it is most likely that the tune used in the *tenor* of the *Canzon di Ruzante* was one of those he had sung on stage. In this case, as in the case of the other Venetian *villanesche,* the model cannot have been a three-voice piece, but just a popular tune.[28]

Neapolitan or Venetian, Willaert's *villanesche* were but a small part of his work and only one of the initial chapters in the long history by which the *villanesca* changed into the *villanella* and then the *canzonetta.* Yet I find in Willaert's *villanesche* some interesting connections with some important features of sixteenth-century music. I have already mentioned their early association with a collection advertising the *misura breve.* This may have been pure coincidence, because I do not see much more than an external resemblance to the trend of the *note nere* and *madrigali cromatici.* In the *villanesche,* fast, nervous rhythms, sudden stops, and new starts express a spontaneous popular verve which I find very different from the self-conscious distortions of rhythm and declamation introduced for the sake of novelty and variety by, for instance, a composer like Corteccia. However, the composers experimenting with the new style must have felt encouraged by its similarities to the rhythms of the *villanesche.*

Of greater interest to me is that the *villanesca* was related to a more general phenomenon which is not easily defined but has many interesting ramifications in various directions. This phenomenon I have come to designate by the term "aria," a term that has acquired very precise connotations deriving from its association with the history of opera, oratorio, cantata, and so on. But none of this had yet happened in the sixteenth century, when the word aria referred to some undefinable quality felt to be present in some pieces of music and missing in others. On more than one occasion I have tried to explain that it meant the feeling that certain melodies or, more generally, certain kinds of music, unfolded phrase after phrase with a coherent sense of direction, with an immediacy that gave to their progress the sense of an inevitable course aimed at a precise goal.[29] Quite often this feeling may have been determined by the fact that the melody or composition was well known to its listeners, so that a permanent mental association had been established between what came first and what followed; but this feeling cannot have been simply one of memory, and the very fact that the piece could be so easily memorized implied the presence in it of qualities that gave it an aria. One basic element, which sixteenth-century theory was still unprepared to recognize and assess, must have been a "logical" sequence of harmonies, either fully realized in a polyphonic composition or merely implied in the statement of a melody, a sequence whose logic was not yet necessarily fully consistent with the logic of tonal harmony. Such logic is what determined the success of a number of bass patterns such as *passemezzo, romanesca, Ruggero,* and the like, which were not melodies and yet were called arie because they dictated typical harmonic sequences and thus imparted to every melody built on them the air of having something in common.

Actually, this is just what I had in mind when I compared the relationship between a four-voice *villanesca* and its model to the relationship between theme and variation. And indeed there is, if not an absolute correspondence, a chronological similarity between the variation-type *villanesca*—one single variation on one theme—and the emergence of sets of *partite,* that is, sets of variations, on *Ruggero, Monica,* or *romanesca,* which variations all had a common aria in spite of their changing melodic traits.

The success of such *arioso* forms marks a transitional phrase in the development of those harmonic habits which were later to be tightly organized in the so-called logic of tonal harmony. It is still a transitional phase, both because their so-called logic did not yet fully coincide with the later system and because the composer was able to recognize its presence but still had no precise criteria to help him control and produce it. Hence the need for recourse to successful *arioso* models, whether found in the *chanson rustique* or in the notorious parallel fifths of the *napolitane*.

Appendix: Willaert's Collections of *Villanesche* and Their Contents

An asterisk (*) indicates pieces in which the main tune is assigned to the higher part. A dagger (†) indicates pieces in which the main tune is assigned to the *tenor*. The two symbols together indicate a composition in which the tune passes from one voice to the other.

1. MADRIGALI A QUATRO VOCE DI GERONIMO SCOTTO CON ALCUNI A LA MISURA BREVE, ET ALTRI A VOCE PARI novamente posti in luce. LIBRO PRIMO. Venetiis, Apud ipsum Authorem. 1542.

   Contains:
   1. Adrian Vuillart, *O bene mio famme uno favore**
   2. Adrian Vuillart, *A quando a quando haveva una vicina**

2. CANZONE VILLANESCHE ALLA NAPOLITANA DI M. ADRIANO VVIGLIARET A QUATRO VOCI, CON alcuni madrigali da lui nuovamente composti & diligentemente corretti, con la Canzona di Ruzante. Con la giunta di alcune altre canzone Villanesche alla Napolitana a Quatro Voci, composte da M. FRANCESCO CORTECCIA non più viste ne stampate, nuovamente poste in luce Venetiis Apud Hieronymum Scotum M.DXLIIII.

   The only extant fragment contains, besides no. 2 of the previous collection (all by Willaert):
   3. *Madonn'io non lo so perché lo fai*† (from Nola)
   4. *Cingari simo venit'a giocare*† (from Nola)
   5. *Madonna mia famme bon'offerta*†
   6. *Un giorno mi prego una vedovella*† (in Venetian dialect)
   7. *Vecchie letrose non valete niente*†

3. CANZONE VILLANESCHE ALLA NAPOLITANA DI M. ADRIANO VVIGLIARET A QUATRO VOCI con la Canzona di Ruzante. Con la gionta di alcune altre canzone villanesche alla napolitana di Francesco Silvestrino ditto

cechin et di Francesco Corteccia novamente stampate con le soe stanze. PRIMO LIBRO A QUATRO VOCI Venetijs Apud Antonium Gardane. M.D.XXXXV.

Contains nos. 1–7 and also:
8. Adriano, *Sempre mi ride sta donna da bene*†
9. Adriano, *O dolce vita mia che t'aggio fatto*† (from Nola)
10. Fran. Silvestrino, *Se mille volte ti vengh'a vedere*†
11. Fran. Silvestrino, *O Dio se vede chiaro che per te moro*†
12. Fran. Corteccia, *Madonn'io t'haggi'amat'et amo assai**
13. Fran. Corteccia, *Madonna mia io son un poverello**
14. Adriano, *Sospiri miei d'oime dogliorirosi*† (in Venetian dialect)
15. Fran. Corteccia, *Le vecchie per invidia sono pazze**
   (The *Canzone di Ruzante* is missing)

4. CANZON VILLANESCHE ALLA NAPOLITANA DI MESSER ADRIANO A QUATRO VOCI. CON la Canzon di Ruzante. Libro Primo in Venetia Appresso di Antonio Gardane 1548.

   Contains nos. 1–11, 14, and 15 (attributed to Willaert), and also:
   16. Adriano, *La Canzon di Ruzante: Zoia zentil*† (in Venetian dialect)
   17. Piersson, *Boccuccia dolce**†

5. CANZON VILLANESCHE ALLA NAPOLITANA DI MESSER ADRIANO A QUATRO VOCI. Con la Canzon di Ruzante. LIBRO PRIMO in Vineggia Appresso Girolamo Scotto. M.D.XLVIII.

   The contents are the same as in the previous edition.

6. CANZON VILLANESCHE ALLA NAPOLITANA DI MESSER ADRIANO A QUATRO VOCI. Con la Canzon di Ruzante A QUATRO VOCI. In Venetia Appresso di Antonio Gardane 1553.

   The contents are the same as in the two previous editions.

7. MADRIGALI A QUATRO VOCI DI ADRIANO WILLAERT CON ALCUNE NAPOLITANE ET LA CANZON DI RUZANTE TUTTE RACOLTE INSIEME Coretti & novamente stampati. In Vinegia, appresso Girolamo Scotto. MDLXIII.

   Contains nos. 3–5, 2, 1, 16 and also:
   18. *Occhio non fu giamai*† (in Venetian dialect?)
   19. *Quando di ros'e d'oro*† (in Venetian dialect?)

13 Notes on Marenzio and Tasso

In an article published in 1945 Luigi Ronga called to the attention of students of music history the conclusion of the dialogue *La Cavaletta, o vero della poesia toscana,* in which the Neapolitan Guest, that is, Tasso, expresses his wish for a reform of music "that would recall it to that gravity in deviating from which it has often fallen at least partially to a state it is better to pass over in silence rather than speak about."[1] Called upon for help in this task are "Striggio and Iacches [Wert] and Lucciasco [Luzzaschi] and some other excellent master of excellent music"; it seems to me that the appended phrase, redundant with excellence, aims only at tempering the Mantuan-Ferrarese accent of the three names specifically mentioned. But Alfred Einstein and Hans Engel—the first decidedly, the second more doubtfully—have suggested that the poet had in mind Marenzio for the fourth name to be included in such great harmony; according to Einstein, his name was omitted to avoid sparking jealousy in the others.[2]

Usually the dialogue on Tuscan poetry is dated 1584; however, Tasso does not in fact speak of it in his letters before the end of 1585, and it was not published until 1587, when it appeared with the *Gioie di Rime, e Prose, Quinta e Sesta Parte,* printed in Venice by Giulio Vasalini. Already in 1584, but even more in 1585 and 1587, Marenzio had consolidated his fame and numbered among his protectors so many and such important members of the houses of Este, Medici, and Gonzaga that no one would have taken offense at the addition of his name to Tasso's list. Similarly, I cannot agree with Einstein when he discerns an influence of the dialogue in the "maniera assai differente dalla passata" (manner very different from the past) and in the "mesta gravità" (sad gravity)—to use Marenzio's own words—of the *Madrigali a Quatro, Cinque, et Sei Voci, Libro Primo*

(Venice, Giacomo Vincenti, 1587). Even if Marenzio had already read the text of the recently published dialogue, how did it happen that his unusual collection of 1587 did not contain a single text by the poet who inspired it?[3]

Quite a bit has been written about Marenzio, but one would like to know more.[4] It is assumed that he was the pupil of Giovanni Contini in Brescia or of Marcantonio Ingegneri in Cremona. But we should perhaps keep in mind Verona, traditional hatchery of musicians, for which he showed a predilection, dedicating a collection of madrigals to the Accademici Filarmonici (1582) and another to one of its most noted members, Count Mario Bevilacqua (1588).[5] One is used to smiling at the title "Maestro di Capella dell'Illustrissimo et Reverendissimo Signor Cardinale d'Este" flaunted on the frontispiece of the *Primo Libro de Madrigali a Sei Voci* (Venice, Angelo Gardano, 1581); it is known in fact that the prodigal and worldly Luigi d'Este did not have a chapel and paid his "maestro" without chapel the meager salary of five *scudi* a month.[6] The origin of that purely honorific title is explained, however, in a letter of one of the cardinal's administrators, Annibale Capello: "He [Marenzio] was chapel master of the Cardinal of Trent [Cristoforo Madruzzo] of blessed memory. He was accepted with the same duties by the cardinal my lord, though not as servant." The last phrase should be seen in relation to the fact that the "messer Luca musico" of the register of the salaried for 1578 is already, in the 1580 register, the "Magnifico Messer Luca Marenzio musico" and appears, moreover, in the list of those whose expenses are paid, while still continuing to figure in the list of the salaried with the same monthly sum.[7] Marenzio could therefore use his monthly salary as pocket money, since the cardinal paid expenses for him and for a servant.

Even more than from his earnings he must have derived satisfaction from having succeeded, despite his humble origins, in attaining status in a society in which, without an aristocratic name, one needed to have notable gifts of mind, manner, and culture to become acceptable. This attitude is particularly evident in the negotiations that took place several times with the Mantuan court. The phrase already cited of the administrator Capello is confirmed by another phrase in the same letter of September 17, 1580: "I believe that if we hire him for the prince's service he would not object to coming to sing in Santa Barbara, but [if we try] to get him simply for singing, I do not know what he will do."[8] Marenzio was able to dictate conditions, even though he was still almost a beginner, having only just published his first collection of madrigals. Six years later similar negotiations were conducted, not by a mere chargé d'affaires but by the patriarch of Jerusalem, Scipione Gonzaga, from whom we learn (May 3, 1586) that Marenzio would perhaps let himself be tempted by the position held by Filippo di Monte at the imperial court. "Messer Luca," the patriarch added a few days later, " . . . would not accept every offer, as one who aims very much at the honorable, neither would he serve where he would have a superior in his profession . . . In short, he demonstrates very noble feelings and does not easily lower himself to every sort of thing; however, neither does he omit to be modest and courteous with those he deals with." There had also been talk of possible employment in the service of the duke of Ferrara, brother of the cardinal, or with the duke of Joyeuse, brother-in-law of the king of France.[9]

An agreement on conditions was finally arrived at with Mantua on July 12, 1586: "150 *scudi* but of gold . . . added to the expenses for himself, servant and horse."[10] But once again nothing was done, perhaps because it was unseemly that Marenzio should leave Cardinal d'Este while the latter's health was worsening (he did, in fact, die on December 30, 1586). But the more profound reason must have been that Marenzio did not like the idea of leaving Rome; in fact, after the death of the cardinal, when asked again, he found pretexts for not going to Mantua. He added to his quibbles "a statement in which he said that he is used to spend here in Rome more than 200 *scudi* beyond expenses, in such a manner that he doubts that with such small provision [the 150 *scudi* accepted before?] he would be able to do honor to the Most Serene Lord Duke as is fitting."[11] It is clear that he envisioned being able to continue the expensive lifestyle to which he was accustomed in Rome. Perhaps he counted upon Cardinal Medici, a great friend of Cardinal Luigi d'Este, and he could not foresee that in a short while, upon the sudden deaths of Francesco dei Medici and Bianca Capello (to whom he had offered musical homage), he would be called upon to transfer to Florence with the "family" of Cardinal Ferdinand, the new grand duke of Tuscany.[12]

Scholars have wondered at the fact that Marenzio, who did not aspire to be a composer of sacred music, should happen upon Rome, where most musicians were employed by the church and, breathing the air of counter-reform, were induced to limit their production of secular music.[13] In any case, this does not mean that there were few occasions for secular music making, and in Marenzio's case we do not know anything of the events that led him to the service of Cardinal Madruzzo, nor do we know how well he did there in the little time it lasted.[14] But we do know that he soon found an ideal patron in Luigi d'Este, who proved "to love him and esteem him very highly and often gave him some valued present,"[15] and because the cardinal was also the representative of French interests in Rome, he had to spend a good deal of his time there. In connection with that very cardinal, being in Rome sometimes meant the villa at Montecavallo, sometimes the Montegiordano palace rented from the Orsini, sometimes, indeed most often, the villa at Tivoli; in any case, it meant being at the center of the splendors, the festivities, the perfidy, and the violence of the Roman "dolce vita."[16]

Then there were trips, which the cardinal, though seriously hampered by gout, had not yet renounced. He was forced to take one in June 1580 when he incurred the anger of Gregory XII (who nevertheless was a great friend of his) following a fight between his people and those of the auditor of the Apostolic Chamber. Banished from Tivoli and Rome, Cardinal d'Este was in Murano on July 7 and in Padua on July 16, but most of his time was divided among Praglia, Abano, and Monte Ortone, perhaps because he was intent on curing his illness. At the beginning of August an emergency called him to Ferrara: his sister Leonora was at the point of death. That crisis happily averted, the cardinal, reconciled on this occasion with his brother Alfonso with whom he had long been in disagreement on matters of inheritance, again departed for Padua.[17] Marenzio did not go to Ferrara that time; on August 8 he was in Rome, where he dedicated to the cardinal his first publication, the *Primo Libro de Madrigali a Cinque Voci* (Venice, Angelo Gardano, 1580); however, he was in Padua on September 10 ("with the other family," wrote Capello from Venice, indicating that the cardinal's "family" was at that time divided between two cities); and from Padua he had a month's leave to go to his native Coccaglio, stopping in Mantua to pay his respects to Duke Guglielmo Gonzaga.[18] By November he must have returned to the cardinal, who spent that winter and a large part of the spring alternating between the "dolce vita" of Venice and that of Ferrara, both scarcely darkened by the death of Leonora d'Este (February 19, 1581). He returned to Rome at the request of the French court, at the end of June.[19]

In Venice on April 10, 1581, Marenzio signed the dedication of the *Primo Libro ... a Sei Voci,* offering it to Duke Alfonso II d'Este as "something that had already been benignly received and appreciated by your judgment."[20] The contents of this second collection, which Einstein called "the book of Roman idylls and elegies," must have been composed in part before he went to Ferrara, since the text of the first madrigal reveals in an acrostic that it is addressed to a Roman beauty, Cleria Cesarini Farnese.[21] But one can easily discern a reflection of Ferrara—perhaps more external than substantive—in the last seven madrigals for six voices (before the very last one for double chorus), which have a notably higher tessitura than the preceding ones and therefore point essentially to a sonority of female voices.[22] The same dualism in vocal registration is also present in the next collection, the *Secondo Libro de Madrigali a Cinque Voci* (Venice, Angelo Gardano, 1581), which Marenzio dedicated from Rome on October 25, 1581, to another figure of the Ferrarese Olympus, Lucrezia d'Este, the duchess of Urbino.[23] But the order and the chronological hypothesis that derives from it are inverted: the first eight madrigals (the less recent?) point to female voices, while the other seven (composed after Ferrara?) return to the usual clefs for soprano, alto, tenor, and bass, with one of the middle parts doubled by the *quinto*. Although Marenzio also in the other collections of his first period often turns to the type of vocal orchestration rendered famous by the ladies of Ferrara (sufficient as examples are the first four madrigals of the *Primo Libro* for five voices), in no case do compositions of this type form such numerous and markedly distinct groups as in the two books connected with the visit to Ferrara.

Luigi d'Este's presence in Ferrara during the summer of 1582—attested to in a recollection of Scipione Gonzaga, who asserted that he had visited him there—seems uncertain, at least to me.[24] Neither am I sure Marenzio accompanied his cardinal on a visit, at the end of 1583, to Paolo Giordano Orsini, who a little while before had secretly married Vittoria Accoramboni.[25] It could be that in the summer of 1584 the cardinal divided again his time among Venice, Abano, and Ferrara, but I do not find confirmation for this in the indirect sources at my disposal. However, Marenzio's dedication of the *Quarto Libro de Madrigali a Cinque Voci* (Venice, G. Vicenzi and R. Amadino, 1584) is signed from Venice and dated May 5, 1584. The possibility that Marenzio then remained for some time in Venice and the surrounding region and that he may even have visited Ferrara is further supported by the Venetian dedication, dated September 1, 1584, of the *Primo Libro delle Villanelle* (Venice, G. Vincenzi and R. Amadino, 1584), even though the signature is that of a certain Ferrante Franchi, to whom Marenzio (who always aimed greatly toward the "honorable") had given the right to collect and publish things of his "composed ... almost as a joke" (composte ... quasi per ischerzo).[26]

Whatever the course and the duration of his travels in 1584, it seems improbable to me that Marenzio's sporadic visits to Ferrara—that of the winter of 1580–81 definite, the others problematic—could have offered him the opportunity to establish personal relations with Tasso, who since March 1579 had been confined in the hospital of Santa Anna; besides, Cardinal Luigi d'Este demonstrated his interest in the poet only in a detached and condescending manner, keeping himself informed but never allowing himself as much as a visit or a personal letter.[27] Marenzio and Tasso could have met later, between November 5, 1587, and March 15, 1588, when the poet was in Rome as the guest of Scipione Gonzaga, who in the same period was made cardinal. But the dedication of the *Madrigali a Quatro, Cinque, et Sei Voci* shows us that Marenzio was in Venice in December 1587, and before that he had been in Verona. Afterward we do not know if he returned to Rome, because the closest firm date is that of his listing in the *Ruolo della Casa* of Ferdinando dei Medici in Florence, September 1, 1588.[28] The meeting with the poet would then be postponed until the period of reunions of the so-called academy of Cinzio Passeri Aldobrandini in Rome from May 1592 to December 1593.[29]

Scarcely more positive is the conclusion to be drawn from the texts Marenzio chose for his madrigals in the first period of his output, which coincides with the time when Tasso's poetic works were stormily appearing in print. In the *Primo Libro* for five voices of 1580, the only text by Tasso is one set for eight voices, *O tu che nelle selve,* which closes the collection; I cannot say how Marenzio would have obtained it to use in the play of echo and dialogue between two equal choruses, and I even have some doubt that it is truly by Tasso.[30] Marenzio's second collection, the *Primo Libro* for six voices of 1581, also contains only one madrigal by Tasso, *Non è questa la mano,* one of the Ferrarese-style compositions that form the second part of the collection; it may have been proposed to Marenzio during his sojourn in Ferrara, or it may have been taken from the *Rime . . . Parte Prima,* which appeared in Venice from the presses of Aldo Manuzio at the very beginning of 1581.[31] Neither the *Secondo* nor the *Terzo Libro* for five voices contains texts by Tasso, even though the *Secondo* (also published in 1581 after the visit to Ferrara) contains a *ballata* by Ariosto, and the *Terzo,* three madrigals by Guarini.

The period in which Marenzio seemed most interested in Tasso's poetry was the first part of 1584, before his departure for Venice.[32] Already the year before he had contributed to the anthology *De Floridi Virtuosi d'Italia Il Primo Libro de Madrigali à Cinque Voci* a composition, *Se tu mi lasci, perfida, tuo danno,* whose text six years later also attracted Monteverdi. In 1584 the *Secondo Libro* for six voices contains the madrigals *In un bel bosco, Io vidi già sotto l'ardente sole,* and *Vita de la mia vita;* the *Madrigali Spirituali* includes the sonnet *Padre del cielo;* and the *Quarto Libro* for five voices opens with a sequence of four octaves from *Gerusalemme Liberata,* to which is added, later in the volume, Tasso's madrigal in two parts *Disdegno e gelosia.* The *Quinto Libro* for five voices, also of 1584, once again knows nothing of Tasso, although it contains a madrigal by Guarini and a sonnet by Ariosto.[33]

Padre del cielo had appeared in 1567 in the Paduan print of *Rime degli Accademici Eterei,* and *In un bel bosco* is part of *Scielta delle Rime . . . Parte Prima,* published in Ferrara by Vittorio Baldini in 1582. For the other texts, musical publication preceded literary publication, so Marenzio must have gotten them from manuscript copies that circulated in his cultural environment; there was certainly no lack of personages great and small in a position to possess them.[34] Among these the first place does not belong to Cardinal d'Este but to the patriarch of Jerusalem, Scipione Gonzaga, Tasso's frequent correspondent even in the darkest times and his counselor in the interminable labor of textual revision.

For more than one reason, the four octaves from *Gerusalemme Liberata* (XII, 96–99), which have a place of honor in the *Quarto Libro* for five voices, require special consideration. First, they are used for the longest and most ambitious madrigal sequence Marenzio had published up to that time (surpassed only by that on Sannazaro's sestina *Non fu mai cervo,* which appeared almost contemporaneously as a conclusion of the *Madrigali Spirituali*). Second, they are quite different from Marenzio's usual idyllic vein, coming to terms with the pathos of Tancredi's visit to Clorinda's sepulcher. And finally, the version of the text used by Marenzio in several instances diverges from the published version of the poem. The last point is the most interesting because it has been taken as proof of the existence of a personal relationship between musician and poet.[35] This is quickly resolved to the extent that in all probability the person who obtained the unusual version of the text from the poet was not Marenzio but Giaches de Wert. Indeed Wert had composed and already in 1581 had published the first two octaves, whose most notable variants are encountered only in manuscripts of the poem; Marenzio took up the text adopted by Wert, adding to them two other octaves that also diverge notably from most of the printed editions but singularly agree with the very first, the one that Malespini had had published in Venice in 1580 as *Goffredo.*[36] Thus it would appear that in choosing these verses, which Tasso considered among the most beautiful of the poems,[37] Marenzio's motive was more musical than literary, because of the impression he had received from the two octaves by the Flemish-Mantuan master.

Wert's and Marenzio's compositions clearly share a few general traits: the same dark sonority, the same tonality (and a similar tonal arc, of ampler dimensions in Marenzio's setting because the length of his sequence is nearly double that of Wert's), the same measure of *brevis* bringing the slower rhythmic pace into harmony with the pathos of the situation.[38] However, Marenzio's intention of distinguishing himself from his predecessor is evident in particulars. For Tasso's octaves Wert had found once again the vein of dramatic recitation which had been suggested to him many years before by some octaves of Ariosto; without completely shunning repetition, he had, on the whole, been rapid and direct and had essentially aimed at the contrast between the petrified tension of the dark recitative and the moving abandon, both lyric and descriptive, of the verse that describes the relief of tears. Marenzio, for his part, does not let the descriptive points go unobserved; his figurative bent is clear from the very beginning, combining an almost heroic theme in the soprano and *quinto* with passages of scales in the other voices that seem to suggest a descent into the depths of a crypt (Ex. 13.1). Nor does he, even in the prevailing texture of declaimed recitation, eschew lingering in textual repetitions and contrapuntal elaborations, such as those that precede the most explicit homage to Wert, the almost exact quotation of Tancredi's first exclamation (Ex. 13.2). And yet he is unusually concise in the verses where Wert lingered longer and with happier expressiveness ("Alfin, sgorgando un lagrimoso rivo . . .").

The motive of voices descending in parallel tenths, with which Wert had expressed the flowing of tears, is echoed by Marenzio in other madrigals and in other situations, beginning with the passage that translates the beginning of the penultimate verse in the following anonymous and less than middling madrigal, also in the *Quarto Libro:*

> Mentre il ciel è sereno
> s'odon ne' campi i grilli,
> e tu, dolce mia Filli,
> col canto fai stupir ninfe e pastori;
> ma io di dolor pieno
> verso da gli occhi el cor che mi sfavilli.
> Tu non odi, crudel, gli acuti strilli.

> While heaven is serene,
> In the fields crickets are heard,
> And you, my sweet Phyllis,
> With your song astound nymphs and shepherds;
> But I, full of pain,
> Shed through my eyes my heart which you enflame,
> You do not hear, cruel one, my piercing cries.

Musically, this little madrigal with the singing crickets is one of Marenzio's most successful miniature *scherzi*. But placed just after the sequence of Tasso's octaves, with the parodistic flavor that phrases like "io di dolor

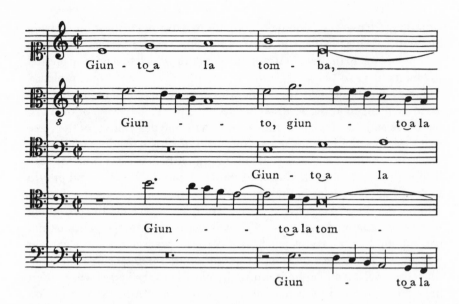

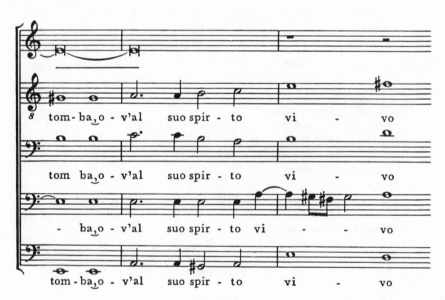

Ex. 13.1   Marenzio, *Giunto a la tomba* (measures 1–6 of Einstein's edition).

Ex. 13.2   Marenzio, *Giunto a la tomba* (measures 28–42 of Einstein's edition).

Ex. 13.2 Continued

pieno" and "acuti strilli" assume there, it is a joke one would gladly do without. Yet it is more easily accepted when one recognizes that it derives more from an inclination toward virtuosic display through contraposition rather than from irreverence. Another example of this is the sorrowful Petrarch sonnet *Oimè il bel viso,* immediately followed by the *sdrucciolo* by Sannazaro, *La pastorella mia spietata e rigida* in the *Terzo Libro* for five voices.[39]

Marenzio's apparent lack of interest in Tasso's poetry and his occasional welcoming of mediocre and even fragmentary texts does not induce me to reject completely Einstein's assessment of Marenzio's refined taste, but only to temper his enthusiasm.[40] I do not doubt that Marenzio had received a solid, cultivated education and that because of it and his environment Tasso's importance and growing fame could not have escaped his notice, even if this is shown very poorly through the only criterion available to us for judging. But the greatness of a poet—which cannot help but be translated into a "typical and singular musicality" all his own[41]—does not always coincide with his "musicability"; and "musicability" is all the more narrowly defined the more distinct and personal is the sensibility of the musician who sets about or renounces the task of making the verses his own. The key to the artistic relationship between Marenzio and Tasso must thus be sought (self-evident truism) in Marenzio's artistic personality and would require a longer discourse than is possible here (even if I felt capable of undertaking it). One element to be considered is that perhaps Marenzio's "classicism" (quite distinct from a "classicity" that may also characterize his output), like other classicisms, must have felt the need to romanticize his models, projecting them into a sphere of mythical, remote perfection, or if you like, conferring upon them a lucid patina of antiquity. To Marenzio's sensitive ear Tasso's musicality, even when to us it appears generated by sensitive images sedately poised in a figurative harmony, must have emitted vibrations that were too modern, too close and compromising, too weighed down with lyric enthusiasms that now escape our ears. More often Marenzio preferred the already crystallized perfection of Petrarchan poetry or Sannazaro's already seasoned arcadicizing, or the mediocre, undemanding poetical vein of anonymous and semianonymous versifiers.

14 ·–·The Orchestra and Stage in Renaissance *Intermedi* and Early Opera

Musical instruments functioned in the Italian theater of the Renaissance in a rather wide variety of ways; in this essay, however, I shall focus mainly upon the relationship between the instruments and the available space in the theater and upon the spatial adjustments necessitated by their presence and their use.

Instruments were either present and "apparent" in the acting area, or they were positioned elsewhere, where they were "not apparent," or at least did not interfere with someone's view of the stage.[1] Their visible presence in the acting area was, as a rule, justified by the fact that any of the characters, whether primary or secondary, could at some point be shown playing an instrument, often to accompany a song or a dance. The rare exceptions we know to this rule became even more rare as time went on. The instrumentalist—almost always a tambourinist—who led the entrance of characters onto the stage in some of the earliest *intermedi* and then remained to provide a rhythmic background without participating in the action, probably perpetuated a custom originating in the *entrées* of convivial *entremets*.[2] The vignette in the 1561 edition of the *Heauton-timoroumenos* of Terence, in which a performer on a bass viol is grouped with two singers at one corner of the stage, while at the center two characters in the comedy carry on a dialogue, is more likely to have been suggested (if it truly represents an actual scene) by antiquarian notions about the presence of instrumentalists on stage in the classical theater. More practicable and more common were the effects which we could call *trompe l'oeil*. They were manifested, for example, when the playing of apparent instruments on the stage was simulated, and the sound came instead from instruments positioned elsewhere, a deceit practiced either to allow the person pretending to accompany himself on an instrument more freedom for virtuosic vocal display or to bring onto the stage a more or less fanciful archeological reconstruction of an ancient instrument that in reality was unfit to produce any sound. (The first verified examples of the first kind are in the Florentine *intermedi* of 1589; for the song of Armonia Doria in *Intermedio* I, and for that of Arione in V, the singers—Vittoria Archilei and Jacopo Peri, respectively—were accompanied from behind the scenes by a chitarrone.)[3] Conversely, in some cases the sound was indeed produced on the stage, but by instruments that were in a sense not apparent because they were concealed within other objects (such as a small rebec behind the head of a hind, or a violin in the body of a swan, with a bow fashioned to resemble a marsh reed). These *trompe l'oeil* effects must always be kept in mind when evaluating the information and possible misinformation provided by pictorial sources.

Complications resulted from the increasing tendency, in the most spectacular court *intermedi,* to multiply the number of singers, instrumentalists, and dancers participating in the onstage action, and to exhibit some of them *ex machina*. This in turn created a desire for dialogues between groups that were distinct and dispersed—on earth, in midair, or in apertures in the heavens—and a consequent demand for effects which today we would call stereophonic. There were no special problems for singers and instrumentalists placed on the floor, provided there was enough space to allow them to distribute themselves in groups that were equally harmonious to sight and hearing. For the second of the Florentine *intermedi* of 1589, niches or alcoves were constructed for the musicians, an interesting solution to the problem of where to place them.[4] A machine (usually a cloud), on the other hand, with its cramped space and precarious stability, was difficult enough to sing in, so most of the instrumentalists who accompanied the singers were prudently transferred to a location offstage. Even though pictorial designs and engravings often show large and crowded groups upon various clouds, they certainly idealize and exalt a more modest reality (which nevertheless was the result of a most remarkable technical boldness).

To maintain the visual perspective, celestial choruses which appeared to be at a lofty distance had to be made up of puppets or cutout models, and the music which supposedly descended from them was produced by instruments and voices placed offstage, a solution that helped to create the appropriate effect of remoteness of the performing forces. They were offstage rather than backstage, because the apparent and not apparent groups, which were engaged in a complex interplay of polychoral polyphony, had to be able to see each other at all times in order to keep the performance going smoothly. In fact, one of the two solutions "for accommodating musicians" suggested in Nicolò Sabbatini's *Pratica di fabricar scene, e machine ne' teatri* (1638) is to "construct two scaffolds, one on each side of the stage, . . . the length of which will reach from the first to the last of the scenic wings."[5] Sabbatini also explains that the two platforms, by raising the instruments above floor level, will leave the entrances onto the scenic area clear. If such a solution were employed on the stage of the Sala delle Commedie in the Uffizi Palace in Florence, a platform about three meters wide could be built on each side.

The above-cited passage continues with two more noteworthy comments. In the first Sabbatini recommends that the beams which support the platforms for instrumentalists "pass through openings in the floor of the stage so as not to touch the floor, since if they terminated on it, the tuning of the organs and other instruments would be upset during the *moresca* [dancing]." He concludes by observing: "Thus will the offstage space for the musicians be constructed so that they will not be seen, which experience tells us is the best solution."[6] A seventeenth-century source thus reaffirms the fondness of the previous century for the sense of mystery created by the remoteness of instruments as well as by the obstructions which sweetened and veiled the sound. In the previous century this fondness had been indicated, for example, by a sentence in Angelo Ingegneri's project for the inauguration of the Teatro Olimpico in Vicenza in 1585, which demands for the beginning of the spectacle: "from behind the scenes, a music of instruments and voices, the sweetest possible, with a plaintive overall effect; and . . . done so that it seems to resound from afar."[7]

Various solutions for the placement of musicians may have been suggested or imposed by diverse circumstances and by the locations selected for spectacles, as well as by the varying nature of the spectacles themselves. One possible constraint might have been a hall so narrow that no space remained for side platforms behind the wings, but in such a circumstance the stage would have been narrowed, the number of performers decreased, and the display of musical resources made more modest. Different solutions may have been suggested, for example, by the availability of a courtyard with loggias, balconies, or parapets suitable for musicians and instruments (but again in that case the readily adaptable stage practice of the time would also have suggested a different type of spectacle based upon the resources of the suggested location). Although it is futile to try to generalize on the basis of such variables, it is clearly possible to affirm that those *balletti* or choreographed *abbattimenti* (battles) in which the stage action spilled over into the *campo di mezzo* (pit) of the theater, as, for example, in the *intermedi* of the *Liberazione di Tirreno* of 1617, required that the instruments, whose sound kept the choreographed action together, be similarly removed from the stage and placed on platforms, scaffolds, or balconies within the hall.

In spectacles whose action spilled over into the pit, the performers on stage tended to be separated from those in the pit by a class distinction, in that the latter were nobles, even the most noble among those present. One example is the *Ballo delle ingrate* (Mantua, 1608) by Rinuccini and Monteverdi, in which the performers in the pit were "the duke and the betrothed prince, together with six cavaliers and eight ladies, chosen from among the most prominent of the city on the basis of nobility, beauty, and grace in dancing."[8] Another, with an even more pronounced distinction of rank, is the above-mentioned *Liberazione di Tirreno:* "In the middle of the auditorium the grand duke danced amid cavaliers, and the archduchess amid ladies, yet with gestures and movements and placements that were always differentiated from those of the others, so that even though they all followed the same music, the masters were always recognized as such."[9] Analogously, all librettos and descriptive passages which refer to *abbattimenti* regularly list the names of cavaliers who took part in the choreographed battle. It is unlikely, however, that the same distinction by social class applied to the musicians who accompanied such performances on their instruments.

Up to this point, our discussion has focused on those kinds of musical spectacle—the most characteristic of which is the *intermedio*—in which the action, chiefly pantomimic and choreographic, was developed principally by groups, and the music was correspondingly polyphonic or polychoral. The invention of opera, which transferred the principal responsibility for action and for musical expression to individual characters, established new relationships and new exigencies; however, the earlier ones were not dropped but were instead incorporated to lend variety to the design of an opera (which needed *intermedi,* or something equivalent, to mark the divisions between acts).

The suppleness of the *stile rappresentativo* or *recitativo* of singing, depending on the subtle nuances of expression and rhythm introduced extempore by the vocal interpreter, intensified the need for direct, close contact between the singer and the accompanying instrumentalists. It furthermore concentrated the function of accompanying the vocal soloists upon a few instruments termed *interi* (self-sufficient), such as the chitarrone, theorbo, harpsichord, organ, or any other which by itself could provide the entire accompaniment (no longer contrapuntal, but instead predominantly chordal). Yet, as the stage directions in the printed score (Venice, 1609) of Monteverdi's *Orfeo* attest, stereophonic effects which underscored the contrast between characters engaged in dialogue were still sought. This may have resulted in greater variety in the utilization of offstage space, with the instruments placed on the sides of the stage as near as possible to the singer for whom they provided a halo of sound, in addition to those located on the raised platforms already described, which were useful for accompanying choral scenes and for purely instrumental passages.

The solution destined to prevail—placing the instrumentalists at the foot of the stage, where they could see the singers and be seen by them, while a partition rendered them invisible to the spectators—was arrived at with difficulty. I believe it may have been tried for the first time in Mantua in 1607, when Monteverdi's *Orfeo* was presented "su angusta scena" (on a constricted stage). This spectacle, which had to be given in a long, narrow hall, thus impeding lateral placement of the musicians behind the scenes, forced the creation of an intermediate area between the stage and the auditorium, which today we call the orchestra pit. (It is already termed the orchestra in a seventeenth-century plan of the Florentine Teatro degli Immobili, built in 1654 by Tacca). Monteverdi, in turn, feeling uneasy about how to arrange the instruments at the Teatro Farnese in Parma, may have suggested a frontal location to Francesco Guitti, who devised it in relation to the construction and operation of the ramps on which squadrons of cavaliers descended from the stage to the pit for their combat in the tournament *Mercurio e Marte* (1628). (He also left a sketch in a letter, claiming to have taken steps to protect the players from the influx of water which submerged the floor of the auditorium for the finale, a sham sea battle.) Guitti repeatedly used the same solution in Ferrarese spectacles during the next decade, all of which combined operatic plots with the spectacular aspects of the tournament, and thus he was perhaps indirectly the means by which the frontal location was transmitted to the public opera houses in Venice.

A particularly instructive passage is found in the *descrizione* of the last spectacle staged by Guitti in Ferrara, *Andromeda* of 1638: "The space before the stage was then entirely filled with a most beautiful and majestic staircase, which formed a noble ornament and enclosed a most capacious area for the instrumentalists who played the *continua armonia* that accompanied the singers. These players, although unseen by the eyes of the spectators, could nevertheless see [the stage] perfectly and were seen by the singers who acted in the representation [see Fig. 14.1]; moreover, in very commodious areas on the sides of the stage, platforms for infinitely more instrumentalists were put up, so that the latter united with the former, who were in front of the stage, played a grand sinfonia at the conclusion of each part of the representation."[10] This description first of all affirms the convenience of a placement in front of the singers, especially for those "self-sufficient" instruments which accompanied them by means of the *continua armonia* (the *basso continuo,* or figured bass). Then it relates that this solution was not yet used exclusively but was added to the usual disposition on offstage platforms, which were particularly useful for the

Fig. 14.1   Francesco Guitti, stage prospect for a Ferrarese opera (*Andromeda,* 1638) with a small pit for the orchestra, encircled by the stairs. (Courtesy of the Fondazione Giorgio Cini.)

"sinfonias" that ended the acts. Such sinfonias may have been purely instrumental (like those played between the acts of Monteverdi's *Orfeo*) or may have also included onstage choruses, and perhaps dancers as well. In any case, an analogy can clearly be drawn with the apparent and not apparent instrumentalists in the *intermedi* of the preceding century, which now became woven into the design of an opera. An operatic finale which combines the above dispositions with apparent instrumentalists is that of the *Nozze degli Dei* (Florence, 1637), an example of extreme richness and splendor (whose extraordinary scenic display was perhaps made possible by the amplitude of the courtyard of the Pitti Palace). Even though it is not really an operatic scene, the third *intermedio* of the *Liberazione di Tirreno* (1617) suggests how the same idea could also be transferred to a more normal scenic display; its most intriguing aspect is the person indicating the beat to the players and dancers by means of a scroll of paper or a short stick.

In opera there was an additional reason to conceal instrumentalists who accompanied the solo singers; the sight of musical instruments would have been enough to spoil the fragile theatrical convention which accepted sung dialogue as an equivalent of spoken discourse by conferring an unlikely appearance of truth upon *recitar cantando* (sung recitation). This aesthetic fetish was punctually observed so long as opera remained in the refined ambiance of the court and had great technical and financial resources at its disposal. It is doubtful, however, whether the observance was so rigorous in the first public theaters, especially those which had originally been created to perform spoken plays. There is reason to believe that the first operatic spectacles given at the Venetian theaters of San Cassiano and San Moisè had instrumental groups situated away from the stage, on platforms or side galleries (of which we can get an idea, or an approximation, in a drawing by Guercino, although it is unlikely that it represents an opera house). In theaters built or rebuilt especially for opera, beginning with the one at San Giovanni e Paolo in Venice, the players were positioned at the foot of the stage, behind a partition which rendered them invisible from the floor of the auditorium; but the preference of the high-ranking spectators for sitting instead in boxes built in tiers must have soon deprived the orchestra, located in the "chasm" under the proscenium, of all its "mysticism." But by then the convention of *cantar recitando* (reciting in song) was so well accepted that no one could be disturbed by the sight of performers manipulating their instruments at the feet of the enchanting vocal divas and their male counterparts.

15 ᚥ Temperaments and Tendencies in the Florentine Camerata

If by chance we come across the source of a mountain stream, we find it difficult to decide whether it is the beginning of a great river or just the modest trickling of a brooklet: it requires a number of tributaries and a broad plain to gather them together to give our tiny, newly risen stream a large volume of water and a long course. Still more difficult is it in the history of any human activity to distinguish the starting point—if there is a starting point—of an epoch-making sequence of events: moments invested with a particular drama or splendor often strike us as less important than appearances led us to suppose; others, of much greater consequence, creep into daily life with no prominent feature to distinguish them from more mundane events. All of us are prepared to agree on that; yet when we try to reconstruct and assess the main features of a historical period, we find it hard to steep ourselves in it and to reconcile our knowledge of later events with its impact upon the men who lived through it and knew nothing of the future.

A very typical example of false perspective and distorted judgment arising from this incapacity is the way we treat the series of events that led to the birth of opera. Unconsciously, we tend to assume that the men of the time foresaw everything that was later to stem from that birth; we tend to regard everything that its protagonists said and did as more important and pregnant with meaning than they themselves did.[1] And it is all the harder to rid ourselves of these errors, because many of them are of long standing: in fact, they were already established in the decades following the performances of the first operas.

The first and perhaps the commonest error lies in the very term we always use nowadays to denote the environment in which the first operas were conceived. Strictly speaking, we ought to limit the term "Camerata" to the meetings that were held in Florence (probably from 1576 to 1581 or 1582) at the house of Giovanni dei Bardi, Count of Vernio. Nearly fifty years ago Angelo Solerti suggested[2] that, besides Bardi's Camerata, we ought also to take into account a second group, with another Florentine nobleman, Jacopo Corsi, at its head, and perhaps also a third, centering around the Roman Emilio dei Cavalieri. However, it is the custom to use the term "Florentine Camerata" to denote the whole movement, which continued after Count Bardi's departure for Rome in 1592 until the first operatic experiments; thus is ingrained in us the idea of a regular institution, an academy almost, which right from the start had certain clearly expressed aims and whose activities were conducted as planned until those aims were realized. It is easy, then, to regard every statement of principles and every practical application of them as the products of common ideas and aspirations. The truth is that the meetings in Bardi's house represented only the first, vague, indeterminate stages of the work that gave rise to opera. This work was not carried out harmoniously; on the contrary, it was achieved through polemics, rivalries, and jealousies and through the clash of outlooks and temperaments which, from both the personal and artistic points of view, were conflicting and irreconcilable.

Giovanni dei Bardi came of an old Guelph family of bankers and businessmen to which Simone dei Bardi, husband of Dante's Beatrice, had also belonged; proud, munificent, and deeply conservative, he represented in Florentine society of the last quarter of the sixteenth century an old-fashioned type of nobleman. He was an erudite philologist and mathematician; he was steeped in Platonic philosophy and affected by linguistic purity associated with enthusiastic love for Dante. Finally, he

took great delight in music and was ... a composer of some reputation; [he] always had about him the most celebrated men of the city, learned in this profession, and inviting them to his house, he formed a sort of delightful and continual academy from which vice and in particular every kind of gaming were absent. To this the noble youth of Florence were attracted with great profit to themselves, passing their time not only in pursuit of music, but also in discussing and receiving instruction in poetry, astrology, and other sciences which by turns lent value to this pleasant converse.[3]

Thus wrote his son Pietro many years later (1634) in a letter to Giovanni Battista Doni which gives us the fullest—and certainly not the most disinterested—account of the Camerata; however, Pietro nowhere lists either dates or the names of members. It is clear, though, that he is writing of what in other times would have been called an intellectual *salon*—that, in fact, is the true meaning of the word "Camerata"; it is clear, too, that the questions thrashed out there were not exclusively musical ones. Indeed, when we remember that the same intellectual climate produced a true literary academy, the Crusca[4] (in which Bardi was *l'Incruscato*), we have reason to doubt that musical discussions loomed as large in the activities of the Camerata as we think they did; perhaps the musical side has been emphasized in later accounts, either deliberately or unconsciously, in order to link it with later artistic developments, which very probably were neither foreseen nor imagined at the time of the true Camerata. Our doubts seem even more legitimate when we find that the link is forged even earlier than Pietro dei Bardi's letter by certain pieces of evidence which we may suspect to be afterthoughts designed to flatter the old count of Vernio.

The document that we might expect to reproduce the musical discussions of the Camerata is the *Dialogo della musica antica e della moderna* by Vincenzo Galilei (father of Galileo), published in Florence in 1581;[5] the interlocutors are Giovanni dei Bardi and Piero Strozzi (who certainly took part in the discussions). But instead it reproduces the disquisitions that Galilei himself gave to the Camerata during the four or five years (from 1576 to 1581) he spent preparing his book. Through the display of rather pedantic erudition and the somewhat petulant arguing over tiny points of detail we can see that the dominant feature of the book is unrelenting criticism of the musical language of the time—a language based on counterpoint. In its place Galilei advances as sovereign cure a return to the simplicity of ancient monody; this seemed to be an essential preliminary to the rediscovery of the emotional and ethical power of ancient music described by Greek and Latin authors.

Galileo's father cuts a poor figure as a theorist and has nothing, or next to nothing, original to say; nor does he ever face up to the real problem of how such a return was to be effected. The idea that the reason for the expressive power of Greek music lay in its being monodic went back at least as far as Glareanus and had been repeated frequently in musical theory; at least twenty years earlier the protagonists of the Counter-Reformation had made counterpoint the stalking-horse in their criticism of religious polyphony. Galilei even took much of his philological and mathematical learning from Zarlino, whose disloyal pupil he was, and also, to a notable extent, from Girolamo Mei and Giovanni dei Bardi himself, both of them better philologists than he was.[6]

More important still, as far as opera is concerned, there is no mention in

Galilei's writings of the problem of tragedy; this is particularly interesting because Galilei must have known that at that time the literary world was loud with heated arguments about tragedy, the educational tendencies it ought to show, and the rules of Aristotle. The idea of reviving classical drama, and with the aid of music too, had already taken root elsewhere: at Ferrara, Reggio, and Vicenza; but it seems to have been far from the thoughts of the earlier members of the Camerata. The reform they proposed affected not music in the theater so much as music in general, in the forms in which they were wont to hear it. The constant preoccupation with madrigals, both in the *Dialogo* and in Galilei's other writings, shows that the Camerata looked upon them as the highest and most complete form of expression in the music—at any rate the secular music—of their day; they criticized madrigals not because they wanted to do away with them but because they wanted to reform them and give them new life.

In this context the practical experiments to which Galilei devoted himself soon after he had published his *Dialogo* are also significant; these were settings for a solo tenor, accompanied by a consort of viols, of Dante's lament of Count Ugolino[7] and the Lamentations of Jeremiah. The two songs were obviously intended to cover the whole field of music, sacred and secular; while the second one can easily be classed as a motet, the first one, however unusual it may seem to have been, takes its place among the madrigals of the time. For some time the madrigalists had tended to abandon merely lyrical expression (in which text and music express, or seem to express, subjective feelings) and had begun to represent sentiments attributed to fictitious characters. An opening narrative would often introduce the psychological situations they wanted to portray. But what pleased them still more was that they could enter into a living situation without wasting time over preliminaries; such an opportunity was offered by the situations of celebrated characters in the great epic poems, which would be familiar to even the most unlettered knight and his lady. Ottavas by Ariosto were often chosen as the texts of madrigals; later on, the pathetic scenes in *Gerusalemme Liberata* were even more popular. However, the madrigalists hardly ever turned to Dante's *Comedia;* when Galilei did so, he showed his lack of critical acumen and perhaps also his desire to conform to the spirit of linguistic purity and burning passion for the supremacy of the Tuscan idiom—in short to the spirit of the Accademia della Crusca—which through Bardi dominated the Camerata. Galilei's two pieces have not survived, and therefore we cannot assess their value as works of art, but the younger Bardi drops his eulogistic tone for a moment to remark that contemporary opinions of them were not very favorable.

But even as innovations, their significance is lessened by the fact that the tendency toward monody was beginning to be felt in practical music independently of Galilei—and even before him. True, this tendency was less marked in madrigals and motets than in the many kinds of composition that made no claims to artistic and technical mastery but that set out to give ready enjoyment and yet were not inelegant: *villanelle*, the new *villotte*, and *canzonette*. Basically these songs continued the tradition of the *frottola* (clarified and refreshed perhaps, by renewed contact with popular music), but the melody in the highest part was now still more conspicuous and was discreetly supported by the other voices, whose parts were very often played on instruments instead. In Rome and Naples—and indeed to a certain extent throughout Italy—singers themselves began to decorate this music with elaborate embellishments; this technique of improvisation even began to invade performances of madrigals and sacred music. Singers liked to sing to the accompaniment of a lute or some string instrument; even in the field of the madrigal, collections of so-called *madrigali ariosi* and "madrigals to be sung and played" (*da cantare e da suonare*) became more and more frequent. In the latter kind the combination of voices and instruments was generally understood to afford contrast between different levels of expression; the dominant voice was the one that had the aria-like (*ariosa*) melody.

This "pseudomonody," as it has been called (to distinguish it from the accompanied monody of the seventeenth century), was well known in Florence. We can trace it back to the *canti carnascialeschi*; Corteccia employed it in the first half of the sixteenth century, and from that time on it turns up with particular frequency in stage music, notably *intermedi*. In the *intermedi* produced in 1539 to mark the wedding of Cosimo dei Medici to Eleanora of Toledo, a singer representing Dawn sang the opening song, *Vattene, almo riposo*, as a solo accompanied by a harpsichord and small positive organs; likewise the conclusion, *Vientene, almo riposo*,[8] was entrusted to a solo singer, this time in the person of Night, accompanied by four trombones. The soft, veiled sound of trombones was constantly associated after this work with the idea of night and, by extension, with the darkness of the underworld. Even after the discussions of the Camerata and the publication of Galilei's *Dialogo* this tradition of pseudomonody was revived in the *intermedi* of 1585, to which Bardi himself contributed a madrigal "to be sung and played," and in those of 1589, which were to a great extent conceived by Bardi.[9] But Galilei's monodic experiments carried so little weight at court that he never figured among the numerous composers who were asked to provide music for the *intermedi*.

It has also been observed that in the *intermedi* of 1589 the monodies, or pseudomonodies, are less frequent than in the earlier ones; brilliant, sonorous polyphony prevails instead. It is clear that the ideas on the monodic reform of music so rigidly formulated by Galilei were in practice much more elastic and that musicians were skeptical about their practical value. Galilei himself published in 1587 a second volume of very conventional madrigals for four or five voices—and he was as ardently in favor of monody as anybody. Count Bardi was more consistent; in his *Discorso mandato a Giulio Caccini . . . sopra la musica antica . . .*[11] he shows that he was convinced of the need to return to monodic expression; but he believed that such a return would be achieved only by degrees in the rather distant future. In the meantime rigid theorizing should give place in musical practice to beauty—or, to use his word, to "sweetness"—no matter what steps were taken to achieve this.

The *intermedi* of 1589 were Bardi's spiritual testament, his swan song; he still had nearly twenty-five years to live, but he seemed an old man now—old not in terms of years, but when seen as a last, lingering representative of the pure, neo-Platonist spirit of the Renaissance, which he had outlived. Music was the main theme of the *intermedi*—or rather, to be more precise, classical myths and the ideas of the neo-Platonists about music, projected in allegories and dignified symbolical stage figures. It is enough to quote the titles of some of the *intermedi*: *The Harmony of the Spheres, The Rivalry of the Muses, The Song of Arion, The Descent of Apollo and Bacchus together with Rhythm and Harmony*. Three of them represent the supreme harmony of the cosmos, three others the power of human harmony. The attention to detail, the magnificent scenery, and the rich fabrics in which the almost motionless characters on stage were clad already show a touch of the baroque; it follows naturally enough that the almost hieratic splendor of the conception required the support of varied and colorful polyphony and the use, for contrast, of ostentatious sound effects and of masses of voices and instruments. These *intermedi* conclude, and in a sense symbolize, a cycle of abstract theorizing and Platonic longings for the music of antiquity, which survived more in fable than reality.[12]

Doubts, uncertainties, no preestablished program, no practical realizations corresponding to the vague ideas of reform—such are the features of a general view of what strictly speaking was the Camerata, the one that met at Bardi's house. We cannot even be certain that its members continued their discussions about music beyond 1581 or 1582. Certainly the ideas they debated were not wholly without influence, but now they began to be discussed and repeated in a less confined society. Only when opera was an accomplished fact did Caccini (a close friend of Bardi's), Severo Bonini (a pupil and admirer of Caccini's), Pietro dei Bardi, and others in their wake attempt, rather self-consciously, to argue the importance of these discussions. Writers in our own time have been too quick to create the legend of a group of theorists and polemicists at whose meetings the theory of the new dramatic music was systematically evolved in the most minute detail before being put into practice.

The last decade of the sixteenth century was much more fruitful and decisive for the birth of opera. Perhaps the time was ripe for the musical language to become more markedly expressive. Certainly this result was stimulated by the bitter conflicts of many differing personalities, who under the cloak of decorum were maneuvering into positions of favor in the Florentine court. A historical account sometimes turns into gossip and has to take the truth where it finds it. The event that touched off the rivalry was the unexpected (and indeed mysterious) death in 1587 of the Grand Duke Francesco I and his wife, Bianca Capello. Francis was succeeded by his brother, Cardinal Ferdinand dei Medici, who had returned to Florence and become reconciled with him only a few days before his death. One of the first things that the new grand duke did was to appoint (in September 1588) a superintendent of all the artists who worked at his court, including "all the musicians of the chapel . . . both singers and instrumentalists."[13] The post went to Emilio dei Cavalieri, whom Ferdinand had probably known in Rome during the fifteen years' exile he had imposed upon himself out of his dislike of Bianca Capello.

The main object of the appointment was probably to limit the authority and influence that Giovanni dei Bardi had hitherto enjoyed at court; Bardi was at loggerheads with Ferdinand because he belonged to a family that in the past had encouraged Francesco's clandestine love affair, and later his marriage, with the beautiful Venetian adventuress. In addition to these reasons for what we may call the political antagonism between Bardi and Cavalieri, we must take into account the conflicting temperaments, literary tastes, and intellectual attitudes which made a clash between the two men inevitable. Cavalieri was younger than Bardi, and he, too, was a proud man in his own capricious and original way; although he showed an independence that precluded any trace of the servility often displayed by courtiers, he could count on the support of the grand duke. It was to his advantage that he also displayed many unusual and pleasing accomplishments which made him a notable figure in the refined atmosphere of the

Florentine court (and which do not always square with the picture drawn by posterity of the composer of the *Rappresentazione di Anima e di Corpo*): he was an urbane, well-informed conversationalist and a "most graceful dancer";[14] he had real talent as a musician; and he was a brilliantly gifted organizer, choreographer, and stage director. His first clash with Bardi[15] occurred as early as the *intermedi* of 1589, which celebrated Ferdinand's marriage to Christine of Lorraine (Ferdinand had had to renounce the purple on becoming grand duke). The new superintendent noted with scrupulous care and not without ulterior motives the immense expense of even the most trivial features of Bardi's sumptuous conception. Later on he did not lose the opportunity of showing that he could organize entertainments quite cheaply—more cheaply, that is, than Bardi did.

Other eminent figures appeared at the Florentine court together with Cavalieri; among them were Vittoria Archilei, one of the most famous singers of Rome, who had long been known in her native city as the principal ornament in Cardinal dei Medici's retinue of musicians, and the poetess Laura Guidiccioni of Lucca, whose close ties with Cavalieri seem soon to have overstepped the bounds of innocent friendship. Cavalieri's share in the *intermedi* of 1589 was not confined to administrative duties; he wrote the music for a madrigal in the first *intermedio* and he was responsible for the choreography and music of the final ballet, which was so successful that it became famous as the "ballo di Firenze." Almost as if to ridicule the ideas of the Camerata, Laura Guidiccioni wrote the words for it only after the music had been composed.

And the challenge continued in other fields: in 1590 Torquato Tasso was in Florence as the guest of Jacopo Corsi—the Tasso who only a few years before had been the victim of a violent diatribe delivered by Bastiano dei Rossi, the secretary of the Crusca Academy and Bardi's faithful collaborator. A performance of *Aminta* was organized that was probably broken up with *intermedi*. Cavalieri, Laura Guidiccioni, and the grand duke himself liked the romantic pastoral manner cultivated by Tasso and Guarini, and in the winter of 1590–91 they very pointedly showed where they stood by producing two pastorales with music, *Il Satiro* and *La Disperazione di Fileno*. Unfortunately, both the words and the music have been lost, as have those of the *Gioco della Cieca*, which was based on an episode in Guarini's *Pastor Fido* and performed at the Pitti Palace in 1595. We shall not gather much idea of what Cavalieri's music was like from the *Rappresentazione di Anima e di Corpo;* the influence of the experiments that Caccini and Peri carried out in the intervening years, as well as its spiritual and moralizing tone, put this work in a different class.

We shall therefore have to guess what Cavalieri's music was like with the help of a few hints dropped by his contemporaries. A phrase of Peri's[16] suggests that Cavalieri, in contrast to the impossible flirtations with the classics indulged in by Bardi's Camerata, was prompted by the desire to show that "our music" (that is to say, the music of his time) could be employed on the stage not only as a static, decorative element but also to interpret and underline action and emotion. In fact, in the preface to *Anima e Corpo* the editor, Guidotti, recalled "the modern staging of *La Disperazione di Fileno* ... in which the singing of Vittoria Archilei ... moved the audience to tears; at the same time the character of Philenus moved them to laughter."[17] Various writers confirm that the musical style that Cavalieri adopted derived from aria-like music such as *villanelle* and *canzonette*, very popular at the time, which based their effect on an incisive, well-defined melodic line repeated unchanged from verse to verse; Doni was later to object that these songs "have nothing to do with true, good theater music" (by which he meant recitative).[18] The little pathetic scenes had to be fitted into a conception that smacked more of pantomime and ballet than real opera and to which aria-like music was well suited. In fact, the preface to *Anima e Corpo* goes on to describe "how in the pastoral of Philenus three satyrs engaged in battle and sang and danced a *moresca* as they fought; and in the *Gioco della Cieca* four nymphs sang and danced playfully around the blindfolded Amaryllis."[19]

Cavalieri alone was responsible for other aspects of what are usually regarded as the common doctrines of the Camerata: consider his advice about the ways of putting on musical spectacles, about the most suitable size of the room to accommodate them, about methods of singing and making gestures, and about the advisability of keeping the musical instruments hidden from the public—this last piece of advice has given rise to innumerable comparisons with the Wagnerian idea of the "mystical gulf." These precepts, too, may be found in the preface to *Anima e Corpo*. We shall see in a moment that they were not really very original: suffice it now to recall that two years before, in 1598, Angelo Ingegneri had expounded them in a treatise published at Ferrara.[20]

Cavalieri's musical and dramatic experience had the effect of directing the activity of Florentine musicians toward stage music, if not toward tragedy itself. Although he has the distinction of being the first man to set to music an entire dramatic text, we may yet understand why Caccini and Peri still claimed priority.

Though already famous as a singer, it seems that by 1589 Giulio Caccini had not yet gained a reputation as a composer; della Valle wrote rather maliciously that his enthusiasm for monody was born of his feeble efforts as a contrapuntist.[21] It is more likely to have been because of his consummate artistry as a singer. Through Alessandro Striggio, Caccini kept himself informed around the years 1584–85 of every detail of the practice of vocal virtuosity for which the three ladies of the rival court of Ferrara were renowned. He is mentioned for the first time as a composer through a solo song, provided with sinfonias and accompanied by instruments, which formed part of the fourth *intermedio* in 1589. But the piece does not appear in the printed score of the *intermedio* which was published, edited by Cristoforo Malvezzi, in Venice in 1591—another indication, perhaps, of the relentless campaign against Bardi and his favorites. We know that Caccini, despite his youth, had attended the meetings of the Camerata in Bardi's house, and he probably entertained his fellow members with his singing; moreover, a letter of Cavalieri's[22] tells us that in 1592 Caccini was acting as Bardi's secretary. He probably went to Rome in this capacity when Bardi moved there in the same year to assume the duties of chamberlain at the court of Pope Clement VIII.[23] Caccini twice mentions[24] as his first essays in his new style of composition the madrigals *Perfidissimo volto, Vedrò'l mio sol*, and *Dovrò dunque morire* and an aria on a text of Sannazaro's, *Itene all'ombra degli ameni faggi*, and says that he sang them in Rome in the house of one Nero Neri. The madrigals appeared later in the collection published in 1602 (1601, old style) with the proud title of *Le Nuove Musiche*; he reinforced his proud claim in a later publication by adding the phrase "e nuova maniera di scriverle" (and a new way of writing them). We must therefore date the inception of the new monodic style between 1589 and 1592.

Among documents dealing with the birth of monody and opera, those written by supporters of either Bardi or Caccini always associate the one with the other; it seems, then, that Caccini was one of the cards Bardi could play (not without a degree of success) to offset Cavalieri's successes in the musical field. There is real originality in Caccini's songs, for they are the first examples of true accompanied monody and are a decided improvement upon anything that had been achieved in the sphere of solo song in Rome or Ferrara. A visible expression of this originality, albeit an external one, is the form in which Caccini set out the instrumental accompaniment, which was designed to support the vocal line. Although its name—*basso continuo*—and the way of writing it down derived from a custom practiced by organists when they accompanied sacred polyphony, Caccini uses it in a different way: when he transferred it from the organ to a "polyphonic" instrument with plucked strings, he "played down" the polyphonic movement of the parts, which was replaced by a series of simple chords. This meant that the melody no longer seemed, in Peri's phrase, "to dance to the movement of the bass"[25] (which still happened in pseudo-monodies or in monodic performances of polyphonically conceived music); it also gave to the melody a relatively stable harmonic basis and a series of, as it were, rhythmic props to its freely flowing line. Moreover, Caccini wrote his *continuo* parts for instruments on which a singer could accompany himself. His own favorite was the chitarrone, or Roman theorbo, a plucked instrument with a large number of strings and a rich, warm tone, which was perfected at that time—and surely not fortuitously—by a colleague of his at the Medici court, Antonio Naldi, called "il Bardella." Not all these matters are just technical ones: they are the foundation of the agogic freedom in performance for which Caccini found the happy phrase "neglect of the song"[26] (*sprezzatura del canto*); thus he added a new meaning to a term already in use to denote the agile suppleness of the ideal dancer. The expressive value that Caccini added to his music through the warmth and spontaneity of his performances was so much appreciated by his contemporaries that Cavalieri (who perhaps was not well versed in playing string instruments) sought to rival him by replacing the chitarrone by a special organ he had had built and whose praises he sang in a letter addressed to Luzzaschi at Ferrara; he called this organ "enharmonic," but in fact it was a tempered instrument on which he tried to emulate the chromatic and enharmonic[27] sounds possible on string instruments.

The texts Caccini chose for his songs show that he was careful to dissociate himself from the composers of facile and banal villanellas and amorous canzonets. He had at least gleaned the following precepts from the confused ideals of the Camerata: the mood of the music must correspond exactly to that of the poetic texts, and he must maintain a constant artistic tension in which the device of repetition, traditional in the canzonet form, is inappropriate or is justified at only a few expressive moments. Another facet of the literary polemics of the time appears in the way Caccini ignores romantic, pastoral poets in favor of more classical ones like Sannazaro, with his echoes of Vergil, and the anacreontic Chiabrera. The success and fame he achieved during his visits to Rome and, a little earlier, to Ferrara enhanced his personal standing at the Medici court; indeed the popularity and high standard of the singing at court were due almost entirely to him, supported by his numerous pupils and the members of his family.

However, one hesitates to decide on the evidence of his songs whether he achieved (to quote his own loftily emotional words) "that complete grace which I can hear in my mind."[28] Taking them just as they appear on the printed page, we can admire their felicitous melodies, the scrupulous declamation, the discreet support given by the bass—in a word, the perfection of the details; but in most cases all this finely chiseled detail does not make for a satisfying whole, and its excessive richness weakens its effect until it soon becomes monotonous. And we may wonder whether Caccini's contemporaries admired his music because of the remarkable, though ephemeral, attraction of his powers as a singer, or whether, to complete the feeling of the printed page one needs the warmth a performer can give by quickening or slackening the tempo, by increasing or abating his voice, and by adding delicate embellishments, which might make the songs more "complete."

At his best, however, Caccini shows outstanding lyrical gifts, but even he will have nothing to do with dramatic music. His innovations contributed to the birth of opera, but they are still really a part of the madrigalian tradition. His two works for the stage confirm that he was temperamentally unable to take the decisive step toward writing dramatic music. The music for *Il Rapimento di Cefalo* (1600) is almost wholly lost, but Chiabrera's text, more decorative than dramatic, virtually justifies the choice of a composer more concerned with beauty of form than with bold and passionate expression. Although the staging of *Cefalo* was much more sumptuous—it was also more "official"—Caccini himself had to accept that of the stage works given in the autumn of 1600, Peri's *Euridice* was the biggest artistic success. His jealous awareness of this showed in the fact that instead of publishing his music for *Cefalo*,[29] he hastily set about imitating his rival with a new *Euridice*, on the same text by Rinuccini, which was published even before it could be performed. But even this opera, although it slavishly follows the outlines of Peri's, is very inferior to it as a genuine work of art. Caccini saps the strength of his work by his preoccupation with various types of exclamation, from the "languid" to the "sprightly," and he tends to transform them into vocal embellishments, which he later codified systematically.[30] His lack of success in this field finally led him to inveigh against the unavoidable tedium of all music written in the *stile recitativo*.[31]

Jacopo Peri, also a singer, but a more solid musician, was probably among the first to understand and follow Caccini in his innovations. And Jacopo Corsi and Ottavio Rinuccini, the first men in Florence to contemplate staging a musical equivalent of Greek tragedy, turned to him, and not to Caccini, for help. Both Corsi and Rinuccini had moved, at any rate in recent years, in the circles associated with Bardi's Camerata; but being more in sympathy with the new fashions in literature and music and less opposed on personal grounds to Cavalieri, they were able to take up a position midway between the old group and the new and to take over, as it suited them, all that was best in the ideas of the one group and in the experiments of the other. Corsi was one of the noblemen who enjoyed greater prestige at court after the arrival of Grand Duke Ferdinand. Of him, too, it was said that "his house was always open—it was almost a public academy—to all who took a lively, intelligent interest in the liberal arts," and it teemed with "noblemen, literary gentlemen, and eminent poets and musicians; Tasso, Chiabrera, Marino, Monteverdi, and Muzio Efrem were some of the famous guests who were entertained there ... 'Carriage-masques' [cocchiate], entertainments, and ballets with music were performed or tried out there; there, too, through the efforts of Ottavio Rinuccini, the famous poet, and Jacopo Peri, a great master of harmony, the stile recitativo, for use in stage music, was born, and their dramatic experiment Dafne was also given there for the first time." This account of Carlo Roberto Dati's[32] clearly sets out to establish a parallel with Bardi's Camerata: Corsi took over from Bardi, especially after the latter's departure for Rome in 1592, as a promoter of meetings and discussions. The date when Dafne was conceived is still a matter for controversy, but it was probably in the winter of 1594–95; Corsi himself had started to compose the music before turning to Peri, and Peri's work, too, had to be touched up and revised. Finally, as happened later with Euridice, it seems that Caccini managed to get some of his own music included in some of the performances that we know took place at carnival time for three years running (1598–1600).[33] Two excerpts, the prologue and an aria, have recently been identified;[34] these are in addition to the two pieces by Corsi which we have known about for some time. But this is still too little for us to judge the work as a whole. However, we do know that "it gave pleasure beyond belief to the few who heard it,"[35] although in Pietro dei Bardi's words, it was "set to music by Peri in few numbers and short scenes and recited and sung privately in a small room."[36]

I have said that Corsi and Rinuccini were the first men in Florence who thought to devise a modern equivalent of Greek tragedy. However, this ambition is still not indicated in the case of Dafne, which was usually described at the time as a fable (favola) or as a sylvan fable (favola boscareccia). In Italy people had been discussing the problems of tragedy (and not only the musical ones) for almost a century; in the second half of the sixteenth century purely literary exercises and discussions about meter, the handling of episodes, and the use of choruses had led, through experiments like *Orbecche*, by Giraldo Cintio of Ferrara, and *Canace*, by Sperone Speroni of Padua, to more and more frequent performances of plays. Although these performances were often provided with music, the outlook for a revival of tragedy seemed to be less promising in the musical than in the literary field. It was generally believed that the ancients had confined the use of music to choruses, and there grew out of this belief a practice that is strikingly similar to one found in the *intermedi* of the time: the tranquil, reflective scenes furnished with music gave relief from the complicated plot, with its recognitions and sudden changes of fortune, whose effect was enhanced by many a bloody deed.

Opinions seem to have been divided, however, about how the choruses should be set to music. Valuable evidence of this is provided by the anonymous chronicler of the performance of the tragedy *Alidoro*, given at Reggio in 1568 in honor of Barbara of Austria, duchess of Ferrara:[37]

I know that in our time choruses have been performed in a number of different ways; some have made a single member of the chorus speak in continuously grave and eloquent tones ... Others have allotted them to a solo singer, unsupported by any accompaniment ... Others still have preferred to let the whole crowd sing together; this method gives pleasure as long as the body of voices is not so large as to render the ideas and the words totally unintelligible ... And I for my part believe that the ancients used all these methods wherever they were most appropriate. This was done in the present tragedy, too; for instance, the chorus was split up for one particular song, so that two verses in honor of Venus were repeated alternately by two women and were finally taken up by the entire chorus ... The obvious reason for there being so many different ways of performing choruses is the difficulty of finding out exactly what the ancients did.

In addition to showing the foolish notions that arise from a too vague and imperfect understanding of an antique model, this passage shows how widespread were the ideas and ambitions commonly thought to have been conceived and nurtured only within the Camerata. None of its members ever expressed them so fully and clearly; and the time, it should be remembered, is still 1568—a decade or so before the meetings held in Bardi's house. The chronicle continues:

An infinite number of singers and instrumentalists started performing together in a truly divine manner; you could hear at once from the gravity of the sound, which was by turns terrible and sad, that the play that was being performed could not be other than tragic.

And "those who put on the play here" wanted

not only the music of the opening but all the music heard later to reflect the terrible and sad qualities of the tragedy and to point to every change of mood. The excellent composers of the music pondered these matters well; they grasped the essential ideas and wrote songs that matched the words so happily that they might almost have been called not songs but reasoned discourses.

For the sake of brevity I am omitting some less significant passages so that I can pass on to other ideas. There is, for example, the idea of the "mystical gulf":

Expert musicians played the bass and the inner parts with infinite taste on delicate, soft-toned instruments, which were placed out of sight some way from the stage. Only the treble part with the words was sung by a woman who was placed among the rest of the chorus at the front of the stage; when she sang to the accompaniment of the instrumental consort, she visible and close at hand, they invisible and remote, it was doubtful if that sweet and distant sound was not the echo of her voice.

And this is how the same writer stresses the need for significant and appropriate acting:

As well as a most mellifluous voice this lady had a natural talent for acting, ruled by art ... And all the time she was singing, her gestures and movements and the expression on her face and in her eyes corresponded exactly to the various conceits with which she so subtly beguiled us; thus she made everyone fear and hope and feel joy and sadness by turns, as seemed to her most fitting.

All this may seem enthusiastic and self-satisfied to a fault—it is probably the author of *Alidoro* himself who is speaking—but it is obvious that in the choruses at least the desire to revive a musical form of classical tragedy had already been satisfied. Among later examples I ought to mention Andrea Gabrieli's choruses for the performance of Sophocles' *Oedipus Tyrannus* which inaugurated Palladio's Teatro Olimpico at Vicenza in 1585.[38]

The Florentines were aiming at once at something more and something less. On the one hand, their liking for pastorales and the example of Cavalieri's diversions, with their mime and their music, led to the performance of plays of a simpler order than tragedy; they thus avoided both the need for a continuous heroic tension and the difficulties inherent in the rather bloodthirsty realism so prevalent in the Italian tragic theater of the time. The unreal, optimistic world of the pastorale afforded the best justification for the use of colorful music and the happy outcome of the action. But on the other hand, the bold power of expression and the immediate impact of the singing stimulated an idea forever latent in the human spirit: that of a scenic action, sung throughout, in which, from the revival of a stylized union of word, gesture, and sound, springs the rediscovery of the exaltation existing in its original association with magic incantation. It is no accident, surely, that Ovid, who sings the prologue to *Dafne*, is the poet of the *Metamorphoses*, which tell of Love's powers of transfiguration. And does not the *nomos* describing Apollo's fight with the Dragon, from which the plot derives (and which had already provided Rinuccini with the theme of the third *intermedio* in 1589), relate the myth of the triumphant, magical power of light and sound? But those who personified the almost unconscious ambitions of which I have spoken sought to rationalize them and to present them on the stage in a plausible manner; later they invented the ideas and theory of "speaking in song" (*recitar cantando*). Peri defined this kind of singing as "an intermediate course, lying between the slow and suspended movements of song and the swift and rapid movements of speech";[39] and certainly "speaking in song" fulfills these practical requirements. But above all it corresponds to a kind of expression that was already coming to maturity in the field of the madrigal and to which Peri's intuition and temperament responded most readily.

Peri was most successful at expressing fervent emotion and at underlining dramatic, even excited, movement. Temperamentally he was inclined, perhaps, to be melancholic, but he did not write in one style so monotonously as to deserve the epithet "lugubrious," which (not without a touch of malice) is what the pupils of the jealous Caccini called him. It is true that the threnody on the death of Eurydice—which is as beautifully proportioned as a fine old sarcophagus—and Orpheus' first invocation in the shadows of Hell are among the finest pages of his *Euridice*; but it cannot be denied that the opera contains other passages, no less successful, expressing the most varied sentiments: consider the description of the joyful wedding day; Orpheus' song, full of anxious and voluptuous expectation; the majestic character of Pluto; the gay pastoral dances. Peri's expressiveness derives from his handling of stresses, the inflections in his writing for the voices, his vibrant declamation, the tension produced by sudden, unexpected discords, and the dying fall of ordinary concords. All this explains—more than do futile arguments about professional jealousy— Caccini's constant hostility toward him; similar leanings in Caccini's tortured makeup were nearly always weakened and frustrated by an ecstatic lyricism which expresses itself in ornamentation, variation, and sensuous vocal writing. Two means of expression come face to face with each other here for the first time; sometimes in the long history of opera they have been reconciled, at other times, they have seemed to be irreconcilable. The second one provides the aesthetic basis of *bel canto*, and it is very difficult for us today to come to terms with it; after two centuries of romantic music we find it alien, unfamiliar, and slow to give up its secrets.

The success of the experimental *Dafne* emboldened Rinuccini to call *Euridice* a tragedy, though he must have been well aware that he was still moving in the world of the pastorale; but his piece is so full of vitality and is so beautifully proportioned, and the *stile recitativo* was such an arresting novelty, that he felt justified in speaking of it in such a rhetorical manner and in laying at the feet of the newly crowned queen the gift of reborn tragedy. And indeed the spirit of the Tuscan Renaissance gives to more than one scene of *Euridice*—not in a philological sense but, more fundamentally, through a similarity of expression—an air of classicism reborn. Such was Peri's boundless confidence in the expressive power of recitative that he even set Orpheus' urgent prayer to the powers of Hell as an impassioned peroration and not as the song that the myth seems to demand and that Monteverdi was later to write; even so, a stream of melody wells up at the more passionate moments. *Dafne* may have been only a fledgling, but with *Euridice*, which treats once more the legend of the power of music, opera is truly and completely established. But it is a mistake to suppose that those who were present when it was performed at the Pitti Palace on October 6, 1600, had even the remotest idea of what it was all to lead to. The performance occupied the humblest place in the series of festivities that celebrated the marriage of Maria dei Medici to King Henry IV of France; the major honors went to the spectacular *Rapimento di Cefalo*. And in the detailed accounts that ambassadors sent as a matter of course to their governments, *Euridice* was either not mentioned at all or was recorded simply as "Sig. Cavaliere Corsi's pastoral"—the performance was Corsi's generous tribute to the new queen. Only later on, when diplomatic considerations gave place to discussions about its merits, did *Euridice* come in for its share of contemporary admiration and become, along with Monteverdi's *Arianna*, the opera whose name was most frequently heard on people's lips.

I have tried to show that the so-called Camerata was not guided—or was guided hardly at all—by predetermined theories. It was not theories and ideas that brought about opera, but the practical attempts of certain men, each following the dictates of his own temperament and sensibility, to realize their own ideals: Caccini that of noble, refined singing, Cavalieri that of elegant and pleasing music appropriate to the stage, Peri and Rinuccini that of dramatic expression. And yet the judgment most often repeated sums up these men, by comparison with Monteverdi, as cerebral manipulators of aesthetic formulas that they were unable to translate into artistic terms. This judgment is doubly unjust: there is no need to magnify Monteverdi's genius by belittling his contemporaries, and the creative activity of the artists of the Camerata was limited only by their own personalities. Each one, like every true artist, deserves and demands to be considered on his merits and not to be measured against the greatness of others.

16 ⃰ Monteverdi and the Problems of Opera

The cautiously generic title of this essay does not state its true purpose. All the same I prefer it to the one that first came to mind, "Monteverdian Heresies," which would have required the clarification that the heretical error is not Monteverdi's but my own. We tend to consider Monteverdi not only the greatest musician of his time, but also the only one with an unerring ability to see through and beyond the prejudices and illusions of that period. It is a heresy not to believe in his infallibility and to love him for his mistakes no less than for his intuitions and successes. Consequently it is heretical of me to explore three moments in Monteverdi's operatic activity in order to see how that activity was rooted in his time and shared some of its false illusions, and how in the greatest accomplishments of his art the shadow and bitterness of defeat were not lacking.

It has been suggested that Monteverdi would have created *Orfeo* just the same even if he had not known the attempts of the musicians of Bardi's circle. This proposition first of all repeats a widespread misunderstanding that I have refuted several times: identifying the first creators of opera with a small circle that had ceased to exist long before the first operatic experiments, and toward which both Rinuccini and Peri had assumed a decidedly antithetical attitude, affirming the validity of "modern music" even in the most arduous field of dramatic expression. Apart from this, the hypothesis is impossible to verify and is part of the common tendency to exalt Monteverdi by belittling the personalities of his contemporaries. Another Monteverdi scholar agrees in exalting the superiority of *Orfeo* over Peri's *Euridice* and cites in support of such superiority that the score for *Orfeo* was printed twice, both times in Venice, in 1608 and 1615. He evidently forgets that Peri's *Euridice* had already gone through two editions, the Florentine of 1600 (actually 1601) and the Venetian (printed by Alessandro Raverii) of 1608. Actually it does not at all detract from Monteverdi to affirm that he was deeply indebted, not to the distant discussions of Giovanni Bardi's Camerata, but to the recent reality of the Florentine performances of 1600. The artist does not create in a vacuum, but is all the greater the more varied and numerous the experiences of his time he succeeds in recreating as his own through the imprint of his taste and personality.

It is not certain whether Monteverdi was in Florence in 1600, but there is no doubt that he was completely familiar with both settings of *Euridice*, that is, Peri's and the one Giulio Caccini, jealous of the artistic success of a potential rival, hurriedly composed and preemptively published a few weeks after the end of the wedding festivities honoring Maria dei Medici. The text of *Orfeo* was certainly the product of a collaboration between Monteverdi and that Alessandrino Striggio who even at the height of his successful political career maintained relations of affectionate friendship with the faraway musician; in its broad outlines it remained faithful to the model provided by *Euridice* and to the poetic style of Rinuccini. One can show a series of similarities and exact correspondences. A single illustration can serve for many: the comparison of the corresponding passages of both works in which the death of Eurydice is narrated to Orpheus.

> Per quel vago boschetto,
> ove, rigando fiori,
> lento trascorre il fonte degli Allori
> prendea dolce diletto
> con le compagne sue la bella sposa.
> Chi violetta o rosa
> per far ghirlande al crine
> togliea dal prato o da l'acute spine,
> e qual posando il fianco
> su la fiorita sponda
> dolce cantava al mormorar de l'onda;
> ma la bella Euridice
> movea danzando il piè su 'l verde prato,
> quando, ria sorte acerba!
> angue crudo e spietato,
> che celato giacea tra fiori e l'erba,
> punsele il piè con sì maligno dente,
> ch'impallidì repente
> come raggio di sol che nube adombri,

e dal profondo core con un sospir mortale
sì spaventoso ohimè! sospinse fuore,
che, quasi avesse l'ale,
giunse ogni Ninfa al doloroso suono.
Et ella in abbandono
tutta lasciossi allor ne l'altrui braccia.
Spargea il bel volto e le dorate chiome
un sudor via più freddo assai che ghiaccio:
indi s'udiò il tuo nome
tra le labbra sonar fredde e tremanti,
e, volti gli occhi al cielo,
scolorito il bel volto e i bei sembianti,
restò tanta bellezza immobil gelo.

By that lovely grove, / where, through rows of flowers, / the brook of
Laurels slowly wends its way, / your most beautiful bride / sweetly enjoyed herself with her companions. / Who violets and roses / to make
garlands about her locks / was picking from the meadow / or from their
prickly stems; / who, lying on her side / on the flowery shore, / softly sang
to the murmuring of the wave; / but your fair Eurydice / danced moving
about the verdant field, / when, evil bitter fate! / a savage, spiteful
snake, / that lay hidden amid the grass and flowers, / bit her foot with such
venomous fangs / that she suddenly turned pale / like the ray of the sun
darkened by a cloud; / then, sighing from the depth of her heart, / she
uttered such a terrifying "alas!" / that, as if they had wings, / all the other
nymphs arrived at her side. / She surrendered herself / completely into the
arms of her companions. / Over her fair face and golden locks / there
spread a sweat colder than ice; / then your name was heard / to sound
between her cold and trembling lips, / and, with her eyes turned toward
heaven, / her face and fair countenance discolored, / such great beauty
was left unmoving ice.

Thus in Rinuccini's *Euridice* (lines 190–222); shorter (not by chance), but
parallel is Striggio's version in *Orfeo* (lines 218–238):

In un fiorito prato
con l'altre sue compagne
giva cogliendo fiori
per farne una ghirlanda a le sue chiome,
quand'angue insidioso,
ch'era fra l'erbe ascoso,
le punse un piè con velenoso dente.
Ed ecco immantinente
scolorirsi il bel viso e ne' suoi lumi
sparir que' lampi ond'ella al Sol fea scorno.

All'hor noi tutte sbigottite e meste
le fummo intorno, richiamar tentando
li spirti in lei smarriti
con l'onda fresca e co' posenti carmi;
ma nulla valse, ahi lassa,
ch'ella, i languidi lumi alquanto aprendo
e te chiamando, Orfeo,
doppo un grave sospiro
spirò fra queste braccia; ed io rimasi
piena il cor di pietade e di spavento.

In a flowery meadow / with her other companions / she went about for flowers / to make of them a garland for her locks, / when a treacherous snake, / lying hidden in the grass, / bit her foot with its venomous fangs. / And behold, suddenly / her fair visage discolored and her eyes / lost that brilliance that put the Sun to shame. / Then dismayed and woeful / we were all about her, trying to revive / the spirits that had left her / with fresh water and with powerful charms; / but all in vain, alas! / for she, opening her languid eyes somewhat / and calling you, Orpheus, / after a heavy sigh / expired in these arms: and I was left / full of pity and of fear in my heart.

In the music of *Orfeo* the ampler and more expansive choral parts reveal the greater richness of Monteverdi's experience with the madrigal, and the frequent use of instruments reveals the variety and flexibility of his invention. But the style of the dialogues and monologues is clearly derived from Peri and, like his, punctuated by the periodic return to phrases of great melodic beauty and touching harmonic intensity. Again let two brief parallel passages serve as example, the passages in which Orpheus' sorrow is expressed, first in interrupted, hesitant phrases of amazed stupor, then in a crescendo of agitation and desperate resolution (Exs. 16.1 and 16.2). Monteverdi follows the suggestions of Peri's musical oratory and his interpretation of *sprezzatura* point by point in both rhythmic and harmonic terms.[1]

No less significant than the similarities are the differences between the two; it is clear that Monteverdi, just as he sometimes avoided the mistakes of his model, at other times proudly held back from treading upon the most successful moments in Peri's score. Both texts are divided classically into five episodes, even though in *Euridice* the division is marked only by the choral conclusions of the various episodes, while in the libretto and the score of *Orfeo* it is expressed graphically by the indication and enumeration of five "acts." But the difference is more apparent than real; in *Orfeo*

Ex. 16.1   Peri, *Euridice* (second episode), Orpheus' lament.

Ex. 16.1   Continued

Ex. 16.2   Monteverdi, *Orfeo* (act II), Orpheus' lament.

Ex. 16.2   Continued

the final chorus is also the true end of each act,[2] and the division into acts does not mean an interruption in the performance. On the contrary, the music for *Euridice* may have had its continuity disrupted after the third episode when the "most lovely glades, both painted and in relief" (selve vaghissime, e rilevate e dipinte) of the woodland scene were changed in sight of the audience and in their place were seen "horrid frightful boulders that seemed real, on which leafless stumps and pale grass appeared" (ivi orridi massi si scorsero e spaventevoli, che parean veri, sovra de' quali sfrondati li sterpi e livide l'erbe apparivano). Another interruption may have been necessary when the "scene as before returned" for the final episode.[3] Also in *Orfeo* after the "falling" of the curtain at the beginning, the sets remained visible until the epilogue;[4] but when the scenery was changed in sight between one act and the next, Monteverdi filled the void with instrumental pieces. These appear in the score at the end of each act, but are actually transitions that lead to the next act, to which they usually refer both in instrumentation and in expressive content.[5]

The first two acts of *Orfeo* repeat the situations of the first two episodes of *Euridice:* the festive morning of the wedding day and the songs with which Orpheus fills the time, interrupted and upset by the sudden announcement of Eurydice's death. Monteverdi could not avoid repeating the narrative of the messenger, which is one of the most vivid pages of Peri's score, but he gave it, perhaps intentionally, a briefer, less intense setting (see the texts above). In compensation he corrected a defect only too evident in his model, almost completely suppressing a weak transition—weak both psychologically and musically—that of the incredulity of Orpheus and his companions and Daphne's reconfirmation, a transition that was probably introduced by Rinuccini and Peri to separate two intensely pathetic passages. A situation which might have compared with the very beautiful threnody, alternating between soloists and polyphonic chorus, that Peri had written for the death of Eurydice, was completely avoided in *Orfeo.*

The third episode of *Euridice* repeats indirectly, through the narrations of witnesses, the description of Orpheus' desperate laments—superfluous repetition, undoubtedly dictated by the necessity of arriving at the traditional number of five episodes. All that is added here is the news of his meeting with Venus. Monteverdi and his docile librettist preferred instead to divide into two acts Orpheus' descent into Pluto's realm, to whose threshold Orpheus is escorted not by Venus but by Hope. Thus the parting from his consoling escort, who cannot penetrate where the souls of the dead reside, acquires greater meaning.[6] Orpheus is left alone to confront

Charon and to persuade him to allow him the use of his bark. For this scene, the most famous of Monteverdi's *Orfeo,* the score gives two different versions without indicating which was used in the 1607 performances in Mantua. In the version which I think came first in order of composition, Orpheus, to convince Charon, applies the same means he will employ in the following act to implore Pluto to restore Euridice, the persuasive force of eloquence, the warmth of moving peroration, translated musically into Peri's intense and concise style. In the second version, with a happy reconsideration of the problem, the text is interpreted no longer as an eloquent declamation, but rather as a fervid and even hieratic prayer—the "righteous prayer" destined to pacify the "powerful spirit," to which Monteverdi himself later pointed as the internal fulcrum around which the entire action of *Orfeo* revolves. Prayer, indeed, but also a triumph of magical force, of the power of song to enchant, that justifies a well-defined formal structure and a richly ornate melody. This idea, which would have pleased Giovanni Bardi, is a realization that the beauty of a virtuosically inflected melodic line adheres to and ennobles the interpretation of *stile recitativo* or *rappresentativo,* in the direction shown in *Le Nuove Musiche* of 1601 by Bardi's most faithful follower, Giulio Caccini.

The fourth act, with Orpheus' entreaties, Pluto's refusals, and the feminine intercession of Proserpine, again approaches the model of *Euridice.* It diverges only in the conclusion, faithful to the myth, which had been suppressed by Rinuccini for the sake of a happy ending. But even Monteverdi's art and psychological acumen are not sufficient to render effectively the moment in which Orpheus finally loses Eurydice. From the very beginning the law is established that only in the very rarest of cases does opera succeed in expressing action musically, not just the aura of affective reactions that accompany action (in this respect even Monteverdi's attempt in *Combattimento di Tancredi con Clorinda* is not completely successful). In the fifth act Orpheus returns alone to the fields of Thrace; the commiserating responses of the echo to his laments are a theme dear, even before the advent of opera, to the pastorale; Apollo's appearance on a cloud and the singer's ascent to heaven and immortality are the pretext for spectacular stage action. They have, indeed, the double advantage of reestablishing the pastoral tradition of the happy ending and providing an opportunity for a musically florid duet, even if deprived of dramatic interest. Perhaps the rustic songs and dances that accompany the joyous return of Orpheus and Eurydice and more cordially conclude Peri's opera are gayer and more natural.

In the last act there survives a trace of a failed attempt on Monteverdi's part to rebel against both the conventions of the pastorale and the even more imperious exigencies of court life. The libretto that was handed out at the performances ends with Orpheus' flight and with a savage dance of furious Bacchantes. But if the music for this Bacchic finale had ever been written, Monteverdi would have included it, as he did the double version of the "righteous prayer"; or at least we would have had some information about it from indirect sources. We do not know how events unfolded, but it is certain that the force of the environment and the tradition behind genres imposed the happy ending and the first of a series of apotheoses, with which the first half-century of opera abounds.[7]

Euridice and *Orfeo*, similar and yet different from each other, are the most significant expressions of the brief pastoral phase of opera. In *Euridice* the touching intensity of feeling is arranged in a picture to which concision and symmetry give a classical composure that does not arise from archeological assumptions but from the sense of balance and clarity that is always present in the Tuscan spirit. In *Orfeo* the emotion is at times, but not always, more deeply affecting, the picture ampler and richer, the structure more complex, the expressive means more varied and more numerous. *Euridice* can be compared to a series of metopes; *Orfeo* ascends toward a high point and descends like the triangular frieze of a temple. The spirit of *Euridice* is gentle and basically serene. In *Orfeo* the interpretation of the pastoral world is more personal, more pathetic, closer to the disturbed spirit of Tasso, Monteverdi's favorite poet. Even in the opening scenes joy is, as it were, veined with melancholy, happy innocence is knowingly caressed as an unreal vision, a nostalgic aspiration, an impossible evasion of the sorrows of humanity.

Historians, and not only students of Monteverdi, attribute to the so-called Florentine Camerata the merit of having created opera but give this creation such legendary form that it is left open to ridicule. Like Columbus in search of a route to the Indies, the Florentine aesthetes had embarked in search of an ancient and famous land—Greek tragedy—only to land instead on the unknown continent of opera, whose immense riches others, such as Monteverdi, would reveal. Columbus's error is made glorious by the dangers he had confronted and by the faith and daring that were necessary to vanquish every obstacle. Not so the error of the so-called Camerata; what sort of perils could ever have disturbed the placidity of the customary gatherings in the salons of Bardi's palace, if not torpid ideological fogs and bland tempests of words? In reality, the creation of opera does not belong to the Camerata of Giovanni Bardi, and none of those who in a partisan spirit connected the origin of the new genre with those old gatherings ever mentioned that the subject of reviving Greek tragedy had been a particularly cherished one there. In 1600 Rinuccini entrusted to the personification of tragedy the task of singing the prologue in *Euridice,* but Rinuccini never had anything to do with Bardi's Camerata, and furthermore his gesture was simply courtly hyperbole, a resplendent compliment to the new queen of France. At that time they used to say that only the noble language of tragedy was suited to the presence of a royal personage.

Euridice and *Orfeo* were called "fables," and the period was too rigidly conscious of genre distinctions to label them otherwise. The libretto of *Arianna,* on the other hand, which was performed in Mantua in May 1608, bears on its title page, in large letters that eclipse both the title and the name of the poet, the qualification "tragedy."[8] In Mantua, therefore, and not in Florence, an attempt was really made to recreate tragedy. No hint remains of who gave birth to the idea. But if it came, as is probable, from Rinuccini, who was then Monteverdi's poet and an ambitious and enterprising man, there is no doubt that to attempt musical tragedy must have appeared a seductive enterprise to the musician who had dreamed of giving an almost tragic ending to the "fable" of Orpheus.

As in *Orfeo,* also in this instance Monteverdi's aspirations were frustrated by the requirements of court life. *Arianna*'s plot was discussed February 27, 1608, in a council presided over by "Madama," the mother of the duke; the decision is reported laconically in a letter dated the same day: "Madama is agreed with Sig. Ottavio [Rinuccini] to enrich it with some 'actions,' it being rather dry." From a glance at the libretto it is easy to recognize the added "actions." One is the conventional and superfluous opening dialogue between Love and Venus; another, the final appearance on stage of Ariadne and Bacchus, united and rejoicing. From the descriptions that have come down to us we learn that at this point "a cloud descended with Jove, who blessed the marriage of Ariadne and Bacchus," and also "a piece was danced by actors dressed like soldiers who were with Bacchus their king . . . and they were sixteen excellent dancers who executed capering steps nearly constantly, a thing very beautiful to behold . . ." Without these *dei ex machina* and their retinues, the action, all of which takes place in the same stage setting ("neither did the scenery change, which was all of mountains, rocks, and seashore") and which is contained within the prescribed twenty-four-hour limit, would have been completely human, except for the final narration of the arrival of Bacchus, by two messengers to the chorus left alone on stage.[9]

In spite of the additions—or perhaps also because of the additions—

Arianna was a great success. Famous singers—including Settimia Caccini, Francesco Rasi, Antonio Brandi, and Lemmo Orlandi—from the school of Caccini participated, lent to the Mantuan court by the Florentine court. But all were surpassed by an actress from the Compagnia dei Fedeli, Virginia Andreini Ramponi, known as Florinda, who "in her musical lament accompanied by violas and violins made many weep over her plight," and who because of her performance merited a place in the most famous poem of the time, Marino's *Adone:*

> E in tal guisa Florinda udisti, o Manto,
> là ne' teatri de' tuoi regi tetti
> d'Arianna spiegar gli aspri martiri,
> e trar da mille cor mille sospiri.
> (VII, *ottava* 88)

> And in such guise you heard Florinda, o Mantua,
> there in the theaters of your royal abode
> disclose Ariadne's bitter torments,
> and draw from a thousand hearts a thousand sighs.

The famous lament, the only piece from *Arianna* that Monteverdi ever decided to publish, was to have been sung by the very young Caterina Martinelli, Monteverdi's pupil, who died from a sudden illness a few weeks before the performance. Beyond being a reminder of the girl who inspired Monteverdi, acute judge of singers and interpreters, it is the sole testimony of a success that must have left in the artist's soul the bitter stamp of defeat.

Not only human but all too human is the plot of *Arianna,* and as such it reflects the prose of humanity along with its poetry. The right to be called tragedy comes, as in the tradition of the genre, from the royal birth and political motivations of its characters. Unlike comedy or pastorale, it does not untangle the personal vicissitudes of private persons, but rather the actions of public personages, which also affect the life and happiness of a state and its citizens. Ariadne is the daughter and betrothed of a king; Theseus is a king; royal duty forces him to abandon the "foreign maid," the "daughter of the enemy king" whom his subjects will never be able either to love or to respect, the "shameless woman . . . deprived of the fair flower of honesty" who betrayed her own kin for love. Theseus inaugurates the motive of the conflict between love and duty imposed by royal station, which later becomes the favorite theme of innumerable operas; he is the first "vincitor di sè stesso" (conqueror of himself). But in substance the dialogue in which Theseus' counselor insists upon the necessity of abandoning Ariadne and suggests furtive departure under cover of darkness is prosaic; the questioning by Ariadne's lady-in-waiting to discover from the chorus of fishermen the nocturnal movements in the camp and down at the ships is prosaic; and prosaic in the end is the comment of the chorus of fishermen representing an insular Arcadia:

> O sorga Febo, o chiugga in mar sua face,
> da' molesti pensieri
> non san posa impetrar regi e guerrieri.

> Let Phoebus rise or shut his torch in the sea,
> From troubled thoughts
> Rulers and warriors never get a pause.

If to this one adds that little happens on stage in *Arianna*—most of it is narrated by messengers or by the chorus—we can hardly wonder that the *tragedia in musica* seemed a failed attempt to the acute eye of Monteverdi and that he never tried to publish the complete score as he had published that of *Orfeo*.[10]

The dream of musical tragedy will be rehearsed again two years later in Bologna with *Andromeda* by Count Ridolfo Campeggi. Girolamo Giacobbi, a musician careful and judicious in dramatic expression, composed the music, also lost, but it is vain to think that he could have succeeded where Monteverdi had failed.[11]

Monteverdi's biographers and panegyrists do not fail to enumerate the long series, between *Arianna* and Monteverdi's last works, of theatrical compositions begun but not completed, or completed but not staged, or staged but unfortunately lost. But they omit that chapter, important as much for the history of music in general as for Monteverdi in particular, which could be titled "Opera from Monteverdi to Monteverdi." Very many things happened between 1608 and 1640, and it is futile to think that an observant, curious, and thoughtful artist was ignorant of them, above all one such as Monteverdi, who was acutely interested in the problems of dramatic expression. The creators of operatic plots tried to broaden the range of their themes and diversify their means of expression. From the idyllic world of the pastorale they passed to the equally unreal, but at least more varied, world of chivalrous poetry. Ottavio Tronsarelli and Domenico Mazzocchi resorted to Marinism with *La catena d'Adone;* the "mockery of the gods" was turned into risqué comedy in *Diana schernita* by Giacomo Francesco Parisani and Giacinto Cornacchioli, who at the same time drew satirical elements from Galileo's recent discoveries in optics. Wondrous scenic inventions were multiplied in *Erminia sul Giordano, Chi soffre speri,* and *Galatea,* taking advantage of the scenographic illusionism of Francesco Guitti and Gian Lorenzo Bernini. Historical opera and the severity of Roman classicism, if only in the context of Christian piety, were attempted in *Sant'Alessio;* and cloak-and-dagger comedy was tried, if somewhat anachronistically, in *San Bonifacio.* Dialectal characters derived from the *commedia dell'arte* were introduced. At the same time and paralleling these developments, composers sought to vary and to hone their musical language and to diversify the types of recitative style, from the most pathetic and affect-laden, to the most violent and impetuous—or, as Monteverdi would have it, *concitato* (excited)—or else to the most discursive manner, almost spoken like prose. But they showed even greater zeal in multiplying the occasions to evade *cantar recitando,* "singing in a recitative manner" (the inversion of the normal order of these words is intentional), and in seeking justifications or pretexts for alternating declamation with pieces in which musical language is made more independent of the word and expands into song, in a word, *cantar cantando,* "singing in a singing manner."

For the sake of verisimilitude there existed tenacious prejudices against the aria, against melodically closed pieces (quite often also strophic), which prejudices had to be overcome or circumvented. The gamut of nuances from recitative to arioso was more consonant with the substantially madrigalian tradition of the language of opera. But the revolution which gave birth to the new monodic language took place on two fronts: on the one hand, it aspired to model melodic accents upon those of speech; on the other hand, having broken the bonds of conventions and contrapuntal constrictions, it enjoyed the freedom thus attained of a melodic arc that soared without any other law or logic than that of pure musical feeling: the aria. Gods and allegorical personifications abound in the operatic plots of this period, even in those that pretend to approach historical realism; they are old, trite conventions from the literary point of view, but they have their own precise function in the musical economy of opera because their supernatural essence exempts the musician from the realism of recitative and permits him to engage in a more florid use of the voice. For prologues and choruses a formal justification—or rather a habit already established before opera—permitted the adoption of set musical forms, often strophic. At the other extreme, the most realistic, prosaic, and popular comic characters often could depart from recitative to express themselves through proverbs or parables set as *canzonette.* For serious characters, occasions for singing arias were offered by the formulas for magical evocations or, as in *Orfeo,* by prayer; from prayer the conquest of melody in all its fullness extends by degrees, with tenacious progress, to moments of solitary meditation, in which the rush of feeling seems to justify the rising wave of lyricism. In a particularly ingenious solution, the moments of most anguished sorrow, the laments, could preserve the freedom and incisiveness of an arioso declamation grafted onto the inexorable musical logic of relentlessly repeated harmonic sequences, the arias on a *basso ostinato.*

These new developments took place for the most part in the Rome of Barberini; hence the chapter could also be entitled "Muses, Piety, and Magic" (having in mind an opera prologue of those years in which Magic, personification of the wondrous inspiration of Bernini's scenographic art, settles in its own favor a garrulous dispute with Poetry, Painting and Music). But even though this is a Roman chapter, we should not forget that Monteverdi's *Armida* responds at the distance of a year to Mazzocchi's Falsirena, who alternates feminine wiles and magical deceptions to try to bind Adonis to her. Nor should we forget that the first musical comedy, *Diana schernita,* coincides in time, if not in type of invention and plot, with the comic *Finta pazza Licori;* nor that the beggar Iro's tragicomic monologue in *Il ritorno d'Ulisse in patria* is preceded two years earlier by the narrative, a dramatic recitative in bergamasque dialect, delivered by a servant in *Chi soffre speri,* about the killing of a cherished falcon sacrificed to the claims of hunger.

Also Roman was the group of musicians and singers who, after an exhibition in Padua in 1636, went to Venice in 1637 and initiated there in the theater at San Cassiano the glorious series of public performances of opera. But already in Padua they had joined with a group of singers from San Marco, among them a Francesco who was none other than a son of Monteverdi. From Rome, in the retinue of Antonio Barberini, came Marco Marazzoli, who, after a sojourn in Ferrara, had an opera performed in Venice in 1642, a year before *L'incoronazione di Poppea.* From Rome also in that year arrived a fanciful poet, author of two librettos for Cavalli the composer and two satires against Cavalli the impresario.[12] But even without these more direct contacts we can be certain that Monteverdi knew, observed, and evaluated all that happened in the world of opera.

A baroque prologue with the allegorical figures of Prudence, Respect, and Ardor could describe symbolically the conflicts that must have arisen in Monteverdi's mind in those years. Creative ardor attracted him to the group that had settled in the theater at San Cassiano, or to the opera houses which then began in 1639 to vie for the favor of the Venetian public. But the respect due his official position as *maestro di cappella* of the Most Serene Republic of Venice and the sacred orders he had entered upon a few years earlier induced him to be cautious—a cautiousness that appears more than justified and that is also evident in the operatic career of Girolamo Rovetta, Monteverdi's immediate successor as *maestro* in San Marco. However, the moment approached for the aged *maestro,* already over seventy years old, to abandon the reserve imposed upon him. He did this with calculated and prudent moves, leaving the first move in 1639 to a young *tenorista* of San Marco, Francesco Cavalli, and limiting himself in that year to having reprinted in Venice, without any changes, the libretto of *Arianna. Arianna,* whether opera or tragedy, was then performed in 1640, as appears in the libretto, slightly pruned in its choruses. Although it was more than thirty years old, it must have made the weight of Monteverdi's presence immediately felt with a wave of classicism that suddenly invaded the operatic theaters of Venice, supplanting the magical and mythological extravaganzas of the first productions.[13] Yet again Monteverdi's caution manifested itself in having *Il ritorno d'Ulisse in patria* presented by Manelli's troupe in Bologna before performing it in Venice. Only after these cautious feelers did Monteverdi "give in" to the pleas of influential persons and have *Ulisse* presented in Venice,[14] followed by *Le Nozze di Enea con Lavinia* and *L'incoronazione di Poppea,* both composed expressly for the Venetian stage.

Classicism does not suffice, however, to explain the singular appearance of Monteverdi's last opera. *L'incoronazione di Poppea* is so different from the two preceding, *Ulisse* and *Enea e Lavinia,* as well as from the earlier libretti by the fatuous Busenello—the verbose *Didone* and the insipid *Amori di Apollo e di Dafne*—that to explain it I would like to suggest a subtle, hidden relationship with an opera that was presented in Rome a year before the appearance of *Poppea* on the Venetian stage. The opera is *Il palazzo incantato di Atlante* by Monsignor Rospigliosi, set to music by Luigi Rossi, and it carried the theme of magic to its extreme consequences. One may suspect that its fundamental idea derived from Bernini because of the prologue referred to above in which the Magic of stagecraft wins out over her sisters Poetry, Music, and Painting in the choice of the theme to be treated. Ariosto provided the point of departure, so that the palace arising suddenly on stage by a double artifice is that in which the magician Atlante attempts to hold Ruggero. Pure magical artifice is the edifice, which in the end dissolves into nothing; pure illusion, or rather a pinwheel of illusions, is the plot, if one can speak of a plot—a carousel of separate episodes that vividly alternate heroics and pathos, coquetry and female devotion, jealousy and cynicism, anger and fear, culminating in dances of phantoms and in turbulent whirling sequences in which each character is in search of the object of his love or his hatred but, misled by the deception of magic, is near the object without recognizing it. It is a merry-go-round to which a Pirandellian moral would be suited, rather than the moral that was tediously tacked onto the prologue in homage to Barberini's piety. But the music, to which the climate of unreality gives free rein, takes advantage of this and expands in luxuriant variety into a kaleidoscope of recitatives and arias, of bass duets, soprano trills, and tenor laments.

What amazes us in *L'incoronazione di Poppea* is Monteverdi's enormous leap in respect to *Ulisse*, although the latter had preceded it by barely two years (of *Enea e Lavinia* only the libretto survives). Except for the appearance of the gods and the singing competition of the suitors, *Ulisse* tends to be a recitative opera. It ends with the triumph of love, but it is conjugal love, old and chaste. In Monteverdi's last opera sensual, torrid, overpowering love predominates. It induces Nero to repudiate Ottavia and suppress Seneca, to marry Poppea and proclaim her empress, in a plot of such vividness that it has been speculated, not unreasonably, that it might have been suggested to Monteverdi by similar immoderate passions witnessed at the Gonzaga court.[15] The nonliterary source of inspiration is even more likely if one considers that no attempt is made in the opera to justify or condemn the morality of the conduct of the principal characters. Like *Il palazzo incantato di Atlante*, *L'incoronazione* is a plot of characters blinded, in the former by magic, in the latter by love: the adolescent love of the page and the lady-in-waiting, Ottone's tormented love, Drusilla's love ready for sacrifice and abnegation, Octavia's disillusioned and mortified love, Nero's violent and choleric love, Poppea's ambitious love, or rather, opportunistic, sensual enticement. The moral, if there is one, is in Seneca's detachment in contemplating such vain desire and raving, almost making his own the motto of one of his predecessors in the history of opera, that of the unattended counselor in *La catena d'Adone:* "Reason loses where sensuality abounds."

But beyond good and bad, the ardor of amorous passion justifies the overflowing expansion of vocal melody. Just as *Il palazzo incantato di Atlante* is a reaction to the excessive dialogue and flat recitative of some earlier operas such as *San Bonifazio,* so too *L'incoronazione di Poppea* reacts against the excesses of verbal rhetoric that characterize *Didone* and to a certain extent *Il ritorno d'Ulisse* as well. In *Palazzo incantato,* however, the climate of unreality justifies the absurdity of "ariettas";

while in *L'incoronazione* Monteverdi's realism rejects (except in a few justified instances) the melodic set piece and lets the melody grow from the psychological "excitement" of the heart, from the ardor of passion that overflows the bonds of language. Luigi Rossi remains on the surface of his text and does not capture its irony, a difficult task; Monteverdi—with eyes open, to be sure, to the vanities of illusions and human passions—was able to identify with them, with a fire and vigor unextinguished either by the years in his heart or by the centuries in his music.

L'incoronazione is a study of characters dominated by passion, and this is what makes it the unique, isolated example of a true historical opera. But it is doubtful that contemporaries grasped its full significance, and the first to feel doubtful about it was the gallant and cynical Busenello, whose hand Monteverdi's driving force had forced. The earliest reflection is found in the first act of Cavalli's *Egisto,* which appeared right after *L'incoronazione* and derived from Monteverdi's model the spreading of the melodic wave that expresses loving ardor. But in *Egisto* the happy, singing lovers are convenient marionettes and almost spectators to the principal action; their only function is to fill the stage with their song. Monteverdi transfigured recitative into winged melody; in *Egisto* verisimilitude was maintained because the lovers *decide* to celebrate their happiness in ariettas and duets. Monteverdi's success was flawed once again by incomprehension of what he had really achieved.

17 ♣ Theater, Sets, and Music in Monteverdi's Operas

The Monteverdi operas that actually reached the stage were all performed, as is known, in Mantua in the period 1607–1608 and in Venice in the last years of Monteverdi's life. This essay attempts to reconsider those operas in light of the manner of performance and the usual theatrical practices at that time, rather than interpreting them through habits of mind acquired in more recent times.

The Mantuan performances fall within a phase of theatrical history that can be said to belong, allowing for a certain breadth of definition, to the Renaissance. *Orfeo* is an example of the tendency toward "perfecting" what the ancients had done, which had its most typical realization in Guarini's *Pastor fido*. *Arianna,* with its strict adherence to the canons of the three unities, and with its division into five episodes marked only by the choruses, aims at recreating the classical tragedy "all in music."

Arianna lends itself better than *Orfeo* to illustrating one of the principal characteristics of the performance technique of the day, namely, continuity of action on stage without interruption or intermission.[1] From the "disappearance of the great curtain that covered the stage" ("sparir della gran cortina che copriva il palco")[2] to the choruses and dances of the final episode (after which the "curtain" was not closed again) the stage always remained open, representing the sequence evening–night–morning–noon, compressed into two-and-a-half hours of performance time, with an effect of temporal perspective having some analogy to its spatial counterpart. During the performance, as well as for some time before and after, it must have been in fact impossible for most of the audience to leave their seats. But the drawbacks of this situation were less serious than those of the performance of Guarini's *Idropica* five days later; what with prologue, five recited acts, and an equal number of *intermedi* set to music (with verse by Chiabrera), the play lasted without interruption for five to six hours.[3] In spite of that, at every performance people crowded at the gate in greater numbers than the building could hold,[4] for a staged performance was a unique event for most, and a fairly infrequent one for the privileged few whose court affiliation offered easier access to such performances.

The first object of curiosity was the theater (a term then used to designate the place assigned to the audience), a magical attraction, and an architectural problem that had long been speculated on. Personally, I tend to give little credence to those traditions which affirm the existence of this or that permanent theater; most often what was involved were halls normally used for other purposes, but whose dimensions, shape, and easy access made them suitable when a performance was being organized. In many cases the same equipment was used over and over, and stored away when not in use. However, this equipment lent itself to variations and innovations with each new use, so that the theater appeared different each time, especially in its painted and molded decorations. The novelty was all the more remarkable when the occasion or the type of performance or some combination of circumstances required selection of a locale different from the usual; the task was then more challenging for the court architects, who had to study and implement from the beginning the division between theater and stage; this engaged the skill of all the artists and artisans who collaborated on decoration and performance, not to mention the literati whose responsibility it was to propose devices and allegories suitable to the circumstance.

It is not for me to judge the degree of permanence of the *scena vecchia* of the ducal palace of Mantua, which had been designed by Giovanbattista Bertani, gutted by fire in 1588, and refurbished about 1594.[5] None of the Monteverdi performances in Mantua that we know about took place in a permanent theater. For *Arianna* (May 28, 1608), for *L'idropica* (June 2), and for *Il ballo delle ingrate* (June 4), all performed for the nuptials of Francesco Gonzaga and the Infanta Margherita of Savoy, the court architect Antonio Maria Viani designed ad hoc, on one side of the Prato di Castello, a theater holding at least five thousand people.[6] Although contemporaries may have exaggerated the figures, their estimates suggest a theater with a seating area of wide half-circular gradins, probably topped by a gallery resting on the walls that encircled the Prato di Castello even then. Stage preparation and equipment were carried out with no less stateliness, and the theater machinery excited the admiration of one expert admitted to see it, the painter Federico Zuccaro; "more than three hundred men" operated the machines.[7]

Once admitted to the theater, the audience was able to observe the decoration of the stage front and the curtain, still closed, separating them from the theatrical world of make-believe in which they would soon be immersed. The following passage describes the start of the performance of *L'idropica*, which I prefer because it mentions a sounding of trumpets that could have been a repetition of the introductory toccata to *L'Orfeo*:

Once the candelabra were lit inside the theater, the *usual signal of the sounding of the trumpets* was given from the area inside the stage, and when it started to sound a third time, the great curtain covering the stage disappeared in the twinkle of an eye, with such speed that even as it was being raised there were few who perceived how it disappeared. So it was that with the sight of the stage revealed to the audience, one started to see . . .[8]

And so the description of the set continues. But here, to apply the account to *Arianna*, we must fill in with the few mentions of it that have been given us. The set in *Arianna* represented "a steep rock surrounded by waves which, in the part of the perspective farthest away, were always seen billowing with great beauty."[9] The importance of the view of the sea in the background is evident, to be related both to the motion of the waves and to the effects of the changing light on it—from twilight to night and then to day. Also Venere (Venus), Settimia Caccini, that is, was to emerge from the sea in the finale. But no less important for the overall architecture was "that part of the rock that bordered on the sea," a conspicuous central element, in relief and practicable, lending the scene the appearance of a sandy open space delimited on each end by rocky and leafy wings and in back by the "steep rock" at the sides of which two wide openings led to the sea. At the start of the performance, Apollo must have landed on the rock to recite the prologue, descending from the sky on a cloud; later on Arianna (Ariadne) must have climbed it to sing her famous lament, but I doubt that the triumphal chariot of Bacco (Bacchus) and Arianna rose there in the finale. The set must have had considerable width and height to allow for a harmonious composition of the final scene with Arianna and Bacco at the center proscenium, Venere rising from the sea, on a shell perhaps, on one side of the central rock, and Giove (Jove) appearing from above for the opening up of the sky—all this above dances of Bacco's soldiers that could even have taken place, classically, in the "orchestra."

The mention of dances in the orchestra is not suggested by the classicizing intentions that make *Arianna* the first real attempt to recreate a tragedy set to music. The semicircular space at the foot of the gradins was often used for seating princes and other notables, but the term "orchestra" that designated it could not fail to suggest its utilization for orchestral activity. Precise confirmation of this comes to us in the account of *Il ballo delle ingrate,* performed in the same theater a few days after *Arianna.*[10] Ten years later Aleotti made a U-shaped seating area in the Teatro Farnese of Parma, thus further expanding the "orchestra."[11]

No need to dwell on the performance of *Il Ballo delle ingrate,* which I treat, albeit briefly, elsewhere.[12] The performance of *Orfeo,* on the other hand, calls for a lengthier discussion. In this case the lack of an account is only partially compensated by the existence of the score and some other documents. To be discredited, first of all, is the myth that other performances preceded that of February 24, 1607, the last Saturday of carnival. This date is verified in a letter by Prince Francesco Gonzaga to his brother Ferdinando. "Tomorrow they'll be doing the sung fable in our academy" (dimani si farà la favola cantata nella nostra Accademia) writes the prince on February 23; but "our Academy" is the location for "doing," and the expression "sung fable" does not mean "previously sung." It is equivalent to "fable ... musically performed" (favola ... musicalmente rappresentata), as Monteverdi later says, or to a play "that will be singular, for all the interlocutors will speak musically," as the nobleman Carlo Magno writes, also on February 23.[13] On the other hand, the Accademia degli Invaghiti, founded in 1562 by Cesare Gonzaga, duke of Guastalla, did not always have an easy time after the death in 1582 of its founder, who had hosted it in his palace; nor did it have a permanent residence until 1610, when Vincenzo Gonzaga assigned it one in the ducal palace.[14] Consequently, the Accademia met in the home of its chief members, among whom could now be counted Vincenzo Gonzaga's two sons, who apparently had taken its future to heart.

Orfeo, then, was rehearsed and performed in the ducal palace with the participation of the singer Giovanni Gualberto Magli, who had arrived several days earlier from Florence. From the letter by Magno we know that it was not performed in "the usual scenic theater" (nel solito scenico teatro), but rather "in the hall of the apartment that Madam Most Serene of Ferrara had previously used" (nella sala del partimento che godeva Madama Ser.ma di Ferrara). Domenico de' Paoli's hypothesis appears to be correct that the place in question was the present-day Galleria dei Fiumi, called at that time, it seems, Sala Nuova.[15] Since the Sala degli Arcieri, which was part of Vincenzo Gonzaga's apartment, is excluded as a possibility, I cannot see a more suitable place in this part of the ducal palace. That is to say, a less unsuitable place: it seems to me in fact that Prince Francesco, along with the Ritenuto Accademico Invaghito (namely, Alessandrino Striggio, librettist of *Orfeo*) and Monteverdi, must have been counting on a more spacious locale, the "usual scenic theater" perhaps, a locale that was denied because the duke had already planned that there be "acted the comedy [a spoken play] ... with the customary magnificence," which did indeed happen two days before the performance of *Orfeo*.[16] The opening sentence of the dedication of the score to Francesco Gonzaga, which would otherwise sound improper, is thus explained: "The fable of Orpheus which was previously musically performed on a *narrow* stage (sopra *angusta* scena) by the Accademia degli Invaghiti under the patronage of V.A. ..." The *angustia* (narrowness) of the place led Magno to doubt whether he would be let in there and was also the reason why a repeat performance of *Orfeo* was given (March 1) "with the presence of all the ladies of this city," who apparently had had to be excluded from the first performance.

In the Sala dei Fiumi, some thirty meters long but less than seven meters wide, it must have been impossible to place musicians and instruments at the sides of the stage, where they would have been hidden by the proscenium and the wings and arranged so as to "see the stage performers' faces so that, better hearing each other, they may proceed together"; the instruments had then to be arranged partly behind the stage and partly in front of it, and it is likely that their number was reduced owing to lack of space.[17] The placement in front of the stage, behind a partition (which later became standard), was aided by the fact that the floor of the stage had to be raised to a man's height and raked up toward the back, so that the audience could view the action from the level of the hall. Everything, in a word, bespeaks a modest, makeshift solution not conforming to the ambitions of the initial plan; if this hypothesis is correct, it could also aid in resolving one of the most controversial problems of *Orfeo*, that of the double finale. I myself had believed that the bacchic finale (sometimes called "tragic") belonged to the original plan and was rejected in favor of the apparition of Apollo as a concession to the taste for stage miracles.[18] The opposite now appears more likely to me: that the *deus ex machina* and the apotheosis of Orpheus were part of the original plan, later modified because the place available for the performance did not allow the use of theater machinery. Various elements bear me out in this hypothesis: the chariot of the sun, besides appearing in a renowned fresco of the Palazzo del Te attributed to Giulio Romano, is found on the ceiling (more or less contemporary with the performance of *Orfeo*) of the Galleria degli

Specchi; the two moralizing strophes of the final chorus correspond to the style of the choral admonitions of the other acts better than the exultation of the bacchantes; finally, the appearance of Apollo befits the heraldic device of the Invaghiti, an eagle gazing at the sun with the motto *Nil pulcherius*. The Apollo finale was restored by Monteverdi when, with the printing of the score, his opera was no longer presented "on a narrow stage" but "in the great theater of the universe."

The devices of the Invaghiti and Gonzaga coats-of-arms must have appeared in the decoration of the proscenium (if there was one) and of the curtain. When the curtain disappeared (either rising up or falling down) at the third blare of the "toccata" of trumpets, the prologue was probably sung by Musica (with artistic devices similar to those described in 1608 for *Dafne*)[19] on the set prepared for act I. To help us picture it, the only data available are offered by two verses of the last strophe of the prologue:

> ... non si muova augellin fra queste piante,
> nè s'oda in queste rive onda sonante ...

> ... let no little bird move among these trees,
> nor a resounding wave be heard on these shores.

In *Orfeo* unity of place is decidedly done away with; its authors had perhaps counted on different settings for each act, but again they had to settle for an expedient solution, because the 1607 libretto indicates changes only at the end of acts II and IV. The settings for the first two acts were supposed to have been sylvan: the first more open, representing perhaps a meadow along the bank of a stream; the second more like the type suggested by Serlio's *scena satiresca*. Whichever setting was selected for both acts, we may apply to it the description given by Michelangelo Buonarroti the younger, of the pastoral setting of *Euridice*: the set "showed quite beautiful woods, both in relief and painted, arranged with a lovely design, and because of the lights well set out, [the woods] full of light as by day"[20]—wings representing trees, therefore, and an analogous backdrop. The setting (or settings) of the two successive acts must have had rocky wings ("horrid boulders ... and fearful, that seemed real, upon which leafless stumps and pale grasses appeared"); in act III Charon's boat (mobile and practicable) was supposed to be seen on the river Styx, with the opposite bank glowing in the distance. For act IV the background was to be framed by two new rocky wings ("and there, further on the inside, through a break in a great cliff one could make out the fiery city of

Dis . . . the surrounding air blazing with a copper-like color"), and it would not have been difficult to have Plutone (Pluto) and Proserpina rise on their thrones from trap doors. For act V the setting must have been another woody one, illuminated at first by twilight and then either by the glowing torches of the Bacchantes or by the radiance of Apollo.

A change of setting is an event we normally think of as taking place during an intermission, behind a closed curtain; at the time of *Orfeo*, though, it was carried out in full view of the audience, without interrupting the continuity of the performance. In *Orfeo*, however, the changes of setting do interrupt, or at least obscure, the continuity of the action, and by introducing a patent lack of verisimilitude into the supposed verisimilitude of the performance, they allow a further compression of temporal values, along with what was mentioned earlier. Even between the first two acts, which I had earlier considered as a continuous sequence performed with just one setting, closer observation reveals a break in continuity. The action of act I concludes with the invitation of a shepherd, "Dunque al tempio ciascun rivolga i passi" (so to the temple let each one turn his steps), with which it would be inappropriate for Orpheus not to comply; he therefore exits from the stage with the others, and we do not know how much time has passed when he returns to greet the "care selve e piagge amate" (dear woods and beloved shores). Furthermore, we soon learn that while he is on stage singing, Eurydice is no longer at the temple but "in un fiorito prato" (in a flowery meadow) gathering flowers. This effect of compression of time had earlier been assigned to the *intermedi,* and it is as *intermedi* that we must consider the choral admonishments in the first four acts of *Orfeo*, being followed by the spectacle of the change of setting in full view. It would please me to think of the choruses as not apparent, which would be particularly suitable for the choruses of "spirits" in acts III and IV; but opposed to that interpretation is the stage direction for the chorus in act II: "Duoi pastori al suono del organo di legno, et un chittarone" (two shepherds to the sound of organ with wood pipes and a chittarone). However, each chorus is preceded and followed by instrumental excerpts designed to provide time—the excerpts preceding the chorus, time for the exit of the main characters and their followers; those following, time for the changing of settings and the entrance of the characters for the new act.[21]

The continuity of the performance is documented by the fact that the instrumental excerpts at the end of each act actually share in the ethos of the following act. The sinfonia at the end of act I is actually the introductory ritornello of Orpheus' first song in act II. The sinfonia at the end of act

II must have required cornetts, trombones, and regals, to which was attributed a nocturnal subterranean ethos; it is repeated in the course of act III and at the end of it, signifying the continuation of the same ethos in act IV as well. At the end of this act we find not one but two instrumental excerpts: a "sinfonia a 7" which concludes the chorus "È la virtute un raggio," and a repetition of the ritornello of the prologue, which symbolizes communion or identity between Music and Orpheus (another "orphic" symbol perhaps is the repetition of the sinfonia that frames the great aria of Orpheus, "Possente spirito," at the moment of Apollo's appearance).[22] Technically, the scene changes in full view must have been accomplished by means of sliding wooden frameworks (*telari*), moved forward or backward according to need (I evidently opt for the *scena ductilis*). That tells us nothing about taste in the staging; we can only hope that it answered the symmetries of the score, its symbolic references, and the strophic classicism of a good number of the arias with a visual realization marked by "broad, serene, solemn expressions, nourished by a sound and flowing calm," as stated in a recent opinion on the architectural activities of the probable author of the Mantuan scene paintings of 1607 and 1608, the "prefetto alle fabbriche" Antonio Maria Viani.[23]

In the libretto to *Arianna* reprinted in Venezia in 1639 by Andrea Salvadori (not one of the usual printers of opera librettos), the text, true to the one printed in Mantua and Florence in 1608, includes the prologue that had been written for Charles Emmanuel of Savoy. In this purely literary publication I see one of the cautious, though not too concealed, moves by which Monteverdi was preparing to return to opera without showing himself too openly anxious about it, out of respect for his ecclesiastic status and his office of *maestro di cappella* of the Most Serene Republic of Venice. During the following carnival, in 1640, *Arianna*— which I would say now belonged to the public—was chosen for the conversion to opera of the third Venetian theater, the San Moisè. Many changes had taken place since the time of the Mantuan performance in the manner of conceiving an "opera to be performed in music" (opera da rappresentarsi in musica; the term itself is indicative of change) as well as in theatrical plot and action in general. But the fame of *Arianna* and of its author allowed it to be revived with no other changes than a slight alteration in the text of the prologue (to adapt it to the Doge Francesco Erizzo) and cuts in the choral passages, to which the formal function of distinguishing the episodes was once again entrusted.[24]

Little is known about the Teatro Giustinian in San Moisè, as is the case for most seventeenth-century Venetian theaters. It made its start as a theater for spoken plays; "its hall was on the small side, but elegant," says G. Salvioli (alias L. N. Galvani).[25] But the "Scherzo avanti il Prologo" of *Sidonio e Dorisbe* (performed there in 1642) speaks of a "narrow and poorly decorated room" and implies that it was used as a meeting place. In the same "Scherzo," Tempo (Time), announcing the performance of the opera, makes a point of taking a place near some ladies, whose gambling he has interrupted, to protect them from any annoyance by indiscreet male members of the audience.[26] There were no boxes, therefore, but gradins (probably running into a gallery at the top) and orchestra; when in 1688 two tiers of boxes were created, the total capacity was barely eight hundred seats.[27] The stage also must have been narrow and inadequately equipped. In fact, after *Arianna,* which did not require set changes or *intermedi,* Ferrari's *Pastor regio* and *Ninfa avara,* both pastorales having few characters and a simple plot, were performed at the San Moisè. Along with them was performed *Sidonio e Dorisbe,* from whose cast divine characters are entirely banned. Slightly more involved is *Amore innamorato* (1642), but there are indications that the lack of machinery was remedied by other means. The stage may have been flanked by two platforms, one of which could accommodate the orchestra, the other as a complement to the stage. The libretto of *La Ninfa avara* informs us: "At the end of the second act as *intermedio,* a squad of nymphs with ingenious measures showed the stars dancing *from a stage.* There then appeared [on the main stage?] the feigned sight of the city of Carthage . . . work of my most ingenious Sir, Gasparo Beccari."[28]

Another move by Monteverdi was, if my conjectures are correct, to compose *Il ritorno d'Ulisse in patria* to be performed in Bologna by the Ferrari and Manelli company in the late autumn of 1639 (even though the sonnets celebrating its performance and that of *Delia* by Manelli were published in 1640). The reserve that Monteverdi showed in Venice, avoiding too close an association with both foreign musicians (he must have encouraged them to begin opera performances) and local ones who had begun to emulate them in 1639 (largely singers of San Marco) did not rule out his composing an opera to be performed in another city and without his direct participation. Wolfgang Osthoff has shown that pressure was brought to bear on Monteverdi to allow *Il ritorno* to be performed in Venice.[29] But the pressure indicates that the opera had been composed to be performed elsewhere; otherwise, composing it would have been to no purpose. *Il ritorno* finally did come to be performed in Venice during the carnival of 1640 and repeated in the carnival of the following year. I am also of the (minority) opinion that the theater was the San Giovanni e Paolo, where performances were given of *Le nozze di Enea in Lavinia* in 1641 and of *La coronatione di Poppea* in 1643 (respective titles of the scenarios). Opinion wavers between the San Giovanni e Paolo and the San Cassiano (with the second predominating);[30] but certain proof is lacking, and it seems to me that Monteverdi always tended to keep those belonging to his chapel—that is, Cavalli and his group—at a distance. It could be that they were allowed only to repeat the Bolognese performance of *Il ritorno* in Venice in 1641.[31]

The Teatro San Giovanni e Paolo, owned by the Grimani family, created or readapted for the opera in 1639, was the most sumptuous of the early Venetian opera houses. A drawing (not prior to 1678; see Fig. 17.1) represents it with a long U-shaped floor plan and five tiers of boxes, but opinions differ as to whether this was the original arrangement or a later modification.[32] It seems impossible for the theater to have had five tiers of boxes in 1639, considering that accounts relating to the Teatro Nuovissimo, built in 1641 to vie in magnificence with the San Giovanni e Paolo, speak above all of the "orchestra," to the point of making it synonymous with the audience, or at least with that part of the audience that counted most.[33] The idea of *palchetti* (diminutive of *palchi,* or boxes) had already been applied in temporary theaters for tournaments or ballets on horseback;[34] some *palchetti,* reserved for persons of authority or those having a part in the management of the theater, may have existed in Venetian theaters before 1637.[35] But the custom by which the *palchetti* became a privileged and sought-after place (even though in most cases they allowed a poorer visual field than the seats in the "orchestra" or parterre) must have become established later, in the course of, rather than at the beginning of, the practice of opera performances with admission fees. The aspiration to emulate the magnificence of court spectacles could be realized in public theaters because the installations and equipment were permanent, and above all because a performance could be and actually was repeated several times as long as it attracted a paying public. Even in the least comfortable of conditions, gaining admission to the unique event of a court spectacle had been an honor; the repeated public opera performances, on the other hand, relieved the more aristocratic members of the audience of the inconvenient obligation of sitting through the performance from beginning to end. Box holders could now have at their disposal reserved seats with easy accessibility, enabling them to come and go as they pleased. The rage for boxes soon followed, though not immediately.

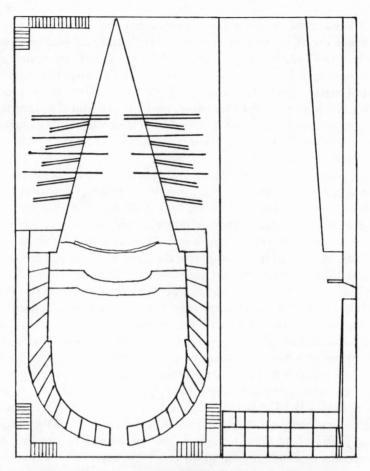

Fig. 17.1   Plan and vertical section of the theater at San Giovanni e Paolo, after a drawing by Tommaso Bezzi. (London, Soane Museum.) In the plan (*left*), from the top: stage with grooves for backdrops and wings; pit for orchestra; corridor in front of parterre; parterre delimited by U-shaped tier of boxes. In the vertical section (*right*), from the top: sloping floor of stage; pit for orchestra hidden by wall; corridor; slightly sloping floor of parterre; profile of five tiers of boxes.

In my opinion, therefore, the San Giovanni e Paolo and the Nuovissimo theaters initially had an "orchestra" with seats for the more select audience and, all around, two or three galleries with standing room, out of which a few boxes (in the proscenium or toward the center of the second gallery, at stage level) may have been created for the specially privileged few. In time the demand for more boxes must have reversed the situation of the San Giovanni e Paolo (the Nuovissimo was destroyed), requiring the conversion of the galleries into tiers of boxes and then the addition of new tiers. But the placement of the orchestra (in the modern sense), which in the drawing is behind a high partition at the foot of the stage (see Fig. 17.1) and is therefore invisible from the "orchestra" (in the classical sense), corresponds to the idea that the "orchestra" was the privileged location in the beginning (while the instruments must have been visible from the second tier of boxes on up).

The most interesting aspect of the drawing, if it indeed reflects the conditions of the San Giovanni e Paolo in 1639, is the ample development of the stage with respect to the hall. Since Venice did not have a court comparable to those of Florence or Mantua or of the Barberini family, the idea of an *opera regia* (royal opera)[36] was the passport for introducing performances in music. The librettos for *Andromeda* and *La maga fulminata* celebrated the beauty of the sets, the ingeniousness of the machines, the innovativeness of the dances, and the richness of the costumes; in addition, the *Maga* libretto praises the author, Ferrari, "who through his efforts, and with the aid of just five fellow musicians, with an expenditure no greater than two thousand scudi, has succeeded in enrapturing the hearts of the listeners through the *royal* performance of that [opera]; *such endeavors cost princes countless sums of money.*"[37] Concerning *Delia,* the first opera performed at the San Giovanni e Paolo, the author explains that it had been conceived "to pay tribute to a great prince, at whose nuptials I thought to present it . . . And it is presented now . . . that it has found a patron of such esteem, such worthy players and such fine machines in the noteworthy theater of the most illustrious Signor Gio. Grimani, *which astonishingly came into being in a few days* for the delight of a long era." The rapidity of construction (repeated by the Nuovissimo in 1641) can be explained if the main effort was at first concentrated on the arrangement and equipment of the stage. The drawing reveals nothing about machines, trap doors, or lights, except to indicate that there was ample room for them, including the space below the stage floor; what is clear, on the other hand, is the layout of grooves for sliding the backdrops and wings (or other stage components), the grooves for the backdrops being parallel to the proscenium and placed at four distances from it, and the five sets of grooves for the wings running slightly slantwise.

The priority given to the problems of the stage is in line with the characteristic features of Venetian opera presentations: a grandiose and composite spectacle in which the pathos of early recitative has been largely overtaken by the pursuit of the *marvelous* in the form of both visual wonder, with aspects derived from the cinquecento *intermedi,* and, to a slightly lesser extent, in the form of singing virtuosity. The tangled and disconnected sequences of Ferrari's first libretto can thus be explained, along with the many episodes and secondary characters that complicate the simple tale of Cavalli's first opera (which, however, gave form, voice, and playing ability to Chiron the centaur, and allowed visualization of the judgment of Paris, with the beauty contest of the three goddesses). With *Il ritorno d'Ulisse,* which made its appearance while Manelli was still immersed in mythology with *Adone,* and Busenello was at play with *Gli amori di Apollo, e di Dafne,* Monteverdi was establishing a criterion, albeit a relative one, of historicity. The fact that the history is pseudohistory is of little importance, since what is evident is Monteverdi's effort to characterize its human characters with notes of humanity and to interpret their psychological processes; on the other hand, Robert Haas has indicated how closely the libretto of *Il ritorno* follows the Homeric model. The same may be said for *Le nozze di Enea in Lavinia* with regard to the Vergilian text. The example of *Il ritorno* was imitated in the season immediately following, in 1641, by Busenello's *Didone,* which has a verbose but intensely dramatic first act, a ridiculous second act, and an absurd third one. A further imitation was Giulio Strozzi's *La finta pazza,* slightly ironic in flavor. As to Monteverdi's influence on his librettists, Badoaro explicitly admits its impact in his verbose prefaces; I have not as yet been able to ascertain how well founded may be the doubts that have recently arisen in connection with *L'incoronazione di Poppea,* but to confirm the efficacy of Monteverdi's role, it seems to me that a quick comparison suffices between *Il ritorno* and *Didone,* between *Le nozze* and *Il pio Enea* by Ascanio Pio di Savoia, or even between *L'incoronazione* and all the other Busenello librettos.

Nearly all the early Venetian operas and many of the later ones generously availed themselves of divine intervention, not only for the opportunity for spectacular events (rivaled only by the opportunity provided by magic scenes), but also because the divinities made possible a vocal floridity rarely granted to human characters and then only under specific conditions and restrictions. Divine characters also appear in the two Monteverdi operas, but their part in the action is authenticated by the sources and therefore is, in a certain sense, historical; it is not to be forgotten, however, that Tasso, a revered model for Monteverdi, had not hesitated to introduce divine personages in an epic poem that made pretenses to historicity. Moreover, it should be noted that Monteverdi almost completely abolishes the characterization of divine personages on a different vocal plane from human characters. True to his madrigalistic training, he does not hesitate to let even the human characters ascend to the most effusive singing wherever an image or sentiment so suggests (it is actually an archaism that places him in the vanguard); if his human characters express themselves in recitative accents more often than his divine ones, it is because the expressive richness of *stile recitativo* (once again an archaism) better lends itself to more intense emotions. As to the libretto for *Le nozze di Enea,* one cannot fail to notice that it must have lent itself to the manner of *stile concitato* to a greater extent than did the libretto for *Il ritorno.*

I am obliged to pass over the scenographic and musical aspects of *Il ritorno* in order to devote at least a few paragraphs to the *Opera Reggia Intitolata La Coronatione di Poppea,* which was performed at Teatro San Giovanni e Paolo during the carnival season of 1643 (including the last days of 1642). The sources for the libretto this time are truly historical, as is the background of imperial Rome (which the Roman *Sant' Alessio* had already made use of ten years earlier). The authors once more did not hesitate to introduce divine characters, but in moderation and in such a way as to stress the meaning of the drama, which is indeed the triumph of Love, but also to underline the higher values of virtue and wisdom. Love's victory is, historically as well, an unstable and temporary victory, and perhaps Monteverdi had a second drama in mind to show its transitory nature.[38] This fits in with another interpretation I have already given: that *L'incoronazione* shows us a humanity blinded by the madness of love, paralleling the portrayal in the contemporary *Palazzo incantato di Atlante,* where the characters are ensnared in magical illusion.[39]

As Badoaro delighted in saying, *Il ritorno d'Ulisse* and *Le nozze d'Enea* were "tragedies with a happy ending" in five acts. The scenario for *Le nozze* describes choruses and ballets that divided the acts; for *Il ritorno,* similar documented testimony is lacking, so that except for a chorus and a dance of naiads after act I (scene 10 of the score), we are left guessing as to what still-fresh ingenuity the Venetian choreographers may have devised. The scenario for *La coronatione* does show that, whatever the intentions of the none too malleable Busenello, the opera was divided into three acts. It does not say, however, just how the audience was informed of the break between one act and another—there is no indication of *intermedi.* It is possible that Monteverdi, demanding and of difficult disposition himself, decided to rebel against the usual grotesque, inopportune additions, yet we have no hint of what may have replaced them. Not choruses, because there is no indication of them, and they were no longer used, even in tragedy;[40] not symphonies, because Monteverdi had become impatient with instrumental pieces that only served to allow time for the action (see the "symphonies" of just one repeated chord in *Il ritorno,* given that he wrote them himself); furthermore, the new way of developing the action as a series of sudden upheavals and contrasts excluded the possibility of symphonies that announced the ethos of the new act, as in *Orfeo.* Therefore, either the task of filling the gap was left to the performers (but their options would be indicated in the scenario), or the curtain was closed and there was singing behind the stage.[41]

The scenario does not refer to the sets by Giovanni Burnacini,[42] but it does at least indicate where there were changes and what places were each time represented. It appears to me that, not having at his disposal the precision machinery devised by Giacomo Torelli for the Nuovissimo, where sets changes took place "turning all the parts around in one swift motion," the scenographer must have found it expedient to alternate some fairly shallow generic sets with others that utilized the full depth of the stage and corresponded to more specific needs. The sequence is the following: "Pallazzo di Poppea" (act I, scenes 1–4), "Città di Roma" (act I, scenes 5–13), "Villa di Seneca" (act II, scenes 1–3), "Città di Roma" (act II, scenes 4–11), "Giardino di Poppea" (act II, scenes 12–14), "Città di Roma" (act III, scenes 1–7), "Reggia di Nerone" (act III, scene 8; the scene numbers are those in *Tutte le Opere,* vol. 13). The city of Rome scene is generic; it was probably a backdrop with a perspective of temples or triumphal arches, placed on the first or second pair of grooves parallel to the proscenium. Behind it the components of the other sets could be changed without having to rush, since the longer sequences of action took place on the generic set. There remains to be examined the problem of the prologue, for which the scenario gives no indication; it seems that the words immediately following "Change of set to the palace of Poppea" must be an error, for in most cases the prologue was performed on the opening set, which even in this case was more suitable for the machine appearances of Fortune, Virtue, and Love than just any backdrop.

Only Minerva's appearance takes place on the generic set. Mercury's flying descent and reascent occur in Seneca's villa; Love appears in Poppea's garden; and the final appearance of Venus, Love, and "Amorini" (putti) in Nero's royal palace. For the first scene, the exterior of Poppea's palace, we have to imagine a façade with a portico, seen from the front and flanked by two streets, one of which must have served as the entrance and exit for Otho, while two soldiers slept, leaning against the other corner; Poppea and Nero must have sung their farewells standing on one or two central steps leading down from the portico to the "street." To visualize the other scenes we can make use of analogous sets conceived by Giacomo Torelli for the Nuovissimo between 1641 and 1644.[43] For Seneca's villa, the villa in *Deidamia* (act I, scene 7)—which perhaps repeats a scene from *La finta pazza*—can be of help to us (see Fig. 17.2); for Poppea's garden, the *dilettoso giardino* from *Bellerofonte* (see Fig. 17.3) may be pictured with a central pavilion, under which Poppea must have lain down to sleep. For Nero's imperial palace we can make use of the *tempio di Bacco* in *La Venere gelosa* (act I, scenes 7–8), replacing the round small temple with a marble baldachin and steps leading up to a throne. But what costumes

Fig. 17.2   Stage setting by Giacomo Torelli for *La Deidamia*, act I, scene 7. (Courtesy of the Fondazione Giorgio Cini.)

Fig. 17.3   Stage setting by Giacomo Torelli for *Il Bellerofonte*, act III, scenes 4–
10. (Courtesy of the Fondazione Giorgio Cini.)

might the figures of Poppea crowned and Nero adoring have been draped
in, as they stood below the rejoicing winged Amorini?

In conclusion, I do not wish to suggest impossible scenic reconstructions
nor generalize on the manner of performance of other operas contemporary to those staged in Mantua and Venice during the first and fifth decades
of the Seicento. It is enough to hope that my attempt at ideal reconstruction may be a help to others, even those in partial disagreement, in order to
better understand the conditions in which Monteverdi's theatrical activity
took place.

18 ⊱ Monteverdi's Poetic Choices

T o make up for the lack of background description of Monteverdi in his youth, we find some help in the printing of the composer's *Sacrae Cantiunculae*. One clue is to be found in the diminutive used in the title ("Claudini Montisviridi") and repeated in the dedication ("Claudinus Monsviridus"), an ostentation of that bit of Latin which could not have just been the work of a fifteen-year-old boy. Another indication is the disproportion between the exiguousness of the subject matter—little more than counterpoint exercises—and the evident affectation of the printing, which must have been paid for by someone, just as someone must have had to see to the printing expenses for *Madrigali spirituali* (1583) and *Canzonette* (1584). What emerges is the picture of a lad made too serious and slightly too conscious of his own qualities by a vocal cluster of relations, friends, even benefactors perhaps, who already were flattering him with the prospects of a brilliant musical career. The fact that the future did confirm their hopes does not negate that their ambitions were, for the time being at least, premature. Such concerned interest must have been judged inopportune by no other than the man entrusted with the task of guiding and developing the talents of the young learner. The fact is that while Monteverdi never failed to proclaim himself a pupil of Marco Antonio Ingegneri as long as the master was alive (and therefore even in the 1587 and 1590 books of madrigals), he never received in exchange that sign of approval that a teacher used to give a promising pupil, namely, including some composition by the pupil in one of his own publications.[1]

So resolute and precocious an orientation toward a musical career, it seems, may have been the cause of a certain deficiency in Monteverdi's literary education, which he must have later regretted when it came to replying to the criticism leveled at him by Giovanni Maria Artusi. What is certain is that the treatise on *seconda pratica*, said by Monteverdi to be ready and only waiting to be revised in 1605, was never published—neither at the time nor when he thought the matter over again in 1633, twenty years after the death of his opponent.[2] We need not speak of university studies: any university curriculum, whether directed toward theological studies and an ecclesiastical career or toward a legal or medical profession, would have represented an unnecessary expenditure of time and energy for a young musician. It was more suitable to concentrate one's efforts, as did Monteverdi, on the practice of performance and the study of composition, so as to acquire a name in each of them. But even in Monteverdi's chosen path there could have been, and perhaps there was not, an effort to methodically develop that first elementary foundation of culture that came to him from his family environment (he was the son of a distinguished Cremona physician) and from the studies of Latin grammar that had to be imparted, even in the Cathedral of Cremona, to the *pueri cantores* along with their musical studies. Monteverdi's letters, so often notable for the acumen of their concepts and for what they reveal about the personality of the writer, are decidedly similar to spoken expression. This does not mean that Monteverdi was uncultured. The way in which he handled the texts chosen for his compositions often gives proof of uncommon penetration of their literary values and, what is more, his poetic choices indicate in each instance decided tastes and tend, more than the compositions of any other musician of his day, to reflect the phases and moods of current poetic production. But his is an episodic culture, irregular, nourished by an unquestionably keen intelligence, by the contacts he had in every phase of his life with persons of a high intellectual and cultural level, and probably by the constant habit of reading and reflection.

It is understandable that this clearness of orientation is not yet present in Monteverdi's initial phase, both because it takes place in a more provincial milieu and because the young musician's early choices must have been determined by musical motivations and suggestions before literary ones. Naturally enough, the texts of *Canzonette a tre voci* (1584) all remain anonymous, given the genre's lack of literary pretensions; all that can be said, despite the fact that the collection is arranged as a mini-*canzoniere*, with a musical dedication (*Qual si può dir*, which embroiders on the name of the person to whom it is dedicated) and an envoi, is that more than half the texts are gathered from other collections of the same type and especially from *Canzonette ... Libro Primo a quattro voci* (Venice,

1581) by Orazio Vecchi.[3] Much more serious is that after close to a century of Monteverdi research, twelve out of nineteen of the texts in *Madrigali a cinque voci ... Libro Primo* (1587) remain anonymous.

Even for these texts musical precedents can be traced. Marenzio had already used the texts of *Ardo sì, ma non t'amo* (Guarini), *Questa ordì'l laccio* (G. B. Strozzi), and *A che tormi il ben mio.*[4] *Ch'ami la vita mia* and *Tra mille fiamme* appear in *De Floridi Virtuosi d'Italia ... Libro Primo* (Venice, 1583), with music by Lelio Bertani and Orazio Vecchi, respectively. *Baci soavi e cari* (Guarini)[5] and, once again, *A che tormi il ben mio* are found in the second and third volumes of the same series (Venice, 1585 and 1586) with music by Paolo Masnelli. *La vaga pastorella* appears in *Secondo Libro di Madrigali A quattro voci* (Venice, 1555) by Vincenzo Ruffo and, twelve years later, as a dialogue in *Primo Libro de Madrigali a sei voci* by Teodoro Riccio. With the exception of Marenzio, the composers from whom Monteverdi could obtain his texts all belonged to the Lombardo-Veneto circle centered around Brescia and Verona: Vincenzo Ruffo, who was Veronese and present in Verona from 1578 to 1580; Riccio, from Brescia and for a time *maestro di cappella* of that city; Masnelli, Veronese and organist first to the Bevilacqua counts and then to Guglielmo Gonzaga, later returning to Verona as organist of the Duomo and of the Accademia Filarmonica; Orazio Vecchi, present in Brescia in 1577 and then *maestro di cappella* of Salò, whose above-mentioned *Canzonette* are dedicated to Count Mario Bevilacqua of Verona; Bertani, *maestro di cappella* of Brescia.

Also from Verona was Ingegnieri, whose texts, however, Monteverdi respectfully avoided repeating. Exceptions are *Ardo sì, ma non t'amo* (Guarini) and *Ardi e gela a tua voglia* (Tasso), which Ingegnieri composed almost contemporaneously with his pupil and published in his *Quinto Libro de Madrigali a cinque voci* (Venice, 1583; dedicated to the members of the Accademia Filarmonica). The texts, in this case, were quite well known, having already been used by Vecchi in *Madrigali a sei voci Libro Primo* (Venice, 1583) and by Masnelli in *Primo Libro de Madrigali a cinque voci* (Venice, 1586). Marenzio limited himself to using just the first text,[6] which had served, however, as the given theme set to music by twenty-eight different composers in the collection *Sdegnosi Ardori* (Munich, 1585).

On the whole there are few texts that Monteverdi may have gotten from composers known to him and nearby; mostly he either must have drawn on some local poet or made use of one of the numerous collections of verse then in circulation. One such collection, *Ghilranda* [sic] *dell'Aurora*

(Venice, 1608) appeared too late for Monteverdi to have used it, but it does enable us to identify Alberto Parma as author of the text *Filli cara ed amata;* it also contains, among many others, texts by Tasso, Guarini, Chiabrera, Marino and, among the minor authors to whom Monteverdi paid fleeting attention, Filippo Alberti, Girolamo Casoni, Livio Celiano, and G. B. Strozzi. Finally there appears as poet Count Marco Verità, Veronese, who could have been the author of several of the anonymous texts of *Libro Primo,* which is dedicated to him.[7] *Fumia la pastorella,* the only madrigal of *Libro Primo* in three parts, is by Antonio Allegretti, a Florentine living in Rome during the first part of the sixteenth century and a friend of Caro; Monteverdi could have taken it from the collection by Dionigi Atanagi, *De le Rime di Diversi Nobili Poeti Toscani . . . Libro Primo* (Venice, 1565), which also contains *Questa ordì il laccio* by Strozzi, but both texts are found in a great many other collections. Monteverdi used the Allegretti text in such a way that the second part is a madrigal (or, if we prefer, an aria) by Fumia within the madrigal by Monteverdi; from Atanagi's index of the collection one learns that Fumia was a certain Neapolitan gentlewoman, Madonna Eufemia, of whom a *canzone,* also by Allegretti, "praises the masterly and utterly sweet way of singing and playing"; Fumia was, then, in a sense a precursor of Adriana Basile, whom Monteverdi later met in Mantua, as, in another sense (for the order of narration-singing-narration), Allegretti's text was a precursor of the *Lamento della Ninfa* in Monteverdi's *Ottavo Libro.*

Always improperly quoted as *Ch'io ami la mia vita,* the first madrigal of *Libro Primo* has some typically Monteverdian features, yet I fail to see it as being "of almost programmatic significance, chosen to indicate the artistic tendency, the stylistic program of the entire book" or that "in every feature it shows the powerful influences of the *canzonetta.*"[8] It begins with three voices as a *canzonetta,* whispering, in something between a trembling and joking manner, the name of the woman for whom it had deserved the prime position in the collection. It goes:

> Ch'ami la vita mia, nel tuo bel nome
> par che si legga ognora . . .

> That you love my life, it seems,
> can always be read in your beautiful name . . .

However, it seems that it ought to read: "Camilla, vita mia . . ." ("Camilla, my life . . ."). Already by the third line, "Ma tu voi pur ch'io mora" ("But you want me to die"), the intentional levity of the opening gives way to a different melodic style, and when the play on the name is repeated in the last line ("Ch'ami la morte e non la vita mia"), the secret (but not too secret) name is brought into focus by a sudden change in vocal orchestration, by the rests (*sospiri*) framing it, and by the repetition.[9] On the whole, the overused contrast between life and death, between happiness and disappointment in love (whether of the twenty-year-old Monteverdi or of Count Verità), rendered with youthful carefreeness, succeeds in having an *aria* without strictly adhering to the model of the *canzonetta*. To place the discussion on a more general plane, it seems to me that the association of melodic spontaneity (*aria*) and the language of polyphony was a widespread aspiration of the time and not a personal goal of Monteverdi's, and that the vogue of the *canzonetta* was not a cause but a symptom, no more important, for instance, than the rich harvest of *madrigali ariosi*.[10] *Libro Primo* offers numerous other samples of arioso quality: for example, the insistence on the impassioned initial gesture of *A che tormi il ben mio,* or the near monody of *Baci soavi e cari.* This does not mean that Monteverdi does not try to associate more varied elements of polyphonism with melodic spontaneity: the rhythmic excitement and the unusual final cadence of *Amor, per tua mercè,* the changing harmonic colors of *Poi che nel mio dolore,* the play of contrasts and the final jubilation of *Fumia la pastorella,* the *legature* (ties) of *Questa ordì 'l laccio,* and even an innocent, expressive madrigalian punning, which in *Se per havervi, hoimé* assigns an interval of a semitone—that is, a *mi–fa*—to the first two syllables of the passage "mi fa di duol morire."[11]

Among the short arioso pieces, evidently aiming at nothing more than an easy immediate success,[12] only the last three texts appear to be more ambitious choices—these are the Guarini text entitled *Foco d'amore,* and the *Risposta* and *Controrisposta* by Tasso, all *rime aspre* (harsh rhymes), which bound the composer to restrain the natural flowing of the *aria,* while a certain display of polyphonic skill was imposed on him to meet the comparison with so many other composers who had already attempted the same texts. To this Monteverdi also added a certain attention to thematic unification, even though the three madrigals were not expressly designated as "parts" of a single composition. Despite all that, the first encounter with Tasso remains a chance one, generated as it was by the sudden vogue of that imaginary poetic context with Guarini; it does not have the programmatic value and significance that the presence of Tasso's texts will assume in the *Secondo Libro* of 1590.

In the preceding decade, numerous other musicians had started to exploit the poetic mine of Tasso's *Rime;*[13] it is rare, however, to find assembled in one collection so many madrigals as in Monteverdi's *Se-*

condo Libro that draw on Tasso's preciously crafted imagery of love and courtly poetry: nine texts out of twenty, plus one which, although by Guarini, often must have been attributed to Tasso.[14] Moreover, two texts are by Filippo Alberti of Perugia, who was Tasso's correspondent and advisor, one is by Enzo Bentivoglio of Ferrara, and three are by Girolamo Casoni, who came from the district of Treviso but was a reader in philosophy at Pavia and could have been one of the people who personally contributed to Monteverdi's new orientation.[15] Only three texts are anonymous; the last of the collection is by Bembo, the father of vernacular poetry of the cinquecento, and it is made particularly conspicuous, not only by its placement at the end but by "an archaistic motet-like style with luxuriant melismas and an uninterrupted flow of the five voices, somewhat in the style of the Rore of 1542 or 1544 or of Willaert's *Musica nova*."[16]

Had *Secondo Libro* appeared just two years later, Tasso's preponderance in it might have been attributed to the influence of the Mantuan milieu, where the poet had stayed for about a year immediately following his release from confinement at Sant'Anna (1586), through the intercession of Vincenzo Gonzaga. However, it appeared at a time when Monteverdi seemed to be gravitating toward Milan and had perhaps established those contacts with the Milanese circle that even later continued to have a notable importance for him.[17] Whether or not there did exist a coterie of Tasso admirers around Girolamo Casoni,[18] one would be inclined to say that Monteverdi had had in mind, besides the poet's verses, the final pages of his dialogue *La Cavaletta overo de la poesia toscana*, in which he calls for leaving aside "all that music which through degeneration has become limp and effeminate" (tutta quella musica la qual degenerando è divenuta molle ed effeminata), proposing to "summon it [music] back to that gravity from which it has strayed, often brimming over into an area about which one would do better to make no mention" (richiamarla a quella gravità da la quale traviando è spesso traboccata in parte di cui è più bello il tacere che il ragionare).[19] Indeed, *Non si levava ancor* (two parts), *Dolcissimi legami*, *Non sono in queste rive*, and *Donna, nel mio ritorno* are all included in *Gioie di Rime, E Prose Del Sig. Torquato Tasso* (Venice, 1587), which is the sole source of *La Cavaletta*; three other texts had appeared a year earlier in *Delle Rime Et Prose Del Sig. Torquato Tasso. Parte Quarta* (Venice, 1586) by the same publisher.

By this time Monteverdi seems determined to establish himself as an artist among artists and to become part of the great current of the cinquecento madrigal. He does not reject "sweetness and suavity" (la dolcezza e la soavità), but rather adds to it that "restraint" (temperamento) which the poet considered necessary to obtain a manner "of magnificence, evenness, and gravity" (un modo . . . il quale è magnifico, costante e grave). Already attesting to this is, at the very opening of the collection, the unusual length, even for a two-part madrigal, of the text to *Non si levava ancor l'alba novella* (Not yet had the new dawn risen): two symmetrical stanzas of ten lines each, within the frame of a four-line exordium and envoi that are symmetrical as well. The scene of the two lovers parting at daybreak includes some bits of impassioned dialogue which Monteverdi effectively translates in brief accents of declamation at the beginning of the second part; still more remarkable is the last farewell, which pours forth in the finale in expressive dissonances, in no way inferior to the celebrated harmonic boldness of the successive books (there is included and repeated an extremely daring downward jump of a major seventh); but in contrast to the notes of sweetness (*dolcezza*) is the attention Monteverdi pays to the musical treatment of the various kinds of poetic imagery in accordance with the madrigalian tradition: "né spiega-van le piume / gli augelli . . ." ("nor were the birds yet opening their wings"; note the negative image and the enjambement), the two charming graceful lovers, the "spiraling" acanthus, and even more remarkable, the treatment of "divise il novo raggio" (the new light "divided"). Command-ing even greater attention is the fresh ascending line of the opening, apparently evoked by the "not yet" rising dawn, which in fact comes back (along with its countersubject) halfway through the second part of the madrigal with the words "E innanzi a l'alba che nel ciel sorgea" (preceding dawn's rising in the sky).[20] It is surprising, though, to find the motif taken up again and developed to form the conclusion to the first part of the madrigal, where its return has no other justification than the return of the opening rhyme of the poem; Monteverdi was aware then that the text is a *ballata* (in a category all its own, as are many *ballate* of the cinquecento),[21] and he emphasized the metrical form at least to the extent of rounding out the musical form of the first part of the composition; his manner of proceeding is irregular, though, from the point of view of madrigalian practice and perhaps can be explained as a result of his having read *La Cavaletta*.

Monteverdi had already found the ascending theme quite winsome in the initial stages of his activity—one need only think of the beginning of the *canzonetta, Raggi dov'è il mio bene,* or of the second line of *Questa ordì 'l laccio* in *Primo Libro*. It is also found in *Secondo Libro,* slightly modified in the upper voice in the opening of *Quell'ombra esser vorrei.* But it may be more than pure coincidence in the case of *Non si levava ancor,* when it calls to mind the opening motif of the first madrigal of *Settimo Libro ... a cinque voci* (Venice, 1581) by Giaches de Wert,[22] the text of which, by Muzio Manfredi, begins:

> Sorgi e rischiara al tuo apparir il cielo,
> Santa madre d'Amor, rimena il giorno ...
>
> Do rise and brighten the sky to your sight,
> Holy mother of Love, bring the day back to us ...

Along with the imitation of nature (the descriptive episodes), we find then the imitation of artistic models—in the present case, of Wert, one of the musicians specifically cited by the *Forestiero Napolitano* (that is, Tasso himself) in *La Cavaletta* (the other two are Striggio and Luzzaschi) in the previously quoted passage on music. "Imitation," it has been shown,[23] was the term most commonly used in the cinquecento to define what modern criticism has taken to calling "parody," that procedure of derivation from already existing compositions, which Monteverdi applied by drawing from a Gombert motet the themes for the fugal episodes of the *Missa da Capella* for six voices (1610); that such imitation did not apply exclusively to sacred polyphony is significantly indicated by a study which combines the consideration of literary and musical parody apropos of Petrarchan and Petrarchesque texts.[24] Future investigation should try to establish how great a part conscious or subconscious imitation of others' compositions had in Monteverdi's works. This is undoubtedly an area of difficult research, both because modern editions of madrigalian literature are far and few between and because it is even more difficult for the music critic than for his literary counterpart to mentally store away references to musical themes and episodes.[25]

The texts selected by Monteverdi, whether Tasso's or those of his imitators, abound in the favorite imagery of flowers, vermilion colors, gems and stars, laughter and song, snares and chains (preferred by Monteverdi for the way they lent themselves to expressive dissonance), sprites and flying kisses. There also creeps in, with a cinquecento echo of a motif of the stil novo (*Mentr'io miravo fiso*), an attempt at going back to the golden century of Italian poetry. But on the whole, even though deliberate adherence to descriptive madrigalism is evident in *Secondo Libro*, one cannot say that the musical imagery chosen by Monteverdi is particularly original or particularly characteristic. The images interest the composer as cells of the musical tissue, which takes its start from them (and which often alters their configurations more for musical reasons than for descriptive ones). More personal is the sense of the overall form of the composition, which we have already seen at work in *Non si levava ancor*. See, for example, the ample development accorded the first three lines of *Non giacinti o narcisi* with a double exposition that insists on the starting tone (D), drawing away from it in a briefer second section that goes from G to F and leads to a (declining) repeat of the initial theme for the last two lines; or see the even greater range of the opening section of *Non m'è grave 'l morire,* equally static tonally and dominated by the obsessive hammering of the initial phrase and of the reply *"anzi il viver m'annoia,"* which Monteverdi has already presented at the beginning, thus anticipating its proper appearance in the third line of the text. See, finally, the most successful of the descriptive madrigals, the orchestral and rhythmic crescendo of *Ecco mormorar l'onde,* once more insistently held for an extended time at a static tonal level (F), to then flow into the characteristically Monteverdian descending progression of the line "L'aura è tua messaggera e tu dell'aura" (Dawn is your messenger and you are dawn's) which, like various other passages of *Secondo Libro,* already foreshadows the sense of the instrumental ritornellos of *Orfeo.* In giving an open form to *Ecco mormorar l'onde,* Monteverdi confirms an intuition on Tasso's part; the poet (but Monteverdi could not have known it) had at first conceived this text as a regular *ballata* but then eliminated every return of rhythm and rhyme, giving the definitive version the form of a free madrigal.[26]

By the time of *Terzo Libro de Madrigali* (1592), the picture had already changed considerably, though only two years separate it from the preceding collection. In place of the texts from *Rime,* Tasso is now represented by two cycles taken from *La Gerusalemme liberata,* two sequences of three madrigals each, corresponding to an equal number of stanzas in *ottava rima* from canto XII (*ottave* 77–79) and canto XVI (*ottave* 59–60 and 63). The first sequence, *Vivrò fra i miei tormenti e le mie cure* (I shall live with my pains and my sorrows), describes Tancredi's grief following the duel in which he has killed Clorinda, and the second, *Vattene pur crudel,* Armida's outbursts of raging invective, alternating with bewildered languor, as she is abandoned by Rinaldo. Surrounding these are less intensely dramatic texts, but still tending toward pathetic or tender expression, mostly by Guarini. The different orientation indicates the readiness with which Monteverdi became a part of the musical tendencies that by the end of the century were to lead, on the one hand, to the expressionistic violence of Gesualdo and the bold expressive and harmonic intensity of Monteverdi himself and, on the other hand, to the monodic formulations of the Florentines and to opera. It is not hard to guess the road by which the invitations that found such a ready response in his temperament reached Monteverdi. In Mantua, Giaches de Wert, who had found dramatic inspiration in Ariosto's epic even before Tasso's, was still active. In nearby Ferrara, Luzzasco Luzzaschi, whose example even the arrogant Gesualdo later claimed to have followed, dominated the musical scene. Nor were contacts with Florence lacking in the Mantuan court, given that Duchess Eleonora was, by birth and in character, a Medici, the sister of the Maria for whom the first "pastorales all set to music" were performed in 1600. Caccini visited Ferrara in 1592, and it is possible, though there is no proof of it, that he also stopped over in Mantua.

A Caccinian gesture opens the madrigal *O com'è gran martire* (in *Terzo Libro*), set to a text by Guarini; at the same time the long exordium entrusted to just three female voices relates the composition to the madrigalian literature inspired by the *concerto* of singing ladies of the Ferrarese court (Monteverdi is once again following in the footsteps of Tasso, who had written rhymes for Lucrezia Bendidio, Laura Peperara, Anna and Isabella Guarini, and Tarquinia Molza). But more important than the outward coincidence with Caccini, even if it is not a chance or isolated one, is that the expressive commitment madrigal composers from Naples to Ferrara and Mantua had in mind was substantially no different from what contemporaneously inspired the Florentine musicians and drove them toward monodic solutions. And even in the case of polyphony, one could legitimately speak, though the term was not historically used, of *stile recitativo* or *rappresentativo,* for we must realize that the fundamental essence of what was then designated by these originally equivalent terms does not consist so much in the adherence to recitation of the text, nor in the fact that the solo singing technically lent itself to the requirements of the stage as, above all, in the vivid immediacy with which a character's inner affective reactions were to be presented live to the audience. To that end the physical reality of the scene was not strictly indispensable; equally adequate and more easily realized was the choice of brief texts that delineated and projected on an imaginary stage a dramatic situation *in nuce.* The throbbing of emotions, whether touching or vehement, desperate or joyful, would then be represented through the music set by the composer, monodist or polyphonist, to those texts.

For such an imaginary performance, I have suggested using the expression *cantare recitando:*[27] *cantare* before *recitare* because the implied form of representation can avoid the practical requirements of realistic speaking that actual representation is usually subject to, but even more because, whether in the case of Monteverdi and a group of five madrigal singers or in the case of Caccini's monodies and the virtuoso soloists of his school, the singing, the representation through the singing, is the declared artistic end.

The imaginary projection of *cantare recitando* was easier when, as in the case of the cycles of Tancredi and of Armida in *Terzo Libro,* it was aided by the general knowledge of the characters, the situations, and the antecedent facts forming the background to the work. In *Quarto Libro* and *Quinto Libro* (published in 1603 and 1605 respectively, but whose madrigals already circulated in handwritten copies before 1600), the heroes and heroines of *Gerusalemme liberata* were replaced by no less noted characters and texts from Guarini's *Il pastor fido,* the pastoral drama that is one of the most direct antecedents of the opera. The beginning of Mirtillo's monologue, *O primavera, gioventù de l'anno,* which opens act III of *Il pastor fido,* had already been used for a madrigal in *Terzo Libro.* We do not know to what extent the new choices were influenced now by Vincenzo Gonzaga's infatuation with the drama and by his attempts at staging it, which failed in 1591 but memorably succeeded in 1598. In any case, the choices were not displeasing to Monteverdi and even included a dramatic dialogue between Dorinda and Silvio from act IV, an authentic duet realized through the five-voice madrigalian group in a series of five madrigals. Monteverdi twice drew on Amarilli's long monologue in act III (scene 4), which foreshadows the future operatic theme of the psychological conflict between love and duty. *Anima mia, perdona,* in *Quarto Libro,* is mostly declaimed, not because considerations of clarity and rapidity in the delivery of the text required it, but because the music makes the word its own, intensifying it with repetitions, with melodic fire, with harmonies vibrating with dissonance, accentuating it with unexpected withdrawals, from imploring exclamations to sudden absorbed concentration. The division in two parts does not serve, as it does at other times, to mark contrast: the tone and dominant sentiment are of a single sort, varied only by the diverse expressions, alternating the exhaustion of discomfort and the intensity of sorrow renewed with every new thought. More concise is the version of the same dramatic situation given by a single madrigal of *Quinto Libro.* It takes as its text the beginning of the monologue with the fervid invocation *O Mirtillo, Mirtillo, anima mia.* The style, once again, is still largely declamatory, but the text is shorter and the intensification through repetition more sparing, so that the unity of the melodic vein running through the various voices of the polyphonic texture proves more concentrated and immediately perceptible.

Such a melodic vein is at times expressed in open singing, at other times carved in a declamation, in which the features of accent and tone of the touching word come to participate in the melody's spontaneity and power of persuasion. Still Monteverdi recognized, as did the Florentines, that the wing of melody has an implied content of harmonic meanings, and it is not true melody unless it is free to express those meanings, even at the cost of violating the cautious rules of consonance or prepared dissonance of traditional polyphony. It is hard to cite a madrigal from *Terzo Libro* that is exempt from the harmonic daring that was to stir the anger of Artusi and provoke repeated attacks by him in 1600. Such daring may be called harmonic *sprezzatura*, for as with the *sprezzatura* of the Florentines, which itself is not without a harmonic aspect,[28] it is dictated by the purpose of expressive immediacy. *O Mirtillo* is one of the compositions against which Artusi leveled his critical darts, on account of the harmonic daring that gives pungency to the emotions expressed in the text. But Monteverdi is no less bold in the wider framework of the composition, in the use of what we now easily recognize as tonal modulation, but which back then, with theoretical definitions still in the future, was almost entirely an uncharted course. Guiding Monteverdi in his exploration was what he once described as "a dim Platonic light,"[29] a recitative sense of the whole that subordinates all the descriptive or recitative details, the harmonic *sprezzatura*, and the vocal ornaments to the expression of the piece as an entirety. Among the many examples that would lend themselves we may choose *Ch'io t'ami* from *Quinto Libro;* also in this collection of three madrigals there is an admirably varied use of expressive dissonance, now discreet and insinuating, now accentuated in the declamation to emphasize opposite senses of cruelty and sweetness. Even more remarkable is the modulation that broadens and renews the musical horizon and so enlivens a text which combines and reassembles various excerpts of Mirtillo's peroration in act III, scene 3 of *Il pastor fido*.[30]

Also present among the various instances of declamation used by Monteverdi is that *parlato* to repeated notes which today we call recitative in a strict sense. This form of *parlato* derived from the madrigal tradition (see the beginning of *Ecco mormorar l'onde*), which had inherited it in turn from sacred polyphony and indirectly from the tones of recitation of the liturgical song. It was also used by the Florentines, who are actually wrongly accused of having used it to excess, and to it Monteverdi applies their concept of *sprezzatura*, prescribing a single chord for the madrigalian chorus and leaving to the performers the choice of rhythmic values that best fit the needs of the recitation. For that reason it is indicative to find this polyphonic *sprezzatura* applied for the first time in *Quarto Libro* to a text by Ottavio Rinuccini, *Sfogava con le stelle* (it will return in some other madrigals and even more noticeably in the compositions set to texts of psalms). But it is also a measure of the latitude of the concept of recitative that such schematic passages of declamation flow into tender vocalization and even into a brief impulse of descriptive madrigal writing suggested by the *vivi ardori* of Rinuccini's text.

The note of more intense and diffused lyricism that appears from *Terzo Libro* on is not new in the history of the madrigal. Examples can be cited as far back as the middle of the sixteenth century, and Monteverdi certainly was referring to them in affirming not only admiration of but even some derivation from Cipriano de Rore, who died even before Monteverdi was born. But this lyricism is reborn after a pause almost of spiritual exhaustion, during which time musical taste fell back on melodic charm and the hedonism of the idyll. Even now the atmosphere of the idyll is not forsaken entirely but is often colored either by more or less open notes of sensuality or by pathetic longings and languors, if not sensual then sensuous, for which it is significant that the choice of texts turns with greater insistence to Guarini than to Tasso. Monteverdi, perhaps alone among the major madrigalists of his time, avoided the elegant, barely disguised obscenity of the famous *Tirsi morir volea,* but certainly not out of an excess of prudery. Just how pleasing mischievous ambiguity was to Vincenzo Gonzaga is indicated by the choice of the anonymous text of *La giovinetta pianta* for the first madrigal of *Terzo Libro,* which is dedicated to him; but a note of even plainer sensuality is sounded in *Sì ch'io vorrei morire* of *Quarto Libro* (also set to an anonymous text), which, between the initial exclamation and its final return in the conclusion, frames a fervid madrigalian description, verbal and musical, of voluptuous and intimate embraces in chains of delicate dissonances and pungent blends and interlockings of the voices.

The new lyricism does not absolutely reject the texture of polyphonic imitations or the traditional and ever-renewed vocabulary of madrigalian imagery; the two idyllic texts of *Quarto Libro, Io mi son giovinetta* and *Quell'augellin che canta* (erroneously attributed to Boccaccio, and both composed, one would be inclined to say, with the Ferrarese trio of noblewomen in mind), lend themselves well to these procedures.[31] But the economy of the composition avoids lingering on them and tends to translate the texts into tension and expectation, finally overflowing into broad tender phrases. In *A un giro sol de bell'occhi lucenti* from *Quarto Libro,* the descriptive attitude of the first part, is reminiscent of the dawn in *Ecco mormorar l'onde;* it lacks the same orchestral crescendo, because in the text by Guarini the description of luminosity emanating from the laughing eyes of his lady love is associated with the sudden calming effect of those eyes on the wind and sea. Monteverdi cannot help but describe positively and successively the whispering of the wind and the heaving of the waves, an approach that was often the target of critics of the madrigal; but he gives it no more thought than so many madrigalists before him, especially since the effect he wants this time is not so much the description of but the contrast between the serenity of the first part and the note of suffering of the conclusion. In *Cuor mio, mentre vi miro,* also from *Quarto Libro* and also set to a text by Guarini, Monteverdi even forgoes the madrigalian characterization of the contrasting imagery of the text. The antithesis "o bellezza mortale, o bellezza vitale" is musically translated into an intensified repetition, and the contrast between "nascere" and "morire" in the conclusion is carried by melodic phrases that are different but not opposite, the first of which naturally leads to the melodic high point of the second. The voices are almost never heard all together; rather, they alternate in various regroupings, dominated by what is in each instance the melody of the upper voice and by the lowest-pitched harmonic support; the effect is *avant la lettre* one of an accompanied monody, spread out in a richer range of timbres than those of a single voice.

In the texts selected, even those outside the epic and pastoral drama, the frequency of exclamations is remarkable, a feature that Guarini was conscious of to the point of using it as a theme for virtuosic exercise in a madrigal that met with a good deal of success among musicians:

> Oimè, se tanto amate
> di sentir dir, oimè, deh perché fate
> chi dice, oimè, morire?
> S'io moro, un sol potrete
> languido e doloroso oimè sentire;
> ma se, cor mio, vorrete
> che vita abb'io da voi, e voi da me,
> n'avrete mille e mille dolci oimè.

> Alas, if you so enjoy
> hearing one say alas, why do you let
> him die who says alas?
> If I die, you will hear
> just one faint, pained alas;

but if, my love, you want
me to get life from you and you from me,
then you shall have a thousand sweet alases.

Monteverdi's version in *Quarto Libro* is among the most elegant. The
beginning, heavy with sorrowful emphasis, is misleading; the composition
is soon back to the polite and slightly ironic jesting that the text demands,
making good use of the usual license of repetition to multiply the "oimè's"
of the text. Monteverdi remembered this virtuosic exaltation of the
exclamation on other occasions and put it to use, for example, with greater
expressiveness in the first part of *Ohimè, il bel volto* (*Sesto Libro*), whose
text is a sonnet by Petrarch on the death of Laura. There the exclamation
(once more "ohimè") occurs several times in the two quatrains, but
Monteverdi turns it into a dominant theme entrusted to the upper voices,
leaving to the others the task of enunciating the rest of the poetic text.
Once again the reference to Caccini's melodic style, in the initial motive
and in restrained touches of melodic ornamentation, is no mere accident.
T'amo mia vita in *Quinto Libro* also entrusts the text to the three lower
voices and could be said to be mostly recitative, except that the declamation expressing trust and subdued fervor is highlighted by the lively
returns of the soprano's melodic theme which interrupts the declamation,
hovering alone over the figurations of the instrumental *basso continuo*. It
is worth quoting the text of the poem by Guarini:

> —T'amo, mia vita!—la mia cara vita
> dolcemente mi dice; e in questa sola
> sì soave parola
> par che trasformi lietamente il core
> per farmene signore.
> O voce di dolcezza e di diletto!
> Prendila tosto, Amore;
> stampala nel mio petto;
> spiri solo per lei l'anima mia;
> —T'amo, mia vita!—la mia vita sia.

> —I love you, my life!—my dear life
> sweetly tells me; and in this one
> so gentle word
> she appears to gladly change her heart,
> to let me be its master.
> Oh sweetest, joyous word!
> Do take it quickly, Love;
> do impress it on my breast;

let all my soul breathe only for her;
let—I love you, my life!—be my life.

More faithful to the spirit than to the letter of the text, Monteverdi makes
the initial exclamation the main theme of the madrigal, repeating it in
continually varied form till it is connected to the repetition in the final line
in which all the voices—including a second soprano which up to this point
has remained silent—take part, joyously exchanging the themes set forth
earlier by the solo soprano.

In another area of expressive madrigalism, the use of chromatic elements in Monteverdi's polyphony is relatively restrained compared to its
more deliberate use by a Gesualdo or even Marenzio; Monteverdi's use
results more from the need to intensify the emphasis of the text through
harmonic surprise than from an explicit chromatic intent. But such an
explicit intent is evident in the choice of chromatic melodic themes that
characterize two madrigals to which Monteverdi assigns positions of
prominence, last place in *Terzo Libro* and *Quarto Libro*, respectively. The
first is *Rimanti in pace* (in two parts) set to a text by Livio Celiano, perhaps
the first sonnet chosen by Monteverdi for a madrigal. The chromaticism,
already anticipated beforehand in the play of false relations, comes to the
fore in the ample elaboration of the lines "Stilland' amar humore" of the
first part and "Di martir in martir" of the second; but I wonder if it should
not also be applied to the soprano beginning of "Rimanti in pace" and to
its repetition on the following page.[32] The text of the other madrigal is
from Tasso's epic repertoire, a stanza in *ottava rima* from the episode of
Erminia, never identified as being by him because, taken from *La
Gerusalemme conquistata* (canto VIII, 6), its beginning, *Piagn'e sospira*, is
different from that of the better-known text of *La Gerusalemme liberata*
("Sovente, allor che sugli estivi ardori," canto VII, 19). Monteverdi
entrusts this beginning, more concentrated in the pathos of the situation,
to a slow ascent of semitones concluded by a brief pause, a sigh (also
present in *Rimanti in pace*), and a sobbing accent. Once more, the
narration that follows is restrained to a muffled tone of recitation. Above
this the chromatic line of the beginning is given great emphasis variously
assigned to one or another voice. A chromatic accent also returns in the
subdued abandon of the final couplet.

The madrigalian way of thinking is based on an exact correspondence
between particular musical figurations and the imagery and concepts
proposed by the text; it is obvious, however, that the true work of the
musician consists not so much in the elementary and all too often

stereotyped process that translates the word into images of sound, as in the elaboration and coordination of these images in a musical discourse that takes its cue from the word. The advent of *basso continuo* did not inevitably imply abandoning the characteristic features of polyphonic madrigalism; on the contrary, it helped to state even more precisely the exact relationship between certain phrases of the text and of the music, since the instrumental harmonic support provided by the *continuo* rescues the voices from those amorphous areas in which some of them, taking turns, must assume the function of harmonic or rhythmic background. An example of madrigal writing as precise as it is transparent is *Tu dormi, ah crudo core* from *Settimo Libro* (1619): transparent because of the restricted number of voices (four) and because the voices, without assuming a monodic posture, stand out in distinct isolation, then withdraw, leaving to the *continuo* the task of assuring an amalgam and, pardon the pun, continuity.[33] The text of *Tu dormi* is anonymous, but it is significant that in the composition immediately following, the return to evidently madrigalian features is once more joined to a text by Tasso, a brief idyll that Monteverdi scholars, relying too exclusively on information provided by Solerti, have failed to recognize:

> Al lume delle stelle
> Tirsi sotto un alloro
> si dolea lagrimando in questi accenti:
> —O celesti facelle!
> di lei ch'amo ed adoro
> rassomigliate voi gli occhi lucenti.
> Luci care e serene
> sento gli affanni, ohimè, sento le pene.
> Luci serene e liete
> sento la fiamma lor mentre splendete.

> By the stars' light
> Thyrsis under a laurel tree
> lamented, weeping, in these words:
> —You heavenly lights,
> you resemble those shining eyes
> of her whom I love and adore.
> Dear serene lights,
> you give me grief, alas, you give me pain.
> Serene and happy lights,
> your shining sets my heart afire.[34]

The bright eyes and the image of the flame allow the shepherd Thyrsis to express himself in open singing, with the usual figurations of the madrigalian convention. We are in Arcadia, where every shepherd is a poet and musician, and the song of Thyrsis is a madrigal within the madrigal by Monteverdi. And precisely to create a distinction between the madrigalism of the introduction and that of the shepherd's song, Monteverdi resorts to unusual figurations for the first. The initial theme ascends in a long, slow arpeggio, then gently descends by degrees, representing perhaps Thyrsis' upward glance toward the stars and the benign light streaming down from them. The inflection of "si dolea lagrimando," intensified by a descending leap to the octave below, is not entirely unusual for Monteverdi, yet it is difficult to justify the unusually extended melodic compass of the theme which should describe the bay laurel. The melodic choices must have been influenced by the desire to contrast the two sections, and the contrast is accentuated by the fact that the themes of the first section stand out in isolation, making their contours even sharper.

The elective affinity between Monteverdi and Tasso was reaffirmed in at least two other instances of returns to the poet's epic production. One of these was the project, perhaps never brought to a successful conclusion, for an *Armida*, mentioned by Monteverdi for the first time in a letter of May 1, 1627, probably addressed to Striggio.[35] But the elusive *Armida*, whatever its form may have been, made way for *La finta pazza Licori*, which so filled Monteverdi with enthusiasm; two letters, of September 18 and 25, 1627, came back briefly to *Armida*, but right after that Monteverdi embarked on the enormous project of the *intermedi* and tournament for Parma. The year 1627 might suggest an opera, stimulated by the precedent of Domenico Mazzocchi's jealous, love-stricken sorceress of *La catena d'Adone* (which had been performed and printed the year before and was perhaps considered for the festivities being put together in Parma); but Monteverdi's words indicate a setting as strictly adherent to Tasso's narrative text as in *Il combattimento*: "I happen to have set many stanzas of Tasso, where Armida begins *O tu che parti* ... continuing with her lament and fury, with Ruggero's replies" (Mi trovo però fatto molte stanze del Tasso ... Armida comincia *O tu che parti, parte tuo di me parte ne lassi* [sic], seguendo tutto il lamento e l'ira con le risposte di Ruggiero [sic]);[36] immediately afterward the letter refers to *Il combattimento*.

Many of Tasso's stanzas—twelve, to be exact—were used by Monteverdi for *Il combattimento di Tancredi e Clorinda* with more than moderate license, as in the change made in the first two lines and the frequent, deliberate contamination of the version of the *Liberata* (canto XII) with that of the *Conquistata* (canto XV).[37] From the fidelity to the narrative form of the text comes a resemblance to the oratorio, which had just then begun to appear as a genre (and which, if one looks to its roots in the "dialogues" of the last decades of the sixteenth century, also indicates a continuity of artistic trends). Yet *Il combattimento* is not a secular oratorio, nor is it an opera, a ballet, or a tournament, though it has something of the features of all these genres. Monteverdi tells us in *Ottavo Libro,* in which *Il combattimento* was later included, that it had been performed in 1624 in Palazzo Mocenigo in Venice "for an evening's entertainment at Carnival time" (in tempo però di Carnevale per passatempo di veglia).[38] It was therefore, in short, an *intermedio,* probably performed without a set, an *intermedio* of the sort placed between the courses of a banquet or an evening's dances and refreshments; among the various forms of *intermedi* it comes closest to those that were called *abbattimenti* because they included an engagement between armed warriors, often stylized with musical accompaniment. The visual stylization explains many features of the music, such as the triple time, imitating in the beginning the trot of Tancredi's horse, and the sinfonia, which shortly thereafter comments on the lines

> E vansi incontro a passi tardi e lenti
> quai duo tori gelosi e d'ira ardenti,
>
> They move toward each other with cautious, slow steps
> like two jealous bulls inflamed by anger

or even the persistent rhythms, the repeated chords and the famous instrumental devices of the tremolo and pizzicato of the strings, all elements having the precise function of regulating the mimetic gesture. Where the rhythm becomes pressing and the voices and instruments thicken with martial figurations of fanfare, which will be characteristic of the "warrior" madrigals, there is born in full armor, as Minerva—doubly armored in fact—the style later called *concitato* by Monteverdi, which made *Il combattimento* a singular work, "canto di genere non più visto né udito" (a song of a kind never heard or seen before). As an *intermedio, Il combattimento* surpasses contemporary operas, which almost never succeeded in representing the actions of characters as effectively as their affective reactions. Still, the exception confirms the validity of the rule adopted by the composers, because even in *Il combattimento* it is the lyric moments which leave the most lasting impression in the heart of the listener: the emotional invocation of the Text (narrator) to the Night,[39] the imploring of the vanquished warrioress after the blind fury of the nocturnal duel, the anguish of Tancredi's recognition of his opponent and, more solemn than any involved spectacular finale, the touching simplicity of Clorinda's spiritual apotheosis.

The laureled shadow of Tasso has taken us ahead of events; let us now turn back to Monteverdi's connections with Ottavio Rinuccini, which in turn will inevitably force us into other digressions. An indication of Monteverdi's awareness of what was happening in Florence has already been seen in his use of a text by Rinuccini. They may have established contact as soon as 1600 if Monteverdi, who had already been part of Vincenzo Gonzaga's personal retinue in the ventures in Hungary and the journey to Spa in 1599, also accompanied the ducal couple to Florence in 1600 on the occasion of the nuptials of Duchess Eleonora's sister, Maria dei Medici. Along with the ducal retinue may also have been, in his capacity as secretary, the librettist of *Orfeo*, the younger Alessandro Striggio.[40] More certain than those conjectures which, though likely, are unsupported by documented evidence, is that the libretto to *Orfeo* closely follows the model of Rinuccini's *Euridice* in the sequence of episodes, and thus broadly echoes its poetic language, as Monteverdi's music echoes the style of both Peri and Caccini.[41]

Striggio never had great literary ambitions and was probably easily molded to Monteverdi's intentions. It is not known to which of the two should be attributed the taste for Dantean reminiscence, which in the third act of *Orfeo* gives particular prominence to Charon and which, in the beginning of the same act, leads to assigning Hope as Orpheus' escort (rather than Venus, as in *Euridice*); on the threshold of Hell she abandons him, after reading and repeating the final line of the inscription placed by Dante on the door of Dis: "Lasciate ogni speranza, o voi ch'entrate." Most certainly Monteverdi's is the firm and intensified adherence to the Guarinian classicism that had guided Rinuccini in *Euridice*. To an even greater extent than *Euridice*, *Orfeo* is Guarinian in its quest for balance between the pathetic intensity of the sentiments and the classical formal composure of the whole; more than *Euridice*, it is a "tragicomedy," a "modern" improvement on the perfection of the classical tragedy.[42]

The well-known symmetries of the first act are the fruit of intended classicism,[43] and it is anachronistic to speak of them as the application of concepts of musical form at a time when the architectonic concept of form was a long way from any conscious formulation, although it was at times hazily perceived by musicians. The admirable result of the first act is equally dependent on the static situation (the festive awaiting of the nuptials of Orpheus and Eurydice) and the vitality of each separate element in and of itself, be it a chorus, solo piece, or instrumental ritornello. More immediately corresponding to the conscious intent of a formal conception (also fundamentally derived or nourished by literary suggestions that had been manifested since the beginning of the cinquecento) is the leaning of each act toward a choral conclusion.[44] Something of a surprise for anyone who still obstinately believes that the *stile recitativo* or *rappresentativo* is necessarily the equivalent of an open manner of proceeding with no formal law is to find ample room for minor closed pieces within the broadest structures (with the exception of the second part of act II[45] and nearly all of act IV, which are necessarily discursive). These structures are not the exclusive prerogative of *Orfeo*, since they are part of the complex game of exchanges and reciprocal reactions between pastoral poetry and music, yet in *Orfeo* they are more evident than ever and mark a phase of keen classicistic concern on Monteverdi's part, culminating shortly thereafter in *Arianna*.

Whether it is a matter of monostrophic or polystrophic structures, of one or more strophe-antistrophe pairs, or of periodic returns of significant phrases, Monteverdi and Striggio must have considered each structure as a sample of pastoral, elegiac, Orphic, Pindaric, or even gnomic (in the case of a few choruses) poetry, incorporated into their classical tragicomedy.[46] Confirming this are the stylistic correspondences, by no means coincidental, between several songs of *Orfeo*, especially those of the protagonist, and the *Scherzi musicali*, which appeared the same year as the performance of the opera (1607); the texts of the *Scherzi musicali* are for the most part by Gabriello Chiabrera, the renewer of Pindaric poetry and the creator of agile strophic forms in which Anacreontic poetry is revived, even more through the grace and lightness of rhythm than through the poetic substance. The formal and stylistic relationships to the *Scherzi musicali* are especially evident in the first half of act II; in the songs and instrumental ritornelli that lead in uninterrupted succession to the song, declared as such, of Orpheus, the polystrophic *canzonetta, Vi ricorda, o boschi ombrosi*. But even aside from these more precise references, in the entire initial part of *Orfeo*, which is the most merry, there is an affinity of tone, if not of spirit, with Anacreontic poetry. Of the various aspects of classicism, it is the carefree mirth of hedonism that, in seizing the joy of the present, intensifies pleasure through the awareness of its transitoriness. In a similar manner, I have always detected a bittersweet grace—whether derived from a presentiment of Orpheus or of the opera's author, or from a nostalgic longing for a lost golden age—in the tenuous shadows veiling the second part of the chorus *Lasciate i monti* (whose long descending progression, after the tonally static first part, repeats with a different poetic meaning an effect already noted in *Ecco mormorar l'onde*), in the instrumental ritornelli of the "chorus" *Alcun non sia* (although the text implies the memory of past sorrows more than the presentiment of future ones),[47] and in the tenor duets of the first part of act II. Their poetic sense is made clearer by the affinity with the tone of nostalgic evocation that veils the joyous description of spring in the first part of the madrigal *Zefiro torna* from *Sesto Libro*, which I like even better than the surprising and more celebrated *ciaccona* with the same incipit.[48]

Much has been written on the *Scherzi musicali* to affirm or deny their identity with the *canto alla francese* which, it is claimed, Monteverdi imported to Italy upon his return from the journey to Spa as part of Vincenzo Gonzaga's retinue (1599).[49] To my knowledge, none of the supporters of the affirmative argument has ever cited in its favor the fact that the principal poet of *Scherzi musicali*, Gabriello Chiabrera, undoubtedly used his knowledge of classically inspired French lyric poetry in his odes;[50] *Amarilli, onde m'assale*, for example, already known in Florence in 1595, is derived from Ronsard and is in turn the nucleus from which derived *Il rapimento di Cefalo*, performed in Florence in 1600.[51] Analogously, it appears to me that the prefatory notes ("Avvertimenti") nearly always have gone unobserved by those who have described the collection and in recent performances of the music it contains. The suggestion that "once the first stanza has been sung à 3, the [line of the] first soprano can be sung à solo or at the lower octave for the following stanzas except the last, which goes back to the same three voices and same violins" (il primo Soprano, cantata che sia la prima stanza à tre voci con i Violini, potrà essere cantato solo, ò vero all'ottava bassa nelle stanze che seguono, ripigliando però l'ultima stanza con l'istesse tre voci, & i violini stessi) produces, when applied, a full chorality dominated by the soprano, alternating with solo singing; this is in fact characteristic of the madrigals *Dolcissimo usignolo* and *Chi vol haver felice* (both set to texts by Guarini) from *Ottavo Libro* (1638), to which is added the statement "cantato a voce piena, alla francese" (sung with full voice in the French style).[52] The conclusion that Monteverdi resolved to imitate exclusively the *musique mesurée à l'Antique* of the Baïf Academy or the less systematic *airs de cour* seems exaggerated; on the other hand, I cannot agree with Schrade's thesis that the *canto alla francese* is just a manner of performance (with full voice and alternation of soloist and chorus).[53] More typical of Monteverdi's manner of proceeding seems to be a flexibility, which, in adapting his music to Chiabrera's classicizing meter, combines the more typically classicistic elements of French and Italian tradition. From the *airs de cour* he is likely to have obtained the measured composure, the prevalence of quaternary rhythm, the frequent inflection of two quavers to one syllable, and perhaps even, unconsciously, a certain indefinable harmonic quality; other rhythms, however, derive from a long Italian tradition that is not, as some would hold, that of the *danza* or of the *balletti* in the manner of Gastoldi, but rather that of the *frottola*, humanistic in origin.[54]

The digression on Chiabrera, the classicism of *Orfeo* and the *Scherzi musicali*, and their relation to French and Italian humanism has not, in point of fact, caused us to wander too far from Rinuccini, who was an emulator of Chiabrera in lyric poetry and of Guarini in the classically inspired pastorale, and like Chiabrera, was open, at least in his conception of ballet, to the suggestions springing from contemporary practice at the Parisian court.[55] Rinuccini's presence in Mantua in 1608 and his contributions to the wedding festivities of that year coincide with the height of Monteverdi's classicistic phase. Of the two spectacles to grow out of the collaboration between Rinuccini and Monteverdi, others may judge which has more fully classical aspirations. The *Balletto delle ingrate* introduces classicism into contemporary court custom by having as participants in the mythological action "the duke and the prince-bridegroom with six knights and eight of the leading ladies of the city as noble as they were fair and graceful in dancing" (il Duca, e il Principe sposo con sei altri Cavalieri e con otto Dame delle principali della città così in nobiltà come in bellezza ed in leggiadria del ballare),[56] and by having Pluto recite a long and wordy speech in courtly praise of the Gonzaga-Savoia newlyweds. It aligns itself with an attitude having a continuous tradition in the French court from the *Ballet comique de la Royne* to the glorifications of the Roi Soleil and to the trifling pastorales for Marie Antoinette. As for *Arianna*, it was (no matter what those who still cling to the traditional commonplaces concerning the mythical Florentine Camerata may think) the first actual and nearly the only attempt at recreating the equivalent of a classical tragedy, music included.[57] In spite of all the musical treasures Monteverdi had to pour out, it was an untimely attempt, for no audience was yet prepared to accept the convention of "speaking musically" outside of the pastoral aura— applied, that is, not to nymphs and shepherds but to men and women in the flesh, beset with practical, realistic, and even political cares.[58]

Arianna and the *Balletto* were quite unlike but had several features in common that are worth observing. One is the preoccupation with caste and rank, which applied only to the performers in *Balletto*,[59] but to the main characters in *Arianna* in accordance with the rule that tragedy required protagonists of royal or princely blood. Another common feature is that the heterogeneous prolixity of the *Balletto* and the untimely realism of *Arianna* were somehow redeemed by the pathos of a lament, sung for both productions by the actress Virginia Ramponi Andreini, the Florinda of the Compagnia dei Fedeli. Finally, the score for *Balletto* was not published by Monteverdi until thirty years later, in 1638; the score for *Arianna* was never published. These are implicit admissions of a less than complete success, also confirmed implicitly by Rinuccini, who returned to the pastoral aura in the libretto for *Narciso*.[60]

Monteverdi kept the text of *Narciso* a long time without ever resolving to set it to music;[61] but attesting to his respect for and favorable recollection of Rinuccini, besides his letters, are two of Monteverdi's best known and most celebrated compositions, certainly conceived after the poet's death (1621).[62] Of *Arianna*'s lament Monteverdi elaborated a well-meditated polyphonic version, the cycle of four madrigals which occupies the place of honor in *Sesto Libro* (1614). This is not a suitable forum for an analysis of the amplifications that the *Lamento d'Arianna* underwent (not only from the viewpoint of musical expression) in the new form; more important is the confirmation by Monteverdi himself of the essential unity during the period 1590-1610 of the expressive lymph that nourished opera, chamber monody, and madrigal polyphony, that is, *recitar cantando* and *cantar recitando*.

And that is not the whole story: the religious *contrafactum* of the lament, the *Pianto della Madonna*, once again placed in a position of prominence in the vast collection of the *Selva morale e spirituale* (1640),[63] leads one to include in the same essential unity of expressive goals even sacred music, and it obliges us to enter into yet another brief digression, one that regards the sacred collection *Sanctissimae Virginis Missa ... Ac Vespere* (1610), the first clear sign of Monteverdi's intention to quit the Mantuan court.[64] I have already mentioned the Mass for six voices on themes by Gombert in regard to the concept of "imitation"; a different kind of imitation is present in the *Introductorium* of the Vespers, *Domine ad adiuvandum*, which is the refashioning and amplification for chorus and instruments of the triple blare of the toccata of trumpets from *Orfeo*. Nor is this the only link between the sacred collection of 1610 and the compositions that had come before it. Many ritornelli of the psalms recall those of *Orfeo*; on several occasions, the choral psalmodic recitation with repeated notes is granted the same liberty, or *sprezzatura*, we have observed in a madrigal set to a text by Rinuccini; instrumental effects similar to those accompanying the aria *Possente spirto* appear several times in the *Magnificat* for seven voices and six instruments and are also transferred to two sopranos similarly adorning the liturgical recitation of the tenor in the *Deposuit.*

One could speak of poetic choices for the way in which Monteverdi elected to set this or that part of the liturgical texts; even more appropriate is to speak of choices for those pieces which, in keeping with the practice of the time, take the place of antiphons and have texts which are, for the most part, paraliturgical.[65] *Pulchra es* is an ornate recitative duet (in the unrestricted sense in which I am interpreting *stile recitativo*) for two sopranos and organ, madrigalian for the choice of text and its anticipation of madrigalian styles of the later books. Even more madrigalian is the treatment of *Duo Seraphim clamabant alter ad alterum,* for *tenor, quinto,* and *alto* (essentially three tenors): it begins with two voices ("Duo Seraphim"); it emphasizes the "clamabant" and then realistically trans-lates it by letting one voice introduce the invocation "Sanctus" and having the other take it up, with both voices bringing it to a close. But the affirmation "tres sunt qui testimonium dant in coelo" is for three voices, and they enter one after the other in the enumeration "Pater, Verbum et Spiritus Sanctus," then resuming in an expanded version for three voices the "Sanctus" of the first part. The influence of the pastorale is evident finally in the first part of *Audi coelum,* a monodic recitative punctuated by the responses of an echo which here is no longer the pagan oracle but instead a celestial confirmation of the Marian praises enunciated by the tenor. The monody expands to six-part polyphony in the conclusion "*omnes* hanc ergo sequamur," in which Monteverdi again finds a way to insert the game of echoed call and response ("consequamur-sequamur," "solamen-amen"), still sung as before by the tenor and the *quinto.*

The beginning of the text to *Audi coelum* was used once more by Monteverdi in *Selva morale e spirituale* for the troped *Salve Regina* (in 1640!) for two tenors, two violins, and *continuo.* It is Monteverdi's last echo of the pastoral echo.

Giambattista Guarini, ubiquitous in all but one of the collections of Monteverdi madrigals, is the undisputed sovereign of *Quinto Libro* (1605) with sixteen texts out of nineteen, eleven of which (two cycles and three isolated madrigals) come from *Il pastor fido.*[66] From the "tragicomic" Guarini, as from the epic Tasso, Monteverdi sought texts that appealed to his most intensely pathetic inspiration and which in fact assumed the form of *cantare recitando*, but the parallel becomes less fitting for the texts that come neither from one or the other *Gerusalemme* nor from *Il pastor fido*. Missing from Guarini's madrigals are those vivid visual illuminations that make those by Tasso seem like so many preciously drawn and distinctly colored miniatures. Guarini rarely uses adjectives that are not generic or hackneyed; rather, he concentrates on the penetrating epigrammatic subtlety of a dominant thought and on the ingenious rounding out of a concept in the space of a few verses.[67] The lyric Tasso sets Monteverdi on the road toward his own versions of descriptive madrigalism; the Guarini of the madrigals leaves to the music the task of supplying the warmth that the words lack, and starts it off more directly on formal pursuits and on a different kind of madrigalism, moderately tender, somewhat ironic and cunning.

In *Ahi, come a un vago sol*, the last line, "Ahi, che piaga d'amor non sana mai" (the epigrammatic point) is anticipated several times, interrupting the orderly exposition and madrigalian illustration of the text by two tenors, before being chorally proclaimed in the finale.[68] Quite similar is the procedure for *E così a poco a poco*. Of a different genre, on the other hand, are the poetic decisions Monteverdi makes when faced with the metrical form and somewhat archaistic taste of a text whose structure brings to mind the reprise and two mutations of a *ballata* that is missing the *volta*:

> Troppo ben può questo tiranno Amore
> poi che non val fuggire
> a chi nol può soffrire.
>
> Quand'io penso talor com'arde e punge,
> i' dico: Ah, core stolto!
> non l'aspettar! che fai?
> fuggilo sì che non ti prenda mai.
>
> Ma poi sì dolce il lusinghier mi giunge,
> ch'io dico: Ah core sciolto,
> perché fuggito l'hai?
> prendilo sì che non ti fugga mai!

Too great a power has this tyrant, Love!/Fleeing him is of no avail/to those who can't endure him.

Thinking at times of his burning and stings,/I say: Oh, foolish heart,/don't wait! what are you doing?/flee him, so that he never may reach you!

But then the tempter catches me so sweetly / that I say: Oh, loose heart, / why have you fled from him? / hold him so that he never may leave you!

All of the voices participate in the apodictic and impersonal beginning; in contrast, the sudden isolation of the soprano at the fourth line underlines the subjective tone of the two symmetrical sections. For these Monteverdi used essentially uniform music, expressing the contrast between them— more apparent than real—only in the different melodic line (on the same bass) of the opening of the solo, hesitant and irresolute in one, serene and confident in the other. In what follows, the correspondence is complete, except for the understandable amplification of the finale; each of the two brief quasi-strophes is an iridescent microcosm in which monody in the Italian manner, choral recitation, a hint of *canto alla francese*,[69] and a spirited madrigalian fugue justified by the text (even though the idea of fleeing is affirmed the first time and denied the second) rapidly succeed each other and are adjusted to each other.

The reader is probably already aware that the examples cited belong to that group of six madrigals in *Quinto Libro* for which the *basso continuo* accompaniment is not *a beneplacito* (left up to the players), but obligatory.[70] The impending transition is already evident in one of the previous madrigals. *M'è più dolce il penar* (*Pastor fido*, act III, scene 6) is still mostly *cantar recitando*, governed by an oratorical line; but the moving intensity of the *sprezzatura armonica* of the beginning gives way almost immediately to a freer and more figurative writing, to some descriptive hints, to a *concitato* rhythmic gesture; four voices join in sonorous dissonance at "Prego il ciel e amor" but immediately disassociate themselves and alternate in duets more typical of *stile concertato*. But more remarkable yet is that at several points the arrangement of the musical discourse is anchored to the line of the lowest voice: to the *tenor* in the second repetition of "E se gioir di lei," to the *tenor* and then to the bass in the repeats of "Prego il ciel."[71] A similar example is the *tenor* of *Era l'anima mia* at the words "Quando anima più bella," and it is likely that one need only look carefully to find other examples even further back.

Recent Monteverdian studies have diminished the importance once attributed to the introduction of the *continuo* in *Quinto Libro* and have rightly reacted to the error of perceiving in it the sign of a break and the advent of a new Monteverdi, a monodist and cantata composer, in place of the polyphonist and madrigalist of the preceding period. The contraposition can only seem absurd to anyone who sees, as I do, in the polyphony and monody of the time parallel rather than contrasting expressions of analogous needs; more absurd yet is to attribute a causal value to something like the adoption of the *continuo*, which was at most a symptom of an inner change. There is nothing wondrous about the fact that there was a change, but even its outward signs show that it was not a radical renunciation of the past but a gradual addition of new interests and needs. The argument could even be reversed by stating that in a certain sense the madrigals with *continuo* accompaniment mark a return to the most varied madrigalian tradition, from which Monteverdi had set himself apart (though never completely) to concentrate on the experience of a tragic classicism. From here on Monteverdi will not renounce *cantare recitando*, the use of passionate tones, dramatic melodic gestures, and intense harmonies, but often he will cease making them an end in themselves and will return to the accents of tenderness, of innocent or mischievous warm-heartedness, of carefree gaiety. And although a master at weaving the nuances of a single affection into finely monochrome compositions, more often he yields to his madrigalistic vocation, aligning episodes of diverse tone and design, which he contrasts or connects, interrupts or takes up anew, at times closely ties or even superimposes. The use of the *continuo* and the thinning, where needed, of the polyphonic texture down to a single melodic line, come into the compositional picture as new means, which do not imply a renunciation of all the colors already available to the artist's palette.

Nine years after *Quinto Libro*, *Sesto Libro* (1614) is Monteverdi's first proud manifestation of independence, having freed himself from the quicksand of the benevolent but despotic employ of the Gonzagas to become "Maestro di Cappella della Sereniss. Sig [noria] di Venetia in S. Marco." *Sesto Libro* is the only one of Monteverdi's published works that lacks a dedication; it does contain a sonnet of uncertain authorship proclaiming the author to be a "Monte Verde, ed altero" (a verdant, proud mountain). But the content of the collection is still in many respects a liquidation of his Mantuan past. It revolves, above all, around two great madrigal cycles, the *Lamento d'Arianna* and the *Lagrime di Amante*, both of which we know Monteverdi had worked on in the early months of 1610;[72] the result is an internal organization in two analogous sections, each having a polyphonic cycle and an unaccompanied madrigal followed by other madrigals "with their *basso continuo* in order to concert them on the harpsichord and on other instruments" (con il suo Basso continuo per poterli concertare nel Clauacembano, et altri stromenti). The structure of each of the two sections is similar to that of *Quinto Libro*, and the overall number of madrigals with *continuo* accompaniment is six, as in *Quinto Libro*, in spite of the fact that between 1605 and 1614 Monteverdi had made extensive use of accompanied monody and *stile concertato* for operas and *balletti*. It is evident, then, that the use of technical means and of old and new styles was not dictated by a criterion of novelty, but solely by how well they served practical and expressive ends.

With *Sesto Libro* we find two poetic nonchoices by Monteverdi. One is the little-to-be-admired sestina of *Lagrime di Amante al Sepolcro dell'Amata* by the young Count Scipione Agnelli;[73] we know that the enamored Glauco of the poem reflects Vincenzo Gonzaga's fatuous protean romanticism and that the text was *imposed* on Monteverdi as homage to the memory of the young singer Caterina Martinelli.[74] The other nonchoice is the third *lamento*, which should also have been part of the collection, but is not. *Leandro*, by Giambattista Marino (*La Lira, Parte II, canzone IX*), would have been better literature (not poetry) than that of Count Agnelli, but it did not lend itself very well to the music, despite Monteverdi's unquestionable interpretive virtuosity. It is likely that when asked to put it to music, Monteverdi used a tactic in which he proved to be quite expert on later occasions: he would agree at first, then let the matter drag on until the request was forgotten.[75] Positive choices, and in my opinion strictly personal ones, that Monteverdi did make are those concerning the two Petrarch texts, two sonnets; as to the rest of the collection of *Sesto Libro*, it comprises four sonnets and a madrigal by Marino and a single anonymous text, *Una donna fra l'altre*, it too a sonnet.

I hold great respect for the knowledge and critical discernment of Alfred Einstein, but I cannot subscribe to, among other things,[76] his opinions of Monteverdi's madrigals. Of the two Petrarch madrigals in *Sesto Libro*, he accuses *Zefiro torna* of being dominated by the baroque preoccupation with contrasts, and *Ohimé, il bel viso* of lacking inner harmony.[77] The key to his views is perhaps given by what he writes of the latter: "How unlike Marenzio's harmonious setting of the same poem (*Terzo Libro*, 1582), written thirty years earlier!" Einstein, who sagaciously followed and analyzed the changing aspects of the madrigal from the beginning to Marenzio, almost sixty years, could not possibly have expected that in as many years of activity, Monteverdi left his style unchanged from the state of the madrigal somewhere around the year 1582! I am of the opinion, on the other hand, that the two Monteverdi collections of 1605 and 1614 group together works that represent the end of a violent digression mainly concerned with content—the *cantar recitando*, the two *lamenti* of

1614[78]—and other works marking the start of a new phase and which, albeit with a different appearance, resume the course he had abandoned shortly after 1590.

Paradoxically, the abandonment of the irregular metrical structures of the madrigal texts is another symptom of a return to madrigalism because the metrical formulas, whatever their nature, tend to lose value in a musical aesthetic entirely dominated by the recitative sense, whereas symmetries and correspondences can more easily be reflected in a manner between lyric and descriptive. External circumstances may have contributed to sparking Monteverdi's interest in the form of the sonnet; but certainly this interest is also in line with his interest in the interplay of metrical correspondences to be found, for example, in the madrigal field, in *Troppo ben può* of *Quinto Libro*.[79] In *Zefiro torna* the two quatrains of the sonnet receive the same music, adjusted to the text with subtle madrigalian devices,[80] but the graceful description of nature is more in the general tone than in the particulars; it is rendered distant and diaphanous by the minor tonality and made nostalgic by the coloratura which interrupts the triple time;[81] it is essentially lyricized. The brusque change of tone (and of tonality) introduced with the tercets is required by the text. In the tercets the respect for symmetry is no longer compatible with the expressive needs dictated by the text; instead, the memory of spring returns again, briefly, adding to the desolation of the musical imagery with which Monteverdi translates the final line: "Sono un deserto e fere aspre e selvagge" (the singing of birds, the blooming of the country, and, from fair good ladies, courteous gestures "are [to me] like a desert, with fierce, wild animals").[82] Monteverdi follows the poet's language and style in a different way in *Ohimé, il bel viso*; as in the text, the first six lines are a continuous progression founded on the theme of the "ohimé's" and flowing into the exalted vision of lines seven and eight. A sense of symmetry, though not absolute symmetry, comes to the two tercets through the similar beginnings of the music; but as the poetic sense requires, the final line is isolated once again.

I am convinced that the two Petrarch madrigals, set to texts chosen from among those on the death of Laura (sonnets CCCX and CCLXVII), can be dated sometime between the end of 1607 and the early days of 1608.[83] They are, with the sole conspicuous exception of the two ample *lamenti* of 1610, the last madrigal compositions in which Monteverdi makes exclusive use of the voices; they reflect, with a more intimate and absorbed tone, the affective as well as the formal experiences of *Orfeo*. Not least of the considerations for determining the date is that it is consistent with

Monteverdi's retiring self-control and dignified reserve to have entrusted the expression of personal moods, the confession of a recent and present sorrow, to a poet still read but classical, still alive and beloved but remote enough to have become a symbol, behind which the most intense and poignant sentiments can find shelter without fear of too crude an exposition. To my mind, Monteverdi's choices of Petrarch are the only ones that provide a peek into his innermost thoughts and secrets.

Among the many causes that contributed to a change in Monteverdi, the external circumstances that affected him cannot be overlooked—the stimulus of new situations that attracted his attention to new problems and created new responses and insights. The musical history of Mantua in this period still has certain gaps;[84] there seems to be no doubt, however, that Vincenzo Gonzaga, a frequent guest at the Ferrarese court, was among those who after 1598 aspired to continuing its traditions of musical excellence.[85] The nine-voice madrigal (*Questi vaghi concenti*) at the close of the *Quinto Libro* turns one's thoughts to a Mantuan restoration of the *concertoni* of voices and instruments at the Ferrarese court (corroborated by the presence of two *sinfonie* for five instruments) and at the same time brings to mind the usual display and predominance of the three female voices.[86] Moreover, and this is particularly important for the *concertato* madrigals of *Quinto* and *Sesto Libro*, one should note the recognition increasingly given in the solo passages to the individuality of each performer. This last trait establishes a subtle difference with respect to Ferrarese madrigalism, a difference that stems in part from the distinction between the Olympian despotism of Alfonso II d'Este and the capricious favoritism of Vincenzo Gonzaga, and is in part the product of the new time and of the growing importance and pretensions of singers of both sexes.

Una donna fra l'altre of *Sesto Libro* ought to be slightly later than the two Petrarch madrigals.[87] It is the only anonymous text of the collection. The other accompanied madrigals, all of them having a text by Marino, appear to be even later, so it is possible that Monteverdi's first artistic encounter with the new star of the Italian Parnassus[88] should be placed in relation to the arrival in Mantua of the diva Adriana Basile, who, like the poet, was Neapolitan.[89] Therefore it is not true that two poets as different as Petrarch and Marino made their appearance in Monteverdi's "workshop" at exactly the same time[90] and, even if they had, there would be no reason to be surprised. As different as they are, they serve different purposes: with Petrarch one identifies Monteverdi the man, in the rare moments in which he abandons himself to what are still cautious and veiled personal revelations; the craftsman Marino is used by Monteverdi the craftsman, no less astute, no less clever, no less controlled than the poet. More ingenious and more sincere than the poet, certainly, but not totally sincere. Starting more or less from this moment, the musician is no longer totally at one with the events and passions of Tancredi, Amarilli, Orpheus, Ariadne, or with those of the poetically unhappy Glaucus. No longer is there *cantar recitando*, but rather *narrar cantando, descriver cantando*; and fairly often, in the telling of a story or in a description, the poet-musician gives voice and life and warmth to the *recitar cantando* of a character while keeping him distinct from himself, in the way a painter does not identify himself with the personage of the portrait he is outlining. All this is done, adapting each time the means and the musical figurations to the subject of the narration, of the description, or of the recitation, and searching for musical images and procedures to suit those of the poetic text. It is madrigalism, even if its means and techniques are different from those of Rore or Marenzio, and its musical language is no longer that of the time of Willaert's Pecorina or of Laura Peperara, but that of the Caccini sisters, of Cardinal Montalto's Ippolita or of "la bella Adriana." Once again let us not mistake the external symptom for the cause; what counts is not Monteverdi's encounter with the poetry of Marino, but the fact that he confidently abandons himself in it, shielding himself in a certain sense, as he will also do with the verses of Guarini, Rinuccini, and other poets.

Monteverdi having missed setting Leandro's lament, the theme of the two artists' first joint venture that is known to us is one of the most exploited themes, with infinite variations, of the poetry of the time: the story-description-representation of the parting of two lovers at daybreak.[91] In *Addio, Florida bella,* it starts out *mediis in rebus* with the words of the lover Floro answered by Florida's farewells; thus the two characters immediately take up their position on the invisible set with two long monodic passages by the tenor and the soprano (the two quatrains of the sonnet), after which the group of five voices narrates (in the tercets) the circumstances of their farewells. The two voices resume the dialogue after the narration, alternating and linking up until reaching a last repeated *addio* in full polyphony; but in contrast with representative realism, which identifies each character with a certain voice, the madrigalian bent is reaffirmed in the descriptive passages suggested to Floro by the image of the "flying dart" (dardo volante), to Florida by the image of the "little bird flying to its favorite nourishment" (augellin che vola al cibo amato). A descriptive vein also stirs the choral narration with the intricate superimposed rhythms which translate the phrase "confuso un suon s'udio / di sospiri, di baci e di parole" (an indistinguishable sound was heard, of sighs, of kisses, and of words). Invisible behind the invisible scene, the author firmly holds the strings guiding the characters: the two quatrains of Floro and Florida, in spite of the diversity of the melody, are carried along the same harmonic base, transposed up a fifth for the soprano. At the end, after the urging and the harmonic crescendo of "Addio, Floro ... Florida, addio," the long inflexible descent of the basses in the final bars resembles the falling of a curtain on the scene.[92]

In another dialogue the situation proceeds from an alleged uncertainty about the reciprocity of feeling to the happy accord of the two lovers, an accord which, in the words of the poet, "matches [past] tears with joys, [past] wars with peace" (pari le gioie ai pianti, alle guerre le paci). It is the seven-voice madrigal *Presso un fiume tranquillo,* the only one of *Sesto Libro,* outside of the two cycles, whose text is not a sonnet; its four stanzas of six lines each, to which Marino had given the title *Numeri amorosi,* are symmetrical also in that the first two lines of each are narration and introduce alternately the words of the two lovers. The formal definition of the composition springs this time not from repetitions of the music or of its harmonic base but from the regular alternation of choral narration and the *recitar cantando* of the solos. Eurillo and Filena are supposed to alternate in the dialogue, but Monteverdi slightly modifies the text of the last stanza so as to attribute to the couple the words that Marino had assigned to Filena.[93] The result is a duet, which then expands, celebrating the reaching of a harmonious consensus, in an ample polyphonic section. Without regard for the tenuity of the poetic motif, Monteverdi gives free rein to his creative fire and to the sonority of the seven voices; but even in the polyphonic tumult the prolonged coloratura inspired by the amorous wars remains entrusted mainly to the soprano and the tenor who were the first to have stated it.

Madrigalian is the freedom with which Monteverdi, while tending to identify the characters with solo voices, easily goes on to a polyphonic rendering of their words any time it suits him; madrigalian is the way the entire polyphonic group can pass from the narrative function to the lyrical one of the two finales described above (or of the beginning to *Misero Alceo,* where it is not clear whether the two words are interpreted as a comment or an exclamation); madrigalian is the freedom with which the composer, though showing a preference for texts rich in metrical symmetries, does not feel obliged to observe them anywhere he sees the possibility of other effects. *Qui rise, o Tirsi,* though a sonnet, is treated as a madrigal. It is reminiscent in different respects of *Ahi come a un vago sol* of *Quinto Libro,* and similarly uses the final line as a recurring choral ritornello; but instead of always assigning the ordered exposition of the text to the same two voices, it begins with the two sopranos and continues with the two tenors, then with a single soprano ("Qui l'angelica voce") with two sopranos and tenor ("Qui le gratie scherzar"), and so on, with choices evidently suggested by a madrigalian mentality.[94] There are authentic madrigalian hyperboles in passages of other compositions, such as ". . . anzi un sol cor, diviso" from the finale of *Misero Alceo,* or the liquid falls of the finale of *Batto, qui pianse Ergasto.*[95] Monteverdi repeats these images insistently, authentic musical Marinisms in which he takes pleasure and which show once again how, independently of the various attitudes and of whether the compositions are his most or least successful, the musical invention always obviously springs from suggestions of the text.

In the arrival in Mantua of Adriana Basile we have recognized the event that probably sent Monteverdi on his way to becoming entangled with the Marinian aesthetic; that he was not averse to the allurements of Marino's muse is demonstrated by his having chosen for the first composition of the *Concerto. Settimo Libro de Madrigali* (1619) Marino's sonnet *Tempro la cetra,*[96] which opens *La Lira. Parte terza* (Venice, 1614). We cannot blame Monteverdi too much for an infatuation that was widespread at the time, and one that was avoided only by those who had some personal resentment toward the poet. The musician's renewed madrigal vein found suitable correspondences in the style of Marino, no less epigrammatic (in the minor poems) and no less verbally musical than the style of Guarini, no less rich in precisely visualized imagery than that of Tasso. Even Monteverdi's remaining classicistic tendencies find nourishment in Marino's classicism, even if in many cases this is reduced to the superficial sensuousness of a smooth polished patina, comparable perhaps (but we shall never know for sure) to the rich and shiny metal of the voice of the Adrianas and their equivalents in the other vocal types and registers.[97] Contrasting with that is Monteverdi's insistent use of coloratura, more as a figurative than as an affective means, a measure of the composer's deep interest in the phonic—we could say instrumental—qualities of the new singing virtuosity.

Just as it is not possible that the madrigals "concertati nel clavicembalo" of *Sesto Libro* may allow one to forget the basically dramatic tone imparted to the collection by the traditional polyphonic part of its content, so it is that conversely, the small number of compositions of *Settimo Libro* still remaining faithful to the aesthetic of *cantar recitando* are unable to counterbalance the sense of noninvolvement emanating from most of the collection, whether because of the lightness of tone, the canzonettistic spirit (if not the form), or the quality of musical compositions destined to "brighten a social evening" (per passatempo di veglia) or any other entertainment, or to display the virtuosity of the singers and the composer himself. Its organization recalls that of the long-past book of the *Canzonette*. The musical dedication is lacking, it is true, but to give the appearance of unity to a miscellaneous content there are *invio* and *congedo* represented by the proem, *Tempro la cetra,* and by the *ballo, Tirsi e Clori;* only the model is no longer a *canzoniere* but a "concerto," ordered (or should I say "concerted") as a collection of "Madrigali a 1. 2. 3. 4. & Sei Voci" and "altri generi de Canti."[98] Leaving aside for the moment the "altri generi" (other genres), only the proem and the last of the actual madrigals (*Con che soavità*) are for one voice (with instruments);[99] just one madrigal, and it appears almost out of place, is for six voices.[100] What is preferred, on the other hand, is the combination of two equal voices and *continuo* with, in this order, four madrigals for two sopranos, one for two contraltos,[101] and no less than eight for two tenors. Following those are a composition for tenor and bass, three for two tenors and bass, and two "A 4. Soprano Alto Tenor e Basso."

The choice of texts essentially is Marinian or pre-Marinian (especially with Guarini),[102] or is Marino-inspired. To this last category also belong the texts which thus far have remained anonymous: two sonnets, four madrigals, the *Partenza amorosa,* two *canzonette* in the manner of Chiabrera, and the text of the *balletto Tirsi e Clori* (often groundlessly attributed to Alessandro Striggio).[103] Besides the text of the proem, Marino is present with another sonnet from *Rime boscherecce* in *La Lira. Parte prima* and with four madrigals from *La Lira. Parte seconda.*[104] Competing with him is Guarini with one sonnet and five madrigals.[105] Chiabrera has two brief nonstrophic odes (included in fact by Monteverdi among the madrigals) from *Le maniere de'versi toscani.*[106] A new name is that of Claudio Achillini, who has been recognized as the author of the text of *Lettera amorosa;*[107] also his is the text of *Ecco vicine, o bella Tigre, l'ore,* a sonnet. Completing the picture are the madrigal *Al lume delle stelle,* which, as has already been mentioned, is by Torquato Tasso,[108] another attributed to F. degli Atti,[109] and an *ottava* by Bernardo Tasso.

In *Settimo Libro* an important part is played by the problems of organization and of formal balance, growing out of the varied metrical form of the texts as well as, in the music, from the alternating, associating, and balancing of two voices of equal color and expressive value. The first two madrigals for two sopranos and *continuo* provide samples of both sets of problems. The text of the first is an almost regular *ballata* by Guarini, with an initial *ripresa* that returns at the end, as occurs in numerous

compositions of the early period of the madrigal,[110] bringing with it the
music of the opening:

> Non è di gentil core
> chi non arde d'amore.
> Ma voi, che del mio cor l'anima sete
> e nel foco d'amor lieta godete,
> gentil al par d'ogn'altro avete il core
> perch'ardete d'amore.
> Dunque non è, non è di gentil core
> chi non arde d'amore.

> He has not a gentle heart
> who's not aflame with love.
> But you, who are the soul of my heart
> and live in love's flames joyously,
> you have a heart as gentle as anyone
> because you burn with love.
> He's not, indeed, he's not a gentle heart
> who's not aflame with love.

The first solo phrase of the first soprano already states the whole *ripresa*,
but Monteverdi adds to it the entrance of the same theme in the second
soprano and expands the musical phrase through progressions sung à 2,
until the phrase is brought to a repetition of the same cadence. In the
second section the formal suggestions come from the voices: the first voice
proposes a recitative phrase concluded in coloratura; the second presides
over a varied and expanded repetition; the two sound together and bring
to a close a new phrase.[111] "Dunque non è" starts off the return of the first
section both in the music and in the text, but Monteverdi adds to it an
anticipation a fifth above it, which makes more pointed the expectation of
a full reprise.[112] In the other madrigal, also by Guarini, *O come sei gentile,*
the repetitive formulation suggested by the equal authority of the two
voices is intensified by the wording of the text:

> ... tu canti, io canto;
> tu canti per colei che t'ha legato,
> et io canto per lei ...

> ... you sing, I sing; / you sing to her who has put you in bonds, / and I,
> too, sing to her ...

Deriving from it is a quadruple (although free, varied, and intensified)
repetition, reflected in turn in the conclusion ("vivi cantando") by an

insistent pealing of the bass, first in minims, then in semibreves—a harmonic invention, in a composition having the appearance of a rhapsodical competition between two singers, that becomes even more sapid for the change of the opening D to a B-flat.

Predominating in the madrigals of *Settimo Libro* is a sense of refinement,[113] related on the one hand to the precise and rarefied madrigalism of the two compositions for four voices,[114] and on the other hand to the detached lightness and miniaturistic perfection of the *canzonetta*. This stems from many factors: from the rhythmic motion which (together with the sense of direction of the melodic lines and the urgency of obvious harmonic resolutions) often unifies the whole course of the composition in a regular and continuous pulse, not even contradicted, on occasion, by a sudden broadening into doubled values; from the largely syllabic treatment of the text, in uniform values, giving the recitation a *staccato*, almost dancelike lightness; last but not least, from the sense of slight but intentional caricature imparted to some emotional passage by contrast with the general context. Among the many examples that could be pointed to, let us consider *Perché fuggi tra i salci* (Marino). The first tenor begins a solo with rapid eighth notes on the uniform motion of semiminims of the *continuo* and outlines, with just a slight pathetic inflection on the double invocation "oh, cruda!" a fluent melody as self-contained as if it were a complete strophe. Monteverdi reopens it, varies it, modulates it in a no less balanced repetition à 2, and then goes on with greater, yet always controlled, pathetic emphasis on "miser" and "morte colsi" (not to mention the *concitato* syncopation of "corsi, corsi"). The final section ("quel bacio che m'ha morto . . .") leads the madrigal back to its conclusion, not with thematic returns but, in spite of some passages of triple time,[115] with the persuasive insistence of the rhythm.[116]

In the madrigals, instances of madrigalism are not lacking, and as usual with Monteverdi they do not attract attention so much for their novelty as for the skill with which they are manipulated and for their function in the general economy of the composition. It is natural for *O come sei gentile* and *Augellin* to be dominated by images of the singer and of the song, since "canto," "riso," "giuoco," "fiori," and "ardori," wherever they are presented in the text, unfailingly give rise to the response of vocal melisma. But more special and spicy cases are not lacking: in *Ah, che non si convien* the spacing of the voices for "lontan" and "appresso," contrasted with the closing on the unison of "fermo come a l'onda immobil scoglio" sustained above the rapid movement of the *continuo;* in *Non vedrò mai le stelle* the graphic visualization of open minims and semibreves for "ch'anzi a tanti occhi e tanti lumi"; in *Ecco vicine, o bella Tigre, l'ore* the quasi-canon in which precipices and steep summits are outlined before coming to the ornate and dancing motion of "l'orme del tuo bel pié leggiadre e sante." After so much recent recitative tradition, whether monodic or polyphonic, exclamations must be counted as madrigalisms. Striking in *Non vedrò mai le stelle* is the able presentation in conspicuous isolation of "o luci belle," and in *Tornate, o cari baci,* the interplay of false harmonic relations at every return of "pascete i miei famelici desiri."[117] The presence of the bass among the voices often acts as a stimulus for Monteverdi to display his own virtuosity in figurations that are pompously and calligraphically rounded to match the virtuosity of the performer; such is the case, for instance, in *Parlo, miser, o taccio* (Guarini) and in *Al lume delle stelle,* the second of which I have already cited several times.

Let us now read the proem, which has been given just passing mention:

> Tempro la cetra, e per cantar gli onori
> di Marte alzo talor lo stile e i carmi;
> ma invan la tento, et impossibil parmi
> ch'ella giamai risoni altro ch'amori . . .

> I tune my lyre, and to sing Mars' triumphs / I try sometimes to raise my style, my songs; / but the attempt is in vain, and I don't see / that it [the lyre] may sound for anything but love.

Whether or not Monteverdi did indeed attempt other themes and a different style as far back as that time, Marino's sonnet is of use to him for affirming that the love themes, the *teneri scherzi* he has necessarily fallen back on, are "the games of a poet's pen, not the real feelings of a pious heart" (scherzi di penna poetica e non sensi di cuor Cattolico.)[118] His emphasis on description, his reserve, refraining from sentimental abandon, are intentional; the proof is that polite restraint, irony, and the pledge to remain uninvolved disappear any time there can be no doubt as to the representative intention of the composition, any time, that is, that the urgency of feeling can be attributed to a character, thus leaving unaffected the composer in charge of the most important, official chapel in Venice.[119] The proem, with its double sinfonia, ritornelli, and strophic treatment, leaves no doubt as to its affinity with the operatic prologues of the time;[120] like those, it is rather formal. But the doubts that could arise for *Con che soavità* are soon dissipated by the spectacular spatial distribution of the two "choruses" of violas, each having its *continuo,* added to the already well-supported group providing the normal accompaniment;[121] the composition is evidently destined for a recital. The "recitative" character of the composition set to Bernardo Tasso's *ottava, Ohimé dov'è il mio ben,* is expressed by the subtitle *romanesca.*[122] Evidently social entertainment is the intended purpose of the two *canzonette* and of the *ballo Tirsi e Clori.* Therefore, in the category of "altri generi de Canti," there are only two pieces for which Monteverdi feels the need to safeguard himself with the direction "a voce sola in genere rappresentativo e si canta senza battuta" (for solo voice in a representative genre and sung without measure); they are *Lettera* and *Partenza,* two variations of the oldest *pièce de resistance* of the operatic repertoire, the *lamento.*

There is a greater difference in years between *Concerto* (1619) and *Libro Ottavo* (1638) than between *Quinto* and *Sesto Libro,* but in both pairs the more recent collection is divided into two parts, each of which resembles the organization of the older collection. In *Libro Ottavo* the section of the *Madrigali guerrieri* and that of the *Canti amorosi* both begin with a proem, end with a *ballo,* and besides madrigals include "altri generi."[123] The parallelism is also accentuated by the fact that the proem of the first section (which also dedicates the entire collection to the new head of the empire, Ferdinand III),[124] imitates, at least in the first quatrain, the sonnet providing the proem to the *Canti amorosi;* this sonnet in turn is nothing other than Marino's *Altri canti di Marte e di sua schiera,* the celebrated proem to *La Lira. Parte Prima.*

Praise for a warlike (in spite of himself) emperor is not unfitting for a dedication nor for an operatic prologue, which *Altri canti d'Amor* clearly resembles, given that prologues had in the meantime assumed a greater variety of forms. An obvious theatrical reference is also the brief sinfonia which introduces the first part of the madrigal.[125] Following that, the composition is carried out on three different musical planes: a tenor and two sopranos sing the first quatrain with brief participation by "doi Violini et una viola da gamba"; the bass ("Di Marte *io* canto"), echoed by the preceding trio and then by all the voices, starts off the warlike description with the aid of the two violins; the full participation of the instrumental chorus of four violas and two violins, in addition to the voices, is reserved to the tercets, in which the bellicose accents sound even more briefly and give way to the idea of singing (with insistent coloratura) and to the concordant choral praise of the conclusion.[126] But the rest of the "warlike" madrigals often sing of amorous wars with a light tone, as in the text *Gira il nemico insidioso, Amore.* It is a *canzonetta,* of which Monteverdi conserves the strophic sense, though he gives different music to each strophe.[127] The musical demiurge reveals himself in a different way in molding to his liking the text of Rinuccini's *Ogni amante è guerriero,* a long series of unrhymed endecasyllables which compares the life of the lover to that of the soldier and manages to find a way, in speaking of wars, to insert new praises for Ferdinand III.[128] Monteverdi illustrates the numerous images in madrigalian manner and tries to put some order into the long rambling speech, dividing it into sections: the first (descriptive) is for two tenors; the second (at first recitative and then "heroic," that is, warlike and eulogistic) is for solo bass; the third is a brief recitative for solo tenor; the last is contrapuntal for three voices. On the whole the most successful piece of this group (leaving aside *Hor che 'l ciel e la terra*) is the madrigal *Ardo, avvampo, mi struggo* (the beginning is Petrarchan, but it is a joke) for eight voices, two violins, and *continuo.* A tumultuous, onomatopoeic scene of fire and sacking is suddenly brought to a halt upon an invocation of mercy; two sopranos announce that "two beautiful eyes are the thieves and love the arsonist" (Son due belli occhi il ladro, e seco Amore / l'incendiario); but the joke is not yet over, and the voices still fling melodic arrows against the heart, till the conclusion declines with a typically Monteverdian trait; the fire languishes and is extinguished in a final tenor duet: "let the heart become ashes, and be silent" (lascia che il cor s'incenerisca, e taci.) The text is a sonnet, anonymous.

Surprisingly, the text of the *ballo Volgendo il ciel—Movete al mio bel suon* is also by Rinuccini.[129] But most of the texts of *Libro Ottavo* remain anonymous: Monteverdi had to resort to local poets to obtain the warlike rhymes and pugnacious loves he needed for the *stile concitato.* In the texts of the *Canti amorosi,* however, more authors are identified. Besides the proem by Marino (some forty years old by then), three madrigals are by Guarini, and a strophic text is by Rinuccini, who is also represented by the text of *Il ballo delle Ingrate* (as Tasso is by the text of *Combattimento*). Of Petrarch we shall speak further on.

Altri canti di Marte, the proem to *Canti amorosi,* does not have a sinfonia or other external sign to make it resemble a theatrical prologue.[130] The explanation for this different treatment is to be found perhaps in Monteverdi's remarks to the reader, "a chi legge," for the entire collection of the *Madrigali guerrieri, et amorosi,* in which he seems to assimilate the bellicose songs to the *rappresentativo* genre (though it is a case, except for the *Combattimento* and the *ballo,* of purely ideal representation), and the amorous songs to the chamber genre; it must be noted, however, that the correspondences mentioned by Monteverdi among a series of groups of three—for example: *concitato, temperato,* and *molle* (agitated, moderate, and soft); *ritmo, melodia,* and *armonia; teatro, camera,* and *ballo* (theater, chamber, and dance music); *musica guerriera, musica amorosa,* and *musica rappresentativa*—are confused, uncertain, and contradictory.[131] Also corresponding well to the idea of chamber music is the text of *Mentre vaga Angioletta,* which in Guarini's collection of the *Rime* has the title *Gorgia di Cantatrice.*[132] It is an unusually long text for a madrigal (twenty-six lines), though not as long as the warlike *Ogni amante,* to which it is a counterpart. Like *Ogni amante* it is rhapsodic (right from the opening, which is for an unaccompanied solo voice) and madrigalian; indeed it is a review of madrigalisms, including descending chromatic lines (pieghevol voce), but it is varied enough so as not to require any musical variety other than that obtained by combining and alternating the two tenors.[133] The idea and the style of chamber music are evoked in another way by the "moderate" expression and by the *canto alla francese* of the other two madrigals set to texts by Guarini which I have already mentioned, *Chi vol haver felice* and *Dolcissimo usignuolo.*

From Prunières to Einstein the idea has been spread in literature on Monteverdi that the advent of the *continuo* in Monteverdi's madrigals marks the beginning of a transition from the madrigal to the cantata, for which Monteverdi is held to be one of those mainly responsible.[134] I have already had occasion to state that in my view the *continuo* is a symptom and not a cause; as for the rest of the proposition, it seems acceptable to me only in its most general terms and exercising due caution, insofar as it underlines the remarkable analogies by which the madrigal prepared the way for the cantata—particularly the resemblance of the poetic themes on which both rest and the effort common to both toward a quasi-representation which "entra per l'orecchie e non per gli occhi" (enters through the ears and not through the eyes).[135] The problem is that the history of the beginnings of the cantata is still not entirely clear,[136] so the name evokes in our mind a standard type that was only arrived at toward the end of the seventeenth century. The madrigal is an open form, under no obligations whatsoever concerning the elements composing it and the order and manner of their concatenation; the mature type of the cantata, on the other hand, tends toward a definite alignment and concatenation of elements and tends to make a complete unit of each, each unit insisting on a determined expressive mood; usually it elaborates a quasi-dramatic situation into a recitative and then expands it lyrically into an aria. Monteverdi may have on some occasions touched on the model of the cantata, but he arrived at it as one of the infinite possible formulations of the madrigal, not because he was guided by a specific cantata outlook.

Cantata-type situations, among others, are those of *Lettera amorosa* and *Partenza amorosa*. But in their music the two pieces are, strictly speaking, recitatives and only indicate Monteverdi's nostalgia for the opera: a cantata composer would have wondered in astonishment where the aria was that so much recitative should have prepared and introduced.[137] Two compositions of *Libro Ottavo*, on the other hand, are set out in a sequence of recitative-aria-recitative, and it is those compositions that I particularly had in mind just now concerning the possibility that the madrigal mentality *also* accidentally hit upon the formula of the cantata. One has as its text the anonymous but graceful sonnet *O sia tranquillo il mare;*[138] the other, better known, is the three-part madrigal(?) *Non avea Febo ancora—Amor, dicea—Sì tra sdegnosi pianti*, to a text by Rinuccini.[139] Here the two recitative texts are choral, and the first of them, even in its brevity, has a tinge of *concitato* madrigalism for the nymph who "walks around, trampling the flowers" (calpestando i fiori / errava or qua, or la). Soloistic, on the other hand, is the *Pianto della Ninfa*, although it is punctuated by the three subdued voices to whom the recitatives are assigned, and it belongs to a type I have previously defined as "recitative aria."[140] The text shows us an uncustomary Rinuccini, one with an almost folksy tone, which may have suggested to Monteverdi a comparison with certain monodic compositions published in Venice between 1620 and 1640 with the name *cantade*. But the relation of the *cantada* to the later cantata is not fully clear, and in any case a single piece would not be enough to turn the madrigalist into a composer of cantatas.[141]

The address of "Claudio Monteverde a' chi legge" placed before *Libro Ottavo* is the composer's major direct theoretical pronouncement and, in spite of its interest, the clearest confirmation of the lack of solid foundations in his learning. More than as a theoretical document, it is important for what it allows us to perceive of the artist's thought on the greatest innovation of the collection, the *stile concitato*. Having considered, he says, the main passions of the soul, "anger, moderation and humility, or supplication" (Ira, Temperanza, & Humiltà o supplicatione), and the voices "high, low, and middle" (alta, bassa & mezzana), and the genres (of the classical tradition) "agitated, soft and moderate" (concitato, molle & temperato), and having found no samples in past composers of the "agitated" genre, "I have therefore set about rediscovering it with considerable solicitude and toil on my part" (perciò mi posi con non poco mio studio, & fatica per ritrovarlo).[142] To me this seems to be a theorization *ex post facto* for manners and movements that Monteverdi must have found spontaneously and madrigalistically (even if it is a vocal-instrumental madrigalism also influenced by the demands of the scenic gesture) for the setting of *Il combattimento*. Other aspects of the *stile concitato* have antecedents going back even further than 1624. Already *concitato* is *Sì ch'io vorrei morire* of *Quarto Libro*, a scherzo in the modern sense, for the pressing insistence of the rhythm;[143] also *concitato* is the superimposition of brief rhythmic designs in a passage of *Addio, Florida bella,* or the pressing imitation in the madrigal preceding it, *Una donna fra l'altre; concitato* must be (to make musical sense, not because the text requires it) the performance of *A quest'olmo* of *Settimo Libro,* which anticipates the rhythmic fragmentation of static harmonies and the intense instrumental collaboration of the warlike madrigals; and *concitato* must be, to do justice to the text, the rhythm of *Eccomi pronta ai baci;* finally, *concitato* is the rhythmic and harmonic obsession in another famous composition on a Rinuccini text, the chaconne *Zefiro torna.*[144]

A detailed discussion of the *stile concitato* is not germane to the aims of this writing, while on the other hand, it is important to explain what may have been the function of the two texts by Petrarch in *Libro Ottavo*. In accordance with the "temperata" and "da camera" mood which prevails in the *Canti amorosi* is *Vago augelletto,* for which Monteverdi used only the quatrains of sonnet CCCLIII, omitting all references to the death of Laura. We may dispense with describing its free treatment of the text and the remarkable analogies with the two madrigals *alla francese.*[145] Different, though, is the case of *Hor che 'l Ciel e la Terra,* both because the pretext placing it among the *Madrigali guerrieri* is quite thin (the phrase "Guerra è il mio stato"), and because one does not find in it that detachment or sentimental half-commitment which seems evident in all of Monteverdi's works starting from the accompanied madrigals of the *Sesto Libro*. Particularly intense is the emotion in the section corresponding to the first quatrain, with the description of the silence heavy with pain, the dramatic burst of "veglio, ardo, piango" (repeated to punctuate the successive declamation of the two tenors), and with the harrowing harmonies of the last line. The *stile concitato* and the intense participation of the violins dominate the quatrain and somewhat justify the madrigal as warlike; but in the *seconda parte,* corresponding to the tercets, emotion and desolation give pathos to the ascending chromaticism of "move il dolce e l'amaro" and to the nostalgic madrigalism of "son lunge."

My conviction that the Petrarchan choices represent a hidden and protected Monteverdian *Secretum,* a screen to the expression of the composer's personal sentiments, is reinforced by the fact that the first two

texts (both labeled "madrigale morale") of *Selva morale e spirituale,*
dedicated to the last of Vincenzo Gonzaga's children still alive, Eleonora,
widow of Ferdinand II of Austria, are by Petrarch. From the *Trionfi,* and
more specifically from the first *capitolo* of *Il trionfo della Morte,* comes the
first, transcribed here in the form in which it was adapted by Monteverdi;
the numbers refer to the lines in the original text:[146]

88	O ciechi, il tanto affaticar che giova?
	tutti tornate alla gran madre antica,
90	e 'l nome vostro appena si ritrova.
	Pur de le mill'è un'util fatica
	che non sian tutte vanità palesi?
	ch'intende i vostri studi si mel dica.
	Che vale a soggiogar tanti paesi
95	e tributarie far le genti strane
	con gli animi al suo danno sempre accesi?
	Dopo l'imprese perigliose e vane,
	e col sangue acquistar terre e tesori,
	vie più dolci si trova l'acqua e 'l pane,
100	e 'l vetro e 'l legno, che le gemme e gli ori.
82	U' son or le ricchezze? u' son gli onori,
	e le gemme, e gli scettri, e le corone,
	e mitre con purpurei colori?
85	Miser chi speme in cosa mortal pone.

Oh, blinded men, so much toil for what? / you shall go back to your great,
ancient mother, / and your names shall hardly be heard again.

Is one labor in a thousand of any avail / to avoid that all be deemed
nothing but vanity? / He who can read your minds should let me know /
what's the sense of conquering many countries, / making so many people
one's tributaries, / whose souls will burn inside, wishing you harm?

After the risks of pointless enterprises, / after buying lands and treasures
with blood, / you'll find more taste in plain bread and water, / more worth
in glass and wood than gold and jewels.

Where are the riches now? where are the honors, / the precious stones, the scepters and the crowns, / the mitres bright with the colors of purple?

Woe is to him who puts hope in mortal things.

As if that were not enough, the second madrigal insists on the "giovanile errore" (youthful error), on "le vane speranze e 'l van dolore" (vain hopes and vain grief)—themes of *Voi ch'ascoltate in rime sparse il suono*, the opening sonnet of Petrarch's *canzoniere*. Expressing the same tone is the anonymous text of the third composition, also a madrigal in meter: [147]

> È questa vita un lampo
> ch'all'apparir dispare
> in questo mortal campo.
> Ché, se miro il passato,
> è già morto; il futuro ancor non nato;
> il presente sparito
> non ben anco apparito.
> Ahi, lampo fuggitivo! e'sì m'alletta,
> e dopo il lampo pur vien la saetta.

Our life is only a lightning, / no sooner seen than canceled / from our world of things mortal.

If I look at the past, / it is dead, and the future still unborn; / the present here is gone / before you've even seen it. / Oh, flashing light! it is so alluring, yet / after the lightning strikes the thunderbolt.

These thoughts are now quite comprehensible if one considers that Monteverdi is in his seventies and for several years has been in the Church. But we have already seen the detachment, or at least the appearance or the will for detachment, in operation for more than a quarter of a century. One might think that age has now attenuated the capacity and intensity of the sentiments while leaving intact the faculties of invention. One might think that Monteverdi is now weary; [148] but the lean figure on the title page of G. B. Marinoni's *Fiori musicali* (of 1644!) is more sprightly and energetic-looking than that of the much earlier portrait in the Ferdinandeum of Innsbruck, in which his brow is knit and his attitude that of a person lacking in willpower. Besides, any tiredness is belied by the intense operatic activity of the last years.

To the last two books of madrigals could be applied the words Monteverdi wrote to Striggio, speaking of *La finta pazza Licori;* to represent it, he thought that the musical imitation ought to rest "on the word and not on the sense of the phrase; therefore, when war is spoken of, war must be imitated; when peace is spoken of, peace; when one speaks of death, death" (sopra la parola et non sopra al senso de la clausola; quando dunque parlerà di guerra bisognerà imitar di guerra, quando di pace di pace, quando di morte di morte).[149] Monteverdi's late madrigalism applies the imitation to single images, combining them with essentially musical means, not because it is dealing with real or simulated madness, but because it refuses to give in too much to the "sense of the phrase." Whether this restraint, this self-control, originated in disgust with the situation of the court in Mantua (and Monteverdi's opening his eyes to the ambiguous complicities he had been involved in during that long and hard service), or in the exalted sense of pride and dignity in the new Venetian situation, or both, it could not have been without conflict, for which Monteverdi's own little Petrarchan *Secretum* could also deserve the other title, *De secreto conflictu curarum mearum.* Certainly, psychological defenses are attenuated whenever (as in the case of the love letters, the *Pianto della Ninfa,* and perhaps the love story of Licori) the explicit representative intent identifies a particular (or unspecified) personage as subject of the passions. But not even the final operatic phase is exempt from checks and inhibitions. In *Il ritorno d'Ulisse* and in *Le nozze di Enea con Lavinia,* the intention to keep mainly to epic themes is clear, the second, more than the first, being full of warlike clangors and furors. Only their success and the certainty of the audience's consent made possible the flourishing of an opera which still found the youthful freshness of sentiment intact and associated it with the clairvoyance of more mature judgment. But even the "scandal" of *L'incoronazione* does not exist, because none of the spectators of the "historical" drama could fail to know that the ephemeral triumph of Nero and of Poppaea would soon be paid for, and "dopo il lampo pur vien la saetta" (after the lightning strikes the thunderbolt).[150] The true triumph is that of the stoic philosopher who joyously meets death, the deliverer from tribulations, from the blindness and toil of life on this earth.

19 &-Early Venetian Libretti at Los Angeles

Curiosity, the seed of science, needs time and favorable conditions to develop into full knowledge. But when, during a recent visit to Los Angeles, my curiosity was aroused by a collection of Venetian libretti preserved there in the music library of the University of California, time was inexorably short. Similar collections exist in some other libraries, but nobody, to my knowledge, has ever undertaken to describe any of them, still less to inquire how much they resemble one another, and whether or not they may have had a common origin. To answer such plain questions would require no little time and labor, and all that I can do is to scatter the seed of my curiosity, hoping, as the farmer does, that it will bear good fruit.

The set at Los Angeles consists of more than one hundred volumes, in all-parchment bindings possibly of the late eighteenth century. On the spine of each volume the title *Raccolta de' Drammi*, lettered in gold on a leather tag, is supplemented by the year or years of the libretti included. Slight variations in the external measurements correspond to variations in the size of the small duodecimo format typical of such libretti (roughly 6 x 3 inches). I had the opportunity to examine only the first four volumes of the collection, which cover the first seven years of operatic activity in Venice. Even this was made possible only by the courtesy and liberality of the U.C.L.A. library system and of its music librarian, Mr. Frederick Freedman.

The spine of the first volume is stamped with the years 1637–38–39. It came as a surprise, therefore, on opening the volume, to find myself confronted with "La Deianira del Sig. Malatesta leonetti. Opera recitatiua in Musica. . . . in Venetia Per Angelo Salvadori Libraro a

San Moisè MDCXXXV." The excitement of a possible discovery quietly subsided, however, when I learned from the editor's dedication that the work had come from Rome, and from the author's original dedication to Cardinal Antonio Barberini, dated Fossombrone, September 8, 1631, that the "opera" had been planned for staging "con suoni, canti, & balli," on the occasion of the Cardinal's visit to that town. Ill health and lack of time had prevented Leonetti from perfecting his text in time and from having it set to music.

Even as an unborn opera, *La Deianira* is remarkable for its use of the term "opera" at least four years (eight, if we consider Leonetti's dedication) before its earliest known occurrence.[1] Also interesting is the ending of the work, which presents six strophes to be sung by a female chorus and danced by youths and damsels, followed by six additional strophes of a "corrente del balletto," and by two final lines for "tutti i chori." For the rest, the opera has some rather archaic features: it is divided into five acts; Hercules' battles backstage are only verbally reported to the audience; and finally, the acts are divided by a moralizing, unidentified "choro," quite distinct from the specific choruses of youths, damsels, priests of Juno, and so on, all of which take an active part in the dialogue and the action.

Following *La Deianira*, the four volumes I examined include all the expected titles for the years 1637 to 1643, each represented by at least one libretto (see the Appendix to this essay). Giacomo Badoaro's texts for *Il Ritorno d'Ulisse in patria* and *Le nozze d'Enea con Lavinia* (nos. 17 and 18) are both in manuscript; comparison with other existing copies might establish whether or not they belong to small manuscript editions (so to speak) that were circulated instead of printed libretti at the time of the original performance.[2] Gian Francesco Busenello, like Badoaro, also seems to have been unwilling to have his texts printed when they were set to music; however, he had them published later in a single volume (*Hore ociose*, Venice, 1656), each with an individual frontispiece and pagination. Abstracts from this print are included in volume 2 (nos. 10, 11, and 14) and volume 3 (no. 30) of the Los Angeles collection. Benedetto Ferrari's *La ninfa avara*, published in 1642 as an individual libretto (although with the date misprinted as 1662), also appears in volume 2 in an abstract from the author's *Poesie drammatiche* of 1644 (no. 16); it is preceded and followed, however, by manuscript pages reproducing title page, dedication, and so on, and an appended *intermedio*, just as they appear in the 1642 libretto. Giulio Strozzi's highly successful *La finta pazza* is present with no less than three different editions (nos. 15, 19, and 20); *L'Arianna* (nos. 9 and 13), *La Venere gelosa* (nos. 32 and 33), and *L'Egisto* (nos. 34 and 35) are each represented by two different editions.

In sharp contrast with such evident striving for completeness, the collection includes very few examples of scenarios: only one in volume 1 (no. 6)[3] and two in volume 3 (nos. 24 and 26).[4] For the rest, a scenario— that is, the description, scene by scene, of what happens on stage—is sometimes incorporated into a libretto, as, for instance, in the first edition of *La finta pazza* (no. 15, pp. 7–21) and in *Amore innamorato* (no. 21, pp. 11–17). Strozzi's *La finta savia* has a general "Argomento Historico" supplemented by extensive individual *argomenti* for the prologue, the *intermezzi,* and every single scene.

We are so used to seeing libretti sold at the doors of our opera houses that we take it for granted that libretti were always printed for or before the first performance of an opera. The evidence we can gather from the libretti now under examination tends to negate such an assumption, at least for the earliest phase. It is well known, for instance, that Ferrari's *Andromeda* and *Maga fulminata* (nos. 2 and 3) contain detailed narratives of the way in which the two operas *had been* staged.[5] A note appended to Strozzi's *Delia* (no. 4) warns the reader that more than three hundred lines of the printed text "*have been* omitted in the performance," these being "the poet's trills," which had to give way to the passages of the singers. Again Ferrari, commending his *Armida* (no. 7) to the doge Francesco Erizzo, expresses hope that the latter's name shall protect her not against adverse reactions of opera goers, but against "the horrors of oblivion." The libretto of Ferrari's *Ninfa avara* (no. 16), performed in 1641, was printed in 1642. Finally, we have seen that both Badoaro and Busenello seem to have prevented the printing of libretti at the time in which their texts were represented with the music of Monteverdi or Cavalli.[6]

Most usual at the time of the performance—or even earlier, judging from the strong advertising flavor of some title pages[7]—was the printing of a scenario, seldom exceeding twenty-four pages, that is, one single duodecimo fascicle. Very few of these small pamphlets have been preserved, but in fact we cannot be sure that none existed, even for operas for which none has survived. Although libretti were evidently conceived as library items, the occasional and utilitarian character of the scenarios, added to their extreme frailty, exposed them all too easily to the danger of obliteration. To be sure, there was some tendency to replace the function of a scenario with the printing of a libretto;[8] even so, the majority of libretti were so much more concerned with the glorification of the poets that even composers' names were usually omitted, not to speak of the names of singers, dancers, or stage designers.

From the latter category a third sort of print originated, which did not appear very frequently, and which is best characterized in connection with the short-lived activities of the Teatro Novissimo (1641–1647). The emphasis these activities placed on stage design and machinery was responsible for such publications—in addition to those of the usual sort— as *Il Cannocchiale per la Finta pazza,* a scenario of fifty-five pages focusing, as the title points out, on the visual aspect of the opera; a folio edition of *Il Bellerofonte,* including ten plates of stage designs; and M. Bisaccioni's *Apparati Scenici Per lo Teatro Novissimo di Venetia Nell'anno 1644,* a narrative of *La Venere gelosa* illustrated by twelve plates (some of them belonging to other productions).[9]

In spite of the diversity of such publications, or perhaps because their publishers' interests and aims were so varied, we can seldom be sure of the precise date of the original performance, or of a repetition, of any given opera. We rely with great confidence on a tradition based on Bonlini's and Groppo's catalogues, without realizing that these authors did not have any better sources of information than we do about operas that had been performed a century before their own time. They, too, when faced with the same difficulties we encounter today, may have been misled by the unconscious projection into the past of customs that prevailed at their own time.[10]

To such misleading projections belongs the view that every printing of a libretto was determined by a new series of performances in a different year or season. Thus the existence of two Venetian libretti of *L'Arianna* has led to the notion, unsupported by any other piece of evidence, that Monteverdi's thirty-year-old opera was first given to inaugurate operatic activity at the theater at San Moisè in the autumn of 1639 and later repeated during the regular season of 1640.

I strongly doubt that the custom of an autumn season was already established in 1639. In fact, a quick glance at the 1639 libretto of *L'Arianna* may suffice to make us realize that its printing was not related to any performance. It was a purely literary publication, reproducing the 1608 text without any mention of theater or composer; nor did it contain any of the marks which in the 1640 libretto were used to indicate numerous lines, mainly in the choruses, that were then omitted in the performance.[11] Quite a different situation is evident just in the title page of the 1640 libretto, "L'ARIANNA DEL SIG. OTTAVIO RINUCCINI Posta in Musica DAL SIG. CLAUDIO MONTEVERDI. Rappresentata in Venetia l'Anno 1640 . . ." Venice was too proud of its most famous musician to let his name pass unnoticed; in addition to the title page, the printer's dedication also mentions the performance and praises Monteverdi, and a sonnet by Ferrari extols him as the "Oracolo della Musica." What is most relevant to our present purpose, however, is that although the 1639 libretto merely reproduces the original prologue,[12] this appears in the 1640 print in a version addressed to the Venetian doge.

More complex is the case of *L'Adone,* which is likewise associated with Monteverdi's last years, even though the traditional attribution of the music to him has recently been rejected.[13] That the composer was Manelli is made clear by the latter's dedication of the libretto to Antonio Grimani (one of the owners of the theater in San Giovanni e Paolo), and particularly by the following passage: "So had I the good fortune, in representing it [*L'Adone*] in music, not to be one of the humblest professors of this art, while the theater of your most illustrious lordship, in which it was performed, is the noblest of all that exist today in Italy."[14] To be sure, the passage also implies that *L'Adone* had already been performed before the date of the dedication, December 21, 1639; but the time during which the performance must have taken place is narrowed down to a few days by a letter from Bologna, also printed in the libretto, in which the poet Paolo Vendramino deplores Manelli's decision to present *L'Adone* in his absence—that is, "without those lights that are most needed for its staging." "It *shall be* your task," he then warns, "to give it that diligence and study that I am not able to give, and which, nevertheless, are deserved by any performance of an opera in Venice."[15] Up to December 16, 1639, the day on which this letter was written, no news of the performance had reached Bologna; it is clear, then, that the presentation on stage of *L'Adone* must have preceded Manelli's dedication by no more than one week. I am inclined to think that the presumed date of the dedication is that of the day following the first performance.[16]

Whatever scant evidence we have seems to indicate that autumn was, at this time, the season in which operatic companies traveled to perform in places other than Venice. As the poet of *L'Adone* had recently moved from Venice to Bologna, so I would suggest that the opposite journey had been made only a few weeks earlier by the Manelli troupe. My reason for believing this is the evidence, recently uncovered by Wolfgang Osthoff, that the troupe had performed Manelli's own *Delia* and Monteverdi's *Ritorno d'Ulisse in patria* in Bologna.[17] Osthoff places the Bolognese performances in 1640, after the first Venetian performance of *Il Ritorno,* which he convincingly dates in 1640 instead of the traditional 1641.[18] It seems more likely to me that Monteverdi's new opera had an "out-of-town" trial before its 1640 appearance in Venice—namely, at Bologna in the late autumn of 1639.

This is no academic shuffling of dates. In both the 1639 Venetian reprint of *L'Arianna* and the Bolognese performance of *Il Ritorno* (in which he had no direct participation) I see Monteverdi's shrewd yet cautious moves toward a full reentry onto the operatic scene. It was not proper for the head of the ducal chapel of San Marco, now a priest, to show any eagerness to become involved in the most thoroughly secular form of musical activity and in the never very reputable milieu of the public stage. Yet Monteverdi, old in years but still young in spirit, must have been thrilled at first by the activity of the "foreign" troupe of Ferrari and Manelli (whom he may have encouraged to settle in the theater in San Cassiano),[19] and even more tantalized in 1639, when his own pupil, Cavalli, and many of his singers in San Marco began their own operatic activity.[20] Cavalli's group obviously established a favorable precedent for the master's still unavowed goal, yet it is remarkable that Monteverdi's operas were all performed in the theaters in which Ferrari and Manelli acted as producers.[21] He probably believed that collaboration with his own dependents would have harmed his lofty position of authority in San Marco.

Badoaro's letter to Monteverdi, missing in the Los Angeles libretto of *Il Ritorno,* but prefacing the corresponding seventeenth-century manuscript in Venice, stresses the pressures exerted on Monteverdi by highly placed persons to have the opera performed in Venice. It also emphasizes the efforts of "private people" (that is, nonprofessionals) to help in the production, as well as the exceptional patronage accorded it.[22] Apparently, all these exceptional circumstances were enough to induce Monteverdi to yield gladly to external pressure, which coincided with the internal urge of his dramatic talent.

Appendix: Contents of Volumes 1–4 of the Los Angeles Collection

In the following list each libretto is identified by its title, printer, and date. (The place of printing, unless otherwise stated, is Venice.) To these elements any other information is added that may help to distinguish between prints having the same title. Whenever possible, reference is made (by the abbreviation LC) to an entry in the Library of Congress *Catalogue of Opera Librettos Printed before 1800,* prepared by O. G. T. Sonneck (Washington, 1914).

Volume 1 ("1637–38–39")
1. *La Deianira,* Salvadori, 1635; 66 [2] pp. (see the text of the essay).
2. *L'Andromeda,* Bariletti, 1637 (LC).
3. *La Maga fulminata,* Bariletti, 1638; 2nd printing, 94 pp.; p. 28, on which other copies are reported to have Ferrari's portrait, is blank.
4. *La Delia O Sia La Sera sposa del Sole,* Pinelli, 1639 (LC).
5. *Le Nozze di Teti, e di Peleo,* Sarzina, 1639 (LC).
6. *Breve espositione* ... (scenario of no. 5), n.i. [Sarzina, 1639]; 23 pp. (see the text of the essay).
7. *L'Armida,* Bariletti, n.d.; 1 preliminary leaf, 58 pp. (LC copy lacks the finely engraved frontispiece).
8. *L'Adone,* Sarzina, 1640 (LC).
9. *L'Arianna,* Salvadori, 1639; 45 pp.

Volume 2 ("1640–41")
10. *Gli Amori d'Apollo, e di Dafne,* Giuliani, 1656 (LC).
11. *La Didone,* Giuliani, 1656 (LC).
12. *Il Pastor regio,* Bariletti, 1640 (LC).
13. *L'Arianna,* Bariletti, 1640; 1 preliminary leaf, 64 pp. (LC).
14. *La Didone,* Giuliani, 1656 (= no. 11, except for one additional engraved preliminary leaf).
15. *La Finta pazza,* Surian, 1641; 108 pp.
16. *La Ninfa avara,* n.i., n.d.; pp. 177–205 of *Poesie drammatiche di Benedetto Ferrari* (Milan, 1644), preceded and followed by respectively 10 and 9 unnumbered manuscript pp., reproducing the missing parts of an earlier libretto (Salis, 1662, but 1642), and including *Proserpina rapita,* an "Intermedio per Musica."
17. *Il Ritorno d'Ulisse in patria,* ms., 1641(?); 116 unnumbered pp., plus blank flyleaves (see the text of the essay).
18. *Le Nozze d'Enea con Lavinia,* ms., 1641(?); 68 pp., plus blank flyleaves (see the text of the essay).
19. *La Finta pazza,* Surian, 1641; 96 [4] pp. ("Seconda impressione").
20. *La Finta pazza,* Surian, 1644; 96 pp. ("Terza impressione").

Volume 3 ("1642")
21. *Amore innamorato,* Surian, 1642 (LC).
22. *La Virtù de' strali d'Amore,* Miloco, 1642 (LC).
23. *Il Bellerofonte,* Surian, 1642 (LC).
24. *Argomento et scenario del Bellerofonte,* Surian, 1642; 19 pp.

25. *Narciso, et Ecco immortalati,* Bariletti, 1642 (LC).
26. *Argomento et scenario di Narciso, et Ecco immortalati,* n.i., n.d.; 18 pp.
27. *L'Alcate,* Surian, 1642 (LC).
28. *Sidonio, e Dorisbe,* Surian, 1642 (LC indicates a mounted notice on p. 106, which is missing here).
29. *Gli Amori di Giasone, e d'Isifile,* Bariletti, 1642 (LC).
30. *L'Incoronatione di Poppea,* Giuliani, 1656 (includes an engraved preliminary leaf not indicated in LC).

Volume 4 ("1643")
31. *La Finta savia,* Leni & Vecellio, 1643 (LC).
32. *La Venere gelosa,* Surian, 1643; 6 preliminary leaves, 92 pp.
33. *La Venere gelosa,* Padua, P. Framo, 1643 (LC. The copy at Los Angeles has only 6 preliminary leaves).
34. *L'Egisto,* Miloco, 1643 (LC).
35. *L'Egisto,* Surian, 1644; 93 pp. ("Seconda impressione"; pp. 25–48 missing.)

20 ᴊ⸺The Lame Horse
and the Coachman:
News of the Operatic Parnassus
in 1642

Francesco Melosio (1609–1670) of Città della Pieve is known to Italian scholars as the seventeenth-century writer who holds the hardly enviable title of king of the punsters, but to his credit, it must be recognized that he did not seem to attach too much importance to his particular talent of stringing together the most extravagant associations of words, usually related by double meanings or assonance. He employed his gift, without much success, to divert or flatter whomever he hoped could be of help to him, but after having tried in vain to make a living in several centers, especially in Rome and Turin, he was obliged at last to return to his native city. Dying there, poor and discontent, he did not suspect that a collection of his poetry and prose would shortly afterward be assembled by admirers even more adventurous than himself and transmitted to posterity in a number of editions.[1]

The editors rounded out their sparse harvest with two libretti, apparently the only works which Melosio himself saw in printed form: *Sidonio e Dorisbe*, "honored by the music of Signor Nicolò Fontè and performed in Venice in the theater of San Moisè in the year 1642,"[2] and *L'Orione*, "produced in the Teatro Regio of Milan in the year 1653."[3] The posthumous editions, designed for the hypothetical approval of posterity, omitted some incidental elements found in the original libretti, especially in *Sidonio e Dorisbe* (Venice, G. B. Surian, 1642), which are of great interest for the history of operatic customs. Omitted is the dedication in which Melosio, in a genealogical vein, offered his libretto "to the most illustrious ... Signor Michele Morosini, son of the most illustrious Signor Andrea, who was son of the most illustrious and most eminent procurator, Signor Barbone," and dated it "at home on February 16, 1642."[4] Omitted also is the address reproduced below, from which we learn that the writing of *L'Orione* had preceded that of *Sidonio e Dorisbe* and that all of Melosio's operatic activity can therefore be dated in 1641 and 1642:

The author to the reader.

I had hoped this year to stage *L'Orione*, an opera already finished, but the sword of this formidable constellation [Orion] has not been able to scare away my misfortunes and to overcome the malignancy of my stars. He who was in charge of producing it has given lack of time as his excuse, trying to tell me that the feeble product of my labor has been injured by the brevity of that elder [Time] who cannot [be content to] harm only by length. But I believe instead that a theater which customarily shelters the most sublime deities of the heavens disdained to welcome poor Orion, who was born within a skin befouled by the urine of three vagabond gods. Perhaps it will be produced some other year, when, purged by a long quarantine of the tainted stench of its birth, it may be admitted to the commerce of humans. The development of the present subject was commissioned to me here in Venice. This will be enough to prove that it cannot be a good thing, because the muses obey unwillingly, and—as with virgins—it is a great sin to violate them. I have borrowed from the Canto degli Errori [*Canto of Errors*] of Marino's *Adone* in order to lay out a drama full of imperfections, and without my saying it you would find out by yourself that it flowed from my pen in a very few days. The music and the [scene] painting will conceal some of my defects, but there will nevertheless be great need for your disposition, O reader, to regard them with indulgence. It will be easy for you to do, and this is how to do it. If you do not see stage engines, you may say that I, being very certain of my disgrace, have deemed it superfluous to engineer it. If a queen appears with but a few attendants, consider that she is outside of her own realm and perhaps must appear incognito. If you are displeased by the meanness of the costumes, remember that she is a widow and that she thinks of displaying nothing other than her vengefulness. Above all, excuse Signora Antonina in the role of Dorisbe; I swear to you that she, not wishing to seem foolhardy, had resolved to appear no more on the stage at a time when the most sublime female singers of our century perform marvels; but then, cheered by the thought that the sun welcomes salutations no less from marsh birds than from song birds, she has changed her mind. A few years ago the voice of this virtuosa could not reach the ear without injuring the heart. She succeeded mortally because she had something divine within herself; therefore I believe that Apollo, the god of medicine as well as of song, must have wanted to diminish her for the benefit of the world, which is precisely what one does with poisons, which need to be prepared with their opposites in order to be made into good medicine. Of me you may say what you like. You need only know that I write from mere caprice and that I do not wish to tie myself to strict observance of rules, nor sell my liberty in order to buy the praise of [being] a good imitator.[5]

The reasons Melosio gives for the cancellation of *L'Orione* are not convincing. In the first place, it is not clear why "lack of time" would have led anyone to prefer, in place of a libretto already written, a work still unwritten that in the end was even longer than the first. Even less satisfactory is the second reason, because *L'Orione*, even more than its substitute, belonged to the class of libretti filled with deities; other than the protagonist (who, though the son of three gods, is mortal), there is only one other human character in the midst of an array of divinities from Olympus, the ocean, and Hades.

The real reasons for the substitution must be sought in the realm of impresarial strategy: Melosio's aim was to assemble in *L'Orione* a sampling of the operatic incidents and characters which had been most in vogue. Even the beginning, when Orion swims to the shore of Delos, where Diana is hunting with her nymphs, reproduces a combined hunting and maritime scene as found in *Le nozze di Teti e di Peleo* (1639). To Delos have come Vulcan and the Cyclopes to celebrate Apollo's victory over the Python; Cupid flies in and asks them to forge new arrows for him. Also at Delos are Aurora, Apollo's assistant, who is followed by the suspicious Titon, and Venus, Apollo's enemy, who wants to be present at the festival and has consequently assumed the disguise of an old woman. Cupid's flights and arrows were plentiful in *Amore innamorato*, the first opera given at the theater at San Moisè that year, 1642, and in an opera given simultaneously at the theater at San Cassiano, *La virtù de' strali d'Amore*, as well as in a distant yet famous Florentine precursor, *Flora*, of 1628. Vulcan and the Cyclopes, formerly seen in *Delia* (1639), were also found in *Amore innamorato*. The infidelity of Aurora and the jealousy of Titon had already been used by Gian Francesco Busenello as a Boccaccian counterpoint to the mawkish sentimentality of *Gli amori di Apollo e di Dafne* (1640). As for Venus, who once again pursues and scolds Cupid and scorns Vulcan, the idea of disguising her as an old woman does anticipate by at least five years a similar treatment of her in Luigi Rossi's *Orfeo*, yet it also relates Venus to a series of caricatures of old hags, the prototype for which is Scarabea in Benedetto Ferrari's *La maga fulminata* of 1638. The scene of Orion sleeping and dreaming, during which Diana and Aurora fall in love with him at first sight and consequently bicker and exchange retorts, is likewise nothing new. We are, as by now is all too evident, in the realm of "scorn of the gods";[6] but even this region, particularly apt for the acidulous talent of Melosio, had already furnished more than one cue to Venetian libretti, ranging from the thievery of Mercury in *Delia* and *Il pastor regio* (1640), to "Di Giove son referendario e spia" (I am Jove's informant and spy) of Hermaphroditus in *Delia*, to the subterfuges of Aurora in *Gli amori di Apollo e di Dafne*.

We cannot say that Melosio's calculated effort to please was mistaken, but it was unfortunately preceded by a work which had the same design: *Amore innamorato*. Moreover, Giovanni Battista Fusconi, the librettist of *Amore innamorato*, had successfully engaged in battle with at least one concurrent opera, *La virtù de' strali d'Amore*, by literally matching its weapons, that is, Love's weapons.[7]

At that time there were, in fact, two main types of operatic strategy in Venice: on the one hand, characters and incidents that had proved successful with the public were exploited as often as possible (any variations being superficial rather than substantial); on the other hand, experiments with new ideas were immediately imitated or even anticipated by rival theaters. A significant example of the latter occurred during the Venetian operatic season of 1641, when the most sensational event was the opening of the Teatro Nuovissimo. Its inaugural opera was *La finta pazza* by Giulio Strozzi, with music by Francesco Sacrati and scenes and machines by Giacomo Torelli. It may have been an accident, but it was more likely a protective measure, that this opera was not advertised in the customary way, by the publication of its scenario. Instead, the scenario was incorporated into the first edition of the libretto, an unusual arrangement,[8] but one that did not prevent the mad scenes of the protagonist[9] from being imitated in concurrent operas: in *Didone* of Busenello and Cavalli at San Cassiano, and in *La ninfa avara* of Benedetto Ferrari at San Moisè.[10] The only stage that remained free of "madness" was that of San Giovanni e Paolo, which produced Monteverdi's *Nozze di Enea con Lavinia*. Since mad scenes can be traced back to Monteverdi's lost *Finta pazza Licori* (intended for Mantua, 1627, but never performed),[11] it would seem that Monteverdi disdained to imitate his imitators.

Even a summary comparison of Fusconi's *Amore innamorato* with Melosio's *L'Orione* clearly manifests the necessity of the hasty drafting of *Sidonio e Dorisbe* to avoid a repetition, on the same stage and almost certainly with the same singers, of situations and characters analogous to those found in the first opera. Gods and mythological personages are banished entirely from the newly drafted work. Just as *Amore innamorato* had dramatized for Venetian spectators the fable of Psyche as told in canto IV of Marino's famous *Adone*, the plot of *Sidonio e Dorisbe* faithfully reproduces that of canto XIV (stanzas 196–396) of the same poem. However, in order to focus primarily on the romance of the desperate and pathetic human events, the story is taken out of its mythological context and happily resolved at the end by means of a sudden reversal.

By emphasizing such a new aspect in an operatic context, Melosio was once again doing nothing more than following a trend which had been established earlier in the season—the very season during which Giovanni Faustini, the "librettist of intrigue," also made his debut. Melosio had the ability, however, to realize it more pointedly, especially by liberating his plot from extraneous elements still present in the libretti of his rivals, such as those from mythology in the *Bellerofonte* by Nolfi and Sacrati and the *Alcate* by Tiraboschi and Manelli, or those from mythology and magic in *La virtù de' strali d'Amore* by Faustini and Cavalli.[12] Prince Sidonio, disguising himself as a gardner to be close to the enemy princess whom he loves, became the prototype for a series of "princely gardeners," including *Il principe giardiniero* (1644) of Benedetto Ferrari.

Another contribution of relative originality in terms of operatic drama- turgy is the character of Vafrino, servant of Sidonio, who, like Filotero, the companion or squire of Orion, is a vehicle for Melosian irony, in that he is cautious and realistic while his master is heroic and bombastic. Vafrino, Filotero, and the timorous Erino, squire of the protagonist of *La virtù de' strali d'Amore*, foreshadow the type of loutish and meddling servants who, though they were omnipresent in spoken and improvised plays, became common in opera only several years later. Masculine comic characters in the first Venetian operas had been either minor mythological figures or *villani* (rustics), like Tacco in *Il pastor regio* and Ghiandone in *La ninfa avara*, both by Ferrari. Or else their comedy consisted primarily of obscenities that might be veiled slightly or not at all, a style exemplified in 1642 by Hermaphroditus and Giraldo in *Gli amori di Giasone e d'Isifile*.

The gods have vanished even from the prologue of *Sidonio e Dorisbe*, where they are replaced, after the contemporary Roman fashion, by allegorical figures: Fortuna and Ardire (Fortune and Courage).[13] The only tie with mythology is a message from Thalia, brought by Time to the bare stage of the theater of San Moisè for a "Scherzo avanti il Prologo, e prima che apparisca il Palco" (scherzo preceding the prologue, before the scenery appears):

> Che si lasci desia
> Libero questo luogo
> A' suoi dotti seguaci;

Che strani avvenimenti
Già sono accinti à palesar al mondo.

She [Thalia] wants
this place opened
to her keen disciples
who are ready to display
strange events to the world.

Thalia does not appear in person and is thus spared the fate which befell Clio in 1643, that of singing *canzonette* on the conduct or misconduct of lovers;[14] but the reply to Time given by a "chorus of gambling ladies" nevertheless introduces mythological fiction into contemporary Venetian reality—a trick analogous to one Giulio Strozzi had played the year before when he had introduced the baroque custom of operatic performances into the fictional Homeric world of his *La finta pazza*:[15]

Di superbi Teatri, e regie Scene
A tal'affar erette
In altre parti la Cittade abonda;
In quest'angusta, e mal'ornata stanza
Né gli Dei, né le Muse hanno ricetto,
E se tu 'l piede vi ponesti o Tempo
È segno che tu sei tempo imperfetto.

Of splendid theaters and regal stages
For such occasions built
In other quarters this city abounds;
In this mean and hardly ornate room
Neither gods nor muses find shelter,
And if you set foot here, O Time,
It means that you are a common Time.

At the end of this dialogue, all of which is similarly adorned with Melosian witticisms, the gambling ladies, divided into two choirs, allow themselves to be convinced:

Al voler di Talia libero il luogo
E noi all'opra spettatrici havrai.

As Thalia wants, you will have free access to this place,
And will have us as spectators at the opera.

And Time replies:

> Andianne: a voi vicino
> Farà dimora il Tempo,
> Perché non osi amareggiarvi il gusto
> Sguardo, né man di spettatore audace.

> Let us start; near to you
> Time will remain.
> Lest your relish be spoiled
> By leers or passes of some impudent spectator.

Even more interesting than this touch of local color is the final stage direction for the "scherzo": "Qui cala il Palco, & apparisce la Scena" (Here the scenery is lowered and the stage setting appears), which clarifies the real intent of this Melosian caprice, that of replacing the usual gods *ex machina* with quite different marvels of "stagecraft." Whatever scenic trick may have been used at the theater at San Moisè, which does seem to have been the smallest of the Venetian theaters, it is worth noting that the sudden appearance of the stage setting at the end of the prologue was an effect devised during the same season by Bernini, in the Roman production of *Il palagio incantato d'Atlante*.[16]

Melosio's *Poesie e prose* include "Recitativi varii, e possono adattarsi per musica" (diverse recitatives, which may be set to music) and "Recitativi ameni" (jocular recitatives).[17] The texts in both categories often suggest settings consisting of ariettas as well as recitatives. In them Melosio indulged his love of word play upon musical terms and comparisons; for example, among the "jocular recitatives" is found a "Cantata non cantata" (song not sung), crammed full of citations from well-known arias, and a "Difesa di un musico castrato amante" (defense of a castrato singer in love).[18] We do not know what contacts he had with musicians other than the two who composed music for his libretti, but he names Marazzoli in a *capitolo* in *terza rima*, and he insults a *maestro di musica* named Pezzi in a sonnet.[19]

Two other *capitoli* refer to Melosio's brief operatic career. One is entitled "To the most illustrious lord, N. Contarini, entreating this influential gentleman upon some indulgence in the matter of an opera by the author, recited in Venice in the theater at San Moisè"; the other is "On the same topic, addressed to the lawyer Pozzi, while he was in bed with the gout."[20] Their common theme is the recompense owed to the poet for his work as a librettist; concerning the identity of the person who refused to pay there can be no doubt, even though a dash supplants his name:

> Voi la mia vita in un sol cenno havete,
>   Perché un sol cenno, che al————ne diate,
>   Darmi soldi per viver lo vedrete.
> Deh, se pure un'Orfeo non mi stimate;
>   Non vogliate Signor, che a i versi miei,
>   In vece di danar, corran sassate.
> Trattato qual Christiano esser vorrei;
>   Se ben son quasi un Turco diventato
>   Nel Teatro del duce degli Hebrei.
> Dal principio mi fu profetizzato,
>   Che un'huom Cavallo, ed un certo Profeta,
>   M'havrian di calci, e corna al fin pagato.
> . . . .
> Mia lingua par sacrilega, se chiede;
>   Che non vuol trar Mosè l'acqua da i sassi
>   Né 'l Cavallo altro fonte aprir col piede.
> Ei sotto il vostro scudo in salvo stassi,
>   Per non uscir con i suoi scudi in Giostra,
>   E di Cavallo, un Saracino fassi.
> Anzi è un miracol ver dell'età nostra;
>   Perché al pagare è Caval zoppo, e lento;
>   E non pagando un Barbaro si mostra.

  You control my life by a single gesture, because if you only gave———— a hint you would see [him] give me money to survive.
  Ah! even if you don't have me for an Orpheus do not desire, sir, that for my verses, instead of money, stones are thrown.
  Treated like a Christian I wish to be, even if I become almost a Turk in the theater of the leader of the Hebrews [the theater at San Moisè].
  From the beginning it was foretold to me, that a horsy man [un' huom Cavallo] and a certain prophet [Moses] would in the end pay me with a kick and a blow.
. . . .

  My tongue may appear sacrilegious in its quest, but Moses refuses to draw water from the stones and the horse [Pegasus-Cavalli] to open another fountain with his foot.
  He remains safe under your protection, so he need not appear in a joust with his shield [scudi, both shields and écus], and shows himself to be a Saracen [the tilting-post in a quintain] rather than a horse.
  Indeed he is a true miracle of our age, because with regard to paying, he

is a lame and slow horse; yet by not paying he shows himself to be a *barbaro* [a Barb and a barbarian].

The *capitolo* addressed to Pozzi similarly aggravated the situation:

Nega il————a i miei sudor mercede,
Né mi fà donation pur d'un quatrino,
Perché mi vuol d'ogni bisogno herede.

Già son privato del furor Divino;
Ché a gir dietro a un Cavallo per danari,
Son fatto di Poeta, un Vetturino.

He,————, denies mercy to my sweat, and will not even donate a
farthing to me, because he wants me to be in need of every necessity.
Already I am bereft of divine fury, because by following a horse for
money, from a poet I am changed into a coachman.

A poor devil he was, yet in ability not inferior to the many poets who were cherished and revered by his contemporaries. His modesty makes him attractive, but perhaps he abused it. Indeed, in "The author to the reader" (given above),[21] it was an excess of modesty, or a bit of malice, that led him far beyond the usual protests of librettists concerning the poverty of their inventiveness and the brevity of time, to denigrate the theater, the scenery, and the singers (or at least the singer who portrayed the principal female character).[22]

In Melosio's two *capitoli*, we read for the first time the "news" that Francesco Cavalli in some way functioned as an impresario at the theater at San Moisè in 1642. We knew already that he had a hand in the administration of the theater at San Cassiano beginning with *Le nozze di Teti e di Peleo* of 1639; his role can be deduced from the scenario of *Le nozze* and from the fact that until 1645 San Cassiano produced only operas composed by him—from 1642 on always based on libretti by Giovanni Faustini. It does seem strange that he would participate simultaneously in the management of two theaters.[23] Yet something analogous had occurred during the two preceding seasons, when Ferrari seems to have been involved in the activities of both the San Moisè and San Giovanni e Paolo theaters, which signifies that it was not easy at that time to find men possessing the diverse abilities needed to organize an operatic spectacle. Moreover, we perhaps define their activities incorrectly by identifying them with those of an impresario, since the real financiers and impresarios were high-ranking persons like Pozzi and Contarini, who did not wish to acknowledge their role officially, and toward whom (as Alessandro Stradella later found out) it was neither prudent nor clever to direct overly pungent retorts.

We do not know whether Melosio's comic invectives against the "lame and slow horse" were successful in that he obtained the payment he claimed. However, even the libretto of *L'Orione* must have remained with Cavalli, for he composed a musical setting for a Milanese production of 1653.[24] Melosio, who was then in Rome or at one of its thankless provincial posts, where he was sent to administer papal justice, had the responsibility of writing a prologue for the occasion, addressed to Emperor Ferdinand III.[25] Perhaps he also revised the "ariette," in which the first line is frequently repeated at the end of a strophe, a format which appears only sporadically in *Sidonio e Dorisbe*.[26]

The final, posthumous homage paid to Melosio's poetic vein was a new *Sidonio*, written by N.N. ("no name," behind which letters Pietro Pariati concealed himself) for a musical setting by Antonio Lotti, produced at the theater of San Cassiano in 1706. In the new libretto (Venice, M. Rossetti, 1706), the usual note to the "Courteous Reader" declares that "the subject of this drama served long ago as an episode in an epic poem, and as the fable of a dramatic poem."[27] In reality, Melosio's *Sidonio e Dorisbe*, which had recently reappeared in Venice in the 1704 edition of his *Poesie e prose* is—much more than Marino's *Adone*—the direct source for the new libretto.

21 Falsirena and the Earliest *Cavatina*

The Roman carnival of 1626 is not remembered for its wealth of festivity. Indeed, from contemporary diaries and chronicles, the major historian of Roman carnivals extracted only one noteworthy event: the performance "in music, in the house of Father Edoardo [*sic*] Conti, of Marino's *Adone*, reduced to a brief pastorale in blank verse, which succeeded extremely well, not only because of the exquisite voices, but also because of the scenic apparatus, diversity of costumes, and diverse ballets."[1] If we recall the immense length of *Adone* (5,625 eight-line stanzas), we can clearly sense a sigh of relief in the word "brief." Yet in actuality, *La catena d'Adone* by Ottavio Tronsarelli and Domenico Mazzocchi, to which the passage refers, dramatized only one episode—albeit one of the most characteristic—of the poem.[2]

The literary acclaim bestowed upon Marino, who had died in his native city of Naples in 1625, was then at its zenith, and as a result his influence was also felt in the field of music. Moreover, his *Lira* and *Zampogna* had begun the fashion of titling collections of poetry with the names of musical instruments. Tribute was paid to this fashion by the *Chitarra*, the *Violino*, and even the *Tromba di Parnaso* of a remarkable adventuress, Margherita Costa,[3] whose career is related in some way to the composition and performance of *La catena d'Adone*. Indeed, Tronsarelli's biographers tell us that he was motivated to write this work by a controversy between the admirers of one Cecca del Padule and those of our Margherita, concerning "which of the two [women] surpassed the other in sweetness of voice and artfulness of singing."[4] This canorous contest was forestalled at the last moment by the intervention of a jealous wife, Princess Aldobrandini. (The composer of *La catena d'Adone*, Domenico Mazzocchi, was then in the service of the Aldobrandinis.) So the two rivals were replaced by castrati, but that does not conceal the fact that *La catena d'Adone* originated amid an aura of undisguised sensuality, which certainly would not have displeased Marino, and which may have been known to the spectators at the seven performances, "a great number of titled and first-rank members of the nobility, men and women."[5]

The plot is well known.[6] Adonis, the lover and beloved of Venus, enters the woods ruled by the sorceress Falsirena while fleeing from jealous Mars. Falsirena falls in love with him and, incited by her counselor Idonia, magically transforms the woods into a beautifully adorned garden to entice him to stay. But Adonis, remaining faithful to Venus, does not respond to either enchantments or blandishments, so the sorceress— against the advice of a second counselor, the wise Arsete—resolves to prevent him from leaving by means of a golden chain forged (in the prologue) by Vulcan and the Cyclopes, and which Adonis alone cannot perceive. Even this is not enough to obtain his love, so Falsirena assumes the appearance of Venus. But then the real Venus arrives, has Adonis freed by Cupid, and has Falsirena bound to a rock with the golden chain. This scene of two opposed Venuses, confronted with whom even the enamored Adonis wavers and is bewildered, was evidently the one designed to decide the contest between the two beautiful earthly rivals. Yet it was certainly a euphemism when the chronicler wrote of a canorous contest, because the authentic Venus makes her first and only appearance in this final scene of the drama and has very little to sing in comparison with Falsirena, who is—even more than Adonis—the true protagonist of the fable.

Although the basis was thus a veritable confrontation between two piquant and certainly thinly disguised beauties,[7] this did not prevent *La catena d'Adone* from having, just like its model, a clever "allegory of the fable," explained at the end of the musical score: "Falsirena, advised to do good by Arsete but persuaded to do evil by Idonia, is Soul advised by reason but persuaded by concupiscence. When Falsirena readily gives in to Idonia, this shows that every affection is easily overcome by the senses. When the wicked Falsirena is at the end bound to an unyielding rock, one must see that punishment is the final consequence of sin." Thus far it works. But what follows, a rarely attained summit of Marinism and hypocrisy, is more difficult to accept: "Adonis, who suffers various afflictions while far from the deity of Venus, is man who falls into many errors while far from God"![8]

Fortunately, neither librettist nor composer gave much thought to the allegory. The text and the music make many concessions to the taste of the time for architectonic and decorative display, yet they do not succumb entirely to marvels of scenography and surprises of scenic machinery (which happened only a few years later, for example, in *Erminia sul Giordano* of 1633). Turning to the dramatic and affective core of the fable, we indeed find that Falsirena does not give a single indication of being a symbol, but is—more than a magician or enchantress—a woman in love who loses patience with obstacles and resistance. Adonis, although more weakly designed, is made real enough in the description of his agitation and distress while suffering afflictions, and these provide expressive opportunities that a composer as sensitive and thoughtful as the elder of the Mazzocchi brothers would not fail to take full advantage of.

With the exception of a single passage in the text, the responsibility for meditating on the hidden and profound truth allegorized in the fable is left entirely, and rather undependably, to the good will of the audience. The sole exception is the monologue at the beginning of act III, in which Arsete deplores the obstinacy with which Falsirena pursues a perilous and errant course of action. Arsete has already fulfilled his dramatic function in the preceding act, by vainly attempting to dissuade Falsirena from using the golden chain to retain and conquer Adonis. His return to the stage is therefore useless with regard to plot development and functions only to spell out the moral meaning, epitomized by a short sentence which he states four times in the course of his monologue: "La Ragion perde dove il Senso abbonda" (reason loses wherever sensuality abounds). It is not much, nor is it particularly well expressed; yet it is enough if one remembers that in *Adone* the entire moral meaning of the poem is similarly encapsulated in a single line (canto I, verse 80): "Smoderato piacer termina in doglia" (immoderate pleasure will end in sorrow).

In this monologue (see Ex. 21.1), the composer is more effective than the librettist.[9] Mazzocchi's Arsete is a bass who is not potent or imperious like the Plutos in Peri's *Euridice* and Monteverdi's *Orfeo*, not a showy virtuoso and rather obsequious wheedler like Pluto in Monteverdi's *Ballo delle ingrate*, not peevish and senile like Charon in *Orfeo*, and not acrobatic and transformative, as the devil was to become in Stefano Landi's *Sant'Alessio* of 1631. Instead, his singing reflects the noble, concerned, and yet disinterested ponderings of a man whose age and wisdom have placed him beyond the reach of the passions, even though he has not lost the ability to be saddened by the folly of others. The role of the philosophic sage, which became a traditional role (and even a stereotyped caricature) in seventeenth-century opera, is here musically delineated for the first time. Monteverdi must have thought of this monologue when he later sketched,

Ex. 21.1 Domenico Mazzocchi, Arsete's monologue from *La catena d'Adone*, act III, scene 1.

Ex. 21.1 Continued

with much greater richness but not with greater dignity, Seneca's role in his *Incoronazione di Poppea*.[10]

This piece is evidently one of those to which Mazzocchi applied the term *mezz'arie*.[11] Each statement of the line which expresses the moral of the fable is marked by a transition from the discursive and unpatterned character of recitative to a more songlike phrase, which has the same "walking" bass but a different vocal figuration for every repetition (two statements are shown in Ex. 21.1). Thus, even though they are short, these melodic phrases embody two of the characteristics which, according to the thought of the time, distinguish arias: support by a patterned and moderately fast-moving bass, and treble variation upon any repetition of the bass pattern.[12] Even if the phrase itself is not particularly expressive, each of its returns punctuates the recitative and thus gives renewed life to the piece.

To designate this piece as "the earliest *cavatina*" may seem anachronistic, yet it is not so far removed in time as it seems at first sight. We customarily associate the *cavatina* with the vaporous and lunatic heroines and the plaintive and choleric heroes of nineteenth-century opera, and we think of it as the fraternal twin of the *cabaletta*, yet both *cavatina* and *cabaletta* have predecessors before the 1800s. For example, an aria in Gluck's *Paride e Elena* of 1767 is known as a *cabaletta*, and the *cavatina* is even older, because Charles Burney gave this designation to some of Handel's operatic arias.[13]

The term from which *cavatina* is derived is *cavata*, which is applied to a melodious piece in Traetta's *Farnace* of 1751,[14] and is discussed as early as 1728 and 1732, by Mattheson and Walther, respectively. No earlier writer, so far as I know, allows us to trace it back still further so as to fill in the century which still separates us from the *Catena d'Adone*; but a bridge over this void is provided by the first part of Walther's definition, which surprisingly describes the procedure employed by Mazzocchi for Arsete's monologue. The passage is approximately as follows: "when the entire content of an extended *recitative* is *concentrated* in a very few words, usually placed at the end, and thus *carved out* [the meaning of *cavare*] from the rest, so that it is necessary (in order to distinguish them) to set such *sententious* words in a measured and *arioso* style."[15]

The second of Walther's definitions is more vague: "when an aria, or some other piece, is so uncommonly well executed that one's wish is fully satisfied." This is so vague as to be obscure, were it not for the passage in Mattheson from which it is derived. Mattheson states that the meaning of the Hebrew word from which "psalm" derives is that of "beschneiden" (approximately, "to cut off" or "to separate"); then, after explaining that this must mean that psalms are separated from other songs because of their greater musical richness, he adds: "And one will not wonder so much over this Hebrew derivation if one considers that even today the Italians name a perfectly well-made, elaborated bravura piece [Kunst-Stück] a *cavata*, which is to say that it is brought out properly."[16] We thus find ourselves with two distinct types of *cavate*, the second of which indeed resembles a *cabaletta* more than what we consider to be a *cavatina*. This second type contradicts the first meaning of *cavata* suggested by Walther, that is, of an arioso, or an aria functioning, we may say, as an epigraph, in which the primary consideration is adding evidence to the text. *Cavata* is, in fact, still in use in the technical jargon of musicians, but it is employed only to describe the ability of the player of a stringed instrument to obtain a rich and full sound *out* of his instrument, in other words, Mattheson's "Wollaut." In the vocal and operatic field, the fullness and richness of a singer's sound may at one time have been similarly described, and therefore *cavata* may have been applied either to indicate the sense of expansiveness that is felt when recitative gives way to the unfurling of singing or, as in the second definition, to distinguish a piece in which full-voiced singing was allowed its greatest display.[17]

I have termed the *cavatina* a fraternal twin of the *cabaletta*. While the *cabaletta* customarily concludes a scene or an act, the *cavatina* often introduces a character. While the *cavatina* is always a solo, the *cabaletta* may also be, and often is, the final section of a duet or an ensemble. While the *cavatina* is inevitably tied to pieces of recitative, the *cabaletta* is always preceded by another aria and thus is a sharper melodic arrow, flashing in its flight toward a goal that is close at hand. Perhaps the image of twins can be strengthened by conceding probability to the hypothesis that the *cabaletta* is a derivation of Walther's second type of *cavata*. It seems clear to me, in any event, that the *cavatina*, as we know it, derives exclusively from the first type: an aria that is limited in scope and perhaps even incompletely developed, and one whose strict connection to a recitative was stressed in every age.

The transition from recitative to arioso and vice versa is suited to the mirroring of inward thoughts, whether meditative (as in the case of Arsete's monologue), doubt-filled, or sorrowful. From this beginning was derived the most common utilization of the *cavatina*: as a monologue which, while revealing the self-questionings of a character, introduces him to the public and defines his role in the drama. At times, this concept degenerated into the idea that a *cavatina* was merely the first aria sung by a character. Whether it is, in structural terms, a *mezz'aria* (arioso), an aria without a second part, or a bipartite aria makes little difference, because the *cavatina* is primarily defined by its dramatic function, of presenting a character's introspective reflection. The *cabaletta*, on the other hand, conveys the sense of exaltation which accompanies a decision already made and going forth to action.

22 ···*Commedia dell'Arte* and Opera

I would prefer that what I am going to say about the two most typical forms of the Italian theater—*commedia dell'arte* and opera—should not take the form of a parallel. For, although my exposition will mainly refer to the analogies and correspondences between them, there are also many different features by which each of these two manifestations of Italian life in the seventeenth and eighteenth centuries preserves its own independent physiognomy. If I may be permitted to make a comparison, I would choose, even though it is old and much abused, that of two branches growing from a common trunk—two branches not quite opposite and divergent, but near each other in their origin, then sometimes separated, sometimes brought nearer by the imponderable factors of air, of light, of the juices running through them and nourishing them.

Of the two branches the *commedia dell'arte* is the older. Its beginning is generally fixed in the first half of the sixteenth century,[1] only the last decade of which will see the first attempts at opera. The term itself, *commedia dell'arte,* requires clarification. We shall never meet any play bearing such a title, as others are called, for instance, tragedies, farces, or operas. It is only a verbal abbreviation to indicate the comedies—in the general meaning of both comic and tragic plays—that were performed by the *comici dell'arte,* professional players who found in spectacle and recitation the essential means and reasons of their life; though often of rustic origin and of low condition, these players came little by little to be accepted and to gain admirers in the most illustrious courts.

The plays performed by such actors were doubly in contrast with the literary comedies of the Renaissance, generally performed by amateur players. The latter represented a kind of work in which, according to its learned, humanistic end, the written text imposed its rules, and the author was always the supreme arbiter of the performance. In the *commedia dell'arte,* on the contrary, we have an essentially popular repertory, often in dialect, in which the dialogue is completely left to the player's capacity for improvisation, only a plot outline, the so-called scenario, having been decided upon in advance. Such a technique certainly originated from the conditions in which the activity of the *comici dell'arte* took place and answered the practical need for a rapid turnover of the repertory. But it proved also to be a special mode of expression in which the vocation and the genius of uncommonly gifted players found their opportunity and their particular convenience.

Being generally devoid of any literary ambition, the *comici* had no other aim than the pleasure of their public. And they had the advantage over the authors and players of regular comedies of long experience as to the most suitable means for arousing the approbation of the audience. Among these means music certainly did not take the last place. But it often happens in the history of music that the more widely diffused and popular are the facts the historian wishes to examine, the fewer precise elements of knowledge are available to him. In this case, at the time of its performance everyone knew the music performed and the ways and means of its execution, but time has swallowed and buried this direct knowledge and has left us only scattered and second- or third-hand documents. We need to gather them together and laboriously interpret them to recover a pale image of a reality that in its own time must have imposed itself with the most obvious power of suggestion.

This is what happened too with the musical settings of the *commedia dell'arte.* Pictorial documents, however, give us evidence of the frequent presence of music; such, for instance, are the many paintings or engravings, sometimes referring to a much earlier phase of the *commedia,* that represent some troupes of mountebanks or peddlers giving their spectacles on platforms in the open air, often without the help of any kind of scenic décor. Each of the groups shows, generally, some musical instrument, such as a harp, a lute, a guitar, or a bowed instrument. Three of these troupes are to be seen, for instance, in an engraving by Giacomo Franco (from his *Habiti d' huomini et donne vinitiani,* Venice, 1610), competing for the attention of the various types of people walking on the Piazza San Marco in Venice (Fig. 22.1). Perhaps a little less realistic, but not less significant, are the fantasies of Jacques Callot, namely his *Balli di Sfessania.*[2] The title of this collection refers to a real Neapolitan entertainment, a popular dance also called *ballo alla maltese;*[3] and the engravings represent some

Ex. 22.1 Comedians and charlatans in the Piazza San Marco, Venice. Engraving by Giacomo Franco, 1610. (Biblioteca Apostolica Vaticana.)

well-known characters of the *commedia*—the so-called *maschere*—giving themselves over to the frenzied and acrobatic dance, accompanied by the sound of musical instruments (Figs. 22.2a, b). A little open-air stage in the background of one of these engravings indicates the relation of the *Sfessania* to the comedy performances; but the main evidence for it is given by the title page (Fig. 22.3) in which the dance takes place in an actual comedy scene.

In another category we can draw the same conclusion from documents referring to musical and theatrical activities by the same people—musicians having familiarity with the stage, or theatrical people practicing music. We can find some authors and players of comedies in the list of the organists of the church of San Marco. As early as the first years of the sixteenth century we meet in this office a *frate* Giovanni Armonio, who was a player and a writer of comedies, only one of which is preserved in

Franca Trippa.   Fritellino.

Fig. 22.2   Characters of the *commedia dell'arte* dancing and playing instruments. Engravings by J. Callot from *Balli di Sfessania*, circa 1622. (Courtesy of the Accademia Nazionale dei Lincei, Rome.)

Fig. 22.2   Continued

print. Many others, the subjects of which were not always quite pious, were often performed in the monastery of the Crocicchieri to which he belonged.[4] Also an organist of San Marco and an author of comedies was Girolamo Parabosco from Piacenza, a pupil of Willaert's and a man of greatly varied gifts. We learn from a Renaissance cookbook that in 1548 one of his comedies was "well played with its proper music and necessary *intermezzi*."[5] Unfortunately neither the music nor the *intermezzi* found their way to us, so we never will be able to appreciate the propriety of the former or the necessity of the latter.

It is likely that Parabosco is portrayed[6] in Titian's *Venus and the Organist* in the Museo del Prado in Madrid. The opulent image of the goddess in this painting is likewise probably borrowed from the real beauty of some Venetian courtesan. Such ladies were very frequent characters in the comedy and, at the time of Parabosco, almost its only feminine public;[7] moreover, they were often talented both in playing and singing, and so found little trouble in passing sometimes from their own profession to that of actress.[8] As a matter of fact, a little musical collection

Fig. 22.3   Title page of J. Callot's series *Balli di Sfessania*. A *commedia dell'arte* performance on a platform, surrounded by spectators, with a simple curtain providing the stage setting. The words refer to songs of the so-called *moresca* type. (Courtesy of the Accademia Nazionale dei Lincei, Rome.)

printed in Venice in 1588, the *Balli d'Arpicordo* by Marco Facoli, contains, after some real dance pieces, a series of instrumental versions of monodic songs, bearing the title of "Arie" accompanied by some feminine names: for instance, "Aria della Signora Livia," "Aria della Signora Fior d'Amore," "Aria della Marchetta Schiavonetta," and so on. Whether they are real or fictitious names, this indicates that each courtesan generally had a personal, favorite song—a custom that the corresponding comedy characters probably reproduced on the stage.[9] Moreover, we find also, in the *Balli d'Arpicordo,* among the *arie* with feminine names and quite similar to them, an "Aria della Commedia" and an "Aria della Commedia nova."

Parabosco, with some other musicians—among whom was Jaquet Buus, also an organist of San Marco—participated in a gay companionship of playwrights such as Antonfrancesco Doni and Ludovico Dolce, and players such as Antonio Molino, called Burchiella, and Andrea Calmo. About all these men there would be something to say regarding the relations between music and comedy. I shall, however, limit myself to the citation of a passage from one of the *Lettere* by Calmo,[10] very famous letters probably reproducing, in the dialect of Burano which they use, the fanciful and extravagant tirades that Calmo himself was accustomed to rumble on the stage. In the passage in question Calmo boasts that he and his friends have restored the language of their fathers—meaning the particular dialect they mainly employed in their plays—and have reestablished the art of singing *strambotti*—of "strambotizare musicalmente."[11] This verb "strambotizare" brings us into contact with all the poetic and musical literature of the *frottole* of the late fifteenth and the early sixteenth centuries, the obscure literary meaning of which, often depending on roguish language and allusions, was certainly completed in the performance by miming and dance.

Venice was not the only center of these performances in which music had a part. In Naples, too, about the middle of the sixteenth century, some performances of comedy took place in which many well-known musicians such as Luigi and Fabritio Dentice, Giulio Cesare Brancaccio, Gian Leonardo dall' Arpa, Giaches da Ferrara, and the famous teacher of Caccini, Scipione del Palla, played important roles.[12] Also from a Neapolitan musician of the court of Munich, Massimo Troiano, we have a document that is considered, somewhat improperly, to be the oldest preserved scenario of the *commedia dell'arte*. It is in fact not the scenario but the report[13] of an improvised comedy that was played in 1568 at the Bavarian court, in the style of the *commedia dell'arte* but by amateur players. The most famous member of the cast was Orlando di Lasso who, probably remembering the comedy experiences of his youth in Italy, played the role of the protagonist, that of the Venetian Magnifico, already endowed with the name and attributes of the mask of Pantalone.[14]

With this performance at the Bavarian court, and with the Neapolitan comedies mentioned earlier, we are no longer dealing with the authentic *commedia dell'arte,* but with its imitation. We shall not be able to avoid using this reflecting mirror to approach at last some musical documents. We can find them in those works by Orazio Vecchi and Adriano Banchieri that are generally known as dramatic madrigals or madrigal comedies. We know that in the title of his *Amfiparnaso* Vecchi intended to emphasize the unity, obtained for the first time in this work, of the Parnasses both of music and of comic poetry. This might sound like a complete negation of all that I have attempted to demonstrate heretofore; but we must consider that the people of that time, when speaking of music, meant both the theory and technique of the art and the actual music created in complete cognizance of its principles. The unity obtained for the first time in the *Amfiparnaso* is therefore, if any, that of the comedy with learned music. But if we examine its text as a comedy text, we will easily perceive that the action and the development of the play are far below the minimum of coherent and logical succession we should expect from the most mediocre comedy. There is in fact only a juxtaposition of scenes and episodes, for the greater part static or accessory from the theatrical point of view. Their connection and integration into a real comedy plot is left in great measure to the listener's imagination; in other words, these episodes are only allusions to an ensemble of situations and developments well known to the listener from the spectacles of the *commedia dell'arte*. So the *Amfiparnaso* is as little a real comedy as the same composer's *Convito musicale* is a real banquet. In this latter we are regaled not with the courses of a real meal, but only with its musical *entremets*.[15] In the same way also in the *Amfiparnaso* the comedy is not the real aim, but only a pretext for a series of more or less picturesque, more or less amusing sketches and genre paintings.

A pretext is effective only for a time, so Vecchi abstained from repeating it and sometimes replaced it with the above-mentioned frame of a banquet, sometimes with that of the *Veglie di Siena,* and so on. Or he actually underlined the character of an amusing and even satirical medley of his works by means of such a title as *A Medley of Varied Amusements* or *The Various Humors of Modern Music* (alternative title of the *Veglie di Siena*). We cannot praise his admirer and imitator Banchieri for equal moderation, because he three times repeated his attempt to join the two Parnasses: with *La Pazzia senile* (1600), with *Il Metamorfosi musicale* (1600), and with *La Saviezza giovanile* (1608).[16] Although also an author of purely literary comedies, Banchieri did not change Vecchi's model and proceedings in his musical comedies. The arguments, characters, and situations of these three works reproduce those of the *Amfiparnaso* with but small changes. At most the roles of the two old men who are the victims of the intrigue are reversed and the place of the action is put in a different town, so that the comedy—or pseudo-comedy—might acquire a new background. For what is essential in each one of Banchieri's musical comedies is the picture of its surroundings, the touches of local color, the masquerade referring to this or that characteristic kind of local profession. Speaking in the language of the *commedia dell'arte*, these musical comedies are but three different realizations of a single scenario, filled each time with different dialogue and, above all, with new musical inventions— Banchieri's musical fancies or *lazzi*. It is not the characters of the plot, but Banchieri himself who is the only real character of his comedies, showing on an ideal stage the resources of his humor and musical imagination.

Such pseudo-comedies, such reflected images of the *commedia dell'arte* allow us, however, at least to know the most suitable occasions for the use of music in the course of the comedies. This use was quite natural in the case of songs, serenades, or dances required by the plot itself; it was less natural in the *intermedi,* which nonetheless seem to have been one of the most often exploited occasions for musical interludes, not unlike the parentheses that choruses and ballets will open later in opera. Finally, both Vecchi's and Banchieri's musical comedies let us catch a glimpse of musical pieces occurring sometimes in the love dialogues or in the monologues, namely those in which a character, speaking to himself, acquaints his public with the most striking features of his own character and condition.

Some further information we owe only to Banchieri. Vecchi had employed in his *Amfiparnaso* the usual resources of the madrigal setting in five parts. Banchieri not only restricted himself in his musical comedies to three-voice writing, but took care to submit his admired model to such a device. His *Studio dilettevole ... dal Amfiparnaso* is in fact nothing more than a reduction for three voices of Vecchi's comedy.[17] We find an explanation of this in the fact that Banchieri's works in five parts—as for instance the *Festino del Giovedì grasso*—are explicitly included and numbered among his madrigal books, while the musical comedies belong to the series of his books of *canzonette* and *villanelle*.[18] It shows Banchieri's consciousness of a traditional relation between the music of the *commedia dell'arte* and the easy, elegant, melodious genre of the *canzonette* and *villanelle alla napoletana*, the forerunners of the accompanied monody and of the baroque aria.

We are once more concerned with that type of authentically or artificially popular music which in different ways runs through all the Italian musical Renaissance. The different names given to such music in the course of the sixteenth century indicate differences in the content and in the dialect of its texts, rather than considerable variations in its form. But once more we are only permitted to know this kind of music in a reflected form, the form we find in the printed collections of polyphonic music— that is, the form by which the learned music tried to assimilate it. The adaptation to the polyphonic chorus, a means of performance different from the original one, is not the last of the deformations to which it was subjected in this process of assimilation. For, since the *frottole*, since the *strambotti* of the singers to the lute and to the lyre—the *cantori a liuto* and *cantori a lira*, among whom was such a famous improviser as Serafino Aquilano[19]—the sonority, the particular expression, and characteristic harmonic features of this music were essentially connected with solo singing, in which the singer generally accompanied himself on a string instrument. It is obvious that this mode of performance was also the most suitable for the musical settings of the *commedia*. To the pictorial documents that I mentioned first we can add some illustrations from the edition of the *Amfiparnaso* showing singers of serenades accompanying themselves; or we may quote the parody of *Vestiva i colli*, a famous madrigal by Palestrina, which is sung in Banchieri's *Pazzia senile* with the interpolation of vocal imitations of a guitar *ritornello*.[20]

Some noticeable correspondences can be found between the subjects and dialects of these more or less popular songs and those of the *commedia dell'arte*. It is impossible, for instance, not to recognize a relationship between the *madrigali alla pavana* sung by the players of the troupe of Ruzzante[21] and the Paduan dialect in which his comedies are written. When we meet some *bergamasche* among the *canzoni villanesche*, or *villotte*,[22] we cannot help remembering that Arlecchino usually spoke in the dialect of Bergamo, and that in general the character of the male servant of the *commedia dell'arte*, the *zanni*, was borrowed from the rustic ingenuousness of the porters from Bergamo, employed in Venice in the meanest and hardest work.[23] A kind of song called *giustiniana*, in Venetian dialect, usually has for its protagonist a sprightly and enterprising old man who has many points of resemblance with the mask of Pantalone. As regards the *greghesche*, this very special kind of song was practiced particularly by musicians, such as Andrea Gabrieli and Claudio Merulo, who were very intimately acquainted with the aforementioned actor Antonio Molino.[24] The *greghesche* owe their name to the use of a half-Venetian, half-Oriental *lingua franca*, which was widely used in the Mediterranean ports, and which Molino introduced and frequently employed in his plays.

It cannot be only a coincidence, at least, that the era of the diffusion of the most widely popular type of song, the *villanella alla napoletana*, corresponds to the period in which, after an initial phase nourished by the contributions of the players and dialects of northern Italy, the *commedia dell'arte* received a considerable injection of southern, particularly Neapolitan, elements. It is the moment in which beside Pantalone, Graziano, and the numberless troop of *zanni*—Arlecchino, Trappolino,

Pedrolino, Burattino, and so on—the characters of southern origin made their appearance: the Maramao, Coviello, Meo Squacquera and, the most universal and most talented, the immortal Pulcinella. About the same time the character of the German soldier, the drunken but jovial *lansquenet*, from which the musical *todesca* had taken its origin, gave way to the *miles gloriosus*, to the much-scorned yet impudently boisterous Capitan Matamoros, or Capitan Spezzaferro, in which the spirit of vengeance of the Neapolitan people ridiculed the hated troops of the Spanish viceroys.

Mutual exchanges and analogies between song and *commedia dell'arte* are only natural. For a song can scarcely obtain wide popularity without sketching either a character or a dramatic or comic situation. And it is useless to ask whether the comedy suggested these characters and situations to the songs, or the songs to the comedy, for they obviously are the product of a similar process of choice, determined in a unique way by the preferences and aversions of an entire society.

What is important for us is to point out that before the rise of the opera the *commedia dell'arte* had already created many of the conditions necessary for the acceptance of opera by the public. This will not be very evident if we limit ourselves to a consideration of the opera in its initial phase, characterized by an aristocratic and highly cultural stamp. Nevertheless, the influence of humanism and of aesthetic theories on its birth has been exaggerated.[25] Even in the earlier phase the distance between opera and *commedia dell'arte* was not so great that it could not be bridged. As a matter of fact it was bridged by the lords of Florence and Mantua when they easily alternated the courtly performances of opera with those of the *zanni*.[26] But we shall pass over the aristocratic opera in Florence and Mantua and its continuation in Rome, for the tradition of the musical theater actually originated from another tendency, the so-called Venetian opera, which we can call democratic only for the sake of contrast.

I do not believe that the opening of the Venetian public opera houses had a decisive influence on the new direction of this genre. I think it was only the most important and most typical episode in a more general operatic activity, to which too little attention has been paid until now: that of the itinerant troupes of singers, generally from Rome or trained in the Roman style of singing. Even before the opening of the first Venetian opera theater in 1637, such towns as Parma, Bologna, and Padua had already seen some opera performances by this type of wandering operatic company.[27] In Venice, too, Benedetto Ferrari and Francesco Manelli, the promoters of the first spectacles in the theater at San Cassiano, arrived at the head of a company that had acted one year before in Padua.[28] And they did not limit their performances to Venice, although this city soon became the most important seat of their activity. We know, for instance, that an attempt by Ferrari to book his troupe into the theaters of Milan,[29] in the same way he had done in Bologna, failed, probably because of the rivalry of another company of singers which enjoyed the support of the Spanish ambassador in Rome, the duke of Oñate. In 1651 this latter company, known as I Febi armonici, introduced opera to Naples, the duke of Oñate being then the Spanish viceroy in that city.[30]

A more thorough investigation into the opera libretti of the middle of the seventeenth century should increase the information we have about the lyric troupes of this time. The opera owes its diffusion to them more than to local theatrical enterprises, and to them too it owes its new direction, which had, at least in earlier times, more a national than a Venetian character; if it was subjected to any particular influence at all, it was that of Roman opera and cantata.

The existence of wandering lyric companies not only marked a point of external resemblance with the itinerant troupes of the *comici dell'arte*, it also started an intense rivalry by the latter, who felt menaced in a realm that until now had belonged only to them. One of the effects of such a competition was a closer resemblance between the two kinds of spectacles. On the one hand the *comici* were induced to give music a greater part than it already had in their plays, and they also tried to appropriate another feature of the musical spectacle, the use of imposing scenic décor and machinery. So, for instance, the *Finta pazza* by Strozzi and Sacrati—an ambiguous work halfway between the comedy with music and dance and the opera with spoken dialogues—was performed at Paris in 1645 by one of the most famous troupes of *comici*, with décors and machinery by Torelli and choreography by Balbi.[31] On the other hand we can find evidence of the musical capacity of the *comici* in a well-known episode of the performance of Monteverdi's *Arianna* in Mantua (1608). The singer for whom the role of Arianna was intended had died and the part was entrusted to Virginia Andreini-Ramponi of the Comici Fedeli troupe, who not only was able to learn it in a few days, but sang it, according to reports of the time, in such a way that she made all the ladies present weep.[32]

As for the lyric companies, it was only natural that they did their best to borrow all the elements suitable for transference into their own brand of spectacle, the precise shape of which was still too recent and uncertain to offer resistance to such injections. Borrowing from the repertory of the *comici* resulted not only from their competition, but also from the fact that since the beginning of the seventeenth century the *comici* had embraced the whole field of dramatic activity, practically overshadowing every literary production. They had a very wide repertory, for which they drew from any Italian or foreign source, simply translating everything to their own mode of performance. That their repertory covered all the theatrical genres is shown even by the classification that we find in almost all the collections of scenarios.[33] There "comedies" include those plots that take place in a bourgeois or popular milieu and that largely employ the traditional characters, the *maschere*, with their particular names, dialects, fashions, and oddities. "Tragedy" is the name given to those scenarios involving killings, horrible vengeances, and thrilling apparitions (thus exaggerating a tendency of the Italian literary tragedy, nearer to Seneca's model than to that of Greek tragedy). There was finally a third category of scenarios, the protagonists of which, like those of the tragedy, were required to be of royal or princely rank; but the plots, although involving entangled and adventurous vicissitudes, nonetheless avoided the horrible and fatal episodes characterizing the tragedies. These plots finally reached a happy close, in which general contentment and recovered serenity were always sealed with a good many more or less well-adjusted marriages radiating an optimistic forecast of eternal happiness. These scenarios, being neither tragedies nor comedies, bore the name of *opera regia*, in short, *opera*.[34] Not only the name but the ingredients were those usually employed in the opera libretti. This was a basic prescription in which thousands of repetitions and variations in the course of about two centuries of opera did not introduce any appreciable change.

The part allotted to the comic element in the opera is small but not devoid of importance. Of the attempts made to transfer the *maschere* into the musical opera we know only a single example, belonging to the aristocratic Roman opera. It is *Chi soffre speri* by Virgilio Mazzocchi and Marco Marazzoli, the libretto of which, by Cardinal Rospigliosi, includes a complete series of masks, namely Coviello, Zanni Moschino, Colillo, and Fritellino. It was performed in 1639, and it probably did not lack some suggestions from a very versatile artist, himself an amateur of the improvised play, the Cavalier Bernini.[35] But it must have been felt very soon in these attempts that the musical *recitativo*, although already very fast and talkative, was not able to keep pace with the recitation of the *comici*, so rich in verbal jokes and so varied in tone. In a later musical comedy also by Rospigliosi, *Dal male il bene*, only one comic character is introduced, the servant Tabacco, who even in his name avoids repeating those of the traditional *maschere*. Nevertheless the comic male servant evolved into a traditional character of the seventeenth-century opera. The variations of his name—Demo, Momo, Simo, Bileno, Falloppo, Lurcano, and even Buffo—must not have produced appreciable change in the character itself, or in the fashion of his dress, probably resembling that of the former buffoons. Whether he is located in the fabulous Colchis, in the Persia of the Satraps, or in imperial Rome, whether he follows Hercules in his descent into Hell or, at the foot of Vesuvius, gives advice in Neapolitan dialect to the Amazons at war with Theseus, he is frightened and boisterous, foolish and mischievous, sometimes drunken but always greedy. His favorite jokes, his *lazzi*, are chosen from those most suitable for underlining by the music: usually he stutters, giving amusing vocal imitations of military fanfares; often his prolonged repetitions of a single syllable make him finish a word when the dialogue has already passed to other subjects, or even when the characters on the stage have changed, giving rise to puzzling mixups.

His equivalent among the feminine characters is the nurse or the old matron, who certainly must have shown in some detail of her dress the station of a former courtesan in retirement. On the musical side her ridiculousness mainly centered in her low contralto or even tenor voice, increasing the absurdity of her love frenzies for some young page with a sharp and clear soprano voice. Frequently she gives mischievous advice to young ladies hesitating in their love affairs because of modesty or pride.

A third comic character, the guardian of the harem, did not find its previous model in the comedy. We have already seen the comic spirit at work in the opera through the inversion of the timbres of voice; Venus herself is given a tenor voice in Luigi Rossi's *Orfeo* when she is disguised as an old woman, while adolescent pages usually sang soprano. But it is also true that the heroes who played the most important roles ordinarily had clear high voices. So it is a little surprising to find such castrati, to whom people rendered honor sometimes with almost hysterical fanaticism, ridiculed in the character of the eunuch, who is scolded, scoffed at, and eluded by the young ladies entrusted to his care. Whence his usual complaints about "the customs of the dames and damsels of today," resembling the occasional allusions of the *comici* to contemporary events and, like them, arousing general hilarity.

But such discussion of the comic characters, though perhaps obligatory, is not the most important argument in our comparison of *commedia dell'arte* and opera. Less evidently, but with more telling effect, the comedy exercised its influence on the whole of opera, especially on its musical form. The first Venetian operas—we refer to them because they are the best known—are still dominated by the recitative style. To be sure, they are not lacking in melody—sometimes very beautiful melody—but it always arises without a break from recitative, as, in an eloquent speech, there surges up at a given moment a rounder and more sonorous wave, which then falls again and dies off. For music is still ruled by the word, is adjusted to it, and tries to interpret, stress, and embellish it, without exceeding the function of an obedient and faithful servant. Somehow the spirit of Monteverdi's *seconda pratica* still lives even after the disappearance of the old hero, even though with that disappearance the last light of a nobler and higher dramatic conception is extinguished. Only about the middle of the seventeenth century does that tendency appear which will give opera its definitive form, a form in which the rules of music will supersede the literary text in a manner that no subsequent reform has been able to temper. It probably became evident for the first time in the work of Antonio Cesti—even in his first opera, *Orontea*, which, achieving an extraordinary success in 1649, brought its author at once to sudden celebrity.[36] From this point on the aria (that is, an autonomous and independent musical organism) becomes the basic element of the operatic structure, while the recitatives tend to be considered only a connective element, necessary to the development of the plot, but secondary, though not completely neglected, from the point of view of musical expression.

It is notable that *Orontea* is also one of the first operas to which we can give the name of a real comic opera, and that this quality allowed the new musical form to be attempted in it without opposition and even with the most considerable success. As a matter of fact, when the same experiment was applied the following year to a serious opera libretto, that of Cesti's *Alessandro vincitor di sè stesso*, the authors felt it could not be presented to the public without explanation. In the preface the librettist Francesco Sbarra writes:

I know that some people will consider the *ariette* sung by Alexander and Aristotle unfit for the dignity of such great characters, but I know also that it is not natural to speak in music, and nevertheless it is not only permitted but even accepted with praise. For today this kind of poetry has only the aim of pleasure, and therefore we need to adapt ourselves to the usage of our time. If the recitative style were not intermingled with such *scherzi*, it would give more annoyance than pleasure.[37]

In this way the establishment of the new form of opera, summoned by the spirit of comedy, is justified by the idea of musical hedonism.

Moreover, the name of *scherzi* given by Sbarra to the *ariette* is only too similar to that of *lazzi*, employed by the *comici dell'arte*. And the *lazzi* were not only the jokes and grimaces springing extempore from the vivid and spirited imagination of the players, but also some form of speech previously agreed upon, even if always susceptible of improvised additions or variations. And this name was also given to some preestablished scheme of monologue or dialogue which resembles actual "closed pieces," based on the effect of persistent repetitions, or on intentional symmetries, or on periodic returns to a fundamental theme.[38] I do not mean that the musical forms were inspired by these "closed" monologues or dialogues, but I believe that their practice in the *commedia dell'arte* had already prepared the public for the acceptance of the closed musical forms in the opera.

Stylization and even mechanical repetition have always been among the most frequently employed means of gaining comic effect. So in the performance of the *commedia dell'arte* the rules of free invention and preestablished form, of realism and stylization, must have alternated in sharp contrast, and with sudden transition, much in the manner of the operatic alternation of recitatives and arias. On the other hand, it has often happened in the history of opera that some given formal elements—as, for instance, the duets and the ensemble pieces, in which everyone is singing and nobody but the public is listening—have been accepted in the serious opera only after having been used and generalized in the comic opera.

To sum up, the analogies in the comic characters, type of plot, and elements of formal structure, are only partial features of a general analogy in conception. Over and above the episodic influences of the *commedia* on the opera and the even more isolated suggestions of the opera to the *commedia*, their analogy is to be explained by the fact that they are both, by different means, the expression of the same society and of the same way of conceiving and realizing the theatrical spectacle. Nobody has ever undertaken a comparison between the scenarios of the *commedia* and the subjects of operatic libretti, because the specialists in each of these fields are usually scarcely interested in the other. But it would be easy to conclude that there is no essential difference between them, except that the operatic subjects embrace a narrower field than those of the scenarios. But in both fields the same apparent variety of situations, characters, and surroundings is swallowed in a gloomy grayness because of the lack of artistic and logical coherency, the arbitrary blending of human and fantastic elements, and the continuous demand for effect by means of extravagant features or sudden transitions.

We may question what real importance such variety had, what value such intrigues had in which surprise abused became no surprise at all. Rather, was it not that the public was attracted and its enthusiasm aroused by the way of acting and animating the play, which was completely entrusted to the ability of the performers? The opera scores, too, of the seventeenth century are only sketches or compendious drawings, the full realization of which was left open to the individual and collective creation of the performers. It was improvised and changed each time, according to the occasion and even to the inspiration of the moment. During this century and the greatest part of the next, we can say that no performance of an opera was ever like another. The history of opera always deals with a continuous modification, addition, or suppression of episodes and characters.

We can see then what was, either in the *commedia* or in the opera, the basic element of the spectacle: the players in the former, the singers in the latter. Of Pantalone, of Arlecchino, of Isabella, of Pulcinella only thin shadows remain, for their life was embodied in the flesh, in the appearance, in the breath of their interpreters. People liked to see them plunging into the strangest and most unexpected adventures and situations. Nevertheless, they did not ask them to give to the characters the verisimilitude of a real merchant, gambler, or honest workman. They did ask them to be only and always Pulcinella, Arlecchino, Pantalone; they liked to recognize behind the most disparate camouflages, the voice, the figure, the particular way of acting and gesturing of the players who were then more closely identified with each of those characters. Almost in the same way the worship of starring singers, born together with opera, made the operatic public ask not for a myth or for a historical description, but for the exhibition of the most admired singers, displaying in that myth or historical description the treasures of their voices. We must admit that in every age a very great majority of the public has gone to the opera house to hear Caccini and Peri rather than Orpheus; Farinello and Senesino rather than Attilio Regolo; even Tamagno and Chaliapin rather than Othello or Boris Godunof. The whole history of opera has always been characterized by such a subordination to the singers, to their personalities and capacities, even to their caprices.

Either about the *commedia dell'arte* or about the opera, the attitude of the public was mainly that of amused incredulity toward the fiction taking place on the stage. An incredulity that becomes patent in the *commedia* when the *comici* slip from their dialogue into a direct address from the player to the audience; it becomes patent in the opera by the break of the scenic illusion occurring when a storm of applause interrupts a climactic scene or induces a Dido returned to life to repeat her suicide. Besides such incredulity, nevertheless, a spirit of popular ingenuousness restored the player to the station of the ancient mime, and the singer to the primitive and almost barbaric prestige emanating from the fascinating suggestion of the singing voice.

This is by no means the most fortunate aspect of opera, of which in general our comparison with the *commedia dell'arte* did not underline the positive qualities—those qualities that often succeeded in turning to the advantage of art an unfavorable social condition. But a total judgment on opera was not the aim of this essay. And we cannot rely either on too enthusiastic praise, or on indiscriminate blame, which almost always only means lack of comprehension. A careful approach to the facts in order to see them in their real essence and to evaluate their condition and necessity would be, I think, a better way to understanding and to dispassionate judgment.

--❧Notes

New notes and additions to the old notes are indicated by brackets.

1 "Musica de sono humano" and the Musical Poetics of Guido of Arezzo

This essay was originally published in *Medievalia et Humanistica,* Studies in Medieval and Renaissance Culture, new series, 7 (1976).

1. See, for instance, Aurelianus Reomensis in Martin Gerbert, *Scriptores ecclesiastici de musica* (St. Blaise, 1784), I, 39a, and Regino Prumiensis, *ibid.,* 246b. The third statement, which I translate from Aurelianus, *ibid.,* 33a, was still reflected by Adam de Fulda in the late fifteenth century; see also Gerbert, III, 347b.

2. Some who were abbots, or became such in the course of their ecclesiastical careers: Regino (d. 915) at Prüm; Odo (d. *ca.* 1030) at St. Maur-des-Fossés; Berno (d. 1048) at Reichenau; Wilhelm (*ca.* 1030–1091) at Hirsau; his pupil Theogerus (1117, bishop-elect of Metz) at St. George in the Black Forest; and Engelbert (*ca.* 1250–1331) at Admont. Aurelian of Réomé dedicated his tract to the *archicantor* and bishop-elect Bernardus; Regino of Prüm to the archbishop of Trier; Guido of Arezzo to his bishop Theodaldus; the *scholastici* Adebold (later bishop of Utrecht) and Aribo to, respectively, Pope Sylvester II (999–1003) and Ellenhard, bishop of Freising. Hucbald of St. Amand (*ca.* 840–*ca.* 930) was a teacher there, as well as at St. Bertin and Reims. Many of these writers, and such others as Notker Balbulus, Notker Labeo, and Hermannus Contractus (not to speak of Bernard de Clairvaux) were also theologians, chroniclers, mathematicians, or astronomers.

3. In Gerbert, II, 34a.

4. Adam de Fulda, *ibid.*, III, 347a. An older statement is that of Berno of Reichenau, *ibid.*, II, 78a.
5. Johannes Affligemensis, *De musica cum tonario*, J. Smits van Waesberghe, ed. (Rome, 1950), p. 52. (I am not fully convinced by the editor's attribution to Johannes Affligemensis, nor by various attempts, more recent, such as those of E. F. Flindell in *Musica disciplina* 20 and 23 [1966 and 1969], to give the work back to Johannes Cotton.) See also the "Summa musicae," no longer thought to be by Johannes de Muris, in Gerbert, III, 195a: "Cui ergo cantorem artis expertem comparare possumus, nisi ebrio versum locum propositum currenti, vel caeco alicui canem verberare volentem?"
6. "Musicae Guidonis regulae rhythmicae," in Gerbert, II, 25.
7. See Berno of Reichenau, quoted above, n. 4.
8. Regino of Prüm, in Gerbert, I, 240a. Similarly, Aurelianus, *ibid.*, 39b.
9. It is worth noticing that several works I have quoted, including Regino's *Epistola* (which I shall presently discuss in more detail), are preambles to *tonaria*. For a perceptive presentation of the problems connected with the transition from oral to written tradition see Leo Treitler, "The Transmission of Epic Poetry and Plainchant," in *The Musical Quarterly* 60 (1974), 333ff.
10. See H. Hüschen, "Regino von Prüm, Historiker, Kirchenrechtler und Musiktheoretiker," in *Festschrift für K. G. Fellerer* (Regensburg, 1962), p. 205ff. O. N. Dorman, "A Study of Latinity in the Chronicon of Regino of Prüm," in *Archivum latinitatis medii aevi* 8 (1933), 173ff., finds the vocabulary rather limited in that work; yet I agree with one bibliophile's report, quoted by Gerbert, c. d 3*v*, stating that from Regino's *Epistola* "eximia eius doctrina in variis disciplinis longe plenius et uberius, quam ex eiusdem chronico & libris de disciplina ecclesiastica publice extantibus, cognosci potest." Very little I found useful to my purpose in E. Oberti, 'L'estetica musicale di Reginone di Prüm," in *Rivista di filosofia neoscolastica* 52 (1960), 336ff.
11. A number of passages I have already quoted are derived from Boethius (see also n. 15 below). In addition, Regino repeatedly quotes Vergil, Cicero, Macrobius, Martianus Capella, occasionally Plato, Philolaus, Cassiodorus, Isidorus, and Aurelius Reomensis. At least once he expressed the typical humanistic longing for the classical past, in comparison with "nostris ... longe inferioribus temporibus." *Chronicon*, Fr. Kurze, ed. (Hannover, 1890), p. 1.
12. His invective can be quite colorful: "Nequaquam autem haec legenda Walcaudo proponimus, aut ad talia discenda eius animum provocamus; frustra enim lyra asino canitur." In Gerbert, I, 247a.
13. *Ibid.*, 246a. Thereupon, Regino embarks on an allegory identifying music with Eurydice, whose name, he says, means "profunda diiudicatio": "Orpheus ... vult revocare de inferno Eurydicem sono citharae, sed non praevalet, quia humanum ingenium conatur profunditatem harmonicae subtilitatis penetrare & discernere, & ad lucem, id est, ad scientiam revocare; sed illa humanam cognitionem refugiens in tenebris ignorantiae latet."
14. *Ibid.*, 245b.

15. I have quoted some Boethian reminiscences which Regino shares with Aurelianus; however, his direct quotations from Boethius' *De institutione musica* (including his own title) are more numerous than Aurelianus' and often independent of them. See G. Pietzsch, *Die Klassifikation der Musik von Boetius bis Ugolino von Orvieto* (Halle, 1929), pp. 24–25. Regino also knew Boethius' *Arithmetica*.

16. Gerbert, I, 233. The description of artificial music, *ibid.*, 236b, includes intriguing ideas: "Artificialis musica dicitur, quae arte & ingenio humano excogitata est, & inventa, quae in quibusdam consistit instrumentis. . . . Omni autem notitiam huius artis habere cupienti sciendum est, quod, quamquam naturalis musica longe praecedat artificialis, nullum tamen vim naturalis musicae recognoscere potest, nisi per artificialem. Igitur quaevis a naturali nostrae disputationis sermo processerit, necesse est, ut in artificiali finiatur, ut per rem visibilem invisibilem demonstrare valeamus." I wonder whether Regino had in mind general procedures of scientific thought or was hinting at the demonstration of pitches through an artificial instrument, the monochord. The latter would be corroborated by a passage by Guido of Arezzo: "Voces, quae huius artis prima sunt fundamenta in monochordo melius intuemur, quomodo eas ibidem ars natura imitata discrevit, primus videmus." *Micrologus,* J. Smits van Waesberghe, ed. (American Inst. of Musicology, 1955), p. 92.

17. My title quotes a later writer, Roger Bacon, whose partition of music, "de sono humano" ("in cantu" and "in sermone") and "instrumentalis," has many points in common with Regino's; see Pietzsch, p. 89.

18. Gerbert, I, 232a. It is worth noticing that Regino relates the modal system only to church music; *musica instrumentalis* does not seem to depend on it.

19. *Ibid.,* 23b.

20. Regino, unlike Aurelianus, never mentions Gregory; yet the *introitus* crediting the latter with having composed "huic libellum musicae artis" is already present in antiphonaries of the late eighth century, and the expression "Gregorianum carmen" had already been used by Pope Leo IV (847–55). For the legend of the Holy Ghost presiding at the creation of the Antiphonary and the evidence in pictorial sources, see Treitler, pp. 337–42 and pl. I–IV.

21. Gerbert, I, 235a.

22. Boethius, *De institutione musica,* G. Friedlein, ed. (Leipzig, 1887), pp. 188–89.

23. Aribo, *De musica,* J. Smits van Waesberghe, ed. (Rome, 1951), p. 46. According to the editor, Aribo was active in Bavaria and Liège. His treatise may be dated *ca.* 1070 (*ibid.*, pp. xxv–xxvi).

24. *Ibid.,* p. 46.

25. *Ibid.,* and then again, p. 58.

26. See, among others, Johannes Affligemensis, p. 51; and Jacobus of Liège, "Speculum musicae," in E. de Coussemaker, *Scriptorum de musica... nova series,* II (Paris, 1867), 312. Most colorful is the language in Arnulphus de Sancto Gilleno, "De differentia et generibus cantoribus" in Gerbert, III. A

small sample concerning instrumentalists (p. 316b) may suffice: "Ex istis nonnullos videmus clericos, qui in organicis instrumentis difficillimos musicales modulos, quos exprimere vix praesumeret vox humana, adinveniunt atque tradunt per miraculosum quoddam innatae in eis inventivae musicae prodigium." How different from the invectives against singers!

27. For Guido's life and works, see J. Smits van Waesberghe, *De musico-paedagogico et theoretico Guidone Aretino* (Florence, 1953). The *Micrologus* was written by Guido *ca.* 1026, on the request of Theodaldus, bishop of Arezzo.

28. They were mainly concerned with the meaning of individual words or scribal errors; see Smits van Waesberghe, pp. 189–93; and his introduction to Aribo, *De musica*, pp. xvi–xxiv.

29. The question is summarized by Smits van Waesberghe, pp. 188–89; G. Reese, *Music in the Middle Ages* (New York, 1940), pp. 140–48; and W. Apel, *Gregorian Chant* (Bloomington, Ind., 1958), pp. 126–32.

30. Gerbert II, 14b.

31. *Micrologus* (quoted above, n. 16), p. 162; Smits van Waesberghe, p. 187.

32. Smits van Waesberghe, *ibid.*, p. 187, n. 2: "Agitur enim de *commoda* i.e. recta et probata modulatione et exponitur quomodo recta vel commoda modulatio *componenda* i.e. coniunctim ponenda (igitur non in sensu posterioris aetatis nempe *modos conficiendi*) sit ita, ut legibus modulationis satisfiat" (italics replace quotation marks of the original). In the next paragraph I shall give a slightly different interpretation of the word *commoda*.

33. P. Ferretti, *Estetica gregoriana* (Rome, 1934), pp. 106–10.

34. The text in *Micrologus*, pp. 162–77. I have taken into account J. Smits van Waesberghe, "Wie Wortwahl und Terminologie bei Guido von Arezzo entstanden und überliefert wurden" in *Archiv für Musikwissenschaft* 31 (1974), 73ff., an analysis of Guido's literary style based precisely on this chapter of the *Micrologus*. I have felt it advisable, however, to leave a number of technical terms untranslated.

35. The adjective *harmonica* is applied by Aurelianus first to that part of *musica humana* which "discernit in sonis acutum & gravem accentum" (a meaning inherited from classical theory) and then to the "nature" of a sound which "ex vocum cantibus constat." After him a number of theorists meant vocal music when they spoke of *musica harmonica*. This, I think, is also the meaning of Guido's *harmonia* in this passage.

36. *Tenor* for *mora vocis* is uncommon, but there are other instances of its meaning the holding or sustaining of a note. Here, as elsewhere in the chapter, the idea is expressed of a *neuma* formed by a number of syllables; we are accustomed by our more restrictive use of this term to think that many *neumae* can be set to a syllable, not the opposite.

37. See, for instance, the beginning of "Musica enchiriadis" by the pseudo-Hucbald in Gerbert, I, 152a.

38. This, too, has an antecedent in "Musica enchiriadis," *ibid.*, 182a. Smits van Waesberghe, *De musico-paedagogico*, pp. 185–96, gives the *tremula* an

intermediate length between long and short notes; he also distinguishes longer *tremulae* from shorter ones with no mark. I think all *tremulae* ought to be long to develop their special effect. Guido's alternative term, *varius tenor*, combining the ideas of length and *varietas*, is better explained by an anonymous commentator quoted by Smits van Waesberghe, *ibid.*, p. 196, n.

39. Only the lower part of the figure in Gerbert, II, 15, resembles the one reproduced in Waesberghe's edition, p. 166 and pl. 10.

40. The text established by Smits van Waesberghe, p. 168, reads: "et cum perpulchrae fuerint duplicatae." I read "tum" instead of "cum."

41. Something in the last clause—either terseness or redundance—caused a number of interpretive interpolations or marginal glosses to be added to the text in many sources.

42. The remarkable consistency of the so-called Gregorian tradition having been constantly stressed in about one century of scholarly research, we need now to be reminded that it did not mean deadly uniformity. It would seem, for instance, that repetition and symmetry were sought and emphasized at certain times and places, obliterated at others, as shown by T. F. Kelly, "Melodic Elaboration in Responsory Melismas," in *Journal of the American Musicological Society* 27 (1974), 461ff.

43. Guido's repeated references to St. Ambrose seems to indicate that he saw many of his requirements embodied in the Ambrosian chant. See the chapter "Ambrosian Chant" by R. Jesson in W. Apel, *Gregorian Chant*, most particularly pp. 481–83.

44. It must be said, however, that a particular ethos (the term itself is never used) was often attributed to each mode.

45. Strangely enough, the suggestion is omitted that different melodies be given different tempi, although such a possibility had already been mentioned by the pseudo-Hucbald; see Gerbert, II, 183 (this section, answering the question "Quid est numerose canere?" probably was the starting point of many of Guido's thoughts).

46. Guido evidently refers to the so-called *distropha* and *tristropha*. Although he clearly asks for *crescendo* or *diminuendo*, his words still reflect the ingrained habit of seeing *accentus* in terms of raise or descent of pitch.

47. Here neumatic notation is clearly referred to, as it had been previously in the requirement that certain *partes* be notated *compresse* or *compressius*.

48. Guido gives as an example the beginning of the introit *Ad te levavi*, whose first syllable has a liquescent neume also in modern editions.

49. Aribo, *De musica*, p. 48. Guido's chapter does not mention the monochord; yet see above, n. 16.

50. *Ibid.*, p. 50. The whole chapter is spent in finding examples in the liturgical repertory for other, less binding prescriptions.

51. See the section of the editor's introduction mentioned above, n. 28.

52. Johannes Affligemensis, *De musica cum tonario*, pp. 117–26.

53. *Ibid.*, p. 117. Compliance with the listeners' taste had already been suggested in chapter 16, where the "cautus musicus" is warned to use such mode "quo

eos maxime delectari videt quibus cantum suum placere desiderat." The "qualitas" of each mode is described in such terms as "curialis vagatio," "modesta petulantia," "mimicos saltus," "matronalis canor," and so on. The need is stressed for the socializing *musicus* to be able to grasp quickly the mode of each song.

54. *Ibid.*, pp. 118–19.
55. *Ibid.*, pp. 120–26. Knowledge of the modes seems to have been Johannes' favorite topic.
56. Smits van Waesberghe's analysis of Guido's literary style, quoted in n. 34, shows its observance of the rules of rhythmic prose. Of course, this is not enough to make Guido's style effective, were it not implemented by an unerring feeling for the sound and rhythmic weight of words, cognate to Guido's striving for quantitative and qualitative balance in the *modulatio*.

2   Dante *Musicus:* Gothicism, Scholasticism, and Music

This essay was originally published in *Speculum* 43 (April 1968).

1. Style and organization of the present writing depend on its having been conceived as a paper for the centennial celebration held on May 15, 1965, in Cambridge, Massachusetts, by the American Dante Society.
2. Erwin Panofsky, *Gothic Architecture and Scholasticism* (Latrobe, 1951).
3. Panofsky, p. 20.
4. On this gap and its consequences, see essay no. 3.
5. Gerhard Pietzsch, *Die Klassifikation der Musik von Boetius bis Ugolino von Orvieto* (Halle, 1929).
6. The aspects of musical creativity are particularly stressed by Jacques Handschin, "Trope, Sequence, and Conductus," *The New Oxford History of Music*, II (London, 1954), 128ff.
7. The well-known passage of Boethius (*De institutione arithmetica libri duo, De institutione musica libri quinque*, G. Friedlein, ed. [Leipzig, 1867], pp. 224–25) is still echoed, for instance, by Englebert of Admont (d. 1321, a student in Padua 1279–1288), who wrote of poets: "Metricus enim modus [docendi & discendi musicam organicam] est histrionum, qui vocantur cantores nostro tempore, & antiquitus dicebantur Poëtae, qui per solum usum rhythmicos vel metricos cantus ad arguendum vel instruendum mores, vel ad movendum animos & affectus ad delectationem vel tristitiam fingunt & componunt," in Martin Gerbert, ed. *Scriptores ecclesiastici de musica* (St. Blaise, 1784), II, 289.
8. *Musica rhythmica* was for a long time the term for the division of *musica organica* that includes the playing of instruments "in pulsu," such as the cithara and lyre; with the insurgence of rhymed poetry it became one type of "musica de sono humano in sermone" (Roger Bacon). See Pietzsch, p. 89.
9. Our basic knowledge of the so-called Notre Dame school comes from a

passage of the anonymous "De mensuris et discantu" (a fragment of a larger treatise) in Charles Edmond Henry de Coussemaker, ed., *Scriptorum de musica medii aevi nova series*, I (Paris, 1864), 342: "Et nota quod Magister Leoninus, secundum dicebatur, fuit optimus Organista, qui fecit magnum librum organi de Gradali et Antiphonario pro servitio divino multiplicando; et fuit in usu usque ad tempus Perotini Magni qui abbreviavit eundem, et fecit clausulas sive puncta plurima meliora, quoniam optimus discantor erat, et melior quam Leoninus erat; sed hic non dicendus de subtilitate organi ... Liber vel libri Magistri Perotini erant in usu usque ad tempus Magistri Roberti de Sabilone, et in choro Beate Virginis Majoris ecclesia Parisiis, et a suo tempore usque in hodiernum diem." The author, an Englishman who evidently had studied in Paris, wrote toward the end of the thirteenth century. An excellent characterization of the role of the cathedral is given by Heinrich Husmann, "Notre-Dame-Epoche," in *Die Musik in Geschichte und Gegenwart*, ed. Friedrich Blume, IX (Kassel, 1961), col. 1700ff., where a logical distinction is made between a Notre Dame period (until *ca.* 1250) and the following Ars antiqua.

10. Although the chronology of the Notre Dame school is largely based on conjectures and to a certain extent is open to conflicting views, there is substantial agreement on the date of Leoninus' *Magnus liber organi*, essentially because it is believed that an identity of purpose existed between the planning of the new cathedral and of its musical liturgy.

11. Unexplained is how *organum* came to be the term for both polyphony in general and for a certain type of polyphonic piece. The instrument we call organ was usually designated with the plural *organa*; see Dante's "quando a cantar con organi si stea, / ch' or sì, or no s'intendon le parole." (*Purgatorio*, IX, 144–145). Accordingly, it is most likely that the poet had polyphony in his mind when he used the singular: "si come viene ad orecchia / dolce armonia da organo" (*Paradiso*, XVII, 43–44).

12. See Heinrich Husmann, "The Origin and Destination of the *Magnus liber organi*," *The Musical Quarterly* 49 (1963), 311ff. A transcription based on the ms. Wolfenbüttel 677 (considered to provide the oldest available version) is given by William G. Waite, *The Rhythm of Twelfth-Century Polyphony* (New Haven, 1954); the latest discussion of criteria of transcription is by Theodore Karp, "Towards a Critical Edition of Notre-Dame Organa Dupla," *The Musical Quarterly* 52 (1966), 350ff. [See also Ernest H. Sanders, "Consonance and Rhythm in the Organum of the 12th and 13th Centuries," *Journal of the American Musicological Society*, 33 (1980), 264ff.]

13. Besides the "holding" aspect, it seems to me that the meaning of direction or rule should also be emphasized, in keeping with the use of *tenor* in the terminology of the church modes, making the transition less abrupt from the older term *vox principalis*. See below the continued influence exerted by the text of the *tenor* on those of the other parts.

14. Unique is Saint Augustine's effort to go beyond the narrowness of the grammarian's consideration of meter and verse to the more general essence of

musical rhythm. He defines the rhythmic process as "legitimis pedibus, nullo tamen certo fine provolvi" (*De musica*, V, 1), a definition that fits perfectly the *modi* of thirteenth-century theory. Also to be stressed is his use of the term *modulatio* for the rhythmic sequence, and the emphasis he placed on the value of pauses (by which *modi* are defined into *ordines* in the thirteenth-century theory and practice). Yet Augustine's influence can only be postulated, nor is the relationship clear, if any existed, between the rhythm of the Notre Dame school and the type of sequence composition represented by Adam of Saint Victor. Heinrich Husmann, "Notre-Dame und Saint-Victor," *Acta musicologica* 36 (1964), 98–123 and 191–221, gives evidence of the strong musical ties between the repertory of *prosae* of the two centers. It would seem, however, that the school of Saint Victor, influential as it was in the field of concepts and ideas, was more on the receiving side as far as the practice of music and composition was concerned.

15. Perotinus, to whom the passage partially quoted above, n. 9, attributes a number of well-known pieces, has been tentatively identified with a Petrus Succentor, active at Notre Dame from 1208 to 1238; this would agree with the fact that he wrote some conductus on texts by Philip the Chancelor (d. 1236). The possibility has also been indicated that he had some connection with Saint Germain l'Auxerrois and Saint Geneviève; see Heinrich Husmann, "St. Germain und Notre Dame," in *Natalicia musicologica Knud Jeppesen oblata* (Copenhagen, 1962), pp. 31–36; and "The Enlargement of the *Magnus liber organi* . . .," *Journal of the American Musicological Society* 16 (1963), 176–203. The identification is opposed by Hans Tischler, "Perotinus Revisited," in Jan LaRue, ed., *Aspects of Medieval and Renaissance Music* (New York, 1966), pp. 813–17, mainly on the ground that Petrus Succentor was not in Paris before 1208 (the evidence in support of this contention, however, is extremely tenuous), while Perotinus' activity as a composer took place, according to Tischler, from 1180 to 1200/05. Personally, I object to seeking an identification for both Leoninus and Perotinus among the *cantores* and *succentores* of Notre Dame, whose offices were largely administrative; furthermore, memory of such titles would have been preserved, while all we know of the two men is that both were called *magister*. On the other side, I do not see why Perotinus' activity should be so definitely confined to the time prior to 1205, nor do I see that his connection with Notre Dame should have necessarily prevented him from composing for neighboring churches.

16. A distinction is made by most thirteenth-century theorists between two-voice *organum duplum* (or *organum proprie sumptum*), which is said to have been a "cantus non in omni parte sua mensuratus," and the category of polyphonic pieces in which at least two parts were subjected to precise modal rhythm, *discantus*. The latter had more *ars* in it, yet the former was praised for a *subtilitas* of which no writer gives a satisfactory account; see n. 9, the sentence in which Perotinus' superiority to Leoninus as a *discantista* is qualified: "sed hic non dicendus de subtilitate organi."

17. This does not mean it was left unchanged, for new pieces were occasionally

added, and old ones reworked; nor is it to be assumed that there were no other composers than the two whose names we know.

18. The manuscripts containing what is broadly defined as Notre Dame repertory often include large sections of substitute *clausulae*. The *organum* itself, in which they could be inserted, represented only the soloistic sections of the responsorial song, and was therefore alternated in performance with sections sung in plainchant by the whole chapter choir.

19. It has often been stressed that medieval polyphony addresses itself not to an audience but to the church or monastic choir that is the agent of the celebration. It is, therefore, listened to, so to speak, from the inside.

20. One typical example is the clausula *Ex semine* from Perotinus' *Alleluja-Nativitas*, of which the *tenor* and one of the upper parts are found in various sources, the first unchanged, the other adjusted to the trope "Ex semine Abrahe divino moderamine ... piscem panem dabit partu sine semine." In some sources new music with the text "Ex semine Rosa prodit spine ... Verbum sine semine" replaces Perotinus' third voice.

21. The earliest collections of motets are prevailingly Latin and sacred in content, and ordered according to the liturgical use of their *tenores*. This is lost in later collections, in which secular vernacular texts become prominent, along with *tenores* for which no proper liturgical use can be determined, or even with definitely secular tenors. However, a persisting amount of musical borrowing indicates that the new motet was still practiced in circles that were acquainted with the repertory of liturgical *organa*. The borrowing worked two ways, for a case has been made for interpreting a number of *clausulae* in the ms. Paris, Bibl. Nationale, f. lat. 15139 (formerly St. Victor 813) as secular motets made into *clausulae*.

22. One example, selected for its brevity and musical interest, is the motet: "Roissoles ai roissoles / de dures et de moles / faites son a biau motes / pour ces biaus clers d'escole / qui dient les paroles / a ces puceles foles / qui chantent as queroles / roissoles ai roissoles." It goes above the tenor *Domino* together with another voice, the text of which begins: "En sce chant / qe ie chant / faz acorder / sanz descorder / ce nouvel deschant ..." Incidentally, the analogy must be noticed between troped texts and the secular troping of the so-called motets *entés*.

23. Again, I can only mention here such obvious examples as the frequent use of *In seculum* or *Aptatur* as tenors for motets of a mundane content. *In seculum*, a fragment of the Easter gradual *Hec dies*, enjoyed much larger popularity than any other tenor derived from the same melody, obviously because of its hint of secularity. *Aptatur* has been tentatively traced to a responsory of the office of Saint Nicholas, patron of students; among the motets, mostly on vernacular texts, using this tenor, one (*Eximie pater-Psallat chorus organico*) is in honor of the saint, another (*Chief bien seans-Entre Adan et Henequel*, attributed to Adam de la Hale) is a characteristic student motet.

24. I may quote as a precedent, however, a passage by the Dominican fra Remigio, who taught in the *studium generale* of S. Maria Novella in Florence,

and may have been one of Dante's teachers. In a chapter on music (Florence, Bibl. Nazionale Centr., Conv. Soppr. C 4 490, fols. 166–167), Remigio transfers the Augustinian concept of *modulatio* to the Church itself: "Ulterius in eccelesia non solum invenitur modulatio sonorum sed etiam modulatio ministeriorum in quantum scilicet secundum quandam proportionem sunt adinvicem ordinata et inter se et respectu dei et respectu subditorum"; quoted from F. Alberto Gallo, *La musica nell'opera di frate Remigio fiorentino* (Certaldo, 1966), p. 4, n. 19.

25. John Freccero, "The Sign of Satan," *Modern Language Notes* 80 (1965), 11ff.

26. The first term can be related to "le sante corde / che la destra del ciel allenta e tira" (*Paradiso*, XV, 5–6).

27. Thomas Aquinas, "De caelo et mundo," II, Lectio XIV, in *Opera omnia*, XIX (Parma, 1866), 112ff.

28. The song itself (*ibid.*, 103–108) is based on the idea of circular motion.

29. The trend arises during the second half of the thirteenth century with the discussion whether the *longa* of three *tempora* should have been called *perfecta* or *ultra mensuram*; see Walter Odington: "Longa autem apud priores organistas duo tantum habuit tempora sic[ut] in metris; sed postea ad perfectionem ducitur, ut sit trium temporum ad similitudinem beatissime trinitatis que est summa perfectio, diciturque longa hujusmodi perfecta," in de Coussemaker, I, 235. Soon the theological considerations obscured the objective reasons of the terminology and applied to the *modi* themselves against the insurgence of binary modes, which were termed not only imperfect but also *lascivi* because their models lay outside artistic practice. See also the pseudo-Aristotle (actually magister Lambertus) in de Coussemaker, I, 270–271, and the pseudo-Johannes de Muris (actually Jacobus de Leodio), *ibid.*, II, 397–398. A subtler justification was given by a Dominican writing in Paris in Saint Thomas' time; Hieronymus de Moravia, *Tractatus de musica*, ed. Simon M. Cserba (Regensburg, 1935), p. 180, equates ternary rhythm with the progression of time from past through present to future: "Prius enim et posterius causant temporis successionem ... Cum igitur tempus harmonicum motui progressivo sit subjectum, oportet omnino in ipso ponere successionem trium scilicet instantiarum."

30. Although I cannot quote any theoretical text supporting such an interpretation, it is made plausible by the existence at a later time of a comparable simile of the voices to the four elements with their different levels of mobility.

31. *Sumer is icumen in* is the most famous example of a *rota*. Of the early Italian *caccia*, resembling the *rota* more than the later type, we have no extant example but a description in an anonymous tract of the early fourteenth century; see my "Piero e l'impressionismo musicale del secolo XIV," in Bianca Becherini, ed., *L'Ars nova italiana del Trecento* (Certaldo, 1962), pp. 57–74.

32. Florence, Bibl. Nazionale Centrale, II.I.122, fol. 142ff.

33. Padua, Bibl. Capitolare, mss. C 55 and C 56; facsimile and transcriptions in Giuseppe Vecchi, *Uffici drammatici padovani* (Florence, 1954). Kurt von Fischer, "Die Rolle der Mehrstimmigkeit am Dome von Siena zu Beginn des

13. Jahrhunderts," *Archiv für Musikwissenschaft*, 18 (1961), 167ff., indicates that polyphony was even more intensively practiced at Siena at that time than in Paris, although probably it was less artistically refined. Various articles by the same author provide information concerning polyphonic settings in Italian sources before the fourteenth century.

34. Saint Augustine, *In Psalmum XXXII Enarratio*.

3 Ars Nova and Stil Novo

This essay was first presented as a lecture at Johns Hopkins University on January 7, 1965. It was published in Italian as "Ars nova e stil novo" in *Rivista italiana di musicologia* 1 (1966).

1. "Music and Cultural Tendencies in Fifteenth-Century Italy," included as essay 7 in this volume.
2. *Epistole inedite di Angelo Poliziano*, ed. L. D'Amore (Naples, 1909), pp. 38–40.
3. I am referring to the polyphonic repertory contained in the mss. once belonging to the Chiesa Collegiata of Cividale, now preserved in the Museo Archeologico of that town.
4. Fausto Torrefranca's book was aimed at a more restricted problem: tracing the origins of the madrigalian style. His title, however, is indicative of a general attitude toward the problems of fifteenth-century music.
5. My thinking on this problem is explained in "Cronologia e denominazione dell'Ars Nova italiana," in *L'Ars nova. Recueil d'études sur la musique du XIVᵉ siècle. Les colloques de Wégimont. II, 1955*, Bibliothèque de la Faculté de Philosophie et Lettres de l'Université de Liège, Fascicule CXLIX (Paris, 1959), pp. 93–104.
6. R. Bacon, *Opera quaedam hactenus inedita*, ed. J. S. Brewer (London, 1859), I, 230–231, beginning with a distinction between instrumental and vocal music: "Omnis igitur sonus vel est ex collisione duri cum duro, vel ex motione spirituum ad vocalem arteriam. Si est ex collisione, tunc est musica instrumentalis ... Si vero sit musica de sono humano, tunc vel est melica, vel prosaica, vel metrica, vel rhythmica."
7. According to Aristide Marigo's comment on Dante's *De Vulgari Eloquentia* (Florence, 1938), paragraph II, viii, 5, p. 236, "Dante sees the composition of *canzoni* without music as being not only possible ... but most usual, and the poet as being distinguished from the musician." As a matter of fact, Dante's main concern in this passage is to establish "utrum cantio dicatur fabricatio verborum armonizatorum, vel ipsa modulatio," that is, beyond the question of names, whether the essence of the *canzone* consists in its text or in its music. His conclusion that the *canzone* is so named even when unaccompanied by a melody, while the melody itself is called "sonus, vel tonus, vel nota, vel melos," does not deny the existence of a melody; on the contrary, the question

could not have arisen without the habit of associating poetry and music in the *canzone*. A different point of view is expressed by W. T. Marrocco, "The Enigma of the Canzone," *Speculum* 31 (1956), 704–13, especially 710: "It appears very unlikely that a *canzone* by Dante Alighieri, the greatest Italian poet of his day, with a musical setting by Pietro (?) Casella or another equally capable musician would have been allowed to disappear." I do not need to repeat here what I think must have determined the silence of written tradition.

8. *De Vulgari Eloquentia*, II, x, 2–4.

9. Dante Alighieri, *Rime*, ed. G. F. Contini (Turin, 1939), pp. 43–44.

10. I do not think that the other version we know of this text (in eleven- and seven-syllable lines) is "di tutta eleganza e correttezza," as it appeared to G. Carducci, "Della varia fortuna di Dante," III, 11, in *Studi letterari* (Leghorn, 1874), p. 354. As for the original version, I am sure it seldom occurs in the sources because of its difficult meter.

11. Dante Alighieri, *Rime*, p. 33: "E priego il gentil cor che 'n te riposa / che la rivesta e tegnala per druda, / sì che sia conosciuda / e possa andar là 'vunque è disiosa." See also *Lo mio servente core* and *Madonna, quel signor che voi portate* (*ibid.*, pp. 35 and 45), two one-stanza *canzoni* with *piedi* and *volta*, that is, with both *fronte* and *sirima* divided into two symmetrical parts.

12. *Ibid.*, p. 46. See also, pp. 101–03, the *ballate, I' mi son pargoletta* (in which, according to Contini, "two typical stil novo themes" are transferred "from the tragic style of the *canzone* ... to the mediocre style, musically more pleasant and accessible, of the *ballata*") and *Perché ti vedi giovinetta e bella*. About Scochetto see N. Pirrotta, "Due sonetti musicali del secolo XIV," in *Miscelànea en homenaje a Monseñor Higinio Anglés* (Barcelona, 1958–1961), II, 654.

13. See F. Liuzzi, *La lauda e i primordi della melodia italiana* (Rome, 1935), and C. Terni, "Per una edizione critica del Laudario di Cortona," *Chigiana* 21 (1964), 111–29.

14. Pirrotta, "Due sonetti musicali." Codex Vatican Barberini lat. 3953 was written for Nicolò de Rossi between 1325 and 1335.

15. See the following passage from his *Rationarium Vitae*, reported by R. Sabbadini, *Giovanni da Ravenna* (Como, 1924), p. 144: "Accedebat vanitati juventus et corporis haud usquequaque contemnenda species, vocis canor ... Canciones balatas sonicia madrigalia ac vulgaris reliqua note deliramenta mira ingenii facilitate pro omnium voto explicaram. Undique cantabar passimque diffamatus eram." This refers to the years during which Giovanni studied in Bologna (1364–1365).

16. This line from the madrigal *Oselleto salvaço*, set to music twice by Iacopo da Bologna, is usually read "tutti enfioran Filipotti e Marchetti." Its correct interpretation is suggested by the variant reading found in Codex Panciatichi 26: "fansi Fioran, Filipotti e Marchetti." For the two letters addressed to Floriano by Petrarch, see the latter's *Poesie minori ... volgarizzate* (Milan, 1831), II, 110–17.

17. This is a *Capitulum de vocibus applicatis verbis*, given this title by S.

Debenedetti, "Un trattatello del secolo XIV sopra la poesia musicale," *Studi medievali* 2 (1906–07), 59–82, and later included in the same author's *Il "Sollazzo"* (Turin, 1922), pp. 179–84. Of the three articles I have written on the *Capitulum*, the following more particularly deal with its nature and the personality of its writer: "Una arcaica descrizione trecentesca del madrigale," in *Festschrift Heinrich Besseler* (Leipzig, 1962), pp. 155–61; and "Ballate e *soni* secondo un grammatico del Trecento," *Bollettino del Centro di studi filologici e linguistici siciliani* 8 (1962), 42–54.

18. Although the identification of the music theorist with the grammarian is not definitely proved, we are sure of their identical name, evidently derived from the name of one section of the university quarters in Paris.

19. This is the *triplum* of the motet *Lonc tens me sui tenu de chanter—Annuntiantes* in Codex Montpellier, Faculté de Médecine, H 196, fols. 273r–275r; its programmatic nature is underlined by the choice of the unusual *tenor*.

4 Polyphonic Music for a Text Attributed to Frederick II

This essay was originally published in *L'Ars Nova Italiana del Trecento*, vol. II (Certaldo, 1968). The translation is by Vanni Bartolozzi.

1. See Ezio Levi, *Francesco di Vannozzo* (Florence, 1908), pp. 324–34; and Ottavio Tiby, "Il problema della siciliana dal Trecento al Settecento," in *Bollettino del Centro de Studi Filologici e Linguistici Siciliani* 2 (1954), 245–70.

2. Alessandro Wesselofsky, *Il Paradiso degli Alberti* (Bologna, 1867), II, 90–91. The conversations, entertainment, and, therefore, the ride itself should have happened around 1389, but there is a belief now that Giovanni da Prato may have written his "novel" much later (*circa* 1425), reflecting, at least in part, changed conceptions and mores. See Hans Baron, *Humanistic and Political Literature in Florence and Venice* (Cambridge, Mass., 1955), pp. 13–37.

3. "Sed ubi pluribus corporibus ac mentis epulis totos, ut dicitur, homines egregie ac solempniter pavimus, remotis mensis, nonnulli florentini adolescentes, qui cenati ad nos inter cenandum ludendi et iocandi gratia concurrerant, paulo post saltare ac coreas ducere ceperunt; quod cum aliquandiu fecissent, ad gallicas cantilenas et melodias conversi ita vocibus suis modulabantur ut pene celestes et quasi angelici cantus cunctis audientibus viderentur. Venetis insuper cantiunculis et symphoniis aliqualem operam navaverunt. Ad extremum juvenis quidam, nomine Cosmas, in Sicilia diutius commoratus, nonnullas siculas symphonias et cantilenas modulari et cantare cepit, atque tanta nimirum suavitate modulabatur, ut omnes audientes incredibili modulandi et canendi dulcedine titillati hanc siculam modulationem ceteris gallicis ac venetis cantibus longe praeferre ac preponere non dubitarent; et, id quod plus aliis ab omnibus laudabatur, expressus quidam et

recensitus, ut ita dixerimus, siculus mulierum preficarum fletus videbatur ... " from *Dialogus in domestico et familiari quorundam amicorum symposio Venetiis habito,* from codex Laurenziano, Plut. XC, sup. 29, quoted by Arnaldo Della Torre, *Storia dell'Accademia Platonica* (Florence, 1902), pp. 282–83. The date of the banquet was October 8, 1448; the dialogue contains other interesting musical references.

4. Levi, p. 329, denies the possibility of singing alternate stanzas, but his argument is not convincing, both because polyphonic singing is improbable during a ride, with one of the performers asked to participate on the spot, and because one cannot otherwise understand why collaboration was necessary. The amoebean singing is the more likely answer.

5. The "siculus fletus" (Sicilian wailing), later called also "tribulus," is but one of the examples of *siciliane* given by Cosma (see the "et" at the beginning of the sentence where it is described). The following passage, where it is said to have produced "so much jeering with so much laughing (tanto risu tantasque cachinnationes ... commovisse) has perplexed all the interpreters. I see a tendency to justify the choice of the "tribulus" as postconvivial music, from which people expected merriment and serenity; anyway, even a grotesque imitation does not deny the pathetic character they used to attribute to *siciliane.*

6. Levi, p. 189, supposes that Francesco di Vannozzo lived in Venice, at least at intervals, between 1373 and 1379. The date seems, though, too far from the year when "young" Andreuolo is supposed to have sung and even farther from the date of the writing of the "novel." I would suggest instead the time between the fall of the "signoria" of the Della Scalas and the poet's assumed move to Milan (1387–1389).

7. A recent description of the codex's three sections and an accurate index of their content are given by Kurt von Fischer, "The Manuscript Paris, Bibl. Nat. Nouv. Acq. Frç. 6771 (Codex Reina = PR)," in *Musica Disciplina* 11 (1957), 38–78. See also Nigel E. Wilkins, "The Codex Reina: A Revised Description," *ibid.* 17 (1963) 57–73; and von Fischer, "Reply to N. E. Wilkins' Article," *ibid.,* 75–77.

8. For the attribution, see n. 10.

9. Kurt von Fischer, *Studien zur italienischen Musik des Trecento und frühen Quattrocento* (Bern, 1956), pp. 228–29; von Fischer, "Manuscript Paris," p. 59.

10. A recent edition of the text is in *La Magna Curia,* ed. Camillo Guerrieri Crocetti (Milan, 1947), pp. 107–8; in *ibid.,* pp. 97–99, the arguments for its attribution to the emperor or to the son are summarized and resolved by Crocetti in favor of the first. Even more resolutely he rejècts the attribution to Jacopo Mostacci. For the Vaticano codex, see n. 11.

11. *Il Libro de varie romanze volgare, cod. Vat. 3793,* ed. Francesco Egidi (Rome, 1908), p. 48. *Ibid.,* p. viiii, the codex is described as "un bel volume di cc. 188, scritto da varj amanuensi in lettera notarile della fine del sec. XIII." In A.

D'Ancona and D. Comparetti, *Le Antiche Rime Volgari secondo la lezione del Codice Vaticano 3793* (Bologna, 1875), I, 172, the version of the *canzone* has some lines strangely mutilated to reduce them to seven-syllable lines, while others remain eight-syllable lines.

12. "Sur la rime italienne et les Siciliens," in *Mémoires de la Societé néophilologique de Helsingfors* 5 (1905), 269–70.

13. Crocetti, p. 107, emends: "membrandome fuor di gioia." The reading of PR gives "mimbrandome de vui, fior di çoia," but the added "de uuy" was probably suggested by mistakenly reading "fuor" as "fior."

14. See the description in the passage of Epistola III of *Diaffonus* by Giovanni del Virgilio, recorded by Vincenzo de Bartholomeis, *Rime giullaresche e popolari* (Bologna, 1926), pp. 73–74.

15. See N. Pirrotta, "Ballate e soni secondo un grammatico del Trecento," in *Bollettino del Centro di studi filologici e linguistici Siciliani* 8 (1962), 47, n. 20. Leonardo Giustinian used the possibility of the double *ripresa* in some of his dialogue *ballate*.

16. See Pirrotta, "Ballate e soni," 48, n. 21.

17. K. von Fischer, *Studien*, p. 49, n. 228.

5 New Glimpses of an Unwritten Tradition

This essay was originally published in *Words and Music: The Scholar's View*, edited by Laurence Berman (Harvard University, Department of Music, 1972).

1. "When I come to pass by, I feel a pain; I see you and cannot greet you. You would believe it is for lack of love; I do so lest people should gossip about you. The eyes of people are like piercing arrows; from far away they can betray one's heart. Listen to what I say, my dearest love; keep being true to me, have no fear." The norm of eight lines with two alternating rhymes (here rhymes 5 and 6 are irregular), known as Sicilian *strambotto* (as opposed to the continental form *a b a b a b c c*), is only a well-balanced optimum $(2 + 2 + 2 + 2)$; the popular practice does not exclude either shorter or longer poems, always with an even number of lines.

2. Alberto Favara, *Corpus di musiche popolari siciliane*, ed. Ottavio Tiby (Palermo, 1957), II, 250–51; I have added the dotted barlines to help delineate rhythmic groups. Rather unusual, and not clearly indicated in the *Corpus*, is the fact that the melody is sung first with lines 1–2 and is then repeated with lines 2–3, 3–4, and so on, thus adding one line at a time instead of two.

3. "(And) in this courtyard there is a rose bush; don't touch it, anybody, for it's mine. Should anyone be thinking about it, he had better quickly give up the idea. He might end up with his head where his feet are; I swear to do this to

him myself. To you I commend myself, o rose, for in your hands is placed all my life." The initial "E" ("and" in the translation) I have put in parentheses, because it does not actually belong to the poem.

4. Favara, *Corpus*, II, 172–73. Although a man is speaking in the poem, both versions are designated "laundress" songs.

5. *Ibid.*, II, 188; "muttettu," like the original French *motet*, means a short text.

6. A recent description of the manuscript and the contents of its three sections are given by Kurt von Fischer, "The Manuscript Paris, Bibl. Nat., Nouv. Acq. Frç. 6771 (Codex Reina = PR)," *Musica Disciplina* 11 (1957), 38–78, to which must be added Nigel Wilkins, "The Codex Reina: A Revised Description," *ibid.*, 17 (1963), 57–73, and Kurt von Fischer, "Reply to N. E. Wilkins' Article on the Codex Reina," *ibid.*, 75–77.

7. Dompnus Paulus, that is, possibly Paolo Tenorista from Florence, well known to us, was not necessarily as well known earlier; very few pieces by the others are known. It is worth noting that only names of obscure composers are given in this section of the manuscript; the works by famous masters are given anonymously, although their authorship was evidently known to the compilers.

8. See essays 3 and 7.

9. See essay 4. No matter how correct the attribution may be, the poem certainly belongs to a representative of the thirteenth-century Sicilian school of poetry.

10. PR, fol. 38v. I shall not attempt to burden the reader with translations that would require discussion and justification. The texts were evidently obscure to the copyists, and the meaning often needs to be guessed at. I have in most cases merely reproduced the text, changing it only by putting in parentheses superfluous elements and in brackets suggestions for needed additions.

11. Oiva J. Tallgren, "Sur la rime italienne et les Siciliens du XIIIᵉ siècle," *Mémoires de la Société néo-philologique de Helsingfors* 5 (1909), 269–70.

12. The transcriptions of the present and following polyphonic pieces conform to the procedures outlined in the foreword to my edition of *The Music of Fourteenth Century Italy*, I (Amsterdam, 1954), ii–iii. A 2/4 signature followed by an asterisk corresponds to a notation in the *octonaria* measure in the original (while an unmarked 2/4 would denote an original in a *quaternaria* measure); the 3/4 signature of Ex. 5.7 corresponds to an original in a *senaria perfecta* measure. The grouping of the resulting modern measures into larger (and largely irregular) rhythmic units is an allegedly subjective interpretation of the editor.

13. Von Fischer and Wilkins agree on the date 1395–1405 for this section of PR and on Venice or Padua as the place where it was copied; see the articles mentioned in n. 6 above, particularly von Fischer, "Reply," p. 76. I have no objection to either the date or the places, although a number of other towns or abbeys might be plausible candidates. I do not dare to enter the game of distinguishing hands (irrelevant to the present topic), because I have had no direct access to the manuscript for many years. I do not, however, agree with the idea that this or any other manuscript may "stem fairly directly from the

manuscripts left by the Carrara family at Padua" (Wilkins, "Codex Reina," p. 65); in my experience, any fairly large collection was usually assembled from a number of smaller sources.

14. Giovanni da Prato, *Il Paradiso degli Alberti*, ed. Alessandro Wesselofsky (Bologna, 1867), II, 90–91. The date of the events described in the "romance" is 1389, but the work itself is later, *ca.* 1425, according to Hans Baron, *Humanistic and Political Literature in Florence and Venice at the Beginning of the Quattrocento* (Cambridge, Mass., 1955), pp. 13–37.

15. Description by Giannozzo Manetti of a real banquet in Venice on October 8, 1448; quoted by Arnaldo Della Torre, *Storia dell'Accademia platonica* (Florence, 1902), pp. 282–83.

16. Santorre Debenedetti, *Il "Sollazzo"* (Turin, 1922), p. 176.

17. The curiosity for exotic specialties and the relish of poets and writers in listing them are, of course, of much older standing; what is worth particular notice at this moment is the insistence on folklore, indicated, for instance, by Sollazzo's repertory. The latter includes local popular songs and dances (*ibid.*, pp. 171, 174), "Calate de Maritima e Campagna, / Canzon de Lombardia e de Romagna" (p. 173), and "Canzon del Cieco, a modo peruscino" (p. 176, certainly not a reference to Landini's music).

18. See Favara, *Corpus*, nos. 51, 120, 127, 138, 145, 152–56, 173, 182–85, 202, 214, 299–301, and 359.

19. In addition to the deletions and insertions suggested by parentheses and brackets (see n. 10 above), I have modified a few passages, the PR readings of which I give here: line 4, "o l'ascossa magiore"; line 16, "par chi luci."

20. See Vittorio Cian, "Ballate e strambotti del sec. XV: tratti da un codice trevisano," *Giornale storico della letteratura italiana* 4 (1884), 41. The manuscript, Treviso, Biblioteca comunale, ms. 43, contains a number of poems that are related to our present topic; furthermore, *Strençì li labri*, as well as *Finir mia vita* (PR, fol. 26), are included in Sollazzo's repertory (Debenedetti, pp. 174, 177, n. 7).

21. Debenedetti, p. 174. For my translation of "suoni" as *ballate* see my "Ballate e 'soni' secondo un grammatico del Trecento," *Bollettino del Centro di studi filologici e linguistici Siciliani* 8 (1962), 42–54.

22. On the problem of the music of the *giustiniana*, see Walter H. Rubsamen, "The Justiniane or Viniziane of the 15th Century," *Acta musicologica* 29 (1957), 172–84. The pieces identified there as *giustiniane*, however, are in a slow rhythm that would have been unsuitable for the poet's long *sirventesi* and dramatic *ballate*.

23. His manneristic ones on French texts are published in *French Secular Music of the Late Fourteenth Century*, ed. Willi Apel (Cambridge, Mass., 1950), pp. 31ff. For the Italian ones see Nino Pirrotta and Ettore Li Gotti, "Il Codice di Lucca," *Musica Disciplina* 3 (1949), 119–38; 4 (1950), 111–52; 5 (1951), 115–42, esp. 133–36.

24. No. 39 in the fragmentary manuscript Lucca, Archivio di Stato (known as the Mancini ms. hereafter cited as Mn), described in Pirrotta and Li Gotti, "Il

Codice." Mn, no. 40, *Or tolta pur mi sei*, also by Antonellus, is more similar from the point of view of rhythm to the examples previously given, with which it has in common the notation in the *octonaria* measure, rendered as 2/4* in my transcriptions.

25. See in Ex. 5.7 the rhythms suggested by broken barlines in the passages corresponding to the words "Segnor mio caro, del vostro partire" and "Via ve n'andate et io."

26. Rubsamen, "Justiniane or Viniziane," p. 184, gives one passage from Ciconia's *Dolçe fortuna* as an example of his use of dissonant seconds, which remained as one of the features of the *giustiniana*; seconds and other dissonances are present to an even greater extent in Ex. 5.8, Mn, no. 54 (also transcribed by Suzanne Clercx, *Johannes Ciconia* [Brussels, 1960], II, 58–60).

27. [Although a few words cannot be read in lines 5–6, the rhyme scheme is clearly the following: *AA BABA AA*.]

28. [G. Cattin, "Ricerche sulla musica a S. Giustina di Padova all'inizio del Quattrocento I: Il copista Rolando da Casale," *Annales musicologiques* 7 (1964–1977), 31ff. I cannot give a precise folio number because the fragment is one of nine leaves found within the binding of ms. 553.]

29. [*Ibid.*, pp. 17–31 and 36.]

30. [F. A. Gallo, "Ricerche sulla musica a S. Giustina di Padova all'inizio del Quattrocento II: Due 'siciliane' del Trecento," *Annales musicologiques* 7 (1964–1977), 43ff.]

31. [*Ibid.*, p. 48; this is Gallo's logical emendation of the punctuation the line is given in S. Debenedetti, "Il 'Sollazzo' e il 'Saporetto' con altre rime di Simone Prudenzani d'Orvieto," *Giornale storico della letteratura italiana*, Supplemento 15 (1913), p. 117, as well as in S. Debenedetti, *Il "Sollazzo"* (Turin, 1922), p. 177.]

32. [I have included a detailed comparison of the two pieces in an essay entitled "Echi di arie veneziane del primo Quattrocento," to be published in a miscellaneous volume honoring Professor Michelangelo Muraro.]

6 The Oral and Written Traditions of Music

This essay was originally published in *L'Ars Nova Italiana del Trecento* (Certaldo, Centro di Studi, 1970). It is more a report on than a reconstruction of my presentation at the Second International Conference on the Fourteenth-Century Ars Nova, held in Certaldo, July 17–22, 1969. The translation is by Lowell Lindgren.

1. See, for example, essays 3 and 7.

2. See essay 4 in this volume.

3. "Paolo da Firenze und der Squarcialupi-Kodex," *Quadrivium* 9 (1968), 6. This most praiseworthy study by my friend von Fischer offers an example of

our attachment to the written tradition: having adroitly identified the artisan who executed the miniatures in the Squarcialupi Codex with the decorator of miniatures in books dated 1406, 1409, and 1423, von Fischer concludes that the decoration of the musical codex was also done *between* 1406 and 1423; he thus disallows the possibility that an artisan who crystallized his style in the decorative formulas he employed over a span of at least seventeen years might have continued to use them during the next decade, for example. My dating of the Squarcialupi Codex at 1440 or later is probably too late (when I gave this date I was influenced by biographical data concerning Squarcialupi and Vespasiano Bisticci), but my conviction that it is a late document of the Ars nova is not altered by von Fischer's arguments.

4. See essay 5.

5. Kurt von Fischer, "The Manuscript Paris, Bibliothèque Nationale, Nouv. Acq. Frç. 6771 (Codex Reina = PR)," *Musica Disciplina* 11 (1957), 47.

6. See the beginning of essay 4.

7. The text has been emended: besides placing superfluous elements (mainly what I have called introductory vowels) in parentheses and a suggested addition in brackets, I have put two verbs into the future tense (*cridarà* in line 7 is *cridava* in the codex, and *amarà* in line 8 is *amara*). The musical setting is given in essay 5.

8. See essay 7.

9. The text is included in Book XII of Poliziano's *Lettere*. This improvised reference came to mind, as usual, because I had cited the text in a book I was writing, which was published a few months later: *Li due Orfei* (Turin, 1969; 2nd ed., 1975), translated as *Music and Theatre from Poliziano to Monteverdi* (Cambridge, 1981), pp. 35–36.

10. See Pirrotta, *Music and Theatre*, p. 155; and also Henry W. Kaufmann, "Music for a Noble Florentine Wedding," in *Words and Music: The Scholar's View*, ed. Laurence Berman (Harvard University, Department of Music, 1972), pp. 167–69.

11. The *oda*, generally considered to be a poem with four-line strophes, in fact consists of strophes made up of two seven-syllable lines plus an eleven-syllable line with an internal rhyme.

12. "Ballata," in *Die Musik in Geschichte und Gegenwart* 1 (1949), col. 1163.

13. The repetition signs in my transcription are reproduced as they appear in the earliest prints, with two dots on either side; in such sources this indicates repetition only of the preceding passage, a custom often misunderstood today. Moreover, the repetition may be limited to only part of the preceding passage, in which case in early sources a vertical line indicates the point where the repetition begins (as in measure 6 of the transcription).

14. The *ripresa* (textually "recommencement") of the *ballata* derives its name from the fact that the refrain was originally stated by a soloist and then immediately repeated by the chorus. In the *frottola* or *barzelletta* the repetition is fully written out, and it is customarily restricted to the first two lines (more rarely to the last two), the second of which—as in the transcription

given—often includes further repetition and cadential amplifications. At the end of each stanza, it is probable that only the abbreviated repetition of the *ripresa* was performed.

7   Music and Cultural Tendencies in Fifteenth-Century Italy

This essay was originally published in *Journal of the American Musicological Society* 19 (1966).

The main text of this article is a slightly revised version of a paper read in Seattle on December 27, 1963, at the annual meeting of the American Musicological Society. As I remarked on that occasion, it sums up the results of a negative—yet useful and necessary—search for musical information in humanistic sources, a search made possible by a fellowship granted to me by the American Council of Learned Societies.

1. "Josquin des Prés, cantore del Duomo di Milano (1459–1472)," *Annales musicologiques* 4 (1956), 55–81.

2. Josquin still served at the Duomo while other singers had already left to become ducal singers (*ibid.*, pp. 66 and 81). For the various lists of the ducal chapel see also Guglielmo Barblan, "Vita musicale alla corte sforzesca" in *Storia di Milano* (Milan, 1961), IX, particularly 826–36.

3. Facsimile in Helmuth Osthoff, "Josquin Desprez," *Die Musik in Geschichte und Gegenwart*, 7, col. 194; transcription of the text in the same author's *Josquin Desprez* (Tutzing, 1962–65), I, 16. Osthoff's contention that Josquin had already been ordained seems to me unsupported by the expression "cantori et capellano nostro" (our singer and a member of our chapel), without any of the titles expected to accompany a priest's name.

4. Franz Xaver Haberl, "Die römische 'schola cantorum' und die päpstlichen Kapellsänger bis zur Mitte des 16. Jahrhunderts," *Vierteljahrsschrift für Musikwissenschaft* 3 (1887), 244.

5. Sforza had arrived in Rome just in time to participate in the election of Innocent VIII (August, 1884). [Josquin's relationship with Sforza finds further confirmation in the documents discussed by E. E. Lowinsky, "Ascanio Sforza's Life: a Key to Josquin's Biography," in *Josquin des Prez. Proceedings of the International Josquin Festival-Conference . . . New York City, 21–25 June 1971*, E. E. Lowinsky, B. J. Blackburn, eds. (London, 1976), pp. 31–75. The whole volume adds precious new information on Josquin.]

6. See the sources listed above, note 2.

7. The situation is generally unclear, both because of the incompleteness and obscurity of the records and because of our tendency to read more into them than is actually present. It should be remembered that churches had no musical chapels at this time, but chapters, whose musical duties, once essential, had come to be delegated mostly to one or two *mansionarii*, who were sort of second-class, locally appointed canons. *Cantor* may have indicated sometimes a polyphonist; more often it had lost its historical meaning of

"leader in the singing of plainchant" and had come to designate one of the officials of the chapter more concerned with administrative than with musical tasks. More specific terms, such as *tenorista, contratenorista*, and *biscantor* (which may have meant either a singer of *discantus* music in general, or of *discantus* parts in particular) are found only occasionally. See, for Padua, Raffaele Casimiri, "Musica e musicisti nella Cattedrale di Padova ... ," in *Note d'archivio per la storia musicale* 18 (1941), 1–31; and Suzanne Clercx, *Johannes Ciconia* (Brussels, 1960), I, 43–50. Florence had no more than two polyphonic singers at a time until the end of 1438, according to Frank D'Accone, "A Documentary History of Music at the Florentine Cathedral ... " (Harvard University dissertation, 1960), pp. 71ff; they were increased to four at the time of the transfer of the Council from Ferrara to Florence, and it is relevant that the new singers were hired in Ferrara, where the Council had been assembled (D'Accone, "The Singers of San Giovanni in Florence during the 15th Century," *JAMS* 14 [1961], 309ff). In Milan the number varied from one to three until 1430, settling on two in the last five years (C. Sartori, "Matteo da Perugia e Bertrand Feragut i due primi maestri di cappella del Duomo di Milano," *Acta musicologica* 28 [1956], 12–27, in which I find objectionable the use of the term *maestri di cappella*). They increased to four from 1430 to 1450, and to seven in the following years, probably due to the influence of Francesco Sforza (see Sartori in *Annales musicologiques* 4, p. 68); but we do not know, of course, how much the added singers actually served the Duomo. Most illuminating about musical practice is a proposal for the reestablishment of a "chapel" in Florence, in a letter addressed in 1469 to Lorenzo dei Medici (D'Accone, *JAMS* 14, p. 324). The writer, a contratenor, proposes himself with one good tenor and three treble singers; a bass might join them to sing *à 4*.

8. See the references in note 7.

9. "Viaggio a Gerusalemme di Nicolò da Este descritto da Luchino del Campo," ed. Giovanni Ghinassi (Turin, 1861).

10. It is significant that the most extensive polyphonic repertory in our possession comes from the *familia* of the bishops of Trent. Another aspect of the impact of the Councils is the opportunity they offered for the diffusion of works by even minor composers. Works originating from the constellation Zacharias—Nicholaus Zacharie—Antonius Zachara, whose components were not clearly separated even in the minds of their contemporaries, found their way to Polish mss. and to the lost Strasbourg ms., and eventually crossed the sea to be included in the English Old Hall ms.

11. On July 17, 1434, "in sacra deputacione pro communibus ... Dominus Abbas de Verona retulit quod dominus episcopus Vincensis ob reverenciam concilii licenciavit cantores quos conduxerat," in Johannes Haller et al., *Concilium basiliense: Studien und Quellen zur Geschichte des Concils von Basel* (Basel, 1896–1926), III, 151.

12. *Ibid.*, III, 115f, 120, 214, 232, 270, 277, 356, 367, 526f, 583, 589; and IV, 12, 73, 86, 96, 118.

13. Frans van Molle, *Identification d'un portrait de Gilles Joye attribué à*

Memlinc (Brussels, 1960), gives detailed biographical information on Joye, discounting, however, his identification with the theologian and poet as suggested by Jeanne Marix, *Histoire de la musique et des musiciens de la cour de Bourgogne* (Strasbourg, 1939), p. 213. The painting is owned by the Sterling and Francine Clark Art Institute, Williamstown, Mass.

14. Haller, III, p. 269. A translation of this record has recently been given by Keith E. Mixter, "Johannes Brassart . . ." *Musica Disciplina* 18 (1964), 49, along with a translation of the original act of incorporation in the Council. Martin Tegen's article, "Basel conciliet och kyrcmusiken omkr. 1440," *Svensk tideskrift för musikforskning* 39 (1957), 126ff, is misleading insofar as it lists as singers of the Council all such members who had titles of *cantor, precentor,* or *succentor.* Such offices were held by their bearers in the churches to which they belonged and had often lost their musical meaning (see above, n. 7); furthermore, it should be remembered that every churchman was expected to be a singer as far as plainchant was concerned.

15. "Les chantres ou chapelains sont presque tous de grands personnages, chanoines, prévôts, doyens, pourvus de nombreuses et grasses prébendes. A la cour, ils sont familiers du prince et cumulent leur office avec ceux de valet de chambre, secrétaire, aumônier, enfin conseiller lorsqu'ils deviennent premier chapelain"; Marix, p. 125.

16. *Ibid.,* p. 139 (also pp. 132–34).

17. *Ibid.,* pp. 242–48.

18. Three boys were sent to Paris in 1409 for at least one year (*ibid.,* p. 135); groups of four were entrusted to Grenon in Cambrai from 1412 to 1415 and again in later years (*ibid.,* pp. 136ff). Their training included grammar and music, but older boys were sent to attend the university in Paris (*ibid.,* p. 141).

19. On October 2, 1444, Maestro Giacomo Barbo or Borbo, "a singer of the royal chapel and the master of five pages also singers in the chapel," is recorded to have accompanied the king with his pupils on a hunting party (Camillo Minieri Riccio, "Alcuni fatti di Alfonso I d'Aragona . . ." in *Archivio storico per le Provincie Napoletane* 6 [1881], 245), and again mentioned as "maestro di canto" on January 27, 1451 (*ibid.,* p. 411). On April 15, 1454, Messer Pietro Brusia is the new teacher, among whose pupils a Francesco Tuppo is listed (*ibid.,* p. 429), possibly the future translator and printer of the vernacular Aesopus published in Naples in 1485. Two short treatises of Giacomo Barbo (preserved in a ms. of the Bibl. Ursino Recupero of Catania) show that his teaching included again grammar and music; he anticipates Tinctoris in humanistic orientation ("*Incipit liber luminator. Cum ergo in libellis marci tullij ciceronis. virgilijque Terencij sepius legi*"), as well as in calling himself "minimus inter musicos"; see Paolo Nalli, "Regulae contrapuncti secundum usum Regni Siciliae tratte da un codice siciliano del sec. XV," in *Archivio storico per la Sicilia orientale* 29 (1933), 280 and 282.

20. As in the case of other similarly constructed titles (including, for instance, the *magister coquine*), the term may have indicated a superintendence of the chapel's activities or may have been occasionally bestowed on an honorary basis. The latter is even more likely if we consider that the title of *capellanus*

(as a member of a pope's or cardinal's chapel, not as the titular of a chapel-altar in a church) was often conferred for honorific purposes; see Bernard Guillemain, *La cour pontificale d'Avignon* (Paris, 1962), pp. 360ff. There was no need of a conductor in the type of performance implied by the letter mentioned above, n. 7, that is, with the lower parts each given to one singer, and doubling limited to the upper part; adult singers could easily keep together, taking a cue whenever needed from the one among them who was in charge of the tenor part. If the chapel included some boys, he who had charge of them was called *magister*, not for whatever guidance he gave to them in the performance, but for teaching them. The term *capella* itself has a long history, originally as a portable shrine (a remnant of this was the custom of having the papal singers marching around the pope's canopy in processions), then as a private place of worship in a royal palace, and only later as the place of a secondary altar in a church. Its musical connotations may derive from the Sainte-Chapelle of the French kings in Paris (the popes created their musical chapel in Avignon as a replacement for the Schola cantorum they had left in Rome). To my knowledge, the earliest event justifying the name of *capella* for a body of singers in a church occurred when Pope Sixtus IV assigned a chapel in St. Peter's to the singers of that church; from his design to endow such a chapel with the revenue needed to support the living expenses of choirboys and their *magister*, the present Cappella Giulia originated. For the sake of objectivity I must, however, mention that both *capella* and *magister capelle* were at least colloquially used for the Florentine cathedral in the documents of 1438–39 referred to by F. D'Accone, *JAMS* 14 (1961), 310-11 and 351.

21. In a letter dated October 22, [1451], Duke Louis of Savoy addressed Dufay as "conseiller et maestre de la chapelle" while asking him to come for a visit. Earlier, on March 21, 1435, the court had paid Dufay his salary as *magister capellae* from February 1434 to January 1435, although he had been away, at least for a time, to visit his mother, receiving gifts to this purpose from both the duke and his son. During the same period payments were made to a *magister puerorum*, Adam Grand (also called *magister cantus*; accordingly, Dufay might have taught grammar). See Gino Borghezio, "La fondazione del Collegio nuovo 'Puerorum innocentium' del Duomo di Torino," in *Note d'archivio per la storia musicale* 1 (1924), 228–30 and 246.

22. See the detailed, penetrating analysis of the papal court in Guillemain, *La cour.*

23. The nonmusical character of this office is stressed by G. Despy, "Notes sur les offices de la curie d'Avignon: Les fonctions du 'magister capelle pape,' " in *Bulletin de l'Institut historique belge de Rome* 28 (1953), 21–30. Quite exceptionally, the title was given under Martin V to the *tenorista* Bertoldus Dauci, but reverted to a nonmusician bishop under Eugene IV; see Franz Xaver Haberl, *Wilhelm du Fay* (Leipzig, 1885), pp. 59–66, as well as my own section of "Rom," *MGG*, XI, col. 695–96 and 704. On February 23, 1437, Brassart is called "Serenissimi Romanorum imperatoris capelle rector"; see J. Haller, V, p. 21.

24. Haberl, *du Fay*, pp. 66 and 115–18.

25. The document, labeled "Cantores cap.nj et clerici seremoniarum," is a cursive copy, or draft of a decree, without indication of date, in the codex Vatican Lat. 3983, fols. 141v–142.

26. Of course, the cathedral schools provided the basis for such an education at Cambrai, as at Tournai, Reims, Liège, or Antwerp; yet it had to be perfected at a university. Concerning music, I doubt that the large numbers of canons and singers in those cathedrals combined forces for the "choral" performance of polyphonic pieces. Choral performances must have been reserved to plainchant, the continued predominance of which is indicated by the scarcity of polyphonic settings for the Proper. But also for the Ordinary, polyphonic performance may have been reserved for internal celebrations in the chapter or for ceremonies at individual chapel-altars more often than for solemn public rites.

27. An example of the latter is the polyphonic setting of hymns. Wherever Dufay may have composed his cycle of hymns, in no other place does their tradition seem to have been as durable as in the papal chapel.

28. See Albert Seay, "The 15th-Century Cappella at Santa Maria del Fiore in Florence," *JAMS* 11 (1958), 45ff. (I need not repeat my objections to such titles); Gino Borghezio in *Note d'archivio per la storia musicale* 1 (1924), 200ff.; and Bramante Ligi, "La cappella del Duomo d'Urbino," *ibid.*, 2 (1925), 1ff., particularly 18–20.

29. Haberl, "Die Romische 'schola cantorum.' "

30. *Ibid.*, 223–24.

31. *Ibid.*, 225–30.

32. The two factors may have been associated, as they were in the case of Johannes Gallicus, a French Carthusian who lived in Mantua, and the author of a *Ritus canendi vetustissimus et novus* (Coussemaker, *Scriptorum de musica medii aevi nova series* [Paris, 1964–76], IV, pp. 298–421). Gallicus' contempt for "modern singers" and secular song stems from the ascetic leaning of his order as well as from the humanistic training he had received under no less a teacher than Vittorino da Feltre. See also note 40 below.

33. It is not my contention that artistic polyphony was never or seldom performed in Italy. It may have been performed even rather frequently, but as one kind of music among many, without any special attention paid to what we consider its special merits and importance in view of future developments. Thus, it happened that while some courts did contend among themselves to obtain the services of certain polyphonic singers, they paid little attention to their creative capacities and usually required (or at least noticed) only music which was already familiar (see, for instance, the recurrent mentions of O *rosa bella* until late in the century; the vogue of quodlibets is also a related phenomenon).

34. See his oration "habita Perusie in templo divi Laurentij pridie Nonas Novembris Mcccclxxxxij principio studij et in commendatione scientiarum" (ms. Vatican Lat. 8750, fol. 136v ff.), as well as his "oratio laudem, et utilitatem Historiae continens, et eius initia repetens" and "oratio de Poetices cum alijs

artibus cognatione, delectatione, utilitateque," both delivered in Vicenza, now in the ms. Vatican Lat. 5358. An earlier example is the "Initio studii MCCCCLV Perusiae oratio" of Giovanni Antonio Campano, in his *Opera* (Rome, 1495).

35. See "Philippi Beroaldi oratio habita in enarratione Questionum Thusculanarum et Oratii flacci continens laudem musices" in his *Orationes et quamplures apendiculae versuum* (Bologna, 1491), fol. 102ff. The section on music is introduced as follows: "Ceterum quantum ciceronis lectio nobis utilitatis est allatura: Tantum carmina oratii flacci *modulata* afferent iucunditatis: et quemadmodum philosophia salubris est: ita musica delectabilis" (italics mine).

36. Besides the obvious example of Paolo Cortese, which we shall soon discuss in more detail, I can quote here the chapter "De Musica & in quo cum re militari commertium eius sit," in Roberto Valturio, *De re militari* (Verona, 1472), fol. 104ff. Giorgio Valla's extensive treatise on music (see n. 41 below) is also part of an encyclopedic work.

37. See Gerhard Pietzsch, *Die Klassifikation der Musik von Boetius bis Ugolino von Orvieto* (Halle, 1929).

38. See, for instance, the following passage, which I translate from Ficino's tract "De rationibus musice" (actually a letter to "Dominico Benivenio claro philosopho et musico absoluto"), in Paul O. Kristeller, *Supplementum Ficinianum* (Florence, 1937), I, 51–56: "I state now that the sesquioctava produces [the interval of] one tone; *if minor, however, one semitone.* And those [notes] that proceed from the low one, which Orpheus names 'hypates,' to the high one, which [he calls] 'neates' . . . progress by grade *according to this proportion* [that is, the sesquioctava, either full or 'minor'; italics mine]." Ficino then goes on to describe the properties of each note in colorful language; the fourth, for instance, "is almost, but not as much dissonant as the second, being evidently spiced by the transition to the forthcoming fifth, and, in the same time, softened by the sweetness of the preceding third." But the succession of notes he describes, with major third and minor sixth, is neither the great system of the Greeks, nor the typical medieval hexachord.

39. " . . . etiam cano, musicus die, nec toto, factus . . . Vacabam et pigebat legere: incurrit casu liber eius artis *infantissimus,* res quidem omnino bonas continens, sed *aliena lingua* scriptus. Conferre coepi graeca cum *barbaris,* et monochordi nomenclatura . . . ad trivialem manum (ita enim modo vocant) accommodare sum conatus . . . Exscriptum id tibi omne mítto ut intelligas *barbarum* a Barbaro iuvari potuisse," in *Epistolae, Orationes et Carmina,* ed. Vittore Branca (Florence, 1943), II, 20 (italics mine). Barbaro had asked many musicians how the "hand" related to the ancient system and was waiting for an answer from a certain Avanitius (possibly a Latinization of a surname such as "Piffero"); but (one more note of distrust), "to urge anybody [into action who belongs] in that discipline, would be, as you well know, a major feat." The letter is addressed from Milan to Gerolamo Donati.

40. " . . . momenta illa sex singulis inclusa syllogismis [the six solmization syl-

lables included in each hexachord], tametsi compendium laboris faciunt et certam in modulando commoditatem afferunt, quia tamen *barbarum* plane sonum et ex cantico *parum latino* derivantur, placere non possunt; nihilominus ferenda sunt tantisper dum absolutius et elegantius aliquid inveniatur" (*ibid.*, p. 21; italics mine). It is interesting to see that at least one branch of humanistically oriented music theorists, from Johannes Gallicus to Ramos de Pareja, was aiming toward elimination of the hexachord system.

41. "De Musica libri V sed primo de inuentione & commoditate eius," in Valla's *De expetendis et fugiendis rebus opus* (Venice, 1501). The books on music follow those on arithmetic and are followed, as one would expect, by those on geometry, astrology, physiology, medicine, and so on, for a total of forty-nine books. The two impressive folio-volumes are protected at the Houghton Library of Harvard University by a contemporary binding of stamped calf on wooden boards, inscribed *Cyclopedia Vallae.*

42. Many such musicians may have been also composers in their own way, which belonged to what I call the "unwritten" tradition of music. Nor do their compositions need to have been all monophonic, for there are strong suspicions of the existence of a polyphonic strain also in the unwritten tradition.

43. Published in *Le rime di Serafino Ciminelli dall'Aquila*, ed. M. Menghini (Bologna, 1894), p. 112, and recently reprinted by H. Osthoff, *Josquin Desprez*, I, 34–35. The date is a minor problem for both Josquin's and Serafino's biographies, for it is unclear from the available information whether the latter's service with the cardinal fell before, around, or after 1490.

44. It might seem that unawareness of or little familiarity with polyphony are contradicted by the fact that several sources of French polyphony toward the middle or in the second half of the fifteenth century again happen to be Italian. It may be noticed, however, that some of them (such as Porto, Bibl. Municipal 714) combine actual music with extensive theory writings, and others make pretence of doing the same by merely prefacing their eminently secular collections of polyphonic pieces with a short elementary tract. I interpret the latter as an attempt to justify the music as a collection of examples, a justification that may have been needed only by monastic or ecclesiastical islands of surviving scholasticism.

45. See, for instance, Giannozzo Manetti's dialogue describing a banquet in Venice in Arnaldo Della Torre, *Storia dell'Accademia platonica* (Florence, 1902), pp. 282–83; or Francesco Filelfo's *Convivia mediolanensia* (1443, printed in Milan, 1498), not to speak of the many later descriptions of banquets with musical *intermedi.*

46. See, for instance, Otto Kinkeldey, "Dance Tunes of the Fifteenth Century," in *Instrumental Music*, ed. David G. Hughes (Cambridge, Mass., 1959), pp. 7ff. The main source of Cornazano's *Sfortiade* is ms. Paris, Bibliothèque Nationale, nouv. acc. ital. 1472.

47. Filelfo (1398–1481), although considerably older, was Cornazano's companion at the Milanese court and one of his models. Filelfo's Homeric

translations were never published, but he was working on a Latin *Sfortias* (24 *canti*; autograph in Rome, Bibl. Casanatense, ms. 415) more or less at the time when Cornazano was writing his own *Sforziade*; he also wrote poems in praise of Lucrezia d'Alagno.

48. He mentions, however (fol. 104 *bis*) that music had already been performed during the banquet: "e accompagnate d'organi et da trombe / venghon, variate, le dive vivande."

49. "el recordar de gli passati guai / a l'animo soccorre in stato ascieso / e il passato dolor gli allenta assai." (fol. 106v of the ms.). Muro Troilo di Rossano is a historical figure.

50. It was published by Michele A. Silvestri, "Appunti di cronologia cornazaniana," in *Miscellanea di storia, letteratura e arte piacentina* (Piacenza, 1915), pp. 155–57.

51. *Ibid.*, particularly p. 143.

52. Cornazano's biography is discussed in detail in the article by Silvestri, where, pp. 154–55 and 158, 1449–59 is given as the time of composition of the whole *Sfortiade*, a date "before 1458" for the passage on Pietrobono, and 1455 for the first redaction of *L'arte del danzare*. Concerning Pietrobono, Emile Haraszti, "Pierre Bono, luthiste de Mathias Corvin," *Revue de musicologie*, 89–92 (1949), 73ff, as well as his "Bono, Piero," in *MGG*, 2, col. 117–19, need clarification. The latter should have been placed under the letter P, for Bono is a middle name; the family name "de Burzeris," "de Bursellis," or even "de Bruxellis" has nothing to do with Brussels. It is incorrect that Pietrobono, born in 1417, "spent his youth at the court of the king of Naples, Ferdinand of Aragon [reigned 1458–94] with Aurelio Brandolini [*ca.* 1440–1497] and Tinctoris [who arrived in Naples *ca.* 1472]"; nor is it true that Tinctoris lists him among ("unter") the German artists. Pietrobono went to Naples in 1473 in the retinue of Sigismondo d'Este, but his musicianship had made him rich in Ferrara already in 1455; similarly, he went to the court of Matthias Corvinus in 1488, in the retinue of Ippolito d'Este. It is possible that he was then lent for a short time to Beatrice of Aragon, wife of Matthias and sister of Eleonora d'Este. Concerning a similar "loan" to Sforza in Milan in 1456, see Barblan, pp. 802–03.

53. This may have been either a shift in Pietrobono's personal activity or the result of changing musical tastes. He is again described as a singer in Cornazano's *De excellentium virorum principibus*, dedicated to Borso d'Este in 1466, where he is shown in the act of singing of Venus' misadventures (Silvestri, pp. 153–54). In later years he appears to have been accompanied by a *tenorista*, that is, another lutenist with whom he could play polyphonic music: "Petrobono del Chirighino [*sic*] con il tenorista, cavalli 3," are listed among those who went to Naples with Sigismondo d'Este in 1473 ("I Diari di Cicco Simonetta," ed. A. R. Natale, in *Archivio Storico Lombardo*, Serie VIII, I [1948–49], 99–100). In 1486 and 1488 Pietrobono's *tenorista* was a certain Francesco de la Gatta (Giulio Bertoni, *L'Orlando furioso e la Rinascenza a Ferrara* [Modena, 1919], p. 421).

54. Benjamin Buser, *Die Beziehungen der Mediceer zu Frankreich während der Jahre 1434–1494* (Leipzig, 1879), p. 374; and Bianca Becherini, "Un canta in panca fiorentino, Antonio di Guido," *Rivista musicale italiana*, 50 (1948), 243–44. A "Chapitolo di messer Antonio buffone fatto pel chonte Francesco i llode d'esser piatoso d'una fanciulla preso a Lluccha" (Florence, Bibl. Nazionale Centrale, Cod. Magliabechi VII. 1010, fol. 112) resembles the story told by Sforza himself in Cornazano's description of the banquet.

55. The episode is discussed by Isidoro del Lungo, *Florentia* (Florence, 1897), pp. 257–62, and two conflicting versions are reported: the first, a passage from Paolo Giovio, *Elogia doctorum virorum* (Basel, 1556), XXXVIII, 89, records a denigratory rumor according to which the poet's last delirious song was inspired by an unnatural love; in the second, a poem by Bembo, "Politiani tumulus," in *Carmina libellus* (Venice, 1552), p. 45, Poliziano dies while singing a lament for the death of Lorenzo dei Medici.

56. Of them, see the last paragraph of Appendix 2 to this essay.

57. "Vita di Serafino Aquilano" in Vincenzo Calmeta, *Prose e lettere edite e inedite*, ed. Cecil Grayson (Bologna, 1959), p. 63. Further information on Coscia, or Cossa, is given *ibid.*, pp. xxi, 90, and 136.

58. See, for instance, the following, which I translate from the "Discorso del Calmeta s'egli è lecito giudicare i vivi o no" in Calmeta, p. 4: "Another new way has been found, besides the printer, by which the poems, especially those in the vernacular tongue, can be brought to [public] light; for, such a profession [the poet's] being much appreciated in our day, many *citaredi* have arisen, who, taking advantage of the works of a few poets, make such works known in all the courts." Biographical information on Calmeta himself is given by Grayson in his introduction; many other writings of Calmeta provide direct or indirect evidence of the custom of singing poetry.

59. Born in Rome in 1465 to a Tuscan family well introduced in the papal court, Cortese was a follower of Pomponio Leto and became his successor as a *scriptor apostolicus* in 1481. Cortese and his older brother, Alessandro (d. 1490), were often hosts to a literary group (the word "academia" used by Calmeta, p. 63, does not need to be taken in a formal sense), including, among others, Aquilano and Calmeta himself. Cortese became a papal secretary in 1498, but resigned in 1503 and retired near S. Gimignano in Tuscany; there he built a beautiful villa, which he named Castrum Cortesium. There, too, he worked at writing his *De cardinalatu*, published soon after his death in 1510, but still printed "in Castro Cortesio." Other works include *De Hominibus doctis dialogus* (Florence, 1734), dedicated to Lorenzo dei Medici (*ca.* 1488), and *In quatuor libros Sententiarum . . . disputationes* (Rome, 1504). See Pio Paschini, "Una famiglia di curiali nella Roma del Quattrocentro: i Cortesi," *Rivista di storia della Chiesa in Italia* 11 (1957), pp. 1–48.

60. I am convinced that the new form and style of the madrigal were shaped in Medicean circles between Florence and Rome, after the death of il Magnifico, but attention should also be paid to Farnese's activity, initially related to the Medici, later more independent. No exhaustive account exists, however, of his life before his pontificate.

61. Evidence gathered from partial investigations of this phase of motet composition and texts seems to stress the nonliturgical (or, at least, not strictly liturgical) and rather occasional nature of this genre. Often conceived for a one-time performance, motets were then collected as models, reworded to fit other one-time occasions, or arranged for instrumental performance. Among the factors contributing to different conditions, musical printing may have had a major role.

62. In the above-mentioned *De hominibus doctis dialogus* Cortese discusses and criticizes "modern" writers in Latin beginning with Dante, but he excludes those who were still alive at the time of his writing. Calmeta was more daring, judging from his "Discorso . . . s'egli è lecito giudicare i vivi o no" (Calmeta, pp. 3–6) and his pungent criticism of Tebaldeo (*ibid.*, pp. 15–19). Nor did Cortese's restraint apply to musicians (see Appendix 2 to this essay).

63. Remigio Sabbadini, *Storia del ciceronianismo* (Turin, 1886), pp. 33–42; and Paschini, pp. 29–31. The dispute was confined to an exchange of letters, but received considerable publicity from the humanistic habit of circulating copies of such letters which were considered to be important for their contents and/or their style.

8 Church Polyphony Apropos of a New Fragment at Foligno

This essay was originally published in *Studies in Music History: Essays for Oliver Strunk*, edited by Harold Powers (Princeton, 1968).

1. I would like to express my gratitude here to all the friends I have consulted for their interest in the Foligno puzzle.

2. It must read "Theophilactus in Euang[elia]," but the abbreviation signs are unclear, and a recent label partially covers the last word. The book protected by the double leaf was therefore by the eleventh-century theologian Theophylact; the work is better known in a Latin translation by Johannes Oecolampadius as *In quatuor evangelia Enarrationes*. Neither the early editions of the Latin version (Basel, 1524 and 1554; Cologne, 1528 and 1541), nor the print of the Greek original (Rome, 1542) match the size of the Foligno fragment, since they are all large, thick folio volumes. That the work in the Foligno library was not a manuscript is indicated by the recent inscription "Duplicato"; it must then have been a more recent (partial?) edition, which I have not been able to identify.

3. See Amédée Gastoué, *Le Manuscrit de musique du Trésor d'Apt* (Paris, 1936), and the review by Guillaume de Van in *Acta musicologica* 12 (1940), 64–69.

4. See the facsimile, ed. Pierre Aubry (Paris, 1907), especially the motet *Quare fremuerunt*, fol. 1r.

5. The full title of the chapter (the sixth of *Pomerium*, Liber II, Tractatus III) is "De nominibus et proportionibus semibrevium de tempore imperfecto modo Gallico et Italico." See also the preceding chapter, "De distantia et differentia

modi cantandi de tempore imperfecto inter Gallicos et Italicos." Both appear in Martin Gerbert, *Scriptores ecclesiastici de musica* (St. Blaise, 1784), III, 175–78; and, in a much improved version, in Marchetus de Padua, *Pomerium*, ed. Giuseppe Vecchi (American Institute of Musicology, Corpus Scriptorum de Musica 6 [Rome], 1961), pp. 172–80.

6. It should be considered, however, in connection with both the date and possible provenance of the piece, that both features appear in an unmistakably French manuscript, the *Roman de Fauvel* (see n. 4), for instance, on fols. 3 and 6.

7. I refer here to a verbal exchange of opinions with Professor Harrison apropos of the Foligno fragment.

8. The music was published in 1962 by the American Institute of Musicology as a one-volume item of the series Corpus Mensurabilis Musicae. A "CompanionVolume" to this, having the same title, publisher, and date, is included in the series Musicological Studies and Documents and contains comments and critical notes. For the sake of a clearer distinction, the two works will be referred to henceforth as CMM 29 (Corpus Mensurabilis Musicae 29) and MSD 7 (Musicological Studies and Documents 7).

9. Attributed in the manuscript to a certain Susay; see Stäblein-Harder, CMM 29, pp. 57–58, and MSD 7, p. 48. In the latter, the view is expressed that the author may have been the same Johannes (or Jehan) Susay (or Suzoy) who composed three pieces in the ms. Chantilly, Musée Condé 564 (olim 1047). Were this true, the fact that a sophisticated composer made his style simple and plain when writing "cathedral" music would provide additional evidence for the discussion of sacred polyphony in the last part of the present study. I suspect, however, that Apt No. 37 may be older than "the beginning of the fifteenth century," and therefore be by a different Susay, despite the parallel sixth chords in the piece—"quite a *modern* effect" (italics replace the quotation marks of the original) according to Stäblein-Harder, but probably quite modern only because we have officially recognized *fauxbourdon* as a new technique originating not earlier than *ca.* 1430.

10. I shall never tire of insisting that normal polyphonic performance required one singer to a part, with occasional doubling only of the superius (not to speak of possible instrumental doublings). Evidence for this is given, for instance, by Frank D'Accone, "The Singers of San Giovanni in Florence during the 15th Century," *Journal of the American Musicological Society* 14 (1961), 307–58, and more extensively in his unpublished "A Documentary History of Music at the Florentine Cathedral and Baptistry during the Fifteenth Century" (Harvard University, dissertation, 1960). Precious information on the number and names of church singers has often been given (by Haberl for St. Peter's in Rome, by Casimiri for Padua, by Sartori for Milan, and by many others for various churches) under the mistaken impression that such singers formed a "chapel." In the papal, as in princely, chapels, the number of singers tended to increase during the second half of the fifteenth century, yet even here one must take into account the many leaves of absence

granted to singers, as well as their justified or unjustified absences. Even when there is evidence that twelve or fifteen were present, this does not mean that they all sang in the same polyphonic pieces, and the continuing need for a plainchant choir must also be considered. The doubling of superius parts performed by boys, which became more and more frequent during the sixteenth century, also increased the need for someone to guide their performance and pull them together. It thus happened that the *magister puerorum*, originally a teacher of grammar and musical theory, gradually became the *magister capellae* or conductor. I suspect that the habit of choral singing may have originated in the imperial Hapsburg court, and later spread, becoming a baroque form of expression.

11. Choruses in early operas are usually performed by characters who have already appeared as soloists, if only for the roles of "una Ninfa" or "un Pastore." (I do not refer, of course, to such gigantic choruses as those of Caccini's *Rapimento di Cefalo*, which are wholly in the tradition of the previous *intermedi*.) In later operas, choruses often provide songs or sound effects backstage, to which all the characters whose presence was not needed on stage were called to contribute. (I have in mind the choral description of a hunt in Cavalli's *Didone*, but often it was merely a short interjection of "Guerra, guerra!" or "Morte, morte!") Finally, the concluding, often moralizing comments, on which most seventeenth-century operas end, are usually cast in the form of short choruses performed by the four principal characters. Slightly different, but also pertinent, is the case of polychoral church performances in which "choruses" including the Caccini girls and other famous soloists of the Medicean court were pitted against other vocal or instrumental groups (see Angelo Solerti, *Musica, ballo e drammatica alla corte Medicea dal 1600 al 1637* [Florence, 1905], pp. 58, 64, 85, 106, 129–30, 144, *et passim*).

12. It seems to me that most of the so-called choral polyphony (see Manfred Bukofzer, "The Beginnings of Choral Polyphony" in *Studies in Medieval and Renaissance Music* [New York, 1950], pp. 176–89) could be explained as an alternation between contrapuntal sections performed by two or three unaccompanied soloists and portions in which the voices of the same performers come together in a more chordal texture supported by instrumental parts. It is true, however, that there are instances in which a superius part, supported by untexted (that is, probably instrumental) parts, is inscribed "Chorus," possibly suggesting a unison performance by two or three singers.

13. In keeping with all that has been said in the preceding notes, I do not think that the whole chapter took part in the performance, but only two, three, or possibly four of its members designated ad hoc.

14. The only intervention of a possibly, but not necessarily, different hand in the Foligno fragment occurs at the end of this contratenor part, where, after the usual illuminated *A*, someone has added (in a lighter and smaller script than that of the other texts) first the syllable "men," then several repetitions of the letters "Am," and a final "Amen."

15. See Stäblein-Harder, CMM 29, nos. 34 (pp. 57–58), 37 (pp. 60–62), and 38 (pp. 63–65).
16. In a private letter Professor Kurt von Fischer, to whom I sent duplicates of the Foligno photographs, expressed the opinion that the two parts belong to two different settings. I hope to convince even him that we are faced with a single, badly corrupted piece.
17. I am not at ease with any of the recently proposed classifications and terminologies which have been variously used and interpreted. The confusion produced in my mind by any proposal of a radical revision or refinement of an already accepted terminology (almost inevitably followed by even subtler counterproposals) leads me to avoid any such attempt and simply describe what I see in the music. I agree that this is easily done when one is dealing with only three (incomplete) pieces.
18. See the description, discussion, and facsimile reproduction by Jacques Chailley, "La Messe de Besançon et un compositeur inconnu du XIVᵉ siècle: Jean Lambelet," *Annales musicologiques* 2 (1954), 90–103.
19. "Studien zur Musik des Mittelalters: I. Neue Quellen des 14. und beginnenden 15. Jahrhunderts," *Archiv für Musikwissenschaft* 7 (1925), 202.
20. For this reason we should reconsider to what extent the arrangement of some manuscripts in which polyphonic settings of the Ordinary are grouped by category (Kyries, Glorias, and so on) depends on their origin as church (polyphonic) choirbooks, rather than on their date. Manuscripts containing one single Mass cycle formed by evidently unrelated pieces can also be placed in the same category. They probably represent all the written-down ordinary polyphony included in the chapter's repertory at the time.
21. Evidence of such practices has not often been brought to the attention of scholars. I can begin by mentioning the passages on performance of plainchant by Hieronymus de Moravia, *Tractatus de musica*, ed. Simon M. Cserba (Regensburg, 1935), pp. 179–87, and then add the occurrence of figural plainchant notation in some of the Cividale manuscripts, the most conspicuous example being the four Passions—all in the hand of one Comucius de la Campagnolla, a canon and imperial notary at Cividale in the first half of the fifteenth century—which form the contents of Codex XXIV. How long the practice survived (along with the usual and more common neumatic notation, to which we do not know what rhythmic interpretation was given) is shown in the ms. St. Gall, Stiftsbibliothek 546, from the first quarter of the sixteenth century, described by Otto Marxer, *Zur spätmittelalterlichen Choralgeschichte St. Gallens* (St. Gall, 1908). The latter source is of great interest not only for its figural notation, but also for the new melodies it gives (particularly Credo melodies, often beginning with the usual formula of Credos I, II, and IV of the *Liber Usualis*, then going their own way), and finally for the inscriptions specifying alternation between an evidently homophonic "Chorus" and "Organum" (Marxer, pp. 149–51, 163–65, 167–68, 175–76, *et passim*) or "Organista" (*ibid.*, pp. 159–60, 161–63, 166). Whether the latter refer to the

organ and its player or to improvised (so to speak) polyphony cannot easily be determined. At any rate, it is worth noting that the performer at times is required to "hold" some notes (*ibid.*, Credo on pp. 163–66, where the "Organum" inscription later becomes, on p. 166, "Organista tenet"), as if some kind of *symphonia basilica* was meant.

22. On December 29, 1964, at Washington, D.C., in a short comment on the Cividale manuscripts concluding a session of the annual meeting of the American Musicological Society that had dealt with "Cathedral Repertories: Worcester and Cividale."

9   Zacara da Teramo

This essay was originally published in *Quadrivium* 12 (1971), an issue honoring Federico Ghisi. The translation is by Vanni Bartolozzi.

1. I translate from Letter 4, "Ad eundem [the cardinal of Pavia] Interamniae seu Terami descriptio," of the *Epistolarum Liber Primus*, in Giovanni Antonio Campano, [*Opera omnia*] (Rome, 1745).

2. "Ordinarii sacerdotes quattuor et viginti, & in praecutinis [*sic*] non inculti. Callent rem divinam ad unguem omnes. Caeremoniarum cultus nusquam solemnior. Ministri sacrorum complures extra ordinem tenent horas: observant momenta: aeque noctibus ac diebus utuntur: student imprimis musicae: servato more majorum: a quibus illustratam praedicant. Zacharum musicum suum dicunt: ostendunt domos: praedia: nepotes: etiam discipulos [.] ejus inventa pro oraculis habentur." *Ibid.*

3. C. Eubel, *Hierarchia Catholica Medii Aevi*, I, 2nd ed. (Munich, 1913), p. 95.

4. *Ibid.*

5. In N. Pirrotta and E. Li Gotti, "Il codice di Lucca," in *Musica disciplina* 3–5 (1949–1951), especially 5, p. 121.

6. Such dissonances, frequent in polyphonic compositions of popular style, can for instance be observed in the *ballata Dolce lo mio drudo:* see essay 4. Such dissonances were discussed, with examples also taken from some of Ciconia's *ballate,* by W. H. Rubsamen, "The Justiniane or Viniziane of the 15th Century," *Acta musicologica* 29 (1957), pp. 172–84.

7. Published, in the fragmentary state in which it is extant, by F. Ghisi, "Italian Ars-Nova Music," p. 13; this is a separate appendix to the article of the same title in *Journal of Renaissance and Baroque Music* (later *Musica Disciplina*), 1 (1946), 173ff. The instrumental two-voice version of the Faenza ms. Biblioteca Comunale 117 has been published by D. Plamenac, "New Light on Faenza Codex 117," in *Report of the Vth Congress of the International Musicological Society. Utrecht 1952* (Amsterdam, 1953), p. 318ff.

8. I published it in "Il codice di Lucca," *Musica disciplina* 4 (1950), p. 151.

9. E. Giammarco, *Dizionario Abruzzese e Molisano* (Rome, 1968), *sub voce.*

The irregular *ballata* has a nonsymmetrical *volta* compared with the *ripresa*, and for this *volta* Zacara wrote a new vigorous musical phrase; the complete text is given by E. Li Gotti in "Il Codice di Lucca," *Musica disciplina* 4, p. 126.

10. No less vivid than Lasso's "extreme" example on the Petrarchan "E col bue zoppo... ," recorded by A. Einstein, *The Italian Madrigal* (Princeton, 1949), I, 232.

11. Published by Ghisi, "Italian Ars Nova Music," pp. 14–15; F. Ghisi, "L'Ordinarium Missae nel XV secolo ed i primordi della parodia," in *Atti del Congresso Internazionale di Musica Sacra, Roma ... 1950* (Tournai, 1952), p. 309, defines the *ballata* as being "d'ispirazione satanico-cabalistica, infarcita di latinismi e barbari nomi tolti dalla mitologia infernale" (of a Satanic-cabalistic inspiration, filled with Latinizing words and barbaric names inspired by infernal mythology). W. Nitschke, *Studien zu den Cantus-Firmus-Messen Guillaume Dufays* (Berlin, 1968), p. 100, follows him, speaking of an "exorcism and a prayer of thanskgiving to the god of hell." Actually, Zacara only mockingly thanks the god of riches for having let him recover some amount of money he had loaned. B. J. Layton calls attention to the unusual accidentals in "Italian Music of the Ordinary of the Mass," Harvard University dissertation 1960, pp. 282–83. Improbable accidentals, such as flats preceding G or C, must be interpreted as mutation signs, meaning that the note must be read as fa, which does not imply the alteration of this particular note, but of others. C flat simply introduces the *hard* hexachord (G–E); but G flat brings in the *hyperhard* hexachord D–B with F sharp; and similarly D flat, which appears twice in the superior part, brings in the *hyper-hyper-hard* (the terms are mine) hexachord A–F sharp with C sharp. It is less certain that more usual accidentals, such as G sharp at the beginning of the superior part, are mutation signs too. The G sharp would bring in the E–C sharp hexachord (with three sharps), and in fact the following C is all right as a C sharp, but such a result could also be obtained through the usual *musica ficta* rules for cadences. Some inconsistencies and redundancies in the use of the sharps make me think they are not Zacara's but have been added by others. [My survey of Zacara's works includes only the pieces I am sure are his, but see the Additional Postscript to this essay for different views.]

12. *Musica disciplina* 5 (1951), p. 133.

13. S. Clercx, *Johannes Ciconia* (Brussels, 1960), I, 49.

14. Perugia would have been the nearest and most obvious city, but it would have been just as easy to reach Padua and Bologna along the Adriatic coast. I thought of Florence because of the presence there of Bishop Giacomo Paladini from Teramo, who died in Poland in 1417 during a legateship entrusted to him by Martin V. See the Additional Postscript for the quotation of a document in which our composer is said to have been a "laicus licteratus."

15. The most conspicuous sign of this orientation is the presence of a madrigal by Antonello Marot da Caserta, which probably refers to the marriage of Queen Giovanna II of Naples to Giacomo de la Marche (1415).

16. See essay 7.

17. Here is how A. L. Antinori describes Marino in *Raccolta di Memorie istoriche delle tre provincie degli Abruzzi* (Naples, 1782), tome III, p. 134: "An. di Gr. 1407 ... vacava ancora in parte la Sede Vescovile; giacchè Antonio Melatino eletto, non era stato mai ordinato Gregorio XII s'avvalse dell'opportunità del tempo. Risiedeva in Roma nell'impiego d'Uditore di Rota Marino di Tocco, Giureconsulto di gran lode nella Corte Romana. Costui fu a' 14 di Febbrajo eletto in Vescovo successore del Corrado [Melatino], morto già del 1405, da Gregorio Papa; si affezionò al suo partito, e vi aderì sempre costante. Egli proseguiva a' 19 di Marzo nel primo impiego; giacché proferì sentenza a favore del Monistero di S. Salvadore del Monte Amiato contro del Vescovo di Chiusi, e si soscrisse bensì col titolo d'Eletto Aprutino. Egli era nativo di Tocco, Terra Diocesana di Chieti, dove poi si stabilirono quelli di sua famiglia." (A.D. 1407 ... the episcopal see was partially vacant; since the bishop elected by Antonio Melatino had never been ordained, Gregory XII seized the right moment. There was in Rome, in the office of an auditor to the Sacra Rota, Marino di Tocco, a much-praised jurisconsult in the Roman court. This man was elected by Pope Gregory on February 14 to succeed Corrado [Melatino], who had been dead since 1405; he became attached to his [the pope's] party and remained always faithful to it. On March 19 he was still continuing [to work] in his previous office, for he decided a dispute in favor of the monastery of St. Salvadore on Mt. Amiato and against the bishop of Chiusi; however, he signed himself the Aprutine bishop elected. He was a native of Tocco, a district of the diocese of Chieti, where his relatives went later to live.) Also, on p. 175, "Marino di Tocco, già deposto dal Vescovado di Teramo, quivi [at the Constance Council] abjurò; e ritornato in grazia, intervenne a quello, fatto Uditore del Concilio." (Marino di Tocco, who had already been deposed from the bishopric of Teramo, abjured there [at the council of Constance], and having reentered [a state of] grace, took part, having been made an auditor, in the Council.) We are certain of the exactness of the information because of the precise reference to a document issued by Marino while he was an auditor to the Sacra Rota. Marino's last seat as a bishop was Chieti, where he died in 1438.

18. Eubel, *Hierarchia*, I, 95 n.

19. On May 5, 1416, he was entrusted, together with Giacomo di Camplo, elected bishop of Penne, with checking the minutes and collecting testimony in the dispute between the chapter and the elected bishop of Strasbourg. In July he was one of the delegates of the Italian nation entrusted with preparing the decisions to be submitted to the Council for the same case. He had similar duties in the dispute between Duke Frederick of Austria and the bishop of Trento, and he expounded the commission's conclusion on that dispute to the Council in the twenty-seventh session (February 20, 1417). He officiated in the Constance cathedral at the beginning of the thirty-first session (March 31, 1417). In June 1417 his name was mentioned among those said to be King Sigismond's partisans, who encouraged the intimidatory maneuvers of two of the "general judges," the bishop of Salisbury and the bishop of Pistoia.

20. C. Eubel, *Hierarchia*, I, 411.

21. See essay 7.

22. The manuscript, dispersed fragments of which are now part of Cividale codices LXIII and XCVIII, was obviously organized so that it reunited in different groups the polyphonic intonations of *Gloria* and *Credo*. Its direct connection with Cividale's major church is confirmed by a *Gloria* that employs as *tenor* the melody of a responsory of local use. Its composer was a "Rentius de Ponte Curvo," beneficed priest in Cividale in 1407–08. Like Zacara, Rentius was a native of the "kingdom," since he came from Pontecorvo near Cassino. He may also have belonged to a family that had two bishops in Aquino in the second half of the fourteenth century (C. Eubel, *Hierarchia*, I, 100). The *Credo* fragment by "Magister A. Dictus Z." appears now on fol. 2' of codex XCVIII.

23. Francesco Zabarella, who was from Padua and was one of the greatest supporters of John XXIII, could have been the link that justifies the presence of a certain number of compositions of Paduan origin in the codex Este, M. 5.24 (olim lat. 568) in Modena, which I have always linked to the sojourn in Bologna of the courts of Alexander V and John XXIII.

24. At least five of them are specifically attributed to him. [See G. Reaney, ed., *Early Fifteenth-Century Music*, CMM 11, vi (n.p., 1977) for a more complete list of sources and attributions as well as a complete edition.]

25. G. De Van, "Inventory of Manuscript Bologna, Liceo Musicale, Q 15 (*olim* 37)," *Musica disciplina* 2 (1948), 231–57.

26. A. Hughes and M. Bent, "The Old Hall Manuscript—A Reappraisal and an Inventory," *Musica disciplina* 21 (1967), 97–147. Later in this essay I discuss the English representatives at the council.

27. For *MüO* see K. Dézes, "Der Mensuralcodex des Benediktinerklosters Sancti Emmerami zu Regensburg," *Zeitschrift für Musikwissenschaft* 10 (1928), 65ff. For the lost Berlin manuscript see J. Wolf, "Eine neue Quelle zur Musik des 15. Jahrhunderts," in *Juhlakiria Ilmari Krohn'ille* (Writings in honor of Ilmari Krohn) (Helsinki, 1927), p. 1544ff.; and L. K. J. Feininger, *Die Frühgeschichte des Kanons bis Josquin des Prez (um 1500)* (Emsdetten, 1937), pp. 22 and 24. The German nation was one of the best represented in Constance.

28. M. Szczepanska, "Nowe zrodlo do historji muzyki sredniowiecznej w Polsce," in *Ksiega pamiatkowa ku czci Prof. Dr. A. Chybinskiego* (Krakow, 1930), pp. 15–56. [See also M. Perz, "Die Einflüsse der ausgehenden italienischen Ars nova in Polen," in *L'Ars nova italiana del Trecento*, III (Certaldo, 1970), 459–83, especially 470–77.] The Polish delegation in Constance included among others the elected bishop of Poznan, the bishop of Kracow, and the dean of the University of Kracow.

29. Together with codex 92, to which it is linked by curious interrelationships, this is the oldest of the Trento codices, although noticeably more recent than the period of Zacara's activity.

30. See Ghisi, "L'Ordinarium Missae." Independently of each other, at the 1950 Congresso we had both decided to speak on the first instances of *missa*

parodia, and we harmonized our communications so that they integrated with each other rather than giving the impression of a nonexistent rivalry. The *Gloria* titled "Zacar Rosetta" and "Zacar Fior gentil" and the *Credo* titled "Zacar Deus deorum" are derived from the respective secular compositions; another *Credo*, titled "Zacar Scabroso," must derive from a lost model. Finally, the *Gloria* titled "Zacar ad ogni vento" probably owes its title to a mistake, since it does not have anything in common with the *ballata Ad ogni vento*. It must be noted that none of these titles refers to Zacharias' secular compositions, and also that the two names are clearly differentiated in the *Kras* manuscript, which marks a *Gloria* as "O[pus] Czakaris mgri Anthonij" and a *Credo* as "Opus Zacharie" (the parallel words in *StP* are "Slowye szacharie mneysche," that is, "Zacharia the minor's work"). On the other hand the two composers share some characteristics that make me think that Zacharias too was a southerner. The dialectal flavor of the text of his only *caccia* contributes to this idea, and the documents referring to Nicolaus Zacharie (if he really was the son of that Zacharias) say that he came from the Brindisi diocese. One last problem concerning the last and minor member of the triad is the name or nickname Nicolaus Gechanc which was given to him. With so many uncertainties it is no wonder that copyists, when unsure of the precise attribution, cut the name to "Zacar."

31. Layton, "Italian Music," tends to doubt my distinction between Zacara and Zacharias; he is led to partially accept it by these two compositions, of which he gives a detailed analysis, concluding that the two do not seem to have much in common with other pieces by Zacara (pp. 251–55). Nitschke, *Studien*, pp. 122–26, also studies the two compositions, but unlike Layton he does not note the fact that the two pieces use as their model the structures of two of Ciconia's compositions, *Gloria* no. 22 and *Credo* no. 29 (Clercx, *Ciconia*, II). [On the distinction between Zacara and Zacharias, see the Additional Postscript.]

32. A recent publication collecting the most interesting documents on the Council is *The Council of Constance*, trans. L. R. Loomis, ed. and ann. J. H. Mundy and K. M. Woody (New York, 1961). Ulrich von Richental's chronicle (*ibid.*, p. 108) mentions the demand of the "English nation," as does, more often and with harsh recriminations, Cardinal Guillaume Fillastre's *Diario* (*ibid.*, pp. 239, 307–8). Fillastre also does not hide his personal dislike of Robert Hallam, formerly chancellor of Oxford University and later bishop of Salisbury (*ibid.*, pp. 372, 389, 392), who was the strongest supporter of English interests and the strongest adversary of the power of cardinals and curia. The count of Warwick, whose life has been outlined in fifty-three extant drawings (London, British Mus., Cotton ms. Julius E IV), made a pilgrimage to the Holy Land, and while crossing Italy fought a duel in Verona against Pandolfo Malatesta. While he was in Constance it was rumored that he enjoyed special favors with the countess of Cilly, wife of King Sigismond.

33. "Und morgens do begiengen sy das fest gar schon und loblich mit grossem gelüt mit grossen brinenden kertzen und mit *Engelschem süssem gesang mit den ordnen* [another ms. has "in den organen"]; *und mit den prosonen,*

darüber tenor, discant und medium ze vesperzit"; Ulrich von Richental, *Das Konzil zu Konstanz*, ed. and comm. Otto Feger (Constance, 1964), vol. II (vol. 1 has the facsimile reproduction), chap. 199. This is perhaps the most ancient known testimony about the impression that English polyphony made on continental listeners. *Das Konzil*, chap. 201, reports on the ceremonies for the return of King Sigismond, during which, after a sermon of the bishop of Salisbury in the cathedral, "sang man Te Deum laudamus in der ordenen" (in this case also the other manuscript clarifies "in organis").

34. I owe this information to the courtesy of Professor Agostino Ziino. The passage is quoted by A. Tulli, *Catalogo di uomini illustri* (Teramo, 1766), pp. 92–93, which had derived it from a preceding *Discorso cronologico sopra i vescovi della città di Teramo*, manuscript of C. Riccanale.

35. I am quoting from N. Palma, *Storia ecclesiastica e civile della regione più settentrionale del regno di Napoli*, new ed. (Teramo, 1893), V, 252: "Zaccarias Teramnensis, Vir apprime doctus in Musicis, composuit quamplures cantilenas, quae nostra aetate per Italiam cantantur, et Gallis et Germanis cantoribus in maxima veneratione habentur: fuit statura corporis parva, et in manibus et pedibus non nisi decem digitos habuit, et tamen eleganter scribebat. In Curia Romana principatum obtinens magna stipendia meruit."

36. Palma, *Storia ecclesiastica*, but on my own I find *zaharella* only with the meaning of ribbon or "fettuccina." In this new light one should examine again the inscriptions "Zacar micinella" and "Slowye czacharie mneysche" already mentioned as ascribed to a *Gloria* and a *Credo* (for the second, see above, n. 30; and also Layton, "Italian Music," p. 285, who assigns it to Zacara because of good stylistic proofs). G. Ginobili, *Glossario dei dialetti di Macerata e Petriolo*, (Macerata, 1965), p. 73, lists *Zaccarì* (a diminutive?) among the nicknames and patronymics in Macerata, but he does not explain either its origin or its meaning.

37. The fact that his given name was Antonio and not Zaccaria is certified by at least three musical manuscripts [but see my Additional Postscript].

38. [A. Ziino, "Magister Antonius dictus Zacharias de Teramo: Alcune date e molte ipotesi," *Rivista italiana di musicologia* 14 (1979), 311–48, includes references to the more recent literature and to the discovery of new sources. Two more documents of 1400 list, respectively, "Zacchara" and "Zacharias" among the singers of Boniface IX; see R. Sherr, "Notes on Some Papal Documents in Paris," *Studi musicali* 12 (1983).]

39. [The qualification as "licteratus" perfectly agrees with the title of "Magister [artium]."]

40. [N. Pirrotta, "Il codice Estense lat. 568 e la musica francese in Italia al principio del '400," in *Atti della Reale Accademia di Scienze lettere e Arti di Palermo*, ser. 4, vol. 5: 2 (1944–45), pp. 101ff.]

41. [Padua, Biblioteca Universitaria, 1225.]

42. [Actually a photographic copy of a lost ms. previously in Poznan, Biblioteka Universitetu.]

43. [Resolved in the sentence "Recomendatione milles cum in omnes Zacharias salutes" (Zacharias [sends] a thousand salutations to all, recommending [himself]). The message is addressed to "karissimi ... patres, ... musici ... fratres," which I surmise to be Zacharias' companions in the papal chapel.]
44. [See, for instance, Perz, "Die Einflüsse."]

10 *Ricercare* and Variations on *O Rosa Bella*

This essay was originally published in *Studi Musicali* 1 (1972). The translation is by Vanni Bartolozzi.

1. "Didici iamdudum ingenium illud tuum agile, ac profecto aureum ea quoque consequutum, quae vulgo, contra veterum consuetudinem, notiora sunt quam eruditis, ut est peritiam cum sono canendi suavissimos modos." A. Traversari, *Latinae epistolae* (Florence, 1795), II, col. 314–15. The letter, which seems to have been written in January 1429, continues with classical examples ("veteres illi, quos admiramur, ... adspernati non sunt")and biblical ones, eventually asking the friend to send his own and other people's "laudi": "Huiusce generis laudes tibi esse familiarissimas, ex pluribus nostri amicissimis sum factus certior; ita ut illas, & instrumentis musicis magna cum suavitate pronunties, partim tuo marte, adiecto eis & abs te melo, partim aliorum. Gratissimum mihi feceris, si ex hisce aliquas miseris una cum melodiis suis." Speaking of Giustinian, Piero Parleone da Rimini gives another interesting indication of the direction followed by humanistic tastes in a letter, written in 1462, to Niccolò Sagundino: "In musica studiose recreabatur ... Scis ... in musicis illum tantam eruditionem habuisse, tantumque ei habitum honorem quantum nec aetate nostra, nec multis ante annis in nemine fuisse, nec habitum esse audivimus. Nam, praeter sacros hymnos, quos extrema aetate composuit, iunior quosdam suavissimos, et miros quosdam vocum et nervorum cantus invenit, qui usque adeo et artis gratia, et numerorum dulcedine omnium aures, mentesque et animos demulcent, alliciunt, ac tenent, ut nec quisquam delectet, nec musicae peritus habeatur, qui Justinianas fidium vocumque modulationes et flexiones, varietatesque ignoret. Nec alii nunc, ut vides, cantus in nuptiis, in conviviis, in triviis, ac vulgo passim adhibentur." From *Miscellanea di varie operette*, coll. G. M. Lazzari, II (Venice, 1740), 87.
2. I have in mind the three studies, all titled "Per l'edizione critica delle canzonette di Leonardo Giustinian": by A. Oberdorfer, in *Giornale storico della letteratura italiana* 57 (1911), 193–217; by G. Billanovich, *ibid.*, 110 (1937), 197–252; and by L. Pini, in *Atti della Accademia Naz. dei Lincei. Memorie. Classe di Scienze morali, storiche e filologiche*, ser. 8, vol. 9: 3 (1960), 419–543.

3. Pini, pp. 419 and 451.

4. Traversari's request (see n. 1) that Giustinian send the *laudi* "una cum melodiis suis" makes us think of some form of musical notation; we do not know if he ever sent them.

5. W. Rubsamen, "The Justiniane or Viniziane of the 15th Century," *Acta musicologica* 29 (1957), 172–83, has obtained very good results in this direction. They can be summarized as follows: *1*) identification of four three-voice compositions of the *Frottole libro Sexto*, by O. Petrucci (Venice, 1505–06), as those referred to as *giustiniane* in the collection's index (the texts of two of them are two isolated stanzas from Giustinian's *sirventesi*); *2*) proof that one of Petrucci's *giustiniane* is a very free and ornate version of a three-voice composition of the second half of the fifteenth century; *3*) identification of some stylistic characteristics shared by these *giustiniane* and some poly-phonic settings of Giustinian's times (the author accepts too easily the attribution to Giustinian of some texts in print collections). The compositions pointed out by Rubsamen are, I believe, only reflections of real *giustiniane*; the setting of a single stanza of a *sirventese* is different from the setting of a long series of stanzas. I recently gave an example of how two different compositions by the same polyphonist used the stanzas of a *sirventese* that already must have had an independent setting ("Two Anglo-Italian Pieces in the Manuscript Porto 714," in *Speculum Musicae Artis. Festgabe für Henrich Husmann* [Munich, 1970], pp. 253–61). Such settings give the impression of a *strambotto* attitude in a period when *strambotti* had not yet achieved literary recognition.

6. My description is influenced by examples belonging to the much later period when *strambotti* were counted by the hundreds in manuscripts and early musical prints; notwithstanding the chronological difference, nothing makes me think the description is not generally correct.

7. A pleasant observation of popular lore on the singing of *strambotti* is the *intermedio* after Act I of *Chi soffre speri* (it is therefore three centuries old, at least, and it is not easy to say if it is by Virgilio Mazzocchi or Marco Marazzoli). Several characters compete in singing seven *strambotti* and repeat the same aria thirty-one times (three *strambotti* have five distichs), always varying the details of the diction and the expressive accent.

8. The current practice at the beginning of the sixteenth century allowed both procedures for the *capitolo*, which is either a derivation or a continuation of the so-called *sirventese*. I have written elsewhere that the term *sirventese* does not match the fifteenth-century usage, in which this type of composition was called *cançone* or even *capitolo*.

9. [According to the Italian system of metrical scanning, the first version of the same line has an accent on the antepenultimate syllable, and the second version has an accent on the last syllable; accordingly, the first is a *settenario sdrucciolo*, the second a *novenario tronco*.]

10. Bembo's statement, fictitiously assigned to his brother Carlo in the first book of *Prose della volgar lingua*, is obviously tendentious: "Non voglio dire ora, se

non questo: che la nostra lingua [viniziana], scrittor di prosa che si legga e tenga per mano ordinatamente, non ha ella alcuno; di verso, senza fallo, molti pochi; uno de' quali più in pregio è stato a' suoi tempi, o pure a' nostri, per le maniere del canto, col quale esso mandò fuori le sue canzoni, che per quella della scrittura, le quali canzoni dal sopranome di lui sono poi state dette e ora si dicono le Giustiniane" (Let this only be said: that our [Venetian] parlance is not represented at this time by any prose writer whom one could regularly read and keep at hand; there are very few such writers of verse, one of whom has been appreciated in his own time as well as in ours *more for the style of singing* in which he made his poems known *than for the style of writing*; such songs were and still are called *giustiniane* after his name). I quote from P. Bembo, *Prose e rime*, ed. C. Dionisotti (Turin, 1960), p. 112.

11. I have not been able to verify B. Wiese's version in "Neunzehn Lieder Leonardo Giustinian's nach den alten Drucken," in *XIV. Bericht vom Schuljahre 1884–1885 über das grossherzogl. Gymnasium zu Ludwiglust* (Ludwiglust, 1885), p. 4; but the order in which the lines are reproduced in *Denkmäler der Tonkunst in Österreich,* vol. 14–15 (Vienna, 1900), 234 (*ripresa, volta, piedi*) makes me think that the prints seen by Wiese (*Canzonette e strambotti d'amore*) derived their text from musical manuscripts. The correct sequence of lines was restored by A. Restori in *Zeitschrift für Romanische Philologie* 18 (1894), 235. The editor of the Italian texts in vol. 14–15 of *DTÖ* refused the correction, because "alle Handschriften gegen sich hat" (thus showing his inexperience of musical procedures). Once again the correct order was reestablished by M. F. Bukofzer, *John Dunstable, Complete Works,* 2nd ed. (London 1970), pp. 201–2, on the basis of two other Venetian prints of 1472(?) and of 1485 (*Il fiore de le canzonete*).

12. S. Clercx, *Johannes Ciconia* (Brussels, 1960), I, 49; *ibid.,* II, 75–77, a transcription of Ciconia's composition, which had already been edited in vol. 14–15 of *DTÖ*, 227–28.

13. Described by J. Wolf, *Geschichte der Mensural-Notation* (Leipzig, 1904), I, 192; and C. Stornaiolo, *Codices urbinates latini* (Rome, 1921), III, 314–15; it bears the inscription "Questo libro de Musicha fu donato a Piero de Archangelo de li Bonaventuri da Urbino dal Mag.ᶜᵒ Piero di Chosimo de Medici di fiorenza." Besides the already mentioned Italian compositions, it contains a small collection of French compositions, mostly by Binchois, copied in Italy around 1440.

14. Summarily described in L. Delisle, *Bibliothèque Nationale. Manuscripts Latins et Français 1875–1891* (Paris, 1891), I, 127–30. For identification of the three fragments of different period and origin that compose it, see K. Jeppesen, *La Frottola II* (Copenhagen, 1969), pp. 86ff.

15. The following are the manuscripts that include O *rosa bella: Porto,* fols. 54v–56; *Pix,* fols. 90v–92; *Pav,* fols. 41v–42; *Cord,* fols. 8v–10; *P,* fol. 30v; and *Sev.,* fol. 50 (two fragments of the same source); *Esc,* fols. 35v–37; *Tr 89,* fols. 119v–120; *Tr 90,* fols. 361v–362; *Tr 93,* fol. 371; *Wolf,* fols. 34v–36; *Dij,* fols. 93v–95; *MC,* fol. 371. For an explanation of the most commonly

used abbreviations, see D. Plamenac, "A Reconstruction of the French Chansonnier in the Biblioteca Colombina, Seville," *The Musical Quarterly* 38 (1952), 89–91; *ibid.*, 248–49, gives more detailed information on variants or omissions in the number of voices (it must be added that the version of *Tr 93* is missing a leaf). For the most important reworkings see the transcriptions in *DTÖ*, vol. 14–15, 229–34, and vol. 22, 1–69; and in Bukofzer, *Dunstable*, p. 135.

16. For this manuscript, in the first part of which there are theoretical treatises, see B. Meier, "Die Handschrift Porto 714 als Quelle zur Tonartenlehre des 15. Jahrhunderts," *Musica disciplina* 7 (1953), 175–97; and also my "Two Anglo-Italian Pieces."

17. The observation is by Bukofzer, in *Dunstable*, p. 200 of the 2nd ed.; the revisers are wrong in asserting that manuscripts *Porto 714* and *Cord* give the correct *ballata* disposition; the impossibility of executing it as a *ballata* is inherent in the music and could not be corrected without altering the musical text.

18. The *signum congruentiae*, present in all manuscripts but *Cord*, is in some cases followed by a breve pause.

19. *Puisque m'amour*; it is included in Bukofzer, *Dunstable*, 2nd ed., p. 136. It seems that Dunstable was active as a musician mostly in France, where he was in the retinue of the duke of Bedford, who died in 1435; in England he was mostly active as an astronomer and a mathematician; M. F. Bukofzer, in *MGG*, 3, col. 949–957, *sub voce*. He is therefore one of those fifteenth-century composers who were better known to their contemporaries in fields other than music.

20. It is not difficult to fill the gap at line 3 ("amore," although I read "a mg°" in the microfilm); *Pix, Cord*, and *Pav* have all eight lines, but in a disposition that suggests the following order (compared with the regular succession given above): 1, 2, 5, 6, 3, 4, 7, 8. Transpositions are made easy by the fact that each distich has a self-contained meaning (as often happens in a *strambotto*).

21. See H. Besseler, in *MGG*, 1, col. 1493–1494, *sub voce*, and my "Two Anglo-Italian Pieces." A sign of Bedingham's presence in Italy is the salutation "Ma dame Florence l'amée" in the French ballad *Grant temps* (arbitrarily included in Walter Frye, *Collected Works*).

22. I mentioned Gilles Joye and a portrait of him by Hans Memlinc in essay 7.

23. I give only the first section of the music in a nondefinitive transcription because of the mediocre quality of the available microfilm and because the microfilm does not let one easily distinguish the use of red notes in the manuscript, forcing the transcriber to guess at their presence. The first section (stanzas 1 and 2) is concluded, after the extension, by vertical bars which are not repeated in the music of stanza 3 and the last stanza. [A recent edition in Galfridus and Robertus de Anglia, *Four Italian Songs for 2 and 3 Voices*, ed. D. Fallows (Antico ed., Newton Abbott, 1977), pp. 5–6, is musically unconvincing.]

24. The following manuscripts contain *Gentil madonna*: *Cord*, fols. 3v–5; *Esc*, fols. 117v–118; *Pav*, fols. 26v–27; *Pix*, fols. 89v–90; *Mel*, fols. 63v–65; *BerK*, fols. 18v–19; *P*, fols. 21v–22; *Mn*, fols. 48v–49; *MC*, fol. 114v. The only one to give the name "Jo. bodigham" is *Mn* (Munich, Bayerische Staatsbibliothek, Cim 351ª; for the other abbreviations, see references in n. 14).

25. I arrive at this result by collating the texts of *P*, *Esc*, *Cord*, *Pix*, and *Pav*, along with the metric pattern of the lauda *Umil Madonna, non m'abbandonare*, in *Laude fatte e composte da più persone spirituali* (Florence, 1458–86). Differences among the versions, already remarkable in this first stanza, make it impossible to reach any conclusion for a second and perhaps a third stanza. In order to sing the two lines of the *ripresa* one must twice repeat the first section of music. However, it is also possible that this was Bedingham's erroneous version and that the author of the poem had conceived a *ripresa* of a line plus a stanza nonsymmetrically divided into two *piedi* but completed by the line given above as the second one of the *ripresa*.

26. At a later time the through-composed handling of the text by Bedingham may have determined the totally different metrical structure of still another *lauda*, whose *ripresa*(?) combines the *ripresa* (one line) and the stanza of the structure I have reconstructed:

> Vergine bella, non mi abbandonare.
> O mia avvocata, o santa margherita,
> Tu sei colei, che reggi la mia vita:
> Degna per me Gesù Cristo pregare.

In *Laude di Feo Belcari* (Florence, *ca.* 1480); this piece is followed by two stanzas of four endecasyllables each and rhymes *x y y x*, without repetition of the rhyme shown in the *ripresa*.

27. Another example could be *Il grant desio* of codex *Esc* (fols. 22v–24), whose text goes back to a *ballata* set to music by Francesco Landini.

28. Going back briefly to my initial "ricercare," I cannot agree with Pini (see notes 2 and 3) who, after quoting a concise, generic, and rhetorical praise paid to Giustinian by Giano Pannonio, comments: "Nessun'altra informazione si può dunque rinvenire più esauriente di quest'ultima per asserire che nelle canzonette l'aspetto contenutistico-letterario è subordinato ed in funzione della forma melodica" (we could not find a more conclusive piece of information to the effect that the literary contents depend on and serve the melodic form). Pannonio's trite image, "plectro celeber Leonardus eburneo," cannot be taken literally, although we know Giustinian really used stringed instruments (see note 1). The melodic form, anyway, whose importance I too have tried to underline, cannot be considered as predominant in the combination of textual, musical, and mimic factors which are aimed at representing an action and therefore a content.

29. See notes 25 and 26.
30. A combination of *O rosa bella* and *He, Robinet* existed, and it is possible to reconstruct it from *Esc,* fol. 3v, adding to *Robinet* the upper part of *O rosa bella.* [See my article "Su alcuni testi italiani di composizioni polifoniche quattrocentesche," *Quadrivium* 14 (1973), 133–34 and 153–54.]
31. I will return to this point later.
32. This edition was prepared by Dr. Kanazawa for the composition of the sacred texts and by Mrs. Pope Conant for the secular ones (see Isabel Pope and Masakata Kanazawa, *The Musical Manuscript Montecassino 871* [Oxford, 1978], pp. 376–77).
33. The most easily accessible sources are A. W. Ambros, *Geschichte der Musik,* 3rd ed., II (Breslavia, 1891); *DTÖ,* vol. 14–15, 229–32; A. T. Davison and W. Apel, *Historical Anthology of Music,* rev. ed. (Cambridge, Mass., 1957), vol. 1, 65–66; Bukofzer, *Dunstable,* 2nd ed., pp. 133–34. Ibid., p. 200, gives other information.
34. I must repeat for this piece the reservations I expressed for the other example (see n. 23) on the reading of some passages where the microfilm does not allow one to determine exactly which notes are red in the original.
35. It is incorrectly interpreted in vol. 14–15 of *DTÖ;* and in Davison and Apel's version, which is derived from *DTÖ;* anyway, the notation is absolutely clear in *Tr 89,* the manuscript taken as the basis of my transcription, which is one of those sources that apply proportional notation and omit every change of measure.
36. The circle, indicating *tempus perfectum,* is used inconsistently in the manuscripts in which it is present, and in one case (*BerlK*) is introduced a measure later than in the other manuscripts.
37. It is edited in *DTÖ,* vol. 14–15, pp. 233–34, with a fourth voice added by Ockeghem.
38. Bukofzer, *Dunstable,* pp. 125–26. For this composition, in fact, Bukofzer employs a criterion of rhythmical interpretation similar to mine.

11 Novelty and Renewal in Italy: 1300–1600

This essay was originally published in *Studien zur Tradition in der Musik. Kurt von Fischer zum 60. Geburtstag,* edited by Hans Heinrich Eggebrecht and Max Lütolf (Munich, 1973).

1. An incomplete list may suffice for the purpose of this essay. Of Florentine origin are the mss. Florence, Bibl. Naz. Centr., Panciatichi 26; London, Br. Mus., add. ms. 29987 (I am aware of an opinion assigning it to Umbria); Paris, Bibl. Nat., it. 568; Florence, Bibl. Laur., Palat. 87 (Squarcialupi codex). Of northern origin are Paris, Bibl. Nat., n.a. frç. 6771 (Codex Reina, from the territory of Venice; the last section belongs to a phase later than the Ars nova)

and Modena, Bibl. Est., M. α. 5.24 (olim lat. 568, probably from Bologna). The major fragments, all of northern origin, are Vatican, Rossi 215, and Ostiglia, Opera Pia Greggiati, both belonging to a disbanded ms. markedly older than all the others; Padua, Bibl. Univ., mss. 1475 and 684, both fragments of a Paduan source to which Oxford, Bodl. Libr., Can.Pat.lat. 229 also belonged. Probably of local origin, but strongly influenced by northern musicians, was the ms. of which a considerable number of leaves are preserved in Lucca, Arch. di Stato. For further reference, see K. von Fischer, *Studien zur italienischen Musik des Trecento und frühen Quattrocento* (Bern, 1956).

2. The plan is strictly observed in the latest source, the Squarcialupi codex, and still detectable in, going back in time, the mss. Paris, Bibl. Nat., it. 568, and London, Br. Mus., add. 29987. The first half of the oldest source, the Panciatichi codex, is entirely dedicated to Landini; the second half begins with Giovanni and Iacopo (plus Piero, named only in this source), and continues as usual, although with fewer works by fewer composers and late additions of older pieces.

3. The latter feature is not easily reconciled with a derivation from conductus, while it better fits an origin in the madrigal texts parallel to that of motet texts.

4. The court referred to by da Tempo is that of Alberto della Scala, lord of Verona with his brother Mastino, and ruler also of Padua (an inept ruler but, according to contemporary sources, a music lover). The repertory of the Vatican and Ostiglia fragments is probably related to the court of the Scala brothers and includes (anonymously) works by Giovanni and Piero. We also have reports, confirmed by some texts of madrigals and *cacce*, that Giovanni and Iacopo competed at the court of Verona; Piero, too, must at some time have entered that contest.

5. Petrarch sojourned, among other places, in Verona, where Iacopo had court connections.

6. This had already been present in cruder ways in the anonymous pieces of the Vatican and Ostiglia fragments, and will be found again in the later madrigals and *ballate* of Bartolino da Padova, the other major representative of the northern tradition, who eventually applied his figural inventiveness to effects of expressive poignancy.

7. As a regular madrigal and as a *caccia*.

8. The *certame coronario* was a poetic contest, held in the Florentine cathedral and presided over by Piero dei Medici, to prove the artistic validity of Italian verse. For this ideological reason more than anything else, I am inclined to give most Florentine sources later dates than those commonly accepted.

9. More particularly, but not exclusively, in the Codex Reina.

10. The aspect of improvisation (the extent of which we tend to exaggerate) also applies to the musical formula, in which the performer could introduce ornamentation and rhythmic change for the sake both of variety and better adjustment to the accentual and expressive needs of each strophe of text.

11. It is a mistaken notion that the existing music of *canti carnascialeschi* originated under Lorenzo dei Medici; most of it belongs to the Medicean restoration, which began in 1513.

12. Even when intended as a joke or a caricature, the *frottola* was meant to be a lyrical poem and had no relation to dance music.

13. Although no settings of *strambotti* exist that are attributed to Serafino, it is known that he received musical training from a Gulielmo Fiamingo, that is, Guillaume Garnier.

14. Of the Este brothers, Alfonso succeeded Ercole in 1505 and continued to improve the chapel; Ippolito became a cardinal; Isabella married Francesco Gonzaga, marquis of Mantua, in 1490; and Beatrice married in 1491 Ludovico Sforza, then still unofficially the lord of Milan. Related to the Este sisters by family ties and a common education was Elisabetta Gonzaga, later the duchess of Urbino.

15. Best known is the institution of the so-called Cappella Giulia in St. Peter's in Rome, followed by chapels in the major basilicas. During the fifteenth century chapels had served the private religious services of great lords; even the papal chapel was essentially meant for private functions.

16. This can also be taken literally if one notices that a number of his parody masses are based on French motets (seldom chansons) of the first part of the century.

17. This is true of the collected poems, for instance, of Cariteo (*Endimione*, 1506) and Sannazzaro (*Rime*, 1530, but mostly written before 1504). In the collection of Tebaldeo's poems (first published in 1498) sonnets still associate with *strambotti* and *capitoli*; in Bembo's *Rime* (collected for publication in 1530) the Petrarchan dosage is applied, but neither madrigals nor *ballate* still observe the old rules.

18. See n. 17 for Bembo's madrigals and *ballate*. The participants of his long dialogues on the subject of platonic love (*Asolani*, 1505) occasionally sing short poems, but always recite the long texts of their (Bembo's) *canzoni*.

19. *Villote* and French *chansons* are often associated in prints and manuscripts of the period preceding the ascent of the madrigal; they probably met the demand for polyphonic pieces to be sung *a libro* by dilettanti, a habit which may have contributed to the all-vocal development of the madrigal.

20. All the surviving Medici had developed sophisticated tastes in the field of music through their education and through long sojourns in France. Giuliano was the owner of the Squarcialupi codex (did this possession affect his ideas about madrigals?) and his nephew, the younger Lorenzo, was the recipient, as a wedding present, of the ms. now called the Medici codex. Above all, the two clergymen in the family, Giovanni (Leo X) and his cousin Giulio (Clement VII) had great impact on Roman musical life. Giovanni, the author of some polyphonic pieces, was quoted by Cortese as a great authority in musical matters. He was the first pope who retained a whole group of *musici secreti* (that is, for private entertainment) in addition to the papal chapel.

12 Willaert and the *Canzone Villanesca*

This essay was originally published in *Studi Musicali* 9 (1980). The translation is by Vanni Bartolozzi.

1. We now know for sure that Willaert was in Ferrara (and later also in Hungary) from 1515 on, at the service of Cardinal Ippolito d'Este; see L. Lockwood, "Josquin at Ferrara: New Documents and Letters," in *Josquin des Prez: Proceedings of the International Josquin Festival-Conference,* New York, 1971, ed. E. E. Lowinsky and B. J. Blackburn (London, 1976), p. 119ff. The information about the trip to Rome, which Willaert probably made when he came to Italy from Flanders at the time of Leo X, is known from an anecdote told by G. Zarlino in the last chapter of his *Dimostrazioni harmoniche,* in the Venice editions of 1558 and 1573.

2. I do not ignore the discussion—originating from M. Menghini's article, "Villanelle alla Napolitana," *Zeischrift für romanische Philologie* 16 (1892), 476–503; and 17 (1893), 441–89—between G. M. Monti, *Le villanelle alla napolitane e l'antica lirica dialettale a Napoli* (Città di Castello, 1925), and, on the other side, F. Novati, *Contributo alla storia della lirica musicale italiana popolare e popolareggiante, in Scritti varii in onore di R. Renier* (Turin, 1912) and C. Calcaterra, "Canzoni villanesche e villanelle," *Archivum Romanicum* 4: 10 (1926), 262–90. On the first side the discussion focuses on the recognition of the Neapolitan background of the *villanelle*; on the second side on a criticism of the romantic concept of "popular origin." I believe in the ethnic origin of the *villanesca*, and I find that the arguments of both sides reduce to a single level (already evident in their use of the generic term *villanella*) phenomena that were different in substance and time. The same fault is found in the very vast bibliography by B. M. Galanti, *Le villanelle alla napolitana* (Florence, 1954), which groups together pieces of very different chronological and geographical origin, ignoring many of the oldest editions because they are in non-Italian libraries.

3. See D. G. Cardamone, "The Debut of the 'canzone villanesca alla napolitana,' " *Studi musicali* 4 (1975), 65ff. For the material here utilized I owe much to the research and publications of Dr. Cardamone, which I had the opportunity to follow closely.

4. *Ibid.,* 65–66.

5. B. D. Falco, *Descrizione dei luoghi antichi di Napoli,* reprinted many times (sometimes with different titles); the first edition, printed in Naples in 1535 by Mattia Cancer and today lost, was dedicated to the emperor.

6. We lack any more precise knowledge of this printer; Cardamone, "Debut," p. 77, having accurately confronted the musical character of two lute tablatures published in Naples in 1536 by the German Johannes Sultzbach, suggests that Johannes de Colonia was associated with Sultzbach.

7. The woodcut is reproduced in Cardamone, "Debut," p. 67.

8. For the relationship between *villanesca alla napoletana* and *strambotto* and for the former's metric and stylistic features, see D. G. Cardamone, "Forme musicali e metriche della canzone villanesca e della villanella alla napolitana," *Rivista italiana di musicologia* 12 (1977), 25–72.

9. The consecutive fifths, of which I will speak later, have often been linked with the anticontrapuntist arguments of the second half of the sixteenth century. Such anachronistic comparisons belittle the aesthetic needs from which that criticism sprang and reduce its content to a mere question of rules and technical procedures.

10. About Nola, who also composed madrigals and motets, see the biographical information and the edition of his music in L. Cammarota, *Giandomenico da Nola*, two vols. (Rome, 1973).

11. D. G. Cardamone gives accurate biographical profiles and careful musical analyses of these composers and Nola in "The 'canzone villanesca alla napolitana' and Related Italian Part-Music: 1537 to 1570," (diss., Harvard University, 1972), pp. 207–28 and 257–310.

12. To them we must add also Francesco Silvestrino, nicknamed Cechin; three four-voice *villanesche* by him are included in Willaert's collection of 1545; see the appendix to this chapter.

13. For the gradual change from the first to the second term, see W. Scheer, *Die Frühgeschichte der italienischen Villanella* (Cologne, 1936). I must add that Antonio Gardane published in 1560 and 1562 a series of five books titled *Villotte alla napolitana,* all three-voice pieces, in which the Venetian term (rendered in Italian) is applied to a content only part of which still has dialectal Neapolitan characteristics, while the rest is Tuscan and therefore similar to the *villanella* and the *canzonetta.* As a northern equivalent of Nola's Neapolitan *villanesche,* published in 1541 by Scotto, we must consider the publication in the same year by Gardane of *Il Primo Libro delle Villote Di Alvuise Castellino chiamato il Varoter da lvi composti li versi et il Canto.* Castellino's are four-voice compositions.

14. A. Calmo, *Le Lettere,* ed. V. Rossi (Turin, 1888), p. 198ff. Calmo also mentions Willaert in other letters.

15. But they were included in his later collections of *Canzoni villanesche*; see the appendix to this essay.

16. A. F. Doni mentions them in *Dialogo della musica* (Venice, 1543), as does Silvestro Ganassi del Fontego, *Lettione Seconda della Prattica di Sonare il Violone d'Arco da Tasti* (Venice, 1543). In the dedication to Neri Capponi he recalls the "sacro & divino collegio" that congregated at the latter's house, "prince of that [holy and divine college] being Messer Adriano whose praise is never adequate, a new Prometheus of the heavenly harmony, glory of the present century and master to future ones."

17. Its text is reproduced by A. Einstein, *The Italian Madrigal* (Princeton, 1949), p. 164; for the music, see J. Arcadelt, *Opera Omnia,* vol. 2 (American Institute of Musicology, 1970), pp. 99–101.

18. It is the six-voice madrigal *Rompi de l'empio cor*, included in Ph. Verdelot, *La più divina, et più bella musica, che si udisse giamai* ... (Venice, 1541); the modern edition is in A. Willaert, *Opera Omnia*, vol. 14, ed. H. Meier (American Institute of Musicology, 1977), 136–42.

19. Maybe it was this procedure that induced Willaert to include Perissone's four-voice *villanesca* in his two collections of 1548.

20. H. M. Brown, *Music in the French Secular Theatre, 1400–1550* (Cambridge, Mass., 1963), pp. 107–8.

21. *Ibid.*; it is the first of a series of prints whose titles make such a distinction; see F. Lesure, "Eléments populaires dans la chanson française au début du XVIᵉ siècle," in *Musique et Poésie au XVIᵉ siècle*," ed. J. Jacquot (Paris, 1954), pp. 169–80.

22. Between 1528 and 1536 almost all of Attaignant's editions used such terminology.

23. The edition given by D. G. Cardamone in the appendix to "Debut of the 'canzone villanesca,' " pp. 97–130 (I specifically suggested that she include the music) hypothetically reconstructs the missing bass part by imitating the bass parts found in many other collections of three-voice *villanesche*.

24. I must say that I realized this only after my choice was made, so this detail did not have any influence on the choice itself.

25. In Jacquot, *Musique et poésie au XVIᵉ siècle*, p. 182ff., I assumed that parallel motion and chords in close position were intended to imitate the sound of a chord instrument (specifically, the *colascione*) used to accompany the singing. Some writers, though, mention a popular, more or less instinctive, custom of singing polyphonic music. See L. Zacconi, *Prattica di Musica* (Venice, 1596), fol. 81v; and S. Cerreto, *Della prattica musica vocale e strumentale* (Naples, 1601), p. 102. One explanation does not exclude the other; the instruments may have derived their chord successions in parallel motion from the model offered by popular singers and their vocal procedures (or vice versa).

26. Naturally this does not refer to the composers who soon started to compose their *villotte* or *villanelle* or *canzonette, ex novo*. In the milieu nearer to Willaert, Perissone Cambio and Donato sometimes took more liberty with the tune of the model; they modified slightly the melodic contours and the rhythm, and they transposed some phrases, but they maintained the fundamental essence, what I will define later as "aria." In doing so they advanced a little in the direction of "parody," but without reaching that "free (often random) variation of an autonomous thematic complex" that should characterize a real parody; see Cardamone, "The 'canzone villanesca alla napolitana,' " pp. 395–414.

27. L. Lockwood, "On 'Parody' as Term and Concept in 16th-Century Music," in *Aspects of Medieval & Renaissance Music*, ed. J. LaRue (New York, 1966), pp. 560–75. For the caution with which the term and concept should be applied to the four-voice *villanesche*, see note 26.

28. *Un giorno mi pregò una vedovella* and *Zoia zentil* (and also Nola's *O dolce*

vita mia and Willaert's *O dolce vita mia* and *Madonn'io non lo so*) are published in *A. Willaert (und andere Meister), Volkstümliche Italienische Lieder*, ed. E. Hertzmann, vol. 8 of *Das Chorwerk*, (Wolfenbüttel, 1930), and now in A. Willaert, *Canzoni villanesche alla napolitana*, ed. D. G. Cardamone, vol. 30 of Recent Researches in the Music of the Renaissance (Madison, Wis., 1979). See also E. Lovarini, *Studi sul Ruzzante e la letteratura pavana* (Padua, 1965).

29. About the term and concept of *aria*, see N. Pirrotta and E. Povoledo, *Music and Theatre from Poliziano to Monteverdi* (Cambridge, 1982), pp. 247ff.

13 Notes on Marenzio and Tasso

This essay was originally published in *Scritti in onore di Luigi Ronga*, ed. Riccardo Ricciardi (Milan, 1973). The translation is by Harris Saunders.

1. L. Ronga, "Tasso e Monteverdi," *Poesia* 2 (April 1945), 272–80, included later in *Arte e gusto nella musica* (Milan-Naples, 1956), pp. 19–32. For the text of the dialogue see E. Raimondi, critical edition of Tasso, *Dialoghi* (Florence, 1958), II, 615–68.

2. A. Einstein, *The Italian Madrigal* (Princeton, 1949), I, 219ff.; II, 663; H. Engel, *Luca Marenzio* (Florence, 1956), pp. 22ff., n. 2.

3. A. Solerti, *Vita di Torquato Tasso* (Turin, 1895), I, 396, assigns to *La Cavaletta* the date of 1584 but then qualifies this in a note on the same page. The dedication of *Gioie di Rime, e Prose*, signed by Vasalini, is March 1587; the dedication of the madrigal collection was signed and dated by Marenzio December 10, 1587.

4. Among recent writings that should be considered, in addition to the two cited in note 2, is the small volume by D. Arnold, *Luca Marenzio* (London, 1965). [The latest are S. Ledbetter, *Luca Marenzio: New Biographical Findings* (Ph.D. diss., New York University, 1971), and Ledbetter, "Marenzio's Early Career," *Journal of the American Musicological Society* 32 (1979), 304–20.]

5. The *Terzo Libro de Madrigali a Cinque Voci* (Venice, A. Gardano, 1582), dedicated to the Accademici Filarmonici, is the first collection published by Marenzio after those destined for members of the house of Este. The following passage from the dedication would not be inappropriate for a young artist addressing his first protectors: "How good a road I have traveled and how much progress I have made thus far in the understanding of the perfect consonance of harmonic numbers, to you alone, most judicious Sirs, belongs the determination." [Ledbetter, "Marenzio's Early Career," convincingly suggests that Marenzio must have followed Contino to Mantua and entered Cardinal Madruzzo's service on Contino's recommendation.]

6. Engel, *Marenzio*, pp. 16ff., 214. The documents here are from 1578 and 1580 and do not justify the assertion that Marenzio was later paid by the day;

even at that time the *companatico* (daily food allowance), which was added to the monthly salary, was computed daily.

7. *Ibid.*, pp. 214, 216.

8. *Ibid.*, p. 216. It is useless to conjecture what would have happened if Marenzio had entered the service of Vincenzo Gonzaga, Monteverdi's future employer.

9. *Ibid.*, pp. 216–17.

10. *Ibid.*, pp. 218–19.

11. The patriarch must have tired of Marenzio's delays, and the negotiations were again taken up by the Gonzaga agent Attilio Malegnani, two of whose letters are reproduced in Engel, *Marenzio*, pp. 219–20. In that of January 24, 1587, to which the cited passage belongs, it is also stated that Marenzio claims to need his father's consent. Duke Guglielmo had this claim verified and perhaps took umbrage because of it, although Marenzio later declared himself ready to accept the Mantuan offer (letter of May 13, 1587).

12. The period from 1582 to 1585 saw a reconciliation of the Medici and Este families, culminating in the marriage of Cesare d'Este to Virginia dei Medici, the negotiations for which were conducted in Rome under the auspices of the two cardinals. Marenzio dedicated to the grand duchess of Tuscany the *Terzo Libro* for six voices, dated February 2, 1585 (Venice, G. Scotto's heir, 1585); beyond this, the madrigal *Real natura* of the *Quarto Libro* for five voices and perhaps also *Il suo vago gioioso* of the *Quinto Libro* for five voices are also addressed to her.

13. Arnold, *Marenzio*, p. 2. The thesis that a great deal of music was performed by dilettanti and that "the true nature of the Roman madrigal indicates that it was intended for dilettante singers" does not seem convincing to me; it is precisely this period for which evidence exists of the presence in Rome of singers like the Neapolitans Giovan Andrea and Giulio Cesare Brancaccio and the Romans Alessandro Merlo and Giovan Luca Conforti (actually from Calabria), who contributed no less than the ladies of Ferrara to the development of vocal virtuosity (for the most part improvised and therefore superimposed on an apparently simple musical script).

14. Little is known about the last years of Cardinal Cristoforo Madruzzo, who died at Tivoli July 5, 1578, while a guest of Cardinal d'Este; before renouncing the duties of bishop-prince of Trent (however, not the cardinalate) he was an animated, picturesque character, protector of artists and men of letters. [Marenzio's master, Contino, had served him from 1541 to 1551, and again from 1558 to 1560; see Ledbetter, "Marenzio's Early Career," p. 309.]

15. Scipione Gonzaga's letter, already cited, May 3, 1586.

16. I am not thoughtlessly applying the phrase to an easy target; a letter of October 7, 1581, printed in V. Pacifici, "Luigi d'Este ... Gli ultimi anni," *Atti e memorie della Società Tiburtina di Storia e d'Arte* 27 (1954), 20, n. 11, records that "Sig. Cardinal d'Este ... was at dinner in the Medici garden where he seemed very much at home; now said Lord Cardinal is back at Tivoli

in the company of Lord Cardinal di Medici, [Cardinal] Santa Croce, and [Cardinal] Collona [Colonna] amid great sweetness." Those years saw no lack of perfidy and violence.

17. Leonora d'Este's letters requested the cardinal to come to Ferrara and to be reconciled with his brother the duke, especially since "it is not the season to get medicated with baths," nor was it "time for mud treatments"; see G. Campori and A. Solerti, *Luigi, Lucrezia e Leonora d'Este* (Turin, 1888), p. 175. The cardinal's movements during that summer are deduced from his letters, from those of his retinue, and from those addressed to him; *ibid.*, pp. 175–202.

18. Capello's letters in Engel, *Marenzio*, pp. 215–16.

19. For Luigi d'Este's sojourn divided between Venice and Ferrara, see Pacifici, "Luigi d'Este," pp. 16–18; the dispatches of June 24, 1581, announcing his return to Rome, are also reported there.

20. Along with the phrases attesting that the madrigals had been performed in the presence of Duke Alfonso, it should be noted that only in this publication did Marenzio flaunt the title of *maestro di cappella* to the cardinal, certainly to indicate the renewed, if only apparent, cordiality between the two brothers.

21. Einstein, *Italian Madrigal*, II, 618–19. It is said that Cardinal dei Medici was interested more than was seemly in the beauty of Cleria Farnese, who had been married at an extremely young age to Giovan Giorgio Cesarini.

22. As I shall also say further on, the increased use of female voices was not limited to the Ferrarese court. Anthony Newcomb has kindly brought to my attention a note from the cardinal to Marenzio (from Tivoli, September 9, 1582) about "certain ladies desiring that you set to music the enclosed madrigal, . . . all the more because you know what type of composition is wont to please them, since they profess to be your disciples." In Marenzio's reply of September 12 (Engel, *Marenzio*, p. 19), which accompanies the already composed madrigal, he hopes "that the excellence of their [the ladies'] singing will make up for every defect and lack in the composition."

23. Also in this dedication Marenzio says of his compositions: "The goodness of Your Most Illustrious Excellency did not disdain to hear them graciously and to commend them." To my knowledge Ariosto is the only Ferrarese poet represented in the collection. [See J. Chater, "Fonti poetiche per i madrigali del Marenzio," *Rivista italiana di musicologia* 13 (1978), 60–104, especially 85–86.]

24. Solerti, *Tasso*, I, 355, affirms this on the basis of a passage in Scipione Gonzaga's *Commentarii*.

25. It is probable that the visit took place during the 1584 carnival, as D. Gnoli, *Vittoria Accoramboni* (Florence, 1870), p. 193, states; but Cardinal d'Este had already in September 1583 (the period of the secret marriage) received Mario Accoramboni, Vittoria's brother, into his entourage. The sonnet *Cedan l'antiche tue* in Marenzio's *Secondo Libro* for six voices (1584) praises a Vittoria.

26. Marenzio dated and signed most of his dedications from Rome, even though nearly all the collections were printed in Venice; thus there is no reason to doubt the genuineness of the dedications dated from Venice. In addition, the dedication of the *Quarto Libro* for five voices (Venice, May 5, 1584) is separated from that of the *Madrigali Spirituali* (Rome, April 24, 1584) by a period of time sufficient for the journey. The same criterion is valid, although with less rigor, for the five books of *villanelle*, all given for publication to keen and enterprising collectors who attached their own dedications; only that of the *Primo Libro* is dated from Venice, while the others are dated from Rome.

27. Tasso was a guest in the palace of Cardinal Luigi d'Este (who was absent from Ferrara) at the time of the wedding of Duke Alfonso to Margherita Gonzaga, when the excesses occurred that led to the poet's imprisonment (Solerti, *Tasso*, I, 306–7). He later imagined that his imprisonment was continued by will of the cardinal, who sent a message by an intermediary to reassure him (*ibid.*, II, document 162).

28. *Commemorazione della riforma melodrammatica* (Florence, 1895), appendix, p. 145.

29. Marenzio dedicated to Cardinal Aldobrandini (Rome, January 1, 1594) the *Sesto Libro de Madrigali a Cinque Voci* (Venice, A. Gardano, 1594), in which, however, there is not a single composition on a text by Tasso. [Actually, Chater, "Fonti poetiche," pp. 72–73, indicates that *Donna de l'alma mia* derives from Tasso's eclogue *Il convito de pastori*.]

30. I do not find it included in any of the old editions of the *Rime*, and it is different from the other Tasso poems based on the echo effect in not incorporating the reply in the meter of the verse.

31. Manuzio's dedication is from December 1583.

32. Documented, as has been stated, by the Venetian dedications. See note 26.

33. I limit my treatment to the first period of Marenzio's output, but his later collections do not alter the situation with respect to Tasso's poetry.

34. Among the small I am tempted to include Giulio Cesare Brancaccio, an expert in military matters, even more noted as a singer associated with the singing ladies of Ferrara; to him both Guarini and Tasso addressed various madrigals. The *Discorso* of Vincenzo Giustiniani documents Brancaccio's presence in Rome at an unspecified period; it is possible that he went there after the disagreement with the duke of Ferrara at the end of July 1583 upon the occasion of the visit of the duke de Joyeuse, which is narrated by Solerti, *Ferrara e la corte Estense* (Città di Castello, 1891), pp. 61ff. Either immediately or sometime later he became a part of the duke of Bracciano's entourage; after the latter's death Brancaccio was summoned, as one of the dead man's familiars, to verify his signature in a controversy over an act of transfer (Padua, December 14, 1585). Finally, Brancaccio was present with Scipione Dentice in the Cavalli palace in Padua the evening of December 22 when assassins burst in to murder Vittoria and Flaminio Accoramboni. See Gnoli, *Vittoria Accoramboni*, pp. 324–25, 360.

35. A. Einstein, introduction to L. Marenzio, *Sämtliche Werke,* II, Publikationen Älterer Musik, VI (Leipzig, 1931), vii.
36. The notable variants of lines 3–4 and 7 of octave 96 and those of line 3 of octave 97 agree with manuscript sources only; those of lines 3 and 6 of octave 99, on the other hand, agree only with the printed edition of *Goffredo* supervised by Malespini; octave 98 is among those with a more consistent tradition. See T. Tasso, *Gerusalemme Liberata,* ed. A. Solerti, vol. III (Florence, 1895), pp. 78–80. Marenzio takes advantage of the variant "Di color, di calor, di moto privo" to create an *Augenmusik* effect, the *note nere* for "color."
37. According to an anecdote collected by Manso and repeated by Solerti (*Tasso,* I, 702), "some gentlemen examined in Torquato's presence the most artful stanzas of his Jerusalem ... [to determine] which was the most beautiful; from among these Salvatore Pasqualoni recited ... *Giunto alla tomba* ... his verdict was confirmed by Tasso."
38. Wert's composition is in Einstein, *Italian Madrigal,* III, 221–29; and now in G. de Wert, *Collected Works,* ed. C. MacClintock and M. Bernstein, vol. VII (American Institute of Musicology, 1967), pp. 38–43. Marenzio's is in *Sämtliche Werke,* II, 1–7. In both compositions the key of A, stated more clearly by Marenzio at the beginning, is reached at the end with a plagal cadence; the tonal *cursus* which goes by way of A and C is normal. An archaic flavor is often attributed to the *alla breve* tactus; it is, rather, a legitimate means for a composer to prescribe a slower rhythmic pace than that of the tactus *alla semibreve;* its *breves* have a longer (though not twice as long) duration than the *semibreves* of the normal tactus.
39. *Sämtliche Werke,* I, Publikationen Älterer Musik, IV (Leipzig, 1929), 98–106.
40. Einstein, *Italian Madrigal,* II, 612, speaks of a "fastidious taste ... evident from first to last in his choice of poems," although he goes on to do Marenzio a disservice in suggesting that he had as *vade mecum* an anthology by Dionigi Atanagi. That meticulous, yet not too meticulous, taste did not prohibit Marenzio from accepting mediocre verses like those mentioned above, even when the text was not imposed by celebratory motives. In the *Quarto Libro* for five voices the obscurity of *Filli, l'acerbo caso* is rendered more strident by the fact that in the second part of the madrigal the female protagonist is addressed with the masculine gender; Marenzio is personally responsible for the confusion, since he changed the first verse of a text, *Scipio, l'acerbo caso,* set to music a little earlier by Rinaldo del Mel and a little later by G. B. Moscaglia. [It had also been set in 1581 by Filippo de Monte and Francesco Soriano; see Chater, "Fonti poetiche," p. 89.] On the other hand, the attention Marenzio paid to the syntactic articulation of texts, establishing or reestablishing continuity even where madrigalistic technique tended to fragment, is remarkable. Finally, the elegant and not entirely conventional Latin of the dedication of the *Motectorum ... Liber Primus* (Venice, 1585) offered

to Scipione Gonzaga, if it is indeed by Marenzio, seems proof of his remarkable culture.

41. Ronga, "Tasso e Monteverdi," p. 273; also "Tasso e la musica," in *Torquato Tasso,* Proceedings of the Convegno di Studi Tassiani, Ferrara, September 1954 (Milan, 1957), pp. 187–207.

14 The Orchestra and Stage in Renaissance *Intermedi* and Early Opera

This essay was originally included in F. Mancini, M. T. Muraro, and E. Povoledo, *Illusione e pratica teatrale,* exhibition catalog (Venice, 1975). The translation is by Lowell Lindgren. All the notes are new.

1. The terms "apparent" and "not apparent" are here applied to musical instruments in the sense in which they were used in Renaissance *intermedi,* that is, they were apparent when they were present on stage, not apparent when they were heard but not seen. Instruments had actually been used in both ways in *intermedi* and had been similarly integrated into or contrasted with the realism of the scenic apparatus.

2. See the various examples cited in Nino Pirrotta, *Li due Orfei,* 2nd ed. (Turin, 1975), pp. 58ff., translated into English as *Music and Theatre from Poliziano to Monteverdi* (Cambridge, 1981), pp. 50ff.

3. Bernardo Buontalenti's sketch for Peri's costume and instrument (an implausible harp) is reproduced in *The New Grove Dictionary of Music and Musicians,* ed. Stanley Sadie (London, 1980), XIV, 402. For examples of archeological reconstructions of musical instruments, see Emanuel Winternitz, *Musical Instruments and Their Symbolism in Western Art* (New York, 1967).

4. Epifanio d'Alfiano's engraving of this scene is reproduced in *New Grove Dictionary,* IX, 264. *Ibid.,* p. 268, an etching by Remigio Cantagallina reproduces the set of the fourth *intermedio* in *Il giudizio di Paride* (1608); various instruments are recognizable on a cloud high in the sky.

5. See the edition by Elena Povoledo (Rome, 1955), p. 50: "Facciansi due palchi, cioè uno per ciascheduno dei lati della scena, ... tanto lunghi quanto sarà dalla prima casa all'ultimo del sito di dietro."

6. *Ibid.*: "trappassino il pavimento del palco [scenico] per buche, acciòche non venghino a toccare esso palco, già che se si fermassero in esso, nel tempo di morescare sconcertarebbono gl'organi, et altri instromenti ... Così si sarà accomodato il luogo di dentro per li musici, mentre non si siano veduti di fuori, secondo che l'esperienza persuade essere più sano consiglio."

7. Alberto Gallo, *La prima rappresentazione al Teatro Olimpico* (Rome, 1973), p. 20: "di dentro una musica di stromenti, et di voci dolce il più che si possa, ma insieme altretanto flebile; et ... far si, ch'ella paia risuonar di lontano."

For the account of a performance of a tragedy in Reggio in 1568, see Pirrotta, *Li due Orfei*, pp. 224–25 (*Music and Theatre*, pp. 201–2).

8. Federico Follino, *Compendio delle sontuose feste fatte l'anno M.DC.VIII. nella città di Mantova* (Mantua, 1608), as cited by Angelo Solerti, *Gli albori del melodramma* (Milan, 1905), II, 249–50: "il Duca, e il Principe sposo con sei altri Cavalieri e con otto Dame delle principali della città cosí in nobiltà come in bellezza e in leggiadria del ballare."

9. From the account by Gioseffo Casato, cited by Angelo Solerti, *Musica ballo e drammatica alla corte medicea dal 1600 al 1637* (Florence, 1905), p. 121: "Nel mezzo del teatro fra li cavalieri ballò il Gran Duca, et fra le dame l'Arciduchessa, ma però con termini et partite sempre et luoghi differenti dagli altri, chè se bene seguivano il medesimo suono, ad ogni modo sempre erano conosciuti i padroni."

10. Ulderico Rolandi, "L'Andromeda musicata da M. A. Rossi (1638)," *Rassegna dorica* 3 (1931–32), p. 54, n. 3: "Quanto poi era il vano della scena tutto era occupato da una bellissima, e maestosa scala, che in se con nobile ornamento chiudeva un capacissimo sito per gli stromenti, che la *continua armonia* formavano in accompagnamento dei musici. Ma questi stromenti non veduti dalle viste degli spettatori vedevano nondimeno perfettamente, ed erano veduti da musici, che rappresentavano l'azione; però in luoghi pure agiatissimi dalle parti della scena erano accomodati palchi per altri infiniti stromenti i quali, uniti con quelli, ch'erano dinanzi alla scena, facevano gran sinfonia nel fine di ciascheduna parte dell'azione."

15 Temperaments and Tendencies in the Florentine Camerata

This essay was published in *The Musical Quarterly* 40 (April 1954). It is a translation by Nigel Fortune (who also added most of the original footnotes) of a slightly modified form of a lecture delivered in Rome on April 30, 1953, and published in *Le Manifestazioni Culturali dell'Accademia Nazionale di Santa Cecilia* (Rome, 1953).

1. [My views on this subject were first expressed in two 1953 texts, a lecture delivered in Rome and published in the original version of this essay, and a paper read in Paris, "Tragédie et Comédie dans la Camerata Fiorentina," in *Musique et Poésie au XVIe siècle*, ed. J. Jacquot (Paris, 1954), pp. 287–97. I have further expanded on the conflicting statements and attitudes of the protagonists in "Early Opera and Aria," in *New Looks at Italian Opera*, ed. W. W. Austin (Ithaca, N.Y., 1968), pp. 39ff., later included as chap. 6 in my *Li due Orfei* (Turin, 1969; 2nd ed., 1975) and in its English edition, *Music and Theatre from Poliziano to Monteverdi* (Cambridge, 1982).]

2. Solerti, *Gli albori del Melodramma* (Milan, 1905), I, 48, 50.

3. Translated in Oliver Strunk, *Source Readings in Music History* (New York, 1951), p. 363.
4. This academy was formed in 1583. Its name, which means "bran" or "chaff," and its emblem, a sieve, were intended to symbolize its function of separating good language and literature from bad.
5. Extracts translated in Strunk, pp. 302–22.
6. See Claude V. Palisca, "Girolamo Mei: Mentor to the Florentine Camerata," *The Musical Quarterly* 40 (1954), 1ff. [I may have been a bit too harsh on Galilei, who has been shown to have displayed a more pragmatic and progressive attitude by Palisca, "Vincenzo Galilei's Counterpoint Treatise: a Code for the Seconda pratica," *Journal of the American Musicological Society* 9 (1956), 81ff. For an exhaustive bibliography on Galilei, see also Palisca's article in *The New Grove Dictionary of Music and Musicians* (London, 1980) 7, 96–98.]
7. *Inferno*, XXXIII, lines 4–75.
8. For these two songs see Robert Haas, *Die Musik des Barocks* (Potsdam, 1928), pp. 19–20; and Alfred Einstein, *The Italian Madrigal* (Princeton, 1949), III, no. 96.
9. Extracts from these *intermedi* have been reprinted several times; the biggest source is Max Schneider, *Die Anfänge des Basso Continuo und seiner Bezifferung* (Leipzig, 1918), pp. 116–57. [All the music for the 1539 wedding festivities has recently been transcribed by A. C. Minor and B. Mitchell, *A Renaissance Entertainment: Festivities for the Marriage of Cosimo I, Duke of Florence, in 1539* (Columbia, Mo., 1968). See also chap. 4 in my *Li due Orfei* (or *Music and Theatre*).]
10. On the Medicis' dislike of Galilei and the Camerata's jealousy of Alessandro Striggio, from whom the Medici commissioned so much *intermedio* music, see Einstein, pp. 233–34.
11. Translated in Strunk, pp. 290–301.
12. [All the music of the 1589 *intermedi* has been published by D. P. Walker, ed., *La Musique des Intermèdes de la "Pellegrina"* (Paris, 1963). See also chap. 5 in my *Li due Orfei* [or *Music and Theatre*.]
13. Decree of September 3, 1588, reprinted in Giovanni Gaye, *Carteggio inedito d'artisti dei secoli XIV, XV e XVI* (Florence, 1840), III, 484.
14. Giovanni Battista Doni, "Trattato della Musica Scenica," in *Trattati* (Florence, 1763), II, 95, and appendix, p. 60. [See also Warren Kirkendale, *L'Aria di Fiorenza id est il Ballo del Granduca* (Florence, 1982), and, for general information and bibliography, C. V. Palisca's article on Cavalieri in *The New Grove Dictionary of Music and Musicians*, 4, 20–23.]
15. See Ulderico Rolandi, "Emilio de' Cavalieri, il Granduca Ferdinando e l'Inferigno," *Rivista Musicale Italiana* 36 (1929), 26–37.
16. In the preface to his *Euridice* [1601]; translated in Strunk, p. 373.
17. Emil Vogel, *Bibliothek der gedruckten weltlichen Vokalmusik Italiens, 1500–1700* (Berlin, 1892), I, 151.

18. Doni, p. 22, and appendix, p. 13.

19. Vogel, I, 151.

20. *Della poesia rappresentativa & del modo di rappresentare le favole sceniche.*

21. Pietro della Valle, *Della Musica dell'età nostra* . . . (1640), in Angelo Solerti, *Le Origini del Melodramma* (Turin, 1903), p. 154.

22. [To my knowledge this letter, which I read in a copy made by Alberto Cametti, has never been published. I hope it is included in the forthcoming book on Cavalieri's life and letters by Warren Kirkendale.]

23. On the other hand, Caccini wrote a letter from Florence on July 25, 1593, explaining that he had quarreled with the grand duke and was contemplating going to Rome; see Riccardo Gandolfi, "Alcune considerazioni intorno alla riforma melodrammatica a proposito di Giulio Caccini, detto Romano," *Rivista Musicale Italiana* 3 (1896), 718. He may have gone to Rome in 1593 and returned to Florence soon after; or did he not go at all?

24. In the prefaces to *Euridice* (1600) and *Le Nuove Musiche*; see Strunk, pp. 370–1, 379. [See also Caccini, *Le Nuove Musiche*, H. W. Hitchcock, ed. (Madison, Wis., 1970), p. 45.]

25. Strunk, p. 374. This definition of Peri's corresponds to the style of Piero Strozzi's madrigal *Fuor dall'humido nido*, printed in Federico Ghisi, *Alle fonti della monodia* (Milan, 1940), p. 46. The version of this pseudomonody for voice and *continuo* is certainly a modernized one, since in 1579 it was sung (by Caccini) to the accompaniment of a consort of viols, as Galilei's monodies had been. The song *Serenissima Donna* that Caccini composed for the *Maschere di Bergiere* (1590, also printed by Ghisi, p. 47) is much more truly monodic; however, Caccini never thought it worth publishing.

26. Strunk, p. 378.

27. This word is used in its modern sense. For Cavalieri's letter, see Henry Prunières, "Une lettre inédite de E. de' Cavalieri," *La Revue Musicale* (1923), 128–33.

28. Strunk, p. 378.

29. The final chorus, which includes three very florid solo songs, was published two years later in *Le Nuove Musiche*. It is not generally known that the text of the last aria in the volume, *Chi mi confort' ahime*, is also from *Il Rapimento di Cefalo*; see Solerti, *Albori*, III, 37.

30. In the preface to *Le Nuove Musiche*; see Strunk, pp. 382–91.

31. See his letter of March 10, 1618, to Andrea Cioli, secretary of the grand duke of Tuscany, quoted in Solerti, *Musica, Ballo e Drammatica alle corte medicea, 1600–1637* (Florence, 1905), pp. 127–28.

32. See Solerti, *Albori*, I, 50.

33. The only authority for this statement is a rather suspicious assertion by Caccini himself made as late as 1614 in the preface to his *Nuove Musiche e nuova maniera di scriverle*; see Vogel, I, 128. On the whole question of the authorship and performances of *Dafne*, see O. G. Sonneck, "*Dafne*, the first opera," *Sammelbände der internationalen Musikgesellschaft* 15 (1913–1914), 102–10.

34. See Ghisi, pp. 9–48.
35. Ottavio Rinuccini, dedication to Maria dei Medici of the libretto of *Euridice*; translated in Strunk, p. 368.
36. Strunk, p. 365.
37. *Il Successo dell'Alidoro* . . . (Reggio, n.d., but probably 1569). The following quotations are taken from Giovanni Crocioni, *L'Alidoro, o dei primordi del melodramma* (Bologna, 1938), pp. 35–39. [The whole text has been reprinted in *Teatro italiano . . . La tragedia del Cinquecento*, Marco Ariani, ed. (Turin, 1977), II, 984–1008; the passages here translated are on pp. 985, 992, and 1000.]
38. [See Alberto Gallo, *La Prima rappresentazione al Teatro Olimpico* (Milan, 1973).]
39. Strunk, p. 374.

16 Monteverdi and the Problems of Opera

This essay was originally a lecture given in 1963 at the Cini Foundation in Venice. It was published in *Studi sul teatro veneto fra Rinascimento ed età barocca*, ed. M. T. Muraro (Florence, 1971). The translation is by Harris Saunders.

1. My transcriptions of the two examples reduce the rhythmic values of the original by half and interpret, where necessary, the variety of accentuations that are masked under the uniform notation in *common time*. The *basso continuo* of Monteverdi's score is not figured; Peri's has a few basic indications for harmonization. Monteverdi requested the use of a chitarrone and an *organo di legno* for the accompaniment; the correspondence of the situations suggests that Peri used a similar instrumentation.
2. More classical, or more classicizing, *Orfeo* gives to the choral conclusions of acts the character of sententious comments; Rinuccini and Peri did not shun making these conclusions an integral part of the action. The difference is due at least in part to the greater breadth that the use of the chorus assumes in *Orfeo*, even in the course of the episodes.
3. The official description of the performance is given in A. Solerti, *Gli albori del melodramma* (Milan, 1904), II, 113.
4. [The curtain was not raised at that time but fell at the foot of the stage, and there was no provision for pulling it up between acts or at the end of the play.]
5. Despite uncertainties and errors in nomenclature, it seems to me beyond doubt that the instrumental pieces destined to accompany a certain scenic action (including the change of scenery) usually were called *sinfonia*; *ritornello* was used for those that introduced or framed a vocal piece, either soloistic or choral.
6. The Mantuan libretto (but not the Florentine one) here cites Dante's well-known verse about the inscription on the doors of Hell.

7. [I have changed my opinion about the two finales and suggested a different sequence of events in essay 17.]

8. Claude Palisca, "Musical Asides in the Diplomatic Correspondence of Emilio de' Cavalieri," *The Musical Quarterly* 49 (1963), 352, has called attention to a letter of November 24, 1600, in which the Florentines who had organized the spectacles of that year are criticized for having "gone into tragic texts." The comment refers to the narrations and laments in *Euridice* and is all the more interesting in that Cavalieri herein refers to and makes his own an opinion expressed by Bardi. The old adversaries had become reconciled, to all appearances, in their aversion to any attempt at "tragedia in musica."

9. Solerti, I, 91–100; the complete text of *Arianna* is in II, 143–87, and should be divided into five episodes and not eight scenes as Solerti does.

10. Claudio Sartori, *Monteverdi* (Brescia, 1953), pp. 113–14, agrees with me in judging *Arianna* an attempt that was not completely successful.

11. *Andromeda* was written in 1610; with *Tancredi* (1615), Campeggi returned to the former usage of having only the choruses or *intermedi* set to music.

12. The poet is Francesco Melosio; see essay 20.

13. Mythology and classicism do not always coincide; in opera, mythological themes often serve to justify scenographic or vocal marvels.

14. See the letter discussed in Wolfgang Osthoff, "Zu den Quellen von Monteverdis 'Ritorno di Ulisse in Patria,' " *Studien zur Musikwissenschaft* 23 (1956), 73–74.

15. Sartori, pp. 228–29.

17 Theater, Sets, and Music in Monteverdi's Operas

This essay was originally published in Raffaello Monterosso, ed., *Claudio Monteverdi e il Suo Tempo*, proceedings of an international congress held in Venice, Mantua, and Cremona, May 3–7, 1968 (Verona, 1969). The translation is by David Morgenstern.

1. The text of *Arianna*, like those of *Dafne* and *Euridice*, has no explicit indication of the division into acts aside from what is provided by the strophic choruses ("Fiamme serene e pure," "Stampa il ciel," "Avventurose genti," "Su l'orride paludi," "Spiega omai giocondo Nume") that conclude the five episodes; other choral participation in the course of the episodes is freer in meter.

2. See Federico Follino, *Compendio delle sontuose feste fatte l'anno MDCVIII nella città di Mantova* (Mantua, 1608); my quotations are derived from Angelo Solerti, *Gli albori del melodramma* (Milan, 1904–1905), II, 147, 187.

3. Also described by Follino, *Compendio*, and Federico Zuccaro, *Il passaggio per l'Italia* (Bologna, 1608), both in Solerti, *Gli albori*, III, 205–234, 235–240.

4. Follino, *Compendio*, in Solerti, *Albori*, II, 145.

5. See Ercolano Marani, "L'architettura" in *Mantova. Le arti,* III (Mantua, n.d., [1965]), 15–16, 50, 92, 118, 170. *Ibid.,* p. 191, mentions a "scena di Castello," for which work was carried out under the direction of A. M. Viani.

6. *Ibid.,* p. 170. For a figure of no less than six thousand people, see Follino, *Compendio,* in Solerti, *Albori,* II, 145.

7. Follino, *Compendio,* in Solerti, *Albori,* III, 240.

8. "Accesi che furono i torchi dentro al teatro, si diede dalla parte di dentro del palco il solito segno del suono delle trombe, e nel cominciar a suonar la terza volta sparì con tanta velocità in un batter di ciglia la gran cortina che copriva il palco ch'ancor ch'ella s'alzasse in alto pochi furono quelli che s'avvidero com'ella fusse sparita. Onde, scopertosi il palco alla vista degli spettatori, si videro ... " Follino, *Compendio,* in Solerti, *Albori,* III, 208. Previously the curtain had "fallen," disappearing into a receptacle at the foot of the stage; the mechanism allowing it to "disappear" upward is described by Nicola Sabatini, *Pratica di fabbricar scene, e machine ne teatri* (Pesaro, 1637), bk. I, chap. 37.

9. "Un alpestre scoglio in mezzo all'onde, le quali nella più lontana parte della prospettiva si videro sempre ondeggiar con molta vaghezza." For this and other details that follow, see Follino, *Compendio,* in Solerti, *Albori,* II, 145ff. N. Sabatini dedicates chaps. 27–34 of bk. II to the sea, to its motion, and to the motion of ships, sea monsters, and so on.

10. Follino, *Compendio,* in Solerti, *Albori,* II, 256. The stage directions of the libretto are quoted (*ibid.,* p. 249): "Here [the ungrateful souls] descend into the theater dancing ... " (Qui scendono [le anime ingrate] nel teatro danzando ...). The fact that the most essential part of the performance was meant to take place in the "orchestra" suggested an arrangement of which no mention is made in the description of other performances: "On that part of the wall, which on the right side of the theater is placed between the end of the seats and the stage, was a grand box where the honorable ambassadors were seated; and opposite that was another box of the same form where there were a large number of musicians with different stringed and wind instruments." It would have been difficult to have the dance in the orchestra accompanied by instrumentalists placed between the wings. Dancers descending into the central part of the hall can be seen in the engraving by Callot that represents the first *intermedio* of *La liberazione di Tirreno e d'Arnea,* performed in Florence in 1617 in the Sala delle Commedie at the Uffizi.

11. The greatest theater of the day was built with tournaments and "ballets on horseback" (balletti a cavallo) particularly in mind and was in fact inaugurated with the tournament *Mercurio e Marte,* which Monteverdi wrote the music for. See its plan reproduced from the libretto of *Le Nozze di Nettuno* in *Enciclopedia dello Spettacolo,* I (Florence, 1954), 275.

12. See essay 18.

13. "[Commedia] che sarà singolare, posciaché tutti li interlocutori parleranno musicalmente." The texts of the two letters along with the March 1 letter by Francesco Gonzaga are given in Solerti, *Gli albori,* I, 68–70.

14. For the little we know about the activity of the Invaghiti, see L. Carnevali, "Cenni storici dell'Accademia Virgiliana," *Atti e Memorie della R. Accademia Virgiliana* 11 (1886–1888), 9–12.

15. D. De Paoli, *Monteverdi*, 2nd ed. (Milan, 1979), p. 72 n. 1. Margherita Gonzaga, sister of Vincenzo and widow of Alfonso II d'Este, seems to have occupied (*ca.* 1600) an apartment in that part of the ducal palace where the apartment called Maria Teresa's was later created. The Galleria dei Fiumi takes its name from the later eighteenth-century painted decorations of Giorgio Anselmi.

16. I do not know what the "usual scenic theater" might have been, whether it was the one restored by Ippolito Andreasi and Antonio M. Viani after the fire of 1558, or the theater used for comedies near Piazza delle Arche, or some other. Alessandro Striggio's academy name is given by the *Lettera cronologica* of Eugenio Cagnoni, published in the appendix to *Mantova. Le lettere* (Mantua, n.d.), vol. II (see p. 621 in particular), where confirmation of Francesco Rasi's participation in *Orfeo*, undoubtedly in the part of the protagonist, is also given.

17. See, in the instructions of the score (Venice, 1609), the divergence between the simple request for particular instruments ("si suona con ...") and the indication of instruments actually used in the performance of 1607 ("fu sonato con ..." or "fu concertato al suon di ..." and so on). The directions regarding *cornetti* and brass instruments all belong to the first group; probably such instruments were excluded in 1607 and the infernal ethos of the instrumentation was reduced to the use of organ with wooden pipes and regal. Only two instructions mention brass instruments: the first is, "Toccata played by all the instruments before the raising of the curtain, and it is played a tone higher if one wishes to play the trumpets with mutes"; and the second indication, a negative one at the end of Act IV, is "*Cornetti*, trombones, and regals tacet." For the toccata one would say that even when the score was printed, Monteverdi found playing "con tutti li strumenti" in C major admissible; it is not clear whether "a tone higher" was prescribed for the trumpets because the mute carried the actual sounds to the pitch of C, or because the "trumpets with mutes" were normally in D. The directions of the "fu sonato con" type also speak of instruments behind the stage (but not alongside it); the directions at the beginning of act V ("Two organs with wooden pipes and two chitarroni harmonized this song, one playing in the left corner of the stage, the other in the right") may also refer to a placement (for echo effect) at the two corners of the front of the stage.

18. See essay 18, note 44.

19. "At fifteen or twenty bars, exit the Prologue, that is, Ovid, making sure to accompany his step with the sound of the symphony; ... after coming to the spot where he thinks it suitable to commence, let him begin without further walking; above all, let the singing be full of majesty, gesticulating more or less according to the emotional pitch of the concerto, watching, however, that every step or gesture be in agreement with the rhythm of the playing and singing." From Marco da Gagliano, *La Dafne* (Florence, 1608), quoted by

Solerti, *Gli albori*, II, 70. See also the "Passeggio" in *Combattimento* and the "entrata e passeggio" of the ballet "Volgendo il ciel"—"Movete al mio bel suon."

20. "... mostrava selve vaghissime, e rilevate e dipinte, accomodatevi con un bel disegno, e per i lumi ben dispostivi, piene di una luce come di giorno." From Solerti, *Albori*, II, 113. Adriano Cavicchi kindly suggested a comparison with the illustration of the prologue to *Il pastor fido* in the 1602 Ciotti edition; it in fact contains (even though adapted to book format) all the elements that may have been part of the sylvan setting of *Orfeo* (especially for act I), that is, the "resounding waves" of a stream, the trees, and the distant view of a temple. It is one more indication of the affinities that link the early operas to Guarini's tragicomedy.

21. Monteverdi never makes a clear distinction between *sinfonie*, which usually accompany any sort of stage action, and *ritornelli*, which ought to introduce or conclude a vocal piece; but he gives the shortest instrumental pieces a repeat sign, probably to be observed when the stage action has not been completed.

22. The two *sinfonie a 7* with *cornetti*, trombones, and regal accompaniment have an infernal ethos; for the sinfonia that frames the aria *Possente spirto* the instrumentation is not indicated, but it shares in the ethos of the orphic enchantment that subdues Charon and ought therefore to be entrusted to strings. Its repetition at the moment of Orpheus' meeting with Apollo is natural; what is unclear, though, is why Music's *ritornello* in the prologue is presented again before the first infernal *sinfonia*, unless the return serves to underscore the two powers set against each other during act III.

23. E. Marani in *Mantova. Le arti*, III, 167. On the various activities of Antonio Maria Viani as a painter as well as an architect and "prefetto alle fabbriche," see also in the same volume the essay "La pittura" by Chiara Perina.

24. Going against the more general opinion, I take the liberty of suggesting that the reasons for the almost complete elimination of choruses were not mainly economic so much as that the newer dramatic conceptions left no room for the chorus as character or as commentator; at the same time the vogue of danced *intermedi* also supplanted the chorus in the formal function of dividing the acts. On the first point, see the defense by Prospero Bonarelli of his *Solimano* (Venice, 1620): "I've been quite far-sighted, I dare say, *in not having choruses* in my *Solimano* ... though later in several other *frottole* of mine I came to introduce choruses: *endeavoring, however, to assign them a role and a scope more than to divide the acts* and to entertain the crowd, being convinced that that can be more worthily accomplished by others, with *intramezzi*, similar to their use introduced today, particularly in Italy." From the letter "Alla Signora Flaminia Atti, ne' Trionfi," in *Lettere in varij generi* (Bologna, 1636), pp. 245–57. For the danced *intramezzi* (that is, *intermedi*) in the opera, see those described by Benedetto Ferrari in the text quoted by Simon T. Worsthorne, *Venetian Opera in the Seventeenth Century* (Oxford, 1954), pp. 168–69.

25. *I teatri musicali di Venezia nel secolo XVII* (Milan, 1878), p. 55.

26. See essay 20.

27. Maria Teresa Muraro in *Enciclopedia dello Spettacolo*, IX (1962), cols. 1545–46.

28. "Nel Fine del Atto Secondo. Per Intermedio, un drappello di Ninfe con ingegnose misure fece vedere da un Palco il carolar de le Stelle. Apparve poi la finta Città di Cartagine . . . Opera del mio ingegnosissimo Signor Gasparo Beccari." The playhouses, frequented by companies used to making the most of chance situations, were probably less respectful than others of the Vitruvian canons. The passage quoted gives us the name of Beccari, who in 1642 also provided his services for *Amore innamorato* and who could have been the scenographer for *Arianna* in 1640; on Beccari, see Per Bjurström, *Giacomo Torelli and Baroque Stage Design* (Stockholm, 1961), pp. 45–46.

29. Wolfgang Osthoff, "Zu den Quellen von Monteverdis *Ritorno di Ulisse in Patria*," *Studien zur Musikwissenschaft* 23 (1956), 69ff.

30. C. Ivanovic assigns the opera to the San Cassiano, but the manuscript libretti (listed in Osthoff, "Zu den Quellen") indicate the San Cassiano in some cases, the San Giovanni e Paolo in others. If my conjecture of a première performance in Bologna is correct, the most natural consequence is to assign the Venetian première performance to the same group (Ferrari and Manelli) and to the Teatro San Giovanni e Paolo, in which the group was active.

31. Other operas were repeated in theaters different from those of the première performance: *Bellerofonte*, staged at the Nuovissimo in 1642, was repeated at the San Giovanni e Paolo in 1645; *Amori di Apollo e di Dafne*, performed at the San Cassiano in 1640, was also performed again at the San Giovanni e Paolo in 1647.

32. The drawing, signed by Tommaso Bezzi, "Ingegniero dell'Ecc.mo Sud.to nel Teatro di Sto. Gio. Grisostomo," now in the Sloane Museum, London, is reproduced by S. T. Worsthorne, *Venetian Opera*, opposite p. 32. Hélène Leclerc, *Les origines italiennes de l'architecture théâtrale moderne* (Paris, 1946), pp. 147, 199, thinks that the theater was thus transformed no earlier than 1650; Worsthorne, on the other hand, is inclined to believe the conjecture that the drawing represents the original structure of 1639. Bezzi, who died in 1729, was active in Venice during the last decade of the seventeenth century; his drawing therefore is quite distant chronologically from 1639. A Tommaso Belli, a fanciful creature, presumed author of the San Gio. Grisostomo, appears to me to be born out of a misreading and built up by the contagious obscurity of footnotes.

33. See M. Bisaccioni, *Il cannocchiale per la Finta Pazza* (Venice, 1641), p. 9: "The *orchestra* filled to capacity with spectators"; *ibid.*, p. 54: "And to induce the audience of admiring onlookers to leave the *orchestra*, for nothing more was left to hear, the curtain fell back [to its place] and the opera came to a close." Similar sentences may be found in *Apparati scenici per lo Teatro Novissimo* (Venice, 1644) by the same author. Concerning the superior view obtainable at orchestra level, see Sabatini, *Pratica*, chap. 40, "which way and in which order the spectators should be seated" (come, et in qual ordine si

debbano accomodare gli spettatori): "One should endeavor to have the feeble-minded and the populace take seats on the main stairs and on the sides, with respect to the imperfection of the machines which at times may be seen from these places, since these people do not pay too much attention to detail. But knowledgeable and well-bred people must be seated *at the parterre level of the hall* ("nel piano della sala"), as near to the center as possible, . . . for in such a location all parts of the stage and the machines exhibit their perfection, and so the details that are, unfortunately, perceived at times from the stairs and the sides as mentioned will not be seen."

34. See "The Forerunners and Origins of the Box Theatre," in Bjurström, *Giacomo Torelli*, pp. 37–39; with regard to this excursus it should be observed: (1) that the sections divided by partitions resemble but are not equivalent to boxes; and (2) that even the drawing reproducing the (temporary) arrangement given by Alfonso Chenda to the Sala della Podestà of Bologna in 1639 refers, once again, to a tournament. Nevertheless, the use of boxes must have met with rapid success, if it is true that the Teatro del Falcone in Genoa was already fitted out with them in 1653. Their use appears definitively established in 1676, date of F. C. Motta's *Trattato sopra la struttura de Theatri e Scene*.

35. If the information given by G. Damerini (and quoted by M. T. Muraro, in *Enciclopedia*, col. 1545) is correct that one Piero Gritti was killed in 1633(?) due to an argument that arose over a box in the Teatro San Luca.

36. Plays "performed in music" had to overcome considerable distrust and tests of credibility wherever they were presented to a public as yet unaccustomed to such performances. Whereas in Rome it had nearly reached the point that one no longer distinguished between acted and sung plays (and the dialogue tended to become that manner of speech which *for us* is typical of the recitative), in Venice the dramatic contributions of Monteverdi himself were an *intermedio* for a *veglia* (evening party) mainly centered on acting (*Combattimento*) and a tale comprising divine characters (*Proserpina rapita*), for whom the usual criterion of verisimilitude was inapplicable.

37. "Quale ha potuto del suo, e con quello di cinque soli Musici Compagni, con spesa, non più di due mila scudi, rapir gli animi à gli Ascoltanti colla reale rappresentatione di quella; operationi simili à Prencipi costano infinito danaro." Ferrari is echoed by M. Bisaccioni, *Apparati scenici*, p. 6: "Venice . . . several years ago introduced the performance in music of great plays with such scenery and machinery . . . as the richest treasures can barely afford in the halls of kings" (Venetia . . . havendo introdotto alcuni anni sono il rappresentare in musica attioni grandi con apparati, e machine tali, che avanzano . . . quello che possono con qualche difficultà nelle Regie Sale gli errarij più abbondanti).

38. A similar thought might later have suggested to Busenello the title of *La prosperità infelice di Giulio Cesare dittatore*, and it is the basis for Nicolò Minato's diptych, *La prosperità d'Elio Sejano* and *La caduta d'Elio Sejano*, performed at the San Salvatore in 1667 with music by Antonio Sartorio.

39. See essay 16.

40. See above, note 24. Badoaro echoes Bonarelli in the "Lettera" preceding the *Argomento et Scenario Delle Nozze di Enea in Lavinia*: "The chorus was an integral part of the old tragedies, entering not only as a character, but mainly singing between the acts with gestures and dances and with corresponding moans and shrieks. But in the modern tragedies it [the chorus] has become less conspicuous . . . While I have also introduced several choruses in the middle of the same acts, I have not made use of them at the end of the acts, for since the entire tragedy is sung, further singing of the chorus would prove too tedious, wherefore to give the audience greater satisfaction though variation, dances have been introduced, originating to some extent from the fable." The passage that follows (pp. 21–22) speaks of a division into acts and of the fact that "between one [act] and the other let one assume a greater passing of time than what actually passes, so that in all, a day's time may be reached."

41. The spiritual madrigals *O ciechi* and *È questa vita un lampo* from *Selva morale e spirituale* (1641) would have been well suited.

42. Alfonso Rivarola, called "il Chenda," the designer of the box arrangement in Sala del Podestà in Bologna in 1639 and first scenographer of the San Giovanni e Paolo, died in Ferrara on January 10, 1640. His place was taken, almost immediately perhaps, by Burnacini, who worked for Giovanni Grimani's theater until 1650, was replaced by G. B. Balbi when he moved to the Santi Apostoli theater, and finally went to Vienna. [The revival of *Bellerofonte* in 1645 at the San Giovanni e Paolo and the insistence on the same subject again in 1650 with the "fall of Bellerofonte" included in *Bradamante,* would seem to indicate a competitive attitude in regard to Torelli.]

43. Most of them are reproduced in the already quoted works by Worsthorne and Bjurström.

18 Monteverdi's Poetic Choices

This essay was originally published as "Scelte poetiche di Monteverdi," *Nuova rivista musicale italiana* 2 (1968), 10–42, 226–54. The translation is by David Morgenstern.

1. One tends much too easily to disregard the influence Ingegnieri may have had on Monteverdi. Is enough of his madrigalian music known to so resolutely discount any influence? In any case, we should bear in mind that besides being a polyphonist, Ingegnieri was a skilled player of the viola (as was Monteverdi) and had formed a "company of musicians" in Cremona that was called upon to join the choristers of the Duomo whenever the occasion arose.

2. See the letter to the "Studiosi Lettori" in *Quinto Libro de Madrigali* (1605) and the two dated October 22, 1633 and February 2, 1634, to an unknown

correspondent, in G. F. Malipiero, *Claudio Monteverdi* (Milan, 1930), pp. 71ff. and 291–97. [Now also in Monteverdi, *Lettere, dediche e prefazioni*, ed. D. de' Paoli (Rome, 1973), pp. 320–28 and 391; see also *The Letters of Claudio Monteverdi*, trans. and intro. D. Stevens (London, 1980), pp. 406–16. *Ibid.*, pp. 406–09, the opinion is maintained that the two letters were addressed to G. B. Doni.]

3. See the *canzonette: Canzonette d'amore, Son questi i crespi crini, Chi vuol veder un bosco, Raggi, dov'è il mio bene, Corse a la morte*, and *I' son fenice*. In addition, *Io mi vivea com'aquila*, in *Canzon napolitane a tre voci* (Venice, 1566; Stefano Lando, composer); *Sù sù che 'l giorno è fore* in *Canzonette alla napolitana*, by Giacopo Moro da Viadana (Venice, 1581); *Come farò, cuor mio*, in *Il primo libro de le napolitane, a quattro voci*, by G. Domenico da Nola (Venice, 1569) and in *Secondo Libro delle Napolitane a tre voci*, by Giovanni Zappasorgo (Venice, 1576); *Corse a la morte*, in *Corona delle napolitane a tre et a quattro voci* (Venice, 1570 and 1572; G. Domenico da Nola, composer); *Tu ridi sempre mai*, in *Il Primo Libro delle Villanelle*, by Alessandro Romano (Venice, 1579).

4. The first two in *Quarto Libro de Madrigali a Sei voci* (Venice, 1587) and the third in *Quarto Libro de Madrigali a Cinque voci* (Venice, 1584). [F. Lesure, C. Sartori, *Bibliografia della musica italiana vocale profana pubblicata dal 1500 al 1700* (Geneva, 1977), 2, p. 1177, give Guarini and Livio Celiano as the authors of, respectively, the texts of *Io mi vivea com'aquila* and *Chi vuol veder un bosco*.]

5. It is the first stanza of a *canzone* later composed in its entirety by Marenzio and published by him in *Quinto Libro de Madrigali a Sei voci* (Venice, 1591), but is not included in the publication of Guarini's *Rime*. For the attribution, see *Rime inedite del Cinquecento*, ed. Lodovico Frati (Bologna, 1918), pp. 142ff.

6. See note 4.

7. It is regrettable that the lacuna in the books of the Accademia Filarmonica of Verona for the period February 1576–May 1601, lamented by Mons. G. Turrini, "L'Accademia Filarmonica di Verona . . . ," *Atti e Memorie della Accademia di Agricoltura Scienze e Lettere di Verona*, ser. 5, vol. 18 (1941), p. 173, prevents us from ascertaining whether or when Monteverdi had dealings with the Accademia Filarmonica itself. *Ibid.*, mention is made of a deliberation of the Accademia concerning the publication of verse "di quelli che nel nostro numero hanno hauto spirito di poesia" (of those numbered among us who have had the spirit of poetry); a more detailed account of this is lacking as well, and we do not know to what extent Count Marco Verità had a part in such things.

8. L. Schrade, *Monteverdi, Creator of Modern Music* (New York, 1950), p. 128, was induced to make such an affirmation by his thesis, which sees in Monteverdi's activity the signs of a conflict between the criteria of Flemish polyphony as received through Ingegnieri's teaching and the suggestions stemming from "native song." Aside from the fact that polyphonic manner-

ism was so deeply acclimated and nationalized in Italy as to make dubious a "Flemish polyphonism," and that even vaguer and emptier still is the concept of "native song" in an Italy so variously regionalistic even today, the phase of compositions that were folkloristic in taste had already faded by the time Monteverdi's creative activity began. What did continue, but cannot be attributed exclusively to Monteverdi, was the quest of melodic spontaneity, generally denied to the melodic lines of a polyphonic composition, and for which the most common term was "aria."

9. Another female name, Maria, emerges in the *canzonetta Vita de l'alma mia* from the phrase, repeated in each of the four stanzas, "Ma ria voi sete . . ."; Monteverdi underlines it by having it begin in the soprano on a brief pause of the other two voices and caressing it with a brief melisma, whereas he does not give particular stress to the name Giulia in *Giù lì a quel petto*.

10. On the concept of *aria* and its importance in the stylistic formulations of the late cinquecento see my essay "On Early Opera and Aria," in *New Looks at Italian Opera*, essays in honor of Donald J. Grout, ed. William W. Austin (Ithaca, N.Y., 1968). [The essay was later a chapter of my *Li due Orfei*, 2nd ed. (Turin, 1975); in English, *Music and Theatre from Poliziano to Monteverdi* (Cambridge, 1982). See also the last part of essay 12.]

11. The same device is present in a madrigal by Willaert, *Amor mi fa morire*, appearing for the first time in *Il secondo Libro de Madrigali di Verdelotto* (Venice, 1537), but republished in 1563 in *Madrigali a quatro voci di Adriano Willaert*, and again in *Musicale Essercitio di Ludovico Balbi* (Venice, 1589).

12. Besides the dedication of *Primo Libro*, also offered to Count Marco Verità were *Giardinetto de Madrigali et Canzonette a tre voci de diversi Auttori* (Venice, 1588) and later *Capricii et Madrigali . . . a due voci* (Verona, 1598) by Paolo Fonghetti of Verona. An indication of the predominant taste of the day is to be found in the observation of Turrini, "L'Accademia Filarmonica," p. 185 n.1, on a list of missing books, a good many of which contained *Napolitane*.

13. On the basis of an examination conducted by A. Solerti, *Le Rime di Torquato Tasso*, vol. I, *Bibliografia* (Bologna, 1898), 389–446, the first Tasso madrigal to appear in print with music was *Stavasi il mio bel sole* in *Terzo Libro del Desiderio* (Venice, 1567; Stefano Rossetti, composer). A number of other madrigals, including *La bella pargoletta*, *Al vostro dolce azzurro*, and *Caro, amoroso neo*, met with some success in the decade 1570–1580, especially, if not exclusively, among composers connected with Ferrara and Padua. It is difficult to explain the presence of twelve texts by Tasso among the twenty madrigals of *Secondo Libro* (Venice, 1584) by Francesco Maria Mazza of Manfredonia. More understandable is the attention given to Tasso by G. B. Gabella in his *Primo Libro* and *Secondo Libro* (Ferrara, 1585, and Venice, 1588; both examined by Solerti but not by Emil Vogel) and by Stefano Felis in his *Sesto Libro* (Venice, 1591), the latter to be considered in connection with the poet's sojourn in Naples.

14. *Crudel, perché mi fuggi,* attributed by Monteverdian literature to Tasso, is actually included with a modification of just the first word ("Lasso, perché ...") in Guarini's *Rime* (Venice, 1598). The version used by Monteverdi is also found in the works of other musicians; it may have circulated under Tasso's name as one of the then frequent cases of mistaken attribution.

15. On Casoni, see G. Ghilini, *Teatro d'uomini letterati,* I (Venice, 1647), 116. He was from Oderzo in Friuli; in 1563 he was nominated "ad lectur[am] Dialecticae et Philosophiae extr[aordinariam]" at Pavia and a short time later, "ad lectur[am] Philosophiae ordinariam" (*Memorie e documenti per la storia dell'Università di Pavia,* parte I [Pavia, 1878], p. 173. He died in 1593. His *Gioie Poetiche di Madrigali* was published in 1587 in Pavia; it includes poems by various other authors and a good thirty-five by Tasso, and imitates the title of *Gioie di Rime e Prose del Sig. Torquato Tasso ... Quinta e Sesta Parte* (Venice, 1587). A madrigal by Casoni for Bembo, *Per questa viva del gran Bembo imago,* may be found in *Il Gareggiamento Poetico* (Venice, 1611).

16. A. Einstein, *The Italian Madrigal* (Princeton, 1949), p. 722. For the choice of Bembo's text, see note 15, above.

17. *Secondo Libro* is dedicated to Sig. Giacomo Ricardi, president of the Milanese Senate; in Milan the three volumes of *Musica di Claudio Monteverde ... Fatta Spirituale,* by Aquilino Coppini, were published in 1607, 1608, and 1609, Coppini being also a reader (of rhetoric) at Pavia; in Milan it appears that Monteverdi visited Don Cherubino Ferrari and, according to rumor, he sought employment there as head of the chapel of the Duomo in the interval between his dismissal from Mantua and his engagement in Venice; he perhaps went to Milan yet again during his journey to Lombardy just a few months before his death. See C. Sartori, "Monteverdiana," *The Music Quarterly* 38 (1952), 399ff.

18. See above, note 15.

19. See the critical edition of Tasso's *Dialoghi,* ed. E. Raimondi, vol. II, tomo II (Florence, 1958), pp. 667–68. The treatment of the various poetic forms— madrigal, *ballata,* and *canzone*—begins on p. 635, but the *Forestiero Napolitano* (that is, Tasso) had already entered into a lengthy discussion of the sonnet earlier.

20. It may be, as Einstein states (*Italian Madrigal,* p. 122), though I am not certain of it, that the descending countersubject has a negative meaning, but in other instances Monteverdi did not hesitate to illustrate negative concepts in a positive way; see, for example, *A un giro sol de belli occhi,* in *Quarto Libro.*

21. The erosion of the metrical form of the *ballata* after the first decades of the cinquecento occurs *pari passu* with the falling from use of the musical repetitions that had determined its symmetries at the outset. A certain number of Luigi Cassola's *Madrigali* (Venice, 1544) are designated as *ballate,* yet I am unable to find a plausible reason of form or content to

warrant setting them apart from the others. Tasso's love rhymes include a
certain number of legitimate *ballate* (for example, *Occhi miei lassi; Io non
posso gioire; Già non son io contento; Lunge da voi, ben mio; Lunge da voi,
mio core; Non son più Belvedere; Vorrei lagnarmi a pieno; Donna, quella
saetta; Non è d'Arabia; Deh, nuvoletta;* and *Stava madonna*), along with
other texts that, though evidently under the influence of the *ballata* meter,
depart in varying ways and degrees from the norm (for example, *Lasciar nel
ghiaccio; Ore fermate il volo; Onde togliesti il foco; Secco è l'arbor gentile;
Solitudini amiche; Non fu dolor;* and *Udite affetto nuovo*). *Non si levava
ancor* is among the latter but is designated as a *ballata* by an indication in the
poet's own hand (see A. Solerti, *Le Rime*, II, 414).

22. In G. de Wert, *Collected Works*, vol. 7, ed. Carol MacClintock and Melvin
Bernstein (American Institute of Musicology, 1967), p. 1.
23. See in particular L. Lockwood, "On 'Parody' as Term and Concept in 16th-
Century Music," in *Aspects of Medieval and Renaissance Music*, Studies in
honor of Gustave Reese, ed. Jan La Rue (New York, 1966), pp. 561ff.
24. J. Haar, "'Pace non trovo': A Study in Literary and Musical Parody,"
Musica Disciplina 20 (1966), pp. 95ff.
25. Most of the observations collected thus far refer to Wert and are usefully
reunited by D. Arnold, *Monteverdi* (London, 1963), particularly on pp.
56ff.
26. See Solerti, *Le Rime*, II, 224–25.
27. See my "Early Opera and Aria."
28. See *ibid.*
29. See the letter of October 22, 1633, in G. F. Malipiero, *Monteverdi*, p. 293.
[Also in Monteverdi, *Lettere*, pp. 319–24, and *Letters*, pp. 406–11.]
30. Other excerpts from *Il pastor fido*, besides those quoted in the text, were
used by Monteverdi for the madrigals *Ah, dolente partita* (act III, end of
scene 3) and *Cruda Amarilli* (act I, scene 2), which were given first place in
Quarto Libro and *Quinto Libro*, respectively.
31. The cinquecento composition of both texts is evidenced by the free madrigalian meter. This observation, which I made while writing these notes,
suggests the necessity of revision and precise definition for all current
ascriptions of authorship of Monteverdi's texts. It may further be noted that
the text for *Quell'augellin che canta* had already been identified by Einstein,
Italian Madrigal, II, 728, as coming from Guarini's *Il pastor fido*.
32. *Tutte le Opere*, Malipiero edition, III, 104, after the first authentic sharp of
the soprano, suggests unnecessary editorial sharps for the three successive
notes of "Rimanti in pace." Similarly, D-B-B flat seems to me to be the
authentic version of the corresponding passage, "Rimanti," also of the
soprano, at the beginning of p. 105.
33. This is particularly evident at the beginning, where the three highest voices
each state their thematic lines and tend to conserve their exclusivity, so that
the melodic line takes place in the shifts from one voice to another. The
delayed entrance of the bass establishes the contrast between the poetic

theme at the beginning, "Tu dormi," and the new theme, "Io piango"; upon the latter the polyphony thickens considerably, elaborating the chromatic ascent, which makes the precipitous drop of "a te che sorda sei" all the more abrupt.

34. It had already been set to music by Marenzio in *Il Settimo Libro de Madrigali a cinque voci* (Venice, 1595).

35. Malipiero, *Monteverdi*, p. 250 [also Monteverdi, *Lettere*, p. 241, and *Letters*, p. 312]. The letter lists *Armida* and *Combattimento* as compositions all finished, and immediately after speaks of "a short opera by Signor Giulio Strozzi, very beautiful and unusual ... entitled 'Licori finta pazza' in love with Aminta" (un operina del Sig.r Giulio Strozzi assai bella et curiosa ... intitolata Licori finta pazza innamorata d'Aminta), which is, however, only a project "much digested in my mind." The letters that follow are among Monteverdi's most stirring and show the alacrity with which he worked and continued to expand the project (from just 400 lines to three acts, and then to five). The letter of September 10, 1627, in which he announces sending the last part of *La finta pazza*, and the letter of the same date to Bentivoglio (pp. 267–71) already speak of the commitments for Parma. The last mention of *Armida* is in the brief letter to Striggio of September 25 (p. 274), but in the immediately preceding letter, of September 18, *Armida* (not *Aminta*) must be read, where Monteverdi writes "I have not finished it all" (non l'ho finita tutta). Apparently the work was supposed to include also the *ottave* already used by Monteverdi for the madrigalian cycle of *Terzo Libro*.

36. The correct version (*Gerusalemme liberata*, XVI, 40; *Gerusalemme conquistata*, XIII, 42) is: "O tu che porte / Teco parte di me, parte ne lassi."

37. It should not seem excessive to state that Monteverdi's judgment, not influenced as Tasso was by preoccupations extraneous to his art, is better than the poet's. The following is a list of Monteverdi's choices, using the *ottave* from canto XII of the *Liberata* as a basis, and giving the main variants suggested for the most part by the *Conquistata*; I have used *La Gerusalemme Liberata e la Gerusalemme Conquistata*, ed. F. Flora and E. Mazzali (Milan, 1952), II, 72–79:

1. XII, 52. The first two lines, left almost unchanged in the *Conquistata*, become, in the text of *Combattimento*: "*Tancredi, che Clorinda un uomo* stima, / *Vuol ne l'armi provarla al* paragone."

2. XII, 53. "*Dàrlati, se la cerchi e fermo attendi*" does not come from the *Conquistata*; the variant is meant to avoid a too brief presence of the Testo (Narrator). The following lines basically conform to the *Conquistata*: "*Né* vuol Tancredi, ch'ebbe a piè veduto / *Il* suo nemico, usar cavallo e scende; / E impugna l'un e l'altro il ferro acuto, / Ed aguzza l'orgoglio, e l'ira accende; / E *vansi incontro a passi tardi e lenti*, / *Quai* duo tori gelosi e d'ira ardenti."

3. XII, 54. The first four lines are those of the *Liberata* but arranged in the

order suggested by the *Conquistata* (3, 4, 1, 2), from which the fifth line derives: "Piacciati *ch'indi* il tragga ..."

4. XII, 55. "Non schivar, non parar, non *pur ritrarsi*."
5. XII, 56. "Stimol novo s'aggiunge e *piaga nova*."
6. XII, 57. "*Di molto sangue*: e stanco ed anelante" does not derive from the *Conquistata*.
7. XII, 58–60. Minor variants are not derived from the *Conquistata*; the only important one is the variant of the last line: "Chi la mia morte, o la *mia vita* onore."
8. XII, 61. "*Rispose* la feroce ..."
9. XII, 62. This follows the *Liberata* but gives greater continuity to the first four lines ("... li trasporta, / Benché deboli, in guerra *a fera pugna*, / U' l'arte in bando ...").
10. XII, 63. The stanza is omitted.
11. XII, 64–68. They substantially follow the more spontaneous version of the *Liberata*. It is an important "choice" to have stopped there, omitting XII, 69, more literary than moving in its crowding together of picturesque adjectives.

38. *Tutte le Opere*, Malipiero edition, VIII, 132ff.
39. *Ibid.*: "The voice of the Narrator shall be clear, steady, and of good pronunciation ... Nowhere shall he make passages or trills, but in the stanza which begins with 'Notte' " (La voce del Testo doverà essere chiara, ferma et di bona pronuntia ... Non doverà far gorghe nè trilli in altro loco, che solamente nel canto de la stanza che incomincia Notte); the stanza addressing Notte is in fact the only point in the *Combattimento* where Monteverdi adds measured touches of coloratura to the part of Testo and there is no need to add others. Monteverdi's writing abounds in coloratura where his taste so warrants; that he has not written in any indicates that its use would be contrary to his intentions. His approach is in line with the aesthetics of the new monodic style, which considered vocal ornamentation one of the more important means of expression (*affetti*) and consequently wanted the composer to be the judge of its application, not the performer. Against the abuses of too many modern performers and publishers (emulators of those opposed by the above-quoted passage), I wish to admonish: "nisi caste caute."
40. Like his father before him, Striggio, a few years younger than Monteverdi, had been to Florence before. His father was a madrigalist, his mother was the Sienese singer and lutenist Virginia Vagnoli. Striggio was a viola virtuoso (as was Monteverdi) and published three posthumous books of his father's madrigals; but above all, he served the various Gonzagas, from Vincenzo I to Carlo of Nevers, first as a diplomat, then beginning in 1627, as "grand chancelor": he was made count around 1613 and then marquis by Carlo of Nevers. Most of Monteverdi's remaining letters are addressed to him; those letters discussing *Armida* and *Finta pazza Licori* come under the brief rule of

Vincenzo II, and it is understandable that the two projects never reached their scenic realization, for the sole memorable undertaking linked to the name of the youngest son of Vincenzo I is the sale of a part of the famous Gonzaga *galleria*. During the war concerning the successor to Vincenzo II, Striggio worked in Madrid and Venice to obtain military and political aid for besieged Mantua. He died of plague in Venice on June 15, 1630, while trying to counter the equivocal and almost hostile conduct of the Venetian ambassador to Mantua, Marco Antonio Busenello, brother of Monteverdi's future librettist; see R. Quazza, *La guerra per la successione di Mantova e del Monferrato* (Modena, 1926), II, 103. His death must have been one of the motives that induced Monteverdi between 1630 and 1632 to receive holy orders.

41. I have mentioned some of the correspondences between the texts of *Euridice* and *Orfeo* in essay 16. For the music, see my essay "Early Opera and Aria."

42. *Orfeo* is called a *favola*, a fable, in the dedication to the score, and similarly Caccini defines as a *favola* his *Euridice*, also in the dedication. It is the most usual term for these early operas; but that one may also speak of *tragicommedia*, the term coined by Guarini for the pastoral genre, would seem to follow from a letter by a certain Carlo Magno (Solerti, *Gli albori del melodramma* [Milan, 1904], I, 69), who, writing on the eve of the performance of *Orfeo* and playing it by ear, uses the term *commedia;* he says "that will be unusual because all the characters speak in music" (che sarà singolare, posciaché tutti li interlocutori parleranno musicalmente). On Guarini's influence on the dramatic art and composition of early operas, see my "Early Opera and Aria."

43. Solos, instrumental ritornelli, and choruses are arranged in inverse order before and after a central point represented by the monodic "madrigal" *Rosa del ciel*, sung by Orpheus, and by a response made by Eurydice, almost to symbolize the crowding of nymphs and shepherds around the happy couple. Contributing to the unity of the opera as well, and also dictated by symbolic intentions, are the various returns of the ritornello, presented for the first time with the stanzas sung by Music in the prologue; when it returns as part of the introduction in act III, Hope is the visible escort of Orpheus, but it is his music which serves as the weapon for liberating Eurydice; similarly, the return of the same ritornello before act V announces Orpheus' return to the "fields of Thracia," where, abandoned by Hope and forever without Eurydice, his art and the unearthly comfort of the echo are all that is left him. With regard to the use of ritornelli and sinfonie at the end of the acts, see my "Early Opera and Aria."

44. The spectacular baroque manner of the *intermedi* already tended toward the use of massive choruses, but the chorus of the opera, both in its realistic presence as a collective character and in its formal participation as observer of represented events, is conceived as the polyphonic combination of the voices of the individual characters who have already variously spoken in the course of the action. That the chorus is formed of single voices is also seen in

the facility with which it divides into duets, trios, or even solos, then reforms
into choral communion. In *Orfeo* the following choruses carry out the
classical function of moralizing over the event, traditional in cinquecento
theater: the one beginning with *Alcun non sia* (preceded by a ritornello) in
act I; *Non si fidi huom mortale* (to which the choral repetition of the
messenger's shout serves as a ritornello) in act II; *Nulla impresa* (framed by
two repetitions of the seven-part sinfonia) in act III; *È la virtute un raggio*
(similarly framed) in act IV; and *Vanne Orfeo* (two stanzas preceded by a
ritornello) in act V. With reference to act V, the divergence is well known
between the so-called "tragic" finale of the libretto (I too have used the
adjective several times, but in reality there is no clear indication that the
Bacchantes kill or have killed Orpheus) and the apotheosis of the score. The
libretto is more in keeping with the myth (and the anger of the Bacchantes is more than justified by the unbearable misogynous proparoxytone
lines that young Striggio gives Orpheus, reminiscent of Sannazaro or
Ariosto); the score, with the presence of the *deus ex machina* and the
"regular" comment of the chorus, is formally more classical. We may never
know whether the music for the Bacchic finale was written and performed;
in order to visualize the "regular" finale, however, it is necessary to allow
that shepherds and nymphs can appear magically in a place which a moment
earlier had been remote and deserted. Another possibility is that the chorus is
sung by celestial entities accompanying Apollo and that the *moresca* is a
reduced version, purely mimic, of the action of the Bacchantes. What is
certain is that *moresca* is more a Bacchic than a pastoral term, or to put it in
Nietzschean terms, more Dionysian than Apollonian.

45. These are parts of the action in which the dialogue is predominant and
obliges the music to follow its open progression; even in these, however,
recitative units can be recognized, separating themselves from the rest, even
if internally they are organized along oratorical lines (like the polyphonic
madrigals of the recitative type); an example can be seen in the narrative of
the (female) messenger, *In un fiorito prato*. A lesser unit of this type is the
immediately preceding phrase, also stated by the messenger, "A te ne vengo,
Orfeo," metrically and musically concluded by Orpheus' "Ohimè!" Its
course (but not its logical and musical continuity) is interrupted by another
exclamation of Orpheus, which creates, with respect to the uninterrupted
continuity, a marvelous superimposition (not succession) of tonal planes.

46. The first part of act II, up to Orpheus' polystrophic "song," no less than the
second part, is all dialogue; but Monteverdi's and Striggio's shepherds, in
strict adherence to the aesthetics of Guarini's "tragicomedy," converse in
song and in precisely defined forms, when their hearts are not agitated by
overly intense emotions. Orpheus' first song is monostrophic, to which the
sinfonia typographically concluding act I acts as an introductory ritornello.
(Sinfonia and song are joined by stylistic and rhythmical analogies, and
both ought to be modernly transcribed in 3/2 with the first two notes on the
upbeat: the instrumental piece is called sinfonia because, besides preparing

Orpheus' song, it is meant to allow time for the exit of Eurydice and her female companions.) What follows, still paired and intercalated with ritornelli, are the brief strophes of one shepherd, of two, and of another two (the response to the last is given by the whole chorus). Though Striggio's lines are far from the metric agility of Chiabrera, Monteverdi does his best to vary the rhythmic modes and maintain an economy and precision of style, similar to that found in *Scherzi musicali*. The brevity of the metric design often leads to concluding the strophe with a repetition of the first line, text and music, already seen with a different style in the first song of act I (*In questo lieto e fortunato giorno*) and later taken up in the first section of Ariadne's lament (*Lasciatemi morire*). There seems no point in using the terms "tripartite form" or "da capo," both because they are associated with more recent forms a good deal broader and more complex, and because it is likely that the procedure initially got its start through a literary suggestion; see, for example, the madrigal *Sí, ch'io vorrei morire*. In the same year that the latter was published, there also appeared the collection *Infidi lumi* (Palermo, 1603), which boasted madrigals by twenty-three different composers, all beginning and ending with the same line from Tasso, "Specchi del cor fallaci, infidi lumi."

47. I find absurd the interpretation of this ritornello as an allusion to a church wedding ceremony (church and organ in Arcadia? Would Monteverdi have admitted them?). It seems much more likely that it serves to establish the tonality and set the form of the gnomic chorus *Alcun non sia* (three strophes: for two, three, and two voices; plus a five-voice conclusion).

48. Further on I discuss the possibility that the two Petrarchan madrigals of *Sesto Libro* are of a date not much later than that of *Orfeo*.

49. See the "Dichiaratione" by Giulio Cesare Monteverdi in *Scherzi musicali*, reproduced by Malipiero, *Monteverdi*, pp. 72–85 (in particular pp. 82–83) and in facsimile in *Tutte le Opere*, X, 69–72 [also in Monteverdi, *Lettere*, pp. 394–404]. The texts of the two "scherzi" by Giulio Cesare included in the collection are by Ansaldo Cebà, he too an admirer and emulator of Ronsard.

50. He was Pindaric in his encomiastic poetry (which he called "heroic" out of courtly adulation); he arrived at the Anacreontic variety with an eye to the translations and reelaborations of the Pléiade, but he also applied its meters and rhythms to satiric and religious poetry. Three of his brief odes, already written by about 1580, found their way into collections of polyphonic *canzonette*: he returned to cultivating the genre after 1590, still declaring that he was doing it at the request of *musici*. A letter of his written in 1595 speaks of a certain number of texts sent to Florence to be shown to Jacopo Corsi, to Rinuccini, and to Caccini (who in turn used Chiabrera's name to give a veneer of respectable classicism to the more frivolous part of his repertoire). In 1599 he was persuaded to publish them in *Rime Parte I* (Genoa, 1599) and to theorize on them in *Le maniere de' versi toscani* (Genoa, 1599), republished in *Canzonette, Rime varie, Dialoghi*, ed. L.

Negri (Turin, 1952), pp. 193–216. He took pleasure in abstruse terminology, but his metrical virtuosity, sustained by indisputable taste, was more analogy than imitation. Not least of his contributions to music history is his introduction, through Monteverdi, Cifra, and Milanuzzi, of the term "scherzo," which later met with varying success. The texts used by Monteverdi come from the *Rime* of 1599, where the Bacchic *Damigella / tutta bella* is specifically dedicated to the Genoese musician G. B. Pinelli; some of Monteverdi's choices come from the examples given in *Le maniere (I bei legami; Quando l'alba; Non così tosto; Dolci miei sospiri; Soave libertate; Vaga su spina)*; *La violetta*, a sample of "giambici dimetri scemi, e trocaici monometri soprabbondanti" (truncated iambic dimeters and augmented trochaic monometers), is among the earliest. Chiabrera's association with the court of Mantua probably dates back to a meeting with the dukes in Florence during the wedding festivities of 1600. He visited Mantua in 1602 and in 1605 received favors from Vincenzo Gonzaga; see A. Neri, "Gabriello Chiabrera e la corte di Mantova," *Giornale Storico della Letteratura Italiana* 7 (1886), pp. 318–19. For the Mantuan nuptials of 1608 Chiabrera provided the text of the challenge for the tournament and the *intermedi* for Guarini's *Idropica*.

51. With most of the music composed by Caccini, it was, from the official point of view, the most important of the spectacles given on the occasion of the nuptials of Maria dei Medici.

52. For the "Avvertimenti," see *Tutte le Opere*, X, 27. The actual rhythmic substance of the *Scherzi* should be extricated from the purely metrical data of the notation.

53. The entire question is summarized by Schrade, *Monteverdi*, pp. 170–78. Neither of the two madrigals of *Ottavo Libro* is strophic, which excludes any formal if not stylistic imitation of the *air de cour*. Also *alla francese* is *Confitebor terzo*, from *Selva morale e spirituale* (in part a readaptation of the music of *Chi vuol aver felice*), of which it is said: "5 voci quali si può concertare se piacerà con quattro viole da brazzo lasciando la parte del soprano alla voce sola" (for five voices, which may be concerted, if it pleases, with four *viole da brazzo*, while leaving the soprano part to the voice *a solo*). The direction "a voce piena" is not repeated. In my opinion *alla francese* and *a voce piena* are distinct characteristics, the first not necessarily being associated with the second; indeed, comparisons between the singing styles of the two nations tend to attribute to the French style a more restrained handling of the voices. The critical literature on *Scherzi musicali* is discussed even more exhaustively by C. Gallico, "Emblemi strumentali negli 'Scherzi' di Monteverdi," *Rivista Italiana di Musicologia* 2 (1967), 54ff. While noting that generally our views coincide, I wish to emphasize the literary origin of the term *Scherzi* and the classicistic meaning attributed in that particular moment of history to what Gallico calls Arcadian flavor (sapore arcadico); finally I wish to add that what Gallico, and others, calls "the singularity, or perhaps anomaly, of the writing in *Scherzi*, in regard to the musical features

of rhythm and meter," is neither singularity nor anomaly, but as general a fact as it is little acknowledged: the rhythm of sixteenth- and seventeenth-century music is independent of the metrical aspects of notation (see note 52).

54. The lines of *Vi ricorda, o boschi ombrosi* in *Orfeo* and of *Amarilli, onde m'assale* and *Quando l'Alba in Oriente* (with rhymes, in this case, ending with paroxytones and proparoxytones) are all octosyllabic, as are others from *Scherzi musicali*; the rhythm of the music is substantially the usual rhythm of the *frottola*, 6/8 or 6/4. The tradition of the *frottola*, which in the form known to us is anything but popular and dancelike, must have survived in some way, and it lived on in Peri and Caccini even before Monteverdi's journey to Spa. It is characteristic that besides Chiabrera, the only well-known author of the texts of *Scherzi musicali* (not counting those by Giulio Cesare) is Sannazaro, author of the proparoxytones of *La pastorella mia spietata e rigida* and contemporary with the flourishing of the *frottola* at the beginning of the sixteenth century.

55. Between 1600 and 1608 Rinuccini was often at the court of Henry IV.

56. Quoted by Solerti, *Gli albori*, II, 249, who in turn takes it from F. Follino, *Compendio delle sontuose feste* ... (Mantua, 1608). The noble performers acted the part of the souls of the *ingrate* and performed the actual ballet, with all the rest—Venus, Cupid, the mouth of Hell—surrounding them like a frame.

57. I have discussed this in essay 16. The word *tragedia* is the element most immediately evident, typographically in relief on the title page of the libretto printed in 1608.

58. These cares are even present in the lament of Arianna: "Volgiti indietro a rimirar colei/che lasciato ha per te la patria e il regno" (turn your head to look at the one who abandoned for you her country and her kingdom); and further on: "Così ne l'alta sede/tu mi ripon de gli avi?/Son queste le corone/onde m'adorni il crine?" (is this the way to place me back on the elevated station of my ancestors? Are these the crowns with which you adorn my head?)

59. The souls of the *ingrate*, played, as has been mentioned, by noble performers, emerged from the infernal abyss onto the stage, where Cupid and Venus had already conversed with Pluto; they did not stop there but descended to audience level, performing their *balletto* in direct contact with the spectators. Only one of the souls remained on stage and did not dance with the others: the soul who at the end had to sing the lament. This part was played by Virginia Andreini, who was admired as an actress and a singer but was kept apart as an outsider from the group of noble performers of the *balletto*. See the continuation of the text quoted in note 56, from Solerti, *Albori*, particularly II, 255–56 and 258.

60. Solerti, *Albori*, I, 107ff., suggests that *Narciso* was written by Rinuccini with the hope of seeing it performed for the Florentine nuptials of 1608. His reasoning is based on the prologue, from which it seems to me, on the

contrary, that one would have to argue a date after the death of Ferdinando I (who is not mentioned, whereas the prologue is addressed to Cristina di Lorena and speaks of "regie tue superbe nuore"). The prologue, furthermore, is spoken by Giulio Caccini, who must have been well along in years, since he is referred to as "cigno canoro più quanto più bianco."

61. "I am sending the present work, *Narciso*, by Signor Ottavio Rinuccini, unpublished, set to music by no one, nor ever performed on any stage; when the said gentleman was alive . . . he was so good . . . as to ask me to take it, for he was most fond of this work of his, in the hope that I would set it to music. I have attacked it several times and have fairly well digested it in my mind, but in all honesty . . . it has not turned out . . . with the kind of forcefulness that I would like it to" (Mando il presente Narciso opera del Sig.r Ottavio Rinuccini non posto in stampa non fatto in musica da alcuno ne mai recitato in scena; esso Sig.re quando era in vita . . . me ne fece gratia . . . di pregarmi che la pigliassi amando egli molto tal sua opera sperando ch'io l'havessi a porre in musica. Holle datto più volte assalti, et l'ò alquanto digesta nella mia mente, ma a confessar il vero . . . mi riuscisse . . . non di quella forza ch'io vorei). Letter of May 7, 1627, in Malipiero, *Monteverdi*, pp. 252–53 [also in Monteverdi, *Lettere*, pp. 243–45, and *Letters*, pp. 314–16].

62. They are the chaconne *Zefiro torna* from *Scherzi musicali* of 1632 and *Lamento de la Ninfa* in *Ottavo Libro*.

63. We have already observed several times the special care with which Monteverdi chose the compositions to conclude his various collections.

64. The declared reason for the journey to Rome in the autumn of 1610 was to deliver to the pontiff the religious collection dedicated to him, but it is evident that Monteverdi was hoping for other results than the admission of his son to the Seminario Romano, a request which appears for the first time in a letter written after his return from Rome.

65. On this subject, as well as on the much-debated question of Monteverdi's Vespers, see the decisive contribution of S. Bonta, "Liturgical Problems in Monteverdi's Marian Vespers," *Journal of the American Musicological Society* 20 (1967), 87–106.

66. The most recent list of Monteverdi's works, that compiled by D. Arnold, *Monteverdi*, pp. 178–84, and the list found at the end of G. Pannain, "Claudio Monteverdi," in *La Musica* (Turin, 1965), III, 383–94, give as anonymous the text of *Ahi, come a un vago sol*, which in fact is in all the printed editions of Guarini's *Rime*. Also by Guarini could be the three anonymous texts: *Amor, se giusto sei*, which has a metrical structure very similar to that of *Troppo ben può*, which immediately precedes it and of which further mention will be made; *Questi vaghi concenti*, which uses as its text two brief symmetrical *canzone* strophes of an unequivocally cinquecento type; and finally *Che dar più*, whose text is shorter and metrically freer.

67. The lyric Guarini does not enjoy good press among today's critics who, especially with an eye toward the sonnets written for the academy of the

Eterei, judge him to be an uninspired Petrarchist, unmindful of even the innocent hedonism (I particularly have in mind the opinion of Toffanin) which became one of the charismatic features of his *Pastor fido*. Apparently there is no room in their judgment for the madrigals, for which it is far too kind to speak of Petrarchism. But the madrigals, more graceful rhythmically and more epigrammatically pointed than his sonnets, in their time met with a success comparable to that of *Il pastor fido*. Literary criticism rarely cares to examine anything connected with music and often arrives at generalizations making a bundle of many facts that are both disparate and chronologically remote from each other.

68. The predominant technique is a quasi-canon a fourth above (or a fifth below) or in unison, which, over the relatively static accompaniment of the *continuo*, aligns the vocalizations suggested by the images of "giro," "stral d'amore," "torna al mio core" and the like. "Lasso" could serve as a classical illustration of the Caccinian *esclamatione*, were it not for the Monteverdian chromaticism on G.

69. Recalling the *canto alla francese* (see above, note 53) are the two exclamations on "Ah core stolto" and "... sciolto" and, to some degree, the solo beginning of the second strophe.

70. See, however, H. F. Redlich, "Claudio Monteverdi: Some Problems of Textual Interpretation," *The Musical Quarterly* 41 (1955), particularly 73ff., on the *continuo* of the madrigals, whose accompaniment is left optional. The fact that the *continuo* doubles the vocal bass in the passages richest in polyphony is not a sign of technical immaturity (which would continue through to the last madrigals!); when needed, besides fulfilling the function of harmonic support, it is able to engage in imitations with the vocal part (for example, in the passage "Anch'ella giusta sia" of *Amor, se giusto sei*), contribute to the madrigalistic rendering of the imagery of the poetic text (see how it emphasizes the rhythmic *sprezzatura* of the tenor in the passage "E per dispreggio" of the same madrigal), or propose meaningful thematic figurations (as the one suggested by "questi poggi solitari e ermi" in *Questi vaghi concenti*).

71. That is all the more remarkable with a dramatic text taken from *Pastor fido*.

72. See the letter published by E. Vogel, "Claudio Monteverdi," *Vierteljahrsschrift für Musikwissenschaft* 3 (1887), doc. 8, p. 430. The writer, the singer Casola, is generally reliable in his accounts, but that is not sufficient to prove that Monteverdi actually did think of writing music for Leandro's lament by Marino, which will receive further consideration in note 75 below.

73. The count was not even able to respect the prescribed order of rhymes in all the strophes.

74. The letter by Casola (see above, note 72) speaks of the text as given to Monteverdi by the duke himself, being about "a shepherd whose nymph is dead, words by the son of Count Lepido Agnelli for the death of Signora Romanina" (di Pastore che sia morta la sua Ninfa, parole del figlio del Sig. Conte Lepido Agnelli, in morte della Signora Romanina.) The blend of

cynicism, ingenuousness, and infatuation in the loves of Vincenzo Gonzaga is too well known for me to have to delve into the episode. Monteverdi fulfilled his task, but that he thought little of the poetic talent of the young Scipione Agnelli (who later became a ponderous historian) is attested by the resistance he put up in 1616–17 (what resistance he could) to the Mantuan requests that he set to music Agnelli's "favola marittima delle nozze di Tetide," or his *Alceste*. He used the same tactic for Marigliani's *Andromeda*, temporizing without ever refusing, until the matter was dropped.

75. See the preceding note. *Leandro* is a *canzone* of eight thirteen-line strophes, plus a brief *congedo*. It amasses description, narrative, a wordy lament by Leandro on the verge of drowning, the story of his death, and a brief plaint by Ero over the corpse brought to shore by the waves; at the close the *congedo* reveals that the entire thing is the tale of an old shepherd reminiscing to his younger companions.

76. Particularly his treatment of the initial and final phases of the madrigal, in regard to which he displays a storehouse of information and erudition but insufficient understanding. That does not diminish my sense of admiration and gratitude for his enormous effort, the fruit of a lifetime of research and intense communion with the subject of his research.

77. *Italian Madrigal*, II, 862.

78. It is a strange but understandable phenomenon that the exaggerated interest in the content and the formal research of the period that follows are both contrasting aspects of a common classicistic aspiration. The two cycles of *Sesto Libro* are the final crowning of the "tragic" phase and a leave-taking from what was becoming in the hands of imitators a facile and abused genre.

79. Text and description have already been given above.

80. Compare the more biting harmonies of "E garrir Progne e pianger Filomena" with the gentler softness of the corresponding verse, "L'aria e l'acqua e la terra è d'amor piena."

81. I find strange the insistence of those who systematically associate the ternary rhythm with the dance, as if musical literature did not offer infinite examples of dances in binary rhythm and of expressions in ternary rhythm having nothing to do with the dance (see, for instance, in the *Sacrae Cantiunculae*).

82. It is characteristic that the idea of the desert, which to us evokes a picture of arid plains or of endless waves of sandy dunes, in Monteverdi's time is always associated with a landscape of rocky and inaccessible slopes.

83. E. Santoro, "Claudio Monteverdi. Note biografiche con documenti inediti," *Annali della Biblioteca Governativa e Libreria Civica di Cremona* 18 (1967), 73–74, quotes a letter by Francesco Gonzaga to his father, from which it follows that on October 9, 1607 (Claudia had died September 10), Monteverdi was already back in Mantua (Davari and Solerti had already given news of this). Rinuccini, on the other hand, arrived on October 23, and a month and a half between Claudia's death and the beginning of work on *Arianna* would have been more than enough for Monteverdi to compose at least one, if not both of the madrigals.

84. Santoro's study, cited in the preceding note, shows that there is still the possibility of adding to our knowledge of the period.

85. Vincenzo Gonzaga visited Ferrara on an almost regular basis between 1581 and 1587; famous among his eccentricities is the sumptuousness of the retinue he later had accompany him to Ferrara in 1598, after the death of Alfonso II and the official takeover by papal authorities.

86. At first sight the composition seems to be in a sphere of Venetian influence because of the imitative and antiphonal interplay of the two choruses à 4 in which the voices are grouped. The two sopranos, one for each chorus, are dominant but are always supported by the rest of the chorus: more autonomous, on the other hand, is the ninth voice, another soprano (which thus recreates the predominance of the three female voices), held in reserve for a long time and only added in the second part of the madrigal to vie with the other two. The complexity of the *concertone* is increased by the fact that the two tenors, as well as the bass of the first chorus, have extended solo passages. "Stile concitato" is foreshadowed in the choral syncopations of "Io bramerei." Furthermore, it should be noted that the second sinfonia, which serves as an interlude between the two strophes, is nothing other than the middle section of the first; held as it is on the dominant, it effectively prepares the return of the principal tonality at the beginning of the second strophe.

87. It was given a new "spiritual" text in *Terzo Libro* by Aquilino Coppini, the dedication of which bears the date May 4, 1609. But it could also be the sonnet referred to by Monteverdi in his letter of July 28, 1607, in which he uncustomarily insists on the necessity of rehearsing the new composition before performing it for the duke, because "it is difficult for the singer to *represent* an aria which he has not rehearsed in advance" (è cosa molto difficile al cantore rappresentare un aria che prima non habbi praticato; notice the use of the terms "rappresentare" and "aria"). In *Una donna* Monteverdi applies techniques already tried in the duos and trios of *Orfeo*, assigning the first quatrain to the two tenors and the bass (with entrances spaced out and solo passages), the second quatrain to the two sopranos mostly as a duo, and the tercets to the five voices, which alternate, however, in changing combinations of three or four. The two tercets are separated by a strong cadence, but related by an intricate interplay of musical correspondences which assimilates the first line of the second tercet to the second line of the first tercet, and the second line of the second tercet to the first line of the first tercet.

88. Marino, arriving in Turin in the early days of 1608, was given the task of writing the "Risposta . . . in persona de' Signori Prencipi di Piemonte, & di Modena con altri avventurieri" to the *cartello di sfida* (challenge for a duel) written by Chiabrera for the tournament held in Mantua in 1608 for the nuptials of Francesco Gonzaga to the Infanta of Savoy ("Cartello" and "Risposta" are included among the "Capricci" of *La Lira. Parte terza*). I am not certain whether he was present in Mantua for the nuptials: in any case he

wrote one of his *Epithalamii* (Milan, 1619) for the occasion, which may in fact be read there on pp. 108–14.

89. The diva arrived, it appears, on May 23, 1610, with an entourage of family members, including her brother, Giambattista Basile, a dialect poet (and follower of Marino for poetry in Italian).

90. This is another criticism of Monteverdi made by Einstein, *Italian Madrigal*, which I am unable to agree with. That Monteverdi should begin to choose sonnets in place of the irregular madrigalian rhymes, often lacking order, is in line with the growing attention he was giving to formal problems, evident from the time of *Orfeo*, if not even earlier.

91. We have already come across it in *Non si levava ancor l'alba novella*; it is found again, besides the other Monteverdi madrigals, in one of the first scenes of *L'incoronazione*, the first duet between Nero and Poppaea.

92. The image is, I must admit, anachronistic and would have been meaningless for Monteverdi; in his day the curtain, if one was used, was lowered and disappeared at the beginning of the performance, leaving the stage open without interruption to the very end.

93. The text is Canzone VII from *La Lira. Parte seconda*. Marino has: "Sì, sì, con voglie accese / la Ninfa allhor riprese" (Oh, yes, started again the nymph with burning desire); Monteverdi modifies it to ". . . l'uno e l'altro riprese" (. . . started again the one and the other).

94. The madrigalisms quoted are only a few of the many to be found in the composition, among which the one suggested by "al suon de le mie canne" deserves special mention because it is anticipated on the word "fiori." I do not know whether the corruption of the line "Qui l'angelica voce e le parole" lies in an error of the modern edition or of the older ones. Marino, *La Lira. Parte prima*, has: "Qui l'angelica voce in note sciolse," which provides the rhyme and verb missing in Monteverdi's version.

95. The falling leaps in the finale are just one of the many madrigalian figurations of the composition, although these become particularly conspicuous not only because of the insistent repetition but also because of the emphasis of the simultaneous final descent in three voices. In contrast to the examples quoted above, in which Monteverdi tends to identify a character with one voice, here the words of the shepherd are entrusted to Canto and Quinto, two sopranos for a male character.

96. If one were able to take the sonnet literally (and the fame of the text and its position of prominence in *Settimo Libro* tempt us to do so) it would seem to indicate that Monteverdi was already thinking of the possibility of a warlike style, and therefore of a *concitato* style.

97. Following Tasso's lead, numerous poems were inspired by singers or by singing. Guarini has a madrigal on *Il basso del Brancazio* (Giulio Cesare Brancaccio, Neapolitan, courtier of Alfonso II d'Este) and another, minutely descriptive, entitled *Gorgia di cantatrice*. Marino finds that "al tremolar del dolce canto e caro, / l'anima trema e le sue fughe fugge. / Da' suoi sospiri a sospirar imparo"; so goes the first of three consecutive sonnets entitled

Canto in *La Lira*. *Parte terza*, immediately followed by the sonnet *Bella suonatrice* and the two madrigals *Bella cantatrice*. Of the many poems dedicated by other poets to this or that famous *cantatrice*, I shall choose only two lines from an ode by Tommaso Stigliani for Settimia Caccini; though they are addressed to a female soloist, they could well apply to a phase of Monteverdi's polyphony: "... ora suole alternar dolci durezze,/ora suol intrecciar dure dolcezze" ("durezze" was often used as a technical term for dissonances).

98. Further investigation is needed to determine whether *concerto* might, even at that time, have had the meaning it has today. Monteverdi certainly suggests such an interpretation with the proem arranged as an operatic prologue and the conclusion of a *ballo*, as in *Orfeo* and in *Arianna* (the finale of the latter must have originally consisted of nothing more than the appearance of Bacchus and Ariadne and a chorus and dance of soldiers).

99. What follows, including the *ballo*, comes under the category of "altri generi de Canti."

100. It is the madrigal set to Marino's sonnet *A quest'olmo*, with, in addition to the six voices, two violins, and two *flautini* or *fifara* (these last two briefly taking part to accompany a bass solo). It strangely interrupts the series of compositions for two voices, begun immediately after the proem, starting with *Non è di gentil core*.

101. *Vorrei baciarti*; but it is never certain that the term *contralto* and the corresponding key necessarily indicate female voices and not a special tenor type (compare the French *haute-contre*). The madrigal is noteworthy for form and rhythms as well as for a certain anticipation of the *stile concitato*, although it is not a warlike madrigal.

102. Guarini, to a much greater extent than Tasso, is a forerunner of Marini in the musical sensuousness of the language, and in the hardly veiled sensuality of the imagery.

103. From a letter of November 21, 1615, addressed to Striggio, it becomes clear that Monteverdi, having been asked for a *ballo* for Mantua without being given particular requisites, expanded one he had already begun to compose on his own the summer before. Monteverdi's remarks to the effect that the duke "take no notice of the present words which can easily be changed" would make little sense if the text had been sent from Mantua, let alone its being by Striggio. Interesting are the directions that the instruments be arranged in a semicircle with a chitarrone and harpsichord on either end to accompany Tirsi and Clori respectively (who were also supposed to have their instruments). From that it may be gathered that the *ballo* must have been performed (during the carnival of 1616) without a stage, otherwise the instruments would have been hidden behind it (perhaps this is the meaning of the phrase "senza inforare li cantori et sonatori," or "without placing the singers and players in a hole.") [D. Stevens, *Letters*, pp. 107–08, thinks that the unnamed addressee of the letter is Annibale Iberti, Striggio's senior as a court secretary, in charge of the Venetian affairs.]

104. These are, in addition to the sonnet *A quest'olmo*, madrigals XVIII, XX, XXI, and XXII (in a different order, though). The texts chosen by Monteverdi tend to be near each other in the poetic collections they are taken from (see the following note).

105. They are sonnet XII (*Interrotte speranze*) and madrigals XLV, LII, LIV, LXXVI, and LXXVII.

106. They are the second and the third odes, examples of "giambici dimetri scemi"; see them in L. Negri, ed. *Canzonette, Rime varie, Dialoghi* (Turin, 1952), pp. 196–97. The first is irregularly divided into two groups of verses by the return of a sort of ritornello (identical only in the last two lines); Monteverdi observes the repetition with even greater freedom than the poet.

107. C. Gallico, "La Lettera amorosa di Monteverdi," *Nuova rivista musicale italiana* 1 (1967), p. 287ff.

108. The text is given above, where I speak of Monteverdi's use of *continuo* in his madrigals.

109. I confess to not knowing who proposed the attribution, nor who F. degli Atti is. It cannot be the fourteenth-century canonist, who does not appear to have written any poetry (no less a sixteenth-century-style madrigal). Arnold, *Monteverdi*, p. 207, gives the name as "Francesca," but I am unable to find any trace of a Francesca degli Atti; it could refer (but it is pure conjecture on my part) to Flaminia Atti nei Trionfi, to whom Count Prospero Bonarelli addressed a letter in defense of his tragedy, *Il Solimano* (1619).

110. See an example by Verdelot in Einstein, *Italian Madrigal*, III, pp. 21–22. We do not know how extensive was Monteverdi's knowledge of the older madrigals, aside from those of Arcadelt, whose Book I he edited in 1627; see E. Vogel, *Bibliothek der . . . weltlichen Vocalmusik Italiens* (Berlin, 1892), I, 33–34.

111. The formal scheme is also underlined by the resemblance of the cadences, which always coincide with the word "amore"; see also the slow plagal cadence of the conclusion.

112. The *ripresa* is identical to the opening, but with the two voices exchanging functions; the last line is repeated again and again, the rhythm slowed and brought to the plagal cadence mentioned in the previous note.

113. The sense of minute precision I wish to suggest with this phrase is also appropriate, oddly enough, in spite of its more ample dimensions, for the six-voice madrigal *A quest'olmo*, which has the same highly polished finish.

114. They are *Al lume delle stelle* (see note 108) and *Tu dormi, ah crudo core*.

115. On the controversial question of the precise value to be attributed to the indications of rhythmic proportions, I hold a middle position between the thesis of a strict interpretation, often made impossible by the obscurity or irrationality of the proportional signs, and one of absolute indifference to their possible meaning. For a long time indications were dictated more out of habit than precise intention; there are, however, some cases, and I believe this to be one of them, in which the intention may have been precise.

116. Also for two tenors, and similar in its tone of contained and somewhat ironic affection, is *Dice la mia bellissima Licori* (Guarini); the actual aria, framed

between the opening narration and the slower rhythm of the conclusion, begins with the words of Licori, "Amore è un spiritello," and it too, with even greater fervor, is intercalated with passages of triple time. In *O viva fiamma* (an anonymous sonnet that imitates Petrarch's *O passi sparsi*) the sense of *canzonetta* comes from the rapid alternating of lines in the two voices in brief phrases spaced every three minims (then restricted to two); the intention is not one of caricature but rather of detachment from the emphasis of the text, a restraint which gives greater expressive strength to the slowing and then double slowing of tempo in the last tercet of the sonnet. In the other anonymous sonnet, *Io son pur vezzosetta*, the tone of *canzonetta* is set by the text (note how the pastoral element is changed from mythical to "sylvan," and the "ninfa" of old becomes a "pastorella," courted by "una schiera di pomposi Citadini"); in this case as well, the levity serves to prepare the contrast of the final tercet. On the other hand, the long recitative, often in unison, of *Interrotte speranze* (another sonnet, by Guarini) prepares the rhythmic hammering of the closing on "saranno i trofei vostri e 'l rogo mio." At least two of the four madrigals for three voices insist on a continuous, persistent pulse of the rhythm; each of the other two has a special feature of its own.

117. False relations play a definite part in the whole piece, beginning with "voi di quel dolce amaro"; I am tempted to accentuate them, anticipating the sharp on G and C already in the passages "di quel dolce amaro" (second time) and "di quel dolce non meno." The dissonant anticipation of notes belonging to the following chord is a common form of harmonic *sprezzatura* in Monteverdi.

118. This is one of the usual formulas with which poets, playwrights, and librettists professed their orthodoxy, although in Monteverdi's case it was not a question of religion but of dignity and personal decorum. The term *scherzi* recurs in the title of the 1632 collection.

119. Monteverdi felt the great sense of responsibility of his office deeply and spontaneously, but certainly that attitude also corresponded to the expectations of the Procuratori di San Marco. Proof of that is the extreme circumspection with which Monteverdi later had to prepare his return to opera, arranging things so as to show he was yielding to a general request.

120. Monteverdi treats the quatrains and tercets of the sonnet as so many quatrains, the most usual meter of prologues, and gives variety of recitation and ornamentation to the voice, while essentially keeping the same order in the harmonies that support it. The ritornelli inserted between the strophes are nothing but the last phrase of the opening sinfonia; this in turn is resumed in the closing sinfonia, to frame with its repetitions a new section in triple time.

121. The most immediate accompaniment is provided by the "Basso continuo per duoi Chitaroni e Clavicembalo e Spinetta" which form a chorus with the voice. The second chorus consists of a solo "viola da brazzo," two other parts (certainly viola da braccio as well) requiring doubling, and *continuo*. The third chorus, consisting entirely of low-pitched instruments, intervenes

(madrigalistically) only at "che soave armonia," and then joins the other two starting from "se foste unitamente." It is a sumptuous instrumentation for the number of instruments taking part and for the implied spatial needs, which transcend those of an almost private performance in a small setting.

122. On the prehistory of this type of "aria per cantare" see J. M. Ward, "Romanesca," in *Die Musik in Geschichte und Gegenwart*, vol. 11. It became a harmonic formula which lent itself to the recitation of poetic texts no less than the "Ruggiero" (see the article of that title by J. M. Ward, also in *MGG*, vol. 11). The text of Monteverdi's *romanesca* is an *ottava*, as is the text by Ariosto from which the name "Ruggiero" comes. Another *ottava* by B. Tasso serves as the text to a *romanesca* by G. Cenci in the collection *Le risonanti sfere* (Rome, 1629).

123. The wording used here is that of *Settimo Libro*; its equivalent in the title of the *Ottavo* is the phrase "Con alcuni opuscoli in genere rappresentativo, che saranno per brevi Episodij frà i canti senza gesto" (with a few small pieces in the *rappresentativo* genre, to serve as short episodes between the songs needing no acting), which makes me feel the possible influence of Giulio Strozzi.

124. The text of the proem is quoted by D. Stevens, "*Madrigali guerrieri, et amorosi*: A Reappraisal," *The Musical Quarterly* 53 (1967), 173–74; one of the many poets active in Venice (see preceding note) could have written it ad hoc for Monteverdi. Stevens emends the text of lines 9–10 to "Tu, cui tessuta han di Cesareo alloro / la corona immortal *Marte e Bellona*, / Gradite il verde ancor novo lavoro ..." (You, whose immortal crown have woven with immortal laurel Mars and Bellona, do also accept this green new work [of mine]) thus giving a subject to the verb "han" (which does not absolutely need one because it can remain impersonal, while what is much more problematic is the agreement "Tu ... gradite"); in so doing, however, he eliminates the only element that could make it possible to date the sonnet. The Monteverdian original "mentr'è Bellona" (You, whose immortal crown has been woven ... while war [Bellona] is with us ...) is perfectly appropriate for an emperor crowned in time of war. Line 11 can be interpreted as a reference to Monteverdi ("*verde* ancor") and to his respectable age; all of the sonnets in praise of the composer work around "monte sempre verde."

125. It has, in fact, the same restricted instrumentation: two violins and tenor viola. The latter drops out after the "tender" opening, but the two violins become extremely active, with the independence and vehement incisiveness that is characteristic of their use in the more mature warlike madrigals. The instrumental terminology of the time is often equivocal, but the nature of the parts shows that Monteverdi had in mind *violini* of a modern type. The violas, on the other hand, when they come in, will above all serve as accompaniment.

126. *Tutte le Opere*, Malipiero edition, vol. 8, p. 26, does not make clear which of the parts the direction "Viole sole toccate con arcate lunghe e soavi" (violas only, played with long and soft bowing) has been taken from.

127. The strophes are unified by the martial shouts at the end of each ("butta la sella!" "Tutti al suo posto," "tutti a cavallo," and so on) sung in arpeggio figurations on the tonic chord; only the last strophe departs from the insistent tonality of C with a sudden, expressive modulation to E major, then wavers between C and A major at the close. [The text is given by F. Lesure, C. Sartori, *Bibliografia*, 2, p. 1193, to Giulio Strozzi, the poet of *La finta pazza Licori*.]

128. It is in Rinuccini's *Poesie* (Florence, 1622), posthumous edition dedicated to Louis XIII, containing only poems pertaining to the French court. *Ogni amante* is another case of classical inspiration (or aspiration); it is entitled "Traduzione di Militat omnis Amans, & habet sua castra Cupido Attice crede mihi &c. Ovid. Eleg. 9 Am. lib. I Al Signor Iacopo Corsi." Monteverdi omitted some sixty of the unrhymed endecasyllables of the translation, but although he still had eighty-three left he chose to have an enlarged repetition of the first distich upon the entrance of the second tenor. Significant omissions are the second line (with which Rinuccini addressed Corsi in place of Attico) and some ten lines alluding to Vergil, Ariosto, and Tasso (the omission produces a seven-syllable verse: "All'hor ... ch'al suon dell' armi"). The variants are numerous, and more than a few are intentional. At the end of the section for two tenors Monteverdi alters the last line, thus creating a rhymed distich (typical literary madrigalism). But then "Senna real" becomes "l'Istro real"; three lines of Rinuccini are replaced by the new distich "di quel Gran Re ch'or sulla sacra testa / posa il splendor del diadema Augusto" (of that great king who is now placing the splendor of the imperial crown on his sacred head; another allusion to a recent coronation); the "Fiorentina cetra" by Rinuccini becomes "questa mia roca cetra"; "quando 'l civil furor" (the religious internal wars in France at the turn of the century) becomes "quando l'hostil furor," referring to the Thirty Years' War; "galliche squille" becomes "belliche squille"; and finally "O glorioso Enrico" is changed to "O gran Fernando Ernesto" (see Stevens, "Madrigali guerrieri," p. 175). "Ardito Amante" in *Tutte le Opere*, VIII, p. 103, should be corrected to "Ardita Musa." One could find both irony and something to philosophize about in the fact that a text written for Henry IV before 1604 (the year of Corsi's death, whose cultural importance is becoming increasingly clear) was revamped once more some thirty years later for the extremely Catholic Ferdinand III.

129. These two sonnets had been written "nel Natale del medesimo" (with reference to Henry IV's "vincitore contr'alla Lega"), and also were included in the edition of Rinuccini's *Poesie* mentioned in the preceding note. In order to serve for the *ballo* celebrating "il Re novo del Romano Impero" (third allusion to the recent coronation) their order was inverted. I will not bother enumerating the "political" variants; what is deserving of mention is that Monteverdi used for the introduction the entire sonnet *Volgendo in ciel* plus the first quatrain of *Movete al mio bel suon*; the latter is then repeated for the actual *ballo*. Once again irony could be found, as well as in the double use of

the texts, in the brusque interruption that takes place after the solemn polyphony of the line "l'opre di Ferdinando eccelse e belle," a gap "to fill which a *canario*, or a *passemezzo*, or any other dance at will is performed without singing" (si fa un canario o passo e mezzo o altro balletto a beneplacito senza canto; *Tutte le Opere*, VIII, 170).

130. The first quatrain and the bellicose description it contains are assigned to all eight voices, although the major contribution of rapidly struck notes comes from the brief interludes of the two violins. In the rest there prevails a thinner contrapuntal texture only occasionally punctuated by brief choral insertions. Evident madrigalisms are those on "Io canto," "un crin mi prese," "fur l'armi," "l'anima afflitta" and, once more with intemperate abundance, on "dà vita al canto." Notable here as well is the use of the two violins (see note 125), whose parts almost never double the vocal ones but at times even vie with their coloraturas.

131. These introductory remarks are reproduced by Malipiero, *Monteverdi*, pp. 89–92, and *Tutte le Opere*, VIII, p. n.n. (facsimile). The confusion I hint at proves the variety and multiplicity of stimuli and impulses, of conscious aspirations and unconscious tendencies, of reflections or mental habits and unexpressed intuitions (at times inexpressible) that contributed to the form and life of every composition.

132. See note 97.

133. Monteverdi divides into three sections (for solo tenor, for two tenors, and for two tenors and bass) the strophic text of *Ninfa che scalza il piede*, combining in one section the last two strophes. The metrical scheme is unusual: $a^{11} b^8 b^{10} b^4 a^{10}$ with the decasyllables divided midway by a strong caesura.

134. See the following passage in B. C. Cannon, A. H. Johnson, and W. G. Waite, *The Art of Music* (New York, 1960), p. 237: "With their dramatic presuppositions and connotations, they provide an artistic bridge to the new category of the cantata, which crystallized as a form of chamber music by the fourth decade of the century." Apart from the fact that I do not know whether the authors are referring to the fourth (1631–1641) or the fifth decade (1641–1650), the proposition is only plausible if one accepts that the "dramatic presuppositions and connotations" of Monteverdi's madrigals had already been in existence from at least the last decade of the sixteenth century and that the "crystallization" of the cantata continues to be quite unstable and changeable up until the end of the seventeenth century. In the minds of less expert readers, on the other hand, such sentences crystallize the conviction (which then becomes impossible to modify) that the type of cantata they know, consisting of a regular succession of recitatives and arias, was born out of the madrigals of Monteverdi.

135. I borrow the phrase, not by chance, from a contemporary of Monteverdi, that is, from the prologue (in music) of *Amfiparnaso* by Orazio Vecchi (1597).

136. In spite of the study by E. Schmitz, *Geschichte der weltlichen Solokantate*

(Leipzig, 1915), which even in the second edition (Leipzig, 1954) treats only summarily the problem of the beginnings.

137. The *Lettera* employs *canto spiegato* almost at the opening with a brief vocalization on the words "il cor stillai," but for the rest concedes only a trill of repeated notes on the final cadence. The conclusion is the only place in which the *Partenza* briefly expands in melody.

138. The piece, after an almost recitative treatment, enlarges into a kind of arietta which carries on through various modulations from F major to D minor. The melodic expansion is started off by the first half of the antepenultimate verse, "Ma tu non torni, o Filli."

139. The text, included in the already cited edition of the *Poesie*, p. 223, consists of ten brief strophes, each followed by the ritornello "Miserella, ahi più, no, no, / tanto giel soffrir non può." Monteverdi uses the first three strophes in his first section, completely omitting the ritornello; he divides the fourth strophe between the soprano and the lower voices (whose text should be corrected: ". . . e 'l piè/mirando il ciel fermò") and only then does he begin the first "miserella" of the ritornello, which is sung just once (with many repetitions of words) by the male voices while the Ninfa sings another five strophes; the last strophe, without ritornello, is used for the third section. On the composition see the comments of Gallico ("Lettera amorosa," pp. 229ff.), with which I agree overall, except perhaps in the overestimation of the "Pianto" as "il momento più acuto dell'arte monteverdiana della rappresentazione musicale degli affetti" (the keenest moment in Monteverdi's art of the musical representation of the affections).

140. The type of aria on *basso ostinato;* I mention it in *Early Opera and Aria.*

141. The folksy tone of the text is certainly not in agreement with the general trend of the cantata.

142. Malipiero, *Monteverdi*, pp. 88–92; see note 131.

143. Only after writing my text did I learn of a contribution by Joel Newman in *Journal of the American Musicological Society* 14 (1961), pp. 418–19, indicating that the text is by the Venetian Maurizio Moro in *Tre giardini de' madrigali* (Venice, 1602, which I have been unable to trace). Newman may also be credited with the identification of Alberto Parma as the author *Filli cara e amata*, which he arrives at from a source different from the one I indicate in the first part of this essay.

144. The text is a paraphrase of the Petrarch sonnet used by Monteverdi in *Libro Sesto*, and that probably explains its exclusion from the *Canti amorosi* of *Libro ottavo;* but in the Rinuccini sonnet the graceful and musical description of spring assumes a pastoral tinge, further reinforced by the names Filli and Clori; the interior Petrarchan desert becomes the seclusion of oneself in physical solitude; and the ending "or piango, or canto" suggests to Monteverdi more song than weeping. The music is a long madrigalian bit of duetting which embroiders into the counterpoint of the two tenors every sort of descriptive cue: the flower dance, the music of Filli and Clori, the gentle breezes, the hills and dales, the echo of the caverns, and the dawn; animating

it all is the *basso ostinato,* repeated no less than fifty-six times, compelling with its elastic rhythm of dance and brief, precise cycle of harmonies. After so much *concitato* treatment, contrast is easily created by a pause and a chromatic accent ("sol io"; is it by chance that here there is a G–G sharp?). The beginning of the line should be corrected, as is evident for reasons of rhyme, to *Zefiro torna, e di soavi odori* (in place of *soavi accenti*).

145. For these madrigals see the first part of this essay.

146. See F. Petrarch, *Le Rime sparse e i Trionfi,* ed. E. Chiorboli (Bari, 1930), pp. 333–34; Monteverdi connects the two fragments by placing together the rhymes "ori" and "onori."

147. More common are spiritual *canzonette,* such as the texts of the fourth and fifth composition of the collection, *Spuntava il dí* and *Chi vuol che m'in-namori.* The latter is reminiscent of the text of *L'Umana fragilità* in the prologue of *Il ritorno d'Ulisse.*

148. It is likely that he was weary physically but not intellectually. I wish to quote, not to adduce as proof, a madrigal by Leonardo Quirini "in morte di Claudio Monteverde padre della musica" (from *Lirici marinisti,* ed. B. Croce [Bari, 1910], p. 332).

> O tu che in nere spoglie
> del gran padre de' ritmi e dei concenti
> l'essequie rinovelli e le mie doglie,
> segui gli uffici tuoi dolenti e mesti,
> ma pian, sì che no 'l desti;
> ch'egli estinto non è, come tu pensi,
> ma stanco dal cantar dà al sonno i sensi.

> You who dressed in black renew at one time the obsequies of the great father of rhythms and harmonies and my own sorrow, do proceed with your mourning sad rituals, but softly, lest you wake him; for he's not dead as you think, but, tired for having sung, he abandons all his senses to sleep.

149. Malipiero, *Monteverdi,* p. 252.

150. That reinforces my interpretation of *L'incoronazione* discussed in essay 16.

19 Early Venetian Libretti at Los Angeles

This essay was originally published in *Essays in Musicology in Honor of Dragan Plamenac,* ed. Gustave Reese and Robert J. Snow (Pittsburgh: University of Pittsburgh Press, 1969).

1. The term is found in both libretto and scenario of *Le nozze di Teti, e di Peleo* (1639); see Donald J. Grout, *A Short History of Opera* (New York, 1947), p. 3.

2. Wolfgang Osthoff, "Zu den Quellen von Monteverdis 'Il Ritorno di Ulisse in Patria,'" *Studien zur Musikwissenschaft* 23 (1956), 69, lists seven manuscript libretti of *Il Ritorno* in various Venetian libraries, of which list he assigns only one, no. 5, to the seventeenth century. Los Angeles no. 17, "1641 Il Ritorno d'Ulisse in Patria di G.B.G.V.," reproduces the title of Osthoff's no. 5 almost literally and seems also to belong to the seventeenth century. The other copies in Venice have longer title pages, giving composer and theater and qualifying Badoaro as "Nobile Veneto," whereas no. 5 and the Los Angeles copy have "G.V." (= Giureconsulto Veneto?). Manuscripts of *Le nozze d'Enea* also exist in Venice, but they have not been thoroughly investigated. An unpaged copy in the Library of Congress is given by the printed catalogue as "probably 17th century." Los Angeles no. 18, written in a minute seventeenth-century handwriting (22 lines of text per page), has both pagination and 8° signatures.

3. "BREVE ESPOSITIONE Della festa Teatrale Del Signor ORATIO PERSIANI, Posta in Musica dal Sig. FRANCESCO CAVALLI Da recitarsi nel TEATRO DI S. CASCIANO. L'Opera è intitolata LE NOZZE DI TETI, e di Peleo" (no imprint, no date). The list of characters on p. 3 reappears with the same typographical setting in the libretto; the latter, however, omits the information that the performers "parte sono stati conceduti all'Auttore da diuersi Potentati. E parte sono stipendiati nella Cappella della Serenissima Republica Veneta."

4. "ARGOMENTO. Et SCENARIO DEL BELLEROFONTE . . . Da rappresentarsi nel Teatro Nouissimo" (Venice, Surian, 1642), and "ARGOMENTO Et SCENARIO DI NARCISO ET ECCO IMMORTALATI . . . Da rappresentarsi in Musica nel Teatro di San Gio. e Paolo" (no imprint, no date).

5. The dedication of *L'Andromeda*, dated May 6, 1637, states that the opera had been represented two months earlier—probably an understatement, since carnival ended that year on February 24. The description of the performance is reproduced by Simon T. Worsthorne, *Venetian Opera in the Seventeenth Century* (Oxford, 1954), pp. 168–69.

6. This is in part a continuation of the courtly habit of publication after the event, for the sake of prestige. It may also be that the printing of a libretto had to wait for at least the first reactions of the audience, lest the dedicatee resent the homage of an unsuccessful opera. Anyway, it was the librettist's business; the poets, not yet a professional lot, were most concerned with their own literary glory and with the benefits to be secured through a well-placed dedication. Thus they always got the lion's share, while the rest received only passing mention, if any at all.

7. See note 3.

8. See *Amore innamorato* (no. 21), "da rappresentarsi in Musica nel Teatro di S. Moisè l'Anno 1642," as well as *Il Bellerofonte* and *La Venere gelosa* (nos. 23 and 32), whose title pages contain similar expressions announcing the performance. The theater at San Moisè seems never to have had scenarios printed for its productions; in the other theaters the habit was discontinued after 1655.

9. None of these items, all reflecting the aggressive personality of Giacomo Torelli, are included in the Los Angeles collection. The last two among them

were dedicated respectively to Ferdinand II of Tuscany and Cardinal Antonio Barberini; plates from both are reproduced in Worsthorne, *Venetian Opera*.

10. Consultation of a microfilm of ms. Cl.VII, 3226 of the Biblioteca San Marco in Venice, containing the expanded version (unpublished) of Groppo's catalogue, made me only more aware of such shortcomings. I want to express here my thanks to Mr. Charles Troy for letting me consult his microfilm.

11. See Library of Congress, *Catalogue of Opera Librettos Printed before 1800*, prepared by O. G. T. Sonneck (Washington, D.C., 1914) I, 141.

12. This is the prologue addressed to Carlo Emanuele of Savoy, printed in the 1608 editions of Florence, Mantua, and Venice, but already modified on the occasion of the Mantuan performance of May 28, 1608, because the duke did not attend his daughter's wedding.

13. See Anna Amalie Abert, *Claudio Monteverdi und das musikalische Drama* (Lippstadt, 1954), p. 128.

14. P. 4: "Così io nel rappresentarla musicalmente hauessi hauuto ventura di non essere uno de gl'ultimi professori dell'arte, come il Teatro di V.S. Illustrissima, nel quale si è rappresentata è il più nobile di quanti hoggidì n'habbia l'Italia."

15. P. 6: ". . . toccherà à lei di darli quello studio, e quella diligenza, che io non hò potuto, e che merita il far recitare un'Opera à Venezia."

16. We can gather, then, from *L'Adone* that fierce competition led to pushing forward as much as possible the opening of the winter season. Placed in the regular 1640 season, *L'Adone* fills the gap that would otherwise exist in the record of the theater in San Giovanni e Paolo. Similarly, if we postpone the date of *L'incoronazione di Poppea*, and anticipate the date of *L'Egisto* (placing both of them in the regular season of 1643, rather than in improbable autumn seasons), the rate of two operas per year, adopted for some time by that theater, is reestablished. (The date 1642 in the 1656 libretto of *L'incoronazione* may indicate an early opening of the winter season.) Puzzling are the opening lines in the preface of *L'Egisto*: "Per non lasciare perire la Doriclea ho formato con frettolosa penna l'Egisto . . . scusa la qualità del suo essere, perchè nato in pochi giorni si può chiamare più tosto sconciatura, che parto dell'intelletto." They do not seem to add any credence to the date 1642 appearing on the Viennese score; furthermore, there is no record of a *Doriclea* before 1645.

17. Wolfgang Osthoff, "Zur Bologneser Aufführung von Monteverdis 'Ritorno d'Ulisse' im Jahre 1640," *Anzeiger der phil.-hist. Klasse der Oesterreichischen Akademie der Wissenschaften* (1958), 155–60.

18. According to Osthoff ("Bologneser Aufführung," p. 155), the title of the pamphlet celebrating the Bolognese performance is the following: "Le Glorie della Musica Celebrate dalla Sorella Poesia, Rappresentandosi in Bologna la Delia, e l'Ulisse Nel Teatro de gl'Illustriss. Guastavillani. In Bologna MDCXXXX. Presso Gio. Battista Ferroni." It seems to me that the date may refer to the printing, not necessarily to the performance.

19. Monteverdi's son Francesco had already collaborated with them in a 1636 Paduan performance of *L'Ermiona*, music by F. Sances. See Bruno Brunelli, *I teatri di Padova* (Padua, 1921), p. 74.

20. See note 3, above.
21. Ferrari and Manelli seem to have assumed control of the theaters at San Moisè and San Giovanni e Paolo in 1639, when Cavalli took over as a kind of artistic director in the theater at San Cassiano.
22. "Gl'habiti ben intesi, le numerose comparse studiosamente elaborate dall' Illmo Malipiero han condotto col maggior segno il possibile di private persone, cosiche per l'avvenire s'affaticherà forse in darno, chi sanza le Protettioni havute dal mio Ulisse cercherà d'uguagliarlo." The full text of the letter is given by Osthoff, "Zu den Quellen" (pp. 73–74).

20 The Lame Horse and the Coachman

This essay appeared in *Collectanea Historiae Musicae*, IV (Florence, 1966) in honor of Guglielmo Barblan. The translation is by Lowell Lindgren.

1. The little that is known about Melosio, which is derived from his own writings and from the epitaph in the cathedral of the Città della Pieve, is summarized by D. Gnoli, "Un freddurista nel Seicento," *Nuova antologia di scienze, lettere ed arti*, ser. 2, vol. 26 (1881), 575–95. Six editions of his works are listed by Gnoli (p. 576); I have been able to see only the second (Venice, 1673) and the last (Venice, 1704). [The first edition, edited by Domenico Bambini and dedicated to Cardinal Flavio Chigi, was issued "In Cosmopoli" [*sic*] in 1672. Neither this nor the 1673 edition includes *Sidonio and Dorisbe*; I do not know which of the following editions it was first entered in.]
2. "Honorato di Musica Dal Signor Nicolo Fontè E rappresentato in Venezia nel Teatro di San Moisè l'Anno 1642," *Poesie e prose* (Venice, 1704) pp. 331–408.
3. "Fatto rappresentare nel Teatro Regio di Milano l'anno 1653," *ibid.*, pp. 221–90. [*L'Orione* is appended to, rather than included in, the 1672 and 1673 editions; that is to say, it is set in the same type but with separate frontispiece and pagination. However, the 1672 (c. 4v, n. n.) has a "Breve indice" listing "L'Orione. Dramma 352" as the last item of the volume; 352 actually refers to the last page of Melosio's "Discorsi accademici," which is immediately followed by the frontispiece of *L'Orione* as p. 1, n. n., of a libretto consisting of 96 pages.]
4. "All'illustrissimo . . . Signor Michele Morosini Dell'Illustrissimo Signor Andrea Fu dell'Illustrissimo, & Eccellentissimo Sig. Barbone Procuratore . . . Di Casa li 16. Febr. 1642." The end date of Melosio's first Roman sojourn is known from the sonnet entitled "Si parte di Corte nel giorno di San Lorenzo l'Anno 1640" (Upon leaving the court on the name day of St. Laurentius [August 10] in the year 1640), *ibid.*, p. 448. We do not know what induced Melosio to make his home in Venice, or how he managed to establish himself there as a librettist; the modest tasks he had accomplished while serving Cardinal Spada in Rome (Gnoli, "Un freddurista," p. 579) had certainly kept him away from the operatic activities of the Barberini family.

5. L'Autore a chi Legge. Io sperava quest'anno di farti vedere su le scene l'Orione opera già compita, ma non ha potuto la spada d'un Astro sì formidabile, spaventar la mia contraria fortuna, né superar la malignità della mia stella. Chi doveva farlo rappresentare s'è scusato con la penuria del tempo, dandomi a conoscere la debolezza delle mie fatighe oppresse colla brevità da un Vecchio, che non può nuocere solo colla longhezza; Ma io credo più tosto, che un Teatro avezzo a dar ricetto a le più sublime Deità del Cielo, si sia sdegnato d'accoglier il povero Orione, che nacque dentro una sozza pelle dall'orina di tre Dei vagabondi. Comparirà forse un'altr'anno, e purgato con una lunga quarantina l'appestato fetore della sua nascita, potrà ammettersi all'humano commercio. La spiegatura del presente soggetto m'è stato ordinato quà in Venetia. Questo ti basti per argomento, che non vi può esser cosa di buono, perché le Muse mal volentieri obediscono, e come Vergini, è gran delitto il violentarle. l'hò tolto dall'Adone del Marino nel canto de gli errori per metterlo in un Drama pieno d'imperfettioni, e senza ch'io te l'avvisi conoscerai da te stesso che m'è precipitato dalla pena in pochissimi giorni. La Musica, e la pittura ricopriranno in qualche parte i miei difetti, ma vi sarà nondimeno gran bisogno della tua cortesia, ò Lettore, in compatirli, Ti sarà facile il farlo, e senti come; Se tù non vedi machine, puoi dire, che essendo io sicurissimo della mia vergogna ho stimato superfluo il machinarmela. Se comparisce una Regina con poco numeroso corteggio, considera, ch'ella è fuori del proprio regno, e che deve forse andarsene incognita; Se ti spiace la povertà degli abiti, sovvengati, che ella è Vedova, e che non pensa ad altre pompe, che a quelle della vendetta. Sopra'l tutto scusa la signora Antonina rappresentante la Dorisbe, la quale ti giuro, che dubitando di non apparir temeraria haveva risoluto di non calcar più la scena, in tempo, che le più sublimi cantatrici del nostro secolo operano meraviglie, ma rincoratasi colla consideratione, che il Sole gradisce non meno i saluti di più palustri, che di più canori Augelli, ha mutato consiglio. La voce di questa virtuosa pochi anni sono, non potea giungere all'orecchio senza offesa del cuore. Ella riusciva mortale, perche haveva in sè del divino; onde mi credo che Apollo Dio, e della medicina, e del canto, habbia voluto diminuirla per benefitio del mondo, come apunto si fa de' veleni, che per renderli giovevoli, è necessario prepararli coi loro contrarij. Di me dì pure ciò che t'aggrada. Ti basti di sapere, che io compongo per mero capriccio, e che non voglio obligarmi alla stretta osservanza delle regole; ne vender la mia libertà per comprarmi la lode di buono immitatore.

6. [Lo scherno degli Dei is the title of a mock-heroic poem published in Rome in 1618 by Francesco Bracciolini (1566–1645), a well-known poet connected with the court of the Barberini Pope Urban VIII.]

7. It is my impression that in this first phase of commercial opera, theater managements were concerned only with the printing of an operatic scenario, that is, a scene-by-scene summary of the action. The printing of the libretto was left to the care and profit of the poet, who, to avoid offering to a patron a work that had been unfavorably received by the public, tended to give the

dedication a date later than the first performance (eventually, the date of the following day). The dedication of the libretto of *Amore innamorato* (Venice, Battista Surian, 1642) is dated "il primo del 1642" (the first day of 1642). Giovanni Faustini, who usually furnished no dedication, did write one for *La virtù de' strali d'Amore* (Venice, Pietro Miloco, 1642), yet avoided the problem by not providing a date; since his opera was the only one presented during the season by the theater at San Cassiano, it was probably first performed during the final days of 1641 or the first days of 1642.

8. The scenario was omitted in subsequent editions, which were printed because of the enormous success of the opera. The scenario and libretto of *La finta pazza* are reprinted in *Drammi per musica dal Rinuccini allo Zeno*, ed. Andrea Della Corte (Turin, 1958), I, 333–430.

9. See *La finta pazza*, act II, scenes 8 and 10; and III, 2, 3, and 6. In II, 10, the madness of the protagonist introduces a dance of "pazzerelli buffoni di corte" (foolish buffoons of the court), which constitutes the *intermedio*.

10. Neither of these texts was printed during the production of the opera. *Didone* was published in Busenello, *Hore ociose* (Venice, A. Giuliani, 1656), while *La ninfa avara* (Venice: heirs of G. Salis) may have appeared in 1642 (with an incorrect year—1662—given on the title page).

11. Although the text as well as the music of *La finta pazza Licori* is lost, we can conjecturally trace back to it similar passages in two possible descendants: compare Iarba in *Didone*: "Meritevole sei / ch'in tuon d'F, fa ut, / ti canti in un l'Arcadia, e il Calicut" (You deserve to be sung at in the key of F-fa-ut by both the Arcadia and the Calicut [old spelling of Calcutta]) with Lilla in *La ninfa avara*: "Cantami un poco in tuono d'effaut / s'è più bella l'Arcadia, ò Calicut" (Do sing to me in the key of F-fa-ut whether Arcadia is more beautiful, or Calicut). Lilla's lines lead to a strophic aria by the rustic Ghiandone ("Amor proprio è una rapa"), which had already been sung by the rustic Tacco in Ferrari's *Pastor regio* of 1640.

12. The plot of another work of 1642, *Gli amori di Giasone e d'Isifile* by Persiani and Marazzoli, is oriented decisively toward comedy. Another work, likewise written by Persiani for the theater of San Giovanni e Paolo in 1642, is the strangely anachronistic fable of *Narciso et Ecco immortalati* (in which, however, the apotheosis of Narciso is reminiscent of that of Psyche in *Amore innamorato* as well as that of the canceled *Orione*). Persiani's dedications in these two libretti are dated significantly later than the probable first performances of these works: January 30, 1642, is given in *Narciso*, and February 22, 1642, in *Giasone*.

13. Such replacement was also a Venetian fashion at the time: in 1641 the prologue of *La finta pazza* was recited by Consiglio Improviso (Sudden Resolve), and that of *La ninfa avara* by Inganno, Artificio, and Ingegno (Deceit, Artifice, and Cleverness); in 1642 *Amore innamorato* was introduced by Bellezza (Beauty), and *La virtù de' strali d'Amore* by Capriccio and Piacere (Caprice and Pleasure). The throng of divinities who otherwise took part in a prologue is exemplified by *Gli amori di Giasone e d'Isifile*, where the gods

despair because Jove, bored and distracted, no longer wants to direct human events; but the song of Armonia (Harmony) rouses him and returns his attention to the affairs of Jason.

14. In the spectacular, but incongruous, story of *La Venere gelosa*, produced at the Teatro Nuovissimo. See, for example, the aria "De ridete / Donne voi de vostri amanti," in act I, scene 4, which has an indecorous refrain, sung after the first three of the four strophes.

15. See III, 2, where Deidamia says: "Che melodie son queste? / Ditemi? che *novissimi* teatri, / che numerose scene / s'apparecchiano in Sciro? / Voglio esser ancor'io / del faticare a parte; / che a me non manca l'arte, ad un sol fischio / di cento variar aspetti, / finger mari, erger monti, e mostre belle / far di Cieli, e di Stelle. . . ." (What melodies are these? / Tell me, what *brand new* theaters, / what numerous stages / have been readied in Skyros? / I too wish / to take part in these labors, / for I do not lack the art, by a single whistle, / in a hundred various ways, / to create seas, raise mountains, and make a show / of beautiful skies and stars); note that the opera was given at the Teatro Nuovissimo. In the same spirit, Torelli introduced familiar Venetian sights into the scene representing the port of Chio; when *La finta pazza* was given in Paris in 1645, they were replaced by views of the Pont Neuf and the Place Dauphine.

16. In the Roman work, Poetry, Painting, and Music argue about which opera to perform, then Magic intervenes and, after determining the subject, summons forth an enchanted palace by means of incantation.

17. *Poesie e prose* (1704), pp. 113–64, 165–220, with addenda to each category on pp. 475–96, 496–537.

18. *Ibid.*, pp. 496–98, 499–501. Compare the former with "Aspettate: adesso canto," in *The Italian Cantata*, I: *Antonio Cesti*, ed. David Burrows (Wellesley, Mass., 1963), pp. 70–93. See also Burrows, "Antonio Cesti on Music," *The Musical Quarterly*, 51 (1965), 518–29.

19. *Poesie e prose*, pp. 106, 436. An unidentified musician is referred to in a letter, written partly in verse and partly in prose, and dated at Capranica on June 4, 1659 (*ibid.*, p. 215): "Hò veduto qui quell'Amico, non sò se dal Violino, ò dalla Tiorba, essendo comparso col suo solito Naso . . . Carico di Doble, gli parea mille Anni di lasciarne il peso sù i Banchi di Roma" (I have seen here that one acquaintance, named either after his violin or his theorbo—I do not know which, for he made his entrance with his usual nose . . . Loaded with doubloons, he could not wait to leave the weight at the banks of Rome).

20. *Ibid.*, pp. 98–99: "All'Illustrissimo Sig. N. Contarini. Si raccomanda all'autorità di questo Signore per una indulgenza, & in occasione d'una sua Opera recitata in Venetia nel Teatro di San Mosè"; and pp. 100–01: "Nel Medesimo soggetto. Al Signor Avocato Pozzi, mentr'era Podagroso in letto."

21. His paragraph serves to confirm the assertion (see note 6) that publication of a libretto was more the concern of the poet than of the management of a theater in which an opera had been produced.

22. [However, Fusconi's address to the reader in the libretto of *Amore in-*

namorato, the first opera given at San Moisè in the same 1642 season, also includes a remark about the weakness of the voices and the visual aspects (comparse), from which "a discriminating spectator will understand that what is made for the sake of profit cannot be perfect."]

23. [In the case of *Amore innamorato* evidence that Cavalli was the composer is provided by Fusconi's address to the reader, where he comes to speak of "la soavità della musica del Signor Francesco Cavalli, che con ragione vien creduto l'Anfione de' nostri giorni" (the sweetness of the music composed by Signor Francesco Cavalli, who is rightly held to be the Amphion of our days). I owe this information to the kindness of Lowell Lindgren.]

24. Cavalli's name does not appear in the extant libretto, found in Washington, D.C., Library of Congress, Schatz 1740, which is lacking pp. 3–4; his name was added by a rather recent hand to the score in Venice, Biblioteca Nazionale Marciana, ms. Ital. IV.444. The musical style, however, seems to confirm the usual attribution to Cavalli. [And he is definitely named as the composer on the title page of the libretto printed in Milan: "L'Orione Dramma del sig. Francesco Melosio posto in musica dal sig. Francesco Cavalli. Fatto rappresentare nel Theatro Regio di Milano dall'ecc.mo marchese di Caracena . . . Milano, Gio. Batt. e Giulio Cesare fratelli Malatesta." The dedication is signed by Gio. Antonio Franceschini and dated from Milan: June 15, 1653. I had no knowledge of this libretto when I first wrote this chapter and owe the information to the courtesy of Lowell Lindgren.]

25. [Professor Lindgren suggests that the prologue may have been written by Gio. Antonio Franceschini, who signed the dedication of the 1653 Milanese libretto; the prologue, however, is included in all the editions of Melosio's works which I have been able to see, including those of 1672 and 1673 (see notes 1 and 3 above).]

26. One must resist the temptation to call them *da capo* arias, because, in comparison with true *da capos*, they lack an exact repetition of the opening music, a full and stereotyped repetition of words, and a clear division into sections. Moreover, no proof of any relationship or continuity between the two types has ever been given.

27. "Cortese Lettore . . . il Soggetto di questo Drama assai prima d'oggi ha servito e di Episodio nel Poema Epico, e di Favola nel Dramatico."

21 Falsirena and the Earliest *Cavatina*

This essay was originally published in *Collectanea Historiae Musicae*, vol. II, (Florence, 1956). The translation is by Lowell Lindgren.

1. Filippo Clementi, *Il carnevale romano nelle cronache contemporanee*, 2nd ed. (Città di Castello, 1939), p. 435, extracted from the "Avvisi di Roma" in the Vatican Library, ms. Vat. Urb. 1095, February 25, 1626, on the performance "in musica, in casa del padre Edoardo [recte: Evandro] Conti dell'Adone del

Marini, ridotto in pastorale brevemente in versi sciolti, che riuscì benissimo, non solo per l'esquisitezza delle voci, ma anche per l'apparato e varietà d'habiti e vestiti e diversi balletti."

2. The plot is derived from Giambattista Marino, *Adone*, 1st ed. (Paris, 1623), second part of canto XII (*La fuga*) and canto XIII (*La prigione*). Although he preserved the general outline, Tronsarelli varied some particulars.

3. See Nino Pirrotta, "Costa, Margherita," *Enciclopedia dello Spettacolo*, III (Rome, 1956), 1555. Erythraeus (see the following note) wrote of Costa: "magis canendi artificio, quam turpi quaestu famosa" (more famous for the art of singing than for her shameful trade).

4. Alessandro Ademollo, *I teatri di Roma nel secolo decimosettimo* (Rome, 1888): "quale cioè delle due superasse l'altra per soavità di voce e arte di canto." [Ademollo reports this sentence as part of a quotation from Gaetano Moroni, *Dizionario di erudizione storico-ecclesiastica* (Venice, 1840–1861), which he defines as a rather literal translation from Tronsarelli's biography in Ianus Nicius Erythraeus (that is, Gian Vittorio Rossi), *Pinacotheca tertia* (Colonia [Amsterdam], 1648). However, I have been unable to find a biography of Tronsarelli in the 103 volumes of Moroni's *Dizionario*.] Ademollo suggests that Cecca del Padule was identical with "Cecca buffona," the protagonist of clamorous scandals. For Costa, see the preceding note.

5. Clementi, *Il carnevale romano*, p. 371: "gran numero di titolati e nobiltà primaria d'huomini e donne." A letter summarized in Alfredo Saviotti, "Feste e spettacoli nel Seicento," *Giornale storico della letteratura italiana* 41 (1903), 70, is less favorable in its judgment of the event, but we know how much any judgment would have been influenced by personal or political rivalries. The same letter identifies the place of performance as the house of Evandro (rather than Edoardo) Conti, duke of Poli. [Further confirmation, plus the information that the stage settings had been designed by Giuseppe Cesari, known as "il Cavalier d'Arpino," comes from Cesari's biography in Giovanni Baglioni, *Le vite de' pittori, scultori, et architetti dal pontificato di Gregorio XIII del 1572 in fino a' tempi di Papa Urbano Ottavo nel 1642* (Rome, 1642), p. 374: "Al Marchese Evandro Conti raggiustò il rinovamento della facciata del suo Palagio à Monti; e diede ordine alle Scene, che in quel Palagio servirono per rappresentare la famosa Catena d'Adone, Favola boschereccia del Signore Ottavio Tronsarelli Romano" (For the Marquis Evandro Conti he arranged the renewal of the façade of Conti's palace at Monti, and planned the stage sets which were used in that palace for the performance of the famous *Catena d'Adone*, a fable of the woods by Signor Ottavio Tronsarelli of Rome). Quoted in Wolfgang Witzenmann, *Domenico Mazzocchi 1592–1665. Dokumente und Interpretation* (Cologne, 1970).]

6. See also Hugo Goldschmidt, *Studien zur Geschichte der italienischen Oper im 17. Jahrhundert* (Leipzig, 1901), I, 8–29, 155–73 (musical examples); and Romain Rolland, *Histoire de l'Opéra en Europe avant Lully et Scarlatti* (Paris, 1895), pp. 129ff.

7. An ample disclosure of feminine beauties, beneath a profusion of veils and precious fabrics, had already been seen in Rome, for example in 1614 in the *Amor pudico* written by Jacopo Cicognini, set to music by several composers, and performed in the residence of the church chancellor on the occasion of the marriage of Don Michele Peretti and Anna Maria Cesi (see Clementi, *Il carnevale romano*, pp. 338–49). The part of Venus in this work was sung by the celebrated "Ippolita of Cardinal Montalto" (Ippolita Marotta). In *Diana schernita* (1629), set to music by Giacinto Cornacchioli, one even finds the undressing of Diana in a risqué scene.

8. *La Catena d'Adone posta in musica da Domenico Mazzocchi* . . . (Venice, Alessandro Vincenti, 1626), p. 126: "Falsirena, da Arsete consigliata al bene, ma da Idonia persuasa al male, è l'Anima consigliata dalla Ragione, ma persuasa dalla Concupiscenza. E come Falsirena a Idonia facilmente cede, così mostra, ch'ogni Affetto è dal Senso agevolmente superato. E se finalmente a duro Scoglio è legata la malvagia Falsirena, si deve anco intendere, che la Pena al fine è seguace della Colpa. Adone poi, che lontano dalla Deità di Venere patisce incontri di varii travagli, è l'Huomo che lontano da Dio incorre molti errori."

9. "A master in the full sense of the word, a master of plastic and expressive invention" is the judgment of Mazzocchi given by Alfred Einstein, who dedicated the closing pages (867–72) of *The Italian Madrigal* (Princeton, 1949) to the composer. Born in Veia, near Civita Castellana, on November 2, 1592, Mazzocchi died in Rome on January 21, 1665. He was a student of G. B. Nanino. Little is known about him save that he was for many years in the service of the Aldobrandinis, and his works have been catalogued in an imprecise and confused manner. Besides the *Catena d'Adone*, only one stage work by him is verified, the *Martirio de' Santi Abondio Prete, Abondantio Diacono, Marciano, e Giovanni suo figliuolo Cavalieri Romani*, whose text (by Tronsarelli) is preserved in a libretto which specifies a performance in Viterbo on September 16, 1641 (see Angelo Solerti, *Le origini del melodramma* [Turin, 1903], p. 248). Mazzocchi was probably also the composer of a "dilettevole opera pastorale composta dal Signor Principe Aldobrandino" (delightful pastoral opera written by Prince Aldobrandini), which was produced by Cardinal Aldobrandini "nella sua delitiosa Vigna di Frascati" (in his delectable vineyard at Frascati), and is mentioned in the "Avvisi di Roma" in the codex Urbinate 1095 of the Vatican Library, under the date of July 1, 1634 (see Ademollo, *I teatri di Roma*, p. 20); but we do not know even the title of this work. The following dialogues, sacred and secular, are also dramatic in character: 1) *Passacaglie* (characters: Silvia, Fileno, Eurilla); 2) *Dido furens* (based on Vergil); 3) *Olindo e Sofronia* (based on Tasso); 4) *Maddalena errante* (text by Prince Aldobrandini); 5) *Nisus et Eurialus* (based on Vergil); 6) *Christo smarrito col Lamento della B. Vergine* (text by Marino); 7) *Aeolus* (based on Vergil). No. 1 is published in the quintus partbook of Mazzocchi's *Madrigali a cinque voci* (Rome, F. Zannetti, 1638);

nos. 2–5 in his *Dialoghi e sonetti* (*ibid.*); no. 6 in his *Musiche sacre e morali, a una, due, e tre voci* (Rome, L. Grignani, 1640); and no. 7 at the end of an *Elegia Urbani Papae VIII* (*ibid.*, 1641). Mazzocchi's comments concerning the use of accidentals, dynamic markings, and so on have often been cited, although not always correctly interpreted; but so far as I know, it has never been noted that he, before Benevoli, exploited the expressive significance of an unexpected silence. [A recent monograph on Mazzocchi, with new documentary evidence and detailed list and analyses of his works, is W. Witzenmann, *Domenico Mazzocchi* (Cologne, 1970).]

10. In this regard, it should be interesting to examine the Venetian libretto of *Adone* (1640), even if the music, as seems probable, was written by Manelli rather than by Monteverdi. [Examination of Paolo Vendramin's libretto has shown that no character has any resemblance to either Arsete or Monteverdi's Seneca.]

11. In a brief note, which is intriguing for several reasons, and is placed at the end of the index of arias and choruses (not in the preface, as stated in Goldschmidt, *Studien*, I, 9) of the score for *Catena d'Adone*: "Vi sono molt'altre mezz'Arie sparse per l'Opera, che rompono il tedio del recitativo" (there are also many ariosos scattered throughout the opera, which break the tedium of the recitative). [Stuart Reiner, "Vi sono molt'altre mezz'arie . . . ," in *Studies in Music History*, essays for Oliver Strunk, ed. Harold Powers (Princeton, 1968), pp. 241–58, is based on this note, and provides the information (p. 248) that Sigismondo d'India had been first asked to set Tronsarelli's text but had had to decline because of sickness; the task thus went to young Mazzocchi for his only opera in a long active life. For the rest I disagree with Reiner's ingeniously contrived arguments on many points. The expression "il tedio del recitativo" need not be interpreted as a wholly negative judgment (d'India's criticism of Mazzocchi notwithstanding, expressive recitative was one of the latter's strong points) but as the realization of a need for variety. It is highly unlikely that the printed score included under Mazzocchi's name additions and / or revisions made by d'India in the part of Adone, although such modifications may have been accepted, or even required, by Lorenzo Sances, a contralto of the papal chapel, who sang the part. Although Mazzocchi's note on *mezz'arie* is rather inaccurate in its wording, it seems unlikely that the term refers to the nine nonstrophic set pieces, which are all labeled "aria" either in the score or in the index or both. Witzenmann, *Domenico Mazzocchi*, pp. 14–15 and 192–96, also rejects Reiner's suggestions and basically agrees with my interpretation of Mazzocchi's *mezz'arie*; his whole study strongly emphasizes Mazzocchi's dramatic bent, which he mainly expressed in his dialogues on secular and sacred texts, moving more in the direction of oratorio than opera.]

12. At this time the most common form for the aria, a form modeled after Caccini's arias and the elaborate song "Possente spirto" in Monteverdi's *Orfeo*, is that in which each strophe contains fresh melodic variations over a bass line that is repeated without change. An instrumental ritornello was

usually placed between the strophes. In the index for the *Catena d'Adone*, headed "Racconto delle arie, e chori a varie voci" (table of the arias, and choruses for diverse voices), even the prologue is termed an "Aria recitativa di sei parti," showing that the most important consideration was the above-mentioned strophic form. The same is true of an "Aria a 6 di cinque parti," in which the first strophe, which is repeated at the end, is choral; the other four strophes, which are preceded and followed by an instrumental ritornello, and which have the same bass line as the first, are respectively for alto and tenor, for soprano, for bass, and for two sopranos (the singers who form part of the chorus à 6). Another category is formed by the two "arie recitative per ottave," employed by Mazzocchi for Falsirena, in the scene in which she invokes Pluto, and for the god's response to her; both examples have a supernatural character. These eight-line stanzas are divided in half, and each half has the same bass line; no ritornello separates the halves. The other soloistic arias in the score are not all in strophic form. Some have only one strophe and no ritornello, but all of them are distinguished by a "walking" motion in the *basso continuo* and, of course, by their melodious character. [Finally, the transition to a short melodic passage, quite often for the final line of a recitative, gives origin to what Mazzocchi termed *mezz'arie*; Witzenmann, *Domenico Mazzocchi*, agrees with my interpretation of this term and lists, p. 95, nine such passages, five to nine measures long (including the ones discussed in this chapter). Similar passages are marked *alla battuta* at the beginning of the anonymous score of *Il pio Enea* (Venice, Biblioteca Marciana, ms. Ital. IV 447), while they are labeled *ariette* in the autograph score of Marazzoli's *Armida* (Vatican Library, ms. Chigi Q 8 189, alternative title *L'Amore trionfante dello Sdegno*). Both operas were performed in Ferrara in 1641.]

13. *A General History of Music*, IV (London, 1789), *passim*. Burney's definition of a *cavatina* (p. 240, note b) is: "an air without a second part," but among the airs which he lists as *cavatinas*, at least one is an exception to this rule: *Duri lacci* in *Arminio* (1736), which, in spite of its brevity and simplicity, is tripartite. By perusing the various examples of the *cavatina* cited by Burney, one may instead define them as monologues (the sole exception is a doubtful example: *Se mai più* in *Poro* of 1731), delivered in solitude (out of doors, in a dark prison, or in a similar situation), and almost always preceded by a short recitative; they almost always possess the character of a serene or somber meditation (excepting Ginevra's monologue addressed to a mirror, *Vezzi, lusinghe, e brio*, in *Ariodante*, which is an antecedent of Norina's *cavatina* in *Don Pasquale*); and their most common tempo indications are *largo* and *larghetto*, with some occurrences of *affettuoso*, and only one (Ginevra's monologue) that is as fast as *andante*. These *cavatinas* are almost always placed at the beginning of an act or scene, a placement that reflects, I think, an attempt to establish an aura or state of mind that prepares the listener for more dramatic incidents. Burney's earliest example of a *cavatina* in Handel's operas is from *Teseo* (1713); his latest is from *Serse* (1738).

14. See *Denkmäler der Tonkunst in Bayern* 25 (Leipzig, 1913), 7. Traetta's piece, like the examples by Handel, is a monologue which ends with a brief bipartite aria. In the same volume (p. 19) is a *cavatina* from Traetta's *I Tintaridi* (1760), which is a funereal meditation, likewise tied to a recitative. These two pieces are not noticeably dissimilar in any way that could imply a difference in the meanings of *cavata* and its diminutive. [*Cavata* is already found in the Viennese score of *Orfeo* by Antonio Sartorio.]

15. Johann Gottfried Walther, *Musicalisches Lexicon* (Leipzig, 1732), p. 150: "*Cavata* (*ital.*) ist ein *Adjectivum*, das *pro Substantivo*, mit Auslassung desselben, gesetzt wird, und heisset: 1) wenn eines weitläufftigen *Recitativs* gantzer Inhalt gemeiniglich am Ende in gar wenig Worten gleichsam *concentrirt*, und dergestalt *herausgeholet* wird, dass es (um einen Unterscheid zu machen) nöthig, solche *sententiösen* Worte nach dem Tact, und *arioso* zu setzen. 2) wenn eine Arie, oder etwas anders, ungemein wohl ausgeführet, und nach Wunsch gelungen ist. *conf. Matthesonii* Ctit [*sic*] Mus. T. 2. p. 146. *It. ejusd.* Musical. Patrioten, p. 254." [Actually, Walther derived his two definitions from the contrasting opinions of Mattheson and an unnamed "Censor" as expressed in the quoted paragraph in *Critica Musica* (Hamburg, 1722–1725; facsimile ed., Amsterdam, 1964), II 146: "Den nechsten Buss bekomme ich wegen des Worts *Cavata*, und meynet mein *Censor*, es bedeute ein kleines *Arioso* hinter einem *Recitativo* ... Aber *Cavato, Cavata,* ist ein *Adjectivum,* das *pro Substantivo,* mit Auslassung desselben/gesetzt wird/und heisst so viel/als ausnehmend/ausbündig/nehmlich/eine ausnehmend-schöne/ausbündige/vor andern heraus- und hervorgezogene *piece,* die starck und fleissig ausgearbeitet ist/als ob sie/so zu reden/recht ausgehölet wäre."] The italicized words are distinguished typographically in the originals.

16. Johann Mattheson, *Der musicalische Patriot* (Hamburg, 1728), p. 254: "Das Grund-Wort, davon *Psalm* herkömmt, heisset *beschneiden;* und wenn jemand frägt, warum diese Kunst-Stücke in der Music solchen Namen tragen, so antwortet *Salomon van Til:* weil sie mit mehr Fleiss *beschnitten* und zugerichtet sind, damit sie in ihrem höchsten Wol-Laut mögten hören lassen ... Und man darff sich über die Hebräische Ableitung nicht so sehr wundern, wenn erwogen wird, dass die Italiäner noch heutiges Tages ein wol-ausgearbeitetes Kunst-Stück in der Music *Cavata* nennen, welches eigentlich *ausgehölet* heist."

17. Burney, *General History*, IV, 340, when discussing the *cavatina* "Grave è il fasto" in *Lotario* (1729), says that it "was probably intended to display the peculiar abilities of the new tenor, Annibale Pio Fabri." Likewise, on p. 358, after describing the closing aria in the first act of *Sosarme* (1732) as "a capital *bravura* air for the Strada," Burney says of "Padre, germano, e sposo": "The second act is opened with a charming cavatina of a truly pathetic and tender cast ... in which the same performer had an opportunity of exhibiting powers of a very different kind from those which the preceding air required." Also significant is the definition of *cavatina* in Jean-Jacques Rousseau,

Dictionnaire de musique (Paris, 1768), pp. 76–77: "Sorte d'Air pour l'ordinaire assez court qui n'a ni Reprise, ni seconde partie, & qui se trouve souvent dans des Récitatifs obligés. Ce changement subit du Récitatif au Chant mesuré, & le retour inattendu du chant mesuré au Récitatif, produisent un effet admirable dans les grandes expressions, comme sont toujours celles du Récitatif obligé" (A kind of aria, usually very short, which has neither *reprise* nor second section, and is often inserted in *obbligato* recitatives. The sudden change from recitative to measured singing, and the unexpected return from measured singing to recitative, produce an admirable effect in the expression of great feelings, as those of the *obbligato* recitative always are.) See also the entries for *cavare il suono* and *cavatina* in Peter Lichtenthal, *Dizionario e bibliografia della musica* (Milan, 1826), I, 149; and for *cavata oder cavatina* in Hermann Mendel, *Musikalisches Conversations-Lexicon*, II (Berlin, 1872), 349.

22 *Commedia dell'Arte* and Opera

This essay was translated by Lewis Lockwood and published in *The Musical Quarterly* 41 (1955).

1. See for general information and bibliography: M. Apollonio, *Storia della Commedia dell'Arte* (Rome, 1930); A. Nicoll, *Masks, Mimes and Miracles* (London, 1931); K. M. Lea, *Italian Popular Comedy* (Oxford, 1934).
2. The date of the *Balli di Sfessania* is about 1622, after Callot's return to France. But he must have attended some actual performance of this dance much earlier, perhaps during his first stay in Rome about 1610. The entire series has been reprinted in facsimile edition by V. Manheimer (Potsdam, 1921).
3. It may have received this name because it was originally danced by Moorish slaves, whose market was Malta, and it is probably the same as the dance called *fiscagne* by Brantôme. See B. Croce, *Saggi sulla letteratura italiana del Seicento*, 2nd ed. (Bari, 1934), p. 195; also G. B. Basile, *Il Pentamerone ossia la Fiaba delle Fiabe*, ed. B. Croce (Bari, 1925), I, 4. Closely related to this *ballo* are the *moresche* by Lasso (and some Italian composers) in which one of the principal characters is Lucia; in fact, still another and more picturesque name given to the *Sfessania* was *Lucia canazza*.
4. *Stephanium*, a Latin comedy by Armonio, was performed some time before its publication in 1502. Giovanni Armonio, a native of the Abruzzi, was appointed organist at San Marco on Sept. 16, 1516. He kept his post until Nov. 22, 1552, when, being old and infirm, he was retired on a pension. His successor was A. Padovano (see G. Benvenuti, in *Istituzioni e Monumenti dell' Arte Musicale Italiana*, I (Milan, 1931), xxv, xxxix, xliii. He was mentioned by F. Sansovino, *Venetia città nobilissima et singulare* (Venice, 1581), fol. 168b, as one of the early players of comedies in Venice. He was also associated with the actor Antonio Molino in the formation of a musical academy, probably that

mentioned by A. F. Doni in his *Libreria* (Venice, 1551). Further on Armonio, see E. A. Cicogna, *Iscrizioni veneziane* (Venice, 1850), V, 551–52; and B. Caffi, *Storia della musica sacra ... in Venezia* (Venice, 1854–55), I, 72–76. The monastery of the Crocicchieri was one of the principal places of theatrical activity in the first half of the sixteenth century; see V. Rossi, *Le Lettere di M. Andrea Calmo* (Turin, 1888), p. 17, and P. Molmenti, *Venezia nella vita privata*, 5th ed. (Bergamo, 1911), III, 293–94.

5. Parabosco succeeded Jaquet Buus as organist at San Marco in 1551 (see Benvenuti, pp. xxxix, xli–xliii. He is the author of eight comedies, a tragedy, a book of *novelle*, some poems, two books of *Lettere*. The comedy to which this passage refers is *La notte*, performed on Feb. 4, 1548, at Ferrara in the house of Cristoforo di Messisbugo, chief cook of the Este court. See C. di Messisbugo, *Banchetti, Compositioni di vivande* (Ferrara, 1549). Further on Parabosco, see Caffi, I, 110–14, and A. Einstein, *The Italian Madrigal* (Princeton, 1949), I, 444–48.

6. This hypothesis was advanced by Benvenuti (p. xxxviii, n. 4) on the basis of Parabosco's known acquaintance with Aretino and other friends of Titian, and it was accepted by Einstein (I, 182).

7. Even at the end of the century the ladies of the nobility were expected to attend comedy performances, if not without pleasure, with at least some sign of prudery.

8. The appearance of feminine players on the stage started in Italy precisely in the second half of the sixteenth century. One of the earliest evidences (1564) is given by Apollonio, p. 93.

9. For the content of the *Balli d' Arpicordo* see C. Sartori, *Bibliografia della musica strumentale italiana* (Florence, 1952), pp. 59–60. Facoli's little collection of songs bearing the names of courtesans may be considered a musical counterpart of the fourth book of the *Lettere* by Andrea Calmo (see note 10). The preceding books of Calmo's *Lettere* contain letters addressed to real people, among whom are a few real courtesans. The fourth book is *completely* devoted to them, but evidently uses fictitious names. It is noteworthy that every letter in this book ends with a *strambotto*.

10. An actor and a playwright, Calmo (1510–1571) appeared not only in Venice but also in other cities, including Padua, Bologna, and Rome. He is considered, together with Angelo Beolco (called Ruzzante), Molino, and Parabosco, one of the forerunners of the *commedia dell'arte*. Following the example of Aretino he published, between 1548 and 1566, four books of *Lettere* (also called *Chiribizzi piacevoli*), the three earlier of which pretend to have been written by fishermen from the islands near Venice (an allusion to Calmo's own humble birth), the fourth by a character resembling Pantalone.

11. See Rossi, p. 29. Rossi does not pay particular attention to this letter (libro I, n. 10), the content of which is probably autobiographical. The letter seems to complain of the Venetians' lack of gratitude toward Calmo and emphatically compares him to many great men mistreated by their fellow citizens. Among the personal qualifications it mentions, the first mockingly refers to the

fisherman who is supposed to be the writer ("Buregheto Canestrin da Lio mazor"), but the following ("chi ha redrezzao la idioma d' i antighi e tornao el strambotizar musicalmente?") evidently are related to Calmo himself ("mi frari e mi, a honor de missier S. Marco"). Likewise, the titles of the four books, with the exception of the second, consistently mention the "lingua antica volgare," or the "vulgar antiqua lengua Veneta." As regards music, the *Lettere* contain frequent references to musical instruments and technique. Some letters are addressed to musicians, such as Giammaria del Cornetto, Ippolito Tromboncino, Parabosco, and Willaert. Other musicians mentioned are Marco da l'Aquila, Arcadelt, Jaquet Berchem, Jaquet Buus, Jaquet de Ferrara, Jusquin, Francesco da Milano, Sigismondo Ongaro, Perisson (Cambio?), Rore, Nicolò Rodioto, Domenico Rosseto, Alvise (Castellin) da Treviso, Verdelot.

12. See B. Croce, *I Teatri di Napoli*, 3rd ed. (Bari, 1926), pp. 22–23, 26.

13. This report is included in Troiano's *Discorsi delli Trionfi . . . nelle sontuose Nozze dell' Ill.mo . . . Duca Guglielmo* (Munich, 1568; reprinted with a different title in Venice, 1569), pp. 183–88. For modern editions (of the so-called scenario only), see Petraccone, *La Commedia dell' Arte* (Naples, 1927), pp. 297–301, and the English translation in Lea, I, 5–11.

14. The performance took place in the Castle of Trausnitz, the favorite residence of Duke Wilhelm V. Pictorial reflections of this performance, as well as of Wilhelm's love of improvised Italian comedy, may still be seen in the frescoes preserved in what was originally the duke's bedroom and on the walls of the spiral staircase called the *Narrentreppe*. For the description of these frescoes and for information about other comedy performances at the Bavarian court, see Lea, I, 11–16, and plates facing pp. 4, 6, 8, 10, 12, 14.

15. Probably it is from the French *entremets* that there arose the Italian *intramesse* (entertainments between courses); from these in turn originated the theatrical and musical *intermedi* or *intermezzi*. On the French *entremets*, see H. Prunières, *Le Ballet de Cour en France* (Paris, 1914), pp. 6–16; on the Italian *intramesse*, see C. di Messisbugo, *passim* (also note 21 below); [also H. M. Brown, "A Cook's Tour of Ferrara in 1529," *Rivista italiana di musicologia* 10 (1975), 256ff.]

16. For the arguments of these works, see E. Vogel, *Bibliothek des gedruckten weltliche Vocalmusik Italiens* (Berlin, 1892), I, 57–61.

17. See Vogel, I, 58–59.

18. The *Pazzia senile* is numbered as *Libro Secondo, a Tre voci* (following the *Canzonette a Tre voci . . . Libro Primo*); the *Metamorfosi musicale* as *Quarto Libro delle Canzonette a Tre voci*; the *Saviezza giovanile* as *Quinto Libro de gli Terzetti*.

19. This type of singer was often required for theatrical performances, as for instance Baccio Ugolini in 1480, and Manetto Migliorotti in 1495 for the role of the protagonist in Poliziano's *Orfeo*; likewise Tommaso Inghirami, called "Fedra" because of his performance of this role in Seneca's *Ippolito* in Rome.

20. Of course this type of parody is a musical *lazzo* or joke, corresponding to the

macaronic and corrupt quotations usually put into the mouth of Dottor Graziano.

21. Ruzzante with five "fellows" and two women sang some "canzoni e madrigali alla pavana" after the sixth course of a banquet in Ferrara on Jan. 24, 1529. We owe this information to C. da Messisbugo (see also Einstein, I, 344). It is one of the earliest mentions of the Renaissance madrigal, but it is hard to believe that in this case real madrigalesque settings are meant, but rather, light songs in dialect. The comedies by Angelo Beolco, called Ruzzante, are among the immediate predecessors of those of the *comici dell' arte*. See A. Mortier, *Ruzzante* (Paris, 1925–26).

22. *Villotta* (as used for instance by Azzaiolo), *canzon villanesca*, and *villanella* are almost synonymous terms insofar as they indicate the setting of a dialect (Venetian, Paduan, Bergamasque, and so on) text. The songs specifically indicated *alla napolitana* stand out in this group for their particular expressive and technical features.

23. See Apollonio, pp. 73–82.

24. See A. Einstein, "The Greghesca and the Giustiniana," *Journal of Renaissance and Baroque Music* 1 (1946), 19–32, which also contains an exhaustive summary of the available information about Molino. He was not only a playwright and actor, but also a composer of madrigals. [For examples of polyphonic *greghesche* see A. Gabrieli, *Complete Madrigals*, A. T. Merritt, ed., II (Madison, 1981).]

25. See essay 15.

26. Much information on performances by *zanni* in Florence is given by A. Solerti, *Musica, ballo e drammatica alla Corte Medicea* (Florence, 1905), see Index under "Zanni, commedia delli."

27. See N. Pirrotta, "Tre Capitoli su Cesti," in *La Scuola Romana* (Siena, Accademia Musicale Chigiana, 1953), pp. 28–31. There (p. 30) the quotation of Carissimi's *Amorose passioni di Fileno* is incorrectly referred to 1635, and must be replaced by that of *Carillo tradito* by Franc. Bonini (of Rome!), performed at Bologna in 1635.

28. The opera performed there in April 1636 was *Ermiona*, text by P. E. degli Obizzi, music by F. Sances of Rome (see B. Brunelli, *I Teatri di Padova* [Padua, 1921], pp. 72–77). Among the singers were Girolamo Medici, Felicita Uga, Maddalena Manelli, Anselmo Marconi, who sang in the following years in Venice, and Monteverdi's son, Francesco. Maddalena Manelli is the wife of Francesco, who was *maestro di cappella* in Tivoli in 1627, but left this town in 1629, probably finding it more profitable to travel with his wife in northern Italy. Its *Delia* had been performed at Bologna before its appearance at Venice in 1639 [see essay 19]. On Manelli, see G. Radiciotti, *L' Arte musicale in Tivoli* (Tivoli, 1921), pp. 41–54.

29. See Pirrotta, "Tre Capitoli su Cesti," p. 31.

30. See Croce, *I Teatri di Napoli*, pp. 80–82. [On the activity of lyric troupes see L. Bianconi and T. Walker, "Dalla *Finta pazza* alla *Veremonda*," *Rivista italiana di musicologia* 10 (1975), 379ff.]

31. Balbi had already collaborated in the first Venetian opera, the *Andromeda* by

Ferrari and Manelli (1637); but from 1641 he was associated with Giacomo Torelli in the productions of a new theater, the Nuovissimo, the brief activity of which was characterized by lavish stage apparatus and machinery (see S. T. Worsthorne, *Venetian Opéra in the Seventeenth Century* [Oxford, 1954], pp. 26, 31). The libretto of *La Venere gelosa*, one of the first operas performed in the Teatro Nuovissimo, was dedicated by Torelli to Cardinal Antonio Barberini (see L. N. Galvani, *alias* G. Salvioli, *I Teatri musicali di Venezia nel sec. XVII* [Milan], p. 68). Further concerning the *Finta pazza* in Paris, see H. Prunières, *L'Opéra italien en France avant Lulli* (Paris, 1913).

32. For further operatic activity of Virginia Ramponi, stage name "Florinda," at the court of the Savoia in Turin, see L. Anglois, *Il teatro alla corte di Carlo Emanuele I di Savoia* (Turin, 1930), p. 120.

33. The most complete lists of existing collections of scenarios and of their contents are to be found in Nicoll, pp. 380–90, and Lea, II, 506–54, followed in the latter (pp. 555–674) by a large selection of scenarios both in Italian and in English translation. Among the other modern editions of scenarios the most extensive are: A. Bartoli, *Scenari inediti della Commedia dell' Arte* (Florence, 1880); F. Neri, *Scenari della Maschere in Arcadia* (Città di Castello, 1913); and Petraccone.

34. "Opera" as a general term was originally applied to *every* type of written or improvised play. Since, however, comedies and tragedies were usually given their specific type names, "opera" came to be used for the third category of plot.

35. Bernini is well known as the designer of machinery, stage effects, and scenic décors for the opera productions of the Barberinis. Characteristically enough, Baldinucci's biography mentions as "Bernini's works" the "commedia della Fiera" (certainly *Chi soffre speri*, which contains the "intermezzo della fiera di Farfa," set to music by Marazzoli), the "commedia della Marina" (probably *Galatea*, libretto and music by Loreto Vittori), the "commedia del Palazzo d' Atlante e d' Astolfo" (evidently the opera by Rospigliosi and Luigi Rossi performed in 1642). A later opera by Rospigliosi and Abbatini, the *Comica del Cielo* performed in 1668, plays with the effect of a simulated opera stage on the real stage, already used by Bernini in his(?) "commedia con due Prologhi, e due Teatri." See F. Baldinucci, *Vita del Cav. G. L. Bernino* (Florence, 1682), pp. 76–77. Bernini was also fond of performing improvised comedies with his assistants (among whom was G. U. Abbatini, brother of the musician) in the Fonderia Vaticana (G. B. Passeri, *Vite de' Pittori Scultori ed Architetti* [Rome, 1772], p. 243). He was able to play every character, comic or serious; sometimes he performed every part of a comedy in order to show the people in the cast how they had to perform their roles.

36. See the second of the above-mentioned "Tre Capitoli su Cesti," which were written for the performance of this opera in Siena in 1953 at the "X Settimana Musicale Senese." The *Orontea* was generally believed to be lost, but scores exist in Rome (Biblioteca Santa Cecilia and Vatican Library), Parma, and Naples.

37. For the Italian text see my "Tre Capitoli su Cesti," p. 47. The music of the

Alessandro, performed at Venice in 1651, is often attributed to Cavalli. From Sbarra's preface we learn that it was inspired by a performance of an opera (*Orontea?*) in Lucca, in which Cesti himself participated. The libretto of *Alessandro* was written in a few days because the same (wandering) troupe had to leave for Venice, where they were scheduled to perform it very soon. Cesti is the only musician named by Sbarra; no mention is made of Cavalli.

38. See Apollonio, pp. 150–63; also the examples of love dialogues and the chapter "Delle chiusette e dei versi" reproduced in Petraccone, from A. Perrucci, *Dell'arte rappresentativa, premeditata e all' improviso* (Naples, 1699).

·Index